deer 126

grape hyacynth
muscari

Horticulture

GARDENER'S DESK REFERENCE

Horticulture

GARDENER'S DESK REFERENCE

Anne Halpin

A Horticulture Book

Macmillan · USA

MACMILLAN
A Simon & Schuster Macmillan Company
1633 Broadway
New York, NY 10019

A *Horticulture* Book

An affiliate of *Horticulture*, the Magazine of American Gardening

Library of Congress Cataloging-in-Publication Data
Halpin, Anne Moyer.
Horticulture gardener's desk reference /Anne Halpin.
p. cm.
ISBN 0-02-860397-4
1. Gardening—Handbooks, manuals, etc. 2. Plants, Ornamental—Handbooks, manuals, etc. I. Title
SB450.96. H35 1996
635—dc20 95-35874
CIP

Manufactured in the United States of America

10 9 8 7 6 5 4 3 2 1

Book design by Rachael McBrearty

CONTENTS

CHAPTER 3: FLOWERS AND FOLIAGE 155

CHAPTER 5: GRASSES AND GROUNDCOVERS 313

INTRODUCTION

This book is intended to provide a handy reference to the information that gardeners need to look up from time to time. Whether you are new to gardening or have been gardening for many years you will, I hope, find much useful information in these pages. Instead of having to page through a shelf full of books and wade through a lot of verbiage to find answers to garden questions or information on plants about which you are curious, or to refresh your memory about how to take soil samples for testing or how to layer a plant, you should be able to find many of the answers here. For more in-depth information on particular aspects of the garden, you can go on to study a book on a specific gardening subject.

The book is organized into sections dealing with general gardening concerns and with particular types of gardens and plants. The first chapter deals with climate, weather, and the garden environment. The second chapter covers basic gardening techniques. If you are new to gardening, these chapters should be especially helpful.

The rest of the chapters deal with particular groups of plants or types of gardens—flowers, trees and shrubs, lawns, ornamental grasses and groundcovers, vines, herbs, vegetables, fruits, and container gardens. Consult these chapters when you are looking for plants for different situations, of different sizes, or with particular qualities. For example, if you are looking for drought-tolerant perennials, annuals that are low in maintenance, bulbs that naturalize well, fragrant rose varieties, or flowers that bloom at night, consult chapter 3. To find trees and shrubs that grow well in your part of the country, see chapter 4. If you need a groundcover for a slope, look in chapter 5. When you want a soothing herbal bath, you'll find a list of herbs to choose from in chapter 7.

The appendices include names and addresses of public gardens, plant societies, and mail-order seed and nursery companies.

Use the table of contents in the front of the book to find listings of topics covered in the book. Use the index to locate more specific information on particular plants or subjects of interest to you.

In addition to providing information in a readily accessible form, the Gardener's Desk Reference also contains bits of interesting and entertaining miscellany. Scattered throughout the pages are such nuggets of information as a list of state trees, flowers of the month, the biggest vegetables ever grown, famous lily breeders and their star hybrids, and herbs believed to have magic powers in folklore.

In the chapters devoted to ornamental plants, plants are listed by botanical name first, followed by common name. See appendix 1 for an explanation of botanical names and the value of using them. Vegetables, fruits, and herbs are listed by their common names, since that is how they are best known in commerce and among gardeners.

If there is information you would like to have seen in this book but that does not appear, please write to me in care of Roundtable Press, 80 Fifth Avenue, New York, NY 10011, and let me know. I will try to include it in a future edition.

Anne Halpin

Chapter 1

THE GARDEN ENVIRONMENT

CLIMATE AND WEATHER

USDA HARDINESS ZONE MAP

The USDA Hardiness Zones are climatic regions defined by their annual average minimum temperature. A plant's hardiness is most often judged by a measure of the coldest temperatures in which the plant is likely to do well. The zone map translates these temperatures into geographic terms.

The map at the end of this book is a revised version of earlier maps; this one was introduced in 1990. This map adds a Zone 11 for the very warmest parts of the country—the Florida Keys, a few places in southern California, and parts of Hawaii. Zones 1 to 10 have now been subdivided into "a" and "b" sections, with the "a" portion of each zone being an average of 5°F cooler than the "b" portion.

Local factors and microclimates (which are discussed below) also play a role in plant survival. A garden in an exposed location may actually have growing conditions similar to those in the next coldest zone: The climate on a windswept hilltop in Vermont may be like that of Zone 3, although the garden is located in Zone 4. If that garden was instead located next to the south-facing wall of a building, and protected on the east and west sides by evergreen shrubs, growing conditions could approximate those found in gardens in Zone 5.

Another important factor in plant hardiness is that many plants have limits to the degree of heat—as well as cold—that they can tolerate. For others, a certain amount of cold is absolutely necessary. For example, many varieties of apples, pears, and other temperate-zone fruits cannot produce their crop unless they receive a certain amount of below-freezing weather. (This is called a "Chilling Requirement," and it is discussed in chapter 9.) *Veronica latifolia*, a popular perennial, is hardy to Zone 3 but will not usually survive south of Zone 8. Iceland poppies, although rated as hardy in Zones 1 to 8, must be grown as annuals in Zones 7 and 8—and sometimes in Zone 6 as well—because the plants are so stressed by hot weather. The cold, however, is no problem for them.

Gardeners in the North, then, must pay special attention to the northernmost limits of a plant's hardiness range. Gardeners in warm climates must be aware of the southernmost boundaries.

HOW LOCAL FACTORS INFLUENCE CLIMATE

In addition to your hardiness zone, here are some local factors that may influence the climate in and around your garden.

Large bodies of water have a modifying effect on local climates. Near the ocean, the climate is milder than in locations at the same latitude farther inland. Summer temperatures are slightly cooler and winter temperatures are slightly warmer. Look at the zone map and note that Long Island and Cape Cod are given warmer zone designations than the mainland nearby.

A large body of inland water, such as a sizable lake, will also have a moderating effect on the climate in nearby gardens. The larger the lake, the farther its influence will be felt.

Elevation. Gardens at high altitudes are colder than those in the same region that are closer to sea level. Mountain climates are characterized by sharp temperature fluctuations—the sun can be quite hot during the day, but air temperatures dip sharply at night. The temperature drops approximately 1°F for every 250 feet above sea level. For gardeners, this means that the higher up they live, the shorter their growing season will be.

A line of hills near where you live will affect your garden's microclimate similarly to the way a range of mountains affects climate on a larger scale.

Humidity and rainfall. Dry cold is very tough on plants. Winter winds *can* seriously desiccate their tissues, and in cold climates, their roots are unable to draw more moisture from the frozen soil to replace what's been lost through the leaves. Much winter injury of broad-leaved evergreens and other plants is due to dryness rather than cold. Gardeners living where cold, dry winters are a problem can turn to antidesiccant sprays to help protect sensitive plants.

Humid air is kinder to plants. The moisture in the atmosphere slows the radiation of heat from the Earth, so temperatures do not drop so rapidly at night. During humid weather temperature swings are less extreme. The danger of humid air is when it's very still, with no wind. Still, humid air is conducive to the development of mildews and fungus diseases, as pathogens sit undisturbed on foliage.

Wind. Strong wind can bend and even break stems and branches, but the worst damage comes from its drying effect. As wind passes over plants, it dries out their tissues—the stronger the wind, the faster it desiccates plants. If a plant's root system cannot replace the moisture lost through leaves as quickly as it evaporates, the plant suffers water stress. The pores in the leaves close and the growth process slows or shuts down entirely in an effort to preserve the plant.

In an exposed hilltop location, plants may suffer from wind damage unless a windbreak is present. Sea air carries salt, and in seashore gardens a windbreak protects plants from salt as well as damage.

Not only gardens in exposed hilltop locations are at risk from winds. Buildings, walls, and other solid structures can concentrate wind and push it into strange patterns. Gardens in cities full of tall buildings are often at the mercy of vagrant winds whipping through the streets. In a suburban or rural locale, a garden seemingly in a sheltered spot—such as tucked up against a stone wall—may suffer damage from wind gusts rushing down over the wall.

Erect windbreaks on the side of your garden facing into the prevailing wind. The windbreak need not be right next to the garden in order to be effective. A windbreak will all but stop the wind for a distance of about twice the height of the windbreak, to the leeward. It will have less dramatic moderating effects over a distance up to ten times its height.

A design should allow for air to pass through it. Instead of a solid wall, put up a fence of open construction, such as a picket fence, or a fence made of vertical wooden slats, that will slow the wind without channeling it into destructive gusts. An evergreen hedge can be an effective windbreak, as can a mixed hedgerow or a row of evergreen shrubs.

A solid wall that is already in place can be modified with the addition of a 1- to 2-foot-high strip of lattice or other material of open construction to make the wall more effective at slowing wind. Attach the strip to the top of the wall, and angle it slightly into the wind. Or, if possible, make holes in the wall to allow for air passage, or reconstruct the top to make it irregular or jagged rather than a straight, smooth surface.

Population density. Cities are generally warmer and windier than less populous places in the same geographic area. The miles of asphalt and concrete, the buildings, and the multitudes of vehicles all contribute heat to the environment. Winds in a big city can be intense, as well, and their patterns capricious. The summer heat, erratic winds, and deep shade cast by tall buildings all make life difficult for plants.

MICROCLIMATES IN THE GARDEN

In addition to local climate, a number of factors can affect the environment in and immediately around your garden.

Microclimate is the term used to indicate the set of local geographic and climatic factors that determine growing conditions in your garden. Your garden's microclimate is determined by the interrelationship of directional exposure, sun and shade, moisture and humidity, slope and elevation, soil type, temperature ranges, day length, and other factors.

Slopes and hillsides. Cold air flows down a slope like water. A spot well up on a hill is a better choice than one near the bottom, which could be in a "cold pocket." An obstacle like a building—or another hill—stops the movement and causes the cold air to collect in a pool. A garden located in a pocket where cold air pools will be subject to later-than-usual spring frosts and earlier fall frosts. Air tends to have less movement at the bottom of a hill, so the chilly air in a cold pocket will be less likely to dissipate on a frosty night—another hazard for plants.

A south-facing slope will be warmer than one that faces north. The warm environment encourages plants to begin growing earlier in spring, which is risky for certain plants. Plants that bloom early in spring, such as fruit trees (especially peaches and apricots) and early perennials, are at risk from late frosts, which could damage early blossoms.

Plants on a north slope will bloom later but be at less risk of damage from a late frost. A southern slope is also less desirable when it is located on the side of a valley, across from a north slope. Cold air may back up behind the north slope and fill the bottom of the valley, affecting gardens on the south slope as well as the north.

Nearby buildings cast shadows that create a darker, colder growing environment for plants. City gardens are most troubled by building shade. Houses, sheds, and garages cast shadows, too, and those shadows move as the seasons change.

Trees create shade, of course, and they cut off sunshine from shorter plants. But trees affect the garden in other ways, too. Trees need lots of nutrients and water to fuel their growth, and they take what they need from the soil, often at the expense of smaller, less vigorous plants growing nearby.

The air is cooler under trees than in the open sunshine, a welcome condition in summer, but one that may not be so welcome in spring and fall (remember, evergreens cast their shade year-round).

What's more, all shade is not alike. The quality of the shade, along with the other growing conditions, determines which plants will grow well in a shady garden. Different trees cast different kinds of shade, some lighter, some denser. Morning shade is different from afternoon shade. A shady place with moist soil is different from a dry, shady spot. See the section on shade, on page 49, for more information.

HOW TO USE PHENOLOGY TO DETERMINE SAFE PLANTING DATES

Thousands of years ago, before the invention of calendars, farmers around the world timed their planting to natural cycles. In ancient Greece, the migration of cranes signaled the time to plant, according to the poet Hesiod. Native Americans in New England in colonial times planted corn when the leaves of local oak trees were as big as the ears of mice.

The study of events that occur in regular cycles in the lives of plants and animals is called *phenology* (from Greek words meaning "science of appearances."). For gardeners, phenology is the awareness of how different stages of plant growth and development in the garden are related to the development of other plants in the landscape, the emergence of insects, and animal behavior such as hibernation and migration.

The phenology of perennial plants in the local landscape—especially trees and shrubs—is related to day length and temperature. Developmental stages of plants can also be related to the life cycles of insects and animals. Gardeners can use local plants as indicators of when weather conditions are suitable for planting vegetables, flowers, and other plants in the garden, and to predict the annual arrival of pest populations.

To choose indicator plants for your garden, note in your garden journal when trees, shrubs and wild plants on and around your property begin to grow, leaf out, develop buds, and reach full bloom. Also keep a running record of weather conditions. After several years you will begin to see a correspondence between the annual development of certain plants and particular weather conditions. You may also recognize a link between the emergence of pests and the growth or flowering of plants. You can then choose likely indicator plants in your neighborhood.

Lilac Calendar

The common lilac *(Syringa vulgaris)* is one of the most widely used indicator plants. Lilacs develop according to a regular schedule that is easy to observe, and grow throughout much of the United States. Here is how to use them:

WHEN LILACS...	IT'S TIME TO PLANT...
begin to leaf out—widest part of the earliest leaves has grown out past the bud scales that had enclosed the leaf bud	hardy annuals such as calendula and sweet alyssum cool-weather vegetables such as peas, lettuce, and spinach cold-tolerant herbs like parsley and chervil
are in full bloom—all flowers on 95 percent of the plant's flower spikes are fully open	tender annuals such as marigolds and geraniums warm-weather edibles like tomatoes, corn, and basil

Here's how to use phenology to predict when major pest populations—Japanese beetles, for instance, or Colorado potato beetles—are likely to occur. Over several years, study the local landscape, the plants and the bugs. If one or more plants are always at the same stage of growth when the pests arrive, they can be used as indicators to predict the insect invasion. You can reduce your use of pesticides by spraying just before a target pest population is likely to be present.

FROSTS AND FREEZES

Many plants that can tolerate light frost will be damaged or killed outright by a severe freeze. It's important to know the difference.

An air temperature of 32°F in the immediate vicinity of plants produces light frost.

The following are widely accepted classifications for frosts and freezes which are used by the National Climatic Data Center in compiling data on frost-free growing seasons around the United States.

Light frost: 32°F (air temperature around plants, as opposed to higher up or on the ground). Tender plants are damaged.

Light freeze: 29° to 32°F. Tender plants are killed, and half-hardy plants are damaged, with little destructive effect on other vegetation.

Moderate freeze: 25° to 28°F. Widely destructive effect on most vegetation, heavy damage to fruit blossoms, and to tender and half-hardy plants.

Severe freeze: 24°F and below. Heavy damage to most nonwoody plants. At these temperatures the ground freezes solid. How deep the soil freezes depends on the duration and severity of the freeze, soil moisture, and soil type.

FROST IS LIKELY WHEN:

Temperature is cool at sunset.

Air is calm.

Sky is clear overnight. If clouds that have been present all day appear to be thinning at dusk, the sky could clear overnight, allowing temperatures to drop.

Soil is cold and dry.

The night is long (the longer the night, the more time there is for temperatures to continue to fall).

An arctic air mass sweeps through the area, following passage of a cold front.

Moon is new or full.

Dew point (the temperature at which dew forms, or moisture condenses out of the atmosphere) in your garden is close to freezing.

FROST IS NOT LIKELY WHEN:

Daytime temperatures are above 75°F (cooler in a moist, mild climate, warmer in dry climates, especially at high elevations).

A good breeze blows throughout the night.

Sky is overcast.

Soil is warm and wet, especially in fall.

Night is shorter (nights before the last spring frost can be up to two hours shorter than nights during the fall frost season).

Moon is neither new nor full.

Dew point in your garden is at least several degrees above freezing.

HOW TO PREDICT FROST

If you know when frost is likely, you can take steps to protect plants at risk. The prediction tables opposite were derived from information found in *The Weather-Wise Gardener* by Calvin Simonds (Emmaus, PA: Rodale Press, 1983).

If the weather forecasts in the newspaper you read or the television news you watch come from a large city which is some distance from where you live, familiarize yourself with the extent to which weather conditions are milder or more severe in your garden, and compensate accordingly in making your predictions.

PLANTS THAT CAN TOLERATE FROST

The plants listed below will tolerate frost. Hardy plants will tolerate a moderate freeze, and their seeds will tolerate severe freezes.

Annuals

Hardy annuals self-sow or can be sown in fall. In northern gardens they will germinate the following spring; in warm climates they will germinate in late fall or winter. Along with true annuals, the list includes some biennials, and perennials that will bloom the first year from seed.

HARDY ANNUALS

Adonis aestivalis, pheasant's eye
Agrostis nebulosa, cloud grass
Amethystea caerulea
Ammi majus, white lace flower
Anagallis arvensis, scarlet pimpernel
Avena species, oat grass
Bellis perennis, English daisy
Brassica oleracea, flowering cabbage and kale
Briza species, quaking grass
Bromus species, brome grass
Calendula officinalis, pot marigold
Carthamus tinctorius, safflower
Cassia fasciculata, golden senna
Catananche caerulea, blue Cupid's dart
Centaurea
 C. americana, basket flower
 C. cyanus, bachelor's button
 C. moschata, sweet sultan
Cerinthe major, honeywort
Chrysanthemum parthenium (*Tanacetum*), feverfew
Cirsium japonicum, plume thistle
Cladanthus arabicus
Clarkia amoena, satin flower
Cnicus benedictus, blessed thistle
Collinsia heterophylla, Chinese houses
Collomia grandiflora
Consolida ambigua, larkspur
Coreopsis tinctoria, calliopsis
Crepis rubra, hawksbeard
Cynoglossum amabile, Chinese forget-me-not
Dianthus barbatus, sweet William
Digitalis purpurea 'Foxy', foxglove
Dyssodia tenuiloba, Dahlberg daisy
Echium vulgare, blueweed
Erysimum perofskianum, wallflower
Eschscholzia californica, California poppy
Gaillardia pulchella, blanketflower
Gilia capitata, Queen Anne's thimble
Glaucium grandiflorum, horned poppy
Helianthus annuus, sunflower
Iberis
 I. amara, rocket candytuft
 I. umbellata, globe candytuft

(continued)

Annuals *(cont'd)*

Juncus bufonias, toad rush
Lagurus ovatus, hare's tail grass
Lamarckia aurea, goldentop
Lathyrus odoratus, sweet pea
Lavatera trimestris, mallow
Layia platyglossa, tidytips
Legousia veneris, mirror of Venus
Limnanthes douglasii, meadowfoam
Linanthus
  L. dianthiflorus, ground pink
  L. grandiflorus, mountain phlox
Linaria maroccana, toadflax
Linum grandiflorum, flowering flax
Lobularia maritima, sweet alyssum
Lunaria annua, money plant
Lupinus, lupine
  L. densiflorus
  L. hartwegii
  L. luteus
  L. texensis, bluebonnet
Lychnis
  L. coeli-rosa, rose of heaven
  L. coronaria, rose campion
Machaeranthera tanacetifolia, Tahoka daisy
Malcolmia maritima, Virginia stock
Malope trifida
Malva verticillata var. *crispa*, musk mallow
Matthiola longipetala, night-scented stock
Mentzelia lindleyi, blazing star
Myosotis sylvatica, wood forget-me-not
Nemophila menziesii, baby blue-eyes
Nigella damascena, love-in-a-mist
Oenothera
  O. drummondii, Texas evening primrose
  O. speciosa, showy evening primrose
Omphalodes linifolia, navelwort
Panicum capillare, witchgrass
Papaver, poppy
  P. glaucum, tulip poppy
  P. rhoeas, field poppy
Phacelia campanularia, California bluebell
Phalaris canariensis, canary grass
Physalis alkekengi, Chinese lantern
Platystemon californicus, creamcups
Polygonum orientale, knotweed
Polypogon monspeliensis, beard grass
Ratibida columnifera, prairie coneflower, Mexican hat
Reseda odorata, mignonette
Setaria italica, foxtail millet
Silene armeria, catchfly
Trachymene caerulea, blue lace flower
Triticum turgidum, bearded wheat
Viola
  V. tricolor, Johnny jump-up
  V. × *wittrockiana*, pansy
Xanthisma texana, star-of-Texas

HALF-HARDY ANNUALS

Agrostemma githago, corn cockle
Antirrhinum majus, snapdragon
Arctotis stoechadifolia, African daisy
Argemone mexicana
Baileya multiradiata, desert marigold
Brachycome iberidifolia, Swan River daisy
Calandrinia umbellata
Callistephus chinensis, China aster
Cheiranthus chrysanthemum
  C. carinatum
  C. cheiri
  C. coronarium, garland chrysanthemum
Cleome hasslerana, spider flower
Dianthus chinensis, China pink
Emilia javanica, tasselflower
Gaura lindheimeri
Gazania rigens, treasure flower
Gerbera jamesonii, Transvaal daisy
Gomphrena globosa, globe amaranth
Gypsophila elegans, annual baby's breath
Helichrysum bracteatum, strawflower
Limonium sinuatum, statice
Lobelia erinus, edging lobelia
Mirabilis jalapa, four-o'clock
Moluccella laevis, bells of Ireland
Nicotiana alata, flowering tobacco
Nierembergia hippomanica, cupflower
Papaver nudicaule, Iceland poppy
Penstemon hartwegii

Petunia × *hybrida*
Phlox drummondii
Rudbeckia hirta, black-eyed Susan, gloriosa daisy
Salvia farinacea, mealycup sage (grown as annual north of Zone 8)
Scabiosa
- *S. atropurpurea*
- *S. stellata*, starflower

Tagetes species, marigold
Xeranthemum annuum, immortelle

Herbs

HARDY ANNUAL HERBS

Borago officinalis, borage
Carum carvi, caraway
Foeniculum vulgare, fennel
Matricaria recutita, German chamomile
Satureja hortensis, summer savory

HALF-HARDY HERBS

Anethum graveolens, dill
Petroselinum crispum, parsley
Salvia sclarea, clary

Vegetables

HARDY VEGETABLES

Broccoli
Brussels sprouts
Cabbage
Collards
Garlic
Kale
Kohlrabi
Leeks
Mustard
Onions
Peas
Radishes
Spinach
Turnips

HALF-HARDY VEGETABLES

Beets
Carrots
Cauliflower
Celeriac
Celery
Chard
Chicory
Chinese cabbage
Endive
Escarole
Globe artichoke
Jerusalem artichoke
Lettuce
Parsnips
Potatoes
Salsify
Scorzonera

HOW FROST HARMS PLANTS

When the temperature dips below 32°F, the fluid inside the membranes within a plant's cells begins to freeze. When that happens, water is forced by osmosis from the protoplasm through the membranes and into the fluid sacs. The transfer of water dries out the protoplasm, and much of the damage we see actually occurs as a result of this dehydration. A hard frost can also rupture the membranes holding the fluid, causing further damage.

If the ice crystals in the fluid sacs have a chance to melt and the water returns to the protoplasm before the rising sun stimulates the plant into its daily activity, tissue damage can be avoided. But if the sun hits the plant while the ice crystals are still frozen, damage will occur. The effect of severe frost damage appears very similar to the effect of a prolonged drought—plants look dehydrated.

PROTECTING PLANTS FROM FROST DAMAGE

The devices listed below can all provide frost protection for plants. Many of them are described in some detail under "Season-Extending Techniques" in chapter 10.

TO PROTECT GROUPS OF PLANTS

"Floating" row and bed covers made of spun-bonded polyester or polypropylene

Plastic tunnels (made of polyethylene)

Homemade plastic tents

Cold frame

Shelter made from bales of hay, "roofed" with plastic or old storm windows

Newspapers (weight down the edges)

Old tablecloths, bed sheets, or other lightweight covers

TO PROTECT INDIVIDUAL PLANTS

Waxed paper hot caps

Bottomless glass or plastic jugs

Plastic tepees or covers

Glass jars (for small plants)

Cylinders made of wire mesh covered with plastic (easiest to use is plastic that has wire mesh already embedded in it)

Peach baskets

Cardboard boxes

Wall O' Water, a cone-shaped plastic device with channeled sides that are filled with water

If you are unable to cover plants, you may be able to save them with water. If the frost will be severe, sprinkle plants during the night so that a coating of ice forms on their leaves and stems. The ice will protect the plants themselves from freezing.

Alternatively, you can sprinkle the plants with water very early in the morning, before dawn. This method is often successful, probably because it replaces moisture in the cellular protoplasm that was pushed inside the pockets of fluid within the cells. Also, as the water on the leaves freezes it releases heat, which slows the rate at which the leaves themselves cool to the freezing point.

THE GROWING SEASON IN THE UNITED STATES

This table shows the average dates of the last spring frost and the first fall frost, and the average number of frost-free days for locations around the United States. It was prepared with data from the National Climatic Data Center.

STATE	CITY	LAST SPRING FROST (average date)	FIRST FALL FROST (average date)	AVERAGE FROST-FREE GROWING SEASON (in days)
Alabama	Mobile	February 27	November 26	272 days
Alaska	Fairbanks	May 17	September 6	112 days
	Juneau	May 16	September 26	133 days
Arizona	Flagstaff	June 13	September 21	99 days
	Phoenix	February 5	December 15	308 days
	Tucson	February 28	November 29	273 days
Arkansas	Pine Bluff	March 19	November 8	234 days
	Fayetteville	April 21	October 17	189 days
California	Eureka	January 30	December 15	324 days
	Palo Alto	February 22	December 7	287 days
	Sacramento	February 14	December 1	289 days
	San Francisco	no frost likely	no frost likely	no frost likely
	San Jose	January 22	December 25	338 days
Colorado	Denver	May 3	October 8	157 days
	Durango	June 4	September 18	105 days
	Telluride	June 28	August 27	59 days
Connecticut	Hartford	April 25	October 10	167 days
	Norwalk	April 24	October 15	173 days
Delaware	Wilmington	April 13	October 29	198 days
District of Columbia	Washington, D.C.	April 10	October 31	203 days

(continued)

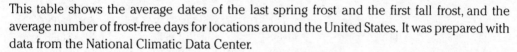

The Growing Season in the United States *(cont'd)*

STATE	CITY	LAST SPRING FROST (average date)	FIRST FALL FROST (average date)	AVERAGE FROST-FREE GROWING SEASON (in days)
Florida	Miami	no frost likely	no frost likely	no frost likely
	Ocala	February 19	December 9	293 days
	Tallahassee	March 12	November 14	246 days
	Tampa	January 28	January 3	338 days
Georgia	Athens	March 28	November 8	224 days
	Savannah	March 10	November 15	250 days
Idaho	Boise	May 8	October 9	153 days
	Pocatello	May 20	September 20	122 days
Illinois	Chicago	April 22	October 26	187 days
	Springfield	April 17	October 19	185 days
Indiana	Indianapolis	April 22	October 20	180 days
	South Bend	May 1	October 18	169 days
Iowa	Atlantic	May 9	September 28	141 days
	Cedar Rapids	April 29	October 7	161 days
Kansas	Manhattan	April 23	October 16	176 days
	Topeka	April 21	October 14	175 days
Kentucky	Ashland	April 27	October 18	173 days
	Lexington	April 17	October 25	190 days
Louisiana	Monroe	March 9	November 7	242 days
	New Orleans	February 20	December 5	288 days
Maine	Bar Harbor	May 4	October 17	165 days
	Portland	May 10	September 30	143 days
Maryland	Baltimore	March 26	November 13	231 days
	Cumberland	April 27	October 12	167 days
Massachusetts	Amherst	May 9	September 29	142 days
	Boston	April 16	October 25	181 days
	Worcester	April 27	October 17	172 days

STATE	CITY	LAST SPRING FROST (average date)	FIRST FALL FROST (average date)	AVERAGE FROST-FREE GROWING SEASON (in days)
Michigan	Ann Arbor	April 28	October 21	175 days
	Lansing	May 13	September 30	140 days
	Marquette	May 12	October 19	159 days
Minnesota	Duluth	May 21	September 21	122 days
	Moose Lake	May 31	September 17	108 days
	Willmar	May 4	October 4	152 days
Mississippi	Columbus	March 27	October 29	215 days
	Natchez	March 10	November 14	248 days
	Vicksburg	March 13	November 18	250 days
Missouri	Jefferson City	April 26	October 16	173 days
	Hannibal	April 15	October 22	189 days
Montana	Bozeman	May 30	September 16	108 days
	Fort Peck	May 5	September 28	146 days
	Helena	May 18	September 18	122 days
Nebraska	Blair	April 27	October 10	165 days
	North Platte	May 11	September 24	136 days
Nevada	Las Vegas	March 7	November 21	259 days
New Hampshire	Concord	May 23	September 22	121 days
New Jersey	Newark	April 4	November 10	219 days
	Somerville	May 2	October 12	162 days
	Trenton	April 6	November 7	214 days
New Mexico	Carlsbad	March 29	November 7	223 days
	Los Alamos	May 8	October 13	157 days
New York	Albany	May 7	September 29	144 days
	Bridgehampton	April 19	October 27	191 days
	Ithaca	May 15	September 28	135 days
	Syracuse	April 28	October 16	170 days
North Carolina	Asheville	April 10	October 24	195 days
	Fayetteville	April 2	October 31	212 days
	Raleigh	April 11	October 27	198 days

(continued)

The Growing Season in the United States *(cont'd)*

STATE	CITY	LAST SPRING FROST (average date)	FIRST FALL FROST (average date)	AVERAGE FROST-FREE GROWING SEASON (in days)
North Dakota	Bismarck	May 14	September 20	129 days
Ohio	Akron	May 3	October 18	168 days
	Cincinnati	April 14	October 27	195 days
Oklahoma	Boise City	April 28	October 16	171 days
	Tulsa	March 30	November 4	218 days
Oregon	Ashland	May 13	October 12	152 days
	Pendleton	April 15	October 21	188 days
	Portland	April 3	November 7	217 days
	Salem	May 5	October 22	169 days
Pennsylvania	Allentown	April 21	October 18	179 days
	Indiana	May 14	October 4	142 days
	Williamsport	April 29	October 15	168 days
Rhode Island	Kingston	May 8	September 30	144 days
	Providence	April 13	October 27	196 days
South Carolina	Charleston	March 11	November 20	253 days
	Columbia	April 4	November 2	211 days
South Dakota	Rapid City	May 7	September 29	145 days
	Hot Springs	May 18	September 20	124 days
Tennessee	Memphis	March 23	November 7	228 days
	Nashville	April 5	October 29	207 days
Texas	Amarillo	April 14	October 29	197 days
	Denton	March 25	November 12	131 days
	San Antonio	March 3	November 24	265 days
Utah	Cedar City	May 20	October 2	134 days
	Logan	May 7	October 12	158 days
Vermont	Burlington	May 11	October 1	142 days
	Woodstock	May 28	September 19	113 days
Virginia	Norfolk	March 23	November 17	239 days
	Richmond	April 10	October 26	198 days

STATE	CITY	LAST SPRING FROST (average date)	FIRST FALL FROST (average date)	AVERAGE FROST-FREE GROWING SEASON (in days)
Washington	Seattle	March 24	November 11	232 days
	Spokane	May 4	October 5	153 days
West Virginia	Parkersburg	April 25	October 18	175 days
Wisconsin	Green Bay	May 12	October 2	143 days
	Janesville	April 28	October 10	164 days
	Milwaukee	May 5	October 9	156 days
Wyoming	Cody	May 18	September 21	125 days
	Laramie	June 9	September 10	92 days

ANCIENT CELTIC SEASONS

The ancient Celtic people of Britain developed a calendar built around the growing of food and the passing of the seasons. This calendar divided the year into eight parts, each of which began with a festival.

Quarter Days marked the solstices and equinoxes, when the seasons begin. Later, as Christianity began to wield an influence, four more festival days were added, corresponding to important holidays in the Christian church. These four Cross-Quarter Days fall about midway between the Quarter Days.

The Celts believed that a period of darkness must precede daylight, just as a seed begins its life in the dark earth before bursting through into the light of the sun. So the Celtic day began at nightfall, and festivals started at sunset.

The four Quarter Days were these:

March 25, Lady Day, which occurred near the vernal equinox, was when farmers hired their workers for the growing season. The early Christians celebrated the Feast of the Annunciation at this time.

June 24, Midsummer Day, which marked the summer solstice, was halfway through the growing season, between planting and harvest. Christians marked the birthday of John the Baptist.

September 29 was Michaelmas. The autumn equinox was a time of celebrating the harvest. Farmers paid their annual rent to the landowners on this date. Christians celebrated this as the feast of the Archangel Michael.

December 25, Christmas, originated as a winter solstice festival in pre-Christian times. It was a time to rest, as the land rested. Farm workers received their yearly wages.

The Chinese Agricultural Calendar

Farmers in ancient China used a calendar that divides the year into twenty-four periods, each beginning on a solstice, an equinox, or a new or full moon. Each period runs until the next new or full moon, whichever comes first. The periods are about two weeks long, except for those beginning with solstices and equinoxes, which are usually shorter, and serve to align a solar-based way of counting the seasons with lunar cycles. In use since at least 200 B.C., the calendar is still used by farmers in some provinces of China.

Below is a list of the names of the periods, and their approximate times. To make a calendar for your own use, match solstices, equinoxes, and moon phases with a conventional calendar to assign dates to each period.

NAME OF PERIOD	APPROXIMATE TIME
Winter Solstice	Winter solstice to next new or full moon
Lesser Cold	New or full moon after solstice to next new or full moon
Greater Cold	New or full moon to next new or full moon
Beginning of Spring	New or full moon to next new or full moon
Rains	New or full moon to next new or full moon
Awakening of Creatures (from hibernation)	New or full moon to next new or full moon
Spring Equinox	Vernal equinox to next new or full moon
Clear and Bright	New or full moon to next new or full moon
Grain Rain	New or full moon to next new or full moon
Beginning of Summer	New or full moon to next new or full moon
Lesser Fullness of Grain	New or full moon to next new or full moon
Grain in Ear	New or full moon to next new or full moon
Summer Solstice	Summer solstice to next new or full moon
Lesser Heat	New or full moon to next new or full moon
Greater Heat	New or full moon to next new or full moon
Beginning of Autumn	New or full moon to next new or full moon
End of Heat	New or full moon to next new or full moon
White Dews	New or full moon to next new or full moon
Autumn Equinox	Autumnal equinox to next new or full moon
Cold Dews	New or full moon to next new or full moon
Descent of Frost	New or full moon to next new or full moon
Beginning of Winter	New or full moon to next new or full moon
Lesser Snow	New or full moon to next new or full moon
Greater Snow	New or full moon to next new or full moon

The Cross-Quarter Days marked the midpoint of each season:

February 2 was Candlemas, when candles and bonfires were lit to welcome the return of the sun from its winter journey. The lambing season began. Christians celebrated the feast of St. Brigid (who is thought to have evolved from Brigit—the Irish goddess of poetry and healing). The Celts believed that if Candlemas Day was fair and bright, spring would be late in coming; if the day was dark and rainy, spring's mild weather would return sooner. Sound familiar? It's where we got our notion of Groundhog Day.

May 1, May Day, was the date of one of the biggest pagan festivals of the year. It was a celebration of fertility and growth, and planting time. To the Druids it was Beltane, when a great bonfire was lit. For the ancient Romans, May Eve, April 30, marked the midpoint of the festival of Floralia, dedicated to the goddess of flowering plants.

August 1, Lammas, marked the beginning of the harvest season. The first of the new grain crop was harvested and bread baked from it was offered in thanks for the bounty of the fertile land. (Lammas is short for loaf mass.)

October 31 was Samhain for the Druids, when the Fire of Peace was lit. It was the beginning of the new year for the Celts. The harvest was now completed, the cattle were brought back from their summer pastures. November 1 was All Saints Day to the Christians (and still is), but people of the older faiths believed the spirits of the dead walked the earth on All-Hallows Eve, along with elves, sprites, and fairies. We see these creatures roaming our own streets on Halloween . . . they are costumed children trick-or-treating.

WEATHER PREDICTION TABLE

This table was adapted from a weather forecasting table originally devised by Dr. Adam Clark, that appeared in a USDA publication from 1903, titled *Weather Folklore and Local Weather Signs*, by Edward B. Garriot.

WIND DIRECTION	BAROMETER READING (adjusted to sea level)	WEATHER FORECAST
SW to NW	30.10 to 30.20, steady	Fair with little temperature change for 1 to 2 days
SW to NW	30.10 to 30.20, rising quickly	Fair and warmer, rain within 2 days
SW to NW	30.20 or above, steady	Continued fair with little temperature change

(continued)

Weather Prediction Table *(cont'd)*

WIND DIRECTION	BAROMETER READING (adjusted to sea level)	WEATHER FORECAST
SW to NW	30.20 or above, falling slowly	Fair with slowly rising temperatures for 2 days
S to SW	30.00 or below, rising slowly	Clearing within a few hours, fair for next few days
S to SE	30.10 to 30.20, falling slowly	Rain within 24 hours
S to SE	30.10 to 30.20, fallinμg quickly	Increasing wind, rain in 12 to 24 hours
S to E	29.80 or below, falling quickly	Severe storm within a few hours, then clearing and colder in 24 hours
SE to NE	30.10 to 30.20, falling slowly	Rain in 12 to 18 hours
SE to NE	30.10 to 30.20, falling quickly	Increasing winds with rain in 12 hours
SE to NE	30.00 or below, falling slowly	Rain continuing 1 to 2 days
SE to NE	30.00 or below, falling quickly	Rain with high winds, clearing and colder in 24 to 36 hours
E to NE	30.10 or above, falling slowly	Light winds in summer, rain in 2 to 4 days. Rain or snow within 24 hours in winter.
E to NE	30.10 or above, falling quickly	Rain probable within 12 to 24 hours in summer. Increasing winds with rain or snow in winter

WIND DIRECTION	BAROMETER READING (adjusted to sea level)	WEATHER FORECAST
E to N	29.80 or below, falling quickly	Severe gale from the NE in a few hours, heavy precipitation. Heavy snow followed by a cold wave in winter.
Swinging to W	29.80 or below, rising quickly	Clearing and colder

Note: To adjust local barometer readings to sea level, add .01 inch for every 10 feet of elevation above sea level. Subtract .01 inch for every 10 feet below sea level.

The Worst Weather for Plants

The worst kind of weather for plants is a prolonged drought followed by an extremely wet spell. Here's why. During a drought, shallow roots die off in the dry soil, and lower roots grow deeper into the soil to find water. A large amount of rain flooding the ground raises the water table. Deep roots sitting in the waterlogged soil "drown" (actually, they suffocate from lack of oxygen), and there are not enough shallow roots left to take over and sustain the plant.

This is why more plants are often lost when a drought ends than were lost during the drought itself.

NATURAL WEATHER PREDICTORS

INDICATORS OF GOOD WEATHER

Cumulus clouds appear to dissolve and vanish

Cumulus clouds are smaller at sundown than they were at noon

Clouds are high—the higher the clouds, the better the weather

The wind is from the west

The sky is red at sunset

Fog comes from the direction of the ocean

(continued)

Natural Weather Predictors *(cont'd)*

Fog rises

Birds fly high in the sky

INDICATORS OF BAD WEATHER

Cumulus clouds increase and ride lower in the sky toward evening

Cirrus clouds merge into cirro-stratus

Clouds travel at different heights and speeds, and in opposite directions

Clouds fly against the wind

The sky is red at sunrise

Yellow streaks are visible in the sky at sunset

Smoke descends instead of rising

Fog comes from a landward direction

Fog settles down toward the ground

The sun looks blurry or hazy, or has a halo

A ring around the moon—the larger the ring, the sooner rain will come

Stars twinkle more than usual

Flowers are especially fragrant

Trees, especially quaking aspens, cottonwoods, and sugar maples, show the undersides of their leaves

Birds fly low or do not fly at all

Birds are noisier than usual

Cows huddle in the field and turn their tails to the coming storm

Bees stay close to the hive and will not swarm

Insects bite more, and the bites itch more

Snakes are more exposed, less hidden than usual

Stone walls feel quite damp

Corns and bunions throb, joints ache

SOIL

SOIL TYPES

Soil is made up of about half solid particles (approximately 10 percent of which in a good, humusy soil is organic matter from decomposed animal and vegetable matter) about one-quarter air, and one-quarter water.

Soil Particle Sizes

Sand

Very coarse sand (or fine gravel), 1.0–2.0 millimeters in diameter

Coarse sand, .50–1.0 mm

Medium sand, .25–.50 mm

Fine sand, .10–.25 mm

Very fine sand, .05–.10 mm

Silt, .002–.05 mm

Clay, less than .002 mm

Three kinds of mineral particles are found in soils—sand, silt, and clay—according to the parent rock from which the soil formed.

Loam. The ideal soil for most plants, loam contains approximately equal amouts of sand, silt, and clay particles, along with animal and vegetable remains (known as organic matter, or humus when it is fully decomposed), water, and air.

Sandy. Sandy soil contains 35 percent or more of sand particles. Sand is the largest of the three types of mineral particles, from .05 to 2.0 millimeters in diameter. Sand particles are classified as very coarse, coarse, medium, fine, or very fine (see table above). Thus, sandy soil is light and porous. Water drains quickly through it, and leaches nutrients as it passes. Sandy soils can have difficulty retaining adequate moisture and nutrients for plants. Because sandy soils contain a lot of air, frost can under some circumstances actually form in them more quickly than in heavier soils. During a cold night the air can act as an insulator, holding the cold air in the soil after the air above ground has begun to warm in the sun.

SOIL COMPOSITION

Sandy Soils: 35% or more sand, less than 15% silt and clay

Coarse sand: 35% or more very coarse or coarse sand, less than 50% fine or very fine sand

Medium sand: 35% or more coarse sand and medium sand, less than 50% fine or very fine sand

Fine sand: 50% or more fine and very fine sand

Very fine sand: 50% or more very fine sand

Loam Soils: less than 20% clay, 30–50% silt, 30–50% sand

Sandy loam: 20–50% silt and clay

Coarse sandy loam: 45% or more very coarse sand and coarse sand

Medium sandy loam: 25% or more very coarse sand or coarse sand and medium sand, less than 35% very fine sand

Fine sandy loam: 50% or more fine sand, less than 25% very coarse or coarse sand and medium sand

Very fine sandy loam: 35% or more very fine sand

Silt loam: less than 20% clay, 50% or more silt

Clay loam: 20–30% clay

Sandy clay loam: less than 30% silt, 50–80% sand, 20–30% clay

Silty clay loam: 20–50% silt, 20–50% sand, 20–30% clay

Clay Soils: 30% or more clay, less than 50% silt, less than 50% sand

Sandy clay: 30–50% clay, less than 20% silt, 50–70% sand

Silty clay: 30–50% clay, 50–70% silt, less than 20% sand

Silty. Silty soil contains a high proportion of silt particles, which are .002 to .05 millimeters in diameter.

Clay. Clay soil contains at least 30 percent clay particles, which are the smallest of the three types of mineral particles, measuring less than .002 millimeter in diameter. Because the particles are so tiny, clay soils are dense and poorly drained. They warm up slowly in spring, delaying the start of planting. Clay soil feels sticky when it is wet; when dry, it turns crusty and can bake hard under a hot sun. Clay soils retain moisture longer than lighter soils, and they usually contain enough nutrients, but the nutrients may not be readily available to plants.

Organic Matter. As it decomposes in soil, organic matter makes certain chemicals available for roots to absorb; improves water-retention capacity, drainage, and aeration; adds nutrients; and feeds soil bacteria. These bacteria in turn release chemicals that might not otherwise be available in a form plants can use.

Adding organic matter improves the texture of both sandy and clay soils. In sandy soils, the particles of organic matter act like sponges, absorbing and retaining moisture, and giving the soil more body. In clay soils the large particles of humus open up the dense soil structure and lighten the texture, allowing excess water to drain more readily, and allowing more air to enter the soil.

pH. The character of some soils is determined largely by their pH. See the section on pH for information on highly acid and alkaline soils.

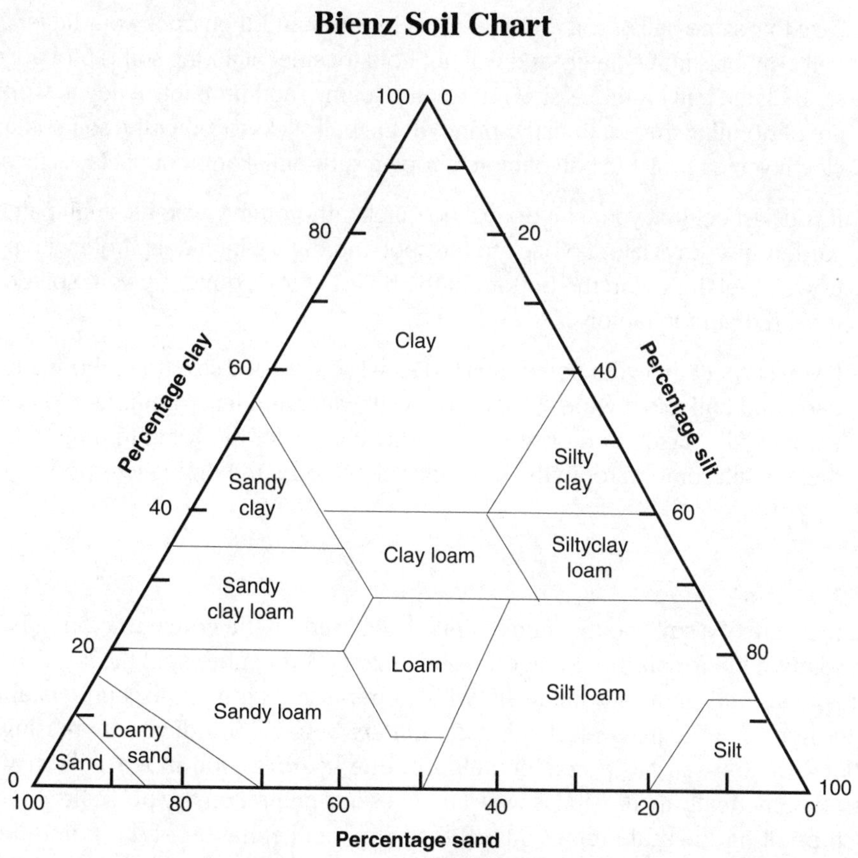

Soil texture. The texture triangle shows the relative percentages of sand, silt, and clay in each textural class. In the United States, the term loam *refers to a soil with more or less equal proportions of sand, silt, and clay. (Courtesy USDA.)*

SIMPLE TESTS TO DETERMINE SOIL TYPE

1. Put a trowelful of soil into a graduated cylinder or other glass container with straight sides. Fill the container almost to the top with water. Cover and shake the container, then watch the soil particles settle out. Stones and pebbles, obviously, will sink first. Sand particles will settle out next, then silt, and finally, clay. Very tiny clay particles may not settle at all, but remain suspended in the water. Dark particles of organic matter will either settle on top of the clay, or will float.

2. A couple of days after a good rain, scoop up a ball of soil small enough to hold in your hand and enclose with your fingers, about the size of a golf ball. Squeeze and slide the soil between your thumb and index finger to feel its texture. Sandy soil will feel gritty, silty soil will feel smooth. Clay soil will feel slippery.

3. Take that same ball of soil and squeeze it in your hand, then open your fingers. If the ball crumbles immediately and will not hold together at all, the soil is probably sandy. If the ball crumbles slowly, the soil is loamy (and probably ready to work if you are performing the test in early spring). If the ball sticks together, the soil contains clay; if you can roll the ball out into a rope, a substantial amount of clay is present.

4. If you suspect that your soil drains too quickly, thoroughly water a small patch of garden. Two days later, go back to the spot and dig a 6-inch-deep hole with a trowel. Feel the soil in the bottom of the hole; if it feels quite dry, your soil does indeed drain too rapidly.

5. If you suspect that your soil drains too slowly, dig a good-size hole, about a foot deep and half a foot wide. Fill the hole with water and let it drain. As soon as it empties, fill it again, and observe how long it takes for the water to drain off. If there is still some water in the hole after eight hours, the drainage is poor.

pH

pH is a measure of a soil's acidity or alkalinity. It is based on the concentration of hydrogen ions in solution in the soil. The higher the concentration, the more acid the soil.

pH is measured on a 14-point scale, with 7.0 representing neutral. Numbers above 7.0 indicate increasing degrees of alkalinity; numbers below 7.0 indicate increasingly acid conditions. Neutral soil has a concentration of one hydrogen ion in ten million, which is expressed numerically as 10. That is why 7.0 represents neutral on the pH scale.

Each point on the scale represents 10 times the concentration of the point preceding it. Thus, pH 8.5 is ten times as alkaline as 7.5; pH 9.5 is 100 times more acid than 7.5.

On the pH scale, a reading of 1.0 to 5.0 indicates strongly acid conditions. Most soils fall somewhere between 5.0 and 8.5, and the pH limits for any plant growth are 4.0 and 9.0. Generally speaking, parts of the country that are largely forested and receive abundant rainfall, particularly the East and Pacific Northwest, have soil with a moderately acid pH. The midwestern prairies, where rainfall is light and grasses and wildflowers provide much of the vegetation, tend to have near-neutral soil. In the arid Southwest, most soils are alkaline.

On the higher end of the scale, at pH 7.5 acid-lovers will suffer, although many shrubs and other plants will perform well. Phosphorus, manganese, and iron start to become less available.

Problematic Alkaline Soils

In parts of the western United States, there is so little rainfall, salts build up in the soil over time. A white crust (of calcium chloride or magnesium chloride) is often visible on the surface of the soil. When the pH is below 8.5, salty soil is called "saline." Salts may be present in amounts that hinder germination and create very difficult conditions for seedlings. Plants that get past the seedling stage may exhibit irregular growth rates and patterns.

Effects of pH on Soils and Plants

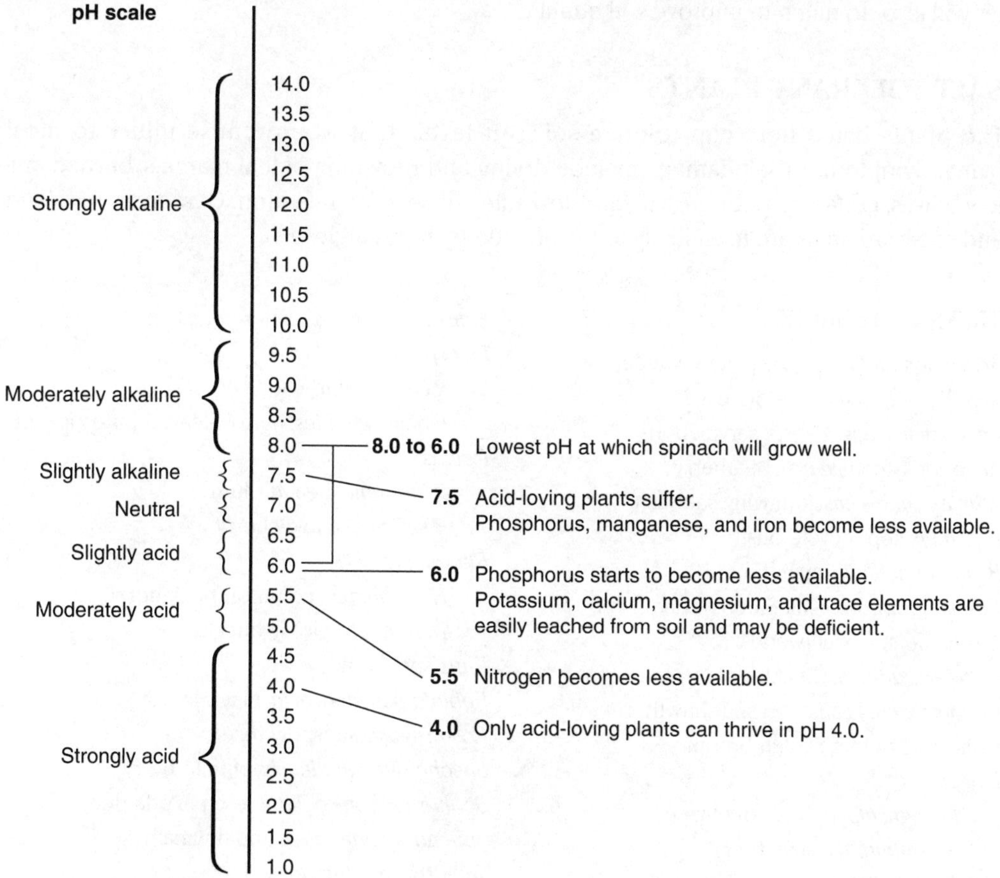

The best way to improve a saline soil is to flush it with clean water that does not contain a lot of salt. For each foot of depth you want to flush, you will need to flood the soil with 8 to 10 inches of water. If poor drainage is also a problem, it may be necessary to install drainage tiles or pipes (see page 45).

Soil with a pH above 8.5 is called "alkali." Such soils have a high sodium content. They are light-colored, likely to develop a salty surface crust, and difficult for water to penetrate. When alkali soil does get wet, it becomes sticky or slippery-looking. Plants in alkali soil may be stunted, and will exhibit burning and drying along the leaf margins that works its way in toward the center of the leaf. Flushing the salt from alkali soil is a two-step process. The first step is to release the sodium from its chemical bonds. Working gypsum into the soil serves the purpose; the magnesium in the gypsum replaces the sodium in the salt molecules. The next step is to flush the soil with water as described above for saline soil.

Gardeners working with saline and alkali soils may do best with salt-tolerant plants until the soil has been improved. Along with periodic flushing of salts, adding lots of organic matter will also do much to improve soil quality.

SALT-TOLERANT PLANTS

The plants listed here can tolerate soil salt levels that would cause injury to most plants. Symptoms of salt damage include drying and browning of leaf margins; burned, yellow leaves; generally poor growth; and low rates of seed germination. Gardeners in desert and seashore areas are most likely to be affected by high salt levels.

TREES AND SHRUBS

Acacia longifolia, Sydney golden wattle
Ailanthus altissima, tree of heaven
Amelanchier canadensis, serviceberry
Arctostaphylos uva-ursi, bearberry
Atriplex canescens, four-wing saltbush
Baccharis spp., coyote bush
Betula populifolia, gray birch
Caragana arborescens, Siberian pea shrub
Casuarina spp., beefwood
Celtis occidentalis, hackberry
Crataegus crus-galli, cockspur hawthorn
Cytisus scoparius, Scotch broom
Elaeagnus
- *E. angustifolia*, Russian olive
- *E. commutata*, silverberry
- *E. umbellata*, autumn olive

Fraxinus excelsior, European ash
Halimodendron halodendron, salt tree
Hippophae rhamnoides, sea buckthorn
Juniperus, juniper
- *J. chinensis* 'Pfitzerana', Pfitzer juniper
- *J. conferta*, shore juniper
- *J. scopulorum*, Rocky Mountain juniper
- *J. virginiana*, eastern red cedar

Koelreuteria paniculata, golden-rain tree
Leucophyllum frutescens, barometer bush
Lonicera tatarica, Tatarian honeysuckle
Maclura pomifera, Osage orange
Myoporum laetum
Myrica pensylvanica, bayberry
Pinus thunbergii, Japanese black pine
Pittosporum
- *P. crassifolium*
- *P. phillyraeoides*, narrow-leaved pittosporum

Prunus
- *P. maritima*, beach plum
- *P. serotina*, chokecherry

Rhamnus
- *R. cathartica*, common buckthorn
- *R. frangula*, glossy buckthorn

Rhus spp., sumac
Robinia pseudoacacia, black locust
Rosa rugosa, saltspray rose
Shepherdia canadensis, buffalo berry
Sophora japonica, Japanese pagoda tree
Spiraea × vanhouttei, bridal wreath
Tamarix spp., tamarisk
Thuja occidentalis, American arborvitae
Ulmus pumila, Siberian elm

GRASSES AND PERENNIALS

Agropyron, wheatgrass
- *A. elongatum*, tall wheatgrass
- *A. smithii*, western wheatgrass

Agrostis palustris, creeping bentgrass
Ammophila breviligulata, American beach grass
Artemisia stelleriana, beach wormwood
Cynodon dactylon, Bermuda grass
Distichlis stricta, salt grass
Elymus canadensis, Canada wild rye
Lathyrus japonicus, beach pea

Opuntia, spp., prickly pear
Puccinellia airoides, alkali grass
Solidago sempervirens, seaside goldenrod
Sporobolus airoides, alkali sacaton
Sedum spp., stonecrop

Altering pH

Changing soil pH to a great degree, or on a large scale, is foolhardy. It is possible, however, to raise or lower pH slightly over a limited area.

Generally speaking, you need about twice as much material to alter the pH for a loamy soil as for a sandy soil. Clay soil needs almost twice as much material as loamy soil to effect a change.

To raise the pH of a slightly acid loam one point requires about 5 pounds of lime per 100 square feet of area. Sandy soil would need less lime; clay soils, or soils with a pH below 6.0 would need more lime, to make a one-point difference.

To raise the pH of acid soil, you can use ground limestone. If your soil is deficient in magnesium, use dolomitic lime; otherwise, use calcitic lime. To raise the pH by one point, add ground limestone in the following amounts:

very sandy soils:	3 to 5½ pounds per 100 square feet
sandy loam:	5 to 7 pounds per 100 square feet
loam:	7 to 10 pounds per 100 square feet
clay soils:	7 to 8 pounds per 100 square feet

It takes six months to a year for limestone to effect the pH change. Wood ashes also raise soil pH—about half as much as lime—and they also add potassium to the soil.

To lower soil pH, use powdered sulfur or peat moss. The pH of sulfur is about 1.2, and peat moss is 4.0, so a greater quantity of peat is needed to make a change.

To lower pH by one point, add 1 to 2 pounds ground sulfur or 1 pound Dispsersul (a blend of elemental sulfur and bentonite clay) per 100 square feet, in any type of soil.

PLANTS FOR ACID SOIL

The following plants all grow well in acid soil. The number indicates the lowest pH in which the plant can be expected to thrive.

Abies spp., fir, 5.0
Aletris farinosa, whitetube star grass, 4.0
Alnus incana, white alder, 4.0
Amelanchier canadensis, serviceberry, 5.0
Androsace spp., 4.0
Anemone nemorosa, European wood anemone, 4.0
Arctostaphylos uva-ursi, bearberry, 4.0
Arethusa bulbosa, 4.0
Arnica montana, mountain arnica, 4.0
Calla palustris, water arum, 4.0
Calluna spp., heather, 5.0
Calopogon pulchellus, 4.0
Camellia spp., 4.0–4.5

(continued)

Plants for Acid Soil *(cont'd)*

Ceanothus americanus, New Jersey tea, 4.5
Chelone spp., turtlehead, 5.0
Chionanthus virginicus, white fringe tree, 5.0
Cimicifuga spp., snakeroot, 5.0
Clethra alnifolia, sweet pepperbush, 4.0–4.5
Clintonia borealis, yellow bead-lily, 4.0
Coptis trifolia, Alaska trifolia, 4.0
Corema conradii, broom crowberry, 4.0
Cornus canadensis, bunchberry, 4.0
Cypripedium spp., lady's slipper, 4.0
Darlingtonia californica, California pitcher plant, 4.0
Dicentra eximia, fringed bleeding heart, 5.0
Dionaea muscipula, Venus's-flytrap, 4.0
Drosera spp., sundew, 4.0
Empetrum nigrum, black crowberry, 4.0
Epigaea repens, trailing arbutus, 4.0
Erica spp., heath, 4.5
Gardenia spp., 4.0–5.0
Gaultheria procumbens, wintergreen, 5.0
Gelsemium sempervirens, Carolina jessamine, 5.0
Habenaria spp., 4.0–5.0
Halesia carolina, Carolina silverbell, 5.0
Helonias bullata, swamp pink, 4.0–5.0
Heuchera americana, American alumroot, 4.0–5.0
Hydrangea macrophylla, 5.0
Ilex, holly
- *I. aquifolium*, English holly, 4.0
- *I. crenata*, Japanese holly, 5.0
- *I. glabra*, inkberry, 4.0
- *I. opaca*, American holly, 5.0
- *I. verticillata*, winterberry, 5.0

Juniperus communis, common juniper, 5.0
Kalmia spp., mountain laurel, 4.0–4.5
Lagerstroemia indica, crape myrtle, 5.0
Ledum groenlandicum, Labrador tea, 4.0
Leiophyllum buxifolium, box sand myrtle
Leucothoe spp., 5.0
Lindera benzoin, spicebush, 5.0
Linnaea borealis, twinflower, 4.0
Lithodora diffusa, 4.0
Loiseleuria procumbens, alpine azalea, 4.0
Lygodium palmatum, Hartford fern, 4.0
Lyonia ligustrina, maleberry, 4.5
Magnolia virginiana, sweet bay magnolia, 4.0
Magnolia, other species, 5.0
Menziesia pilosa, Allegheny menziesia, 4.0
Myrica spp., bayberry, 5.0
Pachysandra terminalis, 4.5
Phyllodoce spp., mountain heather, 4.0
Pieris spp., 5.0
Pinus, pine
- *P. mugo*, mugo pine, 4.5
- *P. palustris*, southern yellow pine, 4.5
- *P. strobus*, eastern white pine, 4.5
- *P. sylvestris*, Scotch pine, 5.0
- *P. taeda*, loblolly pine, 5.0

Polygala paucifolia, fringed milkwort, 4.0
Polypodium aureum, golden polypody, 4.0
Potato, 5.0
Potentilla tridentata, three-toothed cinquefoil, 4.0
Quercus, oak
- *Q. alba*, white oak, 5.0
- *Q. palustris*, pin oak, 5.0
- *Q. phellos*, willow oak, 5.0
- *Q. rubra*, red oak, 4.5
- *Q. virginiana*, live oak, 5.0

Rhexia spp., meadow beauty, 4.0–5.0
Rhododendron spp., 4.0–4.5
Sarracenia spp., pitcher plant, 4.0
Sorbus americana, American mountain ash, 4.0–4.5
Styrax spp., snowbell, 5.0
Vaccinium spp., blueberry, cranberry, 4.0–5.0
Viburnum acerifolium, maple-leaf viburnum, 4.0
Xerophyllum spp., turkey beard, 4.0
Zantedeschia spp., calla lily, 4.0
Zenobia pulverulenta, dusty zenobia, 5.0

PLANTS INDICATIVE OF SOIL TYPE

Wild plants can provide clues to soil type and quality. Spotting one of the plants listed below is not necessarily an indication of a particular soil condition, but where you see several of the plants in one category colonizing an area, you can use them as a guide.

WET, POORLY DRAINED SOIL

Acer rubrum, red maple
Carex spp., sedges
Equisetum arvense, horsetail
Eupatorium purpureum, Joe-pye weed
Lychnis flos-cuculi, meadow pink
Mosses
Podophyllum peltatum, mayapple
Polygonum persicaria, lady's thumb, spotted knotweed
Potentilla argentea, silvery cinquefoil
Prunella
Quercus palustris, pin oak
Rumex acetosella, sheep sorrel
Rumex crispus, curly dock
Solidago canadensis, Canada goldenrod
Spotted spurge
Swamp oak

HEAVY SOIL

Plantago major, plantain
Ranunculus repens, creeping buttercup
Rumex obtusifolius, broad-leaved dock
Taraxacum officinale, dandelion

HARDPAN

Agropyron repens, quack grass
Brassica nigra, wild mustard
Matricaria suaveolens, pineapple weed
Solanum carolinense, horse nettle
Thlaspi arvense, pennycress

SANDY

Centaurea cyanus, bachelor's button
Centaurea melitensis, Maltese thistle
Lactuca pulchella, arrow-leaved wild lettuce
Linaria vulgaris, yellow toadflax
Lychnis alba, white campion
Sheep sorrel

ACID

Cresses
Dandelion
Fragaria vesca, wild strawberry
Hieracium aurantiacum, *H. pratense*, hawkweed, very acid
Kalmia latifolia, mountain laurel
Lady's thumb, spotted knotweed
Leucanthemum vulgare, ox-eye daisy
Mosses
Plantain
Polygonum aviculare, prostrate knotweed
Potentilla monspeliensis, rough cinquefoil
Quercus ilicifolia, scrub oak
Red cedar
Rumex acetosella, red sorrel
Rumex spp., dock
Silvery cinquefoil, very acid
Sonchus arvensis, sow thistle
Tsuga spp., hemlock
Vaccinium, wild blueberry
White birch
White cedar

ALKALINE

Anthemis nobilis, chamomile
Chenopodium spp., goosefoot
Chickweed
Daucus carota var. *carota*, Queen Anne's lace and *Cichorium intybus*, chicory in combination
Lepidium virginicum, field peppergrass

(continued)

Plants Indicative of Soil Type *(cont'd)*

Silene latifolia, bladder campion
Spotted spurge

WELL-DRAINED, HUMUSY
Amaranthus retroflexus, pigweed
Arctium lappa, burdock
Chenopodium album, lamb's-quarter
Chicory
Dandelion
Portulaca oleracea, purslane

SOIL THAT WAS ONCE CULTIVATED
Lamb's-quarter
Plantain
Purslane

POOR QUALITY SOIL
Andropogon virginicus, broomsedge
Anthemis cotula, dog fennel
Red sorrel
Sheep sorrel
Yellow toadflax

TESTING SOIL

Types of Soil Tests

The best results come from reputable private laboratories or from the USDA labs. Private services are more expensive, but some provide a more detailed analysis than the USDA labs. Consult the Laboratories listings in the yellow pages of your telephone directory to find a soil-testing laboratory in your area.

Plants That Indicate Minerals

Some plants can indicate the presence of mineral deposits. Old-time prospectors in various parts of the world used indicator plants to show them where to dig for ores.

Prospectors in nineteenth-century Australia referred to one member of the Pink family, *Polycarpea spirostylis*, as copper plant, because they found copper deposits where the plant was plentiful.

Violets (*Viola calaminaria*) indicate the presence of zinc in Germany.

In Italy, a species of alyssum (*Alyssum bertolonii*) is associated with nickel.

German catchfly (*Lychnis viscaria*) grows in copper-rich ground in Norway.

Here in the United States, a type of moss (*Merceya latifolia*) grows near copper deposits in Montana. Milk vetch (*Astragalus thompsonae*) in Utah indicates selenium and uranium. A different species (*A. pattersoni*) indicates the same minerals in Colorado. An aster (*Aster venustus*) also provides a clue to selenium in various parts of the West. A species of false indigo (*Amorpha canescens*), also known as lead plant, grows in soil containing lead. And rue (*Ruta graveolens*) is a good indicator of zinc.

Information Supplied by USDA Soil Tests

A USDA soil analysis provides measurements of the following levels, along with instructions on what materials and how much to apply to bring the soil to acceptable levels.

pH	iron
phosphorus	manganese
potassium	zinc
calcium	organic matter
magnesium	soluble salts
aluminum	

Test kits sold at garden centers use color charts that indicate levels of pH and the three major nutrients on a simple scale. pH readings may be simply alkaline, neutral, acid, and very acid. Nutrient levels are often listed as high, medium, low, and very low. These readings are approximate at best, and useful primarily as a general indication of soil quality.

The more expensive home test kits are usually more reliable, but they are not cheap, and you must buy new chemicals every year.

If you have several gardens in different locations on your property, such as a woodland garden, a bog garden in a low, wet spot, and an open, sunny flower or vegetable garden, test the soil in one garden at a time. Each kind of garden environment will probably have different needs for soil amendments. Established gardens should be tested every five years or so.

Where to Get Soil Tested

Following are addresses for the USDA soil testing laboratories in the United States:

ALABAMA
Soil Testing Laboratory
Auburn University
118 Funchess Hall
Auburn, AL 36849

ALASKA
Soil Testing Laboratory
Agricultural Experiment Station
University of Alaska
533 E. Fireweed
Palmer, AK 99645

ARIZONA
No soil testing is offered by a public agency.

ARKANSAS
Altheimer/Soil Testing Laboratory
University of Arkansas
276 Altheimer Drive
Fayetteville, AR 72703

CALIFORNIA
No soil testing service is offered by a public agency.

COLORADO
Colorado State University Soil Testing Laboratory
Room 6/Vocational Education Building
Fort Collins, CO 80523

CONNECTICUT
Soil Testing
2019 Hillside Road
University of Connecticut
Storrs, CT 06269

DELAWARE
Plant and Soil Sciences
149 Townsend Hall
Newark, DE 19717-1303
Attn: Soil Testing Laboratory

FLORIDA
Soil Testing Laboratory
University of Florida
Box 110740
Gainesville, FL 32611-0740

(continued)

Where to Get Soil Tested *(cont'd)*

GEORGIA

Soil Testing and Plant Analysis Laboratory
University of Georgia
2400 College Station Road
Athens, GA 30602-9105

HAWAII

Agricultural Diagnostic Service Center
University of Hawaii
1910 East-West Road
Sherman Laboratory/Room 134
Honolulu, HI 96822

IDAHO

Holm Research Center
West 6th Street Extension
University of Idaho
Moscow, ID 83844-2201

ILLINOIS

No soil testing service is offered by a public agency.

INDIANA

Plant and Pest Diagnostic Laboratory
Purdue University
1155 LSPS
West Lafayette, IN 47907-1155
Note: Only tests greenhouse soil.

IOWA

Soil Testing Laboratory
G501 Agronomy Hall
Iowa State University
Ames, IA 50011

KANSAS

Soil Testing Laboratory
Throckmorton Hall
Kansas State University
Manhattan, KS 66506

KENTUCKY

Soil Testing Laboratory
Regulatory Services Building
Lexington, KY 40546-0275

LOUISIANA

Soil Testing Laboratory
125 Sturgis Hall
Louisiana State University
Baton Rouge, LA 70803

MAINE

Soil Testing Laboratory
5722 Deering Hall
University of Maine
Orono, ME 04469-5722

MARYLAND

Soil Testing Laboratory
Agronomy Department
University of Maryland
College Park, MD 20742

MASSACHUSETTS

Soil Testing Laboratory
West Experiment Station
University of Massachusetts/Box 38020
Amherst, MA 01003-8020

MICHIGAN

Crop and Soil Science
Plant and Soil Science Building
Michigan State University
East Lansing, MI 48824

MINNESOTA

University of Minnesota Soil Testing Laboratory
1903 Hendon Avenue
St. Paul, MN 55108

MISSISSIPPI

Soil Testing Laboratory
Box 9610
Mississippi State, MS 39762

MISSOURI

Soil Testing Laboratory
144 Mumford Hall
University of Missouri
Columbia, MO 65211

MONTANA

Soil Testing Laboratory
Plant and Soil Science Department
Montana State University
Bozeman, MT 59717

NEBRASKA

Soil and Plant Analytical Laboratory
Room 139 KEIM
University of Nebraska
Lincoln, NB 68583-0916

NEVADA

Washoe County Extension Office
P.O. Box 1130
Reno, NV 89520

NEW HAMPSHIRE

Analytical Services Laboratory
Nesmith Hall
University of New Hampshire
Durham, NH 03824

NEW JERSEY

Rutgers Soil Testing Laboratory
P.O. Box 902
Milltown, NJ 08850

NEW MEXICO

Soil and Water Testing Laboratory
Box 30003/Department 32
Gerald Thomas Building/Room 269
New Mexico State University
Las Cruces, NM 88003

NEW YORK

Soil Testing Laboratory
Department of Soil, Crop, and Atmospheric Sciences
804 Bradfield Hall
Cornell University
Ithaca, NY 14853

NORTH CAROLINA

Soil Testing Laboratory
Agronomic Division
North Carolina Department of Agriculture
2109 Blueridge Road
Raleigh, NC 27607

NORTH DAKOTA

Soil Testing Laboratory
Waldron Hall
P. O. Box 5575
North Dakota State University
Fargo, ND 58105

OHIO

OARDC-REAL
1680 Madison Avenue
Ohio State University
Wooster, OH 44691

OKLAHOMA

Soil Testing Laboratory
048 North AG Hall
Oklahoma State University
Stillwater, OK 74078-0507

OREGON

Central Analytical Laboratory
3079 AG and Life Sciences Building
Corvallis, OR 97331-7306

PENNSYLVANIA

Agricultural Analytical Service Laboratory
Pennsylvania State University
University Park, PA 16802

RHODE ISLAND

Refer to Massachusetts reference.

SOUTH CAROLINA

Agricultural Service Laboratory
Cherry Road
Clemson University
Clemson, SC 29634

SOUTH DAKOTA

Soil Testing Laboratory
South Dakota State University-Plant Science Department
Box 2207-A
AG Hall 07
Brookings, SD 57007-1096

TENNESSEE

Soil Testing Laboratory
University of Tennessee
P.O. Box 1071
Knoxville, TN 37901

TEXAS

Soil Testing Laboratory
Heep Center/Room 345
Texas A & M University
College Station, TX 77843-2474

UTAH

Soil Testing Laboratory
Utah State University
Logan, UT 84322-4803

VERMONT

Agricultural Testing Laboratory
Hills Building
University of Vermont
Burlington, VT 05405

VIRGINIA

Virginia Tech. Soil Testing Laboratory
145 Smyth Hall
P.O. Box 10664
Blacksburg, VA 24062-0664

WASHINGTON

No soil testing service is offered by a public agency.

WEST VIRGINIA

Soil Testing Laboratory
West Virginia University
P.O. Box 6108
Morgantown, WV 26506

WISCONSIN

Soil and Plant Analysis Laboratory
University of Wisconsin
5711 Mineral Point Road
Madison, WI 53705

WYOMING

Soil Testing Laboratory
Plant, Soil and Insect Sciences
University of Wyoming
P.O. Box 3354
Laramie, WY 82071-3354

How to Take Soil Samples for Testing

The best time to collect soil samples for testing is in midsummer, at the height of the growing season. In spring, cold soil will not yet be fully biologically active. By fall the soil may be exhausted from the summer's growth.

You will need a bucket, trowel, and shovel to collect your samples. The bucket needs to be clean.

Take samples from at least five different places in a small garden, or 10 to 20 places in a large garden. One way to get a good cross-section of the garden is to take the first sample in one corner and work your way diagonally across the garden.

To take a sample, dig a hole 6 to 8 inches deep. Then use the trowel to cut a thin vertical slice, about an inch thick, from one side of the hole. Cut a 1- to 2-inch piece from the middle of the soil slice and put it in the bucket. Toss the ends of the soil slice back into the garden. Put all the samples into the bucket and mix them together.

The USDA likes to have about a pint of soil for each test. Some other laboratories request a cupful.

Pack the sample in a plastic bag or box as directed by the lab. You will also be asked to supply information on what sorts of plants you are growing or would like to grow in the garden you are testing. The lab will also probably want to know when you last added compost, fertilizers, or other soil amendments and what you added.

Review the tips below before collecting your samples, and keep them in mind.

BEFORE YOU TAKE SOIL SAMPLES:

- Make sure the bucket, trowel, and shovel are very clean.
- Do not take samples soon after you have fertilized or amended the soil. Wait several months after applying lime or rock powders; wait four weeks after using fertilizers.
- Do not take samples right after a heavy rain. Biological activity in soil increases after rain and can skew the test results. Wait a few days before collecting your samples.
- If you smoke, do not smoke while collecting soil samples. Ash dropping into the samples could substantially change the test results.

THE 16 ELEMENTS NECESSARY FOR PLANTS

The elements listed below are all essential for plant growth. On the right are the sources from which plants receive these nutrients.

Carbon (C)
Hydrogen (H) } from air and water
Oxygen (O)
Nitrogen (N) from air and soil
Phosphorus (P)
Potassium (K)
Calcium (Ca)
Magnesium (Mg)
Sulfur (S)
Boron (B)
Chlorine (Cl) } from soil (and fertilizers)
Copper (Cu)
Iron (Fe)
Manganese (Mn)
Molybdenum (Mo)
Zinc (Zn)

Plants also contain cobalt, iodine, selenium, and sodium, which are necessary to people (who consume the plants), but which have not to date been proven to be essential for plants. Aluminum and silicon, also present in plants, are not deemed necessary either for plants or the people who eat them.

The elements obtained from soil and fertilizers are grouped into three categories:

- Major nutrients—nitrogen (N), phosphorus (P), and potassium (K)
- Secondary nutrients—calcium (Ca), magnesium (Mg), and sulfur (S)
- Micronutrients or trace elements—boron (B), chlorine (Cl), copper (Cu), iron (Fe), manganese (Mn), molybdenum (Mo), and zinc (Zn).

WHAT NUTRIENTS DO

Major Nutrients

Nitrogen: Needed for strong, vigorous growth, good leaf color, photosynthesis.

Phosphorus: Root growth, ripening of seeds and fruit.

Potassium: Helps in fruit formation, photosynthesis, uptake of other nutrients. Works along with nitrogen. If you add nitrogen to soil, it's wise to add potassium at the same time.

Secondary Nutrients

Calcium: Needed for good growth, especially when plants are young. Helps to build cell walls.

(continued)

Secondary Nutrients *(cont'd)*

Magnesium: Contained in chlorophyll. Needed for photosynthesis, and germination of seeds.

Sulfur: Needed to manufacture chlorophyll.

Trace Elements

Boron: Helps in cell development, helps regulate plant metabolism.

Chlorine: Involved in photosynthesis.

Copper: Helps plants to metabolize nitrogen.

Iron: Assists in the manufacture of chlorophyll, and other biochemical processes.

Manganese: Needed for chlorophyll production.

Molybdenum: Helps plants use nitrogen.

Zinc: Used in development of enzymes and hormones. Needed by leaves. Legumes need it to form seeds.

SYMPTOMS OF NUTRIENT DEFICIENCIES

The deficiency symptoms that show up in plants are confusing and difficult for amateurs to diagnose. However, if the symptoms described below start to appear on your plants, a soil test is in order.

Nitrogen: Lower leaves turn yellow or bluish. Leaves are small. Plant is pale green color, growth is stunted. Stems are thin. Leaves begin to drop, with oldest leaves falling first.

Phosphorus: Stunted growth, thin shoots. Leaves and stems are very small, purple, red or very dark green. Flowering and fruit development are poor. Roots are stunted.

Potassium: Fruit has poor color and flavor. Leaf tips and edges turn yellow, then brown and scorched-looking. Leaves are spotted and curled. Stems are weak.

Calcium: Plants are generally weak. Growing tip, buds, and young leaves may die back. Young leaves may turn yellow.

Magnesium: Leaves turn yellow (chlorotic) between veins, and brownish to purplish patches may develop. Leaves may drop. Growth is stunted.

Sulfur: Leaves, especially young ones, are pale green or yellowish. Growth is poor.

Boron: Young leaves are twisted, thickened, pale green near base. Buds die. Foliage may develop yellow spots.

Copper: Shoots die back. Young leaves turn pale, sometimes mottled white, and wilt; tips brown, leaves develop brown spots. Plants become pale and yellowish. Leaves may not grow.

Iron: Leaves develop chlorosis, turning yellow or very pale between veins. Growth is weak and stunted.

Manganese: Leaves turn yellow and pale between veins, may develop brown spots.

Molybdenum: Leaves turn yellow and pale between veins, or may become bluish green. Overall growth is stunted, leaves do not open completely.

Zinc: Deficiency leads to iron deficiency, which it resembles. Also, leaves are thickened and malformed, small and narrow. Growth is stunted.

PLANT FOODS AND FERTILIZERS

ORGANIC FERTILIZERS

Organic fertilizers are generally agreed among gardeners to mean materials derived from rocks or living things that are put into garden soil in a more or less natural form. These materials break down slowly in the soil to release nutrients in a form plants can use. Microorganisms in the soil convert the organic compounds into soluble forms that roots can absorb. The rate of release is fastest in summer, when the soil is warm and microorganisms are most active.

The drawbacks to organic fertilizers are that their nutrients are not immediately available to plants, they are needed in substantial quantities, and they are not always easily available, although this has been changing with increasing demand from gardeners.

Traditionally, organic materials were added to the soil one at a time, as gardeners tilled animal manures, rock powders, and other materials into the soil. Now, organic fertilizers are also available in pre-blended formulas, in granular or powdered form. These fertilizers are convenient to use, and all-purpose formulas can supply balanced nutrition for the garden. It is important, however, to read fertilizer labels carefully, to be sure the product is really made from organic materials.

In the scientific world, the term "organic" refers to any carbon-containing compound—a very different meaning from the one gardeners assign to the word. And there is no national legal definition of what constituts an organic product. Manufacturers have broad discretion in how they use the term. Organic fertilizers are mild and release their nutrients slowly. Be wary of a fertilizer labeled organic that has an N–P–K ratio adding up to more than 15. If the label does not list ingredients like those in the table of "Organic Nutrient Sources" (see page 38) it is probably not truly organic.

In addition to dry organic fertilitzers, there are also liquid products. Gardeners can purchase concentrates of fish and seaweed products to dilute with water for foliar or root feeding. There are also two time-honored homemade liquid fertilizers—manure "tea" and compost "tea."

SYNTHETIC OR CHEMICAL FERTILIZERS

So-called chemical fertilizers are synthesized from coal, natural gas, or petroleum products or are derived from minerals treated with chemicals to make them more soluble. These fertilizers are in a form that is readily available to plant roots and, unless in a timed-release formulation, can be absorbed as soon as they reach the root zone. Chemical fertilizers are generally far more concentrated than organic materials.

When using synthetic fertilizers, the aim is to supply the immediate nutritional needs of plants as they grow, rather than enhancing the overall health of the soil.

The drawbacks to chemical fertilizers are that they are largely made from nonrenewable resources, some of them can burn plants when allowed to come in direct contact, and their long-term exclusive use can allow soil structure to deteriorate. Overuse of chemical fertilizers allows the excess runoff to cause water pollution.

Synthetic fertilizers are available in dry or granular form, to be worked into the soil near plants, or as granular or liquid concentrates to be diluted with water and used for foliar or root feeding. They are especially convenient for plants growing in containers.

It is important when using any fertilizers, particularly the concentrated synthetic kind, to follow explicitly package directions regarding amount and frequency of application. Overfertilizing causes fast but weak growth of tissue that is very susceptible to damage from pests and diseases.

ORGANIC NUTRIENT SOURCES

NITROGEN SOURCES

Blood meal, dried blood

Coffee grounds (also contain very small amounts of phosphorus and potassium)

Cottonseed meal (also contains small amount of phosphorus and even smaller amount of potassium)

Fish emulsion, fish meal (also contain phosphorus and potassium, in smaller amounts)

Soybean meal (also contains small amount of potassium, and even smaller amount of phosphorus)

PHOSPHORUS SOURCES

Colloidal phosphate

Rock phosphate (contains slightly more phosphorus than colloidal phosphate, but breaks down more slowly)

POTASSIUM SOURCES

Granite dust, granite meal (also contain trace elements)

Greensand (also contains trace elements)

Kelp meal (also contains small amount of nitrogen, smaller amount of phosphorus, and trace elements)

Wood ashes (also contain some phosphorus. Raises soil pH.)

SOURCES OF OTHER ELEMENTS

Boron: borax

Calcium: eggshells, calcitic limestone, dolomitic limestone, gypsum

Magnesium: dolomitic limestone, Epsom salts

What About Bone Meal?

Bone meal has long been a favorite source of phosphorus (and small amounts of nitrogen) among organic gardeners, routinely recommended for bulbs and perennial gardens. But the bone meal marketed today is heavily processed, and much of its nutritional value has been removed. Although bone meal is still widely available, and it certainly is not harmful to plants, many gardeners now have doubts about its efficacy as a fertilizer. You must decide for yourself whether or not to use it in your garden.

ABOUT LIQUID FERTILIZERS

Liquid fertilizers are granules, powders, or liquid concentrates that are dissolved in or diluted with water for use. Liquid fertilizers, whether synthetic or organic, can be sprayed directly onto foliage (this procedure is called foliar feeding), or poured onto the soil around the base of a plant to feed the roots.

In mild form, diluted to one-half or one-quarter the usual strength, liquid fertilizers are a good way to feed young seedlings, especially those growing in soilless potting media.

Synthetic water-soluble plant foods are available in many different formulas, some for all-purpose use and others for particular kinds of plants such as orchids and African violets.

Organic liquid fertilizers include fish emulsions, seaweed concentrates and, as gentle growth enhancers, compost or manure tea.

Manure Teas

These liquids are better regarded as growth enhancers rather than fertilizers.

To make the tea, put a shovelful or two of manure or compost into a burlap bag. Tie the bag shut, and submerge it in a tub of water. Let the bag "steep" for up to a week, until the water turns a dark brown color. Remove the "tea bag" and spread the contents over the garden. Use full strength, or dilute the "tea" until it becomes a light brown color like weak tea.

Water plants with the tea, using about a pint per plant for annuals, perennials, and vegetables, and 1 to 2 quarts for trees and shrubs.

FERTILIZER FORMULAS

The numbers on a bag of fertilizer indicate the percentage composition of the three major nutrients, nitrogen, phosphorus, and potassium. They are always given in the same order: the first number represents nitrogen content, the second number indicates phosphorus, and the third number is the potassium content.

Packaged fertilizers contain nutrient sources and inert filler material. The nutrient sources by themselves would be much too strong for plants.

All-Purpose Fertilizers

All-purpose fertilizers, which contain relatively balanced amounts of the three major nutrients, N, P, and K, are effective for a wide variety of plants. Plants still need all of them in order to grow well. All-purpose synthetic fertilizers include 5–5–5, 5–10–5, 10–10–10, 14–14–14, and 20–20–20. Gardeners who concentrate on a particular type of plant, or who maintain more than one kind of garden, may wish to get more specialized in their choice of fertilizers.

For flowering plants (both herbaceous and woody kinds), bulbs, fruits, root crops, and vegetables that bear their crop in the form of fruits (such as beans, peas, tomatoes, squash, and peppers), you can use a formula that contains more phosphorus, or more phosphorus and potassium than nitrogen. Examples would be an 8–12–4 formula, or 15–30–15. A 5–10–5 formula is also good for flowers. Or use organic nutrient sources such as rock phosphate.

Leafy plants—lawns, foliage ornamentals such as coleus and hostas, and salad greens—benefit from a high-nitrogen fertilizer, such as 12–2–3, or an organic fertilizer such as composted manure, bat guano, or bone meal.

Acid-loving plants such as azaleas (see the section on pH for a list of plants that need acid soil) need specially formulated fertilizers that supply the necessary nutrients in a form their roots can readily absorb.

APPLYING FERTILIZERS

Dry fertilizers can be applied in several ways. Fertilize when plant leaves are dry, so no fertilizer will stick to the foliage and cause burning. Always follow package directions carefully when applying fertilizers.

Broadcasting. This is the easiest way to apply dry fertilizers. Simply scatter the fertilizer evenly over the soil surface and water it in.

Side-dressing. For plants growing in rows, typically in vegetable gardens, spread a band of fertilizer along either side of the row, scratch it lightly into the soil, then water it in.

Individual plants. To feed individual plants, sprinkle fertilizer in a ring around the plant, scratch it in lightly, then water well.

Trees. To get fertilizer down to the root zone, punch several holes in the soil, 8 to 10 inches deep, with a crowbar or soil auger. Make the holes about 2 feet apart, in a circle midway between the truck and the dripline. Pour 1/4 to 1/2 cup of fertilizer into each hole (follow package directions) and fill with soil, or pack each hole with compost. Water well.

There are also a couple of different ways to apply liquid fertilizers, when you have mixed the fertilizers as directed on the package.

Foliar feeding. To foliar-feed, spray the liquid directly onto leaves, continuing until the foliage is dripping wet. To make sure the solution goes on evenly and sticks to the leaves, it is helpful to add a small amount of surfactant, such as a mild liquid soap, to the fertilizer. Apply foliar feeds on a dry, calm day, when rain is not likely.

Root feeding. To root-feed, simply apply the fertilizer solution to the soil at the base of each plant.

COMPOST

Composting is a process by which the gardener assists the natural process by which plant and animal wastes decay and return organic matter and nutrients to the soil. Compost is the gardener's "black gold," the best soil conditioner there is. Compost improves soil texture, fertility, drainage, and moisture retention. Compost is considered a soil conditioner rather than a fertilizer, but plants growing in the kind of fertile soil, rich in organic matter, that regular additions of compost create often need no additional fertilizer.

Use compost throughout the garden, for all kinds of plants. Spread a layer of it over the entire garden, as deep as the amount of compost you have available (the more the better) and till it into the soil. Do this in fall at the end of the growing season, each year. Or use compost to mulch plants, and dig or till it in fall.

Finished compost is dark brown and crumbly.

In the compost pile, microorganisms break down the materials into humus. They need carbon and nitrogen in the right proportions in order to do their work. If too much nitrogen is present, the excess escapes into the air as ammonia; it smells bad, and whatever nitrogen goes into the air is lost to the garden. If the compost pile contains too much carbon, the decomposition process is slowed down, and the nitrogen in the pile becomes depleted.

To achieve a good balance of carbon and nitrogen, build the compost pile from alternating layers of wet (green) materials, such as vegetable peelings and green plant debris, and dry materials such as shredded leaves and dry weeds.

To provide the greatest range of nutrients for plants, make your compost from a variety of materials. You can also add rock powders and bone meal to the compost pile to enrich the finished product.

What Not to Use in Compost

Diseased or pest-infested plant matter

Fats and oils

Fruit pits and seeds (attract scavengers)

Human and pet wastes

Meat scraps and bones

Plant debris treated with herbicides or pesticides

Making Compost

You can make compost in a pile on the ground, or in a container. Homemade bins and pens of wood, concrete blocks, bricks, wire mesh, or hardware cloth panels framed in wood work fine, as do compost bins made of heavy-duty plastic, or wire pens, or barrel-shaped tumblers, which eliminate the need to turn the pile.

A compost pile should be at least 3 feet square and 3 feet high. You can make the pile as long as you wish, but do not build it higher than 5 feet or the materials will pack down and won't get enough oxygen to decompose quickly. The pile will also be practically impossible to turn.

For the decomposition process to work best, a compost pile needs to be constantly moist, but not soggy, and good air circulation is essential. A layer of gravel under the pile can improve drainage, if necessary. To provide air circulation, put down a layer of brush and build the pile on top of it. If the pile dries out, add water until it is as damp as a squeezed-out sponge.

Here are two reliable methods for making compost.

Fast, Hot Compost

This method produces finished compost quickly, but requires more work than the slower method. The heat in the pile will kill some weed seeds and pathogens, but not necessarily all of them. It will also destroy some beneficial microorganisms that protect plants from pathogens.

To make hot compost you will need two enclosures 3 feet square and 3 to 4 feet high.

Spread a 2- to 4-inch layer of green or wet material in the bottom of one container, then add a 2- to 4-inch layer of dry material. Spray with water to moisten. Repeat the layers until the container is full, and cover the top with a tarp. Remove the tarp and turn the pile every day, or at least every two days. Use a pitchfork to transfer the contents of the pile from the full bin to the empty one, moving the material from the outer edges of the pile into the center. If the material seems dry, moisten it with water from a hose or sprinkling can.

If you turn the pile daily, the compost should be ready for use in two weeks. If you turn it less often, the compost will be finished in a month.

Slower Compost

Put down a layer of brush as a base for the pile. Then lay down 6 inches of plant matter, green or dry. Follow with 2 inches of fresh manure, blood meal, or cottonseed meal. Then cover with a $^1/_8$-inch layer of soil. Repeat the layers until the pile is 3 to 5 feet tall. Sprinkle each layer with water as you construct the pile. You can insert a few metal pipes into the finished pile for additional aeration. Cover the pile with a tarp.

After two to three weeks, turn the pile, moving material from the outer edges toward the center. Two to three weeks later, turn the pile again.

The compost should be ready to use in three months.

SOIL MAINTENANCE TIMETABLE

SPRING

- Remove winter mulches and add to compost pile.
- Clean up any garden debris; remove rocks brought to soil surface over winter and large clods of soil.
- Till green manures over cover crops into soil at least three weeks before planting.
- Test soil pH if you added lime or acid materials last fall.
- Apply compost and fertilizers. Organic gardeners can apply nitrogen and potassium fertilizers particularly, if needed.
- Till compost and fertilizers into soil, level and rake smooth to prepare for planting.

SUMMER

- Mulch plants when several inches high, to conserve soil moisture. If pests become a problem in the garden, remove mulch if pests (such as slugs and earwigs) are hiding in it. If grubs and cutworms are hiding in soil, dig up and destroy them, or apply insecticidal soil drench.
- Check soil moisture during dry weather and water when necessary. Test soil if it's been several years since last test.

AUTUMN

- Clean up garden, remove spent plants and debris.
- Plant winter cover crop if desired.
- Test soil in early fall if not done in summer.
- Apply compost, lime if needed, and organic fertilizer, particularly phosphorus sources.
- Prepare soil for new gardens: remove sod, dig or double-dig (see page 44); northern gardeners should leave surface rough over winter.
- When ground freezes, mulch perennials to prevent frost heaving.

WINTER

- Check winter mulches to be sure they don't blow away; replace if necessary.
- In late winter, desert gardeners with salty soil must flush soil with fresh water to leach salts before planting.
- Apply gypsum to sodic (highly alkaline) soils.

HOW TO TELL WHEN SOIL IS READY TO WORK

In spring, when the soil in the garden has thawed, scoop up a handful of soil and squeeze it into a ball, then open your fingers. If the ball of soil stays tightly stuck together, the soil is still too wet to work. Digging now could cause compaction. But if the ball of soil crumbles apart when you open your hand, the soil is dry enough to till and plant.

Double Digging

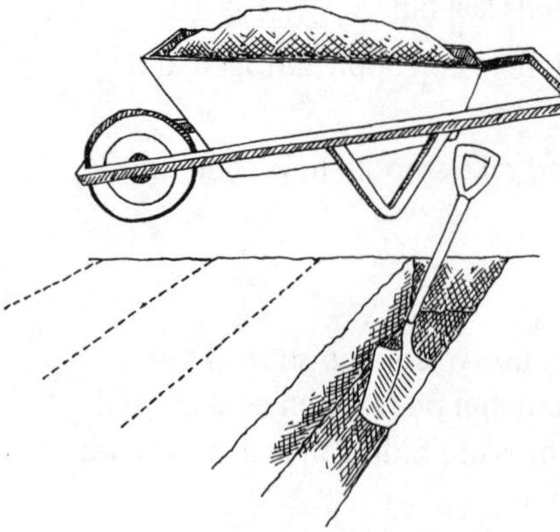

To double-dig the garden, first excavate a foot-deep trench on one end of the garden. Pile the soil into a wheelbarrow.

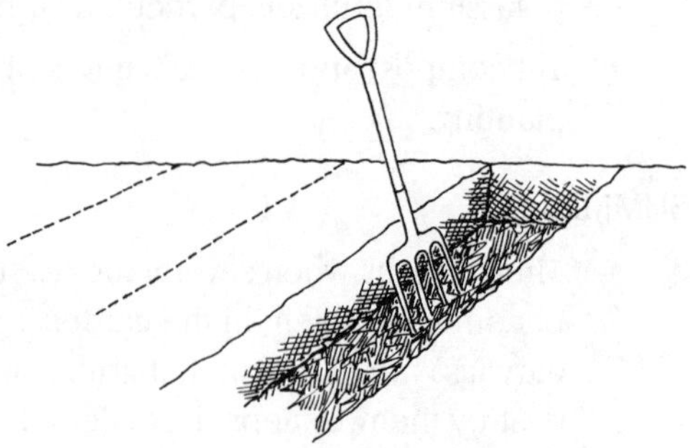

Use a spading fork to loosen the subsoil in the bottom of the trench.

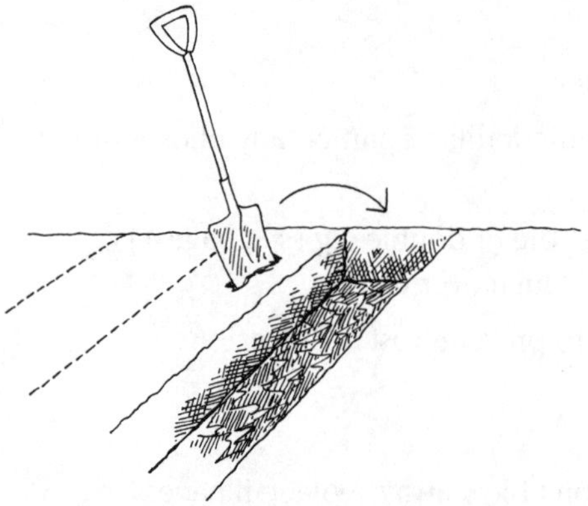

Dig a second trench next to the first one, spading the soil into the first trench. Loosen the subsoil. Repeat the procedure until have worked your way to the other end of the garden.

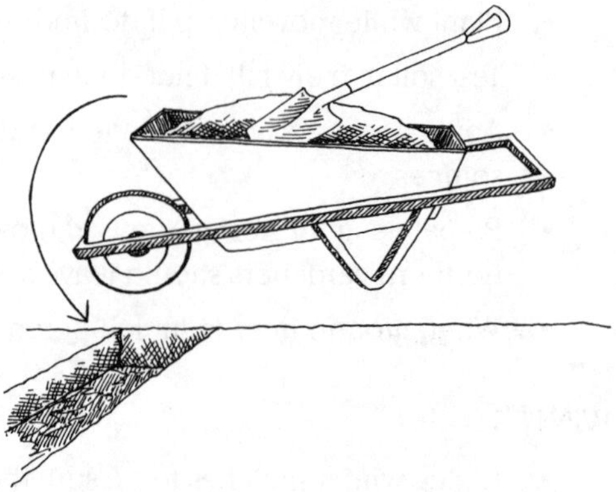

Use the soil from the first trench to fill the last one.

WHAT TO DO WITH POORLY DRAINED SOIL

Good drainage is important for most plants. Without it, plants may suffocate from lack of oxygen, or suffer poisoning from heavy metals leached into water standing in the soil.

It is best to avoid gardening in wet spots if you have a choice. When choosing a site for a garden, avoid low-lying areas, especially at the bottom of a slope. Also steer clear of flat expanses where surface drainage is poor. The best spot for a garden is a gentle slope; such a location will likely be well drained but not dry.

If you are in doubt about soil moisture, look at the weeds growing there. Certain weeds are indicative of wet soil (see page 29). Dig a hole or short trench straight down into the ground so you can examine the subsoil layers. A gray color in the subsoil is another indicator of excessive wetness. Subsoil that appears to be a solid gray color suffers from long-term saturation. Gray mottling in the soil points to periods of saturation. Look instead for subsoil with a rich brown color, possibly with reddish or yellowish streaks.

Ten Ways to Deal with Soggy Soil

If you must garden in poorly drained soil, you can take the following steps to improve conditions for plants:

1. Shape your gardening efforts around the existing conditions and create a bog or water garden. Building raised boardwalks through the wet area will make it easy and comfortable for you to enjoy the garden up close.
2. By far the best solution is to work organic matter into the soil and replenish it on a yearly basis. For soils that are heavy but not compacted, organic matter may be all you need to solve the problem. Organic matter lightens and aerates dense soils, enabling them to drain better while still retaining enough moisture for plants. Spread a 1- to 2-inch layer of compost over the garden and dig or till it in. Thereafter, add 1/2 to 1 inch of compost once a year to maintain the soil in good condition.
3. Maintain a pH between 5.5 and 6.5 if feasible, to improve aggregation of tiny clay particles (that is, encourage them to form clumps with air spaces in between).
4. Lighten the texture by adding coarse sand.
5. Avoid compaction problems by not working the soil when it is wet.
6. Construct raised beds on top of the soil, fill them with a fertile, humusy soil mix, and garden in them.
7. Break up hardpan layers in the subsoil.
8. Install subsurface drainage pipes or tiles to carry off excess water. Lay the pipes or tiles to slope away from the garden (you need a lower spot for the water to drain to), with a drop of at least 4 to 5 inches per 100 feet. Install the drains below the frost line; a depth of 3 to 4 feet is sufficient in most

locations. Keep the drainage lines well away from tree roots that could grow into and clog them. (The roots of willows, poplars, and elms are particularly problematic.) Be sure the drainage lines run straight, without dips or bends where water could collect. Lay 1 inch of gravel in the bottom of the trench before placing the pipes or tiles. Seal any joints with roofing paper, and place gravel, stones, or screening at both ends of the line to keep out soil that could clog the lines.

9. Dig trenches to divert surface water away from the garden.
10. Mulch the garden with black plastic so less water penetrates the soil.

150 PLANTS FOR DRY SOIL

TREES AND SHRUBS

Acacia spp.
Acer ginnala, amur maple
Ailanthus altissima, tree of heaven
Albizia julibrissin, mimosa
Arctostaphylos spp., manzanita
Berberis spp., barberry
Buddleia alternifolia, fountain buddleia
Callistemon spp., bottlebrush
Ceanothus spp., California lilac
Cedrus deodara, deodar cedar
Cercidium floridum, palo verde
Cistus spp., rock rose
Cotinus coggygria, smokebush
Cupressus spp., cypress
Cytisus scoparius, Scotch broom
Echium fastuosum, pride of Madeira
Elaeagnus, spp.
Escallonia spp.
Eucalyptus spp.
Fouquieria splendens, ocotillo
Fremontodendron spp., flannel bush
Ginkgo biloba
Grevillea robusta, silk oak
Jacaranda mimosifolia
Juniperus spp., junipers
Koelreuteria paniculata, golden-rain tree
Lavandula spp., lavender
Ligustrum spp., privet
Mahonia spp., Oregon grape
Melia azedarach, chinaberry
Myrica pensylvanica, bayberry
Nandina domestica, heavenly bamboo
Nerium oleander, oleander
Olea europaea, European olive
Palms
Pinus ponderosa, ponderosa pine
Pinus thunbergiana, Japanese black pine
Pittosporum spp.
Populus alba, white poplar
Prosopis glandulosa, honey mesquite
Raphiolepis indica, Indian hawthorn
Rhus spp., sumac
Robinia pseudoacacia, black locust
Rosa rugosa, saltspray rose
Tamarix spp., tamarisk
Taxus spp., yews
Teucrium spp., germander
Tilia tomentosa, silver linden
Ulmus pumila, dwarf elm
Zizyphus jujuba, jujube

GROUNDCOVERS

Arctostaphylos uva-ursi, bearberry
Arctotis stoechadifolia, African daisy
Coronilla varia, crown vetch

Delosperma spp., *Lampranthus* spp., *Mesembryanthemum* spp., ice plants
Hedera helix, English ivy
Hypericum calycinum, St.-John's-wort
Juniperus horizontalis, creeping juniper
Lantana spp.
Thymus spp., thyme
Verbena spp.

VINES

Bougainvillea spp.
Campsis radicans, trumpet creeper
Lonicera sempervirens, trumpet honeysuckle
Macfadyena unguis-cati, yellow trumpet vine
Polygonum aubertii, silverlace vine
Solanum jasminoides, potato vine
Tecomaria capensis, Cape honeysuckle
Vitis vinifera, grape
Wisteria spp.

ANNUALS, BULBS, AND PERENNIALS

Abronia spp., sand verbena
Achillea spp., yarrow
Agave spp., century plant
Aloe arborescens, candelabra aloe
Ammobium alatum, winged everlasting
Anacyclus spp.
Artemisia spp.
Asclepias tuberosa, butterfly weed
Aurinia saxatilis, basket-of-gold
Baptisia australis, blue false indigo
Brachycome iberidifolia, Swan River daisy
Calandrinia spp., rock purslane
Calendula officinalis, pot marigold
Catharanthus roseus, Madagascar periwinkle
Celosia cristata, cockscomb
Centaurea cineraria, dusty miller
Centaurea cyanus, bachelor's button
Chrysanthemum frutescens (*Argyranthemum frutescens*), Marguerite daisy
Chrysanthemum nipponicum (*Nipponanthemum nipponicum*), Montauk daisy
Clarkia spp., godetia
Coreopsis verticillata, threadleaf coreopsis
Cosmos spp.
Cuphea ignea, cigar flower
Dimorphotheca spp., Cape marigold
Echeveria spp., hen-and-chickens
Echinacea purpurea, purple coneflower
Echinocactus spp., barrel cactus
Echinops ritro, globe thistle
Eryngium spp., sea holly
Euphorbia spp.
Freesia × *hybrida*
Gaillardia grandiflora, blanketflower
Gaura lindheimeri
Gazania rigens, treasure flower
Gerbera jamesonii, Transvaal daisy
Gomphrena globosa, globe amaranth
Hemerocallis spp., daylily
Ipheion uniflorum, spring starflower
Ixia spp., corn lily
Kniphofia uvaria, red-hot poker
Lachenalia spp., Cape cowslip
Lantana montevidensis, trailing lantana
Leucojum aestivum, summer snowflake
Liatris spp. gayfeather
Limonium spp., sea lavender
Lobularia maritima, sweet alyssum
Lychnis coronaria, rose campion
Lyia campestris, tidytips
Mammillaria spp., pincushion cactus
Marrubium vulgare, horehound
Melampodium spp.
Mimulus spp., monkeyflower
Muscari spp., grape hyacinth
Nemophila menziesii, baby blue-eyes
Nepeta × *faassenii*, catmint
Nigella damascena, love-in-a-mist
Oenothera tetragona, stonecrop
Opuntia spp., prickly pear
Ornithogalum umbellatum, star-of-Bethlehem
Osteospermum spp.
Pelargonium × *hortorum*, zonal geranium

(continued)

150 Plants for Dry Soil *(cont'd)*

Penstemon spp.
Phlomis fruticosa, Jerusalem sage
Phlox subulata, mountain pink
Phormium tenax, New Zealand flax
Portulaca grandiflora, moss rose
Romneya coulteri, Matilija poppy
Rudbeckia spp., black-eyed Susan
Salvia spp.
Sempervivum spp., houseleek
Sisyrinchium spp., blue-eyed grass
Stachys byzantina, lamb's ears
Thymus spp., thyme
Tithonia rotundifolia, Mexican sunflower
Tradescantia virginiana, spiderwort
Tropaeolum majus, nasturtium
Verbena spp.
Yucca spp.
Zauschneria spp., California fuchsia

100 PLANTS FOR WET SOIL

TREES AND SHRUBS

Acer rubrum, red swamp maple
Alnus spp., alder
Amelanchier spp., serviceberry
Aronia arbutifolia, red chokeberry
Betula nigra 'Heritage', river birch
Betula spp., birches
Calluna vulgaris, heather
Cephalanthus occidentalis, buttonbush
Chamaecyparis thyoides 'Conica', dwarf white cedar
Clethra alnifolia, sweet pepperbush
Cornus stolonifera, red-osier dogwood
Enkianthus spp.
Halesia carolina, Carolina silverbell
Ilex glabra, inkberry holly
Ilex verticillata, winterberry
Itea spp., sweetspire
Larix laricina, eastern larch
Leucothoe fontanesiana, drooping leucothoe
Lindera benzoin, spicebush
Liquidambar styraciflua, sweet gum
Magnolia virginiana, sweet bay magnolia
Melaleuca quinquenervia, broad-leaved paperbark
Metasequoia glyptostroboides, dawn redwood
Nyssa sylvatica, black gum
Pernettya mucronata
Platanus spp., sycamore
Rhododendron canadense, rhodora
Rhododendron maximum, rosebay rhododendron
Rhododendron viscosum, swamp azalea
Rosa palustris, swamp rose
Sabal minor, dwarf palmetto
Salix discolor, pussy willow
Salix spp., willows
Sambucus canadensis, American elder
Taxodium distichum, bald cypress
Thuja occidentalis, eastern arborvitae
Vaccinium corymbosum, highbush blueberry
Vaccinium macrocarpon, cranberry

GROUNDCOVERS

Asperula odorata, sweet woodruff
Chrysogonum virginianum, goldenstar
Epimedium spp.
Galax urceolata
Houttuynia cordata 'Chameleon', chamaeleon plant
Lamium maculatum, spotted dead nettle
Ruellia makoyana, monkey plant
Salaginella spp.
Xanthorhiza simplicissima, yellowroot

ANNUALS, BULBS, AND PERENNIALS

Acorus gramineus, grassy-leaved sweet flag
Althaea officinalis, marshmallow
Aruncus dioicus, goatsbeard

Asclepias incarnata, swamp milkweed
Aster novae-angliae, New England aster
Astilbe spp.
Calla palustris, water arum
Caltha palustris, marsh marigold
Canna spp.
Cardamine pratensis, cuckooflower
Carex pendula, drooping sedge grass
Chelone spp., turtlehead
Cimicifuga racemosa, black snakeroot
Colocasia esculenta, elephant's ear
Cotula coronopifolia, brass buttons
Cyperus haspans, dwarf papyrus
Eupatorium purpureum, Joe-pye weed
Ferns, many kinds
Filipendula spp., meadowsweet
Geranium spp., cranesbill
Geum rivale, water avens
Gunnera spp.
Habenaria spp., fringed orchid
Helenium autumnale, sneezeweed
Hibiscus moscheutos, rose mallow
Hosta spp., plantain lily
Iris ensata, Japanese iris
Iris pseudacorus, yellow flag
Iris sibirica, Siberian iris
Iris veriscolor, blue flag
Ligularia spp.
Lilium canadense, Canada lily
Lilium superbum, Turk's cap lily
Lobelia cardinalis, cardinal flower
Lobelia siphilitica, great blue lobelia
Lysimachia punctata, yellow loosestrife
Mentha spp., mints
Mertensia virginica, Virginia bluebells
Miscanthus sinensis, Japanese silver grass
Monarda didyma, bee balm
Myosotis scorpioides, forget-me-not
Panicum virgatum, switchgrass
Peltiphyllum peltatum, umbrella plant
Primula japonica, Japanese primrose
Ranunculus spp., buttercups
Rodgersia spp.
Thalictrum spp., meadow rue
Trollius spp., globeflower
Valeriana officinalis, valerian
Viola spp., violets
Zantedeschia aethiopica, calla lily

SHADE

KINDS OF SHADE

Shade conditions vary greatly with location, season, and time of day. Afternoon shade is generally better for plants than morning shade, particularly in summer. In hot climates where the summer sun is intense, many plants appreciate some shade in the afternoon.

The following terms are most widely used to describe different kinds of shade.

Partial shade, semi-shade, or half shade describes a location that receives sun for part—but not all—of the day. Two to six hours of sun per day is considered partial shade. The location may be sunny in either the morning or afternoon, but not both, with light to full shade the rest of the day, or the location may have dappled shade all day. Partial shade can be found in the light, broken shadow of a lattice screen, arbor, or small, very young tree, or east or west of a more solid object. Many plants that prefer full sun will also perform well in partial shade.

Light shade or thin shade exists under mature trees with a high, light canopy of small, open leaves, or under young trees. Shade cast by trees or buildings some distance away from the garden may also be considered light shade. A lightly shaded garden may receive an hour or two of sun a day, and is bright and airy during the rest of the day.

Full shade is found under mature trees with a dense canopy of foliage. No sunlight directly strikes plants growing in full shade.
Heavy or deep shade refers to the day-long shadows found next to buildings, under tall, old evergreens, or in thick woods. Heavily shaded places are most difficult for plants, few of which can thrive in such a dark, cool environment.

WAYS TO COPE WITH SHADE

1. Grow shade-tolerant plants.
2. Modify the shade to let in more light (see below).
3. Get plants out of the shade.
    - Plant seasonal gardens that mature when the area is sunny.
    - Grow climbing plants that can reach up and out of shade cast by a low wall or shrub.
    - Put containers or pocket gardens in small sunny patches where you find them.

WAYS TO MODIFY SHADE

1. Prune low branches from trees in and near the garden to let in more light.
2. Thin out some higher branches to lighten the canopy.
3. Remove a tree entirely if the garden must be located close to it.
4. Bounce light into the garden by painting nearby walls or fences white. Use light-colored paving on driveways or sidewalks adjacent to the garden.
5. Set up reflective panels or mirrors around the garden.

100 PLANTS FOR SHADE

TREES AND SHRUBS

Abeliophyllum distichum, Korean forsythia, partial shade
Amelanchier spp., serviceberry, partial
Aucuba japonica, gold dust plant, light to full
Berberis spp., barberry, partial
Buxus spp., boxwood, partial to light
Clethra alnifolia, sweet pepperbush, partial to light
Cornus spp., dogwood, partial
Daphne spp., partial to light
Enkianthus spp., partial
Fothergilla spp., partial
Fuchsia magellanica, hardy fuchsia, partial
Gaultheria shallon, salal, light to full
Halesia carolina, Carolina silverbell, partial to light
Hamamelis spp., witch hazel, partial to light

Hydrangea quercifolia, oakleaf hydrangea, partial to full
Hypericum calycinum, St.-John's-wort, partial
Ilex, holly, most species, partial to light
I. crenata, Japanese holly, partial to full
Kalmia spp., mountain laurel, light to full
Kerria japonica, Japanese kerria, partial to light
Leucothoe spp., partial to full
Ligustrum spp., privet, partial to light
Magnolia spp., partial
Mahonia spp., partial to light
Oxydendrum arboreum, sourwood, partial
Paxistima canbyi, partial to light
Rhododendron spp., azalea and rhododendron, partial to light
Rhodotypos scandens, jetbead, partial to light
Sarcococca spp., sweet box, light to full
Skimmia spp., partial to light
Styrax japonicus, Japanese snowbell, partial
Symphoricarpos albus, snowberry, partial to light
Taxus spp., yew, partial to dense
Tsuga spp., hemlock, partial to full
Viburnum spp., partial to light

VINES AND GROUNDCOVERS

Ajuga spp., bugleweed, partial to full
Akebia quinata, five-leaf akebia, partial to light
Arctostaphylos uva-ursi, bearberry, partial
Aristolochia durior, Dutchman's pipe, partial to light
Asarum spp., wild ginger, partial to full
Convallaria majalis, lily of the valley, partial to full
Cymbalaria muralis, Kenilworth ivy, light to full
Epimedium spp., bishop's hat, light to full
Euonymus fortunei, wintercreeper, partial to light
Fragaria vesca, wild strawberry, partial to light
Galium odoratum, sweet woodruff, partial to full
Hedera helix, English ivy, partial to dense
Hydrangea anomala var. *petiolaris*, climbing hydrangea, partial to light
Lapageria rosea, Chilean bellflower, partial
Liriope muscari, lilyturf, partial to light
Lonicera spp., honeysuckle, partial to light
Pachysandra terminalis, light to dense
Parthenocissus
P. quinquefolia, Virginia creeper, partial to full
P. tricuspidata, Boston ivy, partial to full
Phlox stolonifera, creeping phlox, partial to light
Pulmonaria spp., lungwort, partial
Vinca minor, periwinkle, partial to full

PERENNIALS, ANNUALS, AND BULBS

Aconitum, spp., monkshood, partial to light
Anemone
A. × *hybrida*, Japanese anemone, partial to light
A. nemorosa, European wood anemone, light to full
Aquilegia spp., columbine, partial to light
Aruncus dioicus, goatsbeard, light to full
Astilbe spp., partial
Begonia
B. grandis, hardy begonia, partial
B. × *semperflorens-cultorum*, wax begonia, partial to light
B. × *tuberhybrida*, tuberous begonia, partial to full
Caladium × *hortulanum*, light to full
Chionodoxa luciliae, glory-of-the-snow, partial to light
Chrysogonum virginianum, goldenstar, green-and-gold, partial to full
Cimicifuga racemosa, black snakeroot, partial to full
Coleus hybrids, partial to full
Corydalis spp., partial to light
Dicentra spp., bleeding heart, partial to light
Digitalis purpurea, foxglove, partial to light
Endymion spp., wood hyacinth, partial to full

(continued)

100 Plants for Shade *(cont'd)*

Erythronium spp., dogtooth violet, fawn lily, partial to light
Eupatorium coelestinum, blue mist flower, hardy ageratum, partial to light
Ferns, many species light to full
Galanthus nivalis, snowdrop, partial to light
Gentiana spp., gentian, partial to light
Geranium spp., cranesbill, hardy geranium, partial to light
Helleborus orientalis, Lenten rose, partial to light
Hesperis matronalis, dame's rocket, partial to light
Heuchera americana, alumroot, partial to light
Hosta spp., plantain lily, partial to full
Impatiens hybrids, bedding impatiens, partial to full
Ligularia spp., partial to light
Lilium, lily
  L. canadense, Canada lily, partial to light
  L. superbum, Turk's cap lily, partial to light
Lobelia spp., partial to light
Mertensia virginica, Virginia bluebells, partial to full
Monarda didyma, bee balm, partial
Muscari spp., grape hyacinth, partial to light
Myosotis spp., forget-me-not, light to full
Nicotiana spp., partial to light
Phormium tenax, New Zealand flax, partial to full
Polemonium caeruleum, Jacob's ladder, partial to light
Polygonatum spp., Solomon's seal, light to full
Primula, spp., primrose, partial to light
Rodgersia spp., partial to light
Scilla spp., squill, partial to light
Smilacina racemosa, false Solomon's seal, partial
Tiarella cordifolia, foamflower, partial to light
Torenia fournieri, wishbone flower, partial to light

PLANTS FOR SEASHORE GARDENS

TREES AND SHRUBS

Acer pseudoplatanus, Sycamore maple
Alnus incana, white alder
Amelanchier spp., serviceberry
Arbutus unedo, strawberry tree
Artemisia californica, California sage, sand hill sage
Baccharis pilularis, coyote bush
Casuarina spp., beefwood
Ceanothus thyrsiflorus, wild lilac
Celtis occidentalis, hackberry
Clethra barbinervis, Japanese clethra
Cotoneaster horizontalis, rockspray cotoneaster
Crataegus × *lavallei*, lavalle hawthorn
Cryptomeria spp.
Cupressus spp., cypress
Cytisus spp., broom
Dendromecon rigida subsp. *harfordii*, island bush poppy
Diervilla sessilifolia, southern bush honeysuckle
Elaeagnus spp., Russian olive, autumn olive
Eucalyptus spp.
Fraxinus excelsior, European ash
Genista sagittalis, arrow broom
Ilex glabra, inkberry
Ilex opaca, American holly
Juniperus conferta, shore juniper
Juniperus virginiana, red cedar
Laurus nobilis, bay laurel
Lavatera assurgentiflora, tree mallow
Melaleuca quinquenervia, broad-leaved paperbark
Mimulus aurantiacus, sticky monkey flower
Myrica pensylvanica, bayberry

Nyssa sylvatica, sour gum
Opuntia spp., prickly pear
Pinus mugo var. *mugo*, mugo pine
Pinus rigida, pitch pine
Pinus thunbergiana (short-lived in some places), Japanese black pine
Pinus torreyana, torrey pine
Prunus maritima, beach plum
Quercus stellata, post oak
Rhamnus californica, coffeeberry
Ribes sanguineum, flowering currant
Robinia hispida, bristly locust
Rosa rugosa, saltspray rose
Salix alba, white willow
Salvia leucophylla, purple sage
Sambucus callicarpa, red elderberry
Schinus molle, California peppertree
Tabebuia chrysotricha, golden trumpet tree
Tamarix ramosissima, tamarisk
Thevetia peruviana, yellow oleander

GRASSES

Ammophila spp., beach grass
Calamagrostis nutkaensis, Pacific reed grass
Deschampsia caespitosa subsp. *holciformis*, coastal hair grass
Elymus glaucus, European dune grass
Erianthus ravennae, ravenna grass
Festuca californica, California fescue
Festuca ovina var. *glauca*, blue fescue
Miscanthus spp., Eulalia grass
Molinia caerulea subsp. *arundinacea*, purple moor grass
Panicum spp., switchgrass
Pennisetum spp., fountain grass
Phragmites australis, reed
Uniola paniculata, sea oats

PERENNIALS, ANNUALS, AND BULBS

Amsonia tabernaemontana, bluestar
Armeria maritima, sea pink
Artemisia stelleriana, beach wormwood
Asclepias tuberosa, butterfly weed
Camissonia cheiranthifolia, beach evening primrose
Cerastium tomentosum, snow-in-summer
Chrysanthemum nipponicum, (Nipponanthemum nipponicum), Montauk daisy
Chrysopsis 'Golden Sunshine', golden aster
Erigeron glaucus, beach aster
Eriogonum spp.
Eriophyllum staechadifolium, lizard tail
Erysimum concinnum, coastal wallflower
Eschscholzia californica var. *maritima*, coastal California poppy
Fragaria chiloensis, coastal strawberry
Hemerocallis, daylily
Lathyrus japonicus, beach pea
Lavandula angustifolia, English lavender
Lupinus spp., lupine
Narcissus spp., daffodil
Santolina spp.
Satureja douglasii, yerba buena
Scrophularia californica, bee plant
Solidago sempervirens, seaside goldenrod
Yucca filamentosa

PRAIRIE PLANTS

There are several types of prairie landscapes: tallgrass, mixed grass, or shortgrass prairies, dry prairies, and wet prairies. The lists below are organized by the amount of moisture available. Since prairies contain few trees and shrubs, the lists are primarily of wildflowers and grasses. At the end of this section is a brief list of trees and shrubs suitable for the drier prairie landscapes.

DRY, SANDY SOILS

Anemone patens, pasqueflower
Aster
- *A. azureus*, sky blue aster
- *A. ericoides*, heath aster
- *A. laevis*, smooth aster
- *A. sericeus*, silky aster

Bouteloua curtipendula, sideoats grama (grass)
Koeleria cristata, June grass
Liatris punctata, dotted blazing star
Lithospermum carolinense, hairy puccoon
Lupinus perennis, lupine
Monarda
- *M. fistulosa*, bergamot
- *M. punctata*, dotted mint

Panicum virgatum, switchgrass
Penstemon grandiflorus, beardtongue
Rudbeckia hirta, black-eyed Susan
Schizachyrium scoparium, little bluestem (grass)
Solidago, goldenrod
- *S. rigida*, stiff goldenrod
- *S. speciosa*, showy goldenrod

Sporobolus heterolepsis, prairie dropseed (grass)
Tradescantia ohiensis, spiderwort

MEDIUM SOILS

Allium cernuum, nodding pink onion
Andropogon gerardii, big bluestem (grass)
Asclepias tuberosa, butterfly weed
Aster
- *A. azureus*, sky blue aster
- *A. laevis*, smooth aster

Baptisia lactea, white false indigo
Ceanothus americanus, New Jersey tea
Dodecatheon meadia, shooting star
Echinacea pallida, pale purple coneflower
Eryngium yuccifolium, rattlesnake master
Heliopsis helianthoides, oxeye sunflower
Liatris, blazing star
- *L. ligulistylis*, Rocky Mountain blazing star
- *L. pycnostachya*, prairie blazing star

Panicum virgatum, switchgrass
Penstemon digitalis, smooth penstemon
Polygonatum biflorum, great Solomon's seal
Ratibida pinnata, yellow coneflower
Rudbeckia subtomentosa, sweet black-eyed Susan
Schizachyrium scoparium, little bluestem (grass)
Silphium terebinthinaceum, prairie dock
Solidago rigida, stiff goldenrod
Sporobolus heterolepsis, prairie dropseed (grass)
Tradescantia ohiensis, spiderwort

MOIST SOILS

Adropogon gerardii, big bluestem (grass)
Asclepias incarnata, red milkweed
Aster novae-angliae, New England aster
Baptisia lactea, white false indigo
Carex, sedge
- *C. hystericina*, porcupine sedge
- *C. vulpinoidea*, fox sedge

Chelone glabra, turtlehead
Eupatorium maculatum, Joe-pye weed
Filipendula rubra, queen of the prairie
Gentiana andrewsii, bottle gentian
Liatris spicata, dense blazing star
Lilium superbum, Turk's cap lily
Physostegia virginiana, false dragonhead
Rudbeckia, black-eyed Susan
- *R. laciniata*, green-headed coneflower
- *R. subtomentosa*, sweet black-eyed Susan

Spartina pectinata, prairie cordgrass
Vernonia fasciculata, ironweed
Veronicastrum virginicum, culver's root
Zizia aurea, golden alexanders

TREES AND SHRUBS FOR PRAIRIE LANDSCAPES

Juniperus, juniper
- *J. davaurica*, dahurian juniper
- *J. excelsa*, spiny Greek juniper

Ligustrum vulgare 'Cheyenne', privet
Picea rubens, red spruce
Prunus besseyi, sand cherry
Prunus hortulana, Hortulan plum
Ribes odoratum, flowering currant

PLANTS FOR DESERT GARDENS

All the plants listed here are suitable for desert gardens, but not all the plants listed will grow in all desert gardens. High desert environments are much colder than deserts at lower elevations, and plants must be chosen according to the particular type of desert environment.

TREES AND SHRUBS

Acacia spp.
Agave spp.
Ambrosia deltoidea, bursage
Bougainvillea spp.
Brachychiton populneus, bottle tree
Caesalpinia spp., poinciana
Callistemon citrinus, lemon bottlebrush
Carnegiea gigantea, saguaro cactus
Cassia spp.
Ceanothus spp., California lilac
Cercidium floridum, palo verde
Cercis reniformis, redbud
Chilopsis linearis, desert willow
Dalea bicolor var. *argyraea*, indigo bush
Enulia farinosa, brittlebush
Erythrina × *bidwillii*, Bidwell coral tree
Forestiera neomexicana, New Mexico locust
Fouquieria splendens, ocotillo
Fremontodendron spp., flannelflower
Justicia californica, chuparosa
Laburnum × *watereri*, golden chain tree
Lantana camara, yellow sage
Larrea tridentata, creosote bush
Lavandula spp., lavender
Leucophyllum frutescens
Lycium fremontii, wolfberry
Melia azederach, chinaberry
Nerium oleander, oleander
Olea europaea, European olive
Pistacia chinensis, Chinese pistachio
Prosopis glandulosa, honey mesquite
Punica granatum, pomegranate
Raphiolepis indica, Indian hawthorn
Robinia hispida, rose acacia
Santolina chamaecyparissus, lavender cotton
Simmondsia chinensis, jojoba
Sophora secundiflora, mescal bean
Tecoma stans, yellow trumpet bush
Teucrium spp., germander
Thevetia peruviana, yellow oleander

ANNUALS, PERENNIALS, AND BULBS

Abronia, sand verbena
Achillea, yarrow
Agave, spp.
Aloe spp.
Anthemis tinctoria, golden marguerite
Arctotis stoechadifolia, African daisy
Baileya multiradiata, desert marigold
Brachycome iberidifolia, Swan River daisy
Cephalocereus spp., old man cactus
Cerastium tomentosum, snow in summer
Coreopsis spp.
Dimorphotheca spp., African daisy
Echinopsis spp., sea urchin cactus
Eschscholzia californica, California poppy
Felicia amelloides, blue marguerite
Gaillardia spp., blanketflower
Gerbera jamesonii, Transvaal daisy
Kniphofia uvaria, red-hot poker
Lampranthus spp., ice plant
Linum perenne, blue flax
Mammillaria spp.
Mesembryanthemum crystallinum, ice plant
Notocactus spp.
Opuntia spp., prickly pear
Osteospermum spp., African daisy
Papaver nudicaule, Iceland poppy

(continued)

Plants for Desert Gardens *(cont'd)*

Penstemon spp.
Ranunculus asiaticus, Persian buttercup
Ratibida columnifera, Mexican hat
Rudbeckia spp., black-eyed Susan, gloriosa daisy
Salvia, sage
  S. coccinea
  S. greggii
Sedum spp., stonecrop
Tecomaria capensis, Cape honeysuckle
Verbena spp., native verbenas
Viola × *wittrockiana*, pansy
Yucca spp.

Chapter 2
GARDENING TECHNIQUES

This chapter provides brief summaries of basic gardening techniques. There is information on planting, propagation methods, caring for plants as they grow, and pruning and training. Techniques that apply only to particular types of plants, such as forcing bulbs, are discussed in the chapters covering those plants.

GROWING PLANTS FROM SEED

ABOUT SEEDS

New plants are produced by two means, sexual and asexual. Asexual propagation methods produce new plants from a single parent, and are used for both woody and herbaceous plants. Trees, shrubs, perennials, bulbs, annuals, and herbs can all be propagated by asexual—or vegetative—methods, such as cuttings, division, and layering. Sexual reproduction occurs when flowers are pollinated and seeds are produced.

Some plants have flowers with both male and female parts that can produce seeds from their own pollen; such plants are called "self-pollinating." Other plants have separate male and female flowers; some of these produce both male and female flowers on the same plant, while others have plants with all male flowers or all female flowers. For these plants—hollies are a good example—the females produce the seed-bearing fruit, but a male plant must be planted nearby to pollinate the flowers. Pollination between two parent plants is called "cross-pollination."

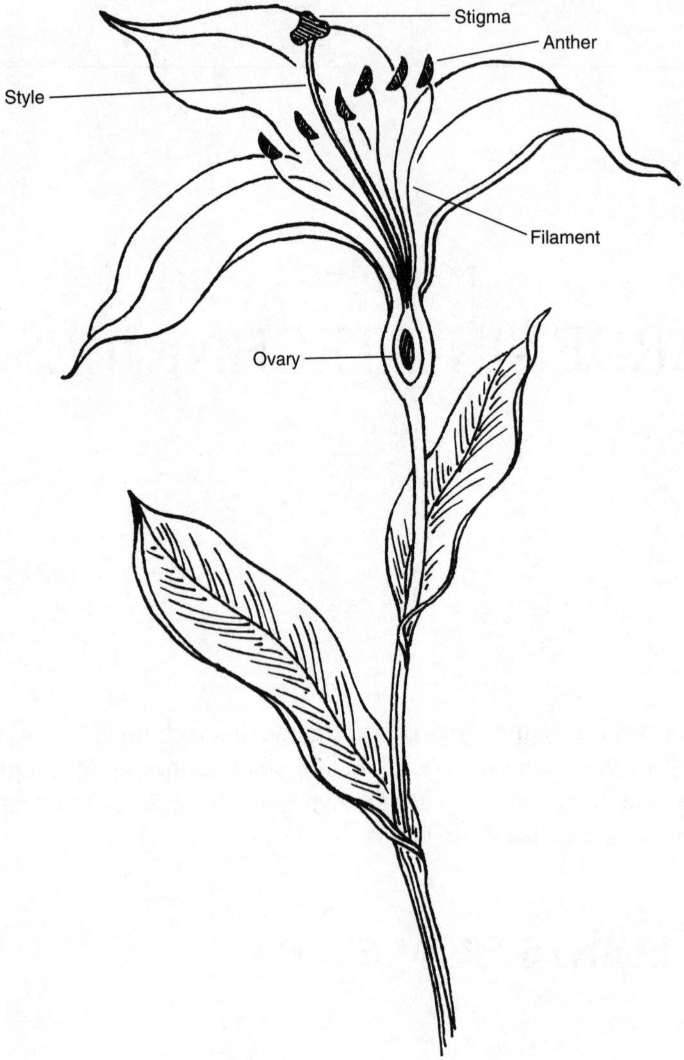

The parts of a flower. The female part, or pistil, consists of stigma, style, and ovary. The male parts, called stamens, are each made up of an anther and filament.

Pollination usually occurs naturally, needing no human intervention. Ripe pollen is carried from flower to flower by a number of natural agents—bees, butterflies and moths, birds, wind, and water. When flowers are pollinated naturally, the process is known as "open pollination." Gardeners who want to collect and save seeds from their plants rely on open-pollinated varieties which can reproduce themselves naturally.

To understand pollination, a basic explanation of flower botany is in order. A flower's female reproductive structure is the pistil, which is made up of the stigma, and a long tube called the style, which supports the stigma. At the swollen base of the style is an ovary containing ovules; after fertilization (pollination), this is where the seeds are produced. The male reproductive parts of a flower are the stamens, consisting of pollen-containing structures called anthers located atop long, slender stalks known as filaments.

When the flower is ready to be pollinated, the stigma becomes sticky. Ripe grains of pollen are transferred by the pollinating agent—a bee, for example—from the anthers to the stigma, where they stick. The pollen grain germinates, sending a hollow tube down through the inside of the style into the ovary. From the pollen grain, sperm cells are launched down the tube and into the ovary, where they fertilize the ovules.

For the seed capsules (the fruit) to mature and produce viable seeds, fertilization must occur. When fertilization does not happen, the fruit falls from the plants without ripening. Some flowers, such as those of strawberries, have many ovaries and stigmas. All the stigmas of these flowers must be pollinated and all the ovaries must be fertilized, or the fruit will not develop evenly and will be misshapen.

A self-pollinating flower produces seeds when its stigma receives pollen from its own anthers, the anthers of other flowers on the same plant, or the flowers of other plants of the same kind. (When plant breeders want to cross two flowers that are self-pollinating, they have to remove the stamens from one flower and the pistil from the other flower.) Edible fruits with self-pollinating flowers are called "self-fruitful." You can plant just one variety of these fruits and get a crop. Blueberries, grapes, peaches, raspberries, and strawberries are all self-fruitful. Other fruits, such as apples and cherries, require cross-pollination between two varieties in order to set fruit.

Cross-pollination occurs between two parent plants, one that supplies the pollen and one that receives it and produces the seeds. For cross-pollination to succeed, the two parent plants must be compatible. That is, the plants must bloom at the same time, and the pistils of one plant must be receptive to the pollen of the other parent, so the pollen grains can germinate on the stigma and fertilize the ovules. Varieties of the same species usually cross-pollinate readily, although some edible fruits can only cross-pollinate with particular varieties. Species within the same genus are able to cross-pollinate in some genera but not in others. Crosses between two genera—known as intergeneric hybrids—also exist, but they are rare.

Seeds produced by cross-pollination contain genes from both parents and are known as first-generation, or F_1 hybrids. F_1 hybrids cannot usually duplicate themselves from the seeds they produce, because the same combination of genes does not occur. To get plants with the exact same qualities of F_1 hybrids, the parent plants must be cross-pollinated anew for each generation. That's why hybrid seeds are more expensive than seeds of open-pollinated varieties.

Seed Structure

Seeds contain all the genetic information needed to produce a new plant. Inside the seed's shell or skin (called the "seed coat") are an embryonic shoot (called a "plumule"), a root (called a "radicle"), and one or more seed leaves (called "cotyledons"), which will be the first leaves that form on the baby plant. Monocotyledonous plants, or monocots, produce one cotyledon. Grasses and onions are examples of monocots. Other plants, called dicots, produce two cotyledons.

The seed leaves, or cotyledons, usually look different from the leaves a plant subsequently produces, particularly in dicots. The leaves with the unique form characteristic of the plant (in other words, the leaves that we recognize as those of a geranium or an oak tree or a tomato) are called "true leaves."

Seeds contain enough nourishment to support the plant until it produces its first true leaves. Thereafter the plant must get its nourishment from soil, air, and water.

How Many Seeds in a Pound?

Seeds come in lots of shapes and sizes. A single coconut can weigh as much as 50 pounds, while rhododendron seeds are so tiny that it can take five million of them to weigh a pound. To give you an idea of the comparative sizes of seeds, here are the approximate numbers of cleaned seeds of some common trees and shrubs that are needed to make up one pound:

Abies balsamea, balsam fir, 59,800
Acer rubrum, red maple, 22,800
Acer saccharum, sugar maple, 6,100
Aesculus hippocastanum, horse chestnut, 109
Alnus incana, white alder, 666,000
Aronia arbutifolia, red chokeberry, 256,000
Berberis thunbergii, Japanese barberry, 27,000
Betula papyrifera, canoe birch, 1,380,000
Cornus florida, flowering dogwood, 4,500
Ilex opaca, American holly, 27,000
Juglans nigra, black walnut, 40
Liquidambar styraciflua, sweet gum, 82,000
Lonicera tatarica, Tatarian honeysuckle, 142,000
Magnolia grandiflora, southern magnolia, 5,800
Nyssa sylvatica, tupelo, 3,300
Oxydendrum arboreum, sourwood, 5,500,000
Picea abies, Norway spruce, 64,000
Populus tremuloides, quaking aspen, 3,600,000
Quercus macrocarpa, bur oak, 75
Ribes aureum, golden currant, 217,000
Symphoricarpos orbiculatus, coralberry, 144,000
Syringa vulgaris, common lilac, 90,000
Thuja occidentalis, American arborvitae, 346,000
Tsuga canadensis, Canadian hemlock, 187,000

SEED GERMINATION

Seeds of different plants need different combinations of environmental conditions in order to germinate, depending on the type of plant they're from, and the climate conditions of their native habitat. In general, seeds require the right light or darkness, moisture, temperature, and dormant period. Seeds of plants native to climates with cold winters need cold periods of varying length and severity to sprout. Some seeds must experience alternating periods of cold and warmth (called double dormancy) before they will sprout.

Seeds do not remain viable (capable of germination) indefinitely. Sooner or later they die. Length of viability varies from a few days for some plants to thousands of years for others.

Storage conditions also affect viability. Most seeds will keep best in cold, dry conditions. A tightly capped glass jar in the refrigerator (*not* the freezer) is a good place to store small quantities of seed.

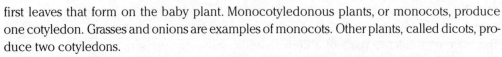

Testing Viability

Here are two simple tests you can use to determine whether seeds you have stored are still viable.

Place 25 seeds on a moist (not sopping wet) paper towel. Roll up the towel and fasten it with rubber bands. Put the towel in a plastic bag, in a warm place away from cold drafts. Open the bag every couple of days to let in fresh air and to check if the paper towel is still damp. Moisten it if it becomes dry. Wait the average number of days the seed takes to germinate (seed packets contain this information), then wait another week. Unroll the towel and count how many seeds have sprouted. Multiply the number by four to find the percentage of germination. If the rate is 75 percent or better, go ahead and plant the seeds. If less than 75 percent of the seeds have sprouted, you should probably buy new seeds or, if the seeds are rare, sow extras to get the number of plants you want.

Another way to test germination is to dump the seeds into a jar of room-temperature water. Viable seeds will tend to sink to the bottom, and nonviable seeds will float.

PRETREATMENTS FOR SEEDS

Some seeds need special treatment before sowing in order to replicate the conditions of their native habitat. Three pretreatments home gardeners may need to use are stratification (providing a cold period), softening a hard seed coat by soaking, or scratching or nicking a hard seed coat so that moisture can enter. This last procedure is known as "scarification."

Stratification

Stratification is a way of imitating the cold winter conditions that seeds of hardy plants need to experience before they can germinate. Most seeds you purchase have already been stratified. But some seeds you buy and those saved from your own plants or received from friends or seed exchanges will need pretreatment. There are a couple of ways to stratify seeds at home.

METHOD #1

- Mix large seeds with moist peat moss, vermiculite, sphagnum moss, or a half-and-half mixture of sand and vermiculite, and place the contents in a plastic bag. Seal or tightly close the bag and place it in a refrigerator or cold frame (in cold climates, insulate the cold frame with old blankets or bags of leaves so the seeds do not freeze).
- Sow fine seeds in a flat of moist potting mix, enclose the flat in a plastic bag, and place in a refrigerator or cold frame.
- Check once a week to make sure the medium stays moist.
- After the required cold period, move flats of fine seeds to a warmer, brighter place to germinate. Remove large seeds from the bag and plant them in moist potting mix for germination.

METHOD #2

- In the bottom of a wooden box, put a layer of damp peat moss, sand, or vermiculite 1/2 to 3/4 inch deep. Spread a thin layer of seeds over the medium, then add another layer of medium. Repeat layers until the box is nearly full or all the seeds are used. End with a layer of the medium.
- Cover the box with plastic and put it where the temperature is about 40°F, perhaps an insulated cold frame, unheated basement, or garage.

STRATIFICATION TIMES FOR COMMON SEEDS

A temperature of about 40°F (the temperature inside most refrigerators) is effective for stratifying seeds of many plants. You will need to consult a book on propagation for more detailed information on the needs of particular plants.

ANNUALS AND PERENNIALS

Aconitum spp., monkshood, 3 weeks
Allium spp., flowering onion, 4 weeks
Antirrhinum majus, snapdragon, 3 to 5 days
Aquilegia spp., columbine, 3 weeks
Cleome hasslerana, spider flower, 3 to 5 days
Dicentra spectabilis, bleeding heart, 6 weeks
Dictamnus albus, gas plant, 6 weeks
Dodecatheon meadia, shooting star, 3 weeks
Echinacea purpurea, purple coneflower, 4 weeks
Felicia amelloides, blue marguerite, 3 weeks
Gentiana spp., gentian, 3 weeks
Helleborus niger, Christmas rose, 3 weeks
Hemerocallis spp., daylily, 6 weeks
Iris kaempferi, Japanese iris, 6 weeks
Lilium auratum, gold-banded lily and *L. martagon*, 6 weeks
Lobelia spp., perennial lobelias, 12 weeks
Mertensia virginica, Virginia bluebell, 6 weeks
Phlox paniculata, summer phlox, 4 weeks
Primula spp., primrose, 4 weeks
Sisyrinchium angustifolium, blue-eyed grass, 4 weeks
Trollius europaeus, globeflower,
Viola spp., pansy, viola, violet, 1 week

TREES AND SHRUBS

Abies spp., fir, 1–3 months
Acer spp., maple, 2–4 months
Aesculus hippocastanum, horse chestnut, 3–4 months
Ailanthus altissima, tree of heaven, 2 months
Alnus spp., alder, 3 months
Amelanchier spp., serviceberry, 3–4 months
Ampelopsis brevipedunculata, porcelainberry, 3 months
Aronia arbutifolia, red chokeberry, 3 months
Berberis spp., barberry, 2–3 months (or sow as soon as seeds ripen, without stratification)
Betula spp., birch, 2–3 months
Calluna vulgaris, heather, 4 weeks (or sow as soon as ripe)
Calycanthus floridus, Carolina allspice, 3 months
Campsis radicans, trumpet creeper, 2 months
Caragana spp., pea shrub, 1 month
Carya spp., hickory, 3–4 months
Cedrus spp., cedar, 1–2 months
Celtis spp., hackberry, 2–3 months
Cercis canadensis, redbud, 3 months
Chamaecyparis spp., false cypress, 2 months
Clematis spp., 2–3 months
Cornus spp., dogwood, 3–4 months
Corylus spp., filbert, 3 months
Cupressus spp., cypress, 1 month
Daphne spp., 2–3 months
Elaeagnus angustifolia, Russian olive, 2–3 months
Fagus spp., beech, 3–5 months

Forsythia spp., 1–2 months
Franklinia alatamaha, Franklin tree, 1 month
Fraxinus spp., ash, 2–3 months
Ginkgo biloba, maidenhair tree, 1–2 months
Ilex aquifolium, English holly, 3 months
Kalmia latifolia, mountain laurel, 3 months
Koelreuteria paniculata, goldenrain tree, 3 months (after scarification)
Larix spp., larch, 3 months
Ligustrum spp., privet, 3–4 months
Lindera benzoin, spicebush, 3 months
Liquidambar styraciflua, sweet gum, 1–3 months
Liriodendron tulipifera, tulip tree, 2–3 months
Lonicera spp., honeysuckle, 1–3 months
Magnolia spp., 3–6 months
Mahonia aquifolium, Oregon grape holly, 3 months
Malus hupehensis and *M. toringoides*, flowering crab apple, 2–3 months (other crab apples are not grown from seed)
Myrica pensylvanica, bayberry, 3 months
Nyssa sylvatica, tupelo, 2–3 months
Paeonia suffruticosa, tree peony, 2–3 months
Picea spp., spruce, 1–3 months
Pinus spp., pine
P. cembra, Swiss stone pine, 3–9 months
P. flexilis, limber pine, 1–3 months
P. strobus, eastern white pine, 2 months
Seeds of *P. mugo*, mugo pine, *P. nigra*, black pine, *P. ponderosa*, ponderosa pine, *P. resinosa*, red pine, *P. rigida*, *P. sylvestris*, Scotch pine, and *P. thunbergiana*, Japanese black pine, need no cold period before planting.
Platanus spp., sycamore, buttonwood, 2 months (or sow immediately when ripe)
Poncirus trifoliata, Mexican orange, 3 months
Prunus spp., cherry, 2–4 months
Pseudolarix spp., golden larch, 1 month
Pyrus spp., pear, 1–3 months
Quercus spp., oak, 1–3 months (or sow immediately when ripe)
Q. macrocarpa, bur oak, 2–3 months
Q. palustris, swamp oak, 1–1½ months
Q. phellos, willow oak, 2–3 months
Q. rubra, red oak, 1–1½ months
Ribes spp., currant, gooseberry, 3 months
Rosa spp., species roses, 4 months or more
Sambucus canadensis, American elder, 3–5 months
Sorbus spp., mountain ash, 2–4 months
Syringa spp., lilac, 1–3 months
Taxus baccata, English yew, 3 months
Thuja spp., arborvitae, 1–2 months
Tsuga spp., hemlock, 2–4 months
Ulmus spp., elm, 2–3 months
Vitis spp., grape, 3 months
Zelkova serrata, Japanese zelkova, 2 months

Double Dormancy

Some seeds must undergo alternate periods of warm and cold dormancy before they can germinate. In nature these seeds typically ripen in fall and do not germinate until a year or two later. To artificially create the necessary dormant periods for such seeds, collect and clean the ripe seeds, then place them in a polyethylene plastic bag of moist peat or sphagnum moss, or a moist mixture of sand and peat. Tightly close the bag and put it in a warm place, with a temperature between 65° and 85°F, for four to six months. Then stratify the seeds at 40°F for three months. Then sow the seeds.

Handling double dormancy is a complicated procedure. If you want to try your hand at it, here are some plants whose seeds need double dormancy:

Double Dormancy *(cont'd)*

Acer, maple
- *A. campestre*, hedge maple
- *A. ginnala*, Amur maple

Amelanchier spp., serviceberry
Carpinus spp., hornbeam
Chionanthus spp., fringe tree
Cornus mas, cornelian cherry
Corylopsis spp., winter hazel
Cotoneaster spp.
Crataegus spp., hawthorn
Davidia involucrata, dove tree
Fraxinus spp., ash
Halesia carolina, Carolina silverbell
Hamamelis spp., witch hazel
Ilex spp., holly
Juniperus spp., juniper
Rhus spp., sumac
Stewartia spp.
Styrax japonicus, Japanese snowbell
Taxus spp., yew
Tilia americana, American linden (if seed is not fresh)
Viburnum spp.

Soaking

Some seeds germinate only when their hard seed coat has been softened. In nature, spring rains do the work. Gardeners can accomplish it by soaking seeds in warm water. Put the seeds in a bowl and pour very hot (about 190°F) water over them. Use at least five to six times as much water as the volume of seeds in the bowl. A smaller amount of water will cool off too quickly, and the seed coats may not be soft enough to allow germination. Let the seeds stand in the water overnight.

If the seeds have swelled noticeably the next day, plant them right away, before they can dry out. If the seeds have not yet swelled, leave them in the water until they do.

The following seeds need or appreciate soaking to soften the seed coat before planting:

Abelmoschus esculentus, okra
Albizia julibrissin, silk tree
Armeria maritima, sea pink
Asparagus
Caesalpinia gilliesii, poinciana
Camellia spp.
Caragana spp., pea shrub
Cercis canadensis, redbud
Coix lacryma-jobi, Job's tears
Cytisus scoparius, Scotch broom
Freesia × *hybrida*, freesia
Gleditsia triacanthos, honey locust
Grevillea robusta, silk oak
Hibiscus spp.
Ipomoea spp., morning glory, moonflower
Lathyrus spp., sweet pea, perennial pea, garden pea
Liriope muscari, lilyturf
Lupinus spp., lupine
Mina lobata, flag of Spain
Petroselinum crispum, parsley
Sophora japonica, Japanese pagoda tree
Thermopsis caroliniana, Carolina lupine
Wisteria spp.

Scarification

Another way to allow water to penetrate a hard seed coat more readily is to scarify the seed. Scarification means nicking or abrading the seed coat with a sharp knife, a file, or sandpaper. Many plants with hard seed coats benefit from either soaking or scarification, or both. Below is a list of some plants whose seeds need scarification.

Albizia julibrissin, silk tree
Baptisia australis, blue false indigo
Camellia spp.
Cercis canadensis, redbud
Cornus florida, flowering dogwood
Cotoneaster spp.
Crataegus spp., hawthorn
Hibiscus spp.
Ilex spp., holly
Ipomoea spp., morning glory, moonflower
Koelreuteria paniculata, goldenrain tree
Lathyrus odoratus, sweet pea
Lupinus spp., lupine
Robinia pseudoacacia, black locust
Sophora japonica, Japanese pagoda tree
Thermopsis caroliniana, Carolina lupine
Wisteria spp.

STARTING SEEDS INDOORS

Starting seeds indoors gives you a head start on the growing season, and allows you to have more control over the environment in which delicate seedlings begin their lives.

A good medium for germinating seeds has three requirements: (1) it must be porous and allow plenty of air to reach the seeds and, later, the young roots; (2) it must retain adequate moisture for seeds while still draining freely; and (3) it must be as free as possible of disease-causing organisms, a state that is achieved by sterilizing, or at least pasteurizing, the medium.

Germination media may or may not contain soil. Soilless mixes offer the advantages of being lightweight, porous, and water-retentive, and the ingredients (peat moss, milled sphagnum moss, perlite, vermiculite, and builder's sand) are sterile when you buy them. The disadvantage is that soilless mixes contain no nutrients for seedlings. When the seedlings develop their first true leaves, you will have to transplant them to a soil-based potting mix or begin regular feedings of dilute fertilizer. It is easy to overfeed young seedlings, provoking rapid growth that weakens the plants. The drawbacks to germinating seeds in a soil-based medium are that the soil, if it came from the garden, may contain pathogens, and the mix may be of too dense and heavy a consistency for delicate roots.

Some Recipes for Germination and Potting Mixes

1. Cornell Mix (developed at Cornell University): equal parts fine peat moss and perlite or vermiculite
2. University of California Mix: equal parts peat moss and sharp builder's sand
3. One part each peat moss, perlite, and vermiculite
4. Equal parts packaged potting soil or pasteurized garden soil, peat moss, and sharp builder's sand (by potting soil I mean a packaged product that is all soil, not a growing mix containing peat moss that is called potting "soil" on the label).
5. Equal parts peat moss and crumbled or sieved compost
6. Equal parts milled sphagnum moss, peat moss, and soil

Sowing Seeds Indoors

You can start seeds in nursery flats, cell packs, peat pots, seed trays, flower pots, or practically any clean container that will hold soil and allow for drainage of excess water from small holes in the bottom. For convenience, set the containers on trays into which excess water can drain. To reduce watering chores, line the trays with *capillary matting* (see the Glossary; matting is available from mail-order garden-supply companies and well-stocked local garden centers). This will provide continuous bottom watering to keep the germination medium evenly moist.

Before filling the containers, you need to moisten the medium. To wet peat moss or a peat-based growing medium, pour it into a big plastic bag or a large tub or dishpan or bucket. Pour some *warm* water into the mix. Close the bag and knead the water into the peat with your hands, or stir with a large spoon or paint stirrer if the mix is in an open container. Keep adding water until the medium is thoroughly moistened but not soggy.

Fill the containers to 1/2 inch from the top if you are using a soilless mix (to allow for watering), or 1 inch from the top if you are using a medium that contains soil. Sprinkle 1/2 inch of a sterile material (perlite, vermiculite, or finely milled sphagnum moss) on top of the soil-containing mix, so the seeds can germinate in the sterile material but send their roots down into the nutrient-containing soil mix.

If planting in a flat, either scatter the seeds evenly over the surface, make tiny furrows, and plant in rows, or place larger seeds individually. In cell packs, peat pots, or other individual containers, place two or three seeds in each pot or compartment, and later thin to leave only the strongest seedling in each one.

For very fine seed, you can place the seeds in a folded piece of paper and tap them out very slowly, or mix the seeds with an equal quantity of fine sand, put the mixture in an old salt shaker, and sprinkle over the surface of the container.

No matter how you sow the seeds, try not to sow too thickly. A dense mass of seeds will turn into a forest of closely packed seedlings. These will be prone to disease until they are big enough to transplant, and will be difficult to transplant without damaging the tangled roots when they do grow large enough.

Unless you know that the seeds you are planting must have darkness, do not cover them. Simply press them gently onto the surface of the soil, and mist them well with a plant mister to settle them in without disturbing them.

Seeds that need darkness to germinate should be covered to the depth recommended on the seed packet. To exclude light, you can cover seeds with finely milled sphagnum moss (which has bactericidal properties) or with some of the planting medium. Alternatively, you can cover the containers with black plastic or place them in a closet.

Cover the containers with plastic to maintain humidity until the seeds germinate.

SEEDS THAT NEED DARKNESS

Seeds of these plants will not sprout in the presence of light.

Armeria maritima, sea pink
Borago officinalis, borage
Calendula officinalis, pot marigold
Catharanthus roseus, Madagascar periwinkle

Centaurea cyanus, bachelor's button
Consolida ambigua, larkspur
Coriandrum sativum, coriander, cilantro
Cyclamen spp., hardy cyclamen
Cynoglossum amabile, Chinese forget-me-not
Delphinium spp.
Echinacea purpurea, purple coneflower
Emilia javanica, tasselflower
Foeniculum vulgare, fennel
Gazania rigens, treasure flower
Lathyrus odoratus, sweet pea
Mesembryanthemum crystallinum, ice plant
Myosotis spp. forget-me-not
Nemesia strumosa
Oenothera spp., evening primrose, sundrops
Papaver nudicaule, Iceland poppy
Papaver rhoeas, Shirley poppy
Phlox spp.
Salpiglossis sinuata, painted tongue
Saponaria ocymoides, soapwort
Schizanthus, butterfly flower
Tithonia rotundifolia, Mexican sunflower
Trachymene caerulea, blue lace flower
Tropaeolum majus, *T. minus*, nasturtium
Verbena spp.
Viola spp., pansy, violet, viola

SEEDS THAT NEED LIGHT

Seeds of these plants must be exposed to light in order to sprout.

Achillea spp., yarrow
Ageratum houstonianum, flossflower
Agrostis nebulosa, cloud grass
Anethum graveolens, dill
Antirrhinum majus, snapdragon
Aquilegia spp., columbine
Arabis spp., rock cress
Aurinia saxatilis, basket-of-gold
Begonia spp.
Browallia speciosa
Campanula spp., bellflower, harebell
Capsicum annuum, ornamental pepper
Coleus × *hybridus*
Coreopsis spp., tickseed
Cortaderia selloana, pampas grass
Cuphea ignea, cigar flower
Digitalis spp., foxglove
Doronicum cordatum, leopard's bane
Exacum affine, Persian violet
Fuchsia × *hybrida*
Gaillardia spp., blanketflower
Gerbera jamesonii, Transvaal daisy
Grevillea robusta, silk oak
Helichrysum bracteatum, strawflower
Hesperis matronalis, dame's rocket
Heuchera spp., coralbells
Impatiens spp.
Kochia scoparia, summer cypress
Lagerstroemia indica, crape myrtle
Lettuce
Leucanthemum × *superbum*, shasta daisy
Lobelia spp., cardinal flower, edging lobelia
Lobularia maritima , sweet alyssum
Lychnis chalcedonica, Maltese cross
Matthiola spp., stock
Moluccella laevis, bells of Ireland
Nicotiana spp., flowering tobacco
Papaver orientale, oriental poppy
Penstemon spp., beardtongue
Perilla frutescens, beefsteak plant
Petunia × *hybrida*
Physalis alkekengi, Chinese lantern
Platycodon grandiflorus, balloon flower
Portulaca grandiflora, moss rose
Primula spp., primrose
Punica granatum, pomegranate
Reseda odorata, mignonette
Salvia splendens, scarlet sage
Sanvitalia procumbens, creeping zinnia
Senecio cineraria, dusty miller
Talinum paniculatum, jewels of Opar
Tanacetum parthenium, tansy
Tithonia rotundifolia, Mexican sunflower

In the northern parts of the country where the growing season is short, gardeners may need to give an early start to squash, beans, melons, nasturtiums, and other plants that do not generally transplant well. For such plants, sow three or four seeds in a 4- or 5-inch plastic pot, and let them all grow. When it is time to transplant to the garden, carefully unpot the whole clump, keep the root ball as intact as possible, and plant the entire group of plants together.

After sowing seeds indoors, label all the containers (it's amazingly easy to forget which seeds you planted where). Keep the potting medium evenly moist until germination occurs. Seeds that need light to germinate can be placed in bright windowsills or about 3 inches below fluorescent lights. Keep plastic-covered seed containers out of direct sun or they could become too hot for the seeds.

Open the plastic covers for an hour or so each day to let in fresh air. Check the planting medium for moisture, and water when necessary. Water from the bottom, by setting containers in a pan of room-temperature water until the soil surface feels moist.

Many seeds sprout more quickly in warm soil. You can supply bottom heat with special electric heating cables installed under the soil in greenhouse benches, or heating mats on which you can set the containers of seeds. The heating cables and mats are low-wattage, and heat the soil to 70°–75°F. Some models have adjustable thermostats. They are meant to be used for seed starting. They are available from mail-order garden supply companies. For safety's sake, do not try to substitute heating pads or electric blankets for the soil heating devices.

If you take care not to plant seeds too deeply, to use a sterile medium and keep it evenly moist, and to give seeds bottom heat, most seeds—at least those of nonwoody plants—will germinate in a week or two.

Caring for Seedlings Indoors

When the first green shoots appear above the soil, give the seedlings all the light you can. Remove plastic covers and increase humidity with once- or twice-daily misting, or by setting the containers atop a layer of pebbles in trays containing water. When you want to water, raise the water level in the trays to touch the bottoms of the containers. The rest of the time the containers should be above the water so that the potting medium does not become soggy and cause your seedlings to rot.

Seedlings growing in sunny windows should be turned daily to keep the stems growing straight. If your seedlings are growing under fluorescent lights, you will need to raise the lamps as the plants grow, to keep the tops of the plants about 4 inches below the lights. Leave the lights on for 12 to 16 hours a day (an automatic timer makes this easy).

Seedlings not getting enough light will be thin and lanky, with leaves far apart on the stems and pale in color. The stems will bend and stretch toward the light source.

Moisture. Seedlings need regular moisture and reasonably high humidity. Soil should be evenly moist but not soggy. Let the soil dry out a bit between waterings (until it feels dry on the surface), then water thoroughly, from above or below. Do not let seedlings stand in water. If you water from the top, pour off any excess water standing in the drainage trays after fifteen minutes. If the trays contain pebbles, just drain off enough water so the bottoms of the pots are not in the water. If you water from the bottom, remove the excess water when the surface of the potting mix feels damp.

Overwatering is the biggest cause of problems for plants indoors. Most people tend to water too often. Seedlings getting too much water will wilt (yes, wilt), and their leaves will turn yellow. Eventually the yellow leaves will drop off. Sometimes the tips of the leaves will become brown and brittle. If overwatering continues, the lower leaves and base of the stem will rot.

On the other hand, when seedlings are not getting enough water, they will also wilt, turning limp and droopy. Unless the seedlings are severely wilted, you should be able to revive them with a thorough watering and a good misting. But try not to let seedlings wilt before you water them; the water stress indicated by wilting slows or shuts down plant growth. Water-stressed seedlings will grow slowly; they will be weaker than seedlings receiving adequate moisture.

Water seedlings with water that is lukewarm or at room temperature. Water that is hot or cold can shock delicate little plants.

To boost humidity levels for seedlings, you can mist them once or twice a day, or enclose the containers in a plastic tent. Use wire hoops made from coat hangers, or wooden dowels placed in the corners of plant trays, as supports to keep the plastic cover from resting directly on the plants. Then simply drape a piece of clear polyethylene over the supports and down over the sides of the containers. You can instead purchase a propagation unit that comes with a plastic domed lid. Plastic covers of either kind are best suited for plants growing under lights—on sunny windowsills, temperatures can become dangerously high under these coverings. If your seedlings are growing on windowsills, remove plastic covers on sunny days.

Temperature. The best temperature for seedlings is dictated by the sort of environment in which the plants thrive when they are mature. Plants such as hardy annuals (like sweet alyssum or pansies) and spring or fall vegetables (like spinach, lettuce, and cabbage), that grow best in cool weather, will respond to cool growing conditions as seedlings. Grow them in a basement, cold frame, or cool room where the temperature is between 50° and 65°F for the sturdiest seedlings.

Tender plants that need warm outdoor conditions, such as petunias, impatiens, tomatoes, eggplant, and tropical trees and shrubs, need a warm indoor environment, with temperatures between 60° and 75°F.

Air. No matter what temperature range seedlings like, they all need plenty of fresh air. Good air circulation helps prevent damping-off, mildew, and other fungal and bacterial ailments. It also promotes efficient transpiration of moisture from leaves, allowing plants to release excess water vapor that builds up in their cells as the plants manufacture food through photosynthesis.

Providing fresh air does not mean exposing the seedlings to cold drafts or strong winds. Make sure the plants are far enough apart that the leaves of neighboring seedlings do not touch one another. If the plants are in a cold frame, crack the lid open on mild afternoons, to let in fresh air. Indoors, especially in a tightly insulated house, you can run a fan on low speed in the room for an hour or two each day to circulate the air. Aim the fan away from the plants; all you want to do is get the air moving.

Fertilizers. Seedlings growing in soilless potting mixes will need regular fertilization when they have developed their first true leaves. For the first three to four weeks, feed once a week with a liquid or water-soluble fertilizer diluted to half the strength recommended on the package. Thereafter, feed every ten days to two weeks with fertilizer diluted at the regular strength.

Organic gardeners can feed seedlings with fish emulsion (look for a deodorized brand for indoor use!), a seaweed–fish mixture, or homemade manure or compost tea. Or you can use one of the all-purpose liquid fertilizers on the market.

Seedlings growing in a potting mix that contains soil will not need to be fertilized for their first four to six weeks. Thereafter fertilize every two weeks with half-strength fertilizer. If seedlings start to look pale before they are six weeks old, begin fertilizing. After eight weeks (if the plants are still indoors), increase to full-strength fertilizer.

SOWING SEEDS OUTDOORS

Prepare the soil in the garden before sowing seeds. Dig or till to a depth of at least 6 inches in a cold frame, or a foot or more in the garden. Remove stones and break up clods and clumps of soil. If you did not already work in compost or other organic matter (see chapter 1), spread a 1-inch layer of compost over the garden and dig or till it in well. Rake the soil to create a level, fine-textured seedbed. Do not till or plant if the soil is wet or you might compact it. (See chapter 1 for information on when soil is ready to work.)

Make furrows for seeds you wish to plant in rows. Shallow furrows are called drills. Follow depth and spacing directions on the seed packet or instructions sent with the seeds. If you are unsure how deep to plant seeds, just cover them lightly; many seeds will sprout under such conditions.

If you are planting in wide rows or bands (a broad row the width of three or four conventional rows, with plants spaced within the band at the normal in-row spacing), or in blocks or intensive beds, you may prefer to broadcast seed over the area. To broadcast, take a handful of seeds and scatter them as evenly as you can over the soil surface as you swing your arm back and forth in a wide arc. Broadcasting is the best way to sow seed over a large area, and is ideal for seeding lawns, meadows, and prairie gardens. Rake some of the soil off the bed before broadcasting seeds, then use it to cover the sown seeds.

To make the most efficient use of space in an intensive bed, block, or wide row, stagger the plants within the planting area, with all the plants spaced the same distance apart that they would be in a conventional single row.

Tap the seeds out of the packet one at a time or pour them into your palm and release them between your thumb and forefinger. Space the seeds as evenly as you can so you will need to do less thinning later on. Cover the seeds to the correct depth and gently firm the soil over them. Then water well with a fine spray of water.

The large seeds of some vegetables, including corn, squash, pumpkins, cucumbers, and melons, have traditionally been planted in hills. To sow in hills, make mounds of soil 6 inches high and 3 to 4 feet apart. Plant five to seven seeds about 3 inches apart in a circle around the top of the mound. When the seedlings come up, thin the weaker ones to leave the three or four sturdiest plants in each hill.

Mark and label the rows or planting areas so you will remember where and what you planted until the seeds sprout and the plants begin to grow.

Thinning

Seedlings will need to be thinned unless you spaced them precisely when sowing. Thinning is important for healthy plants. Crowded plants won't grow as large or vigorous as they would if given enough room. They will produce a smaller crop of flowers or fruit, and they will be more susceptible to pest and disease problems than uncrowded plants.

Thin seedlings as soon as they are big enough to hold with your thumb and forefinger or tweezers. Pull up the unwanted plants to leave the remaining plants at the correct spacing distance. If any soil is loosened when you pull up the plants, pat it back into place. If the plants are crowded together, use manicure scissors to snip off unwanted plants at ground level to avoid damaging the roots of other seedlings nearby.

Vegetable gardeners growing salad crops can thin them twice, once when they are tiny and again a few weeks later, and add the second batch of thinnings to salads.

Hardening Off

Seedlings grown indoors should be gradually acclimated to outdoor conditions before you transplant them to the garden, or the abrupt change in environment could shock them and set back their growth. The process of adjustment is known as hardening off.

Harden off seedlings by moving their containers to a protected location outdoors, perhaps a porch. The first day, leave the seedlings outside for only two or three hours in the afternoon. Over the next week to ten days, leave the seedlings outdoors a little longer each day, until you can leave them outside overnight. After the plants spend a night outdoors, you can plant them in the garden. If the weather turns stormy or unseasonably cold during the hardening-off period, bring the plants indoors and start over when the weather improves.

You can also use a cold frame to harden off seedlings, opening the lid for increasing lengths of time.

When you begin hardening off seedlings, feed them with a half-strength liquid or water-soluble fertilizer solution.

Transplanting

Seedlings growing indoors in undivided flats may need to be transplanted to individual containers to grow larger before it is time to plant them outdoors.

Seedlings from undivided flats will transplant better if you "block" them a few days ahead of time to separate the root systems. To block seedlings, cut through the soil lengthwise and crosswise with a sharp knife, as if you were cutting a pan of brownies. The goal is to have each seedling in its own little block of soil.

The day before you expect to transplant seedlings into the garden, water the seedlings and the part of the garden where you will plant them.

The ideal weather for transplanting is cloudy and mild. If you are planting on a very warm day, do the work in the morning or late afternoon, instead of during the hottest part of the day.

Dig planting holes the appropriate distance apart before removing any seedlings from their containers. Be sure to allow enough space between plants for them to develop fully. The garden will look a bit empty when all the plants are young, but the spaces will quickly fill in as the plants grow.

Make each planting hole large enough to comfortably accommodate the plant's root ball, and deep enough to allow the plant to sit at the same level at which it was positioned in its container. It can, however, be a good idea to plant lanky, spindly seedlings slightly deeper than they grew in the containers, to anchor them more securely in the soil.

When the holes are dug, remove the plants from the containers and plant them one at a time. Handle the small plants carefully; they are fragile and easily damaged. To lift a small plant from a flat, slip a teaspoon or the end of a wooden plant label under its roots, while holding the uppermost leaves between the thumb and forefinger of your other hand. Hold small plants by their leaves, not their stems; a plant can always grow more leaves if you injure them, but if the growing tip of the stem is damaged, growth ceases. Supporting under the root ball, transfer the seedling to the planting hole (or a new container of moist potting mix, if you are transplanting indoors). Firm the soil around the plant and water well.

If you are transplanting seedlings in peat pots to the garden, tear the sides of the pots to make sure the roots will easily be able to grow out into the surrounding soil. Then plant pots and all in the garden. Make sure the upper rim of each peat pot is completely underground. An exposed portion of the peat pot would act like a wick, drawing moisture from the soil around the roots and allowing it to evaporate into the air.

When the new plants are in the garden and duly watered, a bit of special care will help them get off to a good start. If the weather is hot and sunny, cover the plants with floating row covers of spunbonded polyester for their first few days in the garden. Loosely drape these lightweight covers over the plants and weight down the edges with bricks. They are called "floating covers" because the lightweight material rests lightly on plants without damaging them.

Keep the soil evenly moist for the first week or so, while the plants establish themselves in the garden and begin sending new roots out into the soil.

If you have transplanted seedlings to bigger quarters indoors, position them so that the tops are 6 inches below the tubes of fluorescent lights. In sunny windows, pull a sheer curtain between the seedlings and the windowpane for a few days as the plants establish themselves. Water as needed to keep the soil evenly moist but not soggy.

TROUBLESHOOTING GUIDE FOR SEEDLINGS

PROBLEM	CAUSE	TREATMENT	PREVENTION
Poor germination	Old seed	Purchase new seeds and replant	Store seeds in covered container in refrigerator. Purchase new stock of short-lived seeds yearly.
Slow germination	Insufficient heat (*see also* "Lack of Water")	Move to warmer spot (75°F) or use electric soil-heating pad under seedling tray	Check room temperature before planting seeds.
No germination	Seed may require special treatment (stratification or scarification). May also be caused by old seed, improper temperature, or improper light conditions.	Consult seed packets, gardening books, or seed catalogues to determine if special treatment is required.	
Damping-off (seedlings rapidly wilt or rot at base; stem appears girdled and dark, and simply collapses)	Fungus	Apply appropriate fungicide promptly; if losses are great, replant seeds	Use sterilized soil mix designed for starting seedlings. Sterilize containers. Try covering seed with sand, vermiculite, or milled sphagnum.
Wilting	Lack of water (or lack of nitrogen), or too much water	Add water if soil is dry; let soil dry out if it is too wet	Check seedlings daily and water as needed.
Pale yellow leaves	Too much water, or lack of nutrients	Water less frequently, or water with dilute fertilizer	Wait until soil surface is dry to the touch before watering.
Long, pale, spindly growth	Insufficient light	Move closer to source of light, increase time under light, or move to sunnier spot outside	Set seedlings as close as possible to light bulbs, set timer for 12–16 hours per day, or move plants to sunnier, south-facing window.

(continued)

Troubleshooting Guide for Seedlings *(cont'd)*

PROBLEM	CAUSE	TREATMENT	PREVENTION
Leaves mottled or spotted with yellow, red, or purple; spots of dead tissue may appear	Severe nutrient or micronutrient deficiency or imbalance; may be caused by lack of fertilizer or by use of hard water	Feed plants with weak solution of plant food that contains trace nutrients as well as N, P, and K	If using hard (alkaline) tap water to water seedlings, try switching to rainwater or using plant food for acid-loving plants to avoid pH-related deficiencies.
Seedlings go into shock after transplanting outdoors	Seedlings were not hardened off or were hardened off too quickly	Cover seedlings with floating row cover for a few days to shelter from wind and sun; may need to replant	Gradually expose seedlings raised indoors to outdoor conditions over a period of two weeks.

PLANTING NURSERY STOCK

When you receive plants from a mail-order nursery or buy them at a local garden center, look them over carefully for physical damage, signs of pests and diseases, and overall health and vigor. Look closely at the undersides of leaves, and leaf axils (where leaves join stem), where small pests like aphids tend to congregate.

Roots and crowns of bare-root plants should be firm, with no soft spots, fungus, or mold. Canes or branches should be firm and flexible, not shriveled and dry. There should not be new shoots more than a couple of inches long—bare-root plants are supposed to be dormant when they are shipped and planted.

Container plants should look healthy and sturdy, with compact growth of good color. Do not buy plants that look spindly, limp, or pale in color, or with yellowed or damaged leaves.

See "New Procedures for Planting Trees and Shrubs," in chapter 4, for additional planting information.

IF YOU CANNOT PLANT RIGHT AWAY

If you must hold bare-root plants for longer than a couple of days before permanent planting, plant them temporarily in a shallow trench in the garden. This process is called heeling in. Lay the plants in the trench at an angle and loosely cover the roots with soil. Or heel them into an 18-inch-deep bed of pea gravel or similar stone. Water as often as necessary to keep the roots from drying out—constant moisture is essential. Plants held in a gravel bed need an automatic irrigation system.

To hold container-grown plants, put them in a sheltered spot (in the shade in hot weather) and keep them watered until you can plant.

To hold balled-and-burlapped plants for a few days, put them in a shady spot, cover the root balls with loose mulch, and keep the soil in the root balls moist.

Nurseries sometimes grow plants in the field, then dig them and place them in containers for sale. Plants that were not grown in their containers should be treated like bare-root plants. Inquire at the nursery when you buy plants if they are container-grown or field-grown.

PLANTING BARE-ROOT AND DORMANT PLANTS

Bare-root plants are shipped and planted while they are dormant. Deciduous trees and shrubs, small evergreens, roses, nut trees, some fruit and shade trees, and some perennials are sold in bare-root form. The roots of these plants are wrapped in damp sphagnum moss or excelsior to keep them from drying out during shipping. Sometimes the roots are simply covered with a loose packing material. The plants are then packaged in plastic, cardboard, or heavy waxed paper containers.

When a shipment of bare-root plants arrives from the nursery, unpack them immediately and examine them. After checking the plants, immerse the roots in a bucket of water. Let them soak for several hours or overnight before planting. In USDA Zones 5 and north, plant in early spring, as soon as the soil can be worked. In Zone 6, plant in either early spring or fall. In most parts of Zones 7, 8, and 9, autumn is the best time to plant. In Zones 10 and 11, plant in winter.

Loosen the soil in the planting area, and if possible, over the entire future root zone of the plant. In dense, heavy soils, loosening beyond the planting hole encourages roots to grow beyond the planting hole. If your soil is of poor quality and needs to be amended with compost, work it into the soil over the entire root zone, not just in the planting area.

If you are planting trees and shrubs, be sure to allow enough space for them to grow to their full height and spread. The International Society of Arboriculture offers the following guidelines. Generally, plant small trees 10 to 15 feet tall (hawthorn, dogwood, and redbud, for example) 15 to 20 feet apart and at least 8 feet from buildings. Space medium-size trees (such as river birch) approximately 35 feet apart. Plant large trees 50 feet apart. Keep large, strong-wooded shade trees (such as oaks) 20 feet or more from buildings and utility lines, to prevent damage from branches lost during storms. Space shrubs at a distance about half of their ultimate spread away from buildings or other plants. Set tall hedge plants about 3 to 4 feet apart, and low hedge plants (to 4 feet high) about 18 inches apart.

Dig a generous planting hole, twice as deep as the height of the root ball and twice as wide. Remove the plant from the bucket of water and check the roots. If any roots are broken or damaged, use sharp pruning shears to cut them off right above the damaged area. Make a mound of soil in the bottom of the hole on which to set the plant. The plant should sit at the same depth at which it was growing in the nursery field. Set the plant in the hole, and check the depth. If there is a visible soil line on the main stem, it should be even with the soil level around the hole.

When planting perennials, look for the soil line on the old stems. If new shoots are present, they will be lighter in color below the soil level. If the plant has no old stems (oriental poppies, for example, die back and disappear to the ground when dormant), follow planting recommendations sent with the plant, or consult a good reference on planting perennials for the correct planting depth. Planting depth is important, for some plants even critical; bearded irises and peonies will not bloom if planted too deep.

If your plant is sitting on a soil mound, spread the roots out and down the sides of the mound. Otherwise, spread out the roots in the bottom of the hole. Fill in around the roots with soil, working it in around the roots with your fingers. When the hole is half filled with soil, fill the hole to the top with water and let the water drain away. Then fill the hole the rest of the way with soil. Firm the soil around the base of the plant, then water again, to remove air pockets underground. (Roots marooned in an air pocket will dry out and die.)

In dry climates, it is helpful to make a depression in the soil to catch and hold water for roots. Instead of simply making a saucerlike depression around the main stem, make a depressed ring like a donut just inside the circumference of the planting hole, several inches out from the trunk.

Mulch the new plants to conserve soil moisture.

Remove any nursery tags from the plant when you plant it.

Planting Balled-and-Burlapped Stock

Spring and fall are the best times to plant balled-and-burlapped nursery stock, although plants can go into the ground whenever the soil is workable and weather conditions are not too stressful.

Check the soil ball carefully when buying a balled-and-burlapped tree or shrub. Sometimes plants are sold in artificial soil balls made from compressed peat moss. Plants packaged this way are not truly balled-and-burlapped; they are really bare-root plants, and you should handle them that way.

Also take a good look at the burlap around the root ball. Real burlap made of cotton fibers or jute will decompose in the soil and need not be removed during planting. Imitation burlap made with plastic fibers must be completely removed at the time of planting.

When handling balled-and-burlapped plants, lift them by the root ball, not by the trunk. You will need an assistant, or at least a furniture dolly, to move all but the smallest balled-and-burlapped plants—the soil around the root ball makes them heavy.

Dig a planting hole as deep as the root ball and twice as wide. Loosen the soil as for bare-root plants. Lower the plant into the hole. Remove the ropes from the soil ball, loosen the burlap and roll it down partway over the soil ball. Now check for the soil line on the trunk, to see if the plant is positioned at the correct depth. The top of the burlap wrapping is not a reliable guide to planting depth, because it may cover the trunk above the soil line.

If the plant is sitting too deep, lift it out of the hole and put more soil in the hole to raise the level. If the plant is too high, remove some soil. Replace the plant in the hole and roll the burlap back so that it will be completely underground when the hole is filled with soil. Fill in around the root ball with soil. Finish the planting as described under bare-root plants.

Planting Container-Grown Stock

Container-grown plants, whether they are in cell packs (or six packs), or individual pots of any size, can be planted anytime during the growing season when weather conditions are not too stressful.

The procedure for planting container-grown plants is much the same as the procedure for planting bare-root plants. Dig the planting hole before removing the plant from the container.

To remove a plant from a cell pack, push on the bottom of the cell and slide the plant out. To remove a plant from a pot, support the stem and top of the soil ball with one hand as you turn the pot upside down and slide the plant out of the pot. If the plant does not slip out easily, tap on the bottom of the pot with the handle of a trowel. If the plant still does not slide easily from the pot, cut the container and pull it away.

When you have a large plant to transplant—a tree or shrub in a large pot—lay the pot sideways on the ground and tap or press on the sides as you roll the pot to loosen the root ball. Metal containers can be difficult to remove, but upon request, many local nurseries will cut the can for you.

When the plant is out of the pot, take a look at the root ball before setting the plant in the planting hole. If the plant is potbound, with roots coiled around the inside of the pot, the roots may tend to keep the same habit in the garden, never expanding beyond the planting hole. This condition is called "container habit," and plants that have it will survive in the garden only as long as they receive water and nutrients on a regular basis, as if they were still growing in containers. If soil dries out in summer or freezes to the depth of the root ball in winter, the plant can die because it has sent no roots out into the surrounding soil.

To help plants break out of a container habit, loosen the soil in and around the spot where you will dig the planting hole. When the plant is out of its pot, gently untangle and spread out some of the roots. If the roots are in too tight a mass to untangle, take a sharp knife and make two or three vertical cuts up into the root ball from the bottom. Then spread the root ball apart when you put the plant in the hole. Or use a heavy-duty screwdriver to pry some of the longer, tougher roots out of the center of the root ball and cut them off. For plants having a long taproot, straighten the root as much as you can without breaking it before planting. Examine the roots on the top of the soil ball also; if any roots are wrapped around the main stem, cut them off.

If the plant is not rootbound, simply squeeze it to loosen and separate the roots before planting.

Replace any soil that falls out of a dense soil ball before setting the plant in the hole, so there will be no air pockets where roots could dry out. Work quickly so the root ball does not dry out before you get the plant into the garden.

Make the hole a bit bigger than the size of the root ball, and set the plant at the same depth it was growing in the container. Spread out the roots in the hole, and fill in with soil, working it around the root ball with your fingers. Half-fill the hole with soil, water, fill the remainder of the hole and water again.

When planting a tree that has a weak root system (such as a dwarf fruit tree), or that is too tall to stand on its own, it will need staking. Drive three stakes equidistant from one another outside the planting hole. Attach sturdy wire to each stake and wrap it around the tree as low as possible. Pad the wire where it touches the tree by passing it through pieces of old garden hose. Allow some play in the wires so the tree can flex a bit in the wind. Remove the stakes after a year. Stake new trees only if it is absolutely necessary.

It is also a good idea to wrap the trunks of newly planted trees with tree-wrap material (available from garden centers and mail-order garden supply companies) to prevent sunscald. Remove any nursery tags from trees and shrubs.

SPECIAL PLANTING METHODS

PLANTING BY THE MOON

One folklore tradition holds that planting times should correspond to certain phases of the moon. Gardeners who swear the practice works explain it by comparing the moon's effect on ocean tides to its effect upon the movement of fluids within plants (and also within our own bodies).

The simplest approach to planting by the moon is to plant roots and bulbs when the moon is waning, and to plant leafy, flowering, and fruiting plants that grow above ground when the moon is waxing. A further refinement of the scheme calls for planting seeds or transplants of leafy plants, and plants that carry their seeds on the outside of the fruit (such as strawberries and corn) when the moon is between new and first quarter. When the moon is between first quarter and full, sow or transplant plants that produce seeds inside their fruit. Plant bulbs and root crops between full moon and last quarter. Do not plant anything between last quarter and new moon. The week before new moon is, however, a good time to weed the garden.

COMPANION PLANTING

A long-standing gardening tradition is companion planting, in which plants are placed in the garden according to the ways they affect one another. Some plant partners are believed to repel pests or disease-causing organisms, and thus have a protective effect. Some plants are thought to enhance the growth of certain other plants; other plants hinder growth by secreting irritating or even toxic substances into the soil (this effect is known as "allelopathy"). Some plants are good companions because they have different but complementary rooting patterns that make efficient use of garden space; a shallow-rooted plant can be placed next to a deep-rooted one, and the two can coexist happily without competing for room, water, or nutrients. Plants can also be good neighbors when their light requirements are different; a shade-loving plant will thrive in the shadows cast by a taller sun-lover.

Mentions of good and bad plant companions can be found in the works of Pliny and in the great herbals of medieval Europe. More recently, scientific research has been done on various aspects of companion planting, but results have been inconclusive.

Following is a list of various plant associations, good and bad.

Anise: Attracts beneficial wasps; said to repel insects. Plant with coriander and away from carrots.

Apple: Do not plant near potatoes.

Apricot: Do not plant near plums or plants in the nightshade family (tomatoes, potatoes, eggplant, morning glories, petunias, nicotiana).

Asparagus: Plant with parsley, tomatoes, and carrots.

Barberry: Do not plant near wheat or rye.

Basil: Plant with tomatoes, cabbage, or beans.

Beans: Plant with corn, beets, borage, carrots, cabbage, squash, strawberries, marigolds, rosemary, summer savory, or winter savory.

Beets: Plant with cabbage, salad greens, kohlrabi, or onions. Do not plant near pole beans.

Blackberry: Plant near grapes.

Black walnut: Keep most plants outside the tree's canopy by a distance $1^1/_2$ times the distance from the tree's trunk to its dripline. Plants especially susceptible to juglone (a toxic substance secreted by black walnut roots) include apples, azaleas, blackberries, blueberries, lilac, magnolia, mountain laurel, peas, peony, peppers, potatoes, rhododendron, sugar maple, and tomatoes. Less susceptible are beans, beets, corn, forsythia, grapes, onions and raspberries.

Borage: Plant near tomatoes and strawberries. Attracts bees.

Cabbage and relatives (broccoli, brussels sprouts, cauliflower, collards, kale, Chinese cabbage): Plant with mint, dill, sage, hyssop, rosemary, thyme, beans, celery, marigold, nasturtium, onions, or potatoes. Do not plant near grapes.

Caraway: Attracts beneficial wasps. Do not plant near carrots.

Carrot: Plant near tomatoes, cucumbers, radishes, peas, sage, onions, or leeks. Keep carrots away from dill.

Chamomile: Plant near cucumbers, onions, or other herbs.

Chervil: Plant near radishes.

Chives: Plant with carrots, tomatoes, grapes, or roses. Keep away from beans and peas.

Coriander: Attracts beneficial insects. Plant with anise or potatoes, but away from fennel.

Corn: Plant with beans, peas, melons, cucumbers, squash, or sunflowers.

Cucumber: Plant with beans, cabbage, corn, lettuce, radishes, marigolds, tomatoes, broccoli, or onions.

Delphinium and larkspur: Plant near beans, cabbage, or oats; keep away from beets, carrots, parsnips, and turnips.

(continued)

Companion Planting *(cont'd)*

Dendrathema, garden chrysanthemum: Do not plant near lettuce.

Dill: Attracts beneficial insects. Plant near cabbage family members, corn, lettuce, and onions. Do not plant with carrots or tomatoes.

Eggplant: Grow near tarragon or thyme.

Garlic: Plant near roses, cabbage family members, eggplant, or tomatoes; keep away from beans and peas.

Goldenrod: Attracts beneficial insects. Keep away from sugar maple and black locust.

Grape: Plant near beans, peas, hyssop, or blackberry; do not grow near cabbage or radishes.

Hawthorn: Do not plant near apples.

Lettuce: Grow near beets, cabbage, radishes, or strawberries. Keep away from broccoli, fava beans, barley, rye, or wheat.

Marigold: Plant near potatoes, tomatoes, roses, cabbage family members, and peppers.

Mints: Attract beneficial insects. Grow near beans and cabbage family members (but plant in containers because roots are invasive).

Nasturtium: Plant near beans, cabbage family members, peppers, potatoes, or squash.

Onion: Plant with beets, cabbage family members, lettuce, or strawberries; keep away from sage.

Peas: Plant near corn, carrots, cucumbers, eggplant, lettuce, peppers, spinach, tomatoes, or radishes.

Peach: Plant near asparagus, grapes, garlic, or onions; do not grow near potatoes, tomatoes, or raspberries.

Pear: Grow cover crops of clover or alfalfa with pears.

Pepper: Grow near carrots, onions, basil, marjoram, tansy, nasturtium, or oregano. Keep away from beans, fennel, and kohlrabi.

Pine: Do not plant white pine near currants or gooseberries.

Potato: Plant near beans, corn, lettuce, onions, or radishes, marigolds, nasturtiums, catnip, petunias, or coriander. Keep away from apples and pears.

Radish: Plant with beans, cabbage family members, lettuce, tomatoes, peas, onions, and carrots. Do not plant near grapes.

Roses: Plant near garlic, onions, parsley, chives, or geraniums.

Rue: Do not plant near cabbage family members, basil, or sage.

Sage: Plant near cabbage family members, carrots, strawberries, tomatoes, and marjoram; keep away from onions and rue.

Savory: Plant near beans or onions.

Squash: Plant with mint, nasturtiums, radishes, beans, corn, catnip, tansy, or sunflowers. Do not grow near potatoes.

Strawberry: Plant near beans, borage, lettuce, or spinach.

Sunflower: Plant with beans, corn, or squash; keep away from potatoes.

Tansy: Plant near roses, blackberries, raspberries, peppers, potatoes, and squash (but grow in pots because it is invasive).

Tomato: Plant near cabbage family members, asparagus, carrots, onions, dill, basil, parsley, or sage. Do not grow with potatoes or fennel.

Wormwood (Artemisia absinthium): Said to be allelopathic to many other plants.

CROP ROTATION

Crop rotation is a planting system practiced in vegetable gardens to keep soil nutrients from being depleted and to reduce pest and disease problems. Rotate heavy feeders, which require more nutrients, with soil-enriching legumes and light feeders. To minimize pest and disease problems, try not to plant members of the same plant family in the same part of the garden more than once every three or four years.

Here are the major vegetable plant families and some tips on rotating them.

Amaryllis Family, Amaryllidaceae: Garlic, onions, leeks, shallots. Light feeders. Plant to follow heavy feeders. Follow with legumes.

Cabbage Family, Cruciferae: Broccoli, brussels sprouts, cabbage, cauliflower, Chinese cabbage, collards, cress, kale, kohlrabi, radishes, turnips. Heavy feeders. Plant to follow legumes. Follow with a fallow season of cover cropping or soil building with compost or other organic matter.

Composite or Daisy Family, Compositae (Asteraceae): Artichokes, chicory, endive, lettuce. Heavy feeders. Follow, or follow with, legumes.

Goosefoot Family, Chenopodiaceae: Beets, spinach, Swiss chard. Heavy feeders. Follow, or follow with, legumes.

Grass Family, Graminae: Grains—oats, corn, rye, wheat. Follow with nightshade family.

(continued)

Crop Rotation *(cont'd)*

Legume Family, Leguminosae: Beans and peas, clover, vetch. Soil enrichers. Follow, or follow with, any other crops.

Nightshade Family, Solanaceae: Eggplant, peppers, tomatoes, potatoes. Heavy feeders. Plant to follow grass family. Follow with legumes.

Squash Family, Cucurbitaceae: Cucumbers, melons, summer and winter squash, pumpkins, watermelon. Heavy feeders. Plant to follow grass family. Follow with legumes.

Umbellifer Family, Umbelliferae: Carrots, celery, anise, coriander, dill, fennel, parsley. Light to medium feeders. Can follow any other crops. Follow with legumes, onions, or fallow season.

VEGETATIVE PROPAGATION

In vegetative, or asexual, methods of propagation, a piece of a plant is induced to form roots and shoots and grow into a new plant that looks exactly like the parent. Cuttings, layering, budding, grafting, and division are all methods of vegetative propagation.

CUTTINGS

Cuttings can be taken from the stems, leaves, and roots of annuals, perennials, shrubs, and trees.

Stem cuttings are sections of a stem, in some cases taken from the tips of the stems.

Softwood cuttings (also called green cuttings or slips) are taken from young shoots, often sideshoots, of woody plants while the plant is growing actively.

Semi-hardwood (or semi-ripe) cuttings are taken later in the growing season, when the current year's growth has begun to harden (turn woody).

Hardwood cuttings are taken from stems when the plant is dormant and the year's growth has hardened—usually after deciduous trees and shrubs have dropped their leaves in fall.

Root cuttings are pieces of roots.

Other, less commonly used, types of cuttings include leaf cuttings (individual leaves, sometimes with the petiole, or leaf stem, attached) and single-eye cuttings (a single growth bud or eye with just part of a stem attached).

Take cuttings with a sharp, clean grafting knife or pruning shears. Plant hardwood and root cuttings in soil in a cold frame or empty corner of the garden to develop roots. Root softwood, stem, and semi-hardwood cuttings in pots or flats of moist rooting medium indoors or in an insulated cold frame. Three good rooting media are equal parts perlite and vermiculite, equal parts peat moss and perlite, and equal parts peat moss and sand.

To root just a few stem cuttings, you can make your own version of a Forsyth pot. You will need two terra-cotta flowerpots, a small one about 3 inches in diameter and a larger one 6 to 7 inches in diameter (the kind of shallow pot called a "bulb pan" works well). Plug the drainage hole in the small pot, set it inside the larger pot, and fill the space between the pots with moist rooting medium. Plant cuttings in the medium and fill the inner pot with water. As the water passes slowly through the wall of the pot, it provides continuous, even moisture to the cuttings.

Cuttings of woody plants, especially hardwood cuttings, often root more quickly and easily with the aid of an automatic mist system that sprays the cuttings with mist at regular intervals. Few gardeners root enough cuttings to make a mist system worthwhile, but you can mist your cuttings once or twice a day.

Another aid to rooting is rooting hormone powders, which are available from mail-order garden supply companies and local garden centers. To use the powder, pour out a small amount on a clean surface. Dip the cut end of the cutting in the powder, tap off the excess, and then insert the cutting in the rooting medium. Do not pour any leftover hormone powder back into the package or it could contaminate the rest of the powder in the packet. Throw out the leftover powder, and tightly close the package to save the remainder.

STEM, TIP, AND SOFTWOOD CUTTINGS

Stem, tip, and softwood cuttings are usually taken when plants are about midway through the current growing season and the new growth is neither very young and soft nor hardened and woody.

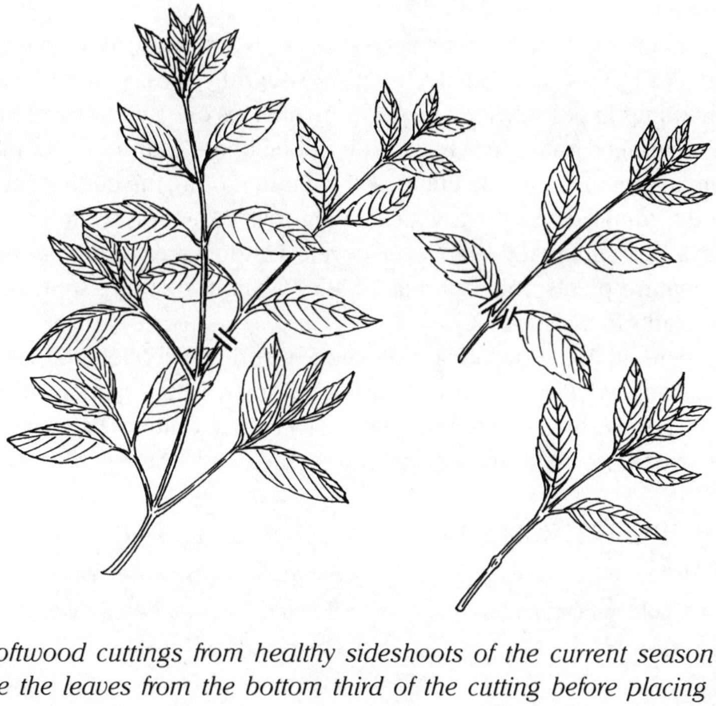

Take softwood cuttings from healthy sideshoots of the current season's growth. Remove the leaves from the bottom third of the cutting before placing in rooting medium.

Stem and tip cuttings are taken from healthy shoots of annuals and perennials. Take cuttings from annuals in early fall to root for winter houseplants. In early spring you can then take cuttings from the indoor plants to raise new plants for the garden. Take cuttings of summer- and fall-blooming perennials in spring, and from spring-blooming perennials in summer. Cut stem tips 2 to 6 inches long, cutting $^{1}/_{4}$ to $^{1}/_{2}$ inch below a node—a dormant growth bud that is usually visible as a small bump on the stem near the point where a leaf attaches to the stem.

With most trees and shrubs, softwood cuttings are taken in summer, generally from healthy sideshoots of medium size. The best shoots to use are firm and flexible, able to bend without crumpling or snapping. A stem that crumples when you bend it is too young to make a good cutting; a stem that snaps is too old.

Cut the shoot where it meets the main stem. (Cuttings of some plants, such as lavender and winter hazel, *Corylopsis* spp., root better if cut to include a "heel"—a piece of the main stem. But for most plants a heel is unnecessary and only damages the parent plant.) Cut off the bottom of the cutting close to a node as described above for tip cuttings, to make the cutting 3 to 6 inches long.

As you cut them, place the cuttings in a plastic bag so they do not dry out. Softwood and stem cuttings wilt quickly and are very prone to drying out. When you collect enough cuttings, place them in moist rooting medium immediately. Remove the leaves from the bottom third of the stem. Insert the stem into the medium up to no more than half its length—one-quarter to one-third of the stem length is best. Set cuttings far enough apart so the leaves do not quite touch.

Keep the medium evenly moist (not soggy) at all times throughout the rooting period. Keep the humidity as high as possible, by misting several times a day or enclosing the containers of cuttings in polyethylene bags. Open the bags once a day to let in fresh air.

Bottom heat supplied from a heat mat (as described under "Starting Seeds Indoors," pages 65–70) is often helpful for softwood cuttings. If you are rooting the cuttings outdoors in the garden or a cold frame, cover them with floating row covers or shade cloth for the first week to ten days. Then gradually remove the covers. Outdoors, give cuttings the kind of light they need as mature plants; root cuttings of sun-lovers in a sunny spot, and cuttings of shade-tolerant plants in the shade.

Cuttings of perennials and woody plants taken in spring will often be rooted by fall and can then be transplated. Plant them 6 to 12 inches apart in the garden. When the plants become crowded, move them to their permanent locations. Cuttings that have not rooted by fall can go into a cold frame for winter, and should be ready for the garden in spring.

PLANTS TO PROPAGATE FROM STEM AND TIP CUTTINGS

Anthemis tinctoria, golden marguerite

Arabis spp., rock cress

Artemisia spp.

Asclepias tuberosa, butterfly weed

Aubrieta spp., false rock cress

Aurinia saxatilis, basket-of-gold

Begonia × *semperflorens-cultorum*, wax begonia

Campanula spp., bellflower, harebell

Cerastium tomentosum, snow-in-summer

Delphinium spp.

Dendrathema spp., garden chrysanthemum
Dianthus spp., garden pinks
Gaillardia spp., blanketflower
Gypsophila paniculata, baby's breath
Iberis sempervirens, perennial candytuft
Impatiens
Lavandula spp., lavender
Linum perenne, blue flax
Oenothera spp., evening primrose, sundrops
Pelargonium spp., bedding geranium, zonal geranium
Phlox
  P. divaricata, wild sweet William
  P. subulata, mountain pinks
Saponaria ocymoides, rock soapwort
Sedum spectabile, showy stonecrop
Veronica spicata, spike speedwell

PLANTS TO GROW FROM SOFTWOOD CUTTINGS

Abelia
Acer, maple
  A. rubrum, red maple
  A. saccharinum, silver maple
Aronia arbutifolia, red chokeberry
Aucuba japonica, gold dust plant
Berberis spp., barberry
Buddleia spp., butterfly bush
Callicarpa spp., beautyberry
Calycanthus floridus, Carolina allspice
Camellia spp.
Campsis radicans, trumpet creeper
Celastrus scandens, American bittersweet
Clematis spp.
Clethra alnifolia, sweet pepperbush
Cornus spp., dogwood
Corylopsis spp., winter hazel
Cotoneaster spp.
Cytisus spp., broom
Deutzia spp.
Elaeagnus
  E. angustifolia, Russian olive
  E. umbellata, autumn olive
Enkianthus campanulatus, redvein enkianthus
Euonymus fortunei, wintercreeper
Forsythia spp.
Fothergilla spp.
Gardenia jasminoides
Hedera spp., ivy
Hibiscus syriacus, rose of Sharon
Hydrangea spp., except for *H. quercifolia*
Hypericum spp., St.-John's-wort
Ilex verticillata, winterberry
Itea spp., sweetspire
Kolkwitzia amabilis, beautybush
Ligustrum spp., privet
Liquidambar styraciflua sweet gum
Lonicera spp., honeysuckle
Magnolia spp.
Malus spp., some flowering crab apples
Nerium oleander, oleander
Pachysandra spp.
Parthenocissus spp., Boston ivy, Virginia creeper
Philadelphus spp., mock orange
Potentilla fruticosa, shrubby cinquefoil
Prunus spp., flowering cherry
Punica granatum, pomegranate
Pyracantha coccinea, firethorn
Rhododendron spp., deciduous azaleas
Rhus spp., sumac
Rosa spp., species roses
Salix spp., willow
Sambucus canadensis, American elder
Spiraea spp.
Styrax americanus, American snowbell
Symphoricarpos spp., snowberry, coralberry
Vaccinium spp., blueberry
Viburnum spp.
Vinca minor, periwinkle
Vitex agnus-castus, chaste tree
Weigela spp.
Wisteria spp.

SEMI-HARDWOOD CUTTINGS

Semi-hardwood cuttings are also taken from the current season's growth of trees and shrubs, but later in the season than softwood cuttings. Semi-hardwood cuttings are typically taken in late summer, when the lower part of the stem has become woody but the tip is still soft.

Choose a sideshoot of medium vigor, and make a cut 1/4 to 1/2 inch below a node. Then cut off the soft tip of the shoot, cutting just above a node. The cutting should be 4 to 6 inches long when you are through.

Plant the cuttings in moist rooting medium as described for softwood cuttings. Move the cuttings into a cold frame for the winter. When roots have developed, transplant the cuttings as described for softwood cuttings.

Plants to Grow from Semi-Hardwood Cuttings

Many shrubs that can be propagated by softwood cuttings also work well as semi-hardwood cuttings. The plants listed here are particularly good candidates for this method of propagation.

Ampelopsis brevipedunculata, porcelain berry
Aucuba japonica, gold dust plant
Buddleia spp., butterfly bush
Buxus spp., boxwood
Chaenomeles spp., flowering quince
Clethra alnifolia, sweet pepperbush
Cytisus spp., broom
Daphne spp.
Euonymus fortunei, wintercreeper
Jasminum nudiflorum, winter jasmine
Kerria japonica, Japanese kerria
Lagerstroemia indica, crape myrtle
Liriodendron tulipifera, tulip tree
Magnolia spp.
Metasequoia glyptostroboides, dawn redwood
Viburnum spp.
Wisteria spp.

HARDWOOD CUTTINGS

Hardwood cuttings are taken from mature shoots of the current year's growth of deciduous trees and shrubs. Take hardwood cuttings in autumn, shortly after the leaves have fallen. The best stems to use are the ends of branches, or canes that have grown from the base of the plant. Do not use late-season growth or spindly, weak canes or branches for hardwood cuttings.

Remove the top inch or so of the stem. Cut the stems into pieces 6 to 10 inches long, cutting the bottom straight across and the top on an angle so you will remember which end goes down when you plant the cuttings. Each cutting should have three or more nodes. If the stems of the plant are hollow or have a spongy center, cut the bottom 1/4 to 1/2 inch below a node. Cut the top 1/4 to 1/2 inch above a bud (that will grow into leaves or shoots next year). Work quickly so the cuttings do not dry out, or cover them with a damp cloth.

Dip the bottom end of each cutting in rooting hormone powder. If you live in a warm climate where the ground does not freeze in winter, you can plant the cuttings in the garden as described below. Gardeners in cooler climates will need to store the cuttings over winter.

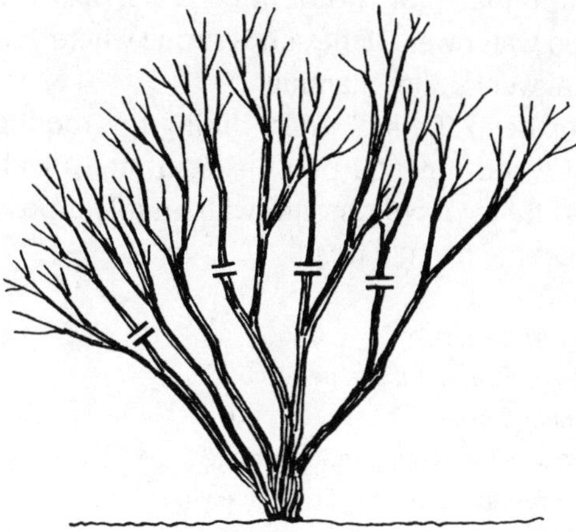

Take hardwood cuttings after leaves drop in fall. Take healthy mature shoots of the current season's growth.

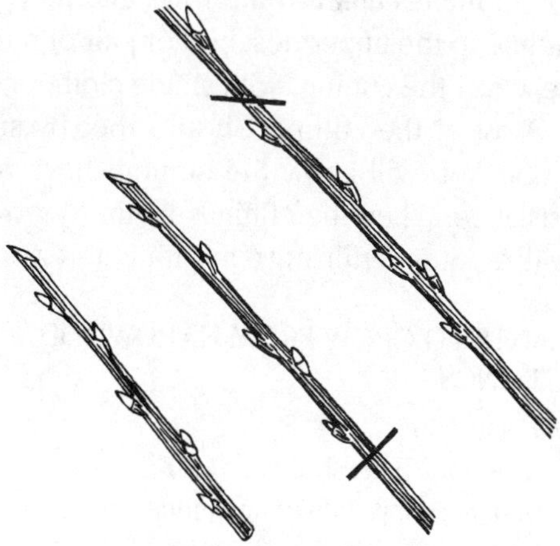

Cut stems into 6- to 10-inch lengths with the top angled and bottom cut straight. Store bundled cuttings in a trench over winter.

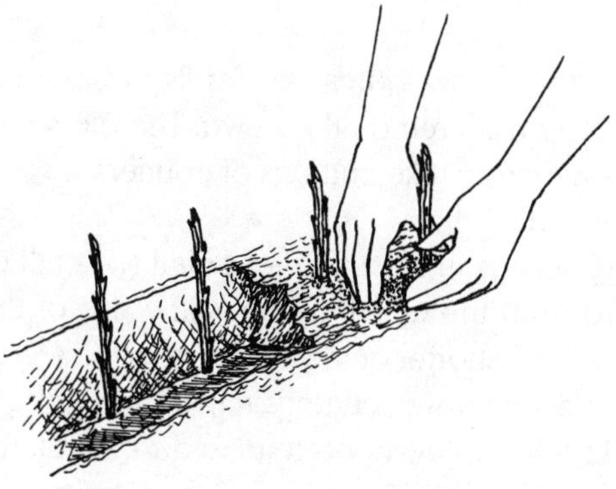

In spring, plant the cuttings, burying them to the uppermost buds.

When the cuttings have rooted and begun to grow, fertilize monthly.

Tie the cuttings in bundles and label each one. Store them in a box of slightly moist sand in an insulated cold frame or an unheated basement or garage, where it will be cold but above freezing during the winter. Or store the bundles in a 1-foot-deep trench in the garden or cold frame. Lay the bundles horizontally in the trench and fill the trench with sand to completely cover the cuttings. Then cover with several inches of a loose mulch.

In spring, as soon as the soil can be worked, plant the cuttings in a part of the garden where you have mixed vermiculite or sand into the soil to lighten it. Set the cuttings at 4- to 6-inch intervals in rows 2 feet apart, and plan to transplant them next year, or set them

9 to 12 inches apart in the rows and leave them in place for two or three years. Bury the cuttings to the uppermost bud or pair of buds, and water well. If the sun is strong where you live, cover the cuttings with shade cloth for several weeks after planting.

Most of the cuttings should root by summer. Keep the soil moist during the rooting period. You will know the cuttings have rooted when a gentle pull on them meets with resistance. When the cuttings begin to grow, feed them once a month with an all-purpose fertilizer. Stop fertilizing a month before you expect the first fall frost.

PLANTS TO GROW FROM HARDWOOD CUTTINGS

Alnus spp., alder
Buddleia spp., butterfly bush
Chaenomeles spp., flowering quince
Cornus sericea, red-osier dogwood
Deutzia spp.
Elaeagnus angustifolia, Russian olive
Forsythia spp.
Hibiscus syriacus, rose of Sharon
Hydrangea spp.
Kolkwitzia amabilis, beautybush
Leucothoe spp.
Philadelphus spp., mock orange
Polygonum aubertii, silver lace vine
Ribes spp., currant
Rosa spp., species roses
Salix spp., willow
Weigela spp.

EVERGREEN CUTTINGS

Evergreen cuttings do not fit exactly into softwood or hardwood categories. They are most like semi-hardwood cuttings, but are probably best considered on their own. There is some disagreement in horticultural circles as to the best time to take cuttings of conifers, so you may need to experiment to see what works best for you.

Generally, you will want to take cuttings of evergreens in late summer or fall (late fall or winter in warm climates). Choose healthy shoots from the current year. At the tips of the branches, make cuttings 3 to 6 inches long (they will be shorter on dwarf conifers). Cut $^1/_4$ to $^1/_2$ inch below a node if possible. On conifers, especially yews, cuttings taken from upright shoots tend to grow into upright plants, and cuttings from sideshoots tend to develop plants with a bushier, more spreading form. Some growers suggest taking a heel with cuttings from conifer sideshoots.

Remove the lower leaves from the cuttings, and any flower buds from cuttings of broad-leaved evergreens. If the plant has large leaves, you can trim the leaves back by as much as half their length to save space when you plant.

Dip the bottom of each cutting in rooting hormone powder and insert it into a flat or pot of moist rooting medium. Root the cuttings in an insulated cold frame, or indoors under lights, enclosed in a plastic bag for increased humidity. Bottom heat from soil heating cables or horticultural heating mats is beneficial. Keep the rooting medium evenly moist.

When the cuttings root, transplant them into individual pots. Cuttings rooted indoors should be ready for transplanting to a nursery bed in the garden in spring, after the last frost. Cuttings started in a cold frame will not be ready for the garden until fall, or even the following spring.

PLANTS TO GROW FROM EVERGREEN CUTTINGS

Abies spp., fir

Berberis spp., evergreen barberries

Buxus spp., boxwood

Camellia spp.

Chamaecyparis spp., false cypress

× *Cupressocyparis leylandii*, Leyland cypress

Ilex spp., holly

Juniperus spp., juniper

Kalmia latifolia, mountain laurel

Pieris spp.

Pinus spp., pine

Rhododendron spp., rhododendrons and evergreen azaleas

Taxus spp., yew

Thuja spp., arborvitae

Tsuga spp., hemlock

ROOT CUTTINGS

Root cuttings are used to propagate some herbaceous perennials, shrubs, and trees. They are especially useful for plants that sucker from the roots (such as raspberries), but cannot be used for plants that are grafted, because the new plants would look like the rootstock rather than the top part of the plant.

Take root cuttings when the plant is dormant. Dig the plant, and cut off a couple of sturdy roots 1/4 to 1/2 inch in diameter and 2 to 3 inches long. It is generally a good idea to have some small, fibrous lateral roots on the root pieces used for cuttings.

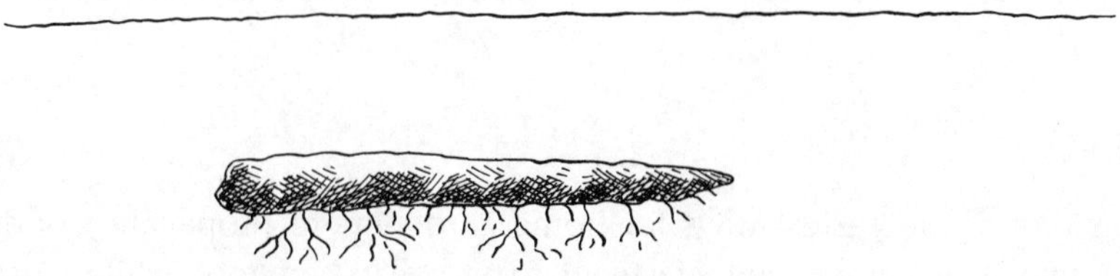

Take root cuttings from dormant plants. Cut roots into 2- to 3-inch pieces. Plant horizontally or vertically.

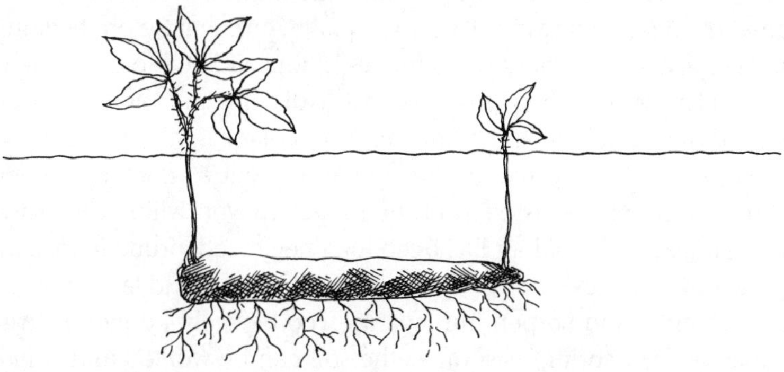

Plant cuttings outdoors in spring and summer, in a cold frame in fall.

Plant the cuttings vertically (or horizontally, if you prefer) in a loose soil or commercially available potting medium. There should be 1/2 inch of medium on top of the cuttings and 3 to 4 inches of medium under them. Keep the medium evenly moist.

Keep cuttings taken in fall in an insulated cold frame, or indoors under lights. Or store them in containers of damp sand in an unheated but frost-free basement or garage. Plant cuttings taken in spring or summer outdoors in loose, crumbly soil.

PLANTS TO GROW FROM ROOT CUTTINGS

Aesculus parviflora, bottlebrush buckeye

Ailanthus altissima, tree of heaven

Albizia julibrissin, silk tree

Campsis radicans, trumpet creeper

Catalpa spp.

Dicentra spp., bleeding heart

Echinacea purpurea, purple coneflower

Echinops spp., globe thistle

Eryngium spp., sea holly

Fothergilla spp.

Gymnocladus dioica, Kentucky coffee tree

Koelreuteria paniculata, goldenrain tree

Limonium latifolium, sea lavender

Papaver orientale, oriental poppy (take cuttings in summer when plants die back after blooming)

Phlox paniculata, summer phlox

Plumbago spp., leadwort

Rhus spp. sumac

Robinia spp., locust

Rubus spp., blackberry, raspberry

Sophora japonica, Japanese pagoda tree

LAYERING

Layering is one of the easiest ways for home gardeners to propagate woody plants. In layering, a stem of the parent plant is fastened to the soil to form roots while it is still attached to the parent plant. When the layered portion of the stem has rooted, it is severed from the parent plant and transplanted.

Layering works best in soil that is loose, porous, and rich in organic matter. Make sure the soil stays evenly moist—but not soggy—while the roots are developing.

If the parent plant is growing in soil of poor quality, enrich it before beginning the layering process. Carefully scoop away several inches of topsoil at the base of the parent in the area where you will be layering the stems. Take care to disturb the roots as little as possible. Mix the soil with sand or vermiculite and compost, then replace it.

Healthy one-year-old stems that are flexible and about as thick as a pencil generally work best. If the parent plant has been pruned regularly, you will have plenty of vigorous young branches to use. If the parent has been long neglected, prune it back and fertilize it to stimulate the growth of new shoots. Then wait until next year to layer any branches.

Simple, compound, and serpentine layering (collectively known as "true layering") are usually done in early spring, as soon as the soil can be worked and while the plant is still dormant. Tip layering is done with the current season's shoots later in spring, when they are long enough to reach the ground, and air layering is usually done in late spring or early summer. Trench or continuous layering is also done in spring, but is less feasible for home gardeners because not many plants can be handled this way. Mound or stool layering is a complicated procedure, used sometimes by nurseries but seldom by home gardeners, and is not covered in this book.

SIMPLE LAYERING

Simple layering is effective for shrubs that have a lot of low-growing, flexible branches.

To begin, insert the tip of a spade or shovel into the ground where the stem will be fastened and push the handle back and forth to make a slit in the ground about 6 inches deep. How far away from the parent plant you make the slit depends on the length of the branch you wish to layer. You will need to bury a portion of the branch that is at least 3 inches, and preferably 5 to 6 inches, from the tip.

Bend the branch down to the ground, keeping it as flat as possible. To prevent the stem from snapping off at the base, bend it in the opposite direction from the way it grows, twisting it slightly as you bend it. Place the stem in the slit and fasten it down with U-shaped pieces of old coat hangers or other heavy wire. You can also use forked twigs or a stone to hold it in place.

Bend the tip of the shoot upward so 3 to 6 inches of it will extend above the surface of the soil. Cover the buried part of the stem with soil and step on it with your foot to pack the soil around the stem. Attach the exposed tip to a small stake to hold it upright.

For faster rooting, you can first remove a strip of bark about an inch wide all the way around the stem at the point where it will be buried. Or instead you can wound the stem at the same point by making a diagonal cut about halfway through the stem on the underside. If the stem is very stiff, insert a wooden matchstick or toothpick into the cut to hold it open. Dust some rooting hormone powder onto the wound if you wish.

How fast the layers root depends upon the type of plant, the age of the shoot, and weather conditions during the rooting period. Many plants layered in spring will have rooted by autumn and can then be severed from the parent plant. One way to tell if a layered shoot has formed roots is to pull on it gently; if you feel resistance, roots have probably formed. After the stem has rooted, you can separate it from the parent plant by cutting it where the stem enters the soil. It is wise to leave the new plant in place over the winter to form a stronger root system. Then dig it up and move it in spring.

Some plants (magnolias, witch hazel, and evergreens are examples) are slow to root and may need to stay connected to the parent plant for as long as three years.

TIP LAYERING

Tip layering is an easy way to propagate shrubs such as forsythia and blackberries with long, arching branches that root easily at the tips. Simply peg the tip of the branch to the ground and cover it with soil until roots form.

SERPENTINE OR COMPOUND LAYERING

For serpentine layering, the stem is covered with soil at several points to produce a number of new plants at once. Use serpentine layering for woody vines—clematis, vining honeysuckles, grapes, ivy, and wisteria.

Make a narrow trench or slit in the soil, about 6 inches deep, starting near the parent plant. Bend the stem in a series of arches so that one node will be underground and the next will be aboveground. Peg the underground nodes into the slit and cover them with soil.

When roots have formed, in fall or the following spring, sever the new plants from the parent.

CONTINUOUS LAYERING

Not many plants respond well to continuous layering, but it has been used with some viburnums, box elder (*Acer negundo*), silver maple (*Acer saccharinum*), apples, cherries, and plums.

If you want to try it, make a narrow trench or slit as for serpentine layering. Lay the branch to be layered flat in the trench, with only 3 to 6 inches of the tip protruding. Fasten down the stem in the bottom of the trench but do not cover it with soil right away. Wait until the dormant buds at the nodes begin to grow into new shoots. Gradually fill in the trench with soil as the shoots grow. When the new plants have rooted, cut them from the parent plant.

AIR LAYERING

If you grow houseplants, you have probably at some time or other used air layering to rejuvenate a rubber plant or dracaena that has developed a long, bare stem. Air layering works for some outdoor shrubs and trees as well. Good candidates for air layering include winter hazel, cotoneasters, hollies, smokebush, tamarisk, wisteria, some rhododendrons and viburnums, and Japanese zelkova.

Strip a ring of bark $^1/_2$ to $^3/_4$ inch wide from the branch you want to air layer. After removing the bark strip, scrape away the thin layer of green, white, or reddish cambium tissue that lies beneath the bark, to expose the inner wood. Sprinkle a bit of rooting hormone powder on the exposed wood on the upper side of the branch.

Wrap the wounded area in moist sphagnum moss. (Soak some fibrous, unmilled sphagnum in water, then squeeze it out like a sponge before using it to wrap the branch.) After applying the sphagnum, wrap it with polyethylene and tape the top and bottom securely to seal out rainwater. Open the plastic from time to time to check that the moss is still damp. Add water when necessary to keep the moss from drying out.

When roots form at the site of the wound (they will be visible through the plastic), cut the new plant from the parent and plant it in a pot or insulated cold frame to pass the winter. Warm-climate gardeners can plant in the garden. Most plants air-layered in spring will root by sometime in fall.

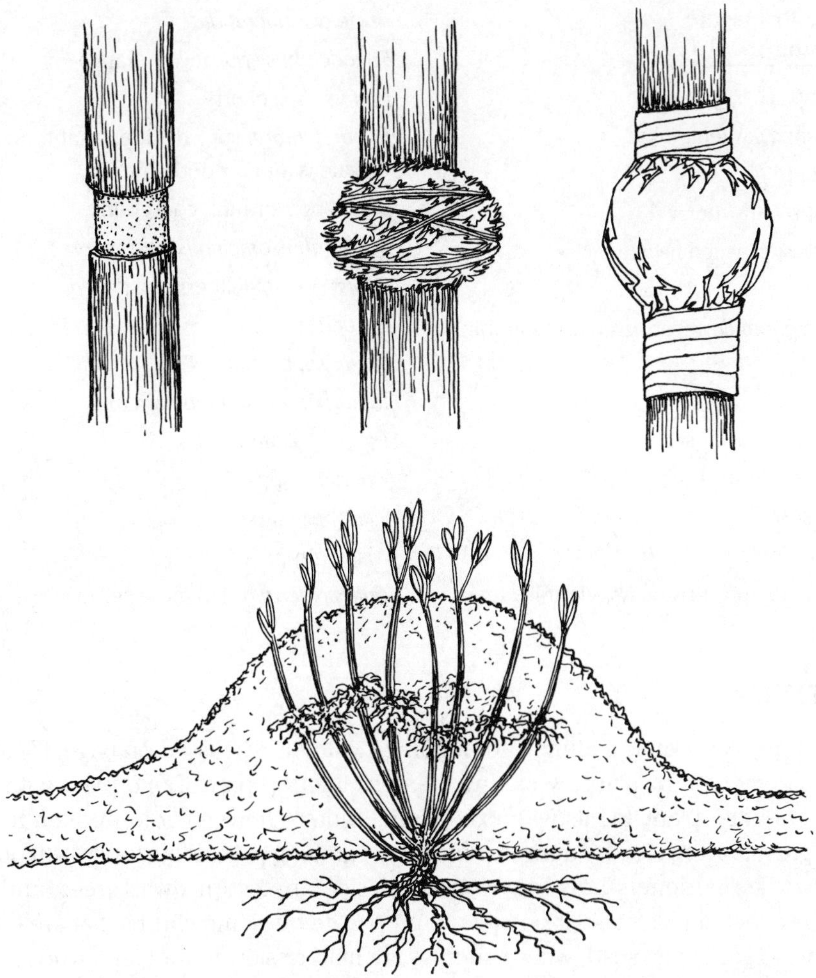

To air layer an indoor plant (top), remove a strip of bark from the stem and cover the injured site with moist sphagnum moss. Cover with plastic and seal the edges. When roots form, sever the rooted portion of the stem from the plant. To air layer outdoor plants (bottom), remove a strip of bark, then mound soil around the plant.

PLANTS TO PROPAGATE BY LAYERING

The plants listed here can be propagated by some form of layering.

Acer, maple

- *A. negundo*, box elder
- *A. saccharinum*, silver maple

Calycanthus floridus, Carolina allspice

Camellia japonica

Chaenomeles spp., flowering quince

Clematis spp.

Corylopsis spp., winter hazel

Cotinus coggygria, smokebush

Cotoneaster spp.

(continued)

Plants to Propagate by Layering *(cont'd)*

Daphne spp.
Dianthus spp., garden pinks
Forsythia spp.
Fragaria spp., strawberry
Hamamelis spp., witch hazel
Hedera spp., ivy
Hydrangea anomala subsp. *petiolaris*, climbing hydrangea
Ilex spp., holly
Jasminum spp., jasmine
Lonicera spp., honeysuckle
Magnolia spp.
Malus spp., apple
Parthenocissus spp., Boston ivy, Virginia creeper
Pernettya mucronata
Philadelphus spp., mock orange
Prunus spp., cherry
Rhododendron spp., deciduous and evergreen azaleas and rhododendrons
Ribes spp., currant, gooseberry
Rosmarinus officinalis, rosemary
Rubus spp., blackberry, raspberry
Spiraea spp.
Syringa spp., lilac
Tamarix ramosissima, tamarisk
Tsuga spp., hemlock
Viburnum spp.
Vitis spp., grape
Wisteria spp.
Zelkova serrata, Japanese zelkova

GRAFTING

The techniques known as grafting and budding (which is discussed on page 97) allow gardeners to create a new plant by joining the desirable top part of one plant with the root system of another plant. Plants with exceptional fruit, or flowers, or form often have weak roots, or grow too large for the desired purpose. By grafting or budding topgrowth onto different rootstocks, gardeners have developed full-size apples on dwarf trees, and hardier roses. These techniques make it possible to propagate trees and shrubs that are difficult or impossible to grow from seed, whose cuttings are hard or slow to root, and whose branches are too inflexible or high above the ground for layering.

Grafting is performed with a piece of stem containing more than one bud. In the nursery industry grafting (as well as budding) is used on fruit trees, roses, tree peonies, some ornamental trees and shrubs, and evergreens. Home gardeners with a yen for experimentation may want to try their hand at grafting and budding deciduous trees and shrubs. Evergreens are too difficult to graft under backyard conditions.

Plants must be close botanical relatives in order to be grafted successfully. In most cases they must belong to the same genus, although some plant families (roses, for instance) are so compatible that plants from different genera can be joined successfully.

The top part of a grafted plant, the stem piece, is known as the scion. Scions are typically slender year-old shoots 1/4 inch or less in diameter and 4 to 6 inches long, with several buds. The root piece upon which the scion is grafted is called the stock, rootstock, or understock. A rootstock can be a seedling, a rooted cutting, a piece of root, or even a mature tree. (Grafting done on a mature tree is called "topworking.") Rootstocks are generally a year or two old, and the same diameter or a bit larger than the scion, although size and age varies with the type of plant.

Rootstock plants are not readily available to home gardeners. You will probably need to grow your own from seeds or cuttings.

When plants are grafted, the cambium tissues of the scion and rootstock are placed together and fastened in place until the tissues intertwine and grow together. For the graft to take hold, the cambium tissue of the two parts must make good contact; pieces must be precisely cut and fitted together.

Once fitted, the two parts must be held securely together until the graft takes hold. Rubber band ties and grafting tape are sold especially for use in grafting, or you can use string to hold the pieces in place.

After the graft is secured, it is sealed with grafting wax or grafting compound, or wrapped in plastic to seal in moisture. The tissues of both scion and rootstock must remain continuously moist for the cells to fuse together.

The best time to perform most grafting is in early spring while the plants are still dormant. But most scion wood is gathered in late autumn or early winter and stored until spring. It is essential that scions be dormant when they are collected and when they are grafted.

For scions, use healthy shoots at least 12 inches long and one to three years old. Tie them in bundles, wrap the bundles in plastic, and pack them in damp peat moss or sawdust. Store over winter in a cold but frost-free location. At grafting time, cut off the top and bottom 2 to 3 inches of each scion, and use the center part.

After making a graft, watch it carefully. If the buds on the scion swell, which should happen in a few weeks, you will know you have succeeded. Several weeks to several months later, when the graft has completely healed, remove the bindings from the graft union.

SPLICE GRAFT

This simple graft is appropriate for deciduous plants less than 1/2 inch thick. Cut the rootstock on an angle, so that the cut is three to four times as long as the diameter of the stock. Cut the bottom of the scion the same way. Match up the exposed cambium layers of scion and rootstock, and fasten the pieces together, then seal.

CLEFT GRAFT

Nurserymen use cleft grafts with small rootstocks growing in containers or nursery beds, or to join a scion to a root cutting.

Cleft grafts are usually done in early spring, when the buds on the rootstock start to swell, but the scion is still fully dormant. Split the top of the rootstock, and cut the bottom of the scion into a wedge shape. Set the scion into the cleft in the stock so the cambium tissues make contact and the two pieces fit tightly together. Bind and seal.

For a cleft graft, cut the end of the scion into a wedge.

Insert the scion into a matching notch in the stock.

Hold the two pieces together with rubber grafting strips or raffia.

WEDGE GRAFT

This graft is used on soft-wooded or herbaceous plants, with both pieces about the same size. Cut the bottom of the scion into a wedge, as for a cleft graft. Make a wedge-shaped cut in the rootstock to hold the scion. Bind and seal.

WHIP-AND-TONGUE GRAFT

Whip-and-tongue grafting is done with young unbranched trees (called whips), grapes, small branches, and roots to produce nursery stock.

A whip-and-tongue graft is like a splice graft with matching notches cut into the scion and rootstock. Cut the two pieces as for a splice graft, then split or cut each piece vertically to about one-third of the way in from the cut end. The scion and rootstock should fit neatly together. Match up the pieces, then bind and seal the graft.

BUDDING

Budding is used for roses, fruit trees (especially stone fruits—cherries, peaches, and plums), and some shade trees. It is performed when mature buds are available and the bark can be easily removed from the rootstock, generally in late summer. At this time growth is finished for the year, but the new wood has not yet hardened for winter.

Rootstocks for budding are usually seedlings in at least their second year of growth.

Use firm, mature buds from the current year's growth, from a firm, woody stem about as thick as a pencil. Cut a piece of the stem 10 or more inches long (called a "budstick").

For a whip-and-tongue graft, cut matching notches in stock and scion.

Match up the notches so the cambiums of the two pieces make good contact.

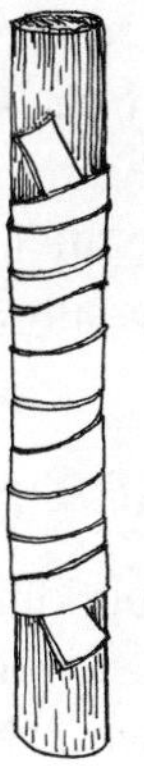

Hold the graft in place with rubber ties or raffia until the two parts grow together.

Remove the blades of the leaves, but leave part of each petiole attached to the stem, to make it easier to handle the buds when you cut them from the stem. (If necessary, you can refrigerate the budstick wrapped in plastic for a few days.)

Cut off the top and bottom 2 to 3 inches of the budstick and discard them. Use the fattest, firmest buds from the middle of the stick. Wrap the stick in a damp cloth while you work, to keep it from drying out.

SHIELD OR T BUDDING

Make a T-shaped cut in the bark of the rootstock, deep enough to cut all the way through the bark but not into the cambium. Twist the knife blade gently under the bark around the cuts in order to loosen it.

Cut a bud from the budstick, starting from below and cutting upward to remove the bud with a shield-shaped piece of bark. Use a shallow, slightly angled cut to remove the bark and most of the cambium layer without cutting into the wood. In the case of fruit trees, you can take a thin strip of wood with the bud.

Insert the shield with the bud under the edges of the T-shaped cut in the rootstock. Push the shield down until the heel of the bud rests against the crosswise cut and the shield fits tightly in the T.

Tie above and below the bud with raffia (soaked in water first), plastic, or rubber budding strips. To tie the bud, first bring the strip over the top of the shield, then start at the bottom of the vertical cut and wind upward. Cover the entire cut and all of the shield except for the bud itself. Remove raffia or plastic ties after 2 to 4 weeks so they do not constrict the growth. Rubber ties can be left in place until they decompose.

After a few weeks, if the petiole shrivels and falls off, the budding has succeeded. If the petiole shrivels but stays attached to the stem, the budding did not work.

Early the next spring, when the bud swells, cut off the top of the stock. On shrubs, cut right above the T. On trees, cut 6 inches above the T, then remove that stub in late summer.

Remove any suckers that may grow from the rootstock.

REVERSE T BUDDING

Reverse T budding is like shield budding except the T-shaped cut in the stock is made upside down. When working with a large bud, make a cross-shaped cut in the stock instead of the upside-down T; it will hold the bud more securely.

JUNE BUDDING

June budding is a type of shield budding used in warm climates where plants do not go totally dormant.

Use the same procedure as for shield budding. Five to 10 days after grafting, bend or partially break the top of the stock to force the bud to grow. When the new shoot has several sets of leaves, cut off the top of the stock right above the bud.

PLATE BUDDING

To make a plate bud, cut three sides of a rectangle into the bark of the stock to form a flap, and bend it down. Cut the bud with a matching rectangle of bark instead of a shield. Match the cambium around the bud to the exposed cambium area on the stock. Bring the flap of bark on the stock back up over the bark attached to the bud (do not cover the bud) and tie it securely.

From this point on, treat the graft like a shield bud.

H BUDDING

H budding is used for trees whose thick bark is difficult to bend for a plate bud. To make an H bud, cut a double rectangle in the bark, with one flap attached at the top and the other at the bottom. Cut the bud with a rectangular shield. Match up the cambiums of the bud and the stock, and close both flaps over the shield. Tie securely and then handle like a shield bud.

PATCH BUDDING

Patch budding is also used for trees with thick bark, such as mangoes and nut trees. It is like plate budding except that no flap of bark is left on the stock—the rectangular area is simply exposed. Patch budding is generally performed in early spring with dormant buds from the previous season, but you can also perform it in summer with buds from the current season.

DIVISION

Division is a fast, easy way to reproduce plants that multiply themselves by suckers, rhizomes, or underground growths or offsets. Most perennials form growth buds (eyes) on the crowns (the points where roots meet stem) that can be separated from the parent plant along with some roots to grow into new plants. When clumps of perennials become crowded, dividing them restores the plants' vigor.

Division is also used with bulbs and some shrubs that form clumps or offsets.

DIVIDING PERENNIALS

Most perennials need periodic division to maintain plant vigor and lush flowering. Some plants need division every year or two, while others can go for many years before they need to be divided. When a clump of perennials looks crowded and the plants produce fewer and smaller flowers, it is time to divide.

Generally, the best time to divide spring-blooming perennials is in early fall. Divide summer bloomers later in fall, and fall bloomers in early spring. When dividing in fall, make sure four to six weeks remain before the first anticipated hard frost, so the divisions have time to establish new roots before the ground freezes.

Cut back to the ground the stems of the plant to be divided. Remove some of the topsoil around the base of the plant, and dig up the entire clump of roots with a shovel or spading fork. Try to leave intact as many of the roots as possible when you lift the plant out of the ground.

Separate the clump of roots into pieces that each contain crowns with dormant buds as well as roots.

If the root system is fibrous and fairly small, as with hardy geraniums (*Geranium* spp.) and primroses, pull the clumps apart with your fingers.

For plants with a cluster of crowns, such as astilbe, use a sharp knife to cut the clump into sections. If the cluster of crowns is large, push two spading forks back to back into the clump. Push and pull the handles back and forth to force the clump apart. Really dense clumps of thick, woody roots, as might be found under long-neglected stands of bearded iris or summer phlox, may have to be chopped apart with a hatchet.

For perennials that have fleshy roots, each with several eyes (daylilies and peonies, for example), cut apart the roots so that each piece has at least two eyes.

When the root clump is divided, discard the tough, old roots and crowns from the center of the clump and replant the younger outer sections.

A less intrusive way to divide plants that seldom need division, such as hostas, or plants that resent being disturbed, such as oriental poppies, is to dig up and remove some of the crowns from the outer edges of the clump without moving the main plant.

Replant divisions right away so they do not dry out. Replant most plants at the same depth they were growing before. Keep the soil evenly moist for the next several weeks as the new plants establish themselves. When the soil freezes in late fall, mulch the divisions to prevent the roots from heaving during the winter.

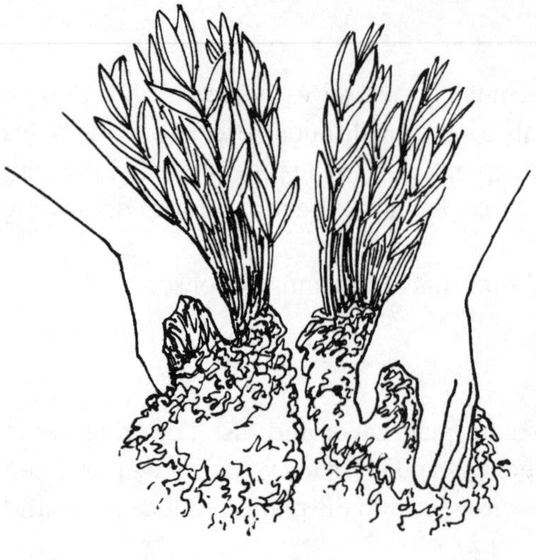

Perennials with fine, fibrous roots can be divided by simply pulling apart clumps of roots.

Cut apart clumps of thicker roots with a sharp knife.

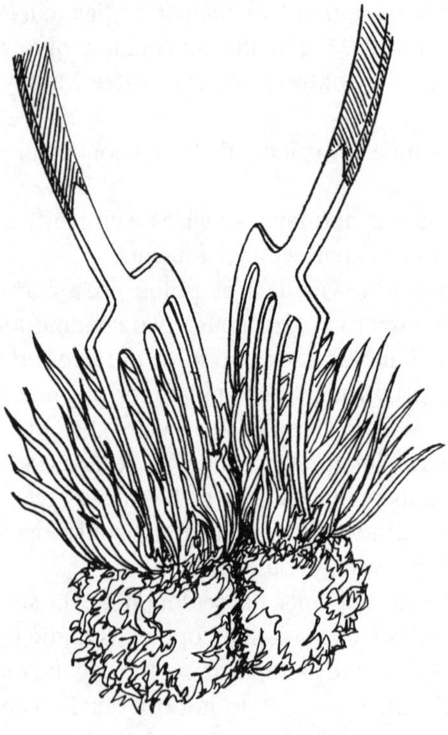

To divide dense clumps of tough roots, push two garden forks into the clump back to back and use them as levers to pry apart the roots.

DIVIDING BULBS

Daffodils, tulips, and many other true bulbs produce offsets that will grow into new plants. When a planting of these bulbs becomes crowded and produces fewer flowers, division is in order. When the leaves die back in summer, dig the bulbs, separate the offsets from the parent bulbs, and replant offsets and parents in loose, deeply dug soil rich in organic matter.

Scaly bulbs like those of lilies, which resemble garlic bulbs, can be divided by pulling off and planting the outer scales. Plant the scales with the pointed end up in a container of moist rooting medium. The scales will grow into little bulblets that can be planted to grow into new plants.

Some lilies produce bulbils on underground parts of the stem or bulblets along the stem in the leaf axils. All these offsets can be removed and planted. Plants will grow to blooming size in one to four years.

Crocuses, gladioli, and some other plants grow from underground structures called "corms." The corm dies and is replaced by the plant each year. Small offsets called cormels develop around the base of the corm. Dig the corms after the plants finish blooming and the leaves die back. Separate the new corm from the old, withered one, and remove the little cormels. Immediately replant the new corms and cormels of hardy plants. Gardeners in cool climates can store the corms and cormels of tender plants until spring (see chapter 3 for information on storing tender bulbs), and plant them out at the appropriate time.

To divide tuberous-rooted plants like dahlias, cut apart the clumps of swollen roots so that each part contains an eye and part of the old stem. Replant roots of hardy plants immediately; store the roots of tender plants to replant in spring.

DIVIDING SHRUBS

Some shrubs, such as mock orange and spiraea, form crowns or clumps, or spread by means of underground shoots. These shrubs can be divided like perennials. In most climates, the best time to divide shrubs is in early spring while the plants are still dormant. Where winters are mild, divide in autumn.

If the shrub is not too large, dig up the entire plant, cut the root clump into sections, and replant the divisions immediately. If the shrub has sent out suckers or rhizomes that have rooted, use a spade to sever them from the main plant without digging up the plant, then dig and replant the severed youngsters. Alternatively, you can dig up the young plants and detach them from the parent with pruning shears or a saw. No matter how you accomplish the division, replant the divided parts right away.

PLANTS TO PROPAGATE BY DIVISION

Achillea spp., yarrow
Aquilegia spp., columbine
Arabis spp., rock cress
Armeria maritima, sea pink
Artemisia spp.
Aster spp.
Astilbe spp.
Aubrieta spp., false rock cress
Aurinia saxatilis, basket-of-gold

(continued)

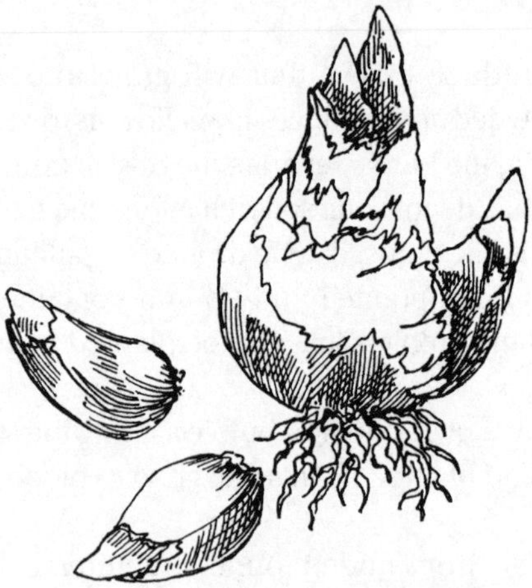

To divide clumps of tunicate bulbs such as daffodils, remove the young offset bulbs and plant them separately.

To divide scaly bulbs such as lilies, remove the outer scales and plant them to grow into blooming size bulbs.

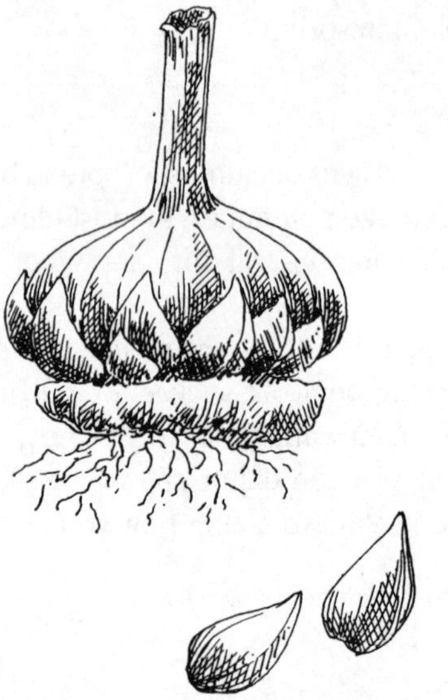

Crocuses and other corms form cormels around the base. Remove and plant them.

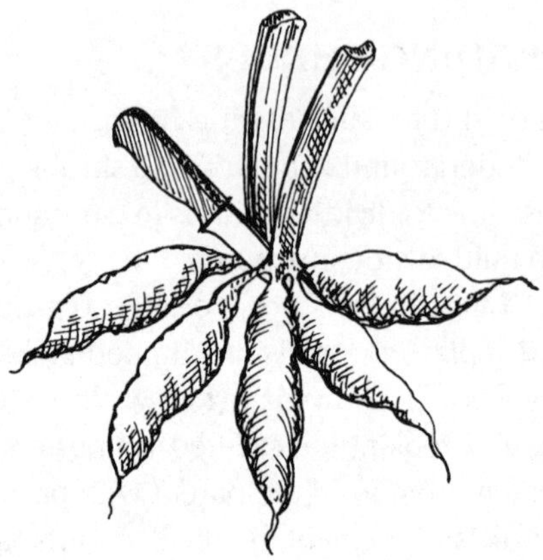

Cut apart clumps of tuberous roots like those of dahlias, making sure each section contains one or more "eyes" (growth buds).

Plants to Propagate by Division *(cont'd)*

Berberis spp., barberry
Bergenia cordifolia, heartleaf bergenia
Campanula spp., bellflower, harebell
Centaurea montana, mountain bluet
Cerastium tomentosum, snow-in-summer
Clethra alnifolia, sweet pepperbush
Convallaria majalis, lily of the valley
Coreopsis spp., tickseed
Cortaderia spp., pampas grass
Crocus spp.
Dahlia spp.
Delphinium spp.
Deutzia spp.
Dendrathema spp., garden chrysanthemum
Dianthus spp., garden pinks
Dicentra spp., bleeding heart
Digitalis spp., foxglove
Echinacea purpurea, purple coneflower
Euonymus spp.
Gaillardia spp., blanketflower
Galanthus spp., snowdrop
Galium odoratum, sweet woodruff
Geranium spp., hardy geranium, cranesbill
Helenium spp., sneezeweed
Heliopsis spp., sunflower
Hemerocallis spp., daylily
Heuchera spp., coralbells
Hibiscus spp.
Hosta spp.
Hyacinthus orientalis, hyacinth
Hydrangea spp.
Iberis sempervirens, perennial candytuft
Iris spp.
Leucanthemum × *superbum*, shasta daisy
Liatris spp., gayfeather
Liriope spp., lilyturf
Lonicera spp., honeysuckle
Lupinus spp., lupine
Lychnis chalcedonica, Maltese cross
Lycoris spp. magic lily
Monarda didyma, bee balm
Narcissus spp., daffodil and narcissus
Oenothera spp., evening primrose, sundrops
Pachysandra spp.
Phalaris spp., ribbon grass
Philadelphus spp., mock orange
Phlox paniculata, summer phlox
Physostegia virginiana, false dragonhead
Primula spp., primrose
Rubus spp., raspberry, blackberry
Rudbeckia spp., black-eyed Susan
Scabiosa caucasica, pincushion flower
Scilla siberica, Siberian squill
Sedum spp., stonecrop
Spiraea spp.
Stachys byzantina, lamb's ears
Syringa spp., lilac
Tradescantia × *andersoniana*, spiderwort
Tulipa spp., tulip
Vaccinium spp., blueberry
Viola spp., violet

WATERING

Water is the medium through which plants receive most of their nutrients; mineral compounds in the soil are dissolved in water and taken up through plant roots. And water fuels the process of photosynthesis. In photosynthesis, water and carbon dioxide combine in the presence of light and produce glucose and oxygen. The water molecules are split and give off the oxygen, which is transpired through the leaves. Excess water vapor is also transpired through leaves to help plants cool themselves.

During a drought plants close their stomata (pores in the leaves) to keep their tissues from drying out. But with the stomata shut tight, the plants cannot take in the carbon dioxide needed for photosynthesis, and they stop growing.

Recently scientists have discovered that plants use water in another way, too. At night, deep-rooted plants draw up water from deep in the soil like pumps, then flush it out into the soil through their shallow roots. These deep-rooted plants actually supply water to other, shallower-rooted plants growing near them. The phenomenon is called "hydraulic lift," and it has been observed in both wet and arid parts of the United States. We have always believed that in times of drought plants growing in close proximity are at risk because they must compete with one another for the available water. But the existence of the pumping action of some plants suggests that plants growing together might actually be better off.

Watering practices change as we learn more about how plants use water. But with water shortages likely to occur more and more frequently in all parts of the country, the best course of action for gardeners is to use water prudently and strive to conserve this most precious of resources. The information in this section is based on efficient water use.

WHEN TO WATER

It is important to know when to water your plants and to water *only* when it is necessary.

Water when the soil is dry. Your hands are a good guide. Don't just touch the surface of the soil, which often dries out quickly. Poke a finger down into the soil. When it feels dry a couple of inches down, it is time to water many plants. Very shallow-rooted plants like annuals may need water more often, and so will plants in containers. During the summer, potted plants need water every day, or twice a day, depending on the size of the pot and how hot and dry the weather is. The smaller the pot, the more it will need watering. Plants in large tubs or barrels don't need to be watered as often.

Soil dries out at different rates, and an understanding of your soil type is essential for gauging watering times. Sandy soil dries out much more quickly than dense clay soil, so plants growing in sandy soil will need watering more often than plants in other types of soil. Adding organic matter improves the texture of both sandy and clay soils. See chapter 1 for more information on the characteristics of different soil types.

Water plants according to their daily and seasonal needs. Don't automatically turn on the sprinkler system or get out the hose for fifteen minutes every day. Unnecessary watering wastes water and is harmful to plants if it is done too often. Learn the water needs of your plants, and treat them accordingly. Shallow-rooted annuals, perennials, and vegetables will need to be watered during spells of dry weather, but trees and shrubs, if they are suited to your growing conditions, should need supplemental watering only during drought or extremely hot weather.

Many plants have the greatest need for water at particular times in their growth cycle. If they receive water at the critical times, they can usually tolerate some dry conditions at other times. Plants have particular need for water when they are young and growing quickly, when they are setting buds, and when fruit is developing. In the vegetable garden, leafy crops need water on a regular basis to form tender, succulent leaves.

While watering every day is not a good idea for most plants, neither is watering too infrequently. Don't wait until plants wilt to water them. If some plants do wilt, you can usually revive them with a thorough drink and a good misting (or, for plants in pots, by submerging the pot in a bucket of water until it stops bubbling). But plants that wilt are severely stressed, and their growth will be set back or slowed. Learn to recognize genuine wilting before rushing off to flood the plants. Some plants, especially young ones, tend to look a bit flaccid on hot afternoons even though they have plenty of water; they perk up again toward evening. But when plants look limp in the morning or evening, they are in trouble and need water right away. Plants may tell you when they are about to wilt by appearing soft and floppy and dull in color.

Give plants enough water. When you do water, water thoroughly. (See "How Much to Water," below.)

Water at the most effective time of day. The best times to water are in the morning or late in the afternoon. Try not to water at midday, when evaporation is greatest, or at night, when wet foliage is susceptible to attack by disease organisms. Another reason not to water at noon is that the water droplets sitting on plant leaves can act like little lenses, focusing the sun's rays onto the leaves and causing burning.

Use moderation and common sense. The guidelines given in this or any other gardening book are just that: guidelines. There are no absolutes in gardening. Use your own judgment in managing your garden. If your garden needs water and you don't get home from work until after dark, go ahead and water. After all, it rains at night sometimes, and plants are usually pretty adaptable. Watering at night is better than not watering at all.

HOW MUCH TO WATER?

The traditional rule of thumb for watering is that gardens need an average of 1 inch of water per week. Whatever doesn't fall from the sky must be supplied by the gardener. That may be fine as a general average, but it is not true at all times for all gardens. Plants in sandy soils will need more than an inch of water a week, while plants in heavy clay soils may need less. Temperature is also a factor. In places where the mercury rises into the 80s, 90s, and beyond, gardens will need more than 1 inch of water, sometimes a lot more.

Use the 1-inch rule as a starting point if you like, but tailor your watering to weather conditions, soil type, and the needs of the plants. It is useful to know how long it takes to put an inch of water on your garden, and there are a couple of ways to determine that.

If you use an overhead sprinkler or an automatic sprinkler or drip system, you can calculate based on the rate at which the equipment emits water and the square footage of the area you have to water. Calvin Simonds, author of *The Weather-Wise Gardener* (Rodale Press, 1983, out of print), suggests the following formula: Multiply the area covered by your sprinkler (in square feet) by the number of seconds it takes your sprinkler to fill a gallon container. Drop the last two digits and you have an approximation of the number of minutes it takes to put an inch of water on an equivalent area of garden space.

A simpler way to measure output is to set out a coffee can in the garden where you are watering and see how long it takes to get an inch of water in the bottom.

Once you know how long it takes to put an inch of water on the garden you can adjust for weather, soil, and plants.

The most important thing to remember about watering is to water thoroughly and deeply each time. Frequent shallow watering encourages plants to concentrate their feeder roots in the top few inches of soil, where they are vulnerable in hot, dry weather if you are not there to water every day. Some plants are naturally shallow-rooted and cannot develop deep roots. Lawn grasses, for instance, go dormant in long, dry periods. But for most plants, watering less often, but more deeply, encourages the plants to send roots deeper into the soil.

Trees are the deepest rooted plants, and it can take several hours to deeply water a tree. If you live where water is scarce, though, it is helpful to know that 80 percent of the root system of most trees is located in the top 18 inches of the soil. If you can water your trees at least that deeply during a drought (it will still take some time), they should be fine.

HOW TO WATER

There are a number of ways to water plants. Gardeners can choose from drip irrigation systems, soaker hoses, conventional hoses with spray nozzles or bubblers, a variety of overhead sprinklers that attach to a hose, automatic sprinkler systems with underground piping, old-fashioned sprinkling cans, and buckets.

Watering at Ground Level

From a water-conservation standpoint, watering methods that deliver water at soil level, directly to the root zone of plants, are best. They make the most efficient use of water, because the water is directed where it is needed, and little is lost to evaporation before it reaches plant roots.

If your garden is very small, you may not need any special watering equipment other than a bucket and a cup or jar. Carry a bucket of water to the garden and dip out water to pour at the base of each plant.

In larger gardens, soaker hoses or drip irrigation systems are both excellent ways to water. Soaker hoses are made either of canvas or porous fabric, or of rubber (some from recycled automobile tires) with small holes punched in the walls. Soaker hoses allow water to seep slowly from the pores in their walls and soak into garden soil. The slow, gradual application lets the water soak into the soil without runoff.

To use soaker hoses, lay them in the garden early in the season, snaking them in and out around and among plants. In rowed vegetable gardens, just stretch the hose down the row right alongside the plants. Connect together as many hoses as you need, and connect the last one to a conventional hose which runs to the water source. Turn on the water at partial

14 Ways to Save Water

1. Mulch. Mulching slows the evaporation of moisture from the soil, and keeps the upper layer of soil cooler. Mulching does not mean you will never have to water, because plants also lose a lot of water through transpiration, which mulch cannot control. In hot, dry weather even mulched gardens will need water.
2. If you prefer not to mulch, keep the garden weeded. Weeds are voracious drinkers that will usually outcompete garden plants for available moisture.
3. Water in the morning on a calm day.
4. Don't water until plants need it.
5. Don't water if rain is likely later in the day.
6. On automatic watering systems, change timer settings according to the weather. Turn off the system if rain is forecast. Or invest in an automatic switch controlled by an underground moisture meter that will turn the system on when it's needed.
7. Check couplings, tubing, hoses, and other equipment for leaks. A leaky connector can waste huge amounts of water.
8. Adjust sprinkler heads to aim water at plants, and minimize watering areas that are not part of the garden.
9. Stop watering if runoff occurs.
10. Capture and recycle water from air conditioners, dehumidifiers, and rain gutters. Catch and save rainwater. Recycle graywater from the household for use in the garden. (Check local regulations governing graywater use. An excellent source of information is *Greywater Use in the Landscape*, by Robert Kourik, available from Edible Publications, P.O. Box 1841, Santa Rosa, CA 95402, for $6.00 + $4.00 shipping and handling, plus tax for California residents.)
11. Try adding a hydrogel to the soil in garden or containers. Available in garden centers, these polymer crystals absorb and hold water, swelling to many times their original size and reducing watering frequency.
12. Grow drought-tolerant plants.
13. In hot climates, give plants some afternoon shade.
14. In windy, exposed locations, plant or build a windbreak to shelter the garden and slow drying.

pressure to operate the soaker hoses. Leave soaker hoses in the garden until fall, then roll them up and store them indoors over winter. If you don't care for the way the hoses look in the garden, cover them with mulch.

Drip irrigation systems use slender plastic tubing with drip emitters at intervals. The tubing is run throughout the garden and emitters are located next to plants. There are all sorts of couplings for linking pieces of tubing together, going around corners, and so forth. The drip emitters come in several sizes intended for use in particular types of soil—larger sizes for sandy soil, smaller sizes for heavier soils. The tubing is meant to be installed underground, although some gardeners just lay it on top of the soil. Most systems are connected to timers that turn them on and off. Drip systems are expensive and a lot of work to install, and the lines sometimes clog. But in areas where frequent watering is essential, they are a tremendous work saver once in place. They also make very efficient use of water.

A good source of information on drip irrigation is *Drip Irrigation for Every Landscape and All Climates* by Robert Kourik (available from Metamorphic Press, P.O. Box 1841, Santa Rosa, CA 95402; $12.00 + $4.00 shipping and handling, plus tax for California residents).

If you're a proponent of the good old-fashioned garden hose, you can convert it to root-zone watering with a bubbler attachment. Lay the hose on the ground in the garden and let it bubble, moving it from place to place to water all the plants.

Overhead Watering

Watering from overhead is not as efficient as watering at ground level. As the water arcs through the air, some of it evaporates before it reaches plants. When the water does get to the plants, it has to filter down through all the foliage before it can reach the soil and soak down to the roots.

Overhead sprinklers that attach to a hose spray their water over large areas—including paths, sidewalks, and driveways. Automatic sprinkler systems with underground pipes are a little better, but not much. The sprinkler heads of these systems are aimed at groups of plants, but in covering a garden or lawn completely, some of the water inevitably ends up on sidewalks and driveways. Sprinkling cans are less wasteful because you pour the water directly onto the plants that need it, but they make sense only for small numbers of plants.

There are some advantages to overhead watering, though, and in some locations these can be considerable. Watering from above cools the air and increases humidity in the vicinity of plants, and it also rinses dirt from the leaves. In some situations, overhead watering may still be the method of choice.

FERTILIZING

Types of organic and synthetic fertilizers and ways to apply them are discussed in chapter 1. Here are some tips on when to fertilize different kinds of plants.

ANNUALS

Add organic fertilizers to the soil when preparing for planting, or when setting out plants. Once they are established, apply fertilizer around the plants on a monthly basis. This is called "top-dressing."

Apply other all-purpose fertilizers when planting, again when plants begin actively growing, then weekly in sandy soils or biweekly in heavier soils.

PERENNIALS

Add organic fertilizers to the soil when preparing for planting, or when planting. Top-dress monthly during the growing season.

Apply other all-purpose fertilizers when planting new plants, when established plants begin growing, then every two weeks in sandy soils or every three to four weeks in heavier soils. Stop fertilizing six weeks before the first expected fall frost.

BULBS

Apply organic fertilizers when preparing the soil for planting, ideally a season ahead of planting (to allow time for phosphorus to become available to plants). Thereafter top-dress once a year, when new shoots emerge.

Apply other all-purpose fertilizers or bulb food at planting time (work it into the soil as deeply as you will plant, and mix it in well), when new shoots emerge, and for hardy bulbs, again when flowers fade, to nourish the leaves.

ROSES

Add organic fertilizers when preparing the soil for planting, a season ahead of planting. Top-dress or side-dress (apply fertilizer alongside roses planted in a row) when new growth begins, and several times during the growing season, stopping 8 weeks before the first expected fall frost.

Apply other all-purpose fertilizers or rose food when growth begins in spring and again after the first flush of bloom. Thereafter fertilize bush roses monthly until six weeks before the first fall frost, shrub roses and climbers just once or twice more in late spring and early summer.

TREES AND SHRUBS

Do not fertilize trees and shrubs during the first year after planting.

Thereafter, top-dress with organics around the dripline when growth begins in spring, and fertilize young trees again in early summer. Work the fertilizer into the top inch of soil.

Apply other all-purpose fertilizers to young trees in spring when growth begins, then monthly until six weeks before the first expected fall frost. Fertilize mature trees once a year in spring. Using a drill or crowbar, make holes 2 feet apart and 12 to 15 inches deep over the root zone (from 2 to 3 feet out from the trunk to the dripline) and put fertilizer into the holes.

VEGETABLES

Work organics into the soil when preparing it for planting. You can also add a small amount to planting holes and furrows. Side-dress monthly during the growing season.

Apply other all-purpose fertilizers after planting, and every two to three weeks when plants are actively growing.

MULCHING

Mulches are useful in summer and winter, for different reasons. Summer mulches keep down weeds by blocking light that enables many of them to germinate. They slow the rate at which moisture evaporates from the soil. They keep the soil from drying excessively and crusting. Earthworms are attracted by mulch, and their tunneling improves soil texture. They also help break down mulch and leave behind nutrient-rich castings that nourish the soil.

As organic mulches break down, they add organic matter to the soil. A number of organic materials make good mulches, and the best are described below.

Spread most summer mulches 2 to 3 inches deep, depending on the coarseness of the material; the coarser the material, the deeper you spread it. Lay mulch around and between plants, but keep it an inch away from the stems of annuals and perennials, or it could cause crown rot. Mulch trees and shrubs from 6 to 12 inches from the base to the dripline. Keep the mulch away from the trunk or it could attract rodents, especially in winter.

Organic mulches keep soil cool in spring, so pull them aside to let the soil warm. Some organic mulches make the soil slightly more acidic. If you are growing plants that prefer neutral or mildly alkaline pH, lime the soil before laying the mulch, or mix some lime with the mulch.

Wood products (bark chips, sawdust) take nitrogen from the soil as they decompose, so add nitrogen fertilizer to the soil before laying down such a mulch. Fresh bark chips contain tannin that may repel slugs. On the other hand, slugs and earwigs love to hide under mulch; if slugs are a problem in your garden, try spreading fresh chips around the perimeter of the garden, frequently replacing them, or avoid mulching altogether.

Black plastic also makes a good summer mulch. Although not aesthetically pleasing, black plastic affords excellent weed control. Black plastic also warms the soil, and makes a good mulch for heat-loving plants such as muskmelons. Lay black plastic mulch before planting the garden. Cut X-shaped slits in the plastic and fold back the flaps to plant. The plant should not completely fill the hole in the plastic, even when mature, or water will not be able to get to the plant roots. In fact, you should cut holes or slits in the plastic to allow passage of water and air. Though a mulch of black plastic retains moisture, it excludes air; soil can eventually grow stale and waterlogged under plastic.

Winter mulches applied before the ground freezes keep the soil from freezing deeply or at all. You can leave carrots, turnips, and other root vegetables in the garden under a 6- to 12-inch-deep mulch of loose organic material, and dig them as needed all winter.

A winter mulch can also be spread over perennials, shrubs, and shallowly planted bulbs (such as crocus) after the soil freezes, to keep the ground frozen all winter. The mulch prevents plant roots from being heaved out of the ground during alternate periods of thawing and refreezing. When soil repeatedly thaws and refreezes, it buckles and heaves, and roots can be pushed out of the soil. Exposed roots are likely to be killed by drought and cold when the mild periods end and the cold returns. Spread these winter mulches 6 to 8 inches deep.

Following is a list of materials to use for mulch. Two things *not* to use as mulch are peat moss and fresh grass clippings. Peat moss repels water and blows around when it is dry. Fresh grass clippings pack down into a slimy, smelly mess unless applied in a very thin layer.

A GUIDE TO MULCHES

Bark (chips): Long-lasting, but can be expensive. The larger the pieces, the longer they last. Spread about 2 inches deep and add nitrogen to the soil before applying the mulch.

Bark (shredded): Long-lasting, and somewhat expensive. Spread 3 inches deep and add nitrogen to the soil before applying the mulch.

Buckwheat hulls: Dark brown-black in color, they last for about two years in the garden. Spread them 2 inches deep.

Cocoa bean hulls: Attractive, brown in color, and smell like chocolate for a short time after you spread them. They are expensive, but a good mulch for formal gardens and flower beds. Spread them 2 inches deep.

Compost: Dark brown in color, nourishes the soil but weeds will grow right through it. It is an excellent soil conditioner. Spread it at least 1 to 2 inches deep as a mulch.

Corncobs (ground): Inexpensive and available in agricultural areas. Add nitrogen fertilizer to the soil before spreading the mulch. Spread 3 to 4 inches thick.

Cottonseed hulls: Add nitrogen to the soil, are effective in suppressing weeds, but tend to blow around. Apply the mulch 3 to 4 inches deep, or use 2 inches of this mulch and cover with another, heavier mulch.

Evergreen boughs: Good winter mulch for perennial gardens, but must be removed in spring; cannot be turned into the soil.

Hay and straw: Lightweight and a good source of organic matter, but compacts with time. Alfalfa and clover hay add nutrients to the soil. Hay may contain weed

(continued)

A Guide to Mulches *(cont'd)*

seeds, especially if it's from the first cuttings. Straw contains no weed seeds, but is coarser in texture. Spoiled hay is often available inexpensively in farm areas. Spread it 4 to 6 inches thick in summer, 8 to 12 inches in winter.

Leaf mold: Decomposed or composted leaves provide good cover and add organic matter to soil. Good choice for woodland and wildflower gardens, or informal flower beds. Spread 2 to 3 inches deep.

Leaves (shredded): Unshredded leaves can pack down and resist water penetration, but shredded leaves are effective as a weed suppressor and insulator. Good for woodland and naturalistic gardens, and as winter mulch. Spread 2 to 3 inches deep in summer, 6 to 8 inches deep in winter.

Paper: Newspaper laid two to four sheets deep suppresses weeds and decomposes in a year or so. Not aesthetically pleasing, so cover with another, more attractive mulch.

Peanut hulls: Lightweight and easy to use where available. Spread 2 to 3 inches deep.

Pine needles: Attractive, light, and long-lasting. Long-term use may lower soil pH; use around acid-loving plants or add lime if used around plants needing neutral or mildly alkaline soil. Spread 3 to 4 inches thick.

Plastic (polyethylene): Warms soil and effectively suppresses weeds, but is impenetrable to moisture except where holes or slits are cut into it. Warms soil. Cover with another, more attractive mulch.

Sawdust: Inexpensive, acidic, takes nitrogen from the soil as it decomposes. Add nitrogen fertilizer before spreading sawdust mulch, or compost it before using. Use around acid-loving plants, or add lime if used around plants needing neutral or alkaline pH. Spread 2 inches thick.

Seaweed: Can be collected from beaches in coastal locations. Good source of organic matter and trace elements, but can be odoriferous. Soak in fresh water before using around salt-sensitive plants. Apply 3 inches deep.

Stone, gravel, or marble chips: Not good at keeping weeds down; use over black plastic for weed control. Stone mulches are best around trees and shrubs or in rock gardens, as permanent mulch. Spread 2 to 3 inches deep, depending on size. You can also use larger stones as mulch; they retain heat.

Weed barrier fabric: Made of polypropylene fibers, this fabric is laid before planting, like black plastic. Unlike plastic, water and air pass easily through it. Cut X-shaped slits for planting. The fabric will break down in the presence of light, so cover it with another mulch.

Wood chips: Reasonably attractive and long-lasting, but decompose more quickly than bark. Add nitrogen fertilizer to soil before spreading wood chips. Apply 2 to 3 inches deep.

PERMANENT MULCH GARDENING

Permanent mulch gardening has been around since the 1970s, but it may be the wave of the future. In the permanent mulch method, the garden is covered with one or more organic mulches as much as a foot deep. As the mulch decomposes, fresh mulch is added. The mulch stays in place all year, and the soil is not tilled or cultivated once the mulch is in place. At planting time, the mulch is pulled aside as plants or seeds are put into the ground, then is replaced as plants grow.

Permanent mulch gardens require little or no weeding, and the soil is continually being improved as old mulch breaks down. Leaving the soil undisturbed, with no digging or tilling, conserves carbon, which is released into the air as carbon dioxide when soil is tilled.

WEEDING

Weeds are the scourge of gardens everywhere. The kindest definition of what constitutes a weed is that it is simply a plant in the wrong place or, as Ralph Waldo Emerson said, "a plant whose virtues have not yet been discovered." But there is more to a weed than just its location or lack of virtue. Weeds are also aggressive, tenacious opportunists that are able to survive in tough conditions. Weeds are bullies, outfighting garden plants for the available space, water, nutrients, and light. Weeds are highly efficient at reproducing themselves. Annual weeds produce amazing quantities of seeds (a single pigweed plant can have millions of them), and perennial weeds have resilient taproots or rhizomes, the smallest piece of which can generate an entire new plant.

Weed seeds ride into our gardens on wind, runoff water, or the feet of animals. Birds drop or excrete them. The hay mulch we spread to control weeds may contain the seeds of more. Worst of all, perhaps, are the weeds that were deliberately introduced here from other countries to serve particular purposes. Free from the controls of their native habitat, they spread totally out of control (see "The Worst Weeds," later in this section).

For better or worse, we're stuck with weeds. Here are some tips on coping with them.

First, be aware that light is an important factor in the germination of many annual weed seeds. One way to keep the weed population down is to disturb the soil as little as possible (a good argument for permanent mulch gardening, as described earlier in the section on Mulching). Another way to minimize weed growth is to mulch the garden.

In a new garden, an empty part of an established garden, or a garden of annuals or vegetables that is replanted every year, try solarizing the soil before planting. Cover the soil with a sheet of clear plastic and leave it in place for several weeks. If you have a reasonable amount of sunny weather during that time, temperatures under the plastic should get hot enough to kill many of the weed seeds in the top few inches of soil.

You can install vertical edging strips of metal or plastic around the perimeter of island beds to keep lawn grasses from invading the garden.

Weed barrier fabrics (described in the Mulching section) are still relatively new, but seem to be effective, especially those with a close weave.

There are also many herbicides on the market for killing weeds. Resort to them if you must, but I would not recommend using them as a matter of course. If you do decide to use an herbicide, look for a product based on fatty acids (glyphosphate), with an applicator that can be precisely aimed. Read and follow directions carefully.

Salt, vinegar, and chlorine bleach have been used by gardeners to kill weeds, but they can affect the soil and damage nearby plants. Confine their use to weeds in the cracks of sidewalks and patios.

Old-fashioned pulling is still an effective way to get rid of weeds, and there are ways to make the most of time spent weeding:

- Pull weeds when they are small. The roots will not yet have gone deep into the soil, and the plants will be easier to uproot.
- If you can't get weeds out of the garden when they are small, at least pull them before they go to seed and start a whole new generation. Do *not* put weeds with seeds on the compost pile. Even a hot pile will not be hot enough to kill all weed seeds. You will end up spreading them through the garden along with the compost.
- Pull weeds when the soil is moist; they will come out of the ground more easily. Don't weed when the soil is wet, though, or you could compact it.
- Frequency is the key. If you pull a few weeds every time you leave the house, or spend just five or ten minutes a day weeding, you can keep things pretty well under control in a garden of modest size. Once you let the weeds get out of control, getting rid of them will be a lot more work, and your garden plants will suffer from the competition.
- Pull or dig by hand perennial weeds with taproots or rhizomes. Hoeing will cut the roots into pieces, and each piece left behind will grow into a new plant. Some of the weeding tools described below under "Tools for Weeding" are meant for digging taproots.

Learn to appreciate the virtues of weeds. Some weeds do have good qualities; some are edible, and others make good cut or dried flowers. See "Useful Weeds" for more information.

Finally, learn to enjoy weeding. It doesn't have to be an onerous chore. Weeding can be a pleasant experience. It can provide a soothingly mindless antidote to a stressful day. And weeding is a splendid opportunity to get out in the garden.

TOOLS FOR WEEDING

A host of hand tools can make weeding easier and faster. If you decide to hoe instead of pull your weeds, just be prepared to do it often. Hoeing exposes more weed seeds to light, and they will germinate into a new crop. You'll have to keep after them. When using a hoe, aim to cut off the weeds just below the soil surface—the deeper you go into the soil, the more seeds you will turn up.

Many types of hoes are available. Hoes with flat-edged blades are good for large areas. There is also a flat-bladed hoe with a curved blade that is good for cutting. Another classic design has two different edges: One side is a flat blade and the other end has two sharp prongs for opening crusted soil or getting into smaller spaces.

A Warren hoe has a flat, triangular blade with a beveled edge that is good for weeding close to plants. For weeding in small spaces or behind plants, a hoe with a narrow, angled blade is effective.

Other hoes are designed to maximize your effort—they cut on both a pushing and a pulling stroke. A scuffle hoe has an open-centered blade with a narrow bottom edge. An action or oscillator hoe is a similar design. The two ends of a narrow band of metal are connected to the handle by means of a simple hinge, which allows the blade to rock back and forth, making it easier to push and pull. There is also a hoe with a flat, wedge-shaped blade with a pointed tip that can either be pushed or pulled.

A number of hand weeders with short handles are also on the market. For weeding small areas and narrow spaces, you can choose a tool with a flat, L-shaped blade with a pointed tip; or a Cape Cod weeder, which has a narrow, L-shaped blade with a sharp cutting edge; or a tool with a flexible curved blade.

For digging tap-rooted weeds like dandelions, use a tool that has a flat blade with a notch in the tip; these tools are available in a couple of different widths.

Hoes and other gardening tools are available from local garden centers and a number of mail-order garden supply companies. One company that specializes in tools for gardeners and nurserymen is:

A. M. Leonard, Inc.
241 Fox Drive
P.O. Box 816
Piqua, OH 45356

THE WORST WEEDS

Some of the most insidious weeds gardeners have to contend with are quack grass, whose tenacious rhizomes can travel hundreds of feet; bindweed, a wild relative of morning glory whose twining stems wrap around other plants for support and routinely suffocate those supporting plants; and horsetail, which grows in wet soils and has roots that can go 60 feet deep.

Other pernicious weeds started out as plants that were introduced from other countries for particular purposes. Out of their native habitats, conditions were so favorable that the plants got out of control. Many of them have become significant threats in parts of the United States. Here are some of these unwelcome visitors—guests that will not leave, however much we'd like them to:

Bermuda grass (*Cynodon dactylon*) and Johnson grass (*Sorghum halepense*): Introduced as livestock forage and became invasive.

(continued)

The Worst Weeds *(cont'd)*

Bouncing bet or soapwort (*Saponaria officinalis*): An ostensibly harmless ornamental, has irritant properties.

Brazilian pepper tree (*Schinus terebinthifolius*), chinaberry (*Melia azedarach*), and cajeput tree (*Melaleuca leucadendron*): Introduced as ornamentals, have pollen that is highly irritating and sap that causes skin rashes and blisters in sensitive people. Cajeput tree was introduced to help dry swampy areas for development, but it is now drying up dangerous amounts of surface water in areas that are important natural wetlands.

Hydrilla (*Hydrilla verticillata*): Introduced as an aquarium plant, now crowds waterways in the Southeast. Crops grown for the trade are believed to have escaped from cultivation.

Japanese honeysuckle (*Lonicera japonica*): Another ornamental, is perniciously invasive in this country.

Kudzu (*Pueraria lobata*): A vine originally planted for erosion control, has taken over many parts of the Southeast. Kudzu can overwhelm even tall trees and can cover entire houses.

Purple loosestrife (*Lythrum salicaria*): Was and is grown in many perennial gardens for its spires of rosy purple flowers. It has escaped from cultivation, and has so clogged wetlands in the Midwest that it is now illegal to grow the plant in some states.

Water hyacinth (*Eichhornia crassipes*): Introduced for its pretty purple flowers but spread so rapidly that it now clogs waterways in Florida, posing a danger to boat traffic, wildlife, and other plants.

Wild roses (*Rosa multiflora, R. bracteata,* and others): Planted as hedges, windbreaks, or simply ornamentals, these roses spread vigorously and are very difficult to eradicate.

USEFUL WEEDS

Some weeds can be appreciated for their good qualities.

Blackberry: Edible fruit

Cattail: Roots and young shoots are edible

Chicory: Roots can be dried, roasted, and ground to use as substitute or additive for coffee

Chickweed: Edible leaves and stems

Dandelion: Edible leaves (best when young, before flowers bloom), flowers can be used to make wine

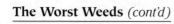

Dock: Edible leaves (remove tough midrib before using)

Goldenrod: Flowers can be used in fresh or dried arrangements

Grasses: Flowers of wild grasses can be used in fresh or dried arrangements

High mallow, or malva: Edible leaves

Lamb's quarters: Edible leaves

Milkweed: Young shoots are edible cooked (do not eat them raw)

Miner's lettuce: Edible leaves

Mints: Edible leaves, flowers can be used in fresh arrangements

Mustard: Edible leaves

Nettles: Leaves and young shoots are edible (cook and strain to remove the sting and the prickly hairs; handle with gloves before cooking)

Pigweed: Young leaves are edible, seeds can be ground and added to bread flour

Plantain: Edible leaves

Prickly pear: Fruit and young pads are edible (peel the pads before using)

Purslane: Edible leaves

Queen Anne's lace: Use flowers in dried arrangements (lay them face down and flat to dry)

Tansy: Use flowers in fresh or dried arrangements

Violet: Young leaves and flowers are edible; flowers can also be candied and used to decorate desserts

Winter cress: Edible leaves, best in fall and winter

Yarrow: Use flowers in fresh or dried arrangements

CONTROLLING PESTS AND DISEASES

It's impossible to get rid of all the bugs, no matter what we spray or dust onto them. The pests develop resistance after a time, and some of the pesticides linger in the environment, where the long-term effects are not yet known. A more reasoned approach to pest control that is gaining many adherents is Integrated Pest Management, IPM. The term is being heard more and more, and all gardeners should be familiar with it.

IPM combines several different means of controlling pests with an overall program of good plant management. The process of IPM begins with careful monitoring of plants, so that when pests attack, you can spot them before the infestation becomes severe. When pests appear, you need to determine the level of injury—how much damage has been done to plants—before setting a course of action. Then take action immediately. Limit control measures to the site of the infestation; if you find pests on a particular part of a plant, focus your efforts there, rather than treating the whole plant, or all the plants in the vicinity. Use the least disruptive means of control first, then evaluate the results. If the pests persist, go on to a stronger control.

IPM aims to take advantage of control measures that already exist naturally, such as plants' resistance to pests, natural predators and parasites of the pests, and the overall health and vigor of plants. Four different kinds of controls are used: cultural, biological, physical, and chemical.

Cultural controls are basically good growing practices that result in healthy, vigorous plants (pests tend to zero in on weak plants first) as well as planting varieties that are resistant to pests known to be a problem in a particular area. Companion planting or planting trap crops are other means of cultural control. Trap crops are plants that are of no interest to the gardener or farmer, but that attract the pest and are planted as decoys to lure the pest away from the valued plants. For example, black nightshade—a weed—can be planted to lure Colorado potato beetles away from potato plants.

Biological controls are effected by predators of the pests, which may be other insects, birds, toads, or other wildlife (insect predators are discussed later, under "Beneficial Insects"), by parasites that attack the pests, and by bacterial agents such as milky spore disease, which sickens and destroys the larvae of Japanese beetles. Another effective bacterial control is *Bacillus thuringiensis*, Bt, which attacks a wide variety of larvae and caterpillars. Insect growth regulators, which mimic the insect's hormones but disrupt their growth cycle, are another form of biological control.

Physical controls include repellents that drive pests away, traps and barriers that keep the pests from reaching the target plants, and the physical removal of the pests from the plants by handpicking or strong sprays of water. There are sticky yellow traps that attract aphids and other flying insects, sticky red traps for codling moths, and numerous ways to use Tanglefoot (the sticky substance used to coat flypaper) to trap crawling insects. Earwigs can be trapped under boards or in crumpled paper, then destroyed. There are barriers to keep slugs out of the garden (see "Slugs," later in this section), and different barriers to exclude deer and other wildlife (see "Deer and Controlling Other Animal Pests," later in this section). Pheromone lures like the bag traps for Japanese beetles combine a biological and a physical control. Mulching plants with aluminum foil repels aphids and other light-sensitive pests.

Chemical controls, the last resort, involve the use of sprays, dusts, and other pesticide or fungicide products. These products may be synthetic or natural (what gardeners usually call "chemical" or "organic"). The term chemical here refers to its mode of action, not what it is made of. For organic gardeners, chemical controls include insecticidal soaps and plant-based pesticides such as pyrethrins (derived from pyrethrum daisies), rotenone, and neem products. Other gardeners may choose products such as Malathion or Sevin. Chemical controls are the last resort because they are the most toxic; they kill beneficial insects along with pests, and thus affect the ecosystem.

Garden centers are stocking an expanding array of environmentally sensitive pest control products, and many more are available by mail. Sources include:

Gardener's Supply Company
128 Intervale Rd.
Burlington, VT 05401

Gardens Alive!
5100 Schenley Pl.
Lawrenceburg, IN 47025

Necessary Trading Company
New Castle, VA 24127

Ringer Corporation
9959 Valley View Rd.
Eden Prairie, MN 55344

COMMON PESTS, SYMPTOMS, AND CONTROLS

PEST	SYMPTOMS	CONTROLS
Aphids	Curled or yellow leaves, sticky honeydew on twigs or leaves, general weakness in plant	Spray plants with strong stream of water. Sticky yellow traps. Aluminum foil mulch. Predatory insects. Horticultural oil sprays. Most general-purpose garden sprays or dusts, including pyrethrins, rotenone, and Malathion.
Borers	Holes in trunks of dogwoods, lilacs, rhododendrons, roses, and other shrubs (frass—gummy sawdust—usually visible by the holes or at base of trunk); brown, mottled foliage on irises	Remove and destroy infested parts of plants where possible. Poke a wire into borer holes in tree trunks to kill borers. Trap with Tanglefoot or burlap wraps around trunks of trees. Cover squash vines with floating row covers except when flowers are blooming. Write or call county cooperative extension office for specific pesticide recommendations. For woody plants, squirt pesticide containing paste into holes, then plug holes. Malathion provides partial control of iris borer.
Caterpillars (cutworms, cabbage worms, etc.)	Chewed leaves; cutworms fell young seedlings	Handpick. Predators and parasites. Dust with *Bacillus thuringiensis* (Bt). Many general-purpose insecticides, including rotenone, pyrethrins, or Malathion.

(continued)

Common Pests, Symptoms, and Controls *(cont'd)*

PEST	SYMPTOMS	CONTROLS
Flea beetles	Small holes all over leaves, tiny insects jump off when you disturb leaves; vegetables (tomatoes, eggplant, potatoes, cole crops, spinach) are the most common targets	Cover crops with floating row covers. Dust with diatomaceous earth. Introduce parasitic nematodes into soil. Insecticides, including neem, nicotine, pyrethrins, sabadilla, Malathion, Sevin.
Japanese beetles (and other beetles)	Large holes in leaves or skeletonized leaves; beetles usually visible near damage	Floating row covers. Handpick. Pheromone traps placed away from plants at risk. Milky spore disease to control grubs in lawn. Insecticides, including rotenone, ryania, carbaryl, Malathion.
Leafminers	Tunnels in leaves (especially columbines, boxwood, birch trees, spinach, and chard)	Remove and destroy damaged leaves as soon as they appear. General-purpose gardening insecticides carefully timed to catch adult flies that lay the eggs. Systemic insecticides.
Mites, spider mites	Speckled yellowish spots progressing to yellow, bronze, and/or curled leaves; fine webs between leaves and stems; small specks visible on webs or on leaf undersides	Keep plants well watered to prevent them. Remove chickweed and other host plants. Spray with strong stream of water. Predatory mites. Insecticidal soaps. Horticultural soil sprays. Insecticides, including nicotine, pyrethrins, rotenone, phosphate insecticides, miticides.
Slugs and snails	Large portions of leaves and flowers chewed (damage generally done at night); shiny trails on soil and plants	Surround beds with copper strips. Trap under boards and destroy. Sprinkle with salt. Slug and snail baits (beer traps lure more slugs to the garden).

PEST	SYMPTOMS	CONTROLS
Whiteflies	Clouds of tiny white insects fly up from foliage when disturbed; plants look generally unhealthy	Sticky yellow traps. Insecticidal soap. Most general-purpose insecticides, including neem, nicotine, pyrethrins, Malathion, Sevin.

Note: Consult your local extension service or garden center for appropriate insecticides for particular pests and particular plants. Some insecticides can damage plants. For example, maidenhair fern is sensitive to several insecticides; Sevin kills both Virginia creeper and Boston ivy (it is also extremely toxic to bees, though relatively safe to fish and wildlife). Read the labels of all insecticide containers and follow directions carefully for best results.

BENEFICIAL INSECTS

Some insects are quite helpful in the garden. Learn to recognize beneficial insects in your garden, and leave them alone to do their work. Predatory and parasitic insects for pest control can be purchased and introduced into the garden. One source is Rincon-Vitova Insectaries, P.O. Box 95, Oak View, CA 93022.

Ant lion or doodlebug: Larva of a fly, traps ants in its burrow in the ground, then eats them

Bees, butterflies and moths: Pollinators

Cryptolaemus, called the mealybug destroyer: A small beetle related to the ladybug. It feeds on mealybugs, but will also eat aphids and immature scale insects when it can't find enough mealybugs.

Dragonflies: Found near water, eat mosquitoes and flies

Encarsia formosa: A parasite of greenhouse whitefly, can be used to control whiteflies indoors

Firefly larvae, or glowworms: Eat a number of small insects, and also snails

Ground beetles: Most of them are dark brown or black, shiny, and rather flat in shape, prey on other insects, and some attack snails

Lacewings and their larvae: Eat many kinds of soft-bodied insects, especially aphids. The larvae are sometimes called aphid lions.

Ladybird beetle, or ladybug: Probably the best known of all predatory insects, consuming mealybugs, scales, and other soft-bodied insects, as well as small worms

(continued)

Beneficial Insects *(cont'd)*

Parasitic wasps, such as Braconids, Ichneumons, and Trichogrammas: Very tiny, they suck the body fluids of their hosts. They lay their eggs on tomato hornworms, tobacco hornworms, and other caterpillars, and the young parasitize the host when they hatch. Trichogramma wasps attack the eggs of moths and butterflies and are helpful in controlling larval pests like corn earworm and cabbage looper.

Praying mantids: Eat all sorts of insects. Unfortunately, they also eat each other, and most of the young that hatch from any given eggcase will never make it to adulthood.

Predatory mites: Consume pest mites or their eggs

Syrphid flies: Small flies that resemble bees or wasps and can be spotted hovering over flowers. Their larvae attack aphids and the larvae of ants, termites, and bees.

Why Do Ants Herd Aphids?

A plant infested with aphids will usually also have a lot of ants. Ants actually herd aphids, and here's why. As aphids suck sap from plant stems, leaves, and buds, they brush against flowers, and nectar gets stuck to their backs. The ants collect the nectar from the aphids and take it back to their nests.

WHAT IS DORMANT OIL?

Petroleum oil sprays afford an excellent means of control for a variety of soft-bodied pests, primarily on trees and shrubs, including various fruit trees. The sprays are solutions of oils (called "horticultural oils") in water, and there are two types.

Dormant oils are heavy oils that are sprayed when plants are dormant, to suffocate overwintering pests such as aphids, scales, and mites. The temperature must be above 40°F for the spray to be effective. Dormant oil is used only on dormant plants because it could damage growth of actively growing plants. Some plants cannot tolerate dormant oil at all; if you are unsure, test the spray on a small section before spraying the entire plant.

Summer oils are lighter oils that may be sprayed while plants are growing, and when the temperature is less than 85°F. In addition to controlling aphids, mites, mealybugs, scales, and some caterpillars, summer oils are effective for controlling mildew. Do not use summer oil on edibles.

PLANTS JAPANESE BEETLES LIKE

These voracious pests aren't very finicky: They'll eat lots of different plants. Listed here are some of their favorite targets.

Acer spp., Japanese maple, Norway maple
Aesculus spp., horse chestnut
Alcea rosea, hollyhock
Asparagus

Betula spp., birch
Cydonia oblonga, quince
Hibiscus syriacus, rose of Sharon
Kerria japonica, Japanese kerria
Ligustrum spp., privet
Malus spp., apple
Malva spp., mallow
Myrica spp., bayberry
Myrtus spp., myrtle
Parthenocissus spp., Boston ivy, Virginia creeper
Prunus spp., cherry, peach, plum
Rhododendron, azaleas
Rhubarb
Rosa spp., roses
Salix discolor, pussy willow
Soybeans
Tagetes spp., marigold
Tilia spp., linden
Vitis spp., grape
Wisteria spp.

Diatomaceous Earth

Diatomaceous earth is a powder made from the ground shells of fossilized diatoms (one-celled, sea-dwelling organisms). The abrasive particles damage the soft tissues of the slugs, and the slugs lose moisture and die.

SLUGS

Slugs and snails are destructive feeders which attack a wide assortment of plants. They will chew on annuals, perennials, groundcovers, foliage plants, vegetables, and fruits. They are active at night, and leave behind silvery, slimy trails as evidence of their passage.

Slugs and snails are especially damaging in spring, when plants are young and tender, but they are active from very early spring to late fall or even into winter. They thrive in moist conditions and are not active in dry periods. During the day, slugs and snails hide under mulch, rocks, boards, bricks, or garden debris.

Slugs and snails do have predators, and welcoming wildlife to your garden may help keep them under control. Beetle grubs, earwigs, birds, toads, turtles, and snakes all eat slugs and snails.

Putting barriers around the garden or especially valued plants can keep out slugs and snails. Diatomaceous earth, wood ashes, fresh wood chips, or copper edging strips are all used as barriers to impede the passage of slugs and snails. One test showed copper strips to be the most effective barrier.

You can also handpick and destroy the creatures. Put out stones, boards, or upside-down flowerpots in the garden to trap them, and empty the traps daily. Or go out at night with a flashlight to catch them on the move. When you catch them, drop them into a pail of soapy water or sprinkle them with salt. Shallow pans of beer sunk into the soil have long been a favorite slug trap, but such traps are actually likely to attract more slugs to the garden than were in residence before.

Pelleted or granular baits containing metaldehyde will attract and kill slugs and snails, but are not recommended for households with young children or pets who might be tempted to eat the bait.

DEER

Deer are a serious garden nuisance in many suburban areas. As habitat areas get built on or paved over, deer have fewer sources of wild food. With hunting strictly limited or prohibited in settled areas, deer populations have grown. With more deer and less food, the plants in home gardens and landscapes are more at risk.

There are two basic approaches to handling deer: repel them from the garden or protect the plants so the deer cannot eat them. Deer seem to behave differently in different places and at different times. The repellents listed below work for some gardeners but not for others, and they work for some gardeners only part of the time. Barriers are more effective, but they are not terribly attractive, although some of the repellents aren't exactly aesthetically pleasing either.

REPELLENTS

- Sprinkle blood meal around the garden; reapply after rain.
- Spray plants with hot pepper solution; reapply after rain.
- Use a commercial deer repellent.
- Suspend bars of soap throughout the landscape, right at grazing level. Ivory, Irish Spring, and heavily perfumed soaps have been reported successful.
- Hang bags of human hair throughout the landscape. Get hair clippings from a local barber or salon, and stuff them into bags made from old pantyhose.
- Hang moving objects from a string that runs around the perimeter of the garden. Strips of aluminum foil, Mylar, or cloth, and aluminum pie pans are some possibilities.
- Set a radio that is tuned to an all-talk station in the garden. This has been reported to scare raccoons more than deer.

BARRIERS

- Erect a fence, at least 8 feet tall (9 to 10 feet is better), around the entire garden. Double-walled constructions of chicken wire or wire mesh, with a second fence 3 to 4 feet high inside the tall fence, are considered best. They are even better if the top is angled outward, and a layer of mesh are laid flat on the ground outside the fence (supposedly deer do not like to put their hooves on it).

Do not touch wild animals in your garden, and transport live-trapped animals with great caution. Especially dangerous are raccoons and skunks, both of which may carry rabies.

Birds: Cover fruiting trees with plastic netting. Scare birds away with scarecrows or inflatable snakes and owls, or hang aluminum pie pans or strips of foil or Mylar to flutter in the wind. Provide alternative food sources elsewhere on the property, away from the garden (see "Trees and Shrubs That Attract Wildlife," in chapter 4).

Gophers, ground squirrels, chipmunks, prairie dogs: Try catch-and-release traps baited with nuts or peanut butter. Surround the garden with a wire mesh or hardware cloth fence that reaches 2 feet above the ground and 2 feet underground. Line bulb planting areas with hardware cloth on the bottom and sides. Flood gopher tunnels with water and kill or trap the animals as they run out.

Groundhogs: Cover young plants with floating row covers. Surround the garden with a fence of chicken wire or wire mesh 3 feet high. If that doesn't solve the problem, try a 4-foot fence with the bottom foot bent outward and buried under soil. Or dig a trench up to a foot deep outside the fence and line the bottom with wire mesh.

Mice, voles: They eat practically anything, but are particularly fond of bulbs. Line bulb planting areas with hardware cloth on the bottom and sides. Plant daffodils and narcissus, which they will not eat, instead of tulips, which are delicacies. Set baited traps in tunnels.

Moles: Moles eat grubs, but they also eat earthworms. Make a barrier around the garden by digging a 2-foot-deep trench and filling it with gravel, ashes, or crushed seashells. Flood their tunnels as described for gophers. Drop castor beans in tunnel entrances. If you can stand it, set up mole traps, which skewer the animals in their burrows with a metal spike.

Rabbits: Surround the garden with a 3-foot-high fence of hardware cloth or wire mesh, that also extends a foot underground. Surround young trees and shrubs with wire mesh cylinders, or use tree wrap or tree guards on trunks of young trees. Sprinkle blood meal around seedlings; sprinkle leaves of other plants with bone meal, rock phosphate, wood ashes, or hot pepper (reapply after rain).

Raccoons: Usually not a problem unless you grow corn. To protect a corn patch, put up an electric fence, scatter sharp stones or ashes on the ground among plants, or cover corn ears with paper bags and secure with tape, string, or rubber bands. Or sprinkle corn silk with hot pepper. You might also try putting a radio tuned to a talk station in the garden at night.

Skunks: Surround the garden with a 3-foot fence. Apply milky spore disease to lawn to kill grubs that skunks eat.

COMMON DISEASES, SYMPTOMS, AND CONTROLS

Disease	Symptoms	Controls
Anthracnose		
(specific types infect roses, sweet peas, beans, melons, shade trees)	Circular spots appear on leaves, usually gray or white in the center edged with red; on trees, leaves appear scorched and defoliation and death of entire limbs may occur	Plant resistant varieties. Maintain overall vigor of plants by building up health of soil. Remove and destroy infected tissues. Bordeaux mixture may be helpful, but may damage roses. Carbamate.
Blights		
(may be fungal or bacterial, includes fireblight, azalea petal blight, late blight, and alternaria or early blight)	Obvious spots or dried leaves appear suddenly, usually without wilting; sudden death of entire branches or plants	Remove and destroy infected plants; rotate plantings. Clear garden of plant debris before winter. Maintain overall plant vigor by building up soil; avoid wetting leaves when watering. Remove and destroy infected limbs or plants (sterilize tools after each cut). Use carbamate or other fungicide (for fireblight use streptomycin or copper fungicides).
Botrytis blight		
(gray mold)	Infected portions of peonies, lilies, dahlias, tulips, gladioli, roses, and begonias rot; peony buds fail to open; tulips and lilies develop blackened and distorted flowers and leaves; eventually a brownish gray mold appears	Improve air circulation by increasing spacing between plants. Improve soil drainage. Remove dead or dying foliage from plant and soil around plant. Remove and destroy infected plant parts. Remove and destroy all plant debris from the beds before winter. Use appropriate fungicides in early spring.
Crown rot		
(fungal)	Shoots suddenly yellow, wither, and dry up; plant crowns and surrounding soil become covered with white strands; usually appears at the onset of warm, humid weather	Remove and destroy all infected plants. In extreme cases, remove infected soil and replace with fresh soil. Drench soil with appropriate fungicide.

Disease	Symptoms	Controls
Damping off		
	Seedlings rapidly wilt or rot at base	Use sterilized soil mix and containers. Don't crowd seedlings. Try covering seed with sand, vermiculite, or milled sphagnum. Apply carbamate fungicide promptly. If losses are great, replant seeds.
Galls		
(includes crown gall, root knot, cane galls)	Woody swelling develops on stems or roots, often an inch or so in diameter	Unattractive but rarely problematic. Prune off and destroy unsightly galls (sterilize pruning tools with crown galls as these are bacterial). Spraying is not effective.
Leaf spot fungi		
(includes black spot on roses)	Round, yellow or yellow-green spots that darken over time	Keep foliage dry (water early in the day and water soil around plant rather than leaves). Remove and destroy infected tissues. Maintain overall plant vigor. For black spot, use baking soda with horticultural oil spray, or dust with sulfur or other appropriate fungicide.
Mosaic viruses		
	Leaves are mottled yellow and green; flowers and new growth are dwarf or malformed	Grow resistant varieties. Practice good garden sanitation. Buy only healthy plants. Destroy infected plants. Control sucking insects that transmit viruses. Fungicides are not effective.
Powdery mildew, downy mildew		
	Grayish white powdery spots appear on leaves, especially in damp or humid conditions	Rarely kills plant, can often be ignored. Improve air circulation, set plants farther apart, water early in the day. Spray with light horticultural oil or carbamate. Use fungicides such as sulfur or copper products.
Rots, bacterial		
(includes iris soft rot)	All or part of plant dies and decays; may be accompanied by ooze and foul odor	Cut away and destroy diseased tissue (for iris, expose remaining healthy portion of tuber to bright sunlight for a couple of days, or disinfect remaining healthy portion of tuber with chlorine).

(continued)

Common Diseases, Symptoms, and Controls *(cont'd)*

Disease	Symptoms	Controls
Rust		
	Powdery rust-colored (or yellowish) spores or jellylike horns on leaves	Remove and destroy infected leaves. Remove plant debris from beds in autumn. Use appropriate fungicide such as carbamate.
Wilts		
(includes fusarium wilt, verticillium wilt, Dutch elm disease)	Plants droop and eventually die (from plugging of vascular system)	Remove and destroy infected plants. Plant resistant varieties. Rotate plantings (or sterilize soil) because disease organisms remain in soil. Fungicides are not effective.

Note: Consult your county cooperative extension office for appropriate fungicides for particular diseases. Some fungicides such as Bordeaux mixture can injure some plants. Also, some fungi have developed resistance to old stand-bys such as Benomyl. Read the labels of fungicide containers and follow directions carefully for best results.

A NEW FUNGICIDE FOR ROSES

Black spot and powdery mildew are the two most common diseases of roses. Many growers spray regularly with fungicides to prevent or control these diseases. Now there's a safer alternative.

Researchers at Cornell University found that spraying roses once a week with a solution of horticultural oil spray and baking soda controlled both diseases. The mixture was tested in 1992 in the rose garden at Longwood Gardens in Pennsylvania. The spray was made with 1 tablespoon of baking soda and $2^1/_2$ tablespoons of Sunspray Ultrafine Horticultural Spray Oil per gallon of water.

The Longwood Gardens rosarians found that the spray controlled powdery mildew almost completely, and afforded moderate control of black spot.

This formula would be worth a try on other plants prone to mildew, as well as roses.

PRUNING

Pruning can be defined as the removal of plant parts for purposes other than harvesting. There are a number of reasons to prune. You may prune to:

- Remove spent flowers from annuals and perennials (an operation known as deadheading)
- Remove dead, damaged, diseased, or weak growth from trees and shrubs
- Rejuvenate overgrown and neglected plants to revitalize them
- Encourage bushier growth, or growth in a particular direction
- Enhance the shape of a plant
- Limit the size of a hedge. (Trees and shrubs should not need to be pruned for size; instead, choose a plant that will mature to an appropriate size for a small space.)

Except in the cases of topiary and espalier, pruning should not attempt to change the basic shape of the plant. If you want a low, rounded shrub, don't plant one with an upright form and try to force it by pruning. Choose plants that will attain in maturity the right size and shape for the location. If you work against a plant's natural inclination, you will have to prune more often to keep the plant in line, and the plant will never achieve its full potential. Consider, for example, the forsythia, which has a place in so many American yards. When forsythias are pruned into neat little globes or boxes, they produce only a fraction of the blossoms they have when left to assume their natural upright, spreading or fountainlike shape.

When pruning it is best to err on the side of caution. Don't overprune. You can always prune a bit more next year.

Most trees and shrubs are best pruned when they are dormant. Late winter or very early spring, before new growth begins, is the best time to prune in most regions. Gardeners in warm climates where winters are mild will do most of their pruning in midwinter. However, when damage from a storm or a disease such as fireblight occurs, you should prune the affected wood immediately, instead of waiting for the tree or shrub to enter dormancy.

Following are brief descriptions of basic pruning techniques.

PRUNING HERBACEOUS PLANTS

Pinching

Annuals and perennials with a branching growth habit develop a bushier, more compact form if the tips are pinched back. Pinching encourages the growth of more sideshoots, and results in increased numbers of flowers. When plants are young, pinch off the growing tips back to the next set of leaves. New shoots will grow in the leaf axils. For greater bushiness, you can pinch the tips of those secondary shoots when they grow long enough. Use your fingernails or a set of flower snips or shears for pinching.

Use the same procedure to encourage bushiness in foliage plants such as coleus, and to remove undesirable flowers.

If you wish to grow exhibition-size flowers on mums, dahlias, and other plants, you must pinch them with the opposite goal in mind. Instead of developing many sideshoots, the plant must develop just one or a few main stems, and concentrate its energy into producing fewer, but larger, flowers. In this procedure, called "disbudding," you pinch out sideshoots that would produce additional flower buds, and pinch all but one or two buds from the remaining stems.

Deadheading

Deadheading is simply removing spent flower heads. Deadheading prevents plants from setting seeds. In annuals this promotes continued bloom, because the mission of annuals is to grow, bloom, produce seeds, then die within a single growing season. Until the plants form seeds, they will keep blooming. Deadheading perennials sometimes induces repeat bloom, and also conserves the plant's vigor, since none of its energy is diverted into seed formation.

To deadhead, pinch or cut back the flowering stem on a branched plant such as chrysanthemum, coreopsis, or salvia to the uppermost leaf or set of leaves. To deadhead a plant that grows in the form of a rosette and produces flowers on individual stems above the basal clump of leaves (coralbells is a good example), cut off the flower stem at its base. If the plant produces clusters of flowers that open over a period of time, such as daylilies and hostas, remove individual flowers when they fade, then cut back the flowering stem when the entire cluster is finished blooming.

Thinning

Some perennials, such as summer phlox, bloom better if some of the stems in the clump are removed. Dense stands of phlox are more prone to mildew and can benefit from thinning even though the root clumps are not crowded enough to warrant division. To thin, just cut back to the ground some of the stems, to open up the plants and allow more space between the remaining stems.

PRUNING WOODY PLANTS

Removing Branches

You should remove tree branches that are dead or damaged, to prevent the spread of a disease. In addition, you may want to eliminate branches that cross one another, to get rid of weak crotches (branches leaving the trunk at too sharp an angle and liable to break), or to remove lower branches to raise the canopy and let more light reach plants growing in the shade of the tree.

To remove a large branch without tearing the bark of the trunk, make a series of three cuts with a saw. Make the first cut 1 to 2 feet out from the branch collar (the raised ridge of bark where the branch joins the trunk), cutting about halfway through the branch from the underside. Next, an inch or two farther out from the first cut, saw completely through the branch from the top, leaving a stub. Remove the stub by cutting flush against the branch collar from the top. The cut will be slightly angled to follow the line of the collar; it will be a bit farther from the trunk at the bottom than at the top. It is important not to cut into the

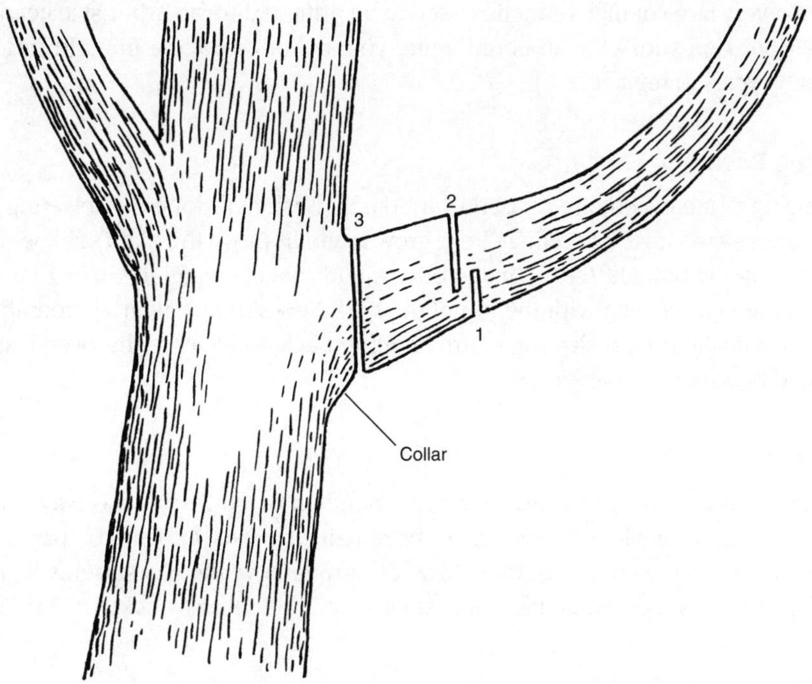

To remove a large branch, make the first cut up from the underside, cutting about halfway through the branch. Make the second cut from the top; the weight of the branch will break the wood, leaving a notched stub. Finally, remove the stub flush with the collar.

collar itself, or to cut farther from the collar and leave a stub; either approach would increase the chance of disease.

To remove smaller branches, cut them off with a pruning saw or pole pruner, cutting right next to the collar as for a large branch.

If you must remove part of a branch, cut back to a smaller branch or a bud. Use a pruning knife, pole pruner, lopper, or clippers, depending on the size and position of the branch. To encourage more open, spreading growth, cut back to a bud facing outward. To encourage denser, more compact growth, cut back to an inward-facing bud. When cutting back to a bud, make the cut 1/4 to 1/2 inch above the bud. Do not cut right next to the bud, or more than 1/2 inch away from it.

When pruning diseased wood, cut back to healthy wood, at least several inches from the site of the infection. Sterilize your tools after each cut by dipping them into rubbing alcohol or a solution of household chlorine bleach and water.

After removing branches, do not paint the cut with wound dressing or tree paint. These materials may actually interfere with the healing process. To help trees recover from pruning, make sure they are well nourished and well watered.

When very large or high branches need to be pruned, hire an arborist instead of attempting the operation yourself. You could injure yourself or damage a fine old tree that would take many years to replace.

Heading Back

Heading back means cutting off part of a branch. It is often done on flowering shrubs that bloom on new wood, to encourage fresh growth and improve the plant's shape. When heading back, cut the branch 1/4 to 1/2 inch above a bud; make an angled cut, with the bottom of the cut being about even with the top of the bud. New shoots will grow from the bud. Step back periodically from a shrub you are heading back, to observe the overall shape of the plant and be sure it pleases you.

Thinning

Thinning is removing crowded or weak branches or canes all the way back to their base. Thinning helps older flowering shrubs remain vigorous, and can be part of the rejuvenation process (see below). Use loppers or a saw to remove the oldest stems at ground level.

When thinning tree branches, cut them back to the collar as described under "Pruning Branches," above.

Rejuvenation

Overgrown, neglected flowering shrubs can be rejuvenated with severe pruning. To rejuvenate the entire plant at once, cut back all the branches or canes to a few inches from the ground. Keep the shrub well nourished and watered throughout the growing season as it begins to send out new growth.

A less drastic way to rejuvenate a shrub is to remove one-third of the old stems each year over a period of three years.

Not all shrubs can tolerate rejuvenation (fothergilla, witch hazel, magnolias, and some viburnums cannot). Those that will respond to rejuvenation generally form clumps by producing suckers from the base; lilac is an excellent example.

Removing Weak Growth

Two kinds of weak growth—suckers and watersprouts—need to be removed from trees and shrubs.

Suckers are vertical shoots growing from the roots or the base of clump-forming shrubs, or from the rootstock of grafted trees and roses. Cut suckers back to the ground or, if they are young, you may be able to pull them up. Remove all suckers from grafted plants. From shrubs remove all suckers except those you will let grow into new stems to replace old ones that were removed.

Watersprouts are weak shoots growing vertically from the branches of trees. Cut them off at the base.

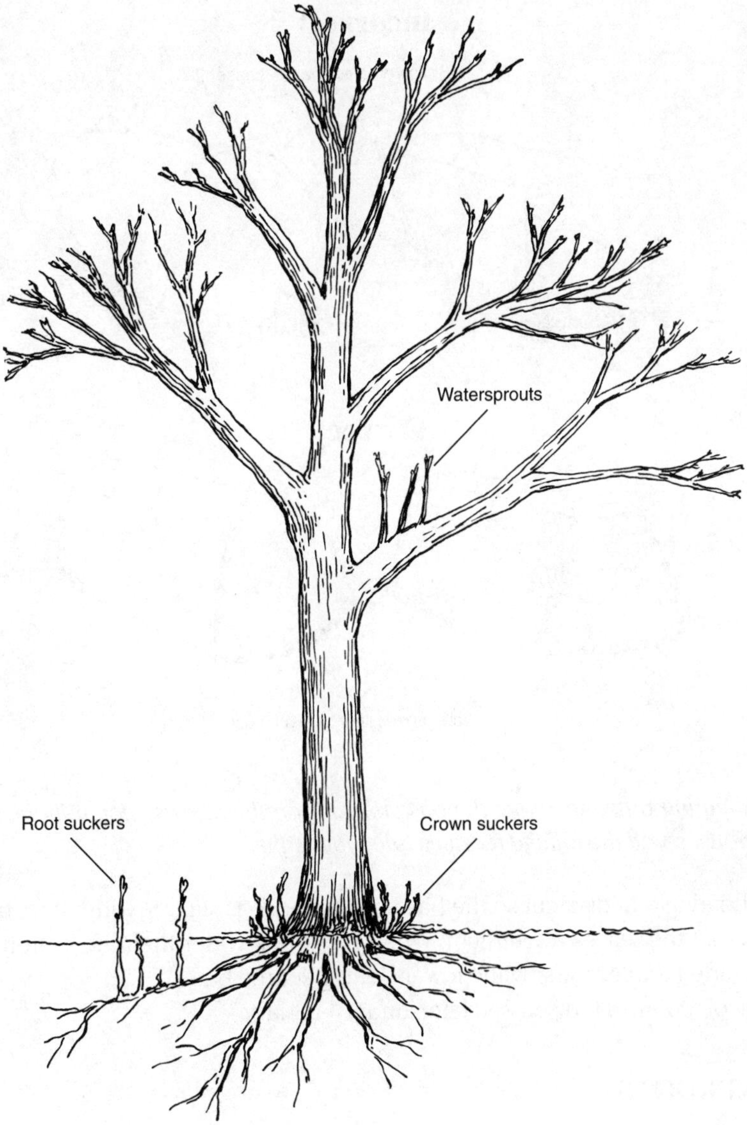

Suckers and watesprouts weaken trees and should be removed when trees are dormant.

Shearing

Shearing is overall clipping of a plant without regard to branch structure or buds, to give the plant a particular shape. Shearing is how hedges are trimmed and topiaries are clipped. Not all plants can tolerate shearing, which is why relatively few plants are suitable for use as formal hedges or topiaries.

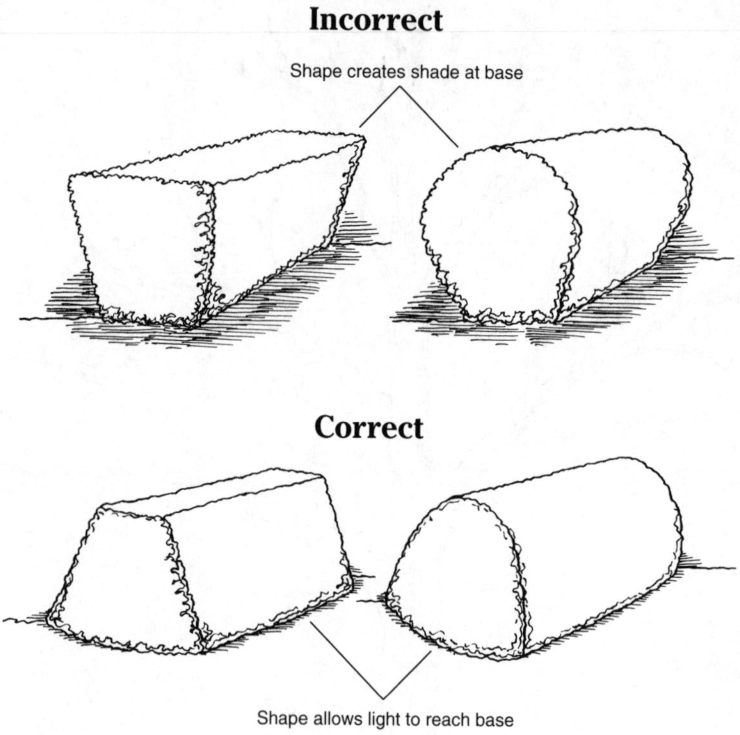
Incorrect
Shape creates shade at base
Correct
Shape allows light to reach base

When shearing a hedge, make the base wider than the top, as shown in the bottom illustrations, so all the foliage receives adequate light.

When shearing a hedge, cut so the base of the hedge is slightly wider than the top. This shape allows all the leaves to get light. When the top is wider than the bottom, the lower leaves are shaded and eventually the lower stems become bare.

Shearing of topiaries is discussed later, under "Topiary."

PRUNING ROOTS

Sometimes roots must be pruned. If you notice on an older tree that a large surface root is growing horizontally over the top of another root or roots, or circling around the base of the trunk (this is called girdling), the crossing portions of the upper root must be removed. Cut off the root in sections to avoid damaging the underlying root.

Girdling roots are often caused by improper practices at the nursery, particularly leaving plants in small containers for too long. Examining new plants carefully when you plant them should enable you to prevent problems later by shortening or removing large roots that have circled around and around the top of the root ball inside the container.

You may also need to remove large roots that grow into water lines or cause a sidewalk to heave. In these cases you will have to dig up the soil to expose the troublesome root, chop off the root, then replace the soil.

PRUNING DIFFERENT KINDS OF PLANTS

DECIDUOUS TREES

Prune fruit trees to encourage central leader, modified leader, or open vase form.

Central leader trees have a dominant vertical branch and an upright form. Choose one branch of the young tree to serve as the leader, and three or four strong lateral branches distributed evenly around the trunk to serve as the primary structural or scaffold branches.

To make the central leader strong, in the first year cut off the top close to the highest bud. Wrap a strip of heavy paper around the bud to force it to grow vertically instead of starting a new lateral branch. If the tree has a cluster or whorl of buds instead of a single bud, as maples do, remove all but one of the buds before attaching the band.

A modified leader begins its growth like a central leader tree. After the scaffold branches have developed and the form is established, the top of the leader is removed.

An open or vase-shaped tree has no central leader. The basic structure is established entirely by the scaffold branches.

As the tree grows, remove new branches that are poorly spaced around or up the trunk, and branches growing from the trunk at too sharp an angle.

To raise the tree canopy higher off the ground, remove some of the lower branches. Do not remove lower branches of young trees until new ones grow at the top to compensate for the loss.

EVERGREEN TREES

Conifers require little in the way of regular maintenance pruning. To give your evergreens an idealized formal shape and dense growth, you can shear them, but once you start down this path you will have to shear the trees every year. If you don't, they will develop looser new growth around the very dense center and will look odd.

Shear conifers in very late spring or early summer, when the new growth is still soft. On conifers that have candles, such as pines, cut back the candles in half. On conifers without candles, cut back the branch tips.

DECIDUOUS SHRUBS

Prune spring-blooming shrubs when they finish flowering. Forsythias, azaleas, lilacs, rhododendrons, flowering quince, and spicebush all bloom on wood produced the previous year, and set next year's flower buds after this year's flowers have finished blooming. If you prune right after they finish blooming, you will not lose any of next year's flower buds.

Shrubs that bloom in summer and fall, such as hydrangea, sweet pepperbush, caryopteris, and beautyberry, bloom on new wood and are best pruned in winter or very early spring when they are dormant.

Of course, there are exceptions to every rule. Not all spring bloomers flower on old wood, and not all summer bloomers flower on new wood. And some shrubs, such as

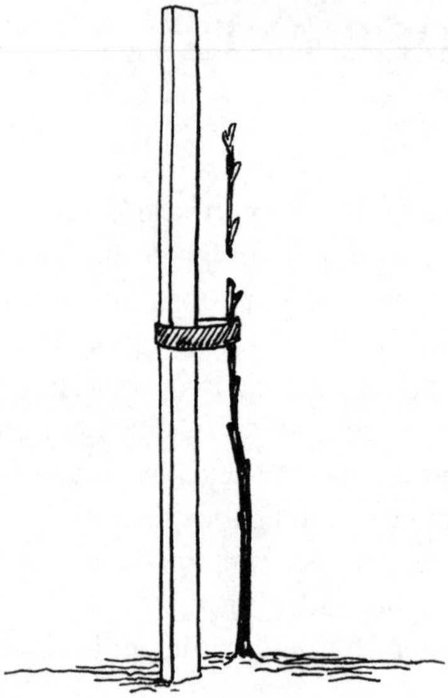

In training a central leader tree, prune the top in the first year.

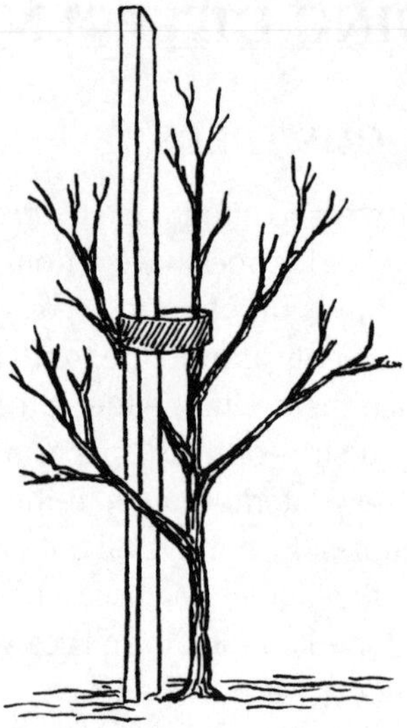

As the tree grows, choose several well-spaced branches to serve as scaffolds.

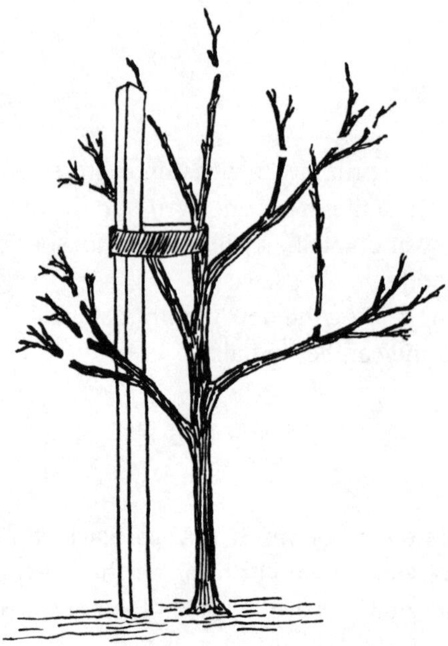

In subsequent years, remove weak growth, poorly spaced branches, and branches growing at a sharp angle from the trunk.

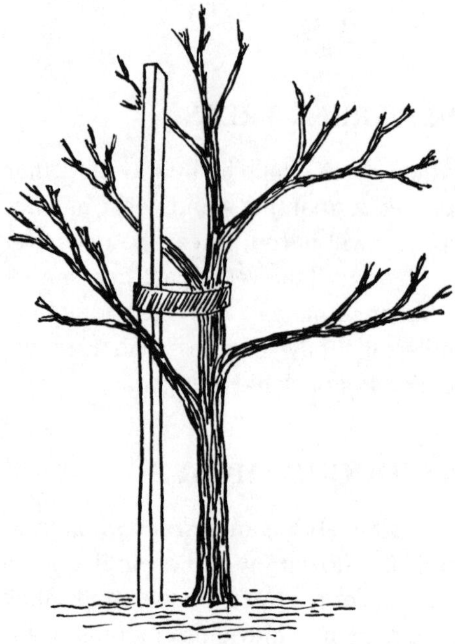

A strong central leader and sturdy structure should result.

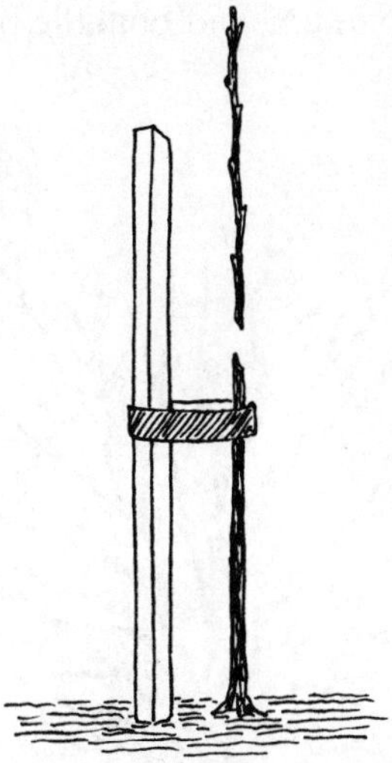

In training an open-center tree, shorten the whip the first year.

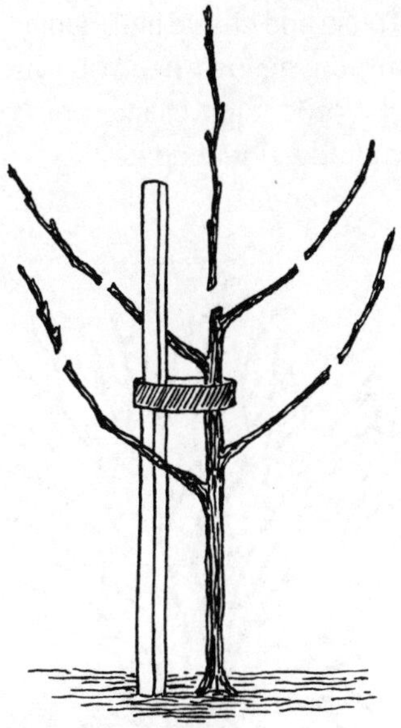

Allow four to six well-spaced scaffold branches to develop. Shorten the branches to create a pleasing shape and encourage development of fruiting spurs.

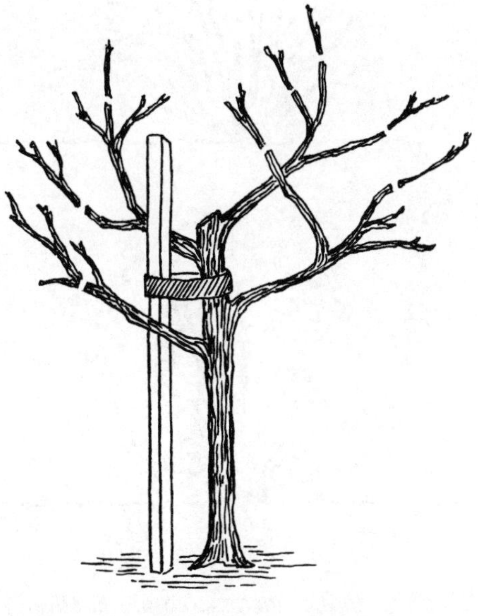

Continue to shorten branches to encourage fruit development in subsequent years.

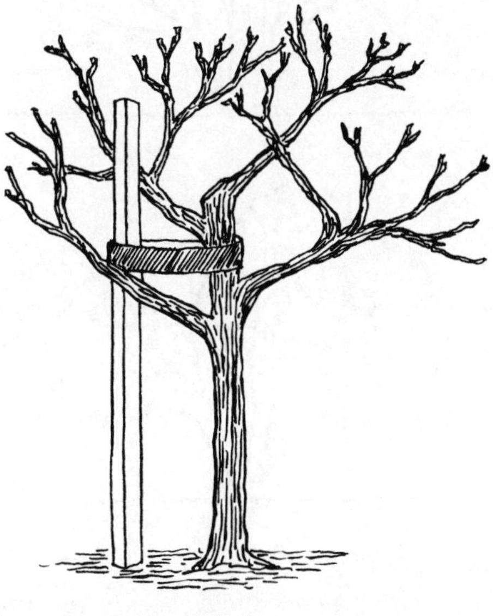

The mature tree has a vaselike form.

butterfly bush and chaste tree, can be cut back to the ground every year at the end of winter. Ask about pruning needs when you purchase any tree or shrub.

Shrubs producing clusters of flowers, such as lilac, viburnum, and butterfly bush, look better when deadheaded.

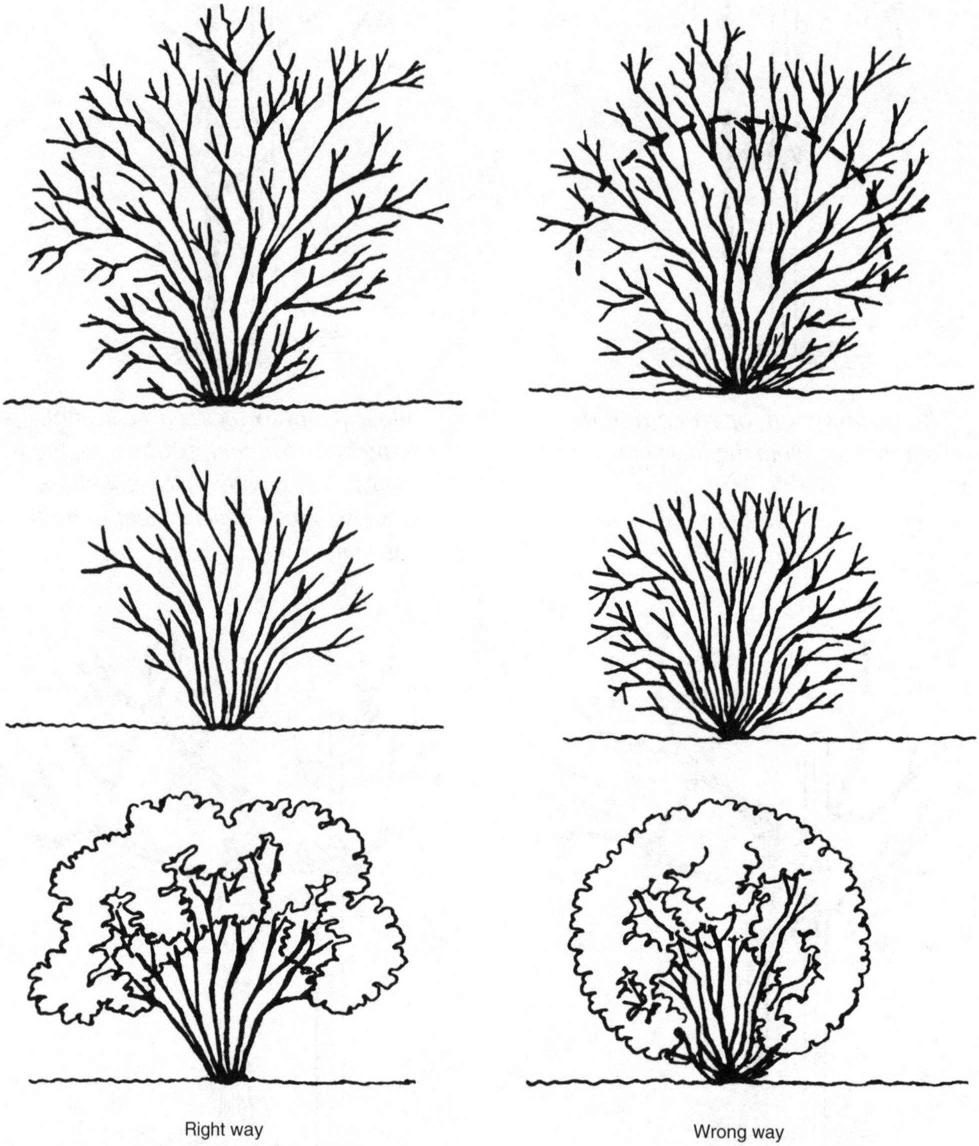

To prune an overgrown deciduous shrub, shorten individual branches to maintain the plant's natural form, as shown at left. Shearing a flowering shrub as shown at right produces unnatural shape and reduces flowering.

Shrubs that produce decorative fruit (hollies, beautyberry, winterberry, and snowberry, for example) should not be pruned after blooming or you will lose the fruit.

Prune other shrubs to thin them, remove suckers, head back long branches, remove dead or damaged growth, or rejuvenate overgrown specimens.

EVERGREEN SHRUBS

Evergreens have particular needs for pruning.

Flowering broad-leaved evergreens such as azaleas and rhododendrons are pruned to improve their flowering. To promote branching (and thus, more flowers), pinch or clip off leaf buds (which are smaller than flower buds), then pinch back the new shoots to get several buds. Rhododendrons also look better when deadheaded.

Broad-leaved evergreens not grown for their flowers, such as boxwood, can be sheared or pruned to a desired shape, or allowed to grow to their natural form.

When pruning conifers, the growth habit determines how you should prune. On many evergreens the older wood closer to the center of the plant loses its foliage with age and is unable to produce new needles if it is cut. When pruning these shrubs, do not cut into the bare part of the branches, for new foliage will not grow there. Confine pruning to the live green part of the plant. Hemlock, arborvitae, and junipers all fit this category.

When pruning a yew, fir, or spruce, cut back to a pair of lateral buds so new branches will develop the next season. These buds are small, but you will find them when you look closely at the branches. Evergreens with these buds can produce new growth on old wood.

Pruning candled evergreens like pines is described above under "Evergreen Trees."

ROSES

Rose pruning is a complicated art; some basic guidelines are included in the section on Roses in chapter 3 (see page 204), but you should consult a good rose book, such as *Roses of America* by Steven Scaniello and Tanya Bayard (New York: Henry Holt, 1990) for more detailed information.

When deadheading roses, cut the stem back to a leaf with five leaflets. When pruning, look for a crescent-shaped scar on the cane with a slight swelling above it. This is a bud eye, and is the point from which a new cane can grow. Cut back to right above a bud eye that faces outward. The new cane will grow outward rather than into the center of the bush. It is important for roses to have an open, well-ventilated form. A dense, crowded form encourages mildew, blackspot, and various other fungal and bacterial ailments.

Remove diseased, damaged, or dead wood from roses as soon as you notice it. Cut back to green, healthy wood with white pith in the center. Remove winter-killed growth at the end of winter before new growth begins.

Use only sharp tools for pruning roses, or you risk crushing the canes. Make cuts on a 45-degree angle, 1/4 inch above a growth bud.

BUSH FRUITS

Prune blueberries, currants, gooseberries, and other bush fruits in very early spring while the plants are still dormant. Remove old, dead, damaged, diseased, or winter-killed growth. To maintain plant vigor, cut to the ground currant and gooseberry stems more than four years old, and blueberry stems thicker than 1 inch in diameter.

BRAMBLE FRUITS

The simplest way to prune blackberries and raspberries is to cut half of all the canes back to the ground in winter or early spring, when the plants are dormant. Other pruning depends upon whether the plants produce all their fruit on second-year canes, or whether the plants produce one crop in early summer on second-year canes and another crop later in summer on new canes.

For the former, cut all the fruit-bearing canes back to the ground when they have finished bearing.

For the latter, cut back the second-year fruiting canes when they have finished bearing the early crop. The canes that produce the later crop are tip-pruned to the desired height early the following spring.

TOPIARY

Topiary is the art of shaping plants into fanciful forms by careful pruning and training. It has been with us since the days of ancient Rome—the Romans were expert topiarists—but it is not often seen these days outside of public gardens, historical sites, formal estate gardens, and Disney World. Topiaries can be simple balls, cones, and other geometric shapes, or they can take the forms of animals, people, or other complex figures.

Topiaries are created by pruning and pinching plants, or by training plants to grow over a form, often a wire form stuffed with sheet moss. Stems and branches are fastened to the form, then regularly clipped to develop the shape. Forms for topiaries can also be hollow, a basic wire shape covered with chicken wire to create more points of attachment for the plants. Maintaining the shape of topiaries requires meticulous, time-consuming clipping.

Plants used for topiary have small leaves and are able to tolerate repeated shearing and clipping. Boxwood, myrtle, yew, arborvitae, privet, and rosemary are all good topiary subjects, as are small-leaved ivies, wintercreeper, baby's tears, creeping fig, and other small-leaved vines. A number of shrubby herbs and houseplants, including thyme, bay, and geraniums, can be trained as standards for a topiary effect.

Simple shapes for topiary include the standard, a straight vertical stem topped by a ball of foliage; poodle, a straight stem with two or three balls of foliage spaced along its length; ring or hoop; and spiral or corkscrew.

Training Topiaries

Plants can be trained on a hollow topiary form in three ways. First, you can tie the stems to the wire frame with string or raffia (available from florist supply companies, craft shops, and garden supply companies). Tying allows you the most control—you can get the stems to closely follow the form. When the plants are old enough that the stems become woody, the stems will hold the shape by themselves and you can remove the ties.

Another method of training, for vining plants, is to wrap individual stems, twining them around the frame. Attach as needed to hold the stems in place. As each stem grows to the top of the frame, clip it off. Twining produces a topiary with a more open, airy look.

The third way to train plants is to weave each stem through the frame. This works best on a wire frame covered with chicken wire. Take one stem and work it through the frame, weaving it in and out and working from the bottom toward the top of the frame. Repeat the procedure for each stem on the plant. As new shoots grow, weave them into the form as well. When the form is completely covered, clip off any additional new shoots to retain the shape of the topiary.

To train vining plants on a form stuffed with moss, you peg the stems to the form with U-shaped wire pins (available from garden, florist, and nursery supply companies and called "greening pins" in the trade). Spread the stems over the form and pin them down at intervals, pinning the stems at points between leaves. As the stems grow, continue pinning until they reach the top of the form, then clip off the tips. At no time should you pin down the growing tip. As new shoots grow, train them to cover bare spots. When the entire form is covered with a single layer of leaves, clip off new shoots to retain the shape.

Caring for Topiaries

Topiaries need light, air, water, and nutrients like any other plants. If your topiary is growing in a pot indoors, turn it regularly so all the sides grow evenly. You may need to hang a topiary upside down periodically to get plants to cover the underside of the form.

Water established topiaries as you would other garden or container plants. Make sure topiaries on moss-filled forms receive enough water to wet the moss as well as the plant leaves, so any roots growing into the moss will also receive moisture. Indoor topiaries appreciate regular misting as well, especially in winter.

Feed garden-planted topiaries like other shrubs or vines. Fertilize container topiaries monthly when in active growth, with an all-purpose liquid or water-soluble fertilizer.

Check the plants often and clip off any stray shoots to maintain a neat shape.

HOW TO MAKE SOME SIMPLE TOPIARIES

To make a standard. Prepare a pot of moist potting medium and a stake that is as tall as you want the stem of the topiary to be. Choose a plant with a straight central leader, and plant it in the pot. Insert the stake next to the plant, and fasten the stem to the stake at intervals to keep it standing straight.

Remove all the sideshoots, but leave the shoots and leaves near the tip of the stem intact. As the plant grows, continue to remove sideshoots and attach the stem to the stake. When the stem reaches the desired height, begin to let sideshoots grow. Pinch off the plant's growing tip. When new shoots grow, pinch them back when they are a few inches long. Always pinch right above a leaf node or dormant bud, so the plant grows bushier. Continue pinching new shoots until you have a bushy ball of foliage on top of the stem. Thereafter, shear and clip the plant as needed to maintain the shape.

To make a poodle form. Let some sideshoots grow where you want the balls of foliage, and pinch to get bushy growth.

To train a spiral. You will need a plant with an upright habit that will eventually develop a woody stem capable of supporting the plant. Begin by planting the plant in a pot or in the garden. Then insert next to the plant a stake as tall as the desired eventual height of the spiral. Attach the main stem to the stake close to the ground, then wind it around the stake in a nicely curved spiral. Attach the stem to the stake at as many points as necessary to hold the correct shape. Trim back any side branches to conform to the spiral shape.

As the plant grows, wrap the new growth around the stake to continue to extend the spiral. When the plant reaches the height you want, pinch or clip off the growing tip. When the stem is woody and strong, remove the stake. Thereafter, clip the plant as needed to maintain the shape.

To make a ring topiary. First, you need to buy a sturdy wire form on which to train the plant. These are available from a number of mail-order firms and at garden centers.

Set the form in the pot, and adjust the base of the form until the stem and ring are standing straight. Fill the pot with moist potting mix and plant an ivy or other vine. As the stems grow, fasten them to the form at intervals, twining them around the ring form. Clip off any long sideshoots to retain the neat form of the plant.

MAIL-ORDER SOURCES FOR TOPIARY SUPPLIES

Garden Magic
1930 Wake Forest Rd.
Raleigh, NC 27608
(919) 821-1997

Kenneth Lynch & Sons, Inc.
84 Danbury Rd.
Wilton, CT 06897
(203) 762-8363
Only large, stainless-steel topiary frames; no other topiary supplies.

Samia Rose Topiary
1236 Urania Ave.
Encinitas, CA 92024
(619) 436-0460

Topiary, Inc.
41 Bering St.
Tampa, FL 33606
(813) 837-2841
Wholesale and retail topiary supplies. Send a self-addressed, stamped envelope for a free brochure.

Vine Arts
P.O. Box 83014
Portland, OR 97203
(503)289-7505

ESPALIER

Espalier is the art of training woody plants to grow in one of several different two-dimensional patterns, with all the growth in one flat plane. Plants can be espaliered against a wall, or on a trellis made of wooden posts and heavy wire. Espalier was developed by the French and has long been used in Europe to grow fruit trees in small spaces. It has never been widespread in the United States, where dwarf trees have provided the answer to space limitations, but good examples of espalier can be seen in the gardens of some colonial estates, such as George Washington's Mount Vernon.

Espaliers are time-consuming to train and maintain, but they do look elegant and graceful, especially trained in front of a white stucco or brick wall. If you have a suitable location and are willing to devote the necessary time to caring for your charges, espaliered trees or shrubs could become a decorative highlight in your garden. Some nurseries sell trees already espaliered, so all you need to do is maintain them.

Fruit trees, especially apples, pears, and peaches, are the classic espalier subjects, but ornamental trees and shrubs can also be trained in this way. See the list, "Plants for Espalier."

ESPALIER PATTERNS

There are numerous shapes for espalier, or you may be inspired to create a shape of your own, perhaps in response to an unusually shaped plant you find at a local nursery. Classic patterns for espalier include the following:

Cordon: A single, unbranched stem that resembles a leafy rope. Cordons are usually grown in groups, and can be trained to grow vertically, diagonally, or horizontally.

U shape: Looks just like it sounds. U shapes are made by training two horizontal cordons, one on either side of the main stem, with the ends trained to grow vertically. There are single U and double U forms.

Palmette verrier: Based on the U shape, except that it has more arms. A palmette verrier has three concentric U shapes, one above the other, all with the ends of the branches turned up 90 degrees to grow vertically.

Palmette oblique: Branches are trained diagonally outward from the main stem, at a 45-degree angle. It is created by training three or four pairs of diagonal cordons, one pair above the other, from a main stem.

Fan: Branches radiate out in a fan shape from the main stem. A fan is essentially three pairs of cordons, each pair trained at a sharper angle to the main stem than the pair below it.

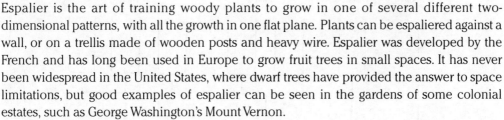

Vertical

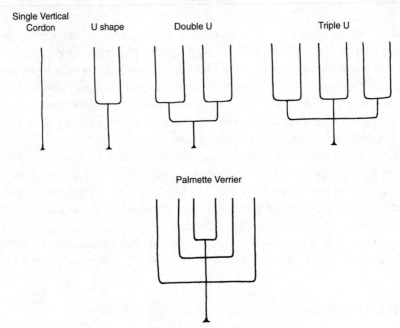

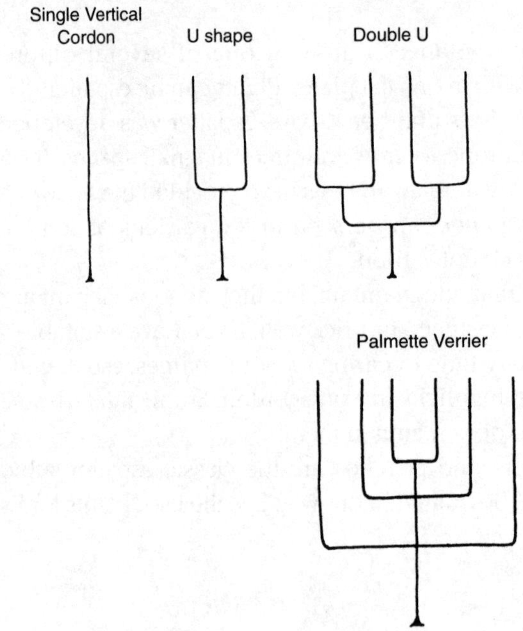

Horizontal

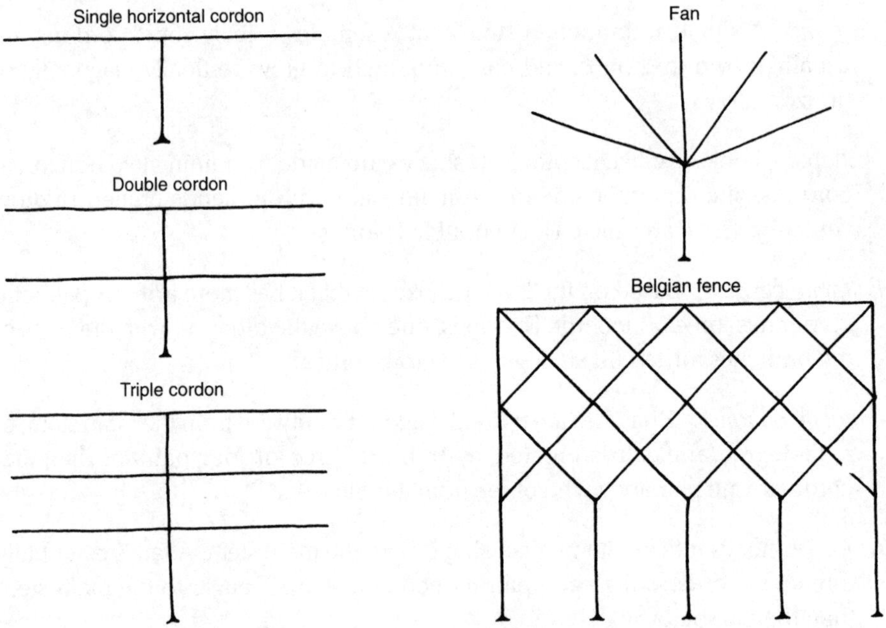

These diagrams show a variety of espalier patterns.

CHOOSING A SITE

Espaliers need the same light and moisture conditions the plants would need when growing in a more natural form. One caveat is to be careful when espaliering plants against a south-facing wall, especially if the wall is white. The additional light and heat reflected by the wall back onto the tender new growth of young plants could cause sunburn. Give the young espaliers next to a white wall some afternoon shade in the summer. When the plants grow larger they will develop enough of their own leaves to provide any necessary shade. Gardeners in warm climates, however, should probably avoid espaliering against a south-facing wall. An eastern exposure would be best.

To grow espaliers for fruit, you should plant them in rich, well-dug soil, and add compost and composted manure every year. To get espaliered trees to produce big crops of fruit, you have to overfeed them and undertake a rather complicated routine of summer pruning. It is better for beginners to content themselves with more modest harvests. Overfeeding causes more vegetative growth that will have to be removed; less heavily fertilized plants can get by with less frequent pruning.

Getting Started

When you have chosen a shape and a site, put the plant supports in place. You can attach supporting wires directly to the wall with special hardware, or construct a wood frame against the wall and attach the wires to that. Or you can set up freestanding frames of wood posts with wires strung between them, to create espaliers that will substitute for a fence or line a driveway.

When planning the design and setting up the training wires, allow enough space between branches so the leaves will be able to develop fully without touching. You have to be able to clearly see the design in order to appreciate it. Two feet is a good spacing distance for cordons and other simple shapes.

Start with a young plant with flexible branches. For the classic formal patterns described above, purchase an unbranched whip, or use a young tree and remove all the side branches. A plant about 3 feet tall is a good size. For an informal design, you may be able to find a somewhat more mature tree with a shape along the lines of what you want, instead of training it from scratch. You might also wish to purchase an already-started espalier from one of the sources mentioned at the end of this section.

If you will be espaliering fruit trees, choose a dwarf variety. You will also need to look into pollination needs for fruit trees. If a self-pollinating variety is not available you will have to plant a second variety that can serve as a pollinator. The nursery from which you buy the trees should be able to give you this information.

Prepare a planting hole that will position the plant at the same depth it was growing at the nursery (see page 75), with the branches about 6 inches away from the wall (if you are espaliering against a wall) so air will be able to circulate behind the branches.

If you are starting with an older plant and need to prune any large branches before beginning the training process, wait until the plant is dormant to prune. Attach the main stem to a wood stake somewhat taller than the intended height of the main stem. When the main stem is tall enough you will begin training sideshoots into the desired pattern.

Plastic-coated wire is the best kind to use for training; it will not rust and will not injure plants.

Bend twigs and young branches to the wires and tie them fast with raffia, string, or the rubber strips used for budding and grafting. Do not use wire to tie stems to the training wires, and do not tie tightly, or growth could be constricted. If you will be making a U shape, in which the branches must be trained horizontally and then bent in another direction, wait until the trained branches have grown a foot or more past the point where the bend will be, then make the bend and tie the branch in the new position.

The ideal thickness for branches being bent is about that of a pencil. Thinner, younger branches may crimp when bent; older, thicker branches may snap. If a branch is the right size but very stiff, bend it gradually over a period of several weeks until it reaches the desired shape.

As the plant grows, remove any shoots that do not conform to the design, pruning them each winter. Or you can remove buds before they have a chance to grow into shoots, if you are able to tell a vegetative bud from a bud that will produce a fruiting spur (a small, gnarly twig that will produce flowers and fruit instead of leaves).

When the branches of the espalier attain their desired height, thereafter prune each year's new vegetative growth back to one bud from the main stem, pruning in winter. If you are growing fruit, thin the crop if necessary to allow each fruit enough space to develop to its full size. Thin when fruits are about the size of marbles.

After a few years, when the trained branches are sturdy enough to stand on their own, you can remove the training wires.

Maintaining Espaliers

Examine espaliered plants regularly. Prune vegetative shoots that grow out of the flat two-dimensional plane. Even better, rub off vegetative buds pointing the wrong way (the direction the bud points is the direction the shoot will grow).

Water the trees in dry weather, and monitor for pests.

Make sure the ties have not become tight and constricting around the branches.

Install tree wrap or tree guards around the trunks of young trees to protect them from rodent damage in winter.

HOW TO MAKE A CORDON

A cordon is a single, straight stem that can be vertical, diagonal, or horizontal. You can train a cordon on a stake, without wires.

Vertical cordon: Plant the whips 2 feet apart. If you want a crop of fruit, the cordoned tree will have to be at least 6 feet tall. At planting, prune all sideshoots back to the first bud or leaves. Do not head back the leader until it reaches the desired height. After a few years, the stems will be strong enough for you to remove the stakes. Continue pruning sideshoots each year so the main stem has lots of leafy growth close to it.

Diagonal cordon: Install the stakes at a 45-degree angle, parallel to one another, and fasten them to a wall or a wire trellis to hold them in place. Plant the whips and fasten them to the stakes. Prune sideshoots as for a vertical cordon.

Horizontal cordon: You can make a horizontal cordon with two leaders trained 180 degrees apart, from a central stem, or you can plant two whips together and bend one leader to the left and the other to the right. You can train more than one set of horizontal branches from the same main stem.

Set up the necessary supports, and plant the whips. Prune back the leader to about 4 inches below the lowest horizontal training wire. Let two shoots grow, and train them on the first wire, going in opposite directions. For a multilevel cordon, allow another bud to remain and grow a new leader. Cut back the one 4 inches below the next training wire, and train sideshoots as you did the first time. When you get to the highest wire, cut off the leader and train sideshoots to make the top cordon.

PLANTS TO ESPALIER

Camellia japonica
Cercis canadensis, eastern redbud
Chaenomeles spp., flowering quince
Citrus limon, lemon
Cornus kousa, kousa dogwood
Cornus mas, cornelian cherry
Cotoneaster spp., especially
  C. horizontalis, rockspray cotoneaster
Euonymus alatus, winged euonymus, burning bush
Ficus carica, fig
Forsythia spp.
Ilex crenata, Japanese holly
Jasminum nudiflorum, winter jasmine
Juniperus chinesis 'Pfitzeriana', Pfitzer juniper
Magnolia grandiflora, southern magnolia
Magnolia × *soulangiana*, saucer magnolia
Magnolia tomentosum, star magnolia
Malus spp., apple, crab apple
Osmanthus fragrans, sweet olive
Philadelphus coronarius, mock orange
Poncirus trifoliata, hardy orange
Prunus perisca, peach
Prunus serrulata and *P. subhirtella*, oriental flowering cherries
Pyracantha spp., firethorn
Pyrus communis, pear
Taxus spp., yew
Viburnum plicatum var. *tomentosum*, Japanese snowball

SOURCES OF ESPALIERED TREES

Arbor and Espalier
201 Buena Vista Avenue East
San Francisco, CA 94117
(415) 626-8880

Leuthardt Nursery
Montauk Highway
P.O. Box 666-R
East Moriches, NY 11940
(516) 878-1387

Long Hungry Creek Nursery
Box 163
Red Boiling Springs, TN 37150

PREPARING FOR WINTER

Winter is a time of rest for gardeners in all but the warmest climates. In South Florida, southern California, and the warmest parts of the Desert Southwest, winter is the time to grow hardy annuals and cool-season vegetables that gardeners farther north will plant in spring or for fall.

Before winter sets in, clean up the garden and put undiseased plant debris on the compost pile. Bring in stakes, row covers no longer in use, and grow netting. Bring clay pots, hoses, and tools indoors for winter storage. Winter is a good time to clean, oil, and sharpen tools, to scrub out and disinfect clay pots.

This section offers a rundown of other things to do to get the garden ready for winter.

ANNUALS

Hardy annuals can be sown in autumn; in cooler climates they will germinate and bloom in spring. In warm climates, plant hardy annuals for winter bloom.

Take cuttings of annuals to pot up for winter houseplants. Wax begonias, geraniums, coleus, and impatiens can all be grown from cuttings. (See page 82 for information on taking cuttings.)

Pull annuals when frost kills them or they fatigue or stop blooming entirely, and put the plants on the compost pile.

PERENNIALS

Cut back perennials at the end of the growing season or, in warm climates, when they finish blooming. In the North cut back stems to 3 to 4 inches from the ground. Do not cut back shrubby plants such as santolina and lavender until early spring; if pruned in fall they could send out new growth that would be very susceptible to winterkill. In warm climates cut back perennials to 2 to 3 inches.

To protect the roots of perennials from heaving out of the ground during alternate periods of freezing and thawing, mulch perennials when the ground freezes (see page 111 under "Mulching").

To protect sensitive plants and young divisions, you can use the same kinds of protective devices used to extend the growing season for vegetables (see "Season-Extending Techniques" in chapter 8).

LIFTING AND STORING TENDER BULBS

Gardeners who live where the ground freezes in winter must dig tender bulbs in fall and store them indoors to replant in spring. Calla lily (*Zantedeschia*), *Caladium*, *Canna*, *Dahlia*, four o'clocks (*Mirabilis*), *Gladiolus*, Peruvian daffodil (*Hymenocallis*), summer hyacinth (*Galtonia*), tuberose (*Polianthes*), tuberous begonia, *Zephyranthes*, *Crocosmia*, *Oxalis*, and *Tigridia* must all be stored indoors over winter except in frost-free climates.

You can wait to dig most bulbs until the foliage has been softened by frost or begun to turn brown. Tuberous begonias and tuberoses are exceptions to the rule; they cannot tolerate any frost at all. Dig them early.

All the tender bulbs must be out of the ground before you get the first heavy frost, or the bulbs themselves may be damaged.

The basic procedure for lifting tender bulbs is as follows:

- Loosen the soil around the plant, then lift the plant from the ground with a spade or spading fork. Retain a good ball of soil around the roots.
- Let the bulbs dry in a cool, dark, ventilated but frost-free place, such as an unheated basement or attached garage.
- Shake off excess dry soil.
- Remove leaves and stems when they wither and fall off.
- Shake or gently brush off any dry soil still clinging to the bulbs.
- Pack bulbs in boxes of dry sand or peat moss, or wrap individually in tissue paper or cotton. Be sure bulbs are dry on the surface before storing, or mildew, mold, or rot may develop.
- Label all containers with type and color of flower.
- Store in dark, dry, airy location where the temperature will not drop below 50°F.

ROSES

Gardeners living where winter temperatures routinely drop below 20°F for extended periods should give roses, particularly hybrid teas and grandifloras, some sort of protection from the cold. You can make the job easier by not encouraging any new growth late in the season. Stop fertilizing roses six to eight weeks before you expect the first frost, and do not prune late in the season.

If winter temperatures seldom dip below zero in your area, you can protect bush roses with a simple mound of soil. After you have had a few frosts in autumn, but before the soil freezes, prune the canes of bush roses back by half, tie the shortened stems together loosely, and make the soil mounds. Hill up soil 8 to 12 inches high around the base of each bush. In spring when the danger of heavy frost is past, gradually remove the soil mounds over a period of a couple of weeks.

Where below-zero temperatures are common, place a foot-tall cylinder of hardware cloth on top of the soil mound when it freezes, and stuff the cylinder with dry leaves. In the coldest climates, where the temperature may go below -15°F in winter, cover the tops of the rose bushes, too. Use styrofoam cones sold for this purpose, or make caps of heavy cardboard covered with plastic, or use upside-down baskets or plastic-covered boxes. On mild days, open or remove the covers to let the plants have some fresh air. Remove the caps when the weather starts to moderate toward spring. Start removing the mulch a little at a time.

Remove winter protection on cloudy days to lessen the risk of sunburn to the canes.

Climbing roses also need winter protection in harsh climates. Unfasten the long canes from their suppports and carefully lay them on the ground. Peg them down. Mound soil over the canes, and when the soil mound freezes, cover it with a mulch of leaves or evergreen boughs, held in place with a tarp or chicken wire weighted down at the corners with heavy stones.

Instead of protecting individual bushes, you can guard a small bed of rose bushes by setting a portable cold frame over them. Open the lid partway on bright, sunny days so the air inside does not get too warm, and to admit fresh air. During spells of extremely cold weather, cover the cold frame with old blankets or rugs, or bags of dry leaves.

SHRUBS

If you are growing tender shrubs in containers outdoors, bring them back inside before the first frost. Move the plants to a shady spot outdoors for a few weeks before bringing them in, to let them begin adjusting to lower light levels. Once indoors, put them in a bright window. Check the plants for signs of pests. Cut back on watering and fertilizing over the winter to let the plants rest.

Make sure outdoor shrubs are well watered going into winter. If your garden is subject to cold, drying winter winds, spray broad-leaved evergreens with an antitranspirant to keep the leaves from drying out. Apply when the temperature is above 40°F. You might also consider planting a windbreak of tall evergreens on the side of your property facing into the prevailing winter winds.

Set up little shelters around shrubs that are not reliably hardy in your climate, to protect them from windburn and from ice and snow buildup. Wrap individual shrubs in burlap and tie loosely with rope, or place four stakes around the shrub and wrap burlap around the stakes to form a shelter. Or surround a smaller shrub with a cylinder of chicken wire and fill it with dry leaves.

To protect a group of shrubs, drive a row of wooden stakes into the ground next to the shrubs on the windward side. Stretch burlap along the stakes to make a windscreen.

Foundation evergreens and other shrubs growing close to the house can be at risk in winter from water dripping out of rain gutters onto the plants and then freezing, or from melting snow and ice sliding off the roof and onto the plants. The best way to protect such plants is to use some scrap lumber to construct a roof over the plants. A better idea is not to place woody plants in such a location. Herbaceous plants, which die to the ground in winter, suffer no damage from falling snow or ice.

TREES

Young trees and trees with tender bark are favorite winter targets of mice and deer, who gnaw the bark. Protect them with tree wrap, plastic tree guards, or cylinders of hardware cloth around the trunks.

Tree wrap also protects against sunscald. Sunscald happens when the tissues of a tree thaw on a bright, sunny winter day, then refreeze at night when the temperature plummets quickly. The rapid expansion of the freezing wood causes the bark to crack. Young trees are particularly at risk. Wrap with tree wrap from ground level to right beneath the lowest branches.

Chapter 3
FLOWERS AND FOLIAGE

ANNUALS

WHAT IS AN ANNUAL?

A true annual is a plant that completes its entire life cycle in one year, going from seed to bloom to setting new seeds within a single growing season. Quite a few plants that are botanically biennials or perennials will also bloom the first year from seed, especially when seeds are started early indoors. Gardeners often consider these plants to be annuals as well, although technically they are not. The lists that follow include true annuals and plants often grown as annuals. Plants that are botanically biennial are marked (B) and perennials (P).

Annuals channel their energy into fulfilling their life cycle by producing seeds; that is why so many of them bloom all summer. Removing their spent flowers before seeds mature stimulates the plants to produce more blossoms.

Annuals are classified as hardy, half-hardy, or tender. Hardy annuals grow best in cool weather, and can tolerate a fair amount of frost. Their seeds survive prolonged exposure to cold temperatures, and many can be sown outdoors in fall to germinate the following spring. Plants can go into the garden in early spring, while there is still a threat of frost. In warm-climate gardens in the American Southeast, Southwest, and West Coast, hardy annuals are planted for winter bloom.

Half-hardy annuals hold up well in cool, damp weather, and most of them can tolerate light frost. But they cannot withstand prolonged exposure to subfreezing temperatures.

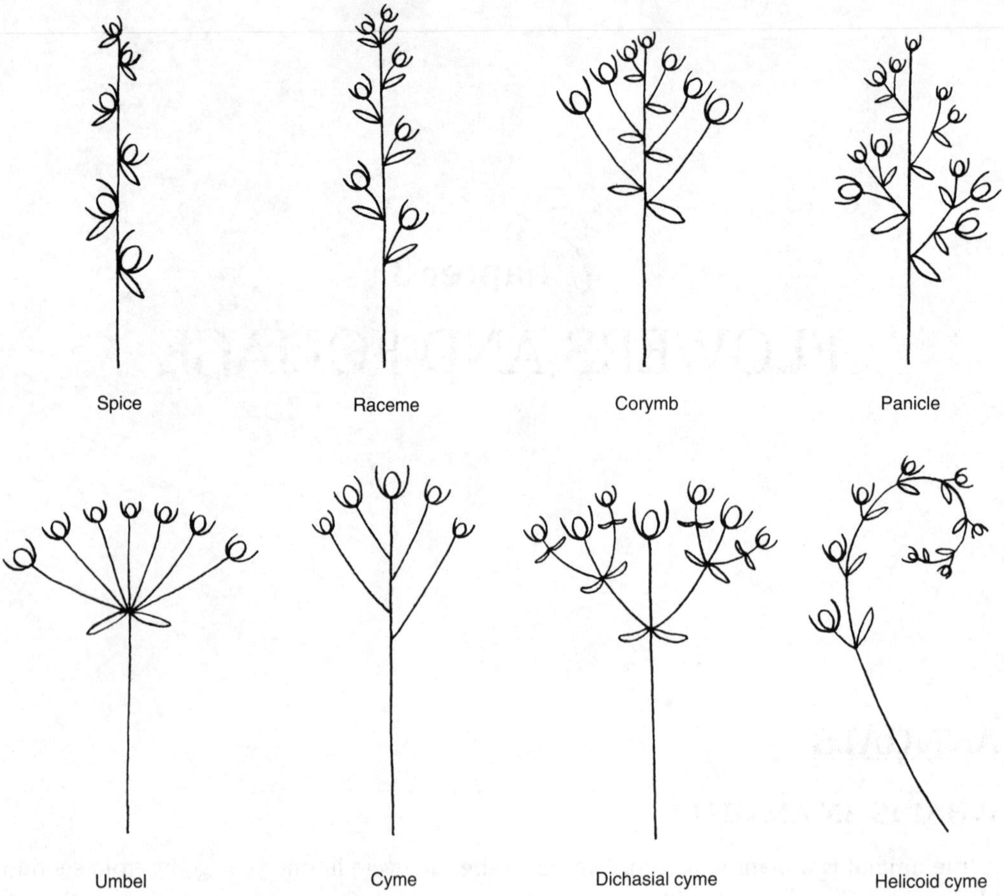

This diagram shows different ways the flowering parts of plants can be arranged.

Tender annuals cannot tolerate any frost at all. They need warm soil and air in order to grow well, and are planted outdoors only after all danger of frost is past.

Hardy Annuals

Note: (P) indicates plants that grow as perennials in some conditions; (B) indicates biennials.

Adonis aestivalis, pheasant's eye
Ammi majus, bishop's weed
Anagallis arvensis, scarlet pimpernel
Asperula orientalis, woodruff
Brassica oleracea, Acephala group, flowering cabbage and kale
Calendula spp., pot marigold
Catananche spp., cupid's dart (P)
Centaurea americana, basket flower
Centaurea cyanus, bachelor's button
Clarkia spp., satin flower
Cleome spp., spider flower

Consolida ambigua, rocket larkspur
Coreopsis tinctoria, calliopsis
Crepis spp., hawksbeard
Cynoglossum amabile, Chinese forget-me-not (B)
Dianthus barbatus, sweet William (B)
Digitalis purpurea 'Foxy', foxglove
Dyssodia tenuiloba, Dahlberg daisy
Eschscholzia californica, California poppy (B or P)
Gaillardia pulchella, blanketflower
Gilia spp., Queen Anne's thimble
Glaucium spp., horned poppy
Helianthus spp., sunflower
Iberis amara, rocket candytuft
Iberis umbellata, globe candytuft
Lavatera trimestris, tree mallow
Layia platyglossa, tidytips
Legousia speculum-veneris, mirror of Venus
Limnanthes douglasii, meadow foam
Linanthus spp., mountain phlox
Linaria maroccana, toadflax
Linum grandiflorum, flowering flax
Lobularia maritima, sweet alyssum (P)
Lupinus subcornosus
Lupinus texensis, Texas bluebonnet
Lychnis coeli-rosa, rose of heaven
Lychnis coronaria, rose campion (B or P)
Malcolmia maritima, Virginia stock
Malope spp.
Malva verticillata var. *crispa*, crisped musk mallow
Matthiola incana, stock (B or P)
Mentzelia lindleyi, blazing star
Myosotis sylvatica, woodland forget-me-not (B, sometimes)
Nemophila menziesii, baby blue-eyes
Nigella damascena, love-in-a-mist
Oenothera drummondii, Texas evening primrose (P, sometimes)
Omphalodes spp., navelwort
Papaver rhoeas, field poppy
Phacelia campanularia, California bluebells
Physalis alkekengi, Chinese lantern (P)
Platystemon californicus, creamcups
Reseda odorata, mignonette
Rudbeckia hirta, black-eyed Susan, gloriosa daisy
Silene armeria, catchfly
  S. gallica
  S. pendula
Viola tricolor, Johnny-jump-up (P, sometimes)
Viola × wittrockiana, pansy (P, sometimes)
Xanthisma texana, star of Texas

Half-Hardy Annuals

Abelmoschus spp. (P)
Abronia spp., sand verbena (P)
Alcea spp., hollyhock (B)
Ammobium alata, winged everlasting (P)
Anchusa carpensis, summer forget-me-not (B)
Antirrhinum spp., snapdragon (P)
Aphanostephus skirrhobasis, lazy daisy
Arctotis spp., African daisy (P)
Arctotis grandiflora, prickly poppy (P)
Argemone mexicana, Mexican poppy
Baileya multiradiata, desert marigold (P)
Brachycome iberidifolia, Swan River daisy
Calandrinia ciliata, *C. grandiflora*, *C. umbellata*, rock purslane (P)
Calceolaria spp., pocketbook plant
Callistephus chinensis, China aster
Campanula isophylla, star-of-Bethlehem, Ligurian bellflower
Celosia cristata, cockscomb, woolflower

(continued)

Half-Hardy Annuals *(cont'd)*

Chrysanthemum carinatum, tricolor chrysanthemum
Chrysanthemum coronarium, garland chrysanthemum
Convolvulus spp., bush morning glory
Cuphea ignea, cigar flower (P)
Dianthus chinensis, China pink (B or P)
Diascia barberae, twinspur
Emilia javanica, tasselflower
Erodium spp., storksbill
Eustoma spp., lisianthus (B)
Felicia amelloides, blue marguerite
Gazania rigens, treasure flower (P)
Gerbera jamesonii, Transvaal daisy (P)
Gomphrena globosa, globe amaranth
Gypsophila elegans, annual baby's breath
Helichrysum bracteatum, strawflower
Hunnemannia fumariifolia, Mexican tulip poppy (P)
Kochia scoparia, summer cypress
Limonium sinuatum, statice (B)
Lobelia erinus, edging lobelia
Lonas annua, golden ageratum
Mirabilis jalapa, four-o'clock (P)
Moluccella laevis, bells of Ireland
Nemesia spp.
Nicandra physalodes, shoofly plant (P)
Nicotiana alata, flowering tobacco
Nierembergia spp., cupflower (P)
Oenothera biennis, *O. missourensis*, *O. speciosa*, evening primrose (B or P)
Papaver nudicaule, Iceland poppy (P)
Penstemon gloxinioides
Petunia spp.
Phlox drummondii
Portulaca spp., moss rose
Proboscidea spp., unicorn plant
Salvia farinacea, mealy-cup sage (P)
Salvia splendens, scarlet sage
Sanvitalia procumbens, creeping zinnia
Scabiosa atropurpurea, pincushion flower
Schizanthus spp., butterfly flower
Senecio cineraria, dusty miller (P)
Tithonia spp., Mexican sunflower
Trachymene caerulea, blue lace flower
Verbena spp.
Xeranthemum annuum, immortelle

Tender Annuals

Ageratum spp., flossflower
Alonsoa spp., mask flower (P)
Amaranthus caudatus, love-lies-bleeding
Amaranthus tricolor, Joseph's coat
Asclepias curassavica, bloodflower (P)
Begonia semperflorens-cultorum, wax begonia (P)
Browallia spp.
Catharanthus roseus, Madagascar periwinkle (P)
Coleus spp. (P)
Cosmos spp.
Datura spp.
Dimorphotheca spp., Cape marigold
Exacum affine, Persian violet (B)
Heliotropium spp., heliotrope (P)
Helipterum manglesii, Swan River daisy
Hypoestes phyllostachya, polka-dot plant (P)
Impatiens spp. (P)
Mimulus spp., monkey flower (P)
Nolana spp., Chilean bellflower (P)
Oxypetalum caeruleum, southern star (P)
Pelargonium spp., geranium (P)
Perilla spp.
Ricinus communis, castor bean
Salpiglossis sinuata, painted tongue
Tagetes erecta, African marigold
Tagetes patula, French marigold
Tagetes tenuifolia, signet marigold
Tolpis barbata, hawkweed
Torenia spp., wishbone flower
Trachelium spp., throatwort (P)
Tropaeolum spp., nasturtium
Vinca major 'Variegata' (P)
Zinnia spp.

Annuals That Self-Sow

These plants often self-sow when grown under ideal conditions. If you do not deadhead all the flowers, they will mature and release their seeds, and new seedlings will come up on their own.

Ageratum spp., flossflower
Amaranthus caudatus, love-lies-bleeding
Antirrhinum spp., snapdragon
Browallia spp.
Centaurea cyanus, bachelor's button
Cleome spp., spider flower
Consolida spp., larkspur
Cosmos spp.
Eschscholzia californica, California poppy
Gaillardia pulchella, blanketflower
Gypsophila elegans, baby's breath
Helianthus spp., sunflower
Iberis umbellata, globe candytuft
Lobularia maritima, sweet alyssum
Malcolmia maritima, Virginia stock
Mirabilis jalapa, four-o'clock
Moluccella laevis, bells of Ireland
Nicotiana alata, flowering tobacco
Nigella damascena, love-in-a-mist
Perilla spp.
Petunia spp.
Portulaca spp., moss rose
Salvia spp.
Tagetes spp., marigold
Viola tricolor, Johnny-jump-up

Low-Maintenance Annuals

These plants are especially durable and easy to care for once established.

Ageratum spp., flossflower
Begonia semperflorens-cultorum, wax begonia
Catharanthus roseus, Madagascar periwinkle (also called—incorrectly—vinca)
Celosia cristata, woolflower
Coleus spp.
Cosmos spp.
Gomphrena globosa, globe amaranth
Helianthus spp., sunflower
Hypoestes phyllostachya, polka-dot plant
Impatiens spp.
Lobularia maritima, sweet alyssum
Portulaca spp., moss rose
Salvia spp.
Senecio cineraria, dusty miller
Tagetes spp., marigold
Tropaeolum spp., nasturtium

Annuals That Bloom All Summer

The following plants will bloom continuously all summer and into fall, especially if deadheaded regularly. Most will flower right up until frost kills them, and sweet alyssum will keep blooming through several frosts. In warm climates, where frost comes late (or not at all), remove the plants when they exhaust themselves.

Ageratum spp., flossflower
Begonia semperflorens-cultorum, wax begonia
Celosia cristata, woolflower
Cosmos spp.
Gomphrena globosa, globe amaranth

(continued)

Annuals that Bloom All Summer *(cont'd)*

Impatiens spp.
Lobelia spp., edging lobelia (if bloom slows in very hot weather, shear back plants for rebloom)
Lobularia erinus, sweet alyssum (if bloom slows in very hot weather, shear back plants for rebloom)
Nicotiana alata, flowering tobacco
Pelargonium spp., geranium
Petunia spp.
Portulaca spp., moss rose
Salvia spp.
Tagetes spp., marigold
Tropaeolum spp., nasturtium
Verbena spp.
Zinnia spp.

Most Popular Annuals

According to the Professional Plant Growers Association, the top ten annuals in terms of sales in 1992 were:

1. Impatiens
2. Petunias
3. Geraniums
4. Marigolds
5. Begonias (fibrous-rooted)
6. Vinca
7. Pansies
8. Dianthus
9. Sweet alyssum
10. Salvia

ANNUAL VINES

Annual vines offer a variety of uses in the garden. Many will provide quick cover to shade a porch or arbor or to camouflage a chain-link fence or screen the compost heap from view. Some, such as black-eyed Susan vine, are happy in a hanging basket. Others, like nasturtiums, are delightful when allowed to ramble about over the ground. See chapter 6 for information on vines that are true annuals or perennials of limited hardiness.

PERENNIALS

WHAT IS A PERENNIAL?

The plants we think of as perennials live for three years or more in the garden. The plants are herbaceous, meaning that their top growth, the part of the plant above ground, is not woody. In the North, most perennials die back to the ground in winter, when cold temperatures cause them to go dormant. In warm climates, perennials may experience dormancy during summer drought. Some are evergreen, keeping their leaves all year.

Most perennials grow from crowns. A crown is the point where stems meet roots, and in most perennials is made up of the bases of stems joined together in a clump. These clumps may be dense and tight, or they may be loose. When the old stems die back in fall, growth buds (or "eyes") that will grow into new stems form on the crowns. When you divide a crowded clump of perennials, it is important that each division have growth buds as well as roots.

WHEN TO PLANT PERENNIALS

The best time to plant perennials depends upon where you live, when the plants bloom, how they grow, and the form in which you buy them.

Local garden centers and nurseries sell perennials that are growing in containers. These can be planted anytime during the growing season when weather conditions are not too stressful for them. Generally speaking, garden centers have the largest selection of plants available in spring. Buying early in the season allows you the widest selection and the healthiest plants, and also enables you to give the plants the longest possible growing season in your garden.

Mail-order nurseries often sell perennials in bare-root form, when they are dormant. As a general rule of thumb, the best time to plant bare-root perennials in Zone 5 and north is in spring. From Zone 7 south, fall is the preferred planting time; the farther south you are, the later you should plant. Gardeners in Zone 6 can plant in either spring or fall. Of course as with all rules, there are exceptions to this one. Here are three:

Oriental poppies go dormant in early summer, after they bloom. This is the time to plant them; they do not transplant well when in active growth.

Bearded irises also are best planted immediately after flowering.

Peonies are best planted in early fall—September in many gardens. When planting peonies, it is imperative that the pink growth buds on the crown are no more than 2 inches below the soil surface. If planted too deeply, peonies will not bloom.

For information on how to plant container-grown and bare-root plants, see chapter 2, "Gardening Techniques."

Perennials to Grow as Annuals

Actinotus helianthi, flannelflower
Alonsoa warscewiczii, mask flower
Angelonia salicariifolia
Arctotis spp., African daisy
Bellis perennis, English daisy
Browallia speciosa, bush violet
Canna spp.
Catharanthus roseus, Madagascar periwinkle
Cheiranthus cheiri, wallflower
Coleus × *hybridus*
Dahlia spp.
Eschscholzia californica, California poppy
Felicia amelloides, blue marguerite
Gazania rigens, treasure flower
Gerbera jamesonii, Transvaal daisy
Helichrysum bracteatum, strawflower
Heliotropium arborescens, heliotrope
Hunnemannia fumariifolia, Mexican tulip poppy
Hypoestes phyllostachya, polka-dot plant
Impatiens spp.
Limonium sinuatum, statice
Mimulus × *hybridus*, monkey flower
Mirabilis jalapa, four-o'clock

(continued)

Perennials to Grow as Annuals *(cont'd)*

Nicotiana alata, flowering tobacco
Nierembergia spp., cupflower
Nolana spp., Chilean bellflower
Papaver nudicaule, Iceland poppy
Pelargonium spp., geranium
Pentas lanceolata, star cluster
Senecio cineraria, dusty miller
Trachelium caeruleum, throatwort
Verbena × *hybrida*, garden verbena

WHEN TO DIVIDE PERENNIALS

Most perennials benefit from periodic division of the root clumps. When a clump of perennials looks crowded, and the quantity and quality of flowers declines, the plant probably needs division. Some plants will appear to grow in a ring around an empty center, because the old central portion of the crown has died out. Dividing the plant will renew its vigor; it will grow and bloom better.

For information on how to divide perennials, see chapter 2, "Gardening Techniques." Here are some guidelines on when to divide.

As a rule of thumb, divide perennials that bloom in spring, such as primroses, in early summer after they finish blooming.

Divide summer bloomers like summer or garden phlox in late summer to early fall.

Divide fall bloomers like mums and asters in spring.

An exception to the rule: in Zone 5 and farther north, it is best to divide all perennials in early spring before they begin putting out new growth.

Perennials That Seldom Need Division

Aconitum spp., monkshood
Adenophora spp., ladybells
Alchemilla vulgaris, lady's mantle
Amsonia tabernaemontana, blue star
Amsonia schmidtiana 'Nana', silver mound artemisia
Aruncus dioicus, goatsbeard
Asclepias tuberosa, butterfly weed
Baptisia australis, blue false indigo
Brunnera macrophylla, Siberian bugloss
Chelone spp., turtlehead
Cimicifuga racemosa, black snakeroot
Dicentra spp., bleeding heart
Dictamnus albus, gas plant
Epimedium spp., bishop's hat
Eryngium spp., sea holly
Euphorbia polychroma, cushion spurge
Geranium spp., cranesbill
Gypsophila paniculata, baby's breath
Helleborus niger, Christmas rose
Hemerocallis spp., daylily
Hosta spp.
Incarvillea delavayi, hardy gloxinia
Iris sibirica, Siberian iris
Limonium latifolium, sea lavender
Paeonia spp., peony
Papaver orientale, oriental poppy
Platycodon grandiflorus, balloon flower
Veronica spp., speedwell

Perennials Needing Frequent Division

These plants need to be divided often—every year or two—to maintain their vigor or, in some cases, to keep them where you want them.

Achillea spp., yarrow
Anthemis tinctoria, golden marguerite
Artemisia lactiflora, white mugwort
Artemisia ludoviciana var. *albula* 'Silver King', silver king artemisia
Aster novae-angliae New England aster, Michaelmas daisy
Aster novi-belgii, New York aster, Michaelmas daisy
Boltonia asteroides
Campanula glomerata, clustered bellflower
Cerastium tomentosum, snow-in-summer
Dendrathema spp., garden chrysanthemum
Eupatorium coelestinum, mist flower
Helenium spp., sneezeweed
Helianthus spp., sunflower
Lysimachia clethroides, gooseneck loosestrife
Physostegia virginiana, false dragonhead, obedient plant
Primula spp., primrose
Rudbeckia fulgida, coneflower
Solidago spp., goldenrod

Perennials That Can Be Invasive

Given conditions they like, these plants can spread like crazy.

Achillea spp., yarrow
Aegopodium podagraria, goutweed
Ajuga spp., especially *reptans*, bugleweed
Anchusa spp., bugloss
Artemisia spp.
Asperula odorata, sweet woodruff
Campanula spp., bellflower
Catananche caerulea, cupid's dart
Convallaria spp., lily-of-the-valley
Echinops spp., globe thistle
Eupatorium purpureum, Joe-pye weed
Euphorbia cyparissias, cypress spurge
Hemerocallis spp., daylily
Lysimachia clethroides, gooseneck loosestrife
Macleaya cordata, plume poppy
Monarda didyma, bee balm
Nepeta spp., catmint
Physostegia virginiana, false dragonhead
Rudbeckia hirta, black-eyed Susan
Tradescantia spp., spiderwort
Verbascum spp., mullein
Viola tricolor, violet, Johnny-jump-up

Perennials with Long Blooming Time

Most perennials bloom for two to three weeks. Those listed below generally flower for at least four to six weeks, or off and on through much of the summer.

Achillea spp., yarrow
Allium spp., flowering onion
Anthemis tinctoria, golden marguerite
Armeria maritima, sea pink
Astrantia major, masterwort
Brunnera macrophylla, Siberian bugloss
Ceratostigma plumbaginoides, plumbago
Chrysogonum virginianum, goldenstar, green-and-gold
Cimicifuga racemosa, black snakeroot
Coreopsis spp., especially 'Moonbeam'
Delphinium spp., Pacific Giants hybrids (rebloom if cut back after first flowering)

(continued)

Perennials with Long Blooming Time *(cont'd)*

Dendrathema spp., garden chrysanthemums, cushion type

Dicentra eximia, fringed bleeding heart

Digitalis purpurea, foxglove (reblooms if cut back after first flowering)

Echinacea purpurea, purple coneflower

Gaillardia spp., blanketflower

Geranium spp., cranesbill

Heliopsis spp., sunflower

Hemerocallis spp., 'Stella de Oro' and 'Black-eyed Stella', daylily

Linum perenne, blue flax

Lysimachia clethroides, gooseneck loosestrife

Monarda didyma, bee balm

Nepeta × faassenii, catmint

Nipponanthemum nipponicum, Montauk daisy

Physostegia virginiana, false dragonhead

Platycodon grandiflorus, balloon flower

Rudbeckia fulgida, coneflower

Sanguisorba canadensis, American burnet

Sedum 'Autumn Joy'

Stokesia laevis, Stokes' aster

Tanacetum parthenium, feverfew

Tradescantia × andersoniae, spiderwort

50 Perennials for Different Regions

When looking over the list for your region, bear in mind that within each region there exist different climates, and many kinds of local microclimates. For example, a perennial garden near Phoenix, Arizona, would contain plants different from those in a garden high in the mountains near Flagstaff. The particular set of environmental conditions in and around your garden will determine what will grow there.

The following lists offer broad suggestions for plants that grow well in different parts of the country, but not every plant will grow in every garden in the region.

NORTH

Achillea, yarrow

Aconitum, monkshood

Adenophora, ladybells

Ajuga, bugleweed

Anaphalis, pearly everlasting

Anthemis, golden marguerite

Aquilegia, columbine

Arabis, rock cress

Aruncus, goatsbeard

Aster, heath aster, white wood aster

Boltonia

Brunnera, Siberian bugloss

Campanula, bellflower

Centaurea, knapweed

Chelone, turtlehead

Chrysanthemum, arctic daisy, *C. weyrichii*, shasta daisy

Cimicifuga, bugbane

Coreopsis, threadleaf coreopsis

Delphinium

Dianthus, maiden pink, *D. knappii*

Dicentra, bleeding heart, Dutchman's breeches

Doronicum, leopard's bane

Echinops, globe thistle

Erigeron, Oregon fleabane

Eryngium, sea holly

Filipendula, Siberian meadowsweet

Gentiana, bottle gentian, crested gentian

Geranium, cranesbill

Hemerocallis, daylily

Heuchera, coralbells

Hosta
Iberis, perennial candytuft
Iris, bearded iris
Liatris, gayfeather
Ligularia
Lychnis, Maltese cross
Nepeta, catmint
Paeonia, peony
Papaver, oriental poppy
Penstemon
Phlox, creeping phlox, summer phlox
Physostegia, false dragonhead
Polemonium, Jacob's ladder
Primula, auricula primrose, polyanthus primrose
Rudbeckia, black-eyed Susan
Saponaria, bouncing bet, rock soapwort
Solidago, goldenrod
Trollius, globeflower
Veronica, speedwell
Yucca, soapweed

EAST AND MID-ATLANTIC

Achillea, yarrow
Aconitum, monkshood
Alcea, hollyhock
Amsonia, blue star
Anemone, Japanese anemone
Aquilegia, columbine
Artemisia
Aruncus, goatsbeard
Aster, Michaelmas daisy
Astilbe
Aurinia, basket-of-gold
Bergenia
Boltonia
Brunnera, Siberian bugloss
Campanula, bellflower
Centranthus, red valerian
Cimicifuga, black snakeroot
Coreopsis
Delphinium
Dendrathema, garden chrysanthemum
Dianthus
Dicentra, bleeding heart, Dutchman's breeches
Digitalis, foxglove (biennial)
Echinops, globe thistle
Geranium, cranesbill
Heliopsis, sunflower
Hemerocallis, daylily
Heuchera, coralbells
Hibiscus
Hosta
Limonium, sea lavender
Lupinus, lupine
Macleaya, plume poppy
Mertensia, Virginia bluebells
Monarda, bee balm
Nepeta, catmint
Paeonia, peony
Papaver, oriental poppy
Phlox, creeping phlox, mountain pinks, summer phlox, wild sweet William
Platycodon, balloon flower
Polemonium, Jacob's ladder
Primula, primrose
Salvia
Sedum, stonecrop
Sidalcea, false mallow
Stachys, lamb's ears
Thalictrum, meadow rue
Tradescantia, spiderwort
Veronica, speedwell
Viola, violet

SOUTHEAST

Achillea, yarrow
Agapanthus, lily-of-the-Nile

(continued)

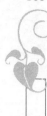

50 Perennials for Different Regions *(cont'd)*

Ageratum, flossflower
Allium, flowering onion
Amsonia
Anemone, pasque flower
Aquilegia, columbine
Asclepias, butterfly weed, blood flower
Aster, Michaelmas daisy
Astilbe
Baptisia, false indigo
Begonia, hardy begonia
Belamcanda, blackberry lily
Campanula, bellflower
Chrysogonum, green-and-gold
Convolvulus, ground morning glory
Coreopsis
Corydalis
Dianthus, cottage pink
Dictamnus, gas plant
Euphorbia, spurge
Gaillardia, blanketflower
Gerbera, Transvaal daisy
Hedychium, ginger lily
Helenium, sneezeweed
Helleborus, Christmas rose, lenten rose
Hemerocallis, daylily
Heuchera, alumroot
Hibiscus, rose mallow
Hosta
Hypericum, St.-John's-wort
Iris, Japanese, Louisiana, Siberian iris
Liriope, lilyturf
Lycoris, magic lily
Mertensia, Virginia bluebells
Monarda, bee balm
Phlox, wild sweet William
Physostegia, obedient plant
Platycodon, balloon flower
Primula, primrose
Rudbeckia, coneflower
Salvia
Sedum, stonecrop
Stokesia, Stokes' aster
Thalictrum, meadow rue
Thermopsis, yellow lupine
Tradescantia, spiderwort
Veronica, spike speedwell
Viola, horned violet, sweet violet
Zephyranthes, atamasco lily

MIDWEST

Achillea, yarrow
Aquilegia, columbine
Artemisia
Asclepias, butterfly weed
Aster
Astilbe
Centaurea
Cimicifuga, black snakeroot
Coreopsis
Dendrathema, garden chrysanthemum
Dicentra, bleeding heart
Digitalis, foxglove
Dodecatheon, shooting star
Echinacea, purple coneflower
Erigeron, fleabane
Eupatorium, Joe-pye weed, mist flower
Filipendula, Queen-of-the-prairie
Gaillardia, blanketflower
Gypsophila, baby's breath
Helenium, sneezeweed
Hemerocallis, daylily
Heuchera, alumroot, coralbells
Hosta
Iris, bearded iris
Liatris, gayfeather
Lithospermum, hairy puccoon
Lobelia, cardinal flower
Lupinus, lupine
Lychnis, Maltese cross
Macleaya, plume poppy

Mertensia, Virginia bluebells
Monarda, dotted mint
Myosotis, forget-me-not
Oenothera, evening primrose, sundrops
Paeonia, peony
Papaver, oriental poppy
Penstemon
Phlox, summer phlox
Physostegia, false dragonhead, obedient plant
Platycodon, balloon flower
Polygonatum, great Solomon's seal
Ratibida, yellow coneflower
Rudbeckia, black-eyed Susan
Sedum, stonecrop
Sisyrinchium, blue-eyed grass
Solidago, goldenrod
Thalictrum, meadow rue
Tradescantia, spiderwort
Viola, bird's foot violet, sweet violet

SOUTHWEST

Achillea, yarrow
Agapanthus, lily-of-the-Nile
Agave
Aloe
Anigozanthus, kangaroo paw
Argyranthemum, marguerite daisy
Armeria, sea pink
Aster × frikartii
Bergenia
Campanula
Clivia, Kaffir lily
Coreopsis
Crassula
Dianthus, pinks
Dietes
Echeveria
Echinocereus, hedgehog cactus
Echinops, globe thistle
Erigeron, fleabane
Eryngium
Euphorbia, spurge
Felicia, blue marguerite
Gaillardia, blanketflower
Gaura
Gazania
Gerbera, Transvaal daisy
Geum, avens
Helichrysum, curry plant
Hemerocallis, daylily
Iberis, perennial candytuft
Iris, bearded iris, Siberian iris, winter iris
Kniphofia, red-hot poker
Lampranthus, ice plant
Lavandula, lavender
Limonium, statice
Liriope, lilyturf
Mammillaria
Mesembryanthemum, ice plant
Nepeta, catmint
Opuntia, prickly pear
Perityle, Mexican rock daisy
Phormium, New Zealand flax
Romneya, Matilija poppy
Rudbeckia, black-eyed Susan
Salvia, Mexican sage
Scabiosa
Sedum, stonecrop
Tacitus
Valeriana, valerian

WEST COAST

Acanthus, bear's breeches
Achillea, yarrow
Agapanthus, lily-of-the-Nile
Aloe
Alstroemeria, Peruvian lily
Anigozanthus, kangaroo paw
Anthemis, golden marguerite
Arabis, rock cress
Armeria, sea pink

(continued)

50 Perennials for Different Regions *(cont'd)*

Asclepias, blood flower
Astilbe
Aurinia, basket-of-gold
Bletilla, Chinese ground orchid
Campanula, chimney bellflower
Clivia, Kaffir lily
Convolvulus, ground morning glory
Coreopsis
Delphinium (Pacific Northwest)
Dianthus (*D. knapii* especially in high altitudes)
Diascia, twinspur
Elhium, pride of Madeira
Erigeron, Mexican daisy
Euphorbia, spurge
Gaillardia, blanketflower
Gerbera, Transvaal daisy
Gypsophila, baby's breath
Helianthus, sunflower
Helichrysum, curry plant
Hemerocallis, daylily
Hosta, plantain lily
Iris, Pacific Coast iris, winter iris
Lavandula, lavender
Linum, flax
Lupinus, lupine
Osteospermum, freeway daisy
Papaver, oriental poppy
Penstemon
Phlomis, Jerusalem sage
Phlox, creeping phlox, mountain pinks
Phormium, New Zealand flax
Primula, primrose
Romneya, Matilija poppy
Salvia, Mexican bush sage, Texas sage, others
Santolina, lavender cotton
Saxifraga, London pride
Scabiosa, pincushion flower
Trollius, globeflower
Yucca
Zantedeschia, calla lily
Zauschneria, California fuchsia

Long-Lived Perennials

Perennials may live for three years or for generations. The plants listed here, if given the kind of growing conditions to which they are best suited, and divided when they become crowded, will usually live for a good, long time.

Aconitum spp., monkshood
Agapanthus africanus, African lily
Amsonia spp., blue star
Anemone spp., Japanese anemone
Asclepias spp., butterfly weed
Astilbe spp.
Baptisia spp., false indigo
Belamcanda chinensis, blackberry lily
Centaurea spp., knapweed
Chelone spp., turtlehead
Cimicifuga racemosa, black snakeroot, bugbane
Convallaria spp., lily of the valley
Coreopsis spp.
Dicentra spp., bleeding heart (except in warm climates)
Dictamnus albus, gas plant
Doronicum spp., leopard's bane
Echinacea purpurea, purple coneflower
Echinops spp., globe thistle
Epimedium spp.
Erigeron spp., fleabane
Eryngium spp.
Euphorbia spp., spurge
Filipendula spp., meadowsweet
Gaillardia spp., blanketflower
Geranium spp., cranesbill
Geum spp., avens
Heliopsis spp.
Helleborus spp., hellebore
Hemerocallis spp., daylily

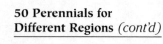

Heuchera spp., alumroot, coralbells
Hosta spp.
Iris spp.
Liatris spp., gayfeather
Linaria spp.
Nipponanthemum spp., Montauk daisy
Oenothera spp., evening primrose, sundrops
Paeonia spp., peony
Phlox spp., creeping phlox, wild sweet William
Platycodon spp., balloon flower
Polemonium spp., Jacob's ladder
Polygonatum spp., Solomon's seal
Potentilla spp.
Sempervivum spp.
Smilacina spp., false Solomon's seal
Tanacetum spp., feverfew
Thalictrum spp., meadow rue
Tradescantia spp., spiderwort
Uvularia spp., merry bells
Veronica spp., speedwell
Viola spp., violet
Yucca spp.

Drought-Tolerant Perennials

Acanthus spp., bear's breeches
Achillea spp., yarrow
Anaphalis spp., pearly everlasting
Anthemis tinctoria, golden marguerite
Arabis spp., rock cress
Armeria maritima, sea pink
Artemisia spp.
Asclepias tuberosa, butterfly weed
Aurinia saxatilis, basket-of-gold
Catananche caerulea, cupid's dart
Centaurea macrocephala, globe centaurea
Cerastium spp.
Coreopsis spp.
Dianthus spp., cottage pink
Echinacea purpurea, purple coneflower
Echinops 'Taplow Blue', globe thistle
Eryngium spp., sea holly
Euphorbia spp., spurge
Gaillardia spp., blanketflower
Hemerocallis spp., daylily
Kniphofia spp., red-hot poker
Lavandula angustifolia, English lavender
Liatris spp., gayfeather
Linum perenne, blue flax
Lychnis chalcedonica, Maltese cross
Potentilla spp., cinquefoil
Ratibida columnifera, Mexican hat
Rudbeckia fulgida, coneflower
Salvia spp.
Santolina spp., lavender cotton
Sedum spp., stonecrop
Sempervivum spp.
Stachys byzantina, lamb's ears
Yucca spp.

Earliest Blooming Perennials

The perennials listed here are among the earliest to bloom. Time of bloom varies with location, but generally speaking, these plants flower in early spring; some bloom in winter in warm climates.

Adonis amurensis, amur adonis
Anemone blanda, Grecian windflower
Arabis spp., rock cress
Aubrieta spp., false rock cress
Aurinia saxatilis, basket-of-gold
Bergenia spp.
Helleborus spp., hellebore
Hepatica spp.
Iberis sempervirens, perennial candytuft
Iris cristata, crested iris
Iris unguicularis, winter iris

(continued)

Earliest Blooming Perennials *(cont'd)*

Myosotis scorpioides, forget-me-not
Petasites japonicus var. *gigantens*, Japanese butterbur
Phlox subulata, mountain pink, moss pink
Primula × polyantha, polyanthus primrose
Pulmonaria spp., lungwort
Sanguinaria canadensis, bloodroot
Tussilago farfara, coltsfoot
Vinca minor, periwinkle

BULBS

WHAT IS A BULB?

A bulb is a modified shoot or flower bud that usually forms underground. It has swollen leaf bases or thick scales that protect the bud and store food to nourish it during a rest period in which the plant's top growth dies back. The bulb contains nearly everything the embryonic bud will need to grow and bloom. The bud rests in the center of the bulb. It is surrounded by scales, which resemble the layers of an onion in bulbs such as narcissus and tulips, or are like the cloves of a garlic bulb in the bulbs of lilies. The scales are anchored to a tough basal plate (the flat end of the bulb) from which the roots will grow. Some bulbs are called "tunicate," which means the scales are covered by a thin skin known as a tunic. Bulbs reproduce by means of underground offsets called bulblets, or in some lilies, by small, round bulbils that develop in the leaf axils. Both will eventually grow into full-size bulbs if planted. Daffodils and narcissus, tulips, hyacinths, and lilies all grow from true bulbs.

In addition to true bulbs, there are a number of other underground storage organs which in informal usage are also thought of as bulbs because the plants grow in much the same way. These other structures are corms, rhizomes, tubers, and tuberous roots.

A corm is the swollen underground base of a stem, which stores food in the same way a bulb does, although corms store most of it in the basal plate instead of in scales. Corms are usually flatter than bulbs. The corms reproduce by forming small cormels or cormlets at the base of the parent plant, or, less commonly, on aboveground stems. Crocus and gladiolus are two common plants that grow from corms.

Rhizomes are swollen underground stems that grow horizontally through the soil instead of vertically down into the ground. They can produce new roots and shoots, and many plants spread by means of their creeping rhizomes. The rhizomes can be divided or cut up to propagate new plants. Bearded iris is probably the best-known rhizomatous plant.

Tubers are swollen stems that are also located underground in most cases. Tubers contain buds or "eyes" from which new plants can grow.

Tuberous roots are swollen roots, like those of dahlias, which have become modified into storage organs. Tuberous-rooted plants have the growth buds in the crown, the base of the plant where stems and roots meet.

Bulbs and the other bulblike structures can be hardy and able to withstand below-freezing temperatures, or they may be tender, and damaged or killed by frost. The bulbs that

Types of Bulbs

Tunicate-true bulb (daffodil)

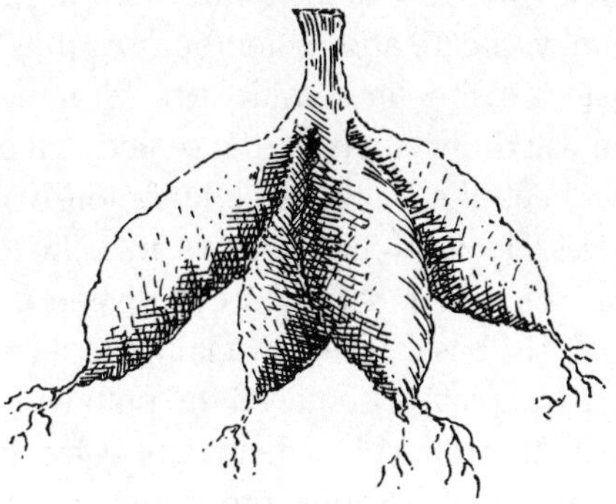

Tuberous root (dahlia)

Corm (crocus)

Scaly bulb (lily)

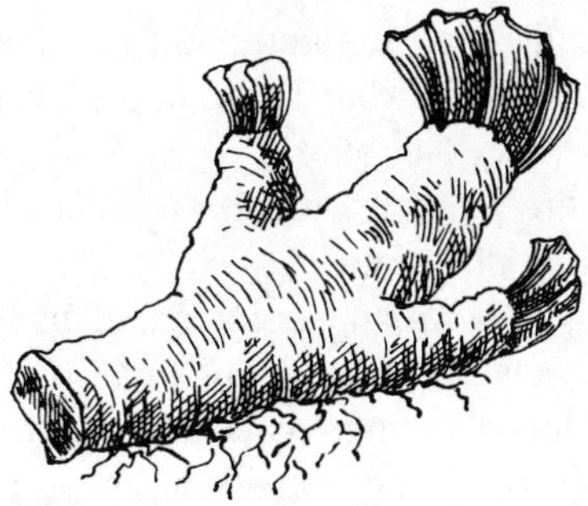

Rhizome (iris)

Tuber (begonia)

bloom in spring—crocuses, daffodils, scilla, tulips, hyacinths, and the rest—are hardy. Many summer bulbs—gladiolus, tuberous begonias, dahlias, and Peruvian daffodils, for example—are tender. But not all summer-blooming bulbs are tender. Many lilies, for example, are quite hardy.

HANDLING BULBS

When you bring bulbs home from the garden center or receive them in the mail, handle them with care and remember that they are alive, even when dormant. Although they may not look it, they are sensitive to environmental conditions. Hot sun will shrivel them, too much rain will drown them, being sealed in a plastic bag will suffocate them.

Check the bulbs carefully before you buy them, or as soon as a mail-order shipment arrives. Healthy bulbs will be firm to the touch (except in some special cases, such as anemones, which look shriveled even when healthy). They should not have soft, rotten spots, or mold. The basal plate, especially, should feel solid and show no evidence of mold or damage. If the basal plate is damaged the bulb will bloom poorly or not at all.

If you cannot plant them right away, store the bulbs in a cool place out of direct sun, where air circulation is good. Spread them out on open shelves, or put them in mesh bags or roomy paper bags. You can use the same storage method in winter to keep tender bulbs for replanting next year.

PLANTING HARDY BULBS

In cold climates, hardy spring-blooming bulbs go into the ground in early to mid-autumn, before the first hard frost. In warmer climates, plant later in the fall—November or even December where winters are mild. Depending upon how far south you live, you may need to refrigerate hardy bulbs for 6 to 8 weeks before planting to ensure that they receive the necessary cold period.

Hardy bulbs will grow in most well-drained soils of reasonable fertility, in full sun or partial shade. Dig the soil to appropriate depth for the bulbs you are planting (see the table, "Planting Depths for Bulbs"). Loosen the soil and work in compost and bulb fertilizer or an all-purpose fertilizer. Bone meal has traditionally been the nutriment of choice for bulbs, but the quality of the bone meal being sold today is not what it used to be. If your soil is dense and clayey, add sand, as well. Rake the soil surface smooth.

If you are planting lots of bulbs, prepare the entire planting area at once. For smaller numbers you can dig individual holes with a trowel or bulb planter.

Place the bulbs in the soil where you want them to grow with the pointed end up. For the most effective display, plant in drifts or clusters of twelve or more. Plant small bulbs like crocuses or grape hyacinths by the score—you need lots of them to make an impact.

Set the bulbs firmly in the soil, cover them with soil to the correct depth, and water thoroughly. Mulch with 2 to 3 inches of shredded leaves.

PLANTING TENDER BULBS

The procedure for planting tender bulbs is basically the same as the procedure for planting hardy bulbs, except it takes place in spring, after the danger of frost has passed and the soil has warmed. Prepare the soil as for hardy bulbs and plant at the recommended depth.

Planting Depths for Bulbs

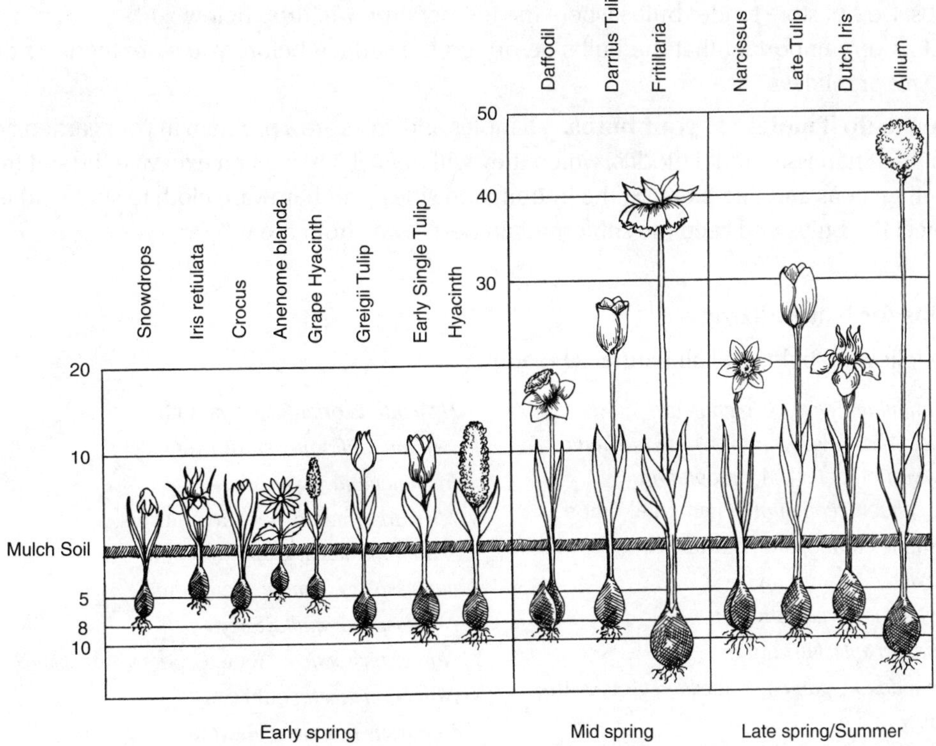

Gardeners in the North, where the outdoor growing season is short, can start tuberous begonias in pots indoors, and move them outdoors when conditions permit. Other tender bulbs can go right into the garden at the appropriate time.

LIFTING AND STORING TENDER BULBS

Gardeners in regions where winters are cold must dig up tender bulbs in autumn and store them indoors over winter. You can wait to dig most bulbs until the leaves have started to turn brown or soft from frost, but get them out of the ground before heavy frost or the plant crowns or bulbs could be damaged. Two exceptions are tuberous begonias and tuberoses, which cannot tolerate any frost at all. Dig them before you get the first frost.

Loosen the soil around the plant, then lift the entire plant from the ground with a digging fork or spade. Leave a good amount of soil around the roots. Spread the bulbs out to dry in a cool, dark basement or root cellar that is frostproof but airy. Sort the bulbs by type and color when you dig them, and keep them labeled throughout the storage process so you know which is which at planting time.

When the stems and the leaves dry out, remove them. Shake off the dry soil clinging to the bulbs, then let the bulbs dry for a few more days. Pack them in boxes of dry peat moss or wrap them individually in newspaper, and store as described earlier for newly purchased bulbs. Do not store tender bulbs where the temperature will drop below 50°F.

It is very important that the bulbs be dry on the surface before you store them, or they may rot or mildew.

What to do if moles eat your bulbs. If moles and voles are a problem in your garden, you can plant narcissus and daffodils, which they will not eat. Or you can excavate the soil from planting areas and line them on the bottom and sides with hardware cloth to surround and protect the bulbs and keep the subterranean pests away from them.

Bulbs for Naturalizing

The following bulbs will all naturalize readily.

Allium aflatunense, A. giganteum, A. karataviense, A. moly, A. neapolitanum (warm climates), *A. oreophilum, A. sphaerocephalum*, ornamental onion

Anemone blanda and cultivars, Grecian windflower

Brodiaea lactea, starflower

Camassia cusickii, camass

Chionodoxa gigantea, C. luciliae, glory-of-the-snow

Colchicum autumnale, meadow saffron

Crocus ancyrensis, C. chrysanthus cultivars, *C. tomasinianus* cultivars, *C. vernus* cultivars

Endymion hispanicus, Spanish bluebell

Erythronium albidum, E. americanium, E. californicum, E. grandiflorum, trout lily

Erythronium dens-canis, dogtooth violet

Fritillaria meleagris, guinea hen flower

Galanthus nivalis, snowdrop

Hyacinthus orientalis, hyacinth

Ipheion uniflorum, starflower

Iris reticulata, dwarf iris

Muscari armeniacum and cultivars, *M. botryoides*, grape hyacinth

Narcissus cyclamineus cultivars

Narcissus jonquilla 'Suzy'

Narcissus poeticus 'Actaea', poet's narcissus

Narcissus tazetta cultivars

Narcissus triandrus 'Hawera'

Narcissus 'Barrett Browning', 'Birma', 'Canton', 'Flower Record', 'Fortune', 'Ice Follies', 'Mount Hood', 'Salome', and 'Thalia', hybrid daffodils and narcissus

Ornithogalum umbellatum, star-of-Bethlehem (can become invasive)

Puschkinia scilloides, striped squill

Scilla siberica, Siberian squill

Bulbs Endangered in the Wild

Many of the bulbs sold commercially are propagated in nurseries, but some are collected from the wild in Turkey and other countries, and distributed overseas. Continued collection is decreasing wild populations to the point where some have become endangered.

Between 1990 and 1995 Dutch companies have been phasing in a program of labeling packages of bulbs as "grown from cultivated stock" or "from wild sources." The agreement covers only Dutch companies, however; bulbs exported by other countries will not carry these labels.

As a general guide, avoid buying species bulbs that are offered at very low prices; cheap bulbs are often collected from the wild. Also exercise caution when buying the bulbs listed below to make sure you are buying bulbs that were propagated rather than collected. The bulbs listed below are covered under the Dutch bulb industry agreement.

Anemone blanda, Grecian windflower
Arisaema spp.
Cardiocrinum giganteum
Cyclamen spp., except for florist's cyclamen, *C. persicum*
Cypripedium, all North American species, lady's slipper
Dracunculus spp.
Eranthis cilicica
Eranthis hyemalis, winter aconite
Galanthus spp., except for *G. nivalis*, snowdrops
Iris acutiloba
Iris kopetdaghensis
Iris paradoxa
Iris persica, Persian iris
Iris sibirica subsp. *elegantissima*
Iris tuberosa (*Hermodactylus tuberosus*)
Leucojum aestivum, summer snowflake
Leucojum vernum, spring snowflake
Narcissus asturiensis
Narcissus bulbocodium var. *conspicuus* and *N. bulbocodium* 'Tenuifolius' hoop-petticoat daffodil
Narcissus cyclamineus
Narcissus juncifolius
Narcissus rupicola
Narcissus scaberulus
Narcissus triandrus var. *albus* and *N. triandrus* var. *concolor*, angel's tears
Pancratium maritimum, sea daffodil
Sternbergia, all species, lily of the field
Trillium, all species
Urginea maritima, sea onion
Uvularia spp., merrybells

The Natural Resources Defense Council also recommends avoiding the following as collected in the wild:

Erythronium, all North American species, as well as *E. japonicum*. The hybrid 'Pagoda' is propagated and thus acceptable.

Fritillaria, uncommon North American species. The commonly grown types are propagated.

Tulipa praecox, which is rare in its native Turkey and not widely propagated by growers.

NARCISSUS CLASSIFICATION

Hybrid narcissus and daffodil cultivars are classified by the Royal Horticultural Society of England into 12 groups according to their size, shape, and color. The groups are as follows:

Division 1: Trumpet Narcissus. Classic daffodil form. The corona, or "trumpet," is as long as or longer than the perianth segments ("petals"). Plants bear one flower per stem.

Division 2: Large-Cupped Narcissus. The corona, or "cup," is more than one-third, but less than equal to, the length of the perianth segments. Plants have one flower to a stem.

(continued)

Daffodils/Narcissus

Trumpet

Double

Small cup

Large cup

Poeticus

Split corona

Triandrus

Cyclamineus

Jonquilla

Tazetta

Narcissus Classification *(cont'd)*

Division 3: Small-Cupped Narcissus. The corona is not more than one-third the length of the perianth segments. One flower per stem.

Division 4: Double Narcissus. Perianth segments or the corona, or both, are doubled. One or more flowers to a stem.

Division 5: Triandrus Hybrids. Flowers are pendent (drooping downward) with reflexed (backward-curving) perianth segments. Corona is at least two-thirds the length of the perianth segments. Generally two or more flowers per stem.

Division 6: Cyclamineus Hybrids. Flowers point downward at an acute angle to the stem, have a very short pedicel ("neck"). Perianth segments are strongly reflexed. Usually one flower per stem.

Division 7: Jonquilla Hybrids. Small flowers have spreading perianth segments, are fragrant, and are usually one to three to a stem. Narrow, dark green leaves.

Division 8: Tazetta Narcissus. Clusters of three to twenty fragrant flowers on each stem. Spreading perianth segments, broad leaves. Not as hardy as other narcissus.

Division 9: Poeticus Narcissus. Pure white perianth, small, disc-shaped corona with red edge and green or yellow center. Flowers are fragrant.

Division 10: Species, Wild Variants, and Wild Hybrids. Includes all species, along with variants and hybrids that developed in the wild.

Division 11: Split-Corona Narcissus. Corona is split, usually for more than half its length.

Division 12: Miscellaneous Narcissus. All narcissus that do not fit into any of the other eleven divisions.

LILY CLASSES

This varied genus can be extremely confusing. There are many species, a bewildering array of hybrids, and flowers in several forms: trumpet, pendent, upward-facing, outward-facing, bowl-shaped, sunburst, and reflexed. The following classes have been established to group the hybrids.

Division 1: Asiatic Hybrids. Based on species native to the Orient, although the parentage is distant at this point. The popular Mid-Century Hybrids belong to this division.

Division 2: Martagon Hybrids. Martagon lilies, also called Turk's cap lilies, have reflexed petals and come in shades of pinkish purple, also white.

Division 3: Candidum Hybrids. Hybrids of the Madonna lily, *L. candidum*. Flowers are white and fragrant.

Division 4: American Hybrids. Hybrids derived from native North American species.

Division 5: Longiflorum Hybrids. These are the Easter lilies, with large, fragrant, trumpet-shaped flowers.

Division 6: Aurelian Hybrids. Derived from several Asian species, formerly called Trumpet and Olympic hybrids.

Division 7: Oriental Hybrids. This group is mostly hybrids of *L. auratum* and *L. speciosum*, also *L. japonicum*, *L. rubellum*, and *L. henryi*. Flowers are fragrant.

Division 8: Miscellaneous Hybrids. This division includes hybrids that do not fit into the other divisions.

TULIP CLASSIFICATION

The Royal Horticultural Society of England and the Royal Dutch Bulb Growers together established categories for tulips, based primarily on appearance. Some classes, particularly Breeder and Mendel tulips, are seldom grown in the United States. The rest will be familiar to gardeners in North America.

Single Early tulips: Large flowers in red, pink, yellow, or white, on stems 10 to 16 inches tall, bloom early in the tulip season.

Double Early: Double flowers in shades of red, pink, yellow, and white, 10 to 12 inches tall, bloom early.

Triumph: Hybrids between Single Early and Darwin tulips, Triumph hybrids flower in midseason, after Single and Double Earlies but before Single Lates. Usually under 22 inches tall. Colors include red, pink, purple, yellow, white, and bicolors. Many lovely pastels.

Single Late: This group combines two hybrid groups that were formerly separate—Darwins and Cottage tulips. Large oval flowers with squarish bases, 24 to 30 inches tall, in shades of red,pink,maroon,purple, lavender, mauve, orange, yellow, and white. Late blooming.

Lily-flowering: Although officially considered part of the Cottage hybrid group, these are now given their own category in grower catalogs. The graceful flowers have pointed petals that curve outward. About 24 inches tall, shades of red, pink, purple, orange, yellow, and white.

Parrot: Flowers are fringed and ruffled, some flamed, streaked or feathered in a contrasting color. Shades of red, purple, pink, yellow, and white. Late blooming.

Rembrandt: Similar to Darwins, except streaked or variegated rather than solid colors. True Rembrandts are now illegal to grow in the United States because the "broken" color is caused by a virus. Single Late cultivars with broken (not solid) color are called Rembrandts in the trade because they resemble the originals.

Fringed: Developed from Single Early, Double Early, and Darwin tulips, these have petals with fringed edges. Colors include rose, pink, lavender, and white. They are sometimes called orchid flowering.

Viridiflora: Flowers in shades of red, rose, yellow, cream, and white, edged and flushed with green.

Multiflowering: Flowers come in clusters of 3 to 6, in shades of red, pink, yellow, and white, to 27 inches tall.

Breeder: Large flowers, round to oval on tall stems to 40 inches. Shades of orange, bronze, and purple.

Mendel: Single flowers bloom between Single and Double Early tulips and Darwins. To 20 inches tall. Shades of red, pink, orange, yellow, and white.

Tulips

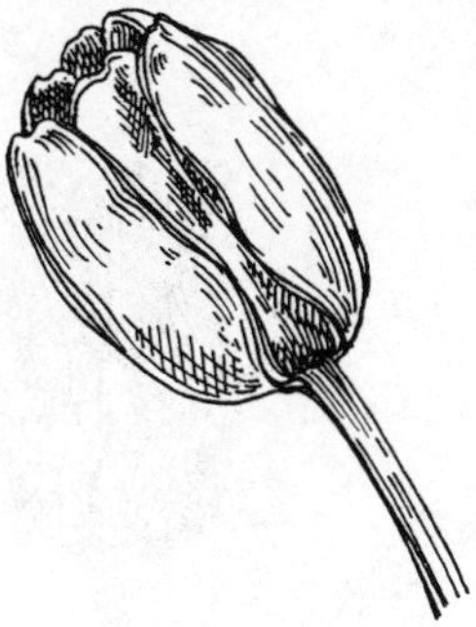

Single Early

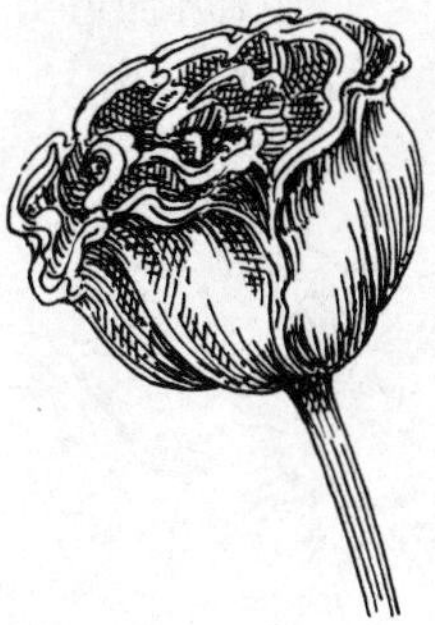

Double Early

Single Late

Peony-flowered (unofficial variety)

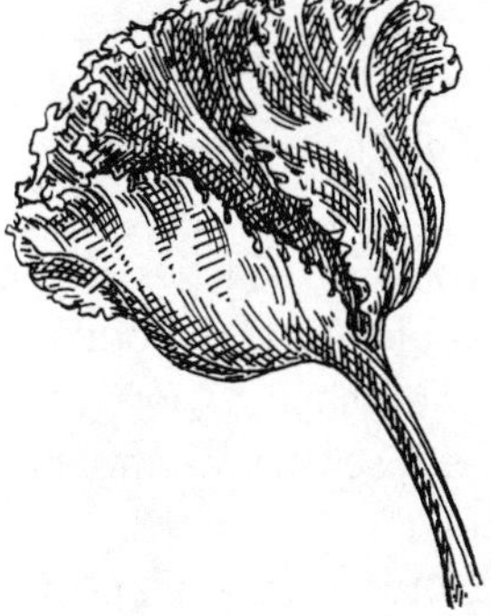

Parrot

Lily-flowered

SPECIES HYBRID GROUPS

These three groups were developed from the species forms, and generally do well in mild climates, as well as farther north.

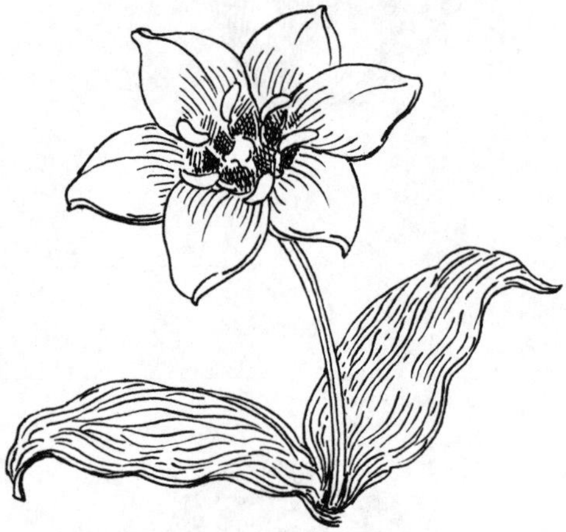

Kaufmanniana

Greigii

Fosterana: Very large flowers, in stems to 20 inches tall, in red, yellow, and cream. Early blooming.

Greigii: Large midseason blossoms in shades of red, pink, and orange. Plants are noted for their leaves, which are mottled and splashed with burgundy. Low to medium height.

Kaufmanniana: Also called waterlily tulips, these have pointed petals that open wide. Yellow streaked with red is typical; there are also shades of yellow, red, and salmon-pink. Short stemmed and very early blooming.

HOW TO FORCE BULBS

Many bulbs can be coaxed into bloom indoors in winter if given special treatment. To force bulbs, begin by buying the highest quality bulbs.

The forcing process begins in autumn. Plant the bulbs in pots 5 to 6 inches in diameter, with drainage holes in the bottom. A 6-inch pot holds three double-nosed daffodil bulbs, five to six tulip bulbs, or three hyacinths. Use a 5-inch bulb pan (a wide, shallow pot) to force smaller bulbs such as crocuses, squills, grape hyacinths, or netted irises. Leave enough space between bulbs when you plant them so water can pass through.

Be sure the pots you use are clean. If reusing old pots, scrub them out and soak them in a solution of 1 part liquid chlorine bleach to 9 parts water for an hour. Drain and rinse with clear water before filling with soil.

How to Force Paperwhite Narcissus

Fragrant paperwhites *(Narcissus tazetta* 'Paperwhite') are practically foolproof. Plant the bulbs in pots of soil or perlite, or in bowls of pebbles. Set the bulbs about 1/2 inch apart, and cover them about 1/3 of the way with the medium of your choice. Water soil or perlite thoroughly; add water to pebbles until it just touches the bottom of the bulb.

The plants will bloom in 3 to 4 weeks. Plant in succession 2 weeks apart for extended bloom. Warm climate gardeners can plant the bulbs outdoors after they bloom; elsewhere they are discarded.

Two close relatives of the paperwhite that can be forced in the same way are the yellow-flowered 'Soleil d'Or' and the Chinese sacred lily (*N. tazetta* var. *orientalis*).

Use a porous, moisture-retentive potting medium; a mix of equal parts potting soil, peat moss, and sand is one good medium. Most bulbs should be buried only to their tips. Allow 1/2 inch between the soil line and the top edge of the pot to permit watering.

For flowers over a longer period, stagger the plantings. A good rule of thumb is to plant in September for flowers in late December or January, in October for February flowers, and in November for flowers in March. Label the pots as you plant them so you remember which kind of bulb is in each pot.

Water thoroughly after planting. Then set the pots in a cold frame, or an unheated shed, bulkhead, or garage. If you have only a couple of pots, you can cover them with foil and put them in the refrigerator for their cold period. The bulbs need 8 to 12 weeks of cold temperatures (from about 35°F to 45°F) to form roots before they can be forced into bloom. Keep the soil moist but not wet during the cold period. Check the pots weekly and water when necessary.

At the end of the cold period, bring the pots into bright light but not direct sun. Cover the top of each pot with tissue paper (remove any foil first) for a few days to ease the transition to brighter light.

When the shoots are 2 to 3 inches high and bright green, put the pots on a sunny but cool windowsill. If the temperature is too warm, the bulbs may produce leaves but no flowers. Give the plants as much light as you can. Turn the pots every day so the stems grow straight. Stake the stems if necessary. Water with room-temperature water when the potting mixture dries out.

To get the longest life from the flowers when they bloom, put them in a cool—not cold—place at night, and keep them out of cold drafts.

When the flowers fade, clip them off and keep watering as needed for a month or two to let the leaves grow to nourish the bulbs. Then gradually taper off watering and allow the foliage to die back. You can then store hardy bulbs until fall, when you can plant them out in the garden (anemones and freesias are not hardy outdoors in the North).

COLD PERIOD NEEDED TO FORCE BULBS

Florist's anemone: 6 to 8 weeks, at 45° to 50°F. Soak tubers in water before planting.

Crocus: 8 weeks. Plant 1 to 2 inches deep and 1 inch apart, in a pot at least 3½ inches deep.

Daffodil and Narcissus: 8 weeks

Freesia: 6 to 8 weeks, at 50°F. Plant just below soil surface, 2 inches apart. After rooting period, place in bright location 65° to 70°F during the day, with a 10 degree drop at night.

Hyacinth: 6 to 8 weeks

Iris: 8 weeks. *Iris reticulata* and *I. danfordiae* work best.

Lily of the valley: Pips from mail-order nurseries should bloom with no cold period prior to forcing.

Tulips: 12 weeks

EARLIEST-BLOOMING BULBS

Many of us look for hybrid crocuses as the harbingers of spring, but some bulbs flower even earlier. The blooming times given below vary with location—the farther south your garden, or the more protected the site, the earlier the plants will bloom.

Anemone blanda, Grecian windflower	Late winter to early spring.
Chionodoxa species, glory-of-the-snow	Late winter to early spring.
Crocus species: *C. ancyrensis*, *C. biflorus* (Scotch crocus), *C. imperati*, *C. susianus* (cloth-of-gold), *C. tomasinianus* (tommies)	Bloom in late winter to very early spring.
Eranthis hyemalis, winter aconite	Late winter to early spring. These bulbs are usually wild-collected, so avoid buying them unless nursery-propagated bulbs are available.
Galanthus nivalis, snowdrop	Late winter to early spring.

Iris:	
I. danfordiae	Late winter to early spring.
I. reticulata, netted iris	Late winter to early spring.
I. unguicularis, Algerian or winter iris	Midwinter. For warm climates.
Dutch iris hybrids	Bloom in winter in the Deep South and along the West Coast if planted in fall.
Narcissus hybrids:	
'February Gold'	Late winter to early spring.
'February Silver'	Late winter to early spring.
'Paperwhite'	Blooms outdoors in winter in warm climates.
Scilla tubergeniana, Persian squill	Late winter to early spring.

MOST POPULAR BULBS

The top-selling bulbs in 1990 (the most recent year for which statistics are available) were, according to the Netherlands Bulb Information Center:

1. Tulip
2. Gladiolus
3. Iris
4. Crocus
5. Lily
6. Narcissus
7. Anemone
8. Hyacinth
9. Freesia
10. Allium

The Most Expensive Bulb

The record price paid for a single tulip bulb was 3,000 Dutch guilders (equivalent to about $1,500). This occurred when tulipmania was at its peak in nineteenth-century Europe.

ROSES

HOW TO PLANT ROSES

Pick a location in full sun—roses grow best with six hours of direct sunlight a day. They need deeply dug soil that is moist but well-drained, rich in organic matter, and of at least average fertility. Drainage is especially important; roses will not thrive in soggy soil. The ideal soil pH is 6.5, but roses will generally tolerate a range of 5.5 to 7.0.

If possible, prepare the soil for planting a season ahead of when you will actually plant.

Plant bare-root roses, roses packaged in biodegradable cartons, and roses preplanted in cartons in early spring, as soon as the soil can be worked. Cut slits into the sides and bottom of biodegradable cartons intended to be planted along with the roses. This ensures that the roots grow out into the surrounding soil. Be careful when cutting the box that you don't damage the plant.

Container-grown roses can be planted anytime from spring to fall when the weather is mild and not stressful for plants.

If possible, plant bare-root plants within 24 hours of receiving them. You can hold the roses in a cool, shady spot for 2 to 3 days, but open the package and sprinkle them with water so they don't dry out. If you must hold bare-root roses longer than 3 days, take them out of their packages and heel them into a shallow trench in the ground. If you must hold container roses, put them in a shady spot and keep the soil in the containers moist.

Soak the plants overnight in a bucket of muddy water. Before planting bare-root roses, cut off any broken, damaged, or shriveled canes, any canes thinner than a pencil, and any canes that cross over one another.

Dig a hole deep and wide enough to comfortably accommodate the roots without bending them. Loosen the soil in the bottom of the hole and mix in a shovelful of compost. Make a mound of soil in the bottom of the hole and set the plant on it so that the bud union (the knob where the greenish top meets the brown roots) is at the correct depth for your area. In Zones 3 to 7, the bud union should be 1 to 2 inches below the soil surface. In Zones 8 to 11, plant with the bud union 1 to 2 inches above the soil surface.

Spread the roots down over the soil mound and begin filling with soil. Carefully work the soil around the roots with your fingers. When the hole is two-thirds full, fill it to the top with water. When the water drains away, fill the hole the rest of the way with soil, firm it around the base of the plant, and water again.

If weather conditions are stressful—hot, cold, or dry—make a mound of soil about 8 inches high around the stem. Gradually remove the mound over a period of a week or so as you see signs of growth.

To plant container-grown roses, dig a hole at least 6 inches deeper and wider than the container. Loosen the soil in the bottom and sides, and add a shovelful of compost, so the soil level after planting is even with the surrounding soil. Water the new plants regularly during the first 3 weeks after planting, as the plants are establishing themselves in the soil and sending out new roots.

If you are planting climbing roses, have the supports in place before you plant.

Spacing is very important for roses. They require good air circulation to minimize the threat of disease. Follow these guidelines:

Zone 3, the coldest parts of New England and the North Central states: Plant hybrid teas, grandifloras, and floribundas $1^1/_2$ to 2 feet apart.

Zone 4, North Central and parts of the Northeast: Plant hybrid teas, grandifloras, and floribundas 2 to $2^1/_2$ feet apart.

Zones 5 to 7, East Coast, mid-South, and South Central: Plant hybrid teas and grandifloras $2^1/_2$ to 3 feet apart, floribundas 2 to 3 feet apart.

Zones 8 to 11, Deep South, Southwest, West Coast, and Pacific Northwest: Plant hybrid teas and grandifloras 3 to 4 feet apart, floribundas $2^1/_2$ to $3^1/_2$ feet apart.

All zones: Plant climbing roses 6 feet apart, miniatures 1 to 2 feet apart, and shrub roses to be grown as hedges 2 to 3 feet apart.

Many gardeners find it helpful to mulch newly planted roses with 2 inches of buckwheat or cocoa bean hulls, or shredded bark, to keep down weeds, conserve moisture, and prevent water from splashing onto stems (which can promote disease).

TYPES OF ROSES

Hybrid Teas

Hybrid tea roses are bush roses that have been introduced to the marketplace since 1867 (the variety L France, which is considered to be the first hybrid tea, was introduced in that year). Hybrid teas have long, narrow buds on long stems, that open into flowers with many petals. Plants are upright, and grow 3 feet or taller.

The hybrid tea roses listed below are rated excellent or outstanding for gardens by the American Rose Society, as reported in *Parks Rose Guide* by John Parks, published in 1993 by the American Rose Society (P. O. Box 30,000, Shreveport, LA 71130). The ARS ratings are averages based on nationwide performance.

Bride's Dream, pink
Captain Harry Stebbings, pink
Century Two, pink
Color Magic, pink blend
Dainty Bess, pink
Double Delight, red blend
Dublin, red
Elegant Beauty, yellow
Elina, yellow
Elizabeth Taylor, pink
First Prize, pink blend
Folklore, orange
Fragrant Cloud, orange-red
Garden Party, white
Jema, apricot
Keepsake, pink blend
KORlingo, red
Lady X, mauve
Marijke Koopman, pink
Miss All-American Beauty, pink
Mister Lincoln, red
Olympiad, red
Paradise, mauve
Pascali, white
Paul Shirville, orange-pink
Peace, yellow blend
Peter Frankenfeld, pink
Pristine, white
Red Jacket, red
Royal Highness, pink
Suffolk, white
Swarthmore, pink blend
Tabriz, pink
Thunderbolt, pink blend
Tiffany, pink blend
Touch of Class, orange-pink

Floribundas

Derived from hybrid teas and classified since the 1940s, floribundas produce clusters of flowers through the summer. Bushes are compact and 2 to 3 feet tall. They are easy to grow.

These floribunda roses are rated excellent or outstanding by the ARS.

Anabell, orange
Angel Face, mauve
Anna Wheatcroft, orange-red
Apricot Nectar, apricot
Betty Prior, pink
Bridal Pink, pink
Cherish, orange-pink
Dairy Maid, yellow
Dicky, orange-pink
English Miss, pink
Escapade, mauve
Europeana, red
Gene Boerner, pink
Grüss an Aachen, pink
H. C. Andersen, red
Kanegem, orange-red
Lavaglut, red
Lichterlo, red
Liverpool Echo, orange-pink
MElbalbika, red
Natali, pink
Orangeade, orange-red
Orange Sensation, orange-red
Pink Grüss an Aachen, orange-pink
Playgirl, pink
Poulsen's Pearl, pink
Rob Roy, red
Royal Occasion, orange-red
Sarabande, orange-red
Sexy Rexy, pink
Showbiz, red
Simplicity, pink
Stadt den Helder, red
Sun Flare, yellow
Sunsprite, yellow
Tony Jacklin, orange-pink
Traumeri, orange
Travemunde, red
Trumpeter, orange-red
Vera Dalton, pink

Grandifloras

Grandifloras produce clusters of flowers on long stems, blooming through the summer. The hardy bushes grow 5 to 6 feet tall. The first grandiflora was Queen Elizabeth, introduced in 1955.

These grandiflora roses are rated as excellent or outstanding by the ARS.

Aquarius, pink
Earth Song, pink
Gold Medal, yellow
Pink Parfait, pink
Queen Elizabeth, pink
Sonia, pink
Tournament of Roses, pink

Miniatures

Miniature roses have small flowers, and most do not grow more than 2 feet tall. They can be grown in the ground or in containers.

These miniature roses are rated as excellent or outstanding by the ARS.

Acey Deucy, red
Amorette, white
Angelita, white
Anytime, orange-pink
Arizona Sunset, yellow blend
Baby Katie, pink blend
Beauty Secret, red
Berkeley Beauty, mauve
Black Jade, red
Blushing Blue, mauve
Cherry Magic, red
Cinderella, white
Coral Sprite, pink
Crazy Dottie, orange
Dixie Dazzle, orange
Dreamglo, red blend
Fancy Pants, red blend
Finesse, yellow
Fresh Pink, pink
Golden Gardens, yellow
Gourmet Popcorn, white
Grace Seward, white
Heartbreaker, pink blend
High Spirits, red
Hurdy Gurdy, red blend
Jean Kenneally, apricot
Jennie Ann, red blend
Jennifer, pink blend
Just For You, pink
KINgig, pink
Kitty Hawk, pink blend
Little Artist, red blend
Little Jackie, orange
Loving Touch, apricot
Magic Carousel, red blend
Mary Marshall, orange
Millie Walters, orange-pink
Mini Magic, red blend
Minnie Pearl, pink blend
My Sunshine, yellow
Olympic Gold, yellow
Orange Rosamini, orange-pink
Orange Sunblaze, orange-pink
Orange Twist, orange
Our Town, pink
Over the Rainbow, red blend
Pacesetter, white
Party Girl, yellow blend
Peaches n' Cream, pink blend
Peggy "T", red
Pierrine, orange-pink
Pink Diddy, pink
Pink Meillandina, pink
Pink Petticoat, pink blend
Popcorn, white
Pucker Up, orange-pink
Rainbow's End, yellow blend
Ramapo, pink
Red Beauty, red
Red Rosamini, red
Renny, pink
Rise n' Shine, yellow
Robin Red Breast, red blend
Rose Hills Red, red
Ruby Pendant, mauve
Shortcake, red blend
Simplex, white
Single's Better, red
Snow Bride, white
Spitfire, red
Starina, orange-pink
Summer Cloud, white
Swiss Bliss, yellow
Tennessee, orange-pink
Tiffany Lynn, pink blend
Toy Clown
Tutti-Frutti, yellow blend
Virginia Lee, yellow blend
Wanaka, orange-pink
White Mini-Wonder, white
Whiteout, white
Why Not, red blend
Winsome, mauve
Wow, orange

Large-Flowered Climbers

Climbing roses have flexible, arching canes to 10 feet long which the gardener must fasten to a trellis, arbor, fence, or other support; the plants do not actually climb on their own. Climbing roses bloom on and off through the summer or continuously all season. Rambler roses are similar, but have smaller flowers in clusters, and longer, more slender canes. They bloom just once, in late spring to early summer.

These climbing roses are rated excellent or outstanding by the ARS.

Altissimo, red
America, orange-pink
Belle Portugaise, pink
City of York, white
Clair Matin, pink
Compassion, orange-pink
Don Juan, red
Dublin Bay, red
Galway Bay, orange-pink
Handel, red blend
Iceland Queen, white
Pink Perpetue, pink
Rhonda, pink
Rosarium Ueteresen, pink
Royal Sunset, apricot

Shrub Roses

Shrub roses, as the name implies, grow like shrubs, with arching canes. Most are about 5 feet tall and as wide, although some varieties reach heights of 10 to 12 feet. Many bloom throughout the summer. They are very hardy and easy to maintain.

The following shrub roses are rated excellent or outstanding by the ARS.

Alba Meidiland, white
Alchymist, apricot blend
All That Jazz, orange-pink
Applejack, pink blend
AUScot, orange-pink
AUSwhite, white
Ballerina, pink
Belinda, pink
Belle Story, pink
Blanc Double de Coubert, white
Buff Beauty, apricot blend
Carefree Beauty, pink
Cerise Bouquet, pink
Champlain, pink
Charles Austin, apricot
Chaucer, pink
Cocktail, red blend
Cymbaline, pink
Distant Drums, mauve
Dornroschen, pink blend
Dortmund, red
Dove, pink
Elmshorn, pink
Elveshorn, pink
Erfurt, pink blend
Fair Bianca, white
Felicia, pink blend
Fisherman's Friend, red
Frau Dagmar Hartopp, pink
Gartendirektor Otto Linne, pink
Hansa, red
Heidelberg, red
Henry Hudson, white
Heritage, pink
Immensee, pink
Jens Munk, pink

John Cabot, red
John Davis, pink
Kathleen, pink
King Crimson, red
Lavender Dream, mauve
Leander, apricot
Lillian Austin, orange-pink
Linda Campbell, red
Marie Bugnet, white
Mary Rose, pink
MELdomonac, pink
Moonlight, yellow
Morgenrot, red blend
Nevada, white
Paulii Rosea, pink blend
Penelope, pink
Pink Meidiland, pink blend
Prairie Flower, red blend
Prairie Princess, orange-pink
Prosperity, white
Prospero, red
Raubritter, pink
Robin Hood, red
Robusta, red
Rosenresli, pink
Roseraie de l'Hay, red
Rugosa Magnifica, mauve
Running Maid, mauve
Sally Holmes, white
Seafoam, white
Serendipity, orange
Sparrieshoop, pink
Stretch Johnson, red blend
Therese Bugnet, pink
The Reeve, pink
The Squire, red
The Wife of Bath, pink blend
Vanity, pink
Wandering Wind, pink
Weisse au Sparrieshoop, white
White Meidiland, white
William Baffin, pink
Will Scarlet, red
Wise Portia, mauve

Old Garden or Heritage Roses

This group generally consists of roses in existence before 1867, when the first hybrid tea was introduced, although later varieties with similar qualities are often included as well. Old garden roses include many traditional favorites, such as the extravagantly fragrant damask and musk roses, albas, bourbons, centifolias, Chinas, gallicas, noisettes, rugosas, and tea roses. The old roses are shrubby, and most have very thorny canes. Flowers may be single or double.

The roses listed below are rated good, excellent, or outstanding by the ARS.

ALBAS

Alba Maxima, white
Alba Semi-plena, white
Belle Amour, pink
Celestial, pink
Felicite, Parmentier, pink
Great Maiden's Blush, white
Königin von Danemark, pink
Mme. Legra de St. Germain, white
White Rose of York, white

BOURBONS

Boule de Neige, white
Coquette des Alpes, white
Gipsy Boy, red
Grüss an Teplitz, red
Honorine de Brabant, pink blend
La Reine Victoria, pink
Louise Odier, pink
Mme. Ernst Calvat, pink

(continued)

Old Garden or Heritage Roses *(cont'd)*

Mme. Isaac Pereire, pink
Mme. Pierre Oger, pink blend
Souvenir de la Malmaison, pink
Variegata di Bologna, red blend
Zephirine Drouhin, pink

CENTIFOLIAS
Burgundian Rose, pink blend
Cabbage Rose, pink
Fantin-Latour, pink
Petite de Hollande, pink
Rose de Meaux, pink
Rose des Peintres, pink
Shailer's Provence, pink

CHINAS
Archduke Charles, red blend
Cramoisi Superieur, red
Green Rose, white
Hermosa, pink
Louis Phillippe, red blend
Mutabilis, yellow blend
Old Blush, pink
Pink Pet, pink
Pompon de Paris, pink
Serratipetala, pink blend
Slater's Crimson China, red

DAMASKS
Autumn Damask, pink
Bella Donna, pink
Celsiana, pink
Ispahan, pink
Kazanlik, pink
La Ville de Bruxelles, pink
Leda, white
Marie Louise, pink
Mme. Hardy, white
Mme. Zoetmans, white
Pink Leda, pink
Rose de Rescht, pink
St. Nicholas, pink
York and Lancaster, pink blend

GALLICAS
Alain Blanchard, mauve
Alika, red
Apothecary's Rose, pink
Belle de Crecy, mauve
Belle Isis, pink
Camaieux, mauve
Cardinal de Richelieu, mauve
Charles de Mills, mauve
Complicata, pink blend
Désirée Parmentier, pink
Duc de Guiche, mauve
La Belle Sultane, red
Narcisse de Salvandy, pink
President de Sèze, mauve
Rosa gallica, pink
Rosa Mundi, pink blend
Superb Tuscan, mauve
Tricolore de Flandre, pink blend
Tuscany, mauve

HYBRID PERPETUALS
Anna de Diesbach, pink
Baron Girod de l'Ain, red blend
Baronne Prevost, pink
Baroness Rothschild, pink
Candeur Lyonnaise, yellow
Captain Hayward, pink
Duchess of Sutherland, pink
Ferdinand Pichard, red blend
Frau Karl Druschki, white
General Jacqueminot, red blend
Henry Nevard, red
La Reine, pink
Mable Morrison, white
Marchesa Boccella, pink

Marchioness of Londonderry, pink
Marchioness of Lorne, pink blend
Mme. Gabriel Luizet, pink
Mrs. John Laing, pink
Mrs. R. G. Sharman-Crawford, pink blend
Oskar Cordel, pink
Paul Neyron, pink
Paul's Early Blush, pink
Reine des Violettes, mauve
Roger Lambelin, red blend
Souvenir d'Alphonse Lavallée, red
Souvenir du Docteur Jamain, red
Ulrich Brunner Fils, pink
Victor Hugo, red
Waldfee, red

MOSSES

Alfred de Dalmas, red
Blanche Moreau, white
Celina, mauve
Communis, pink
Comtesse de Murinais, white
Crested Jewel, pink
Crested Moss, pink
Crimson Globe, red
General Kleber, pink
Henri Martin, red
Jeanne de Montfort, pink
Little Gem, pink
Marie de Blois, pink
Mme. de la Roche-Lambert, mauve
Mme. Louis Lévèque, pink
Old Red Moss, red
Salet, pink
White Bath, white
William Lobb, mauve

NOISETTES

Blush Noisette, white
Celine Forrestier, yellow
Champney's Pink Cluster, pink
Crepuscule, apricot
Lamarque, white
Mme. Alfred Carriere, white
Nastarana, white
Rève d'Or, yellow

TEAS

Bon Silene, pink
Catherine Mermet, pink
Devoniensis, white
Duchesse de Brabant, pink
Lady Hillingdon, yellow blend
Maman Cochet, pink blend
Marie van Houtte, pink blend
Mme. Lombard, orange-pink
Mons. Tillier, orange-pink
Mrs. B. R. Cant, pink
Mrs. Dudley Cross, yellow blend
Safrano, apricot

Species Roses

These are the wild roses that are found in nature. Most are hardy and vigorous growers, and some make good hedges. Most of our wild roses (there are approximately 150 species in the Northern Hemisphere) bloom in shades of pink, but there are also reds, yellows, and whites.

Rosa banksiae var. *lutea*, Lady Banks rose, yellow
R. carolina, pasture rose, pink
R. eglanteria, sweetbriar, pink
R. foetida var. *bicolor*, Austrian copper rose, orange-red with yellow
R. hugonis, Father Hugo's rose, yellow
R. laevigata, Cherokee rose, pink
R. moyesii, red
R. multiflora, white (invasive)

(continued)

Species Roses *(cont'd)*

R. palustris, swamp rose, pink
R. roxburghii var. *plena*, chestnut rose, pink
R. rubrifolia, pink
R. rugosa, saltspray rose, pink
R. rugosa var. *alba*, white
R. spinosissima, Scotch rose, white or light yellow
R. wichuraiana, memorial rose

Fragrant Rose Varieties

Roses have always been loved for their delicious scents. Many modern varieties were bred for form and color, and have little discernible fragrance, but breeders are again considering fragrance as they work to develop new varieties. Many of the old garden roses are exquisitely scented, and the roses listed below are also noted for their scent. Some rose fragrances contain elements of other scents; these qualities are noted wherever possible in the list below.

Alec's Red
Aloha
American Beauty
American Home
Angels Mateu (fruity)
Anna Pavlova
Arthur Bell
Blue Moon
Chrysler Imperial (clove)
City of London
Condesa de Sastago (violet)
Conrad Ferdinand Meyer (nasturtium)
Crimson Glory (clove)
Curly Pink
Daybreak (musk)
Deep Secret
Double Delight
Dusky Maiden
Eden Rose (apple, clove, and lemon)
English Miss
Forgotten Dreams
Fragrant Cloud
Georg Arends (nasturtium)
Golden Dawn (violet)
Golden Masterpiece (orris)
Golden Wings
Hansa (rose and clove)
Heart's Desire (nasturtium)
Iceberg
Kazanlik
Kordes Perfecta (fruity)
La France (lemon)
Lawrence Johnston
Luna (clove)
Madame Alfred Carriere
Madame Jules Bouche (violet)
Madame Louis Lévèque (lily of the valley)
Madame Victor Verdier
McGredy's Sunset (orris and violet)
Margaret Merril
Mirandy (lemon)
Mojave
Moriah
Nymphenberg (apple)
Papa Meilland
Parfum de l'Hay
Paul Neyron
Paul's Himalayan Musk (musk)
Paul's Lemon Pillar
Penelope (musk)
Perfume Delight
Reichspresident von Hindenburg
Rosalyn Carter
Rosemary Harkness
Rouge Meilland
Rubáiyát (lemon)
Sarah Van Fleet (nasturtium)
Sir Frederick Ashton

Sunsprite
Sutter's Gold (fruity)
Symphonie (lemon)
Tiffany
Veilchenblau (orange)
Velvet Fragrance
Whiskey Mac
Zephirine Drouhin

ALL-AMERICA ROSE SELECTIONS

The All-America Rose Society (AARS) is a nonprofit organization of rose producers that was established in 1938 to test new roses and determine which ones are the best and most suitable for home gardens. New roses are evaluated for two years in AARS-accredited test gardens all over the United States and are judged according to a set of rigid standards. Each rose is known only by a number; the breeder and producer of the rose is kept a secret. Roses being tested receive a level of care that a good gardener—but not necessarily an expert or rosarian—could give them. At the end of the two years, the roses are evaluated by AARS judges (each test garden has a judge assigned to it). In evaluating roses, the judges consider novelty, bud form, flower form, bud color, color of open blossoms, aging quality, flowering effect, fragrance, stem/cluster, plant habit, vigor, foliage, disease resistance, repeat bloom, and personal opinion. Scores are compiled and compared, and the winners are chosen by AARS members.

Roses chosen as All-America Rose Selections winners are given a green and white tag to identify them to consumers.

AARS ACCREDITED PUBLIC GARDENS

All these gardens are open to the public.

ALABAMA	
Birmingham:	The Formal Rose Garden at Birmingham Botanical Gardens
Fairhope:	Fairhope City Rose Garden
Mobile:	David A. Hemphill Park of Roses
	Battleship Memorial Park Rose Garden
Theodore:	Bellingrath Gardens Rose Garden
ARIZONA	
Glendale:	Sahauro Historical Ranch Rose Garden
Phoenix:	Valley Garden Center Rose Garden
Tucson:	Gene C. Reid Park Rose Garden
ARKANSAS	
Little Rock:	State Capitol Rose Garden

(continued)

AARS Accredited Public Gardens *(cont'd)*

CALIFORNIA	
Citrus Heights:	Fountain Square Rose Garden
Corona del Mar:	Roger's Gardens
LaCanada:	Descanso Gardens Rose Garden
Los Angeles:	Exposition Park Rose Garden
	Watts Senior Citizen Center Rose Garden
Oakland:	Morcom Amphitheater of Roses
Pasadena:	Tournament of Roses Wrigley Garden
Palos Verdes Peninsula:	James J. White Rose Garden
Riverside:	Fairmont Park Rose Garden
Sacramento:	Capitol Park Rose Garden
	McKinley Park Rose Garden
San Diego:	Inez Parker Memorial Rose Garden
San Francisco:	Golden Gate Park Rose Garden
San Jose:	San Jose Municipal Rose Garden
Santa Barbara:	A. C. Postel Memorial Rose Garden
Westminster:	Westminster Civic Center Rose Garden
Whittier:	Pageant of Roses Garden
COLORADO	
Littleton:	War Memorial Rose Garden
Longmont:	Longmont Memorial Rose Garden at Roosevelt Park
CONNECTICUT	
Norwich:	Norwich Memorial Rose Garden
Stratford:	Boothe Park Wedding Rose Garden
West Hartford:	Elizabeth Park Rose Garden
DISTRICT OF COLUMBIA	
Washington, D.C.:	The George Washington University
FLORIDA	
Lake Buena:	AARS Display Garden at Walt Disney World
Largo:	Sturgeon Memorial Rose Garden
Winter Haven:	Florida Cypress Gardens

GEORGIA	
Athens:	Elizabeth Bradley Turner Memorial Rose Garden
Atlanta:	Atlanta Botanical Rose Garden
Thomasville:	Thomasville Nurseries Rose Test Garden
HAWAII	
Kula, Maui:	University of Hawaii
IDAHO	
Boise:	Julia Davis Rose Garden
ILLINOIS	
Alton:	Nan Elliott Memorial Rose Garden at Gordon F. Moore Community Park
Evanston:	Merrick Park Rose Garden
Glencoe:	Bruce Krasberg Rose Garden at Chicago Botanic
Libertyville:	Lynn J. Arthur Rose Garden at Cook Memorial Park
Peoria:	George L. Luthy Memorial Botanical Garden
Rockford:	Sinnissippi Rose Garden at Rockford Park District
Springfield:	Washington Park Rose Garden
INDIANA	
Ft. Wayne:	Lakeside Rose Garden at Lakeside Park
Richmond:	Richmond Rose Garden at Glen Miller Park
IOWA	
Ames:	Iowa State University Horticultural Gardens
Bettendorf:	Charles Liebestein Memorial Rose Garden
Davenport:	Vander Veer Park Municipal Rose Garden
Des Moines:	Greenwood Park Rose Garden
Dubuque:	Dubuque Arboretum Rose Garden
Muscatine:	Weed Park Memorial Rose Garden
State Center:	State Center Public Rose Garden
KANSAS	
Topeka:	E. F. A. Reinisch Rose Garden

(continued)

AARS Accredited Public Gardens *(cont'd)*

KENTUCKY	
Louisville:	Kentucky Memorial Rose Garden
LOUISIANA	
Baton Rouge:	Burden Research Plantation AARS Rose Garden
Many:	Hodges Gardens
Shreveport:	American Rose Center
MAINE	
Portland:	City of Portland Rose Circle at Deering Oaks Park
MASSACHUSETTS	
Boston:	James P. Kelleher Rose Garden
Westfield:	Stanley Park
MICHIGAN	
East Lansing:	Michigan State University Horticulture Gardens
MINNESOTA	
Chanhassen:	Palma Wilson Rose Garden at Minnesota Landscape Arboretum
Minneapolis:	Lyndale Park Municipal Rose Garden
MISSISSIPPI	
Hattiesburg:	Hattiesburg Area Public Rose Garden at University of S. Mississippi
Jackson:	The Jim Buck Ross Mississippi Agriculture and Forestry Museum Rose Garden
MISSOURI	
Kansas City:	Laura Conyers Smith Municipal Rose Garden at Jacob L. Loose Memorial Park
St. Louis:	Gladney & Lehmann Rose Gardens at Missouri Botanical Gardens
MONTANA	
Missoula:	Missoula Memorial Rose Garden

NEBRASKA	
Boys Town:	Boys' Town Constitution Rose Garden at Father Flanagan's Boys Home
Lincoln:	Lincoln Municipal Rose Garden at Antelope Park
Omaha:	Memorial Park Rose Garden
NEVADA	
Reno:	Reno Municipal Rose Garden
NEW HAMPSHIRE	
North Hampton:	Fuller Gardens Rose Gardens
NEW JERSEY	
East Millstone:	Rudolf W. van der Goot Rose Garden at Colonial Park
Lincroft:	Lambertus C. Bobbink Memorial Rose Garden at Thompson Park
Tenafly:	Jack D. Lissemore Rose Garden at Davis Johnson Park & Gardens
NEW MEXICO	
Albuquerque:	Prospect Park Rose Garden
NEW YORK	
Bronx:	The Peggy Rockefeller Rose Garden at New York Botanical Garden
Brooklyn:	Cranford Rose Garden at Brooklyn Botanic Garden
Buffalo:	Joan Fuzak Memorial Rose Garden at Erie Basin Marina
	Delaware Park Casino
Canandaigua:	Sonnenberg Gardens Rose Garden
New York:	United Nations Rose Garden
Old Westbury:	Old Westbury Gardens
Rochester:	Maplewood Park Rose Garden
Schenectady:	Central Park Rose Garden
Syracuse:	E. M. Mills Memorial Rose Garden at Thornden Park

(continued)

AARS Accredited Public Gardens *(cont'd)*

NORTH CAROLINA

Asheville:	Biltmore Estate
Clemmons:	Tanglewood Park Rose Garden
Fayetteville:	Fayetteville Rose Garden at Fayetteville Technical Community College
Raleigh:	Raleigh Municipal Rose Garden
Winston-Salem:	Reynolds Rose Gardens of Wake Forest University

OHIO

Akron:	Stan Hywet Hall and Gardens
Bay Village:	Cahoon Memorial Rose Garden
Columbus:	Columbus Park of Roses
Mansfield:	Charles E. Nail Memorial Rose Garden
Youngstown:	Fellows Riverside Gardens

OKLAHOMA

Muskogee:	J. E. Conrad Municipal Rose Garden
Oklahoma City:	Charles E. Sparks Rose Garden
Tulsa:	Tulsa Municipal Rose Garden at Woodward Park

OREGON

Coos Bay:	Shore Acres Botanical Garden/State Park
Corvallis:	Corvallis Rose Garden at Avery Park
Eugene:	Owen Memorial Rose Garden
Portland:	International Rose Test Garden

PENNSYLVANIA

Allentown:	Malcolm W. Gross Memorial Rose Garden
Hershey:	Hershey Gardens
Kennett Square:	Longwood Gardens
McKeesport:	Garden Club of McKeesport Arboretum at Renziehausen Park
Philadelphia:	The Morris Arboretum Rose Garden at University of Pennsylvania
West Grove:	Robert Pyle Memorial Rose Garden

SOUTH CAROLINA	
Orangeburg:	Edisto Memorial Gardens
SOUTH DAKOTA	
Rapid City:	Rapid City Memorial Rose Garden
TENNESSEE	
Chattanooga:	Warner Park Rose Garden
Memphis:	Memphis Municipal Rose Garden
TEXAS	
Austin:	Mabel Davis Garden at Zilker Botanical Gardens
Dallas:	Samual-Grand Municipal Rose Garden
El Paso:	El Paso Municipal Rose Garden
Fort Worth:	Fort Worth Botanic Garden Rose Garden
Houston:	Houston Municipal Rose Garden
Tyler:	Tyler Municipal Rose Garden
UTAH	
Fillmore:	Territorial Statehouse State Park Rose Garden
Nephi:	Nephi Federated Women's Club Memorial Rose Garden
Salt Lake City:	Municipal Rose Garden
VIRGINIA	
Alexandria:	All-America Rose Selections Garden
Arlington:	Bon Air Memorial Rose Garden at Bon Air Park
Norfolk:	Norfolk Botanical Gardens Bicentennial Rose Garden
WASHINGTON	
Bellingham:	Fairhaven Rose Garden at Fairhaven Park
Chehalis:	City of Chehalis Municipal Rose Garden
Seattle:	Woodland Park Rose Garden
Spokane:	Manito Park, Rose Hill
Tacoma:	Point Defiance Rose Garden

(continued)

AARS Accredited Public Gardens *(cont'd)*

WEST VIRGINIA

Huntington:	Ritter Park Rose Garden
Moundsville:	The Palace Rose Garden

WISCONSIN

Hales Corners:	Boerner Botanical Gardens
Madison:	Olbrich Botanical Gardens

All-America Rose Selections Winners

1994	Caribbean
	Midas Touch
	Secret
1993	Child's Play
	Rio Samba
	Solitude
	Sweet Inspiration
1992	All That Jazz
	Brigadoon
	Pride 'n' Joy
1991	Carefree Wonder
	Perfect Moment
	Sheer Elegance
	Shining Hour
1990	Pleasure
1989	Class Act
	Debut
	New Beginning
	Tournament of Roses
1988	Amber Queen
	Mikado
	Prima Donna
1987	Bonica
	New Year
	Sheer Bliss
1986	Broadway
	Touch of Class
	Voodoo
1985	Showbiz
1984	Impatient
	Intrigue
	Olympiad
1983	Sun Flare
	Sweet Surrender
1982	Brandy
	French Lace
	Mon Cheri
	Shreveport
1981	Bing Crosby
	Marina
	White Lightnin'
1980	Cherish
	Honor
	Love

1979 Friendship
Paradise
Sundowner

1978 Charisma
Color Magic

1977 Double Delight
First Edition
Prominent

1976 America
Cathedral
Seashell
Yankee Doodle

1975 Arizona
Oregold
Rose Parade

1974 Bahia
Bonbon
Perfume Delight

1973 Electron
Gypsy
Medallion

1972 Apollo
Portrait

1971 Aquarius
Command Performance
Redgold

1970 First Prize

1969 Angel Face
Comanche
Gene Boerner
Pascali

1968 Europeana
Miss All-American Beauty
Scarlet Knight

1967 Bewitched
Gay Princess
Lucky Lady
Roman Holiday

1966 American Heritage
Apricot Nectar
Matterhorn

1965 Camelot
Mister Lincoln

1964 Granada
Saratoga

1963 Royal Highness
Tropicana

1962 Christian Dior
Golden Slippers
John S. Armstrong
King's Ransom

1961 Duet
Pink Parfait

1960 Fire King
Garden Party
Sarabande

1959 Ivory Fashion
Starfire

1958 Fusilier
Gold Cup
White Knight

(continued)

All-American Rose Selections Winners *(cont'd)*

1957	Golden Showers
	White Bouquet
1956	Circus
1955	Jiminy Cricket
	Queen Elizabeth
	Tiffany
1954	Lilibet
	Mojave
1953	Chrysler Imperial
	Ma Perkins
1952	Fred Howard
	Helen Traubel
	Vogue
1951	No Winners
1950	Capistrano
	Fashion
	Mission Bells
	Sutters Gold
1949	Forty-Niner
	Tallyho
1948	Diamond Jubilee
	High Noon
	Nocturne
	Pinkie
	San Fernando
	Taffeta
1947	Rubaiyat
1946	Peace
1945	Floradora
	Horace McFarland
	Mirandy
1944	Fred Edmunds
	Katherine T. Marshall
	Lowell Thomas
	Mme. Chiang Kai-shek
	Mme. Marie Curie
1943	Grand Duchesse Charlotte
	Mary Margaret McBride
1942	Heart's Desire
1941	Apricot Queen
	California
	Charlotte Armstrong
1940	Dickson's Red
	Flash
	The Chief
	World's Fair

THE MOST POPULAR ROSE VARIETIES

The American Rose Society does regular surveys to track which roses are most popular in America. The list below is from the most recent survey, compiled in December 1992. These are the top fifteen varieties, along with the type of rose and the name of the breeder.

1. Touch of Class, hybrid tea (Michel Kriloff)
2. First Prize, hybrid tea (Eugene S. Boerner)
3. Mister Lincoln, hybrid tea (Herbert Swim and O. L. Weeks)
4. Double Delight, hybrid tea (Herbert Swim and Ellis)
5. Pristine, hybrid tea (William A. Warriner)
6. Peace, hybrid tea (Francis Meilland)
7. Queen Elizabeth, grandiflora (Dr. Walter E. Lammerts)
8. Olympiad, hybrid tea (Sam McGredy IV)
9. Fragrant Cloud, hybrid tea (Mathias Tantau)
10. Gold Medal, grandiflora (J. E. (Jack) Christiensen)
11. Jean Kenneally, miniature (Dee Bennett)
12. Paradise, hybrid tea (O. L. Weeks)
13. Garden Party, hybrid tea (Herbert Swim)
14. Color Magic, hybrid tea (William A. Warriner)
15. Tropicana, hybrid tea (Mathias Tantau)

The most popular floribunda rose is French Lace (developed by William A. Warriner), but it did not make the top fifteen for all categories. The list is dominated by hybrid teas.

CARING FOR ROSES

Water roses regularly and deeply in dry weather, whenever the soil feels dry 1 to 2 inches below the surface. If you water from overhead, with a hose or sprinkler, do it early in the day. In any case, be sure the leaves are dry before sundown—wet leaves at night encourage fungus diseases, to which roses are very susceptible.

Deadhead—remove faded flowers—regularly. Cut off the spent blossoms about 1/4 inch above the nearest leaf with five leaflets. On reblooming roses, a dormant bud located just above a 5-part leaf will produce a new flowering shoot.

Top-dress roses with aged manure once a year, and feed with an all-purpose fertilizer in spring after growth begins, and again in midsummer. Occasional foliar feeding with a diluted liquid fertilizer gives plants an additional boost.

Roses are prone to a number of diseases, including mildew, blackspot, and various fungal problems. Remove mildewed leaves as soon as you notice them, and hose down the plants regularly to keep mildew in check. Many gardeners spray regularly with fungicides to prevent disease problems; follow package directions explicitly if you use such products.

Researchers at Cornell University have found that spraying roses once a week with a solution of 1 tablespoon of baking soda and 2 1/2 tablespoons of ultrafine horticultural spray oil to 1 gallon of water controlled both blackspot and powdery mildew.

Roses need winter protection in cold climates. In fall, make a mound of soil 6 to 8 inches high around the base of each bush. When the soil mound freezes, top it with a foot of loose mulch (a cylinder of hardware cloth will hold the mulch in place).

To protect climbers and ramblers, remove the long canes from their supports and carefully lay them on the ground. Cover with a soil mound, and mulch when the soil freezes.

Pruning Roses

Roses also need pruning, but pruning is complicated, and different for different kinds of roses. It is important to use sharp pruning shears that will cut cleanly without crushing the stems. Cut about 1/4 inch above a bud, and make cuts on a 45-degree angle. Look for buds on the outside of the stem and make cuts there; outward-facing buds will produce shoots that grow outward, instead of in toward the center of the bush.

Prune roses while the plants are dormant. The best time is generally in late winter, before new growth begins. Remove any wood that is damaged, diseased, or dead—severe winter weather often causes damage. Winterkill shows up as gray or brown areas on the stems. When pruning, cut back to healthy white pith (the tissue in the center of the cane).

In addition to the general pruning described above, note the following for particular types of roses:

Bush Roses—Hybrid Teas, Grandifloras, and Floribundas: Thin old bushes, removing one or two of the oldest canes to the ground each year. Cut the rest of the canes on hybrid teas and floribundas back to 1 to 1 1/2 feet; cut back grandifloras to 2 feet.

Climbers and Ramblers: Cut back stem tips by 6 inches after the plants bloom. When plants go dormant in fall, remove dead and damaged wood, and one or two of the oldest canes.

A Bit of Rose Miscellany

Attar of roses, the perfume oil distilled from damask roses since the days of ancient Persia, costs almost $10,000 a pound—it's more precious than gold. It takes about 4,000 pounds of rose petals to produce 1 pound of attar.

FLOWERS FOR DIFFERENT PURPOSES

Flowers for Cutting

The following flowers are all good for cutting. The list includes annuals, perennials, bulbs, shrubs, and vines.

Acanthus, bear's breeches
Achillea, yarrow
Agapanthus, lily-of-the-Nile
Ageratum, flossflower
Alcea, hollyhock
Alchemilla, lady's mantle

Allium, flowering onion
Alstroemeria, lily of Peru
Ammi
Anaphalis, pearly everlasting
Anemone
Anthemis, golden marguerite
Antirrhinum, snapdragon
Aquilegia, columbine
Argyranthemum, marguerite daisy
Armeria, sea pink
Asclepias, butterfly weed
Aster, Michaelmas daisy
Astilbe
Begonia
Bellis, English daisy
Bergenia
Brunnera, Siberian bugloss
Buddleia, butterfly bush
Calendula, pot marigold
Callistephus, China aster
Camellia
Campanula, bellflower
Catananche, cupid's dart
Celosia, cockscomb
Centaurea, bachelor's button
Centranthus, red valerian
Chaenomeles, flowering quince
Cheiranthus, wallflower
Chrysanthemum
Clarkia, godetia
Clematis
Cleome, spider flower
Consolida, larkspur
Convallaria, lily of the valley
Coreopsis
Cosmos
Crocus
Cytisus, Scotch broom
Dahlia
Delphinium
Dendrathema, garden chrysanthemum
Deutzia
Dianthus, carnation, garden pink
Dicentra, bleeding heart
Digitalis, foxglove
Doronicum, leopard's bane
Echinacea, purple coneflower
Echinops, globe thistle
Emilia, tasselflower
Endymion, Spanish bluebell
Eremurus, foxtail lily
Erica, heath
Eryngium, sea holly
Eschscholzia, California poppy
Eustoma, lisianthus
Filipendula, meadowsweet
Forsythia
Freesia
Fritillaria, crown imperial, fritillary
Gaillardia, blanketflower
Galanthus, snowdrop
Gazania, treasure flower
Genista, broom
Geranium, cranesbill
Gerbera, Transvaal daisy
Geum, avens
Gladiolus
Gomphrena, globe amaranth
Grasses—many ornamental grasses are useful in arrangements
Gypsophila, baby's breath
Hamamelis, witch hazel
Helenium, sneezeweed
Helianthus, sunflower
Helichrysum, strawflower
Heliopsis
Heliotropium, heliotrope
Helipterum
Helleborus, hellebore
Hemerocallis, daylily
Herbs—many herbs are useful in arrangements

(continued)

Flowers for Cutting *(cont'd)*

Hesperis, dame's rocket
Heuchera, coralbells
Hosta, plantain lily
Hyacinthus, hyacinth
Hydrangea
Hypericum
Iberis, candytuft
Impatiens
Iris
Kniphofia, red-hot poker
Lantana
Lavandula, lavender
Lavatera, mallow
Leucanthemum, shasta daisy
Leucothoe
Liatris, gayfeather
Lilium, lily
Limonium, statice
Linaria, toadflax
Lobelia, cardinal flower
Lobularia, sweet alyssum
Lunaria, money plant
Lupinus, lupine
Lychnis, Maltese cross, rose campion
Lycoris, magic lily
Lysimachia
Lythrum, purple loosestrife
Matthiola, stock
Mertensia, Virginia bluebell
Moluccella, bells of Ireland
Monarda, bee balm
Muscari, grape hyacinth
Myosotis, forget-me-not
Narcissus, daffodil
Nicotiana, flowering tobacco
Nigella, love-in-a-mist
Nipponanthemum, Montauk daisy
Ornithogalum, star-of-Bethlehem
Paeonia, peony
Papaver, poppy
Pelargonium, geranium
Penstemon
Petunia
Philadelphus, mock orange
Phlox
Physalis, Chinese lantern
Physostegia, false dragonhead
Pieris
Platycodon, balloon flower
Polemonium, Jacob's ladder
Polianthes, tuberose
Polygonatum, Solomon's seal
Primula, primrose
Ranunculus, Persian buttercup
Reseda, mignonette
Rhododendron, azalea
Rose, rose
Rudbeckia, black-eyed Susan
Salpiglossis, painted tongue
Salvia, sage
Santolina, lavender cotton
Scabiosa, pincushion flower
Schizanthus, butterfly flower
Scilla, squill
Sedum, stonecrop
Silene, catchfly
Solidago, goldenrod
Spiraea
Stokesia, Stokes' aster
Syringa, lilac
Tagetes, marigold
Tanacetum, feverfew, pyrethrum
Thalictrum, meadow rue
Tithonia, Mexican sunflower
Torenia, wishbone flower
Trachymene, blue lace flower
Trollius, globeflower
Tropaeolum, nasturtium
Tulipa, tulip
Verbena
Veronica, speedwell
Viburnum
Vinca, periwinkle
Viola, pansy, violet, Johnny-jump-up
Zantedeschia, calla lily
Zinnia

HOW TO DRY FLOWERS

Harvest flowers you wish to dry on a warm, sunny day, when the plants are dry. For the best results when dried, most flowers should be cut just as they mature—older flowers will not dry or hold their color as well.

The easiest way to dry flowers is to air-dry them. Strip off the leaves and tie the stems in small bunches with string or rubber bands (rubber bands work well because they contract as the stems dry and continue to hold them tight). Hang the bunches upside down in a dark, dry, airy place, such as a well-ventilated attic. The flowers will take from one or two to several weeks to dry, depending on the thickness of the flower and the temperature and humidity of the drying area.

Flowers with many petals, such as marigolds, or with delicate petals, such as roses, often dry better in a desiccant powder; silica gel works well for this purpose (you can buy it in craft shops). Cut off the stems an inch or so below the flower head (when the flowers are dry you can insert florists' wire to substitute for the stems). In the bottom of an airtight container, spread 1/2 inch of silica gel if the flowers will be dried face down, or 1 1/2 to 2 inches if you will dry the flowers face up.

Flat flowers like daisies dry best facing downward; most other flowers dry better face up. Lay the flowers carefully on top of the silica gel, and do not let the petals of adjoining flowers touch. Lay long spikes or sprays of flowers horizontally. Sprinkle more silica gel between and among the flowers, then cover them completely. Work gently to avoid disturbing the petals, and try to sift the gel in between petals so the flowers dry evenly.

When all the flowers are covered, close the container and label with the contents and date. Put the container in a warm, dry place.

The flowers will dry in a couple of days to a week. Check one flower to see if it has dried; when it has, you can uncover the entire batch. If the crystals of silica gel have turned pink after use, you can dry them out and reuse them. Spread them on a cookie sheet and place it in a warm oven (250°F) until they turn blue again—it may take 30 minutes or longer. When the crystals cool, store them in an airtight container.

Flowers for Drying

The flowers listed here all dry well:

Acacia, mimosa
Acanthus, bear's breeches
Achillea, yarrow
Ageratum, flossflower
Allium, flowering onion
Amaranthus, love-lies-bleeding
Ammobium, winged everlasting
Anaphalis, pearly everlasting
Armeria, sea pink
Artemisia (foliage)
Asclepias, butterfly weed, milkweed
Astilbe
Astrantia, masterwort
Baccharis, groundsel
Baptisia, blue false indigo (seedpods)
Calendula, pot marigold
Calluna, heather
Carthamus, safflower
Catananche, cupid's dart

(continued)

Flowers for Drying *(cont'd)*

Celastrus, bittersweet ("berries")
Celosia, cockscomb
Centaurea, bachelor's button, basket flower, sweet sultan
Clematis (seed heads)
Consolida, larkspur
Convallaria, lily of the valley
Dahlia, small to medium-size varieties
Daucus, Queen Anne's lace
Delphinium
Dictamnus, gas plant (seedpods)
Dipsacus, teasel
Echinops, globe thistle
Epilobium, fireweed
Erica, heath
Eryngium, sea holly
Eucalyptus
Eupatorium, Joe-pye weed, boneset
Ferns (foliage)
Filipendula, meadowsweet
Gomphrena, globe amaranth
Grasses, many ornamental grasses dry well
Gypsophila, baby's breath
Helianthus, sunflower
Helichrysum, strawflower
Helipterum, Swan River everlasting, sun ray
Heuchera, coralbells
Humulus, hops
Hydrangea
Lavandula, lavender
Leontopodium, edelweiss
Liatris, gayfeather
Limonium, sea lavender, statice
Lunaria, money plant (seedpods)
Moluccella, bells of Ireland
Monarda, bee balm
Narcissus, daffodil
Nigella, love-in-a-mist (seedpods)
Papaver, poppy (seedpods)
Physalis, Chinese lantern
Polemonium, Jacob's ladder
Polygonum, silver lace vine
Proboscidea, unicorn plant (seedpods)
Protea
Ranunculus, buttercup
Rosa, rose (buds, partially open flowers, hips)
Rudbeckia, black-eyed Susan, gloriosa daisy
Salvia, sage
Sanvitalia, creeping zinnia
Sedum, stonecrop
Silene, catchfly (seedpods)
Solidago, goldenrod
Spiraea
Stachys, lamb's ears (flower stalk)
Tagetes, marigold
Tanacetum, tansy, feverfew
Thalictrum, meadow rue
Trifolium, rabbit's foot clover
Tulipa, tulip
Verbascum, mullein
Veronica, speedwell
Xeranthemum, immortelle
Zinnia

Fragrant Flowers

This list includes annuals, bulbs, and perennials. For lists of shrubs and woody vines, with fragrant flowers, see the appropriate chapters.

Abronia, sand verbena
Acidanthera
Allium, daffodil garlic
Brugmansia, angel's trumpet
Centranthus, red valerian
Centaurea, sweet sultan
Cheiranthus, wallflower
Convallaria, lily of the valley

Crinum

Crocus chrysanthus

Datura

Dendrathema, garden chrysanthemum (strongly aromatic flowers)

Dianthus, clove pink, carnation

Dictamnus, gas plant

Erysium, Siberian wallflower

Eucharis, Amazon lily

Filipendula, meadowsweet

Freesia

Galanthus, snowdrop

Galium, sweet woodruff

Hedychium, butterfly lily

Heliotropium, heliotrope

Hemerocallis, daylily. Most are not fragrant, but these are:

- *H. lilioasphodelus*, lemon daylily
- *H.* 'Classic Simplicity'
- *H.* 'Hyperion'
- *H.* 'Lexington'
- *H.* 'Mary Todd'

Hesperis, dame's rocket

Hosta, plantain lily. A few have fragrant flowers:

- *H. plantaginea*
- *H.* 'Honeybells'
- *H.* 'Royal Standard'

Hyacinthus, hyacinth

Hymenocallis, Peruvian daffodil

Iberis, rocket candytuft

Ipomoea, moonflower

Iris

- *I. danfordiae*
- *I. reticulata*
- Bearded iris hybrids

Lathyrus, sweet pea

Lavandula, lavender

Leucojum, spring snowflake

Lilium, lily (Many—but not all—species and hybrids are fragrant.)

Linnaea, twin flower

Lobularia, sweet alyssum

Lycoris, magic lily

Matthiola, common stock, evening-scented stock

Mirabilis, four-o'clock

Monarda, bee balm

Muscari, grape hyacinth

Narcissus, daffodil, narcissus (Many—but not all—species and hybrids are fragrant.)

Nicotiana, flowering tobacco

- *N. alata*
- *N. sylvestris*
- White dwarf hybrid form (mildly fragrant at night)

Oenothera, evening primrose

Ornithogalum, star-of-Bethlehem

Paeonia, peony

Pancratium

Petunia

Phlox

Polianthes, tuberose

Polygonum, fragrant Solomon's seal

Primula, primrose

Reseda, mignonette

Rosa, rose (Many—but not all—species and hybrids are fragrant.)

Saponaria, bouncing bet (fragrant at night)

Scabiosa, pincushion flower

Silene, catchfly

Tagetes, marigold (strongly aromatic flowers and leaves)

- *T. tenuifolia*, signet marigold, has most pleasant scent

Tropaeolum, nasturtium

Tulipa, tulip. Most are not fragrant, but these are:

- 'Angelique'
- 'Apricot Beauty'
- 'Bellona'
- 'Bestseller'
- 'Celsiana'

(continued)

Fragrant Flowers *(cont'd)*

'Cheerleader'
'Orange Bouquet'
'Peach Blossom'
'Princess Irene'
'United States'

Valeriana, valerian
Verbena, garden verbena
Viola, sweet violet
Yucca

Flowers That Bloom at Night

In addition to the plants listed here, white flowers belong in moonlight gardens.

Abronia, sand verbena
Epiphyllum, orchid cactus (Houseplant. Some are night-blooming.)
Gaura
  G. coccinea, scarlet gaura
  G. lindheimeri, white gaura
Gladiolus tristis
Hemerocallis, daylily (Some daylilies are nocturnal, opening or remaining open in the evening.)
  H. citrina, citron daylily
  'After the Fall'
  'Alice Gibson'
  'American Bicentennial'
  'Angel's Tears'
  'Apple Tart'
  'Betty'
  'Border Giant'
  'Born Yesterday'
  'Butter Curls'
  'Coastal Empire'
  'Cosmic Treasure'
  'Country Club'
  'Crystal Chandelier'
  'Dee Dee'
  'Erin Prairie'
  'Evening Bell'
  'Fairest Love'
  'Green Dragonfly'
  'Guardian Angel'
  'Ishmael'
  'Java Sea'
  'Jewel of Hearts'
  'Kazuq'
  'Lemon Mint'
  'Little Brandy'
  'Louise Latham'
  'Lullaby Baby'
  'Master Blend'
  'May May'
  'Meadowbrook Green'
  'Moon Frolic'
  'Neon Yellow'
  'Our Love Song'
  'Pardon Me'
  'Purity'
  'Southern Nights'
  'Toltec Sundial'
  'Treasured Bouquet'
  'Witches Dance'
Hesperantha, evening iris
Hesperocallis, desert lily
Hosta plantaginea, fragrant plantain lily
Hylocereus, night-blooming cereus (houseplant)
Ipomoea, moonflower
Matthiola, evening stock
Mentzelia decapetala, evening star
Mirabilis, four-o'clock

Nicotiana, flowering tobacco
- *N. alata*
- *N. sylvestris*
- *N. suaveolens*

Nymphaea, waterlily (Many are night blooming.)
Oenothera, evening primrose
Pardanthopsis, vesper iris
Silene, catchfly
- *S. alba*, white campion
- *S. noctiflora*, night-flowering catchfly
- *S. nutans*, Nottingham catchfly

Yucca (Flowers turn upward at night for pollination.)

Edging Plants

The annuals, bulbs, and perennials listed here grow 18 inches tall or less. Plant them in the front of the garden or as edgings.

Abronia, sand verbena
Aeonium, several species
Aethionema, stone cress
Ageratum, flossflower
Ajuga pyramidalis, bugleweed
Anacyclus, Mt. Attas daisy
Androsace, rock jasmine
Anemone,
- *A. blanda*, Grecian windflower
- *A. coronaria*, poppy anemone
- *A. pulsatilla*, pasqueflower

Antirrhinum, snapdragon, dwarf varieties
Arabis, rock cress
Arctotheca, capeweed
Armeria, sea pink
Artemisia 'Silver Mount'
Astilbe chinensis 'Pumila'
Aubrieta, false rock cress
Aurinia, basket-of-gold
Baileya, desert marigold
Begonia, tuberous begonia, wax begonia
Bellis, English daisy
Bletilla, Chinese ground orchid
Brachycome, Swan River daisy
Brunnera, Siberian bugloss
Callistephus, China aster, dwarf varieties
Campanula, bellflower
- *C. carpatica*, Carpathian bellflower
- *C. portenschlagiana*
- *C. poscharskyana*
- *C. rotundifolia*, bluebells

Cardamine, lady's smock
Catharanthus, Madagascar periwinkle
Celosia, plumed varieties
Cerastium, snow-in-summer
Ceratostigma, plumbago
Chionodoxa, glory-of-the-snow
Chrysogonum, goldenstar, green-and-gold
Colchicum, autumn crocus
Convallaria, lily of the valley
Convolvulus, dwarf morning glory
Corydalis lutea
Cotula, brass buttons
Crepis, hawk's beard
Crocus
Cuphea, cigar plant
Cyclamen
Dahlia, dwarf varieties
Dendrathema, cushion chrysanthemum
Dianthus, garden pinks
Dicentra
- *D. cucullaria*, Dutchman's breeches
- *D. eximia*, fringed bleeding heart

Dyssodia, Dahlberg daisy
Epimedium, barrenwort
Eranthis, winter aconite
Erigeron, fleabane

(continued)

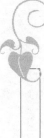

Edging Plants *(cont'd)*

Erythronium, trout lily
Eschscholzia, California poppy
Evolvulus
Exacum, Persian violet
Felicia, blue marguerite, kingfisher daisy
Galanthus, snowdrop
Galium, sweet woodruff
Gazania, treasure flower
Gentiana, gentian, numerous species
Geranium, cranesbill, numerous species
Geum, avens
Gomphrena, globe amaranth
Gypsophila, annual baby's breath, creeping baby's breath
Helianthemum, rock rose
Helleborus, Christmas rose
Hosta, plantain lily, dwarf varieties
Hyacinthus, hyacinth
Hypoestes, polka-dot plant
Iberis, candytuft
Impatiens, bedding impatiens, busy Lizzie
Iris, numerous species, also: bearded iris, miniature dwarf and standard dwarf varieties
Lamium, spotted dead nettle
Leontopodium, edelweiss
Leucojum, snowflake
Lewisia
Limnanthes, meadow foam
Liriope, creeping lilyturf
Lobelia, edging lobelia
Lobularia, sweet alyssum
Malcolmia, Virginia stock
Malephora, ice plant
Mesembryanthemum, ice plant
Mimulus, monkey flower
Myosotis, forget-me-not
Narcissus, *Cyclamineus*, *Jonquilla*, and *Triandrus* varieties
Nemophila, baby blue-eyes
Nierembergia, cupflower
Nolana
Omphalodes, navelwort
Osteospermum, freeway daisy
Oxalis
Pelargonium, ivy-leaved geranium
Petunia
Phacelia, California bluebell
Phlox
  P. divaricata, wild sweet william
  P. drummondii, annual phlox
  P. stolonifera, creeping phlox
Platystemon, creamcups
Polygonum, Himalayan fleeceflower
Portulaca, moss rose
Primula, primrose, numerous species
Prunella, self-heal
Pulmonaria, lungwort
Ranunculus, Persian buttercup
Reseda, mignonette
Ruellia, monkey plant
Salvia, scarlet sage, dwarf varieties
Sanguinaria, bloodroot
Sanvitalia, creeping zinnia
Saponaria, rock soapwort
Scilla, squill
Sedum 'Ruby Glow'
Sempervivum, hen-and-chickens
Senecio, dusty miller
Setcreasea, purple heart
Shortia, oconee bells
Silene, wild pink
Stachys, lamb's ears
Tagetes, French marigold, signet marigold
Tiarella, foamflower
Tolpis, yellow hawkweed
Torenia, wishbone flower
Tropaeolum, nasturtium (when allowed to sprawl)
Tulipa, tulip, numerous species and varieties
Verbena, garden verbena
Viola, Johnny-jump-up, pansy, violet
Zinnia, dwarf varieties

Background Plants

These plants are all at least 4 feet tall when in bloom, and are best used in the back of most gardens.

Acanthus mollis, bear's breeches
Aconitum carmichaelii, azure monkshood
Agave americana, century plant
Alcea, hollyhock
Alpinia, ginger lily
Anigozanthos flavidus, kangaroo paw
Artemisia lactiflora, white mugwort
Aruncus, goatsbeard
Boltonia
Campanula pyramidalis, chimney bellflower
Cimicifuga racemosa, black snakeroot
Cleome, spider flower
Cosmos, garden cosmos
Crambe cordifolia, colewort
Dahlia, tall varieties
Delphinium, Pacific hybrids, Blackmore and Longdon hybrids
Echium, pride of Madeira
Eremurus, foxtail lily
Eryngium yuccifolium, rattlesnake master
Eupatorium purpureum, Joe-pye weed
Euphorbia characias var. *wulfenii*
Filipendula rubra, queen-of-the-prairie
Gunnera
Hedychium, ginger lily
Helenium autumnale, common sneezeweed
Helianthus, sunflower
Heliopsis, false sunflower
Hibiscus moscheutos, rose mallow
Iresine, bloodleaf
Lavatera, tree mallow
Ligularia 'The Rocket'
Lilium, lily, numerous species and varieties
Macleaya, plume poppy
Martynia, unicorn plant
Nicotiana sylvestris
Phormium, New Zealand flax
Ricinus, caster bean
Romneya, Matilija poppy
Rudbeckia laciniata, cutleaf coneflower
Sanguisorba canadensis, Canadian burnet
Thalictrum rochebrunianum, lavender mist meadow rue
Tithonia, Mexican sunflower
Veratrum viride, false hellebore
Veronica, ironweed
Veronicastrum, bowman's root
Yucca (flower stalks)

Edible Flowers

These flowers are edible. You can toss them into salads, use them to flavor butters, slip them into sandwiches, and float them on soups or glasses of punch or iced tea. Some can be candied and used to decorate cakes, puddings, and other desserts. If you purchase flowers instead of growing your own, make sure they were grown organically and not treated with chemical preservatives or toxic pesticides.

Agastache, anise hyssop
Alcea, hollyhock
Allium, chives, garlic chives
Anethum, dill
Begonia, tuberous begonia
Bellis, English daisy
Borago, borage
Brassica, mustard
Calendula, pot marigold

(continued)

Edible Flowers *(cont'd)*

Citrus, lemon, orange
Coriandrum, coriander
Cucurbita, squash
Dendrathema, garden chrysanthemum
Dianthus, carnation, garden pinks
Foeniculum, fennel
Gladiolus
Hemerocallis, daylily (buds)
Hyssopus, hyssop
Lavandula, lavender
Lonicera, honeysuckle
Matricaria, German chamomile
Monarda, bee balm
Ocimum, basil
Origanum, oregano, marjoram
Pelargonium, scented-leaved geraniums
Phaseolus, beans
Pisum, peas
Rosa, roses
Salvia, sage, pineapple sage
Sambucus, elderberry
Syringa, lilac
Tagetes, marigold, especially signet marigold (*T. tenuifolia*)
Thymus, thyme
Tropaeolum, nasturtium (leaves are also edible)
Tulipa, tulip
Viola, Johnny-jump-up, pansy, violet

Poisonous Plants

Edible flowers are delightful, but not all flowers are edible. The plants listed here are poisonous, and should never be consumed or used as garnishes.

Aconitum, monkshood
Aesculus, buckeye
Amaryllis, naked ladies
Anemone
Caladium
Clematis
Colchicum
Consolida, larkspur
Convallaria, lily of the valley
Datura, jimsonweed and all other species
Delphinium
Gelsemium, jessamine
Gloriosa, gloriosa lily
Hippeastrum, amaryllis
Hydrangea
Iris
Lantana
Lathyrus, sweet pea
Lobelia, cardinal flower
Lupinus, lupine
Narcissus, daffodil, narcissus
Nerium, oleander
Ornithogalum, star-of-Bethlehem
Ranunculus, buttercup
Rhododendron, azalea, rhododendron
Strelitzia, bird of paradise
Tanacetum, tansy, feverfew
Wisteria

Flowers by Color

If you are looking for flowers of a particular color for your garden, these lists may prove helpful. They include many common annuals, bulbs, and perennials that are readily available from mail-order suppliers and local garden centers.

RED FLOWERS

Abutilon, flowering maple
Actaea, red baneberry (berries)
Alcea, hollyhock
Alstroemeria
Amaranthus, love-lies-bleeding

Anemone, poppy anemone
Anigozanthos, kangaroo paw
Antirrhinum, snapdragon
Aquilegia, columbine
Asclepias, bloodflower
Astilbe
Begonia, tuberous begonia, wax begonia
Belamcanda, blackberry lily
Bellis, English daisy
Canna
Celosia, woolflower
Centaurea, sweet sultan
Cosmos
Crocosmia
Cuphea, cigar flower
Dahlia
Dendrathema, garden chrysanthemum
Dianthus, carnation, garden pink, sweet William
Dicentra, fringed bleeding heart
Emilia, tasselflower
Epimedium
Fritillaria, fritillary
Fuchsia
Gaillardia, blanketflower
Gerbera, Transvaal daisy
Geum, avens
Gladiolus
Helianthemum, rock rose
Helianthus, sunflower
Helichrysum, strawflower
Hemerocallis, daylily
Heuchera, coralbells
Hibiscus, rose mallow
Hyacinthus, hyacinth
Impatiens
Iris
Lantana
Lathyrus, sweet pea
Lilium, lily
Limonium, statice
Lupinus, lupine
Lychnis, Maltese cross
Mimulus, monkey flower
Monarda, bee balm
Nicotiana, flowering tobacco
Oxalis
Paeonia, peony
Papaver, poppy
Pelargonium, geranium
Penstemon
Petunia
Phlox, annual phlox
Portulaca, moss rose
Potentilla
Primula, polyanthus primrose
Ranunculus, Persian buttercup
Salpiglossis, painted tongue
Salvia, scarlet sage
Sedum, stonecrop
Sparaxis, harlequin flower
Tanacetum, pyrethrum
Tigridia, tiger flower
Tropaeolum, nasturtium
Tulipa, tulip
Verbena, garden verbena
Viola, pansy
Watsonia
Zinnia

PINK FLOWERS

Abronia, sand verbena
Achillea, yarrow
Alcea, hollyhock
Allium, flowering onion
Anemone, Grecian windflower, Japanese anemone
Antennaria, pussytoes
Antirrhinum, snapdragon
Aquilegia, columbine
Arctotis, African daisy

(continued)

Flowers by Color *(cont'd)*

Armeria, sea pink
Aster
Astilbe
Aubrieta, false rock cress
Begonia, wax begonia
Bellis, English Daisy
Bergenia
Calandrinia, rock purslane
Callirhoe
Callistephus, China aster
Catharanthus, Madagascar periwinkle
Celosia, woolflower
Centaurea, bachelor's button
Centranthus, red valerian
Chelone, turtlehead
Clarkia
Cleome, spider flower
Colchicum
Cosmos
Crepis
Crocus
Cyclamen
Dahlia
Dendrathema, garden chrysanthemum
Dianthus, carnation, garden pinks, sweet william
Dicentra, bleeding heart
Dictamnus, gas plant
Digitalis, foxglove
Echinacea, purple coneflower
Epimedium
Erigeron, fleabane
Erythronium
Filipendula, meadowsweet, queen-of-the-prairie
Fritillaria
Fuchsia
Galega, goat's rue
Geranium, cranesbill
Gladiolus
Gomphrena, globe amaranth
Gypsophila, baby's breath
Helleborus, hellebore
Helianthemum, rock rose
Hemerocallis, daylily
Hesperis, dame's rocket
Heuchera, coralbells
Hibiscus, rose mallow
Hyacinthus
Iberis
Impatiens
Incarvillea, hardy gloxinia
Ipomoea, morning glory
Lantana
Lathyrus, sweet pea
Lavatera, mallow
Liatris, gayfeather
Lilium, lily
Limonium, statice
Linaria, toadflax
Linum, flowering flax
Lobularia, sweet alyssum
Lunaria, money plant
Lupinus, lupine
Lychnis, German catchfly, rose campion
Lycoris, magic lily
Lythrum, purple loosestrife
Malcolmia, Virginia stock
Malope
Malva, hollyhock mallow
Matthiola, stock
Mesembryanthemum, ice plant
Mimulus, monkey flower
Mirabilis, four-o'clock
Monarda, bee balm
Nemesia
Nerine
Nicotiana, flowering tobacco
Oenothera, evening primrose
Oxalis
Paeonia, peony
Papaver, Iceland poppy
Pelargonium, geranium

Petunia
Phlox
Physostegia, false dragonhead
Polygonum, knotweed
Portulaca, moss rose
Primula, primrose
Prunella, self-heal
Saponaria, bouncing bet, rock soapwort
Saxifraga, London pride
Scabiosa, pincushion flower
Schizanthus, butterfly flower
Sedum
Shortia, oconee bells
Sidalcea, checkerbloom
Silene, moss campion
Stachys, betony
Teucrium, germander
Thalictrum, meadow rue
Tradescantia, spiderwort
Tulipa, tulip
Valeriana, valerian
Verbena
Veronica, speedwell
Viola, pansy, violet
Xeranthemum, immortelle
Zephyranthes
Zinnia

ORANGE FLOWERS

Asclepias, butterfly weed
Begonia, tuberous begonia
Calendula, pot marigold
Celosia, woolflower
Clivia, Kaffir lily
Cosmos
Crocosmia
Dahlia
Dendrathema, garden chrysanthemum
Epimedium
Eremurus, foxtail lily
Eschscholzia, California poppy
Euphorbia, spurge
Fritillaria, fritillary
Gerbera, Transvaal daisy
Geum, avens
Gladiolus
Haemanthus, blood lily
Helianthemum, rock rose
Helichrysum, strawflower
Hemerocallis, daylily
Kniphofia, red-hot poker
Lilium, lily
Mimulus, monkey flower
Osteospermum
Papaver, poppy
Physalis, Chinese lantern
Portulaca, moss rose
Primula, polyanthus primrose
Ranunculus, Persian buttercup
Tagetes, marigold
Tithonia, Mexican sunflower
Tropaeolum, nasturtium
Tulipa, tulip
Veltheimia
Viola, horned violet, pansy
Zinnia

YELLOW AND YELLOW-GREEN FLOWERS

Abelmoschus, okra
Achillea, yarrow
Adonis
Alchemilla, lady's mantle
Allium, flowering onion
Anthemis, golden marguerite
Antirrhinum, snapdragon
Arcotheca, African daisy
Argemone, Mexican poppy
Argyranthemum, marguerite daisy
Aurinia, basket-of-gold
Baileya, desert marigold
Calceolaria, pocketbook plant

(continued)

Flowers by Color *(cont'd)*

Caltha, marsh marigold
Cassia, partridge pea
Celosia, woolflower
Centaurea
Cheiranthus, wallflower
Chrysogonum, goldenstar, green-and-gold
Coreopsis
Corydalis
Crocus
Dahlia
Dendrathema, garden chrysanthemum
Dianthus
Disporum
Doronicum, leopard's bane
Dyssodia, Dahlberg daisy
Eranthis, winter aconite
Erythronium
Euphorbia, spurge
Freesia
Fritillaria, fritillary
Gaillardia, blanketflower
Gazania, treasure flower
Helenium, false sunflower
Helianthus, sunflower
Heliopsis
Helleborus, hellebore
Hemerocallis, daylily
Hibiscus
Hunnemannia, Mexican tulip poppy
Hyacinthus, hyacinth
Inula
Iris
Ixia
Lachenalia, Cape cowslip
Ligularia
Lilium, lily
Limnanthes, meadowfoam
Limonium, statice
Linum, golden flax
Lysimachia, yellow loosestrife
Mentzelia, blazing star
Mimulus, monkey flower
Narcissus, daffodil
Nemesia
Oenothera, evening primrose, sundrop
Opuntia, prickly pear
Oxalis
Paeonia, peony
Phlomis, Jerusalem sage
Platystemon, creamcups
Portulaca, moss rose
Potentilla, cinquefoil
Primula, primrose
Ranunculus, buttercup
Reseda, mignonette
Rodgersia
Rudbeckia, black-eyed Susan
Ruta, rue
Salpiglossis, painted tongue
Sanvitalia, creeping zinnia
Sedum, stonecrop
Sisyrinchium, blue-eyed grass
Solidago, goldenrod
Sternbergia, winter daffodil
Stylophorum, celandine poppy
Tagetes, marigold
Tanacetum, feverfew
Thalictrum, meadow rue
Thermopsis, Carolina lupine
Tigridia, tiger flower
Trollius, globeflower
Tropaeolum, nasturtium
Tulipa, tulip
Uvularia, merrybells
Viola, horned poppy pansy
Zinnia

BLUE, VIOLET AND PURPLE FLOWERS

Aconitum, monkshood
Adenophora, ladybells
Agapanthus, lily-of-the-Nile

Ageratum, flossflower
Allium, flowering onion
Amsonia, blue star
Anagallis
Anchusa, Italian bugloss
Anemone, pasqueflower
Aquilegia, columbine
Aster
Baptisia, false indigo
Borago, borage
Brachycome, Swan River daisy
Browallia
Brunnera, Siberian bugloss
Callistephus, China aster
Camassia, camass
Campanula, bellflower
Catananche, cupid's dart
Centaurea, bachelor's button
Ceratostigma, plumbago
Chionodoxa, glory-of-the-snow
Cleome, spider flower
Consolida, larkspur
Convolvulus, dwarf morning glory
Crocus
Cynoglossum, Chinese forget-me-not
Delphinium
Dendrathema, garden chrysanthemum
Echinops, globe thistle
Echium, viper's bugloss
Endymion, Spanish bluebell
Eryngium, sea holly
Eupatorium, mistflower
Eustoma, lisianthus
Exacum, Persian violet
Felicia, blue marguerite, kingfisher daisy
Freesia
Gentiana, gentian
Geranium, cranesbill
Gladiolus
Heliotropium, heliotrope
Hosta, plantain lily
Hyacinthus, hyacinth
Impatiens, balsam
Ipheion, spring starflower
Ipomoea, morning glory
Iris
Lathyrus, sweet pea
Lavandula, lavender
Lavatera
Limonium, statice
Linum, perennial flax
Lobelia
Lupinus, bluebonnet, lupine
Mertensia, Virginia bluebell
Muscari, grape hyacinth
Myosotis, forget-me-not
Nemophila, baby blue-eyes
Nepeta, catmint
Nierembergia, cupflower
Nigella, love-in-a-mist
Omphalodes, navelwort
Penstemon
Perovskia, Russian sage
Phacelia, California bluebell
Phlox, creeping phlox, mountain pink, wild, sweet William
Physostegia, false dragonhead
Platycodon, balloon flower
Polemonium, Jacob's ladder
Primula, primrose
Pulmonaria, lungwort
Salpiglossis, painted tongue
Salvia
Torenia, wishbone flower
Trachelium, throatwort
Trachymene, blue lace flower
Tradescantia, spiderwort
Tricyrtis, toad lily
Tulipa, tulip
Verbena, garden verbena
Veronica, speedwell
Viola, pansy, violet

(continued)

Flowers by Color *(cont'd)*

WHITE FLOWERS

Acanthus, bear's breech
Achillea, yarrow
Acidanthera
Actaea
Ageratum, flossflower
Allium, flowering onion
Ammobium, winged everlasting
Anaphalis, pearly everlasting
Anemone
Antherium, St. Bernard's lily
Antirrhinum, snapdragon
Arabis, rock cress
Arenaria, Irish moss
Argemone, prickly poppy
Armeria, thrift
Aruncus, goatsbeard
Astilbe
Begonia, tuberous begonia, wax begonia
Boltonia
Campanula, bellflower
Catharanthus, Madagascar periwinkle
Celosia, woolflower
Cerastium, snow-in-summer
Cimicifuga, snakeroot, bugbane
Cleome, spiderflower
Consolida, larkspur
Convallaria, lily of the valley
Cosmos
Crambe
Crinum, swamp lily, atamasco lily
Crocus
Datura
Delphinium
Dendrathema, garden chrysanthemum
Dianthus, carnation, garden pinks
Dicentra, Dutchman's breeches
Dictamnus, gas plant
Dietes, African iris
Dimorphotheca, Cape marigold
Disporum, fairy bells
Dodecatheon, shooting star
Endymion, wood hyacinth
Epimedium
Erythronium, fawn lily
Eucharis, Amazon lily
Euphorbia, flowering spurge, poinsettia
Filipendula, meadowsweet
Freesia
Fritillaria, fritillary
Galanthus, snowdrop
Galax, wandflower
Galium, sweet woodruff
Galtonia, summer hyacinth
Gaura
Gladiolus
Gypsophila, baby's breath
Helleborus, hellebore
Hesperocallis, desert lily
Hibiscus
Hyacinthus, hyacinth
Hymenocallis, Peruvian daffodil
Iberis, candytuft
Impatiens
Ipomoea, moonflower
Iris
Ixia
Lamium, spotted dead nettle
Lathyrus, sweet pea
Leontopodium, edelweiss
Leucanthemum, shasta daisy
Leucojum, snowflake
Liatris, gayfeather
Lilium, lily
Limonium, sea lavender, statice
Lobularia, sweet alyssum
Lysimachia, gooseneck loosestrife
Macleaya, plume poppy
Malva, musk mallow

Mesembryanthemum, ice plant
Narcissus, daffodil, narcissus
Nicotiana, flowering tobacco
Nipponanthemum, Montauk daisy
Omphalodes, navelwort
Ornithogalum, star-of-Bethlehem
Osteospermum, ice plant
Paeonia, peony
Papaver, poppy
Physostegia, false dragonhead
Polianthes, tuberose
Polygonatum, Solomon's seal
Potentilla
Primula, primrose
Reseda, mignonette
Rodgersia
Romneya, Matilija poppy
Salvia
Sanguisorba, Canadian burnet
Saxifraga, strawberry geranium
Smilacina, false Solomon's seal
Tanacetum, feverfew
Tiarella, foamflower
Trillium
Tulipa, tulip
Viola, horned violet, pansy, violet
Watsonia
Zantedeschia, calla lily
Zephranthes
Zinnia

SEASONAL BLOOMING SCHEDULES

These blooming schedules list common plants that bloom in each season. Blooming times vary with location, microclimate in the garden, and yearly weather conditions. These schedules are geared loosely to gardens near 40 degrees North latitude; however, you may find that plants in your garden bloom a bit earlier or later, even if you live in this region. Gardeners farther north will find that their flowers will bloom later, and gardeners farther south will have earlier bloom. The schedules include annuals, bulbs, perennials, and roses.

EARLY SPRING

Adonis, amur adonis
Anemone, pasqueflower
Arabis, rock cress
Aubrieta, false rock cress
Aurinia, basket-of-gold
Calochortus, white globe lily
Chionodoxa, glory-of-the-snow
Claytonia, spring beauty
Clivia, Kaffir lily
Crocus, species and hybrid crocuses
Erythronium, fawn lily
Fritillaria, checker lily, guinea hen flower, fritillary
Helleborus, Lenten rose
Hepatica
Ipheion, spring starflower
Iris, *I. danfordiae*, netted iris, Algerian iris
Lachenalia, Cape cowslip
Leucojum, spring snowflake
Mertensia, Virginia bluebells
Muscari, grape hyacinth
Myosotis, forget-me-not
Narcissus, daffodils and narcissus
Ornithogalum, star-of-Bethlehem
Primula, polyanthus primrose
Pulmonaria, blue lungwort
Puschkinia, striped squill
Ranunculus, Persian buttercup
Scilla, Siberian squill, twinleaf squill

(continued)

Seasonal Blooming Schedules *(cont'd)*

Early Spring *(cont'd)*

Trillium, purple trillium
Tulipa, lady tulip, Fosterana hybrids, Single Early hybrid tulips, waterlily tulips
Tussilago, coltsfoot
Veltheimia, unicorn root
Vinca, periwinkle
Viola, pansy
Zephyranthes, atamasco lily

MID-SPRING

Actaea, red baneberry
Alchemilla, lady's mantle
Allium, daffodil garlic
Anemone, poppy anemone
Aquilegia, columbine
Arcotheca, capeweed
Armeria, sea pink
Bergenia
Brunnera, Siberian bugloss
Caltha, marsh marigold
Centaurea, mountain bluet (may bloom again in fall)
Convallaria, lily of the valley
Dicentra, Dutchman's breeches, common bleeding heart, fringed bleeding heart
Disporum, fairy bells
Doronicum, leopard's bane
Draba
Endymion, Spanish bluebell, wood hyacinth
Epimedium
Erythronium, dogtooth violet
Euphorbia, cushion spurge, cypress spurge, myrtle euphorbia
Fritillaria, crown imperial
Galium, sweet woodruff
Geranium, cranesbill
Geum, avens
Hedyotis, bluets, Quaker ladies
Hesperocallis, desert lily
× *Heucherella*
Hyacinthus, hyacinth
Iberis, perennial candytuft
Iris, crested iris, fringed iris, dwarf bearded iris
Lathyrus, perennial pea, sweet pea
Lilium, Easter lily (in warm climates)
Lloydia
Lobularia, sweet alyssum
Narcissus, hybrid daffodils and narcissus, late varieties
Omphalodes, navelwort
Paeonia, Japanese tree peony, fernleaf peony
Phlox, creeping phlox, ground pink, wild sweet William
Polemonium, Jacob's ladder
Polygonatum, Solomon's seal
Primula, auricula primrose, cowslip, Himalayan primrose, juliana hybrid primrose
Pulmonaria, lungwort, Bethlehem sage
Rosa, Cherokee rose
Saxifraga, London pride, strawberry geranium
Shortia, oconee bells
Smilacina, false Solomon's seal
Trillium, snow trillium
Trollius, globeflower
Tulipa, Darwin hybrid tulips, Double Late hybrid tulips, Greigii hybrid tulips, lily-flowered tulips, Triumph hybrid tulips
Viola, horned violet, pansy

LATE SPRING

Amsonia, blue star
Anemone, garden anemone, snowdrop windflower
Aquilegia, columbine, hybrid columbines, American columbine, Rocky Mountain columbine
Arenaria, Irish moss
Astrantia, masterwort
Baptisia, false indigo

Campanula, Carpathian harebell, Dalmatian bellflower
Centaurea, bachelor's button, sweet sultan
Cerastium, snow-in-summer
Chrysogonum, goldenstar, green-and-gold
Dianthus, allwood pink, cheddar pink, grass pink, maiden pink, sweet William
Dodecatheon, shooting star
Geranium, *G. endressii*, bigroot cranesbill, blood-red cranesbill, Johnson's blue cranesbill
Hemerocallis, lemon daylily
Heuchera, coralbells
Incarvillea, hardy gloxinia
Iris, bearded iris hybrids, Louisiana iris hybrids, Pacific Coast irises, roof iris, yellow flag
Lathyrus, sweet pea
Leucojum, giant snowflake
Lilium, Turk's cap lilies
Linaria, toadflax
Lychnis, German catchfly
Lysimachia, yellow loosestrife
Myosotis, annual forget-me-not
Nemesia
Nigella, love-in-a-mist
Paeonia, Chinese peony, common peony
Papaver, Iceland poppy, oriental poppy
Physalis, Chinese lantern
Potentilla, staghorn cinquefoil
Primula, Japanese primrose
Ranunculus, creeping buttercup
Saponaria, rock soapwort
Stylophorum, celandine poppy
Thalictrum, meadow rue
Thermopsis, Carolina false lupine
Tradescantia, spiderwort
Tulipa, Fringed tulips, Parrot tulips, Single Late hybrid tulips, Viridiflora hybrid tulips
Uvularia, big merrybells
Valeriana, valerian
Veronica, Crater Lake blue speedwell
Viola, sweet violet, Johnny-jump-up
Zantedeschia, calla lily

EARLY SUMMER

Achillea, yarrow (some bloom all summer)
Ageratum, flossflower (all summer)
Allium, giant garlic
Amorpha, false indigo
Anthemis, golden marguerite
Anthericum, St. Bernard's lily
Antirrhinum, snapdragon
Armeria, sea pink
Aruncus, goatsbeard
Astilbe
Baptisia, blue false indigo
Calendula, pot marigold
Campanula, clustered bellflower, peach-leaved bellflower
Centaurea, globe centaurea, mountain bluet
Cleome, spider flower
Consolida, rocket larkspur
Coreopsis, dwarf-eared coreopsis, lance-leaved coreopsis
Dictamnus, gas plant
Digitalis, foxglove (reblooms in late summer if cut back)
Eremurus, foxtail lily
Erigeron, fleabane
Filipendula meadowsweet, queen-of-the-prairie, queen-of-the-meadow
Gaillardia, blanketflower (all summer)
Galega, goat's rue (all summer)
Geranium, Armenian cranesbill, Iberian cranesbill, *G. cinereum*
Gypsophila, creeping baby's breath
Hemerocallis, hybrid daylilies (early to late summer, depending on variety)
Hesperis, dame's rocket
Iberis, globe candytuft
Inula, swordleaf inula
Iris, Japanese iris, Siberian iris
Kniphofia, red-hot poker
Lavandula, lavender

(continued)

Seasonal Blooming Schedules *(cont'd)*

Early Summer *(cont'd)*

Leucanthemum, shasta daisy
Lilium, coral lily, Japanese Turk's cap lily, meadow lily, Madonna lily, Mid-Century hybrid lilies, regal lily
Linum, blue flax (all summer), golden flax
Lobelia, edging lobelia (early summer to fall, bloom slows in hot weather)
Lupinus, lupine
Lychnis, Maltese cross, rose campion
Lysimachia, gooseneck loosestrife
Malva, hollyhock mallow
Oenothera, evening primrose, sundrops
Opuntia, prickly pear
Petunia (early summer to fall)
Potentilla, shrubby cinquefoil, Nepal cinquefoil (both early to late summer)
Rosa, floribunda roses (all summer), grandiflora roses (all summer), hybrid tea roses (early to midsummer, some repeat bloom), miniature roses (all summer), climbing roses (off and on all summer), rambler roses (may bloom again in early fall), shrub roses (some bloom once in early summer, others bloom all summer)
Scabiosa, pincushion flower (early summer to early fall)
Sidalcea, prairie mallow
Tagetes, marigold (early summer into fall)
Tanacetum, pyrethrum
Tropaeolum, nasturtium (all summer)
Verbascum, mullein
Verbena, garden verbena (early to late summer), vervain
Veronica, germander speedwell, spike speedwell (early to late summer), woolly speedwell
Zinnia (all summer)

MIDSUMMER

Acanthus, bear's breeches
Achillea, woolly yarrow
Adenophora, lady bells
Agapanthus, lily-of-the-Nile
Alcea, hollyhock
Allium, various flowering onions
Anaphalis, pearly everlasting
Asclepias, butterfly weed
Belamcanda, blackberry lily
Callistephus, China aster
Campanula, Canterbury bells, milky bellflower
Celosia, woolflower
Centaurea, basket flower, Persian centaurea
Chelone, turtlehead
Cimicifuga, black snakeroot
Coreopsis, threadleaf coreopsis, 'Moonbeam' coreopsis
Dahlia (midsummer to early fall, depending on variety)
Delphinium, hybrid delphinium
Dianthus, carnation
Echinacea, purple coneflower
Echinops, globe thistle
Erigeron, fleabane (much of the year in warm West Coast climates)
Eryngium, sea holly
Euphorbia, flowering spurge
Fuchsia, hybrid fuchsia
Gentiana, willow gentian
Gladiolus (midsummer to frost, depending on planting date and variety)
Gypsophila, annual baby's breath, perennial baby's breath
Helianthus, sunflower
Heliopsis, false sunflower
Hemerocallis, tawny daylily, hybrid daylilies
Hosta, plantain lily (mid to late summer, depending on species or variety)
Hypericum, St.-John's-wort
Lamium, spotted dead nettle
Liatris, gayfeather
Lilium, many hybrid lilies, scarlet Turk's cap lily, gold-banded lily
Limonium, sea lavender, statice

Lobelia, cardinal flower
Lythrum, purple loosestrife
Macleaya, plume poppy
Malva, musk mallow
Monarda, bee balm
Penstemon
Phlox, annual phlox, garden or summer phlox
Physostegia, false dragonhead
Platycodon, balloon flower
Rudbeckia, black-eyed Susan
Salvia, mealy-cup sage, scarlet sage, violet sage
Saponaria, bouncing bet
Sedum, stonecrop
Stachys, big betony
Stokesia, Stokes' aster
Tanacetum, feverfew
Veronica, *V. incana*, *V. longifolia*
Yucca

LATE SUMMER

Aconitum, monkshood
Anemone, Japanese anemone
Aster, *A.* × *frikartii*
Chelone, pink turtlehead
Coreopsis, pink tickseed
Dendrathema, garden chrysanthemum
Eryngium, Mediterranean sea holly
Gentiana, *G. septemfida*, *G. sino-ornata*
Helenium, sneezeweed
Hosta, plantain lily (some species and varieties bloom in late summer)
Hyssopus, hyssop
Ligularia
Lilium, various hybrid lilies, tiger lily, late-blooming forms of *L. formosanum*
Lobelia, great blue lobelia
Salvia, blue sage, azure sage
Sanguisorba, great burnet
Sedum, 'Autumn Joy' sedum, *S. maximum*
Thalictrum, lavender mist meadow rue
Zauschneria, California fuchsia

AUTUMN

Aconitum, azure monkshood
Allium, garlic chives
Arum, Italian arum (berries in fall)
Aster, New England aster, New York aster
Boltonia
Ceratostigma, plumbago, leadwort
Cimicifuga, Kamchatka snakeroot
Colchicum
Crocus, autumn crocus, saffron crocus
Cyclamen, hardy cyclamen
Dendrathema, garden chrysanthemum
Eupatorium, mistflower, Joe-pye weed
Gentiana, bottle gentian
Helenium, *H. hoopsei*
Leucojum, autumn snowflake
Lycoris, magic lily (early autumn, late summer in some locations)
Nerine, nerine lily
Oxalis, *O. boweii*
Polianthes, tuberose
Salvia, azure sage
Schizostylis, crimson flag
Sedum (some species bloom in early autumn)
Sternbergia, winter daffodil
Tricyrtis, toad lily
Urginea, ironweed, sea squill
Yucca, Spanish dagger (warm climates)

WINTER

Adonis, amur adonis (late winter to early spring, depending on location)
Anemone, Grecian windflower (late winter in warm climates)
Bulbocodium, spring meadow saffron (late winter to very early spring)
Calendula, pot marigold (can be grown for winter flowers in warm climates)
Chionodoxa, glory-of-the-snow (late winter to early spring, depending on location)

(continued)

Seasonal Blooming Schedules *(cont'd)*

Winter *(cont'd)*

Consolida, rocket larkspur (can be grown for winter flowers in warm climates)
Crocus, species crocuses (late winter to early spring)
Eranthis, winter aconite (late winter to early spring, depending on location)
Galanthus, snowdrop (late winter to early spring)
Helleborus, Christmas rose (late winter in warm climates)
Iberis, perennial candytuft (blooms late winter in the South)
Iris, netted iris, Algerian iris, *I. danfordiae* (all late winter to early spring), Dutch iris hybrids (winter in Deep South and along West Coast if planted in fall)
Lobularia, sweet alyssum (can be grown for winter flowers in warm climates)
Matthiola, stock (can be grown for winter flowers in warm climates)
Narcissus, February Gold and February Silver narcissus (both late winter in the South), Paperwhite narcissus (winter, outdoors in the South, indoors in the North)
Primula, polyanthus primrose (winter in the South and on West Coast), English primrose (late winter to early spring, depending on location)
Scilla, Persian squill (late winter to early spring)
Viola, pansy (can be grown for winter flowers in warm climates)

THE LANGUAGE OF FLOWERS

During the Victorian era, people used flowers to send messages to others. Flowers could express love, friendship, jealousy, or other emotions, or reflect some quality of the receiver's or sender's personality.

Here are the meanings that tradition has associated with some popular flowers.

Aster, Michaelmas daisy: Farewell
Calla lily: Magnificent beauty
Camellia
  Red: Excellence
  White: Perfect loveliness
Canterbury bells: Acknowledgment
Carnation: Bonds of affection
Chrysanthemum: Cheerfulness in adversity
China aster: Variety
Clove pink: Resignation
Coreopsis: Always cheerful
Cornflower: Quarrel
Cyclamen: Diffidence
Daffodil: Regard
Dahlia: Instability
Daisy: Innocence
Foxglove: Insincerity
Gardenia: Secret untold love
Goldenrod: Treasure
Hawthorn: Hope
Heather: Admiration, protection
Heliotrope: Devotion
Hyacinth: Game, sport
Hydrangea: Heartlessness
Iris: Message
Ivy: Eternal friendship
Jasmine: Grace
Larkspur: Attachment
Lavender: Mistrust
Lilac, purple lilac: First feelings of love
Lily: Pure in heart
Lily of the valley: Happiness returns
Lupine: Imagination
Marigold: Grief, jealousy
Monkshood: Chivalry
Myrtle: Sincere love

Narcissus: Self-importance
Nasturtium: Patriotism
Oleander: Beware
Orchid: Beauty
Pansy: Thinking of you
Sweet pea: Departure
Peony: Shyness
Phlox: Sweet dreams or proposal of love
Poppy, red poppy: Consolation
Ranunculus: You are charming
Rhododendron: Danger
Rose
- Red rose: Love
- White rose: I am worthy of you
- Yellow rose: Friendship or jealousy

Rosemary: Remembrance
Rudbeckia: Justice
Salvia: Esteem
Snapdragon: Desperation
Snowdrop: Hope
Stock: Lasting beauty
Sunflower: Pride, haughtiness
Sweet William: Gallantry
Tuberose: Dangerous pleasure
Tulip: Fame
- Red tulip: Love
- Yellow tulip: Hopeless love

Violet: Loyalty or modesty
Wallflower: Faithfulness in adversity
Zinnia: Thinking of absent friends

STATE FLOWERS

Alabama: Goldenrod
Alaska: Forget-me-not
Arizona: Saguaro cactus
Arkansas: Apple blossom
California: California poppy
Colorado: Rocky Mountain columbine
Connecticut: Mountain laurel
Delaware: Peach blossom
District of Columbia: American Beauty rose
Florida: Orange blossom
Georgia: Cherokee rose
Hawaii: Hibiscus
Idaho: Mock orange
Illinois: Native violet
Indiana: Zinnia
Iowa: Wild rose
Kansas: Sunflower
Kentucky: Goldenrod
Louisiana: Magnolia
Maine: Pine cone and tassel
Maryland: Black-eyed Susan
Massachusetts: Trailing arbutus
Michigan: Apple blossom
Minnesota: Showy lady's slipper
Mississippi: Magnolia
Missouri: Red haw
Montana: Bitterroot
Nebraska: Goldenrod
Nevada: Sagebrush
New Hampshire: Purple lilac
New Jersey: Violet
New Mexico: Yucca
New York: Wild rose
North Carolina: Flowering dogwood
North Dakota: Wild prairie rose
Ohio: Red carnation
Oklahoma: Mistletoe
Oregon: Oregon grape
Pennsylvania: Mountain laurel
Rhode Island: Violet
South Carolina: Yellow jessamine
South Dakota: Pasqueflower
Tennessee: Iris
Texas: Bluebonnet
Utah: Sego lily

(continued)

State Flowers *(cont'd)*

Vermont: Red clover
Virginia: Flowering dogwood
Washington: Rhododendron
West Virginia: Rhododendron
Wisconsin: Violet
Wyoming: Indian paintbrush

FLOWERS OF THE MONTH (BIRTHDAY FLOWERS)

January: Snowdrop
February: Primrose
March Violet
April: Daisy
May: Hawthorn
June: Rose
July: Waterlily
August: Poppy
September: Morning glory
October: Hops
November: Chrysanthemum
December: Holly

ALL-AMERICA SELECTIONS FLOWER AND BEDDING PLANT WINNERS

1933 Canterbury bell, Annual Mixed
Delphinium, Cambridge Blue
Lupine, Giant King Mixed
Marigold, Guinea Gold
Nasturtium, Golden Gleam
Pansy, Dwarf Swiss Giants
Verbena, Beauty of Oxford Hybrids
Verbena, Lavender Glory

1934 Aster, Los Angeles
Aster, Silvery Rose
Calendula, Sunshine
Canterbury bell, Angelus Bell
Canterbury bell, Liberty Bell
Chrysanthemum, Eldorado
Hunnemannia, Sunlite
Larkspur, Blue Bell
Larkspur, Rosamond
Linaria, Fairy Bouquet
Marigold, Monarch Mixed
Petunia, Victorious Mixed

1934 *(cont'd)* Petunia, Pink Gem
Petunia, Pink Sensation
Scabiosa, Giant Hybrids
Verbena, Cerise Queen
Verbena, Dannebrog
Verbena, Spectrum Red

1935 Anchusa, Blue Bird
Calendula, Orange Shaggy
Celosia, Flame of Fire
Cosmos, Orange Flare
Dianthus, Laciniatus Splendens
Marigold, Golden Beauty
Marigold, Primrose Queen
Marigold, Scarlet Glow
Marigold, Yellow Beauty
Marigold, Yellow Supreme
Nasturtium, Glorious Gleam Mixture
Nasturtium, Scarlet Gleam
Petunia, Martha Washington

1935 (cont'd) Phlox, Gigantea Art Shades
Verbena, Violet Bouquet
Zinnia, Fantasy Mixture

1936 Aster, El Monte
Cosmos, Sensation
Marigold, Dixie Sunshine
Nasturtium, Golden Glove
Petunia, Dainty Lady
Petunia, Flaming Velvet
Petunia, Improved Rose King
Petunia, Rose Gem
Snapdragon, Royal Rose
Snapdragon, St. George

1937 Cornflower, Jubilee Gem
Iceland poppy, Yellow Wonder
Marigold, Dwarf Royal Scot
Marigold, Crown of Gold
Petunia, Burgundy
Snapdragon, White Spire
Stock, Giant Excelsior/Rose Pink
Verbena, Floradale Beauty
Zinnia, Fantasy Star Dust

1938 Aster, Enchantress
Aster, Illusion
Calendula, Orange Fantasy
Calliopsis (Coreopsis), Golden Crown
Marigold, Chrysanthemum Flowered
Marigold, Golden West
Myosotis, Ingrid
Pansy, Coronation Gold
Petunia, Blue Gem
Petunia, Salmon Supreme
Petunia, Topaz Rose

1938 (cont'd) Petunia, Victorious Gaiety
Petunia, Victorious Orchid Beauty
Snapdragon, Celestial
Zinnia, Navajo Mixed

1939 Aster, Early Giant Light Blue
Celosia, Royal Velvet
Chinese Forget-me-not (Cynoglossum), Firmament
Hollyhock, Indian Spring
Marigold, Early Sunshine
Marigold, Golden Glow
Morning glory, Scarlet O'Hara
Petunia, Hollywood Star
Petunia, Lady Bird
Petunia, Velvet Ball
Petunia, Victorious Apple Blossom
Phlox, Salmon Glory
Scabiosa, Blue Moon
Snapdragon, Guinea Gold
Verbena, Blue Sentinel
Zinnia, Fantasy White Light

1940 Ageratum, Midget Blue
Aster, Rose Marie
Marigold, Limelight
Marigold, Yellow Pygmy
Morning Glory, Lavender Rosette
Petunia, Cream Star
Salvia, Royal Blue
Scabiosa, Heavenly Blue
Snapdragon, Rosalie

(continued)

All-American Selections Flower and Bedding Plant Winners *(cont'd)*

1940 *(cont'd)*
- Sweet pea, Spring Blue
- Sweet pea, Spring Lavender
- Sweet pea, Spring Rose Pink

1941
- Marigold, Goldsmith
- Marigold, Spry
- Petunia, Blue Brocade
- Petunia, First Lady
- Petunia, Radiance
- Petunia, Violet Gem
- Phlox, Rosy Morn
- Scabiosa, Peace
- Zinnia, Black Ruby

1942
- Cleome, Pink Queen
- Cosmos, Yellow Flare
- Marigold, Butterball
- Marigold, Golden Bedder
- Marigold, Melody
- Marigold, Yellowstone
- Morning glory, Pearly Gates
- Nierembergia, Purple Robe
- Petunia, Glamour
- Phlox, Red Glory
- Rudbeckia, Starlight
- Zinnia, Royal Purple

1943
- Aster, Extra Early Giant
- Aster, Victory Giants Mixed
- Cosmos, Giant Sensation Dazzler
- Marigold, Sunkist
- Petunia, Alldouble America
- Petunia, English Violet
- Petunia, Igloo

1944
- Marigold, Mammoth Mum
- Petunia, Cheerful

1945
- Marigold, Flash
- Marigold, Real Gold
- Petunia, Shades of Rose

1946
- Dianthus, Westwood Beauty
- Petunia, Bright Eyes
- Petunia, Colossal Shades of Rose
- Petunia, Peach Red

1947
- Marigold, Naughty Marietta
- Petunia, Mrs. Dwight D. Eisenhower
- Petunia, Rose Marie
- Snapdragon, Velvet Giant

1948
- Cosmos, Radiance
- Marigold, Red Head

1949
- Hollyhock, Indian Summer
- Morning Glory, Blue Star
- Petunia, Silver Medal

1950
- Petunia, Fire Chief

1951
- Marigold, Glitters
- Tithonia, Torch

1952
- Cosmos, Fiesta
- Petunia, Ballerina
- Phlox, Globe Mixed
- Zinnia, Persian Carpet

1953
- Alyssum, Royal Carpet
- Petunia, Comanche

1954
- Zinnia, Blaze

1955
- Celosia, Toreador
- Columbine, McKana Giant
- Petunia, Paleface
- Petunia, Prima Donna

1956
- Petunia, Fire Dance

1957 Petunia, Glitters
Petunia, Red Satin
Phlox, Salmon Glory Twinkle
Snapdragon, Vanguard

1958 Marigold, Petite Gold
Marigold, Petite Harmony
Marigold, Petite Orange
Petunia, Maytime

1959 Alyssum, Pink Heather

1960 Marigold, Spun Gold
Marigold, Toreador
Phlox, Glamour
Snapdragon, Rocket Bronze
Snapdragon, Rocket Golden
Snapdragon, Rocket Orchid
Snapdragon, Rocket Red
Snapdragon, Rocket Rose
Snapdragon, Rocket White

1961 Alyssum, Rosie O'Day
Petunia, Coral Satin
Rudbeckia, Gloriosa Double

1962 Basil, Dark Opal
Dianthus, Bravo
Zinnia, Old Mexico
Zinnia, Red Man

1963 Delphinium, Connecticut Yankee
Zinnia, Firecracker
Zinnia, Thumbelina

1964 Celosia, Fireglow
Salvia, Evening Glow
Zinnia, Bonanza
Zinnia, Tom Thumb Pink Buttons

1965 Petunia, Appleblossom
Snapdragon, Floral Carpet Rose
Zinnia, Yellow Zenith

1966 Cosmos, Sunset
Marigold, Spun Yellow
Pansy, Giant Majestic Mixed
Pansy, Majestic White Blotch
Snapdragon, Bright Butterflies
Sweet William, Red Monarch
Verbena, Amethyst

1967 Foxglove, Foxy
Marigold, Golden Jubilee
Sweet pea, San Francisco

1968 Celosia, Golden Triumph
Geranium, Carefree Bright Pink
Geranium, Carefree Deep Salmon
Geranium, Carefree Scarlet
Marigold, First Lady
Marigold, Orange Jubilee
Verbena, Blaze
Zinnia, Wild Cherry

1969 Cornflower, Snow Ball
Vinca, Polka Dot
Zinnia, Cherry Buttons
Zinnia, Rosy Future
Zinnia, Torch

1970 Dianthus, China Doll
Marigold, Bolero
Morning glory, Early Call
Snapdragon, Madame Butterfly

1971 Dianthus, Queen of Hearts
Hibiscus, Southern Belle

(continued)

All-American Selections Flower and Bedding Plant Winners *(cont'd)*

1971 *(cont'd)*
- Hollyhock, Silver Puffs
- Snapdragon, Little Darling
- Zinnia, Peter Pan Pink
- Zinnia, Peter Pan Plum

1972
- Hollyhock, Summer Carnival
- Marigold, Gold Galore
- Petunia, Circus
- Zinnia, Carved Ivory

1973
- Marigold, Happy Face
- Zinnia, Peter Pan Scarlet

1974
- Celosia, Red Fox
- Cosmos, Diablo
- Dianthus, Magic Charms
- Marigold, Showboat
- Zinnia, Peter Pan Orange
- Zinnia, Scarlett Ruffles

1975
- Carnation, Juliet
- Dahlia, Redskin
- Pansy, Imperial Blue

1976
- Hollyhock, Majorette

1977
- Geranium, Showgirl
- Marigold, Primrose Lady
- Petunia, Blushing Maid

1978
- Dianthus, Snowfire
- Zinnia, Cherry Ruffles
- Zinnia, Peter Pan Cream
- Zinnia, Peter Pan Ruffles

1979
- Marigold, Queen Sophie
- Nicotiana, Nicki Red
- Pansy, Orange Prince
- Zinnia, Peter Pan Gold

1980
- Marigold, Janie
- Ornamental pepper, Holiday Time
- Verbena, Sangria
- Zinnia, Peter Pan Flame

1981
- Celosia, Apricot Brandy
- Impatiens, Blitz

1982
- Carnation, Scarlet Luminette
- Zinnia, Fantastic Light Pink
- Zinnia, Small World Cherry

1983
- Kochia, Acapulco Silver
- Ornamental pepper, Candlelight
- Marigold, Red Picotee

1984
- Zinnia, Border Beauty Rose

1985
- Celosia, Century Mixed
- Gazania, Mini-Star Tangerine
- Geranium, Rose Diamond
- Verbena, Trinidad
- Zinnia, Yellow Marvel

1986
- Cosmos, Sunny Red

1987
- Basil, Purple Ruffles
- Petunia, Purple Pirouette
- Sanvitalia, Mandarin Orange
- Snapdragon, Princess White Purple Eye

1988
- Celosia, New Look
- Petunia, Ultra Crimson Star
- Shasta daisy, Snow Lady

1989
- Coreopsis, Early Sunrise
- Dianthus, Telstar Picotee
- Impatiens, Tango
- Marigold, Golden Gate
- Petunia, Orchid Daddy

1989 (cont'd) Torenia, Clown Mixture
Verbena, Novalis Deep Blue
Verbena, Sandy White

1990 Achillea, Summer Pastels
Celosia, Castle Pink
Pansy, Jolly Joker
Petunia, Burgundy Star
Petunia, Polo Salmon
Zinnia, Scarlet Splendor

1991 Gaillardia, Red Plume
Geranium, Freckles
Pansy, Maxim Marina
Pansy, Padparadja

1991 (cont'd) Vinca, Parasol
Vinca, Pretty in Rose

1992 Canna, Tropical Rose
Dianthus, Ideal Violet
Salvia, Lady in Red
Verbena, Peaches & Cream
Vinca, Pretty in White

1993 Verbena, Imagination

1994 Lavender, Lady

1995 Petunia, Celebrity Chiffon Morn
Petunia, Purple Wave
Rudbeckia, Indian Summer

FOLIAGE PLANTS

Plants with Colored or Variegated Leaves

In addition to the plants listed below, a number of ornamental grasses also have colored and patterned foliage.

Acalypha, copperleaf: Greenish bronze leaves with red, copper, or purple mottling

Acorus, sweet flag: 'Variegata' has leaves striped with yellow

Aegopodium podagraria 'Variegatum', goutweed: White-edged leaves

Aeonium: Several cultivars have purple leaves

Agave, century plant: Cultivars have leaves striped or edged with yellow

Ajuga, bugleweed: Cultivars have bronze or purple leaves, some variegated with cream

Aloe: Some cultivars have white-variegated or pink-edged leaves

Alternanthera, Joseph's coat: Leaves are green with purple-bronze and red

Amaranthus: Leaves are a mixture of red, yellow or orange, purple, and brown

Arum, Italian arum: Cultivars have leaves with white markings

Atriplex, orach: Cultivars have deep red, light red, or coppery foliage

Begonia, rex begonia: Metallic green leaves are marbled, splotched, and spotted with rose, purple, silver, and bronze, with red undersides

(continued)

Leaf Shapes

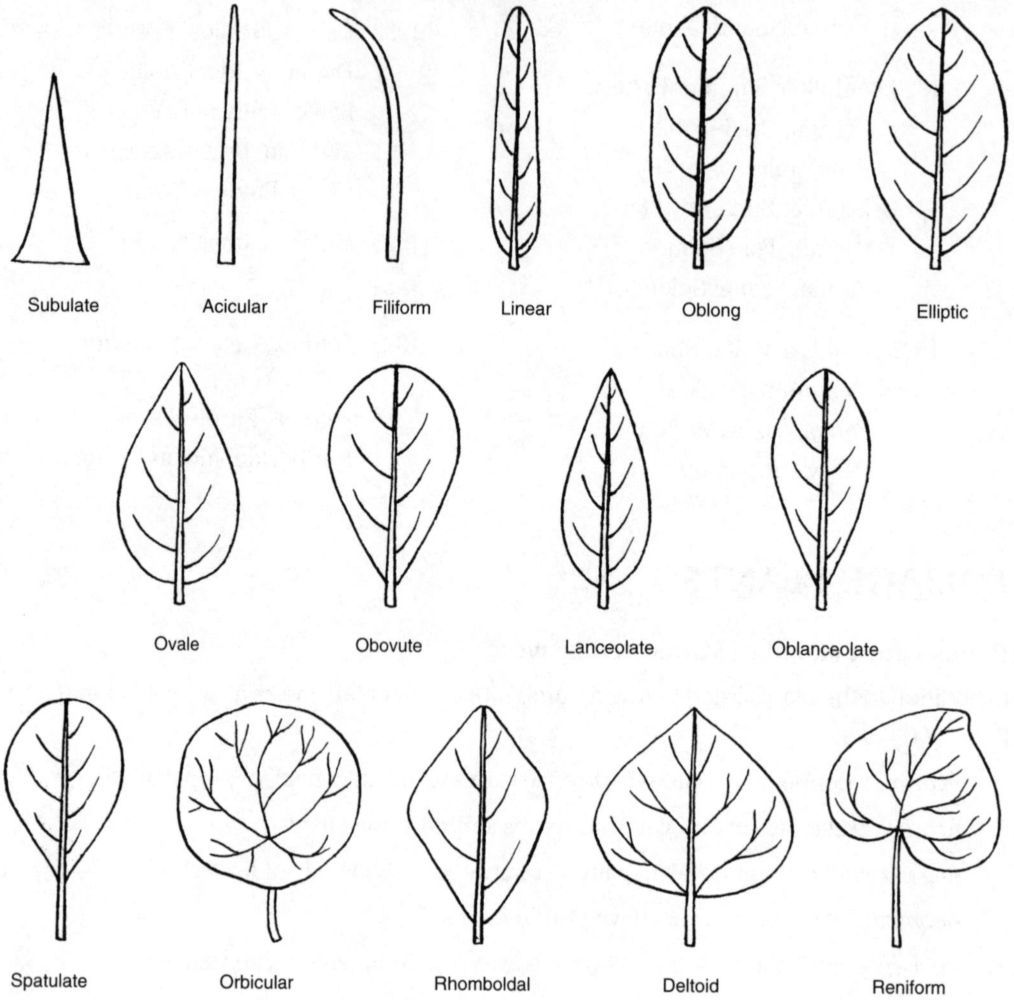

Plants with Colored or Variegated Leaves *(cont'd)*

Bergenia purpurascens: Leaves turn deep red in winter

Brassica, flowering kale and cabbage: Heads of blue-green leaves turn creamy white or red-violet from the center outward in fall with cold weather. Flowering kale has frilly-edged leaves, the leaves of flowering cabbage have smooth edges.

Caladium, elephant ears: Leaves are light green flushed, veined, and blotched with red or pink, or white veined and patterned with green

Canna: Cultivars have purple, bronzy, or green-and-yellow or green-and-ivory-striped leaves

Leaf Margins

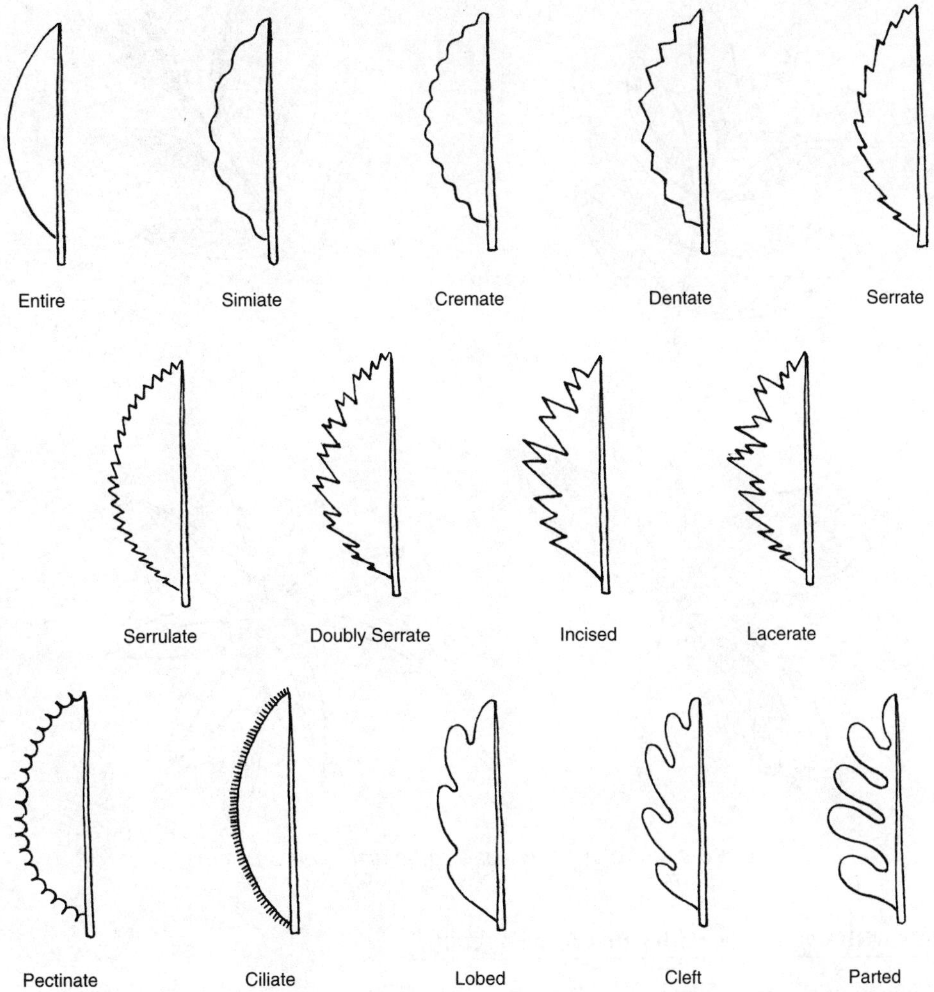

Cimicifuga, kamchatka bugbane: 'Atropurpurea' has dark purple leaves

Coleus: Various combinations and shades of green, yellow-green, red, maroon, orange, brown, pink, bronze, and yellow

Convallaria, lily of the valley: One cultivar has ivory-striped leaves

Euonymus, wintercreeper: Some cultivars have foliage with white or yellow edges, or that turn purple in fall

Euphorbia, snow-on-the-mountain: Grayish green leaves striped and edged with white

(continued)

Leaf Position

Here are some ways leaves can be arranged on stems.

Plants with Colored or Variegated Leaves *(cont'd)*

Filipendula, queen-of-the-meadow: 'Aurea' has golden leaves

Foeniculum, fennel: 'Bronze' has purple-bronze foliage

Hedera, English ivy: Cultivars have yellow or white variegation

Heuchera, coralbells: Cultivars have bronzy purple leaves, or green leaves marked with silver or bronze

Hosta, plantain lily: Many cultivars, with blue-green, chartreuse, or golden yellow foliage, or leaves striped, banded, streaked, or blotched with yellow or white

Houttuynia cordata: 'Variegata' has green leaves mottled with red-violet and cream

Hypoestes, polka-dot plant: Small, dark green leaves are splashed and spotted with pink

Iresine, beefsteak plant: Bloodleaf, dark burgundy leaves

Iris: Several cultivars have yellow or white variegation on green leaves

Kochia, summer cypress: Leaves turn red in fall

Lamiastrum, yellow archangel: Green-veined leaves overlaid with white

Lamium, spotted dead nettle: Cultivars have leaves with white splotches

Ligularia, leopard plant: Leaves of 'Aureo-maculata' are splotched with pink, white, or yellow

Liriope, big blue lilyturf: 'Variegata' has leaves striped with yellow

Mentha, pineapple mint: Leaves are variegated with white

Ocimum, basil: 'Dark Opal' and 'Fluffy Ruffles' have deep purple leaves

Origanum vulgare, pot marjoram: 'Aurea' has golden leaves

Pachysandra, Japanese spurge: 'Variegata' has white-variegated leaves

Pelargonium, zonal geranium: Some have leaves banded with purple-brown, cream, and red; others have green leaves with white edges

Peltiphyllum, umbrella plant: Leaves turn bright red in fall

Perilla: Reddish purple or deep purple foliage with bronze overtones

Phormium, New Zealand flax: Cultivars are striped or marked with red, purple, orange, bronze, ivory, or yellow

Polygonatum, fragrant Solomon's seal: 'Variegatum' has white-striped green leaves

Pulmonaria, lungwort, Bethlehem sage: Cultivars have various patterns of silver spots

Ricinus, castor bean: Cultivars have deep purple or dark red leaves

Rodgersia podophylla, bronzeleaf rodgersia: Metallic bronze leaves

Ruta, rue: 'Variegata' has blue-green leaves marked with white

Salvia, culinary sage: Cultivars chartreuse-edged or purple leaves; leaves of 'Tricolor' are a blend of green, cream, and purple

Setcreasea, purple heart: Cultivars have purple leaves with small silver hairs

Silybum, St. Mary's thistle: Deep green leaves with white veins and spots

Tanacetum, feverfew: 'Aureum' has feathery golden leaves

Thymus, thyme: Cultivars have golden or ivory-edged leaves

Vinca major 'Variegata', variegated vinca: Green leaves edged with ivory

Yucca: Cultivars have foliage with centers, edges, or stripes of cream or light yellow

Plants with Bold, Dramatic Foliage

The plants listed here have large, sculptural leaves that add dramatic focal points or background interest to garden settings.

Acanthus, bear's breeches
Agave, century plant
Bergenia, heart-leaved bergenia
Canna
Colocasia, elephant ear
Crambe, sea kale
Cynara, cardoon
Eryngium, rattlesnake master
Gunnera
Heracleum, giant hogweed
Kirengeshoma
Macleaya, plume poppy
Onopordum, Scotch thistle
Peltiphyllum, umbrella plant
Phormium, New Zealand flax
Podophyllum, Mayapple
Polygonatum, giant Solomon's seal
Rheum, rhubarb
Ricinus, castor bean
Rodgersia
Rohdea, nippon lily
Salvia argentea, silver sage
Silphium, prairie dock
Silybum, St. Mary's thistle
Xanthosoma, elephant ear, taro
Yucca

Plants with Delicate Foliage

These plants have small or narrow leaves, or compound leaves made up of small leaflets. Use them in small gardens, or to create lacy, feathery, ferny textural effects in contrast to bolder leaved plants.

Achillea, yarrow
Anthemis
- *A. anthemis*, golden marguerite
- *A. sancti-johannis*, St. John's chamomile

Artemisia
- *A. absinthium* 'Lambrook Silver', wormwood
- *A. canescens*
- *A.* 'Powis Castle'
- *A. schmidtiana* 'Silver Mound'

Astilbe
Centaurea cineraria, dusty miller
Dicentra, fringed bleeding heart
Ferns
Festuca ovina var. *glauca*, fine fescue
Ficus pumila, creeping fig
Foeniculum, fennel
Galega, goat's rue
Galium, sweet woodruff
Geranium, cranesbill, numerous species
Ipomoea quamoclit, cypress vine
Mentha, Corsican mint
Myrrhis, sweet cicely
Polemonium foliosissimum, leafy polemonium
Senecio cineraria, dusty miller
Soleirolia, baby's tears
Tagetes filifolia, Irish lace
Thymus, thyme
Vancouveria, barrenwort

Plants with Fragrant Foliage

Plants with scented leaves are delightful at the edge of paths, where passersby brush against them and release the scent. This list includes some trees and shrubs, as well as nonwoody plants. Some herbs with ornamental value are listed, but many other herbs also have scented leaves. And don't overlook the refreshing fragrance of conifer needles when searching for scented foliage.

Achillea, yarrow, aromatic

Aloysia, lemon verbena, lemony

Anthemis, golden marguerite, aromatic

Artemisia, aromatic

Buxus, boxwood, aromatic, resiny

Calamintha, calamint, minty

Calendula, aromatic, pungent

Calycanthus, Carolina allspice, spicy

Caryopteris, blue mist

Chamaemelum, Roman chamomile, fresh, applelike

Choisya, Mexican orange, pungent

Cinnamomum, camphor tree

Cistus ladanifer, rock rose, sweet

Comptonia, sweetfern, aromatic

Cymbopogon, lemongrass, lemony

Dendrathema, garden chrysanthemum, strongly aromatic

Dictamnus, gas plant, citrusy

Dracocephalum, dragon plant, lemony

Eucalyptus, gum tree, menthol-like

Foeniculum, fennel, sweetly aromatic, anisey

Galium, sweet woodruff, fresh, hay-scented

Hyssopus, hyssop

Illicium, Florida anise bush, aromatic

Lantana

Laurus, sweet bay, refreshing, aromatic

Lavandula, lavender, refreshing and somewhat sweet

Lindera, spicebush, spicy

Magnolia salicifolia, anise magnolia, aniselike

Matricaria, German chamomile, fresh, applelike

Melianthus, honeybush, sweet

Melissa, lemon balm, lemony with hint of mint

Mentha, mint

- *M.* × *piperita*, peppermint
- *M. pulegium*, pennyroyal, citrusy
- *M. requienii*, Corsican mint, pepperminty
- *M. spicata*, spearmint
- *M. suaveolens*, apple mint, applelike
- *M. suaveolens* var. *variegata*, pineapple mint, pineapplelike

Monarda, bee balm, citrusy

Myrica

- *M. cerifera*, southerm wax myrtle, aromatic, resiny
- *M. pensylvanica*, bayberry, aromatic, resiny

Myrtus, myrtle, aromatic, resiny

Nepeta, catmint, citrusy

Ocimum, basil, most are spicy; cinnamon, licorice, and lemon-scented varieties also available

- *O. sanctum*, holy basil, is sweet-scented

Pelargonium, scented-leaved geraniums. Available with peppermint, rose, lemon, ginger, coconut, nutmeg, apple, orange, cinnamon, and other scents.

Perovskia, Russian sage, aromatic

Rosmarinus, rosemary, piney

Ruta, rue

Salvia, sage

- *S. elegans*, pineapple sage, pineapplelike
- *S. officinalis*, culinary sage, aromatic

(continued)

Plants with Fragrant Foliage *(cont'd)*

Santolina, lavender cotton, aromatic
Sassafras, citrusy
Skimmia, pungent
Tagetes, marigold, strongly aromatic, pungent
Tanacetum, tansy, feverfew, aromatic
Thymus, thyme
  T. × *citriodorus*, lemon thyme, lemony
  T. herba-barona, caraway thyme, caraway-scented
  T. herba-barona 'Nutmeg', nutmeg-scented
  T. vulgaris, common thyme, aromatic
Vitex, chaste tree

FERNS

FERNS FOR COOL AND TEMPERATE CLIMATES

Adiantum pedatum, northern maidenhair fern
Asplenium
  A. platyneuron, ebony spleenwort
  A. trichomanes, maidenhair spleenwort
Athyrium
  A. filix-femina, lady fern
  A. goeringianum 'Pictum', Japanese painted fern
  A. thelypteroides, silvery spleenwort
Blechnum, deer fern
Botrychium
  B. dissectum, lace-leaved grape fern
  B. virginianum, rattlesnake fern
Camptosorus, walking fern
Cheilanthes, lip fern
Cystopteris
  C. bulbifera, bulblet fern
  C. fragilis, brittle fern
Dennstaedtia, hay-scented fern
Dryopteris
  D. austriaca, fancy fern
  D. cristata, crested wood fern
  D. dilatata, broad shield fern
  D. filix-mas, male fern
  D. goldiana, giant wood fern
  D. marginalis, marginal wood fern
  D. spinulosa, toothed wood fern
Gymnocarpium, oak fern
Lygodium, Hartford fern
Matteuccia, ostrich fern
Onoclea, sensitive fern
Osmunda
  O. cinnamomea, cinnamon fern
  O. claytoniana, interrupted fern
  O. regalis, royal fern
Pellaea, purple cliff brake
Polypodium, common polypody
Polystichum
  P. acrostichoides, Christmas fern
  P. lonchitis, holly fern
Pteridium, bracken
Thelypteris
  T. noveboracensis, New York fern
  T. palustris, marsh fern
  T. phegopteris, northern beech fern
Woodsia
  W. ilvensis, rusty woodsia
  W. obtusa, blunt-lobed cliff fern
Woodwardia
  W. areolata, net-veined chain fern
  W. virginica, Virginia chain fern

FERNS FOR WARM CLIMATES

Adiantum
  A. capillus-veneris, southern maidenhair fern
  A. hispidulum, rough maidenhair fern
Asplenium, hen-and-chicks fern
Cibotium, tree fern
Cyathea, tree fern
Cyrtomium, holly fern

Cystopteris, bulblet bladder fern
Davallia trichomanoides, squirrel's foot fern
Dicksonia, tree fern
Nephrolepis
- *N. cordifolia*, sword fern
- *N. exaltata*, Boston fern, lace fern, fluffy ruffles fern

Phegopteris, southern beech fern
Platycerium, staghorn fern
Polystichum munitum, sword fern
Pteris, brake fern
Rumorha, leatherleaf fern
Woodwardia
- *W. areolata*, net-veined chain fern
- *W. fimbriata*
- *W. virginica*, Virginia chain fern

Chapter 4
TREES AND SHRUBS

WHAT'S A TREE? WHAT'S A SHRUB?

Trees and shrubs are woody plants that remain in the garden year after year. A tree is defined by botanists as a woody plant that has one main stem (the trunk) and usually a discernible head (the canopy), and that is at least 12 to 15 feet tall. A shrub is a woody plant that branches from the base and has more than one main stem. A bush is a low shrub that has at least several and often many stems, with no distinct main stem or trunk.

By definition there are obvious differences between trees and shrubs, but in reality the differences are not always so obvious. Some trees, such as white birches, tend to grow in clumps and appear to have several trunks. Large shrubs are sometimes grown like trees, with all but one main stem removed. Even with all the stems left intact, large shrubs may function like trees in the landscape, especially a small landscape, providing height and basic structure in the overall design, and offering the benefits of summer shade and colorful autumn foliage. Similarly, small trees may act like shrubs in some situations, often becoming part of mixed borders, or serving as screens or dividers in the landscape.

Because the distinctions between large shrubs and small trees can be subtle, trees and shrubs are treated together in this chapter.

NEW PROCEDURES FOR PLANTING TREES AND SHRUBS

The traditional way to plant woody nursery stock, whether it was in bare-root, balled-and-burlapped, or container-grown form, has been to dig a hole twice as deep as the rootball and improve the soil in the planting hole by adding compost or fertilizer. But the rules for planting trees and shrubs are changing. Research has taught us that the old method isn't always successful. For example, improving the soil only in the planting hole sometimes discourages roots from growing out into the surrounding soil. Plants grow as if they are pot-bound—their roots circling around in the rich soil—even though they are not in containers.

Now the experts recommend some different procedures for planting trees and shrubs. Here are the old rules and their new replacements.

OLD RULE	NEW RULE
Dig the planting hole deeper than the rootball.	Better than digging a deep planting hole, it is now believed, is to dig a wide hole. For balled-and-burlapped or container-grown stock, dig the hole no deeper than the rootball, but make it at least twice as wide. Most trees and shrubs have wide-spreading root systems that grow more horizontally than vertically. Most of the roots of many woody plants are concentrated in the upper 18 inches of the soil. The roots of many trees range well past the dripline (an imaginary line that marks the boundary of the outermost branches of the tree, the edge of its canopy). For the best results, particularly in heavy soil, loosen the soil over the entire area that will eventually be filled with roots. For example, if you are planting a 3-inch caliper tree ("caliper" is a measure of trunk size) that will eventually mature into a 10-inch caliper tree, you are advised to cultivate the soil to a depth of about 10 inches over an area covering a 10-foot radius from the trunk of the tree. Then dig the planting hole.
Improve the soil in the planting hole with compost and fertilizers.	The new rule is *not* to enrich the soil at planting time unless it is in very poor shape. If your soil is of extremely poor quality, work in compost or other soilbuilders over the entire future root zone of the plant. And do not fertilize until the plant has been in the ground for at least one full growing season. Nice, fertile soil in the planting hole encourages the roots to stay confined there and not grow out into the surrounding soil. Fertilizers are now to be avoided because we have learned that nitrogen hinders the growth of new roots on newly planted stock.

OLD RULE	NEW RULE
Make a saucer in the soil around the trunk to catch water.	Constant moisture can cause the trunk to rot. In dry areas, a better approach is to make a depression a few inches deep in the soil in a ring 2 to 3 feet out from the trunk. The depressed ring will capture water for roots without harming the trunk. Even more important for getting the tree or shrub off to a good start is mulch. Spread 2 to 3 inches of an organic mulch from the trunk over the entire root zone, starting six inches out from the trunk, and renew it when it grows thin. The mulch helps conserve soil moisture, and adds organic matter and nutrients to the soil (to help nourish shallow feeder roots) as it decomposes.
Prune the tree or shrub when you plant it to encourage good shape and strong structure.	It is still necessary to prune at planting time to remove dead or damaged branches and broken or injured roots, but wait until the tree is established to do all other pruning. If you do need to prune damaged top growth, do not seal the cuts with tree wound paint—it can hinder the plant's natural healing process.
Stake newly planted trees to keep them upright.	Staking is now recommended only for windy locations. Guy wires connecting the tree to the stakes should have some play in them to allow the trunk to flex in the wind, which strengthens it.

See chapter 2, "Gardening Techniques," for a rundown of the basic procedures for planting bare-root, balled-and-burlapped, and container-grown plants from the nursery or garden center.

CARING FOR TREES AND SHRUBS THROUGH THE YEAR

Planting a tree or shrub is making an investment in the future. To make your investment pay off, take care of your trees and shrubs after you have put them into the ground. Mature plants need care just as newly planted specimens do.

Here is a basic schedule of maintenance for trees and shrubs. The guidelines are given in three very broad regional categories: Cool Climates (corresponding to climates from USDA Plant Hardiness Zone 2 to northern Zone 5), Temperate Climates (Zones 5 to 7), and Warm Climates (Zones 8 to 11).

No matter where you live, examine every tree and shrub at least once a year. Look at the new shoots that have grown this year, and compare them to the growth from the previous two or three years. If this year's shoots are markedly smaller, even at the end of the season, and less healthy-looking, or if the leaves are smaller than they were in the past, something is wrong. Dead branches in the crown of a tree, loose bark, and abnormal growths also signal problems. The plant may have improper growing conditions, or may be suffering from disease or pests. If you cannot diagnose the problem yourself, call in a professional arborist while there's still time to save the plant.

To keep trees and most shrubs well nourished, fertilize once a year, in spring or fall, with an all-purpose fertilizer.

Mulch trees and shrubs in summer with 2 to 4 inches of loose, organic material (see chapter 2 for information on mulches). Spread the mulch from close to (but not touching) the base of the trunk out to the dripline or even beyond, if possible.

Prune trees and shrubs as needed to remove damaged or dead growth, and to shape the plant and enhance its growth pattern. Prune trees and nonflowering shrubs while the plants are dormant—in winter or very early spring—so the wounds heal quickly. Your goal should be to prune as little as possible. Overpruning weakens plants, so if in doubt, it is better to err on the side of caution. See chapter 2 for information on basic pruning.

COOL CLIMATES

Spring. Continue to remove snow accumulation from evergreens if necessary in early spring. When the weather begins to moderate, you can start removing burlap windscreens, mouse guards, and other winter protection from trees and shrubs.

In early spring, fertilize established trees and shrubs before they break dormancy and begin to show new growth. Fertilize evergreens if you did not do so last fall.

Prune trees and shrubs that need it when the wood thaws but while plants are still dormant. Remove any winter-damaged growth.

When the temperature rises above 40°F for a few days, spray trees and shrubs with dormant oil spray if you see signs of overwintering pests.

As soon as the ground thaws, plant bare-root trees and shrubs. Wrap trunks of young trees with tree wrap to guard against sunscald and pests later on. Water newly planted stock regularly if the weather is dry.

As established trees and shrubs begin to grow, watch for signs of winterkill; remove any winter-killed growth. Also remove growth damaged by late frosts.

When the soil becomes workable, layer shrubs that you wish to propagate by this method.

In midspring, plant balled-and-burlapped and container-grown stock.

Deadhead and prune spring-blooming shrubs as soon as they finish flowering.

As the weather warms, water newly planted trees and shrubs regularly during dry weather. Water established plants only when necessary.

Mulch drought-sensitive trees and shrubs when the soil has warmed.

Summer. Continue to water newly planted trees and shrubs regularly during dry weather. Water established plants only when necessary.

Mulch drought-sensitive trees and shrubs.

Prune and deadhead flowering shrubs as soon as they finish blooming.

You can fertilize established trees and shrubs if you have not already done so, but stop fertilizing six weeks before you expect the first frost, so new growth has a chance to harden before winter.

Take softwood cuttings of trees and shrubs you wish to propagate.

Watch for signs of pests and disease; take prompt action if you notice symptoms.

Autumn. Water new and established trees and shrubs deeply if the weather is dry, to make sure they have plenty of moisture going into winter. If rodents often trouble your trees in winter, surround the trunks of young trees with cylinders of hardware cloth to keep mice from gnawing the bark, or wrap the trunks with tree wrap.

If your location is very windy in winter, set up windbreaks for shrubs that may be damaged, and be sure young trees are staked. Spray broad-leaved evergreens with antidesiccant while the temperature is still 40°F or above.

You may also want to set up wooden shelters over evergreens located under rain gutters or elsewhere. Otherwise, ice may build up on the branches over winter and cause them to snap.

Continue to watch for signs of pests and disease while the weather is warm, and take prompt action if you notice any symptoms.

Winter. Check windbreaks, mouse guards, tree wraps, mulches and other winter protection periodically to make sure all remain securely in place.

In windy locations, spray broad-leaved evergreens with antidesiccant while the temperature is above 40°F if you have not already done so.

When the weather permits, check for signs of overwintering pests; remove and destroy any you find. If a winter thaw brings the temperature above 40°F for a few days, you can spray trees and shrubs with dormant oil spray to destroy borers and the overwintering egg masses and cocoons of other pests.

After heavy snowfall, brush snow from the branches of evergreen trees and shrubs to prevent damage to branches. If wet snow has frozen to ice, let it melt naturally from tree and shrub branches; trying to knock it off could cause branches to snap.

When weather permits, start pruning trees and shrubs that need it.

TEMPERATE CLIMATES

Spring. As the weather moderates going into spring, remove burlap windscreens, mouse guards, mulches, and other winter protection from trees and shrubs.

While established trees and shrubs are still dormant, you can spray with dormant oil if you see evidence of overwintering pests.

Prune trees and shrubs as needed while they are still dormant. As established plants begin to grow, watch for signs of winterkill; prune away any winterkilled growth.

Deadhead and prune spring-blooming shrubs when they finish flowering.

Fertilize established trees and shrubs before they break dormancy. Fertilize evergreens if you did not do so last fall.

Water newly planted trees and shrubs regularly in dry weather. Water established plants only when necessary.

Mulch drought-sensitive trees and shrubs when the soil warms.

Watch for signs of pests and disease; take prompt action if you notice any symptoms.

Anytime after the soil can be worked in spring, layer shrubs you wish to propagate by this method.

Summer. Plant container-grown trees and shrubs as long as the weather is not too hot.

Water newly planted trees and shrubs regularly during dry weather. Water established plants only when necessary.

Prune and deadhead flowering shrubs when they finish blooming.

Watch for signs of pests and diseases; take prompt action when you notice symptoms.

Take softwood cuttings of trees and shrubs you wish to propagate.

Order nursery stock for fall planting.

Autumn. Water new and established plants deeply if the weather is dry, to help prepare them for winter.

Fertilize trees and shrubs growing in nutrient-poor soils; do not fertilize less than six weeks before you expect the first fall frost.

Watch for signs of pests and disease; take prompt action if you notice any symptoms.

Install winter protection for trees and shrubs of borderline hardiness. Wrap trunks of young trees with tree wrap to prevent sunscald and pest damage. If your location is windy, you may wish to install windbreaks or burlap windscreens. Also check to see that new trees in windy locations are securely—though loosely—staked. You may also wish to spray broad-leaved evergreens with antidesiccant.

When deciduous trees and shrubs drop their leaves, take hardwood cuttings of those you want to propagate.

Winter. Where the soil is not yet frozen, water new and established shrubs thoroughly if the weather is dry, so they will have plenty of moisture going into winter. When the ground freezes, mulch new plantings to prevent winter thaws and refreezes from damaging roots.

Water shallow-rooted evergreens and young trees and shrubs during spells of mild, dry weather in late winter. Pull aside mulch to water, and replace it when you finish.

Check winter protection periodically to make sure all remains securely in place.

In warmer areas, take hardwood cuttings in early winter from deciduous trees and shrubs you wish to propagate.

Look for signs of overwintering pests; remove and destroy any you find. If plants are dormant and the temperature is 40°F or above for a few days, you can also spray with dormant oil.

If cold winter winds are a problem in your garden, spray broad-leaved evergreens with antidesiccant spray as winter begins if you did not do so in fall.

Brush heavy accumulations of snow from the branches of evergreen trees and shrubs to prevent damage to branches. Allow ice to melt naturally from branches; trying to knock it off could cause branches to snap.

Order nursery stock for spring planting.

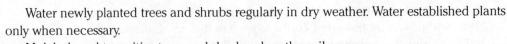

WARM CLIMATES

Spring. Water trees and shrubs as needed in dry climates; elsewhere, water newly planted stock regularly in dry weather, established trees and shrubs when necessary.

Fertilize established trees and shrubs growing in nutrient-poor soils.

Deadhead and prune spring-blooming shrubs when they finish flowering.

When the weather starts to warm, begin mulching broad-leaved evergreens and drought-sensitive trees and shrubs.

Layer or take softwood cuttings of trees and shrubs you wish to propagate.

Watch for signs of pests and disease; take prompt action when you notice symptoms.

Summer. Prune and deadhead flowering shrubs when they finish blooming.

Water newly planted trees and shrubs regularly in dry weather; water established plants when they need it.

Be sure drought-sensitive trees and shrubs are well mulched.

Watch for signs of pests and disease; take prompt action if you notice any symptoms.

Take softwood cuttings of trees and shrubs you wish to propagate.

Autumn. Water new trees and shrubs regularly in dry weather; water established plants as needed.

Fertilize trees and shrubs growing in nutrient-poor soils when temperatures begin to moderate after summer's heat.

Watch for signs of pests and disease; take prompt action if you notice any symptoms.

Wrap the trunks of young trees to prevent sunscald.

When deciduous trees and shrubs drop their leaves, take hardwood cuttings of those you wish to propagate.

Winter. Wrap trunks of young trees with tree wrap to prevent sunscald.

Water newly planted trees and shrubs in dry weather; water established plants when necessary.

Take hardwood cuttings from dormant trees and shrubs you wish to propagate.

Check for signs of pests and disease; take prompt action if you notice any symptoms.

In late winter, prune deciduous trees and shrubs that need it while they are still dormant. Prune broad-leaved evergreens if necessary. If you must prune conifers to adjust their shape, do so while they are still dormant. Prune from subtropical plants any growth that has been damaged by frost.

When the temperature is above 40°F, spray trees and shrubs with dormant oil spray to destroy borers and overwintering cocoons and egg masses of other pests.

Fertilize broad-leaved evergreens in late winter if you did not fertilize last fall.

In dry climates, water trees and shrubs as needed.

TREES AND SHRUBS FOR DIFFERENT REGIONS

Here are some trees and shrubs that are well suited to growing conditions in different parts of the United States.

Trees and Shrubs for Different Regions *(cont'd)*

NORTHEAST (NEW YORK TO MAINE)

Abies, fir
- *A. balsamea*, balsam fir
- *A. concolor*, white fir

Acer, maple
- *A. ginnala*, Amur maple
- *A. griseum*, paperback maple
- *A. pensylvanicum*, striped maple
- *A. rubrum*, red maple
- *A. saccharum*, sugar maple
- *A. spicatum*, mountain maple

Alnus incana, white alder

Aronia spp., chokeberry

Berberis, barberry
- *B. koreana*, Korean barberry
- *B. thunbergii*, Japanese barberry

Betula, birch
- *B. jacquemontii*, white-barked Himalayan birch
- *B. lenta*, sweet birch
- *B. nigra*, river birch
- *B. papyrifera*, paper birch (susceptible to leaf miners and borers)
- *B. populifolia*, gray birch (susceptible to leaf miners and borers)

Carpinus spp., hornbeam

Carya ovata, shagbark hickory

Celtis occidentalis, hackberry

Cercidiphyllum japonicum, katsura tree

Chamaecyparis, false cypress
- *C. lawsoniana*, Lawson false cypress
- *C. obtusa*, Hinoki false cypress
- *C. pisifera*

Chionanthus virginicus, white fringe tree

Cladrastis, yellowwood

Clethra spp., sweet pepperbush

Cornus
- *C. alba*, Tatarian dogwood
- *C. controversa*, giant dogwood
- *C. mas*, Cornelian cherry
- *C. sanguinea*, bloodtwig dogwood
- *C. sericea*, red-osier dogwood

Crataegus spp., hawthorn

Deutzia gracilis, slender deutzia

Elaeagnus angustifolia, Russian olive

Euonymus alatus, burning bush

Evodia danielii, bebe tree

Fagus grandifolia, American beech

Forsythia
- *F.* × *intermedia*, border forsythia
- *F. mandchurica*
- *F. ovata*, early forsythia
- *F. suspensa*, weeping forsythia

Fothergilla
- *F. gardenii*, dwarf fothergilla
- *F. major*, large fothergilla

Fraxinus, ash
- *F. americana*, white ash
- *F. pennsylvanica*, green ash

Hydrangea
- *H. arborescens*. smooth hydrangea
- *H. paniculata* 'Grandiflora', peegee hydrangea
- *H. quercifolia*, oakleaf hydrangea

Ilex verticillata, winterberry

Juniperus, juniper
- *J. chinensis*, Chinese juniper
- *J. communis*, common juniper
- *J. sabina*, Savin juniper
- *J. scopulorum*, Rocky Mountain juniper
- *J. virginiana*, eastern red cedar

Kerria japonica

Kolkwitzia amabilis, beautybush

Larix laricina, larch, eastern tamarack

Ledum groenlandicum, Labrador tea

Liriodendron tulipifera, tulip tree

Malus spp., flowering crab apple. Hardy hybrids include Dolgo, Hopa, Mary Potter, Radiant, Royalty, and Flame.

Nyssa sylvatica, black gum, tupelo

Philadelphus spp., mock orange

Physocarpus opulifolius, ninebark
Picea, spruce
  P. abies, Norway spruce
  P. glauca, white spruce
  P. pungens, blue spruce
  P. rubra, red spruce
Pinus, pine
  P. banksiana, jack pine
  P. cembra, Swiss stone pine
  P. densiflora, Japanese red pine
  P. mugo, mugo pine
  P. parviflora, Japanese white pine
  P. strobus, white pine
  P. sylvestris, Scotch pine
Populus, poplar
  P. alba, white poplar
  P. deltoides, eastern cottonwood
  P. tremuloides, quaking aspen
Potentilla fruticosa, bush cinquefoil
Prunus
  P. americana, Newport plum
  P. maritima, beach plum (coastal areas)
  P. tomentosa, Manchu cherry
  P. virginiana, Canada red cherry
Quercus, oak
  Q. alba, white oak
  Q. bicolor, swamp white oak
  Q. macrocarpa, bur oak
  Q. rubra, red oak
Rhamnus spp., buckthorn
Rhododendron, azalea and rhododendron
  R. canadense, rhodora
  R. catawbiense
  Exbury Hybrid azaleas
  Gable Hybrid azaleas
  Girard Hybrid azaleas
  R. maximum, rosebay rhododendron
  Northern Lights Hybrid azaleas
  R. periclymenoides, pinxterbloom azalea
  Weston Hybrid azaleas
Rhus glabra, smooth sumac
Ribes alpinum, alpine currant
Robinia pseudoacacia, black locust
Rosa, rose
  R. blanda, meadow rose
  R. carolina, pasture rose
  R. foetida, Austrian brier rose
  R. rubrifolia, redleaf rose
  R. rugosa, saltspray rose
  R. spinosissima, Scotch rose
  R. virginiana, Virginia rose
Rubus odoratus, flowering raspberry
Salix, willow
  S. alba, white willow
  S. caprea, goat willow
  S. pentandra, laurel willow
  S. purpurea, purple osier willow
Sassafras albidum
Sorbus, mountain ash
  S. alnifolia, Korean mountain ash
  S. aucuparia, rowan
  S. decora, American ash
Spiraea
  S. × *bumalda*
  S. nipponica 'Snowmound', bridal wreath
  S. × *vanhouttei*, bridal wreath
Stewartia pseudocamellia, Japanese stewartia
Symphoricarpos spp., snowberry
Syringa spp., lilac
Tamarix ramosissima, five-stamen tamarisk
Taxus canadensis, Canadian yew
Thuja occidentalis, American arborvitae
Tilia
  T. americana, basswood, linden
  T. cordata, littleleaf linden
  T. × *euchlora*, Crimean linden
  T. tomentosa, silver linden
Tsuga canadensis, Canadian hemlock
Vaccinium
  V. angustifolium, lowbush blueberry
  V. macrocarpon, cranberry

(continued)

Trees and Shrubs for Different Regions *(cont'd)*

Viburnum

- *V. americanum*
- *V. × bodnantense*
- *V. × burkwoodii*, Burkwood viburnum
- *V. carlesii*, Korean spice viburnum
- *V. dentatum*, arrowwood
- *V. opulus*, European cranberry bush
- *V. plicatum* var. *tomentosum*, doublefile viburnum
- *V. sieboldii*, Siebold viburnum
- *V. trilobum*, American cranberry bush

MID-ATLANTIC/PIEDMONT (PENNSYLVANIA TO VIRGINIA, WEST TO INDIANA AND KENTUCKY)

Abelia × grandiflora, glossy abelia

Acer, maple

- *A buergeranum*, trident maple
- *A. ginnala*, Amur maple
- *A. griseum*, paperbark maple
- *A. palmatum*, Japanese maple
- *A. rubrum*, red maple
- *A. saccharum*, sugar maple

Aesculus × carnea, red horse chestnut

Amelanchier

- *A. arborea*, downy serviceberry
- *A. laevis*, Allegheny serviceberry

Aronia spp., chokeberry

Berberis, barberry

- *B. × chenaultii*
- *B. julianae*, wintergreen barberry
- *B. thunbergii*, Japanese barberry
- *B. triacanthophora*, threespine barberry
- *B. verruculosa*, warty barberry

Betula, birch

- *B. jacquemontii*, whitebarked Himalayan birch
- *B. lenta*, sweet birch
- *B. nigra*, river birch
- *B. papyrifera*, paper birch (susceptible to leaf miners and borers)
- *B. populifolia*, gray birch (susceptible to leaf miners and borers)

Buddleia spp., butterfly bush

Buxus, boxwood

- *B. microphylla*, littleleaf boxwood
- *B. sempervirens*, common boxwood

Carpinus caroliniana, ironwood

Carya ovata, shagbark hickory

Caryopteris × clandonensis, blue mist shrub

Celtis occidentalis, hackberry

Cercidiphyllum japonicum, Japanese katsura tree

Chamaecyparis, false cypress

- *C. lawsoniana*, Lawson false cypress
- *C. obtusa*, Hinoki false cypress
- *C. pisifera*, sandra false cypress

Chionanthus virginicus, white fringe tree

Cladrastis lutea, yellowwood

Cornus, dogwood

- *C. alba,* Tatarian dogwood
- *C. controversa*, giant dogwood
- *C. florida*, flowering dogwood
- *C. kousa*, kousa dogwood
- *C. mas*, cornelian cherry
- *C. × rutgersensis*, hybrid dogwood
- *C. sericea*, red-osier dogwood

Corylus, hazel

- *C. avellana* 'Contorta', Harry Lauder's walking stick
- *C. colurna*, Turkish hazel

Cotinus obovatus, American smoke tree

Crataegus, hawthorn

- *C. crus-galli*, cockspur hawthorn
- *C. phaenopyrum*, Washington thorn
- *C. viridis*, green hawthorn

Deutzia gracilis, slender deutzia

Elaeagnus

- *E. angustifolia*, Russian olive
- *E. pungens*, thorny elaeagnus

Enkianthus campanulatus, redvein enkianthus
Evodia danielii, bebe tree
Fagus, beech
- *F. grandifolia*, American beech
- *F. sylvatica*, European beech

Forsythia
- *F. × intermedia*, border forsythia
- *F. ovata*, early forsythia
- *F. suspensa*, weeping forsythia

Fothergilla
- *F. gardenii*, dwarf fothergilla
- *F. major*, large fothergilla
- *F. monticola*

Franklinia alatamaha
Fraxinus, ash
- *F. americana*, white ash
- *F. pennsylvanica*, green ash

Ginkgo biloba, maidenhair tree (plant male trees only; females produce smelly fruit)
Gleditsia triacanthos var. *inermis*, thornless honey locust
Gymnocladus dioica, Kentucky coffee tree
Halesia carolina, Carolina silverbell
Hovenia dulcis, Japanese raisin tree
Hydrangea
- *H. arborescens*, smooth hydrangea
- *H. macrophylla*, bigleaf hydrangea
- *H. paniculata*, peegee hydrangea
- *H. quercifolia*, oakleaf hydrangea

Ilex, holly
- *I. aquifolium*, English holly
- *I. × attenuata*, hybrid holly
- *I. × meserveae*, Meserve hybrid hollies
- *I. opaca*, American holly
- *I. verticillata*, winterberry

Koelreuteria
- *K. bipinnata*, Chinese flame tree
- *K. paniculata*, goldenrain tree

Leucothoe fontanesiana, fetterbush, drooping leucothoe
Liquidambar styraciflua, American sweet gum
Liriodendron tulipifera, tulip tree
Magnolia
- *M. denudata*, Yunan magnolia
- *M. × soulangiana*, saucer magnolia
- *M. tomentosa*, star magnolia
- *M. virginiana*, sweet bay magnolia

Mahonia bealei, leatherleaf mahonia
Malus, flowering crab apple, many species and cultivars, including:
- *M. floribunda*, Japanese flowering crab apple
- *M. hupehensis*, tea crab apple
- *M. sargentii*, Sargent crab apple

Nyssa sylvatica, tupelo
Osmanthus heterophyllus, hollyleaf osmanthus
Oxydendrum arboreum, sourwood
Paxistima canbyi
Philadelphus spp., mock orange
Pieris
- *P. floribunda*
- *P. japonica*, Japanese pieris

Pistacia chinensis, Chinese pistachio
Platanus × acerifolia, London plane tree
Poncirus trifoliata, hardy orange
Populus deltoides, eastern cottonwood
Potentilla fruticosa, bush cinquefoil
Prunus, oriental flowering cherries
- *P. serrulata*, Japanese flowering cherry
- *P. subhirtella*, Higan cherry
- *P. × yedoensis*, Yoshino cherry (the famous cherry blossoms of Washington, D.C.)

Pyracantha spp., firethorn
Pyrus calleryana, callery pear
Quercus, oak
- *Q. alba*, white oak
- *Q. bicolor*, swamp white oak
- *Q. imbricaria*, shingle oak
- *Q. macrocarpa*, bur oak
- *Q. phellos*, willow oak
- *Q. rubra*, red oak
- *Q. shumardii*, Shumard oak

(continued)

Trees and Shrubs for Different Regions *(cont'd)*

Rhododendron, azalea and rhododendron

- *R. arborescens*, sweet azalea
- *R. calendulaceum*, flame azalea
- *R. carolinianum*, Carolina rhododendron
- *R. catawbiense*, catawba rhododendron
- Dexter Hybrid rhododendrons
- *R. fortunei*
- Gable Hybrid azaleas
- Ghent Hybrid azaleas
- Glenn Dale Hybrid azaleas
- Knap Hill Hybrid azaleas
- *R. mucronulatum*, Korean rhododendron
- North Tisbury Hybrid azaleas
- P. J. M. Hybrid rhododendrons
- Robin Hill Hybrid azaleas
- *R. schlippenbachii*, royal azalea
- *R. yakusimanum*

Salix, willow

- *S. alba*, white willow
- *S. babylonica*, weeping willow
- *S. purpurea*, purple osier willow

Sassafras albidum

Sophora japonicus, Japanese pagoda tree

Sorbus, mountain ash

- *S. alnifolia*, Korean mountain ash
- *S. aucuparia*, rowan

Stewartia pseudocamellia, Japanese stewartia

Styrax

- *S. japonicus*, Japanese snowbell
- *S. obassia*, fragrant snowbell

Syringa spp., lilacs

Tilia, linden

- *T. cordata*, littleleaf linden
- *T.* × *euchlora*, Crimean linden
- *T. tomentosa*, silver linden

Ulmus parviflora, lacebark elm

Viburnum

- *V. acerifolium*, mapleleaf viburnum
- *V.* × *burkwoodii*, Burkwood viburnum
- *V.* × *carlecephalum*, fragrant snowball
- *V. carlesii*, Korean spice viburnum
- *V. dilatatum*, linden viburnum
- *V.* × *juddii*
- *V. opulus*, European cranberry bush
- *V. plicatum* var. *tomentosum*, doublefile viburnum
- *V. sieboldii*, Siebold viburnum

Vitex agnus-castus, chaste tree

Zelkova serrata, Japanese zelkova

SOUTHEAST (NORTH CAROLINA TO FLORIDA, WEST TO ARKANSAS AND LOUISIANA)

*Indicates plants suited to southern Florida and the warmest parts of the Southeast

Abelia × *grandiflora*, glossy abelia

*Acacia baileyana**, Cootamundra wattle

Acer, maple

- *A. buergeranum*, trident maple
- *A. ginnala*, Amur maple
- *A. griseum*, paperbark maple
- *A. japonica*, full moon maple
- *A. palmatum*, Japanese maple
- *A. rubrum*, red maple
- *A. saccharum* 'Legacy', sugar maple

Aesculus × *carnea*, red horse chestnut

Albizia julibrissin, silk tree

Amelanchier spp., serviceberry

Arbutus unedo, strawberry tree

Aucuba japonica, gold dust plant

Berberis, barberry

- *B. julianae*
- *B. thunbergii*, Japanese barberry

Betula nigra, river birch

*Bougainvillea** spp. and hybrids

Buddleia spp., butterfly bush

Buxus spp., boxwood

*Callistemon citrinus**, lemon bottlebrush

Camellia

- *C. japonica*
- *C. sasanqua*

Carpinus caroliniana, ironwood
Carya ovata, shagbark hickory
Caryopteris × clandonensis, blue mist shrub
*Cassia fistula**, crown of gold
Cedrus spp., cedar
Celtis occidentalis, hackberry
Cephalotaxus spp., Japanese plum yew
Cercidiphyllum japonicum, katsura tree
Cercis
    C. canadensis, eastern redbud
    C. chinensis, Chinese redbud
Chaenomeles spp., flowering quince
Chionanthus virginicus, white fringe tree
*Chorisia speciosa**, floss-silk tree
*Cinnamomum camphora**, camphor tree
Cladrastis kentukea (*C. lutea*), yellowwood
Clethra alnifolia, sweet pepperbush
Cornus, dogwood
    C. florida, flowering dogwood
    C. kousa, kousa dogwood
Cotinus obovatus, American smoke tree
× *Cupressocyparis leylandii*, Leyland cypress
Daphne odora, winter daphne
Diervilla sessilifolia, southern bush honeysuckle
Elaeagnus pungens, thorny elaeagnus
*Eucalyptus ficifolia**, red-flowering gum
Euonymus
    E. alatus, burning bush
    E. japonicus
Euscaphis japonica
Evodia danielii, bebe tree
Fagus grandifolia, American beech
Fatsia japonica, Japanese aralia
Feijoa sellowiana, pineapple guava
Fothergilla gardenii
Franklinia alatamaha
Fraxinus, ash
    F. americana, white ash
    F. pennsylvanica, green ash
Gardenia jasminoides
Genista spp., broom
Ginkgo biloba, maidenhair tree (plant male trees only)
Halesia carolina, Carolina silverbell
Hamamelis virginiana, common witch hazel
Hibiscus
    H. rosa-sinensis
    H. syriacus, rose of Sharon
Hovenia dulcis, Japanese raisin tree
Hydrangea
    H. macrophylla, bigleaf hydrangea
    H. quercifolia, oakleaf hydrangea
Ilex, holly
    I. aquifolium, English holly
    I. × attenuata, hybrid holly
    I. cornuta, Chinese holly
    I. opaca, American holly
    I. verticillata, winterberry
    I. vomitoria, yaupon
Illicium floridanum, Florida anise tree
Itea virginica, sweetspire
*Jacaranda mimosifolia**
Jasminum spp., jasmine
Juniperus, juniper
    J. chinensis, Chinese juniper
    J. communis, common juniper
    J. conferta, shore juniper
Kalmia latifolia, mountain laurel
Koelreuteria
    K. bipinnata, Chinese flame tree
    K. paniculata, goldenrain tree
Lagerstroemia indica, crape myrtle
Lantana camara
Ligustrum, privet
    L. japonicum, Japanese privet
    L. sinense, Chinese privet
Liquidambar styraciflua, sweet gum
Liriodendron tulipifera, tulip tree
Magnolia
    M. denudata, Yulan magnolia
    M. grandiflora, southern magnolia

(continued)

Trees and Shrubs for Different Regions *(cont'd)*

- *M.* × *soulangiana*, saucer magnolia
- *M. tomentosa*, star magnolia
- *M. virginiana*, sweet bay magnolia

Malus, many species and cultivars, flowering crab apple

- *M.* 'Callaway' is especially good for the southeast

Myrica cerifera, southern wax myrtle

Nerium oleander, oleander

Nyssa sylvatica, black gum, tupelo

Osmanthus

- *O. fragrans*, sweet olive
- *O. heterophyllus*, holly osmanthus

Oxydendrum arboreum, sourwood

Photinia serrulata, Chinese photinia

Picea pungens 'Foxtail', foxtail Colorado spruce

Pieris

- *P. floribunda*
- *P. japonica*, Japanese pieris

Pinus, pine

- *P. taeda*, loblolly pine
- *P. thunbergiana*, Japanese black pine

Pistacia chinensis, Chinese pistachio

Pittosporum tobira

Platanus × *acerifolia*, London plane tree

Poncirus trifoliata, hardy orange

Populus deltoides, cottonwood

Prunus

- *P. caroliniana*, Carolina cherry laurel
- *P. mume*, Japanese apricot
- *P. persica*, flowering peach
- *P. serrulata*, Japanese flowering cherry

Pyracantha spp., firethorn

Quercus, oak

- *Q. agrifolia**, Coast live oak
- *Q. alba*, white oak
- *Q. bicolor*, swamp white oak
- *Q. falcata*, southern red oak
- *Q. imbricaria*, shingle oak
- *Q. myrsinifolia*, Chinese evergreen oak
- *Q. phellos*, willow oak
- *Q. virginiana**, live oak

Raphiolepis indica, Indian hawthorn

Rhamnella franguloides

Rhododendron, azalea and rhododendron

- Belgian Indica hybrid azaleas*
- *R calendulaceum*, flame azalea
- *R. catawbiense*, catawba rhododendron
- Dexter Hybrid rhododendrons
- Glenn Dale Hybrid azaleas
- Kurume Hybrid azaleas
- Pennington Hybrid azaleas
- *R. prunifolium*, plumleaf azalea
- Robin Hill Hybrid azaleas
- Southern Indica Hybrid azaleas
- *R. yakusimanum*

Rhus spp., sumac

Rosa, rose

- *R. banksiae*, Lady Banks rose
- *R. laevigata*, Cherokee rose
- *R. wichuraiana*, memorial rose

Rosmarinus officinalis, rosemary

Sambucus canadensis, American elder

Sassafras albidum

*Tabebuia chrysotricha**, golden trumpet tree

Taxodium distichum, bald cypress

Ulmus parviflora, lacebark elm

Vaccinium ashei, rabbiteye blueberry

Viburnum

- *V.* × *burkwoodii*, burkwood viburnum
- *V. davidii*, david viburnum
- *V. japonicum*, Japanese viburnum
- *V. odoratissimum*
- *V. prunifolium*, blackhaw viburnum

Yucca gloriosa, Spanish dagger

Zelkova serrata, Japanese zelkova

Zenobia pulverulenta, dusty zenobia

MIDWEST (NORTH DAKOTA TO OKLAHOMA)

*Indicates plants that can withstand the cold, dry conditions of the upper Midwest

Abelia × *grandiflora*, glossy abelia
Acer, maple
- *A. buergeranum*, trident maple
- *A. ginnala**, Amur maple
- *A. griseum*, paperbark maple
- *A. japonicum*, full moon maple
- *A. palmatum*, Japanese maple
- *A. rubrum*, red maple
- *A. saccharinum**, silver maple
- *A. saccharum**, sugar maple

Aesculus
- *A.* × *carnea*, red horse chestnut
- *A. parviflora*, bottlebrush buckeye

*Amelanchier alnifolia**
Aronia, chokeberry
- *A. arbutifolia*, red chokeberry
- *A. melanocarpa*, black chokeberry

Baccharis halimifolia, groundsel bush
Betula, birch
- *B. nigra*, river birch
- *B. papyrifera**, paper birch
- *B. pendula**, European white birch

Buxus spp., boxwood
Callicarpa spp., beautyberry
Calluna vulgaris, Scotch heather
Calycanthus floridus, Carolina allspice
Carpinus caroliniana, ironwood
Carya ovata, shagbark hickory
Caryopteris × *clandonensis*, blue mist shrub
Celtis occidentalis, hackberry
Cercidiphyllum japonicum, katsura tree
Cercis canadensis, eastern redbud
Chaenomeles spp., flowering quince
Chamaecyparis obtusa, Hinoki false cypress
*Chamaedaphne calyculata**, leatherleaf
Chionanthus virginicus, white fringe tree
Cladrastis lutea, yellowwood
Clethra alnifolia, sweet pepperbush
Corylus avellana 'Contorta', Harry Lauder's walking stick
Cotinus obovatus, American smoke tree
*Cotoneaster multiflorus**, many-flowered cotoneaster
Crataegus, hawthorn
- *C. crus-galli*, cockspur hawthorn
- *C. phaenopyrum*, Washington thorn
- *C. viridis*, green hawthorn

Daphne
- *D.* × *burkwoodii*
- *D. cneorum**, garland flower

Deutzia gracilis, slender deutzia
*Elaeagnus angustifolia**, Russian olive
Enkianthus campanulatus, redvein enkianthus
Euonymus alatus, burning bush
Evodia danielii, bebe tree
Fagus grandifolia, American beech
Forsythia
- *F.* × *intermedia*, border forsythia
- *F. ovata**, early forsythia

Fothergilla major, large fothergilla
Fraxinus, ash
- *F. americana**, white ash
- *F. nigra*, black ash
- *F. pennsylvanica**, green ash

Ginkgo biloba, maidenhair tree (plant male trees only; females produce smelly fruit)
Gleditsia triacanthos var. *inermis*, thornless honey locust
Holodiscus discolor, cream bush
Hydrangea
- *H. arborescens**, smooth hydrangea
- *H. paniculata* 'Grandiflora', peegee hydrangea
- *H. quercifolia*, oakleaf hydrangea

Hypericum calycinum, Aaron's beard St.-John's-wort
Ilex, holly
- *I.* × *attenuata*, hybrid holly
- *I. crenata**, Japanese holly
- *I. opaca*, American holly

(continued)

Trees and Shrubs for Different Regions *(cont'd)*

*Juniperus**, juniper, many species are suited to this region, including the following:
- *J. chinensis*, Chinese juniper
- *J. virginiana*, eastern red cedar

*Kalmia** spp., mountain laurel
Koelreuteria paniculata, goldenrain tree
Kolkwitzia amabilis, beautybush
Lagerstroemia indica, crape myrtle (lower Midwest)
*Ledum groenlandicum**, Labrador tea
Leucothoe fontanesiana, fetterbush, drooping leucothoe
Liriodendron tulipifera, tulip tree
Magnolia
- *M. denudata*, Yulan magnolia
- *M. tomentosa*, star magnolia

*Malus**, flowering crab apple, the following are among those suited to the Midwest and upper Midwest:
- *M. baccata* and cultivars
- *M. ioensis* and cultivars
- hybrid cultivars Albright, Arctic Dawn, Dolgo, Donald Wyman (not hardy in the upper Midwest), Flame, Hopa, Pink Cascade, Radiant, Red, Silver, Royalty, Rudolph, Snowdrift, Sparkler, Thunderchild, White Candle

Oxydendrum arboreum, sourwood
*Paxistima canbyi**
Philadelphus coronarius, mock orange
Picea, spruce
- *P. glauca* 'Densata'*, Black Hills spruce
- *P. pungens*, Colorado spruce

Pieris japonica, Japanese pieris
*Pinus**, pine. The following are all hardy in the upper Midwest
- *P. flexilis*, limber pine
- *P. mugo*, mugo pine
- *P. ponderosa*, western yellow pine
- *P. resinosa*, red pine
- *P. sylvestris*, Scotch pine

Populus, poplar
- *P. canescens**, gray poplar
- *P. deltoides*, eastern cottonwood
- *P. tremula* 'Erecta'*, European aspen
- *P. tremuloides**, quaking aspen

*Potentilla fruticosa**, bush cinquefoil
*Prunus**, the following are all hardy in the upper Midwest
- *P. maackii*, Amur chokecherry
- *P. tomentosa*, Manchu cherry
- *P. virginiana*, chokecherry

Pseudolarix amabilis, golden larch
Pyracantha spp., firethorn
Pyrus calleryana, callery pear
Quercus, oak
- *Q. alba**, white oak
- *Q. macrocarpa**, bur oak
- *Q. rubra*, red oak

Rhododendron, azaleas and rhododendron
- *R. carolinianum*, Carolina rhododendron
- *R. catawbiense**, catawba rhododendron
- Dexter Hybrid rhododendrons
- Exbury Hybrid azaleas
- Gable Hybrid azaleas
- Ghent hybrid azaleas
- *R. japonicum*, Japanese azalea
- *R. maximum*, rosebay rhododendron
- *R. mucronulatum*, Korean rhododendron
- P. J. M. Hybrid rhododendrons*
- *R. schlippenbachii*, royal azalea

Ribes odoratum, flowering currant
Rosa, rose
- *R. rugosa**, saltspray rose

Salix discolor, pussy willow
Sambucus canadensis, American elder
Skimmia spp., Japanese skimmia
Sophora japonica, Japanese pagoda tree
*Sorbus americana**, American mountain ash
Spiraea
- *S. × bumalda**
- *S. prunifolia*, bridal wreath
- *S. × vanhouttei*, bridal wreath

*Staphylea trifolia**, bladdernut

Syringa, lilac

- *S. meyeri**, Meyer lilac
- *S. reticulata*, Japanese tree lilac
- *S. vulgaris**, common lilac

*Thuja occidentalis**, American arborvitae

Tilia, linden

- *T. cordata*, littleleaf linden
- *T. × euchlora*, Crimean linden

*Viburnum**, the following are all hardy in the upper Midwest

- *V. carlesii*, Koreanspice viburnum
- *V. dentatum*, arrowwood
- *V. lentago*, nannyberry
- *V. prunifolium*, blackhaw viburnum
- *V. trilobum*, American cranberry bush

Weigela florida

*Yucca**

- *Y. filamentosa*, Adam's needle
- *Y. glauca*, soapweed

MOUNTAIN REGION (MOUNTAINOUS PARTS OF WYOMING TO NEW MEXICO AND ARIZONA)

*Indicates plants that grow at elevations of 10,000 feet

Acer ginnala, Amur maple

*Caragana arborescens**, Siberian pea shrub

Celtis occidentalis, hackberry

Chaenomeles speciosa, flowering quince

Corylus colurna, Turkish hazel

Cotinus obovatus, American smoke tree

Crataegus viridis, green hawthorn

Elaeagnus angustifolia, Russian olive

Forsythia

- *F. mandchurica*
- *F. ovata*, early forsythia

Gleditsia triacanthos var. *inermis*, thornless honey locust

Juniperus, juniper

- *J. communis*, common juniper
- *J. scopulorum*, Rocky Mountain juniper
- *J. virginiana*, eastern red cedar

Koelreuteria paniculata, goldenrain tree

Larix, larch

- *L. decidua*, European larch
- *L. kaempferi*, Japanese larch
- *L. laricina*, tamarack

*Lonicera tatarica**, Tatarian honeysuckle

Mahonia aquifolium, Oregon grape holly

Philadelphus coronarius, mock orange

Pinus, pine

- *P. cembroides*, Mexican piñon pine
- *P. flexilis*, limber pine

Populus

- *P. deltoides*, eastern cottonwood
- *P. tremuloides*, quaking aspen

*Potentilla fruticosa**, bush cinquefoil

Quercus, oak

- *Q. alba*, white oak
- *Q. macrocarpa*, bur oak
- *Q. rubra*, red oak

Ribes, currant

- *R. aureum*, golden currant
- *R. cereum**, wax currant

Sorbus alnifolia, Korean mountain ash

*Syringa**, lilac

- *S. × persica*, Persian lilac
- *S. vulgaris*, common lilac

Tilia cordata, littleleaf linden

Viburnum

- *V. carlesii*, Koreanspice viburnum
- *V. lantana*, wayfaring tree
- *V. opulus**, European cranberrybush viburnum

SOUTHWEST (TEXAS TO ARIZONA AND NEVADA)

*Indicates plants suitable for desert gardens

Acacia spp.*

Acer, maple

- *A. griseum*, paperbark maple
- *A. japonicum*, full moon maple

(continued)

Trees and Shrubs for Different Regions *(cont'd)*

- *A. macrophyllum*, bigleaf maple
- *A. palmatum*, Dissectum group, cutleaf Japanese maple

Albizia julibrissin, silk tree

Araucaria

- *A. araucana*, monkey-puzzle tree
- *A. heterophylla*, Norfolk Island pine

Arctostaphylos spp., manzanita

Baccharis halimifolia, groundsel bush

*Bauhinia variegata**, orchid tree

Bougainvillea spp.*

Buddleia davidii, butterfly bush

Buxus spp., boxwood

Caesalpinia spp.* (Poinciana), bird of paradise bush, dwarf poinciana

Callicarpa japonica, beautyberry

Callistemon spp.*, bottlebrush

Calocedrus decurrens, incense cedar

Calycanthus

- *C. floridus*, Carolina allspice
- *C. occidentalis*, spicebush

Camellia

- *C. japonica*
- *C. sasanqua*

Carissa microcarpa, natal plum

Caryopteris × *clandonensis*, blue mist shrub

Cassia spp.*, senna

Catalpa

- *C. bignonioides*, common catalpa
- *C. speciosa*, western catalpa

Ceanothus spp., wild ceanothus

Cephalanthus occidentalis, buttonbush

Cercidiphyllum japonicum, katsura tree

*Cercidium floridum**, palo verde

*Cercis reniformis**, redbud

Cercocarpus

- *C. ledifolius*, mountain mahogany
- *C. montanus*

Chamaecyparis spp., false cypress

*Chilopsis linearis**, desert willow

Cistus spp., rock rose

Cupressus arizonica, Arizona cypress

Erythrina × *bidwillii**, Bidwell coral tree

Eucalyptus spp.

Ficus spp., fig

Fothergilla gardenii

Fouquieria splendens, ocotillo

Fuchsia spp.

Grevillea spp., silk oak

*Hibiscus rosa-sinensis**

Jacaranda mimosifolia

*Jasminum mesnyi**, primrose jasmine

Juniperus spp., juniper

Lantana

- *L. camara**, red or yellow sage
- *L. montevidensis*

*Leucophyllum frutescens**, Texas silverleaf

Magnolia grandiflora, southern magnolia

*Melianthus major**, honeybush

Myrica cerifera, wax myrtle

Nandina domestica, heavenly bamboo

*Nerium oleander**

Olea europaea, olive (many people are allergic to the pollen; the cultivar 'Swan Hill', a.k.a. 'Oblonga', releases only a small amount of pollen)

Parrotia persica, Persian parrotia

Paxistima spp., spindle tree

Philadelphus coronarius, mock orange

Phlomis fruticosa, Jerusalem sage

Phoenix spp., date palm

Photinia serrulata, Chinese photinia

Pieris floribunda

Pinus, pine

- *P. edulis**, piñon pine
- *P. flexilis*, limber pine

*Pistacia chinensis**, Chinese pistachio

Pittosporum tobira, Japanese pittosporum

Populus

- *P.* × *acuminata*, lanceleaf cottonwood
- *P. fremontii**, western cottonwood

*Prosopis glandulosa**, honey mesquite
*Punica granatum**, pomegranate
Pyracantha spp.
Quercus, oak
Q. emoryi
Q. gambelii, Rocky Mountain white oak
Q. shumardii *, Shumard oak
Q. virginiana, live oak
*Rhaphiolepis indica**, Indian hawthorn
Rosa, rose
R. banksiae, Lady Banks rose
R. foetida, Austrian brier
R. harisonii, Harison's yellow rose
R. wichuraiana, memorial rose
Salix, willow
S. discolor, pussy willow
S. matsudania, Hankow willow
Sambucus canadensis, American elder
Sarcococca spp.
*Sophora secundiflora**, mescal bean
Tamarix spp., tamarisk
*Tecoma stans**, yellow trumpet bush
*Tecomaria capensis**, Cape honeysuckle
*Thevetia peruviana**, yellow oleander
Ulmus, elm
*U. crassifolia**, cedar elm
U. parviflora, Chinese elm
Viburnum davidii
Vitex, chaste tree
*V. agnus-castus**
V. negundo
Washingtonia spp. fan palm
Yucca spp.

WEST COAST

*Indicates plants suitable for the Pacific Northwest

Abelia × grandiflora, glossy abelia
*Acacia baileyana**, Cootamundra wattle
*Aesculus × carnea**, red horse chestnut
*Arbutus unedo**, strawberry tree
*Arctostaphylos**, manzanita
A. columbiana, hairy manzanita
A. manzanita, common manzanita
Bauhinia blakeana
*Berberis**, barberry
B. darwinii, Darwin barberry
B. × stenophylla, rosemary barberrry
B. triacanthophora, three-spine barberry
Bougainvillea spp.
Buxus spp.*, boxwood
Calliandra spp., powderpuff
Callicarpa spp.*, beautyberry
Calluna spp.*, heather
Calycanthus spp., Carolina allspice
Camellia spp.*
Carissa spp., natal plum
*Carpenteria californica**, tree anemone
Cephalanthus occidentalis, button bush
Cercidiphyllum japonicum, katsura tree
Chaenomeles spp.*, flowering quince
Chamaecyparis, false cypress
C. lawsoniana, Lawson false cypress
*C. nootkatensis**, Nootka false cypress
Chilopsis linearis, desert willow
*Chionanthus retusus**, white fringe tree
*Choisya ternata**, Mexican orange
Chorisia speciosa, floss-silk tree
Cinnamomum camphora, camphor tree
Cistus, rock rose
Cornus nuttallii, Pacific dogwood
Cotoneaster
*C. lacteus**
C. salicifolius, willowleaf cotoneaster
Cytisus spp.*, broom
*Daphne**
D. cneorum, garland flower
D. odora, winter daphne
D. retusa
*Davidia involucrata**, clove tree
*Enkianthus campanulatus**, redvein enkianthus

(continued)

Trees and Shrubs for Different Regions *(cont'd)*

Erica spp. *, heath
Erythrina spp., coral tree
Escallonia spp.
Eucalyptus spp. *
Eucryphia × *nymansensis* *
Fatsia japonica, Japanese aralia
Feijoa sellowiana, pineapple guava
Ficus spp., fig
Franklinia alatamaha
Fraxinus spp., ash
Fremontodendron californicum, flannelbush
Fuchsia spp.
Garrya elliptica *, silk tassel
Gaultheria shallon, salal
Genista spp. *, broom
Ginkgo biloba *, maidenhair tree
Hebe spp.
Hibiscus
  H. rosa-sinensis
  H. syriacus *, rose of Sharon
Hovenia dulcis, Japanese raisin tree
Hydrangea *
  H. macrophylla
  H. paninculata 'Grandiflora', peegee hydrangea
  H. quercifolia, oakleaf hydrangea
Ilex *, holly
  I. × *altaclarensis*, camellia-leaved holly
  I. aquifolium, American holly
  I. crenata, Japanese holly
Jacaranda mimosifolia
Jasminum spp., jasmine
Juniperus spp., juniper
Kalmia spp. *, mountain laurel
Koelreuteria bipinnata *, Chinese flame tree
Laburnum spp., goldenchain tree
Lagerstroemia spp., crape myrtle
Lantana
  L. camara, yellow sage
  L. montevidensis
Laurus nobilis, sweetbay
Leptospermum spp., tea tree
Ligustrum japonicum *, Japanese privet
Lithocarpus densiflorus, tanbark oak
Magnolia grandiflora, southern magnolia
Mahonia aquifolium *, Oregon grape holly
Malus floribunda *, Japanese flowering crab apple
Metasequoia glyptostroboides *, dawn redwood
Michelia figo, banana shrub
Myrtus communis *, myrtle
Nandina domestica, heavenly bamboo
Nerium oleander, oleander
Olea europaea, olive
Osmanthus heterophyllus *, holly osmanthus
Paxistima myrsinites *, Oregon boxwood
Pernettya mucronata *
Philadelphus spp. *, mock orange
Phoenix spp., date palm
Photinia *
  P. × *fraseri*
  P. serrulata, Japanese photinia
Pieris spp. *
Pinus, pine
  P. attenuata *, knobcone pine
  P. bungeana, lacebark pine
  P. contorta var. *latifolia*, lodgepole pine
  P. monticola, western white pine
  P. mugo *, mugho pine
  P. radiata, Monterey pine
  P. thunbergiana *, Japanese black pine
Pistacia chinensis *, Chinese pistachio
Pittosporum tobira
Podocarpus macrophyllus, maki
Potentilla fruticosa, bush cinquefoil
Prosopis glandulosa, honey mesquite
Prunus laurocerasus *, cherry laurel
Pyracantha spp.
Quercus, oak
  Q. agrifolia *, Coast live oak
  Q. coccinea, scarlet oak
  Q. douglasii, blue oak
  Q. palustris, pin oak

Rhaphiolepis
- *R. indica*, Indian hawthorn
- *R. umbellata*, yeddo rhaphiolepis

*Rhododendron**, azalea and rhododendron
- *R. luteum*
- *R. schlippenbachii*, sweet azalea
- *R. vaseyi*, pinkshell azalea
- *R. yakusimanum*
- *R. yunnanense*

*Ribes odoratum**, flowering currant

Rosa, rose
- *R. banksiae*, Lady Banks rose
- *R. foetida*, Austrian brier
- *R. harisonii*, Harison's yellow rose
- *R. wichuraiana*, memorial rose

Salix, willow
- *S. discolor*, pussy willow
- *S. gracilistyla*, rosegold pussywillow
- *S. matsudana*, Hankow willow

Sambucus canadensis, American elder

*Sarcococca**
- *S. confusa*, sweet box
- *S. hookerana*

Solanum rantonnetii, blue potato bush

Sophora secundiflora, mescal bean

Spartium junceum, Spanish broom

Spiraea spp.

Tabebuia chrysotricha, golden trumpet tree

Tecomaria capensis, Cape honeysuckle

*Thuja plicata**, western red cedar

Tibouchina urvilleana, glory bush

*Umbellularia californica**, California laurel

*Viburnum**, many species

Vitex negundo, chaste tree

Xylosma congestum

Yucca spp.

TREES AND SHRUBS FOR SEASONAL INTEREST

SPRING

Abeliophyllum distichum, Korean forsythia, white forsythia: Fragrant white flowers resembling those of true forsythia in mid-spring. Zones 4–8.

Acer ginnala, Amur maple: Fragrant flowers. Zones 2–8.

Aesculus spp., horse chestnut: Upright clusters of white, pinkish, or red flowers in spring. Zones 3–7.

Amelanchier arborea, serviceberry: Clusters of white flowers in early spring. Zones 4–9.

Aronia arbutifolia, red chokeberry: White flowers. Zones 4–9.

Buddleia alternifolia, fountain buddleia: Clusters of small purple flowers in mid-spring. Zones 5–9.

Callistemon citrinus, lemon bottlebrush: Red flowers consisting mostly of clusters of bright red stamens. Zones 9–11.

Calycanthus floridus, Carolina allspice: Aromatic red-brown flowers in mid-spring. Zones 4–9.

(continued)

Trees and Shrubs for Seasonal Interest *(cont'd)*

Camellia spp.: Large, waxy flowers of rosy red, pink, or white in early spring, fall, or winter. Zones 7–9.

Caragana spp., pea shrub: Yellow pealike flowers in mid-spring. Hardiness varies; many are hardy in Zones 3–7.

Ceanothus spp., California lilac: Clusters of blue-violet flowers in early to mid-spring. Hardiness varies with species.

Cercidium floridum, palo verde: Yellow flowers spring to early summer. Zones 7–11.

Cercis canadensis, redbud: Red-violet buds opening to purplish pink flowers in early spring. Zones 4–9.

Chaenomeles spp., flowering quince: Red, pink or white flowers in early spring. Zones 4–8.

Chionanthus virginicus, white fringetree: Panicles of small, white to greenish, fringelike flowers in late spring. Zones 3–9.

Cinnamomum camphora, camphor tree: Clusters of fragrant greenish white flowers in mid-spring. Zones 9–11.

Cladrastis kentuckea, yellowwood: Drooping clusters of fragrant white flowers in late spring to early summer. Zones 4–8.

Cornus spp., dogwood: Showy star-shaped white, pink, or pale yellow bracts look like flowers in spring.

- *C. mas*, cornelian cherry: Fuzzy clusters of little yellow flowers in early spring. Zones 4–8.

Cotoneaster multiflorus, many-flowered cotoneaster: Clusters of white flowers in mid-spring. Zones 3–7.

Corylopsis spp., winter hazel: Drooping clusters of small, mildly fragrant yellow flowers in early spring. Zones 5 or 6–8.

Corylus colurna, Turkish hazel: Drooping catkins in early spring. Zones 4–7.

Crataegus spp., hawthorn: White, red, or pink flowers in late spring. Hardiness varies with species.

Cytisus, broom

- *C.* × *praecox*, Warminster broom: Pale yellow flowers in late spring. Zones 7–9.
- *C. scoparius*, Scotch broom: Yellow flowers in late spring. Zones 6–8.

Daphne

D. × *burkwoodii*, Burkwood daphne: White flowers flushed with pink in mid-spring. Zones 4–8.

D. cneorum, garland flower: Clusters of small, fragrant pink or red flowers in mid-spring. Zones 4–7.

D. mezereum, February daphne: Fragrant rosy purple flowers in early spring. Zones 4–8.

Davidia spp., dove tree: Showy white bracts in mid to late spring look like birds or handkerchiefs perched on the branches. Zones 6–8.

Deutzia gracilis, slender deutzia: Clusters of white flowers in late spring. Zones 4–8.

Dirca palustris, leatherwood: Yellow flowers in early spring. Zones 4–9.

Elaeagnus angustifolia, Russian olive: Fragrant white flowers. Zones 2–7.

Enkianthus campanulatus, redvein enkianthus: Clusters of small, bell-shaped yellow or orange flowers veined with red, in mid to late spring. Zones 4–7.

Forsythia, numerous species and cultivars: Golden yellow flowers in early spring. Hardiness varies with species.

Fothergilla gardenii: Fluffy clusters of small white flowers in early to mid-spring. Zones 5–8.

Fremontodendron californicum, flannel bush: Orange-yellow flowers. Zones 7–11.

Halesia carolina, Carolina silverbell: Small, bell-shaped white flowers dangle from the branches in spring. Zones 4–8.

Hamamelis spp., witch hazel: Fragrant, ribbony yellow or orange flowers in late winter or very early spring. Hardiness varies; most are hardy in Zones 5–8.

Jasminum nudiflorum, winter jasmine: Small yellow flowers (not fragrant) in late winter to early spring. Zones 5 or 6–10.

Kalmia latifolia, mountain laurel: Clusters of pink or white flowers in late spring to early summer. Zones 4–9.

Kerria japonica, Japanese kerria: Yellow flowers in late spring. Zones 4–9.

Kolkwitzia amabilis, beautybush: Small, bell-shaped blossoms of soft pink in late spring or early summer. Zones 4–8.

Laburnum × *watereri*: Golden chain tree, long clusters of yellow flowers in late spring or early summer. Zones 5–7.

(continued)

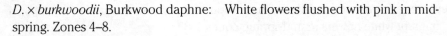

Trees and Shrubs for Seasonal Interest *(cont'd)*

Leucothoe fontanesiana, fetterbush, drooping leucothoe: Hanging clusters of fragrant white flowers in mid-spring. Zones 5–8.

Magnolia spp.: Large flowers, white, pink, or reddish purple in early to mid-spring. Evergreen species bloom in late spring or summer. Hardiness varies with species.

Malus, flowering crab apple: Pink or white flowers, many opening from red buds, in mid to late spring. Hardiness varies with species.

Paulownia spp., empress tree: Large clusters of fragrant, light purple flowers similar to foxgloves in mid-spring. Zones 5–9.

Philadelphus spp., mock orange: Clusters of white flowers, scented in some varieties, in late spring. Zones 4 or 5–8.

Photinia spp.: Clusters of white flowers in mid-spring. Hardiness varies with species.

Pieris spp.: Drooping clusters of white flowers in mid-spring. Hardiness varies with species.

Poncirus trifoliata, hardy orange: Small white flowers in early spring. Zones 5–9.

Potentilla fruticosa, bush cinquefoil: Yellow, ivory, or white flowers in spring. Zones 2–7.

Prunus spp., flowering cherry: Trees are covered with pink or white flowers in early spring. Hardiness varies with species.

Prunus spp., flowering plums and peaches: Pink or white flowers in early spring. Hardiness varies with species.

Prunus glandulosa, flowering almond: Clusters of many-petaled pink or white flowers in mid-spring. Zones 4–8.

Pyrus calleryana, callery pear, Bradford pear: Clusters of small white flowers cover the trees in early to mid-spring. Zones 5–8.

Rhododendron spp., azaleas and rhododendrons: Spring flowers in shades of red, pink, white, yellow, or orange; color and time of bloom depends on species and cultivar. Hardiness varies.

Rhodotypos scandens, jetbead: White flowers in late spring. Zones 4–8.

Ribes odoratum, flowering currant: Fragrant yellow flowers in mid-spring. Zones 4–7.

Salix discolor, pussy willow, *S. caprea*, goat willow: Both are grown for their soft, fuzzy, gray-white flower buds in early spring. Zones 4–8.

Skimmia japonica: Faintly fragrant, cream-colored flowers in mid-spring. Zones 4–8.

Sorbus spp., mountain ash: Clusters of white flowers in mid-spring. Zones 3–6 or 7.

Spiraea × *vanhouttei*, bridal wreath: Bushes are covered with small white flowers in mid to late spring. Zones 3–8.

Styrax

S. japonicus, Japanese snowbell: Drooping clusters of slightly fragrant white flowers in late spring. Zones 5–8.

S. obassia, fragrant snowbell: Drooping clusters of fragrant white flowers in mid-spring. Zones 5–8.

Syringa spp., lilac: Upright clusters of deliciously fragrant small flowers, purple, lilac, red-violet, yellow, or white, in late spring. Zones 3–7 or 8.

Tilia cordata, littleleaf linden: Fragrant but inconspicuous flowers in late spring. Zones 3–7.

Viburnum spp.: Clusters of white, greenish, or pinkish flowers, some fragrant, some full and round like snowballs, in mid to late spring. Hardiness varies with species.

SUMMER

Abelia 'Edward Goucher': Purple-pink flowers from early summer until frost. Zones 6–9.

Aesculus parviflora, bottlebrush buckeye: Long clusters of white flowers with prominent pink stamens in early summer. Zones 4–8.

Albizia julibrissin, silk tree: Fluffy round clusters of pink and white flowers with prominent stamens in midsummer. Zones 6–9.

Baccharis halimifolia, groundsel bush: Clusters of white fruits in summer. Zones 5–9.

Buddleia davidii, butterfly bush: Slender clusters of mildly fragrant small flowers in shades of pink, purple, or white, from midsummer to frost. Zones 5–9.

Caesalpinia gilliesii, bird-of-paradise bush: Yellow flowers with red stamens in summer. Zones 9–11.

Callicarpa spp., beautyberry: Small pink, blue, or white flowers in midsummer. Hardiness varies with species.

Calluna vulgaris, Scotch heather: Spikes of small, mostly pink flowers in summer. Zones 4–6.

Caryopteris incana, blue mist shrub: Blue flowers in late summer. Zones 6–9.

(continued)

Trees and Shrubs for Seasonal Interest *(cont'd)*

Catalpa spp.: Clusters of white flowers in late spring to early summer, depending on location. Zones 4 or 5–8.

Ceanothus ovatus, inland ceanothus: Clusters of small white flowers in late spring, red fruit in summer. Zones 4–7.

Cephalanthus occidentalis, button bush: Small white flower clusters in midsummer. Zones 5–10.

Chilopsis linearis, desert willow: Fragrant bell-shaped white to lavender flowers all summer. Zones 8–11.

Chionanthus virginicus, white fringe tree: Develops black berries in late summer. Zones 3–9.

Cistus spp., rock rose: White, rose, or lilac flowers in summer. Zones 8–9.

Clethra alnifolia, sweet pepperbush: Slender clusters of fragrant white flowers in mid to late summer. Zones 3–9.

Cornus spp., dogwood: Red berries in late summmer. Zones 5–9.

Cotinus spp., smokebush: Fluffy fruiting panicles through the summer look like a cloud surrounding the tree. Zones 4 or 5–8.

Cyrilla racemiflora, swamp cyrilla: Hanging clusters of white flowers in summer. Zones 5–11.

Delonix regia, royal poinciana: Clusters of bright red and yellow flowers in summer. Zones 10–11.

Deutzia scabra hybrids, fuzzy deutzia: White or light pink flowers in early summer. Zones 5–8.

Eucalyptus ficifolia, red-flowering gum: Clusters of pink to red flowers in mid to late summer. Zones 9–11.

Evodia danielii, bebe tree: Clusters of small white flowers from early to late summer. Zones 4–8.

Franklinia alatamaha, Franklin tree: Large, fragrant white flowers resembling those of camellias in late summer to fall. Zones 5–8.

Fremontodendron californicum, flannel bush: Large yellow-orange flowers in summer. Zones 9–10.

Hibiscus

H. rosa-sinensis, Chinese hibiscus: Large red, pink, orange, yellow, or white flowers in summer. Zones 10–11.

H. syriacus, rose of Sharon: Red, pink, or white flowers in summer ('Blue Bird' has blue flowers). Zones 5–8.

Hydrangea

H. arborescens, smooth hydrangea: Clusters of white flowers in early summer. Zones 3–9.

H. macrophylla: Round heads of blue or pink flowers in summer. Lacecap varieties have flowerheads consisting of a central disk of small true flowers surrounded by an outer ring of petal-like bracts. Zones 6–9.

H. paniculata 'Grandiflora', peegee hydrangea: Large clusters of white flowers that turn purplish with age, in midsummer. Zones 3–8.

H. quercifolia, oakleaf hydrangea: Large pyramidal clusters of creamy white flowers in midsummer. Zones 5–9.

Hypericum, St.-John's-wort: Yellow buttercup flowers in summer. Hardiness varies with species.

Itea virginica, sweetspire: Spikes of fragrant white flowers in early to midsummer. Zones 5–9.

Jacaranda mimosifolia: Large clusters of lavender-blue flowers from mid-spring to early summer. Zones 9–11.

Koelreuteria

K. bipinnata, Chinese flame tree: Large clusters of fragrant yellow flowers in late summer to early fall. Zones 7–10.

K. paniculata, goldenrain tree: Upright clusters of yellow flowers in midsummer. Zones 5–7.

Kolkwitzia amabilis, beautybush: Pale pink flowers in early summer. Zones 4–8.

Laburnum × watereri, goldenchain tree: Drooping clusters of yellow flowers in early summer. Zones 5–7.

Lagerstroemia indica, crape myrtle: Slender clusters of red, rose, pink, white, purple, or lavender flowers from midsummer to early fall. Zones 7–9.

Liriodendron tulipifera, tulip tree: Pale yellow cup-shaped flowers in early summer; tree only blooms when it reaches maturity, which can take as long as 20 years. Zones 5–9.

Lonicera tatarica, Tatarian honeysuckle: Sweet-scented flowers of white, pale yellow, or pink in early summer, followed by red fruits in midsummer. Zones 3–8.

Magnolia

M. grandiflora, southern magnolia: Large fragrant ivory flowers in late spring and summer. Zones 7–9.

M. virginiana, sweet bay magnolia: Fragrant white flowers in late spring and early summer, and periodically throughout the summer. Zones 5–9.

(continued)

Trees and Shrubs for Seasonal Interest *(cont'd)*

Nerium oleander, oleander: Red, pink, purple, yellow, or white flowers from spring through summer. Zones 8–11.

Oxydendrum arboreum, sourwood: Clusters of small white flowers in midsummer. Zones 5–9.

Philadelphus spp., mock orange: White flowers, some fragrant, in late spring or early summer. Zones 4 or 5–8.

Potentilla fruticosa, shrubby cinquefoil: Yellow buttercup flowers all summer. Zones 2–7.

Rhododendron, azaleas and rhododendrons

R. maximum, rosebay rhododendron: Rosy pink flowers in early summer. Zones 3–7.

R. viscosum, swamp azalea: Fragrant white flowers in early summer. Zones 3–9.

Robinia pseudoacacia, black locust: Hanging clusters of very fragrant white flowers in late spring or early summer. Zones 3–8.

Rosa spp., roses: Red, pink, white, yellow, or orange flowers, many very fragrant, in early to midsummer; some bloom continuously or off and on through the summer. Hardiness varies with species.

Rhus typhina, staghorn sumac: Red fruits in mid to late summer, seed heads in late summer to fall. Zones 3–8.

Sambucus canadensis, American elder: Large clusters of small white flowers in early summer, blue-black fruits in late summer. Zones 3–9.

Sophora japonica, Japanese pagoda tree: Clusters of white flowers in mid to late summer, followed by green pods. Zones 4–8.

Stewartia pseudocamellia: Large, creamy white flowers in summer to early fall. Zones 5–7.

Styrax japonicus, Japanese snowball: Mildly fragrant, bell-shaped white flowers in late spring or early summer. Zones 5–8.

Syringa reticulata, Japanese tree lilac: Large clusters of fragrant white flowers in early summer. Zones 3–7.

Tilia tomentosa, silver linden: Fragrant but inconspicuous ivory flowers in early summer. Zones 4–7.

Vitex agnus-castus, chaste tree: Slender clusters of lavender to purple flowers from midsummer to early fall. Zones 6–9.

Yucca spp.: Tall spikes of bell-shaped white flowers in early to midsummer. Hardiness varies with species.

AUTUMN

Abelia × grandiflora: Bronzy red to purple leaves in fall. Zones 5–9.

Acer, maple

A. campestre, hedge maple: Yellow leaves. Zones 4–8.

A. ginnala, Amur maple: Orange and red leaves. Zones 2–8.

A. griseum, paperbark maple: Dark orange leaves. Zones 4–8.

A. palmatum, Japanese maple: Red or brilliant orange leaves, depending on variety. Zones 5–8.

A. palmatum 'Sango-kaku', coralbark maple: Young stems are bright red-orange in fall and winter. Zones 6–8.

A. rubrum, red maple: Orange and yellow leaves. Zones 3–9.

A. saccharum, sugar maple: Red and orange leaves. Zones 4–8.

Aesculus

A. × carnea, red horse chestnut: Yellow leaves. Zones 4–7.

A. parviflora, bottlebrush buckeye: Yellow leaves. Zones 4–8.

Amelanchier

A. arborea, serviceberry: Red-orange leaves. Zones 4–9.

A. laevis (a.k.a. *A. larmarckii*): Orange leaves. Zones 4–8.

Arbutus

A. unedo, strawberry tree: Red fruit forms in fall, the year after plants bloom, and persists all winter. Zones 7–9.

A. andrachne, madrone: Red-orange fruit in fall, remaining into winter. Zones 8–9.

Aronia arbutifolia, red chokeberry: Orange to red leaves and red fruits. Zones 4–9.

Berberis spp. barberry: Many species have bronze to orange to reddish leaves in fall; small red, yellow, or blue-black fruits persisting into winter. Hardiness varies with species.

B. gilgiana, wildfire barberry: Especially beautiful autumn foliage. Zones 5–7.

Betula, birch

B. nigra, river birch: Yellow leaves. Zones 4–9.

B. pendula, weeping birch: Yellow leaves. Zones 2–6.

B. populifolia, gray birch: Yellow leaves. Zones 3–6.

(continued)

Trees and Shrubs for Seasonal Interest *(cont'd)*

Buddleia davidii, butterfly bush: Continues blooming in early fall, until frost. Zones 5–9.

Callicarpa spp., beautyberry: Clusters of lavender to violet berries, leaves also turn purplish. Hardiness varies with species.

Calluna vulgaris, Scotch heather: Often blooms into early autumn. Zones 4–6.

Camellia spp.: Some varieties bloom in autumn, depending on location. Zones 7–9.

Carpinus betulus, European hornbeam: Yellow and orange leaves. Zones 4–7.

Caryopteris spp., blue mist shrub: Still blooming in early autumn. Zones 6–9.

Ceanothus spp., California lilac: Some bloom into early fall. Zones 8–10.

Cercidiphyllum japonicum, katsura tree: Red to yellow leaves. Zones 4–8.

Cladrastis kentuckea, yellowwood: Yellow leaves. Zones 4–8.

Clethra alnifolia, sweet pepperbush: Yellow leaves. Zones 3–9.

Cornus, dogwood

C. alba, Tatarian dogwood: Red to purplish leaves. Zones 2–7.

C. florida, flowering dogwood: Red to orange leaves, red fruits. Zones 5–9.

C. kousa, kousa dogwood: Red to orange leaves, red fruits. Zones 5–9.

C. mas, Cornelian cherry: Yellow leaves, red fruits. Zones 4–8.

C. sericea, red-osier dogwood: Yellow leaves. Zones 2–8.

Cotinus coggygria, smokebush: Fluffy flower panicles may persist into autumn; orangey-yellow leaves. Zones 4 or 5–8.

Cotoneaster spp.: Red berries in fall, persist into winter. Hardiness varies with species.

Crataegus, hawthorn: Yellow or orange leaves

C. 'Autumn Glory' has especially beautiful autumn foliage. Zones 5–7.

Davidia involucrata, dove tree: Yellow leaves. Zones 6–8.

Enkianthus spp.: Red to yellow leaves. Zones 4 or 5–7.

Escallonia spp.: Blooms into early fall. Zones 8 or 9–11.

Euonymus alatus, burning bush: Brilliant red leaves. Zones 4–8.

Fagus sylvatica, European beech: Golden bronze leaves. Zones 4–7.

Fothergilla major: Red to orange to yellow leaves. Zones 4–8.

Fraxinus, ash

F. americana, white ash: Maroon to reddish purple to rich purple leaves. Zones 3–9.

F. oxycarpa: Leaves turn purple in fall if tree is grown in full sun. Zones 5–8.

(continued)

Famous Hybridizers and Their Noteworthy Cultivars

Joseph B. Gable, Stewartson, Pennsylvania, developed a whole class of azaleas, the Gable hybrids. Perhaps the best known is 'Stewartsonian', a vivid fiery red.

Peter Girard Sr., Geneva, Ohio, developed the Girard hybrid azaleas. Exceptional cultivars include 'Purple Robe' (clear purple), 'Border Gem' (hot pink), and 'Girard's Rose'. He also developed 'Hot Shot' (reddish orange flowers).

Ben Morrison, former director of the National Arboretum, developed the Glenn Dale hybrid azaleas. Three of the best of these are 'Buccaneer' (early-blooming, reddish orange), 'Ben Morrison' (pink and white bicolor with very large flowers), and 'Martha Hitchcock'.

Dr. Charles Fischer, Linwood, New Jersey, developed what are known as the Linwood hybrids, best suited for southern gardens. Two widely available cultivars are 'Linwood Blush' (light yellow-pink) and 'Linwood Lavender' (light purple).

Polly Hill, Martha's Vineyard, Massachusetts, developed the North Tisbury hybrids. The best known of these is 'Joseph Hill', an outstanding dwarf with vibrant orange-red flowers.

Edmund V. Mezitt, Hopkinton, Massachusetts, developed the purple P. J. M. hybrid rhododendrons. Three different clones, 'Elite', 'Regal', and 'Victor' are probably the most widely planted rhododendrons in New England in recent years. Other notable rhododendron introductions include 'Olga Mexitt', 'Aglo', and 'Weston' (a Dexter hybrid).

A. M. (Tony) Shammerello, of South Euclid, Ohio, bred the popular 'Hino Red', as well as 'Elsie Lee' (double orchid flowers) and its sister cultivar, 'Helen Curtis' (white). He also bred hardy, large-leaved rhododendrons, including 'Yaku Princess' and 'Spring Dawn'.

Anthony Waterer Sr., a British grower, was responsible for many rhododendron and azalea hybrids in the early twentieth century. Rhododendrons include 'Roseum Superbum', 'Caractacus', and 'Catawbiense Album'. He also developed the Knap Hill hybrid azaleas.

Lionel de Rothschild developed many of the Exbury hybrid azaleas at his Exbury estate in Southampton, England, after World War I. These are sometimes grouped with the Knap Hill hybrids, from which they were developed. 'Golden Sunset' is one noteworthy cultivar.

Charles Owen Dexter of Cape Cod developed 'Scintillation', one of the best of his Dexter hybrids and a very popular rhododendron. 'Brown Eyes' is another of his outstanding cultivars.

Robert Gartrell developed the late-blooming Robin Hill hybrid azaleas. 'Betty Anne Voss' has huge flowers; others include 'Olga Niblett' and 'Nancy of Robinhill'. These excellent plants, relatively recent introductions, are becoming increasingly popular.

Trees and Shrubs for Seasonal Interest *(cont'd)*

Fuchsia hybrids: Continue blooming into early fall. Zones 10–11.

Gymnocladus dioica, Kentucky coffee tree: Yellow leaves. Zones 3–8.

Halesia carolina, Carolina silverbell: Yellow leaves. Zones 4–8.

Hamamelis spp., witch hazel: Yellow-orange leaves. Hardiness varies; most are hardy in Zones 5–8.

Holodiscus discolor: Seed heads persist well into autumn. Zones 6–9.

Hydrangea

H. paniculata 'Grandiflora', peegee hydrangea (Zones 3–8), and *H. quercifolia*, oakleaf hydrangea (Zones 5–9): Flower clusters persist into fall, gradually turning pinkish, drying, and fading to brown.

Hypericum calycinum, St.-John's-wort: Continues blooming into fall. Zones 5–8.

Ilex spp., holly: Red, yellow, or orange berries produced in autumn and persist well into winter. Hardiness varies with species.

Koelreuteria paniculata, goldenrain tree: Yellow leaves. Zones 5–9.

Lagerstroemia indica, crape myrtle: Red, orange, and yellow leaves. Zones 7–9.

Leucothoe fontanesiana, fetterbush, drooping leucothoe: Red to purplish leaves. Zones 5–8.

Liquidambar styraciflua, sweet gum: Red to orange leaves. Zones 5–9.

Liriodendron tulipifera, tulip tree: Yellow leaves. Zones 4–9.

Lonicera fragrantissima, winter honeysuckle: White to yellow flowers begin blooming in late fall. Zones 4–8.

Magnolia grandiflora, southern magnolia: Still blooming in early autumn. Zones 7–9.

Mahonia aquifolium, Oregon grape holly: Purplish leaves and blue-black fruit. Zones 5–8.

Malus spp., crab apple: Yellow or red fruit in early fall (ornamental flowering varieties do not usually have very showy fruit). Hardiness varies with species.

Nandina domestica, heavenly bamboo: Reddish orange leaves. Zones 6–9.

Nerium oleander, oleander: Continues blooming into fall. Zones 8–11.

Nyssa sylvatica, tupelo, black gum: Red and orange leaves. Zones 3–9.

Oxydendrum arboreum, sourwood: Red and orange leaves. Zones 5–9.

Pernettya mucronata, Chilean pernettya: Red, pink, or white fruits persist through fall and into winter. Zones 7–9.

Photinia villosa: Orange and yellow leaves, red fruits in late summer or early fall. Zones 4–7.

Populus, poplar

P. alba, white poplar and *P. nigra*, black poplar have yellow leaves in fall. Zones 3–9.

Prunus, flowering cherry

P. sargentii, Sargent cherry: Yellow and orange to red leaves. Zones 4–7.

P. serrulata: Yellow to orange leaves, 'Amanogawa' has brighter colors than most. Zones 6–9.

Punica granatum, pomegranate: Yellow-green leaves. Zones 8–11.

Pyracantha spp.: Clusters of red, orange, or yellow fruits in early autumn, persisting into winter. Hardiness varies with species.

Pyrus calleryana, callery pear, Bradford pear: Orange to red leaves. Zones 4–8.

Rhododendron, azaleas and rhododendrons

Exbury and Knap Hill hybrid azaleas: Red, orange, and yellow leaves. Zones 5–7.

R. kaempferi hybrids: Reddish leaves. Zones 5–8.

R. mucronulatum, Korean rhododendron: Yellow and red-bronze leaves. Zones 4–7.

P. J. M. hybrid rhododendrons: Purple leaves. Zones 4–8.

R. schlippenbachii, royal azalea: Red, orange, and yellow leaves. Zones 4–7.

R. vaseyi, pinkshell azalea: Red leaves. Zones 4–8.

Rhodotypos scandens, jetbead: Shiny black fruit like beads in late summer to early autumn.

Rhus spp., sumac: Golden to red and orange leaves, seed heads persist through autumn and well into winter. Zones 3 or 4 to 8 or 9.

Robinia pseudoacacia, black locust: Yellow leaves and grayish green seedpods in fall. Zones 3–8.

Rosa spp., roses: Many shrub roses develop bright orange to red fruits (called hips) in late summer or fall. Hardiness varies with species.

Sassafras albidum: Red-orange leaves. Zones 4–9.

Skimmia japonica: Female plants produce clusters of red fruit in fall if planted near a male. Zones 4–8.

(continued)

Trees and Shrubs for Seasonal Interest *(cont'd)*

Sorbus, mountain ash

S. americana, American mountain ash: Orange and yellow leaves, clusters of red or, in some varieties, yellow fruits. Zones 2–6.

S. aucuparia, rowan: Orange to yellow leaves, clusters of red fruit. Zones 3–6 or 7.

Stewartia spp.: Orange to red leaves. Hardiness varies with species.

Symphoricarpos

S. albus, snowberry: Clusters of white berrylike fruits through fall. Zones 3–7.

S. orbiculatus, coralberry: Clusters of red fruits in mid-autumn. Zones 2–7.

Symplocos paniculata, sapphire berry: Bright blue to turquoise berrylike fruits in fall. Zones 4–8.

Tilia spp., linden: Yellow leaves. Hardiness varies with species.

Vaccinium spp., blueberry, cranberry: Red to orange leaves. Hardiness varies with species.

Viburnum: Many produce blue-black fruits in fall.

V. × *carlcephalum*, fragrant snowball viburnum: Reddish purple leaves. Zones 6–8.

V. cassinoides, witherod viburnum: Orange-red to deep red or purplish leaves. Zones 3–8.

V. dentatum, arrowwood viburnum: Yellow to reddish or purple leaves. Zones 2–8.

V. dilatatum, linden viburnum: Rusty red or bronze leaves, red fruits in fall. Zones 5–7.

V. opulus, European cranberry bush: Clusters of red or yellow fruits in fall. Zones 3–8.

V. plicatum var. *tomentosum*, doublefile viburnum: Red-purple leaves. Zones 5–8.

V. trilobum, American cranberry bush: Yellow to purple-red leaves, red fruit. Zones 2–7.

Vitex agnus-castus, chaste tree: Continues blooming into early fall. Zones 6–9.

Zelkova serrata, Japanese zelkova: Purplish to red, orange, and yellow leaves. Zones 5–8.

Zenobia pulverulenta, dusty zenobia: Reddish leaves. Zones 5–9.

WINTER

Acacia: Begins blooming in late winter. Zones 9–10.

Acer, maple

A. griseum, paperbark maple: Brown outer bark peels to reveal golden red-brown inner bark which is especially striking in winter. Zones 4–8.

A. palmatum, Japanese maple: Young stems of young specimens of 'Sango Kaku' (a.k.a. 'Senkaki'), coralbark maple, are coral-colored, stunning in winter; as plants age, their foliage becomes their main asset. Zones 6–8.

Alnus spp., alder: Dark brown to black catkins form in winter and persist until spring, when they open into small yellow flowers. Hardiness varies with species.

Arbutus

A. andrachne, madrone: Peeling orange-brown bark. Zones 8–9.

A. unedo, strawberry tree: Peeling orange-brown bark; the red autumn fruits persist into winter. Zones 7–9.

Berberis spp., barberry: Many cultivars retain their autumn foliage colors and berries into winter. Hardiness varies with species.

Betula spp., birch: Many species have catkins that remain through winter, and interesting bark. The white birches are especially beautiful in winter, but are plagued with borers and leaf miners in many areas. Hardiness varies with species.

Calluna vulgaris, Scotch heather: Grayish seed heads in winter. Zones 4–6.

Camellia spp.: Blooms from late fall to spring, depending on location; red, rose, pink, or white flowers. Zones 7–9.

Catalpa spp.: Long seedpods remain into early winter. Zones 4 or 5–8.

Chimonanthus praecox, wintersweet: Fragrant yellow flowers bloom in winter in warmer parts of its range. Zones 6–9.

Cornus, dogwood

C. alba, Tatarian dogwood: Red stems in winter. Zones 2–7.

C. mas, cornelian cherry: Yellow flowers in late winter to very early spring. Zones 4–8.

C. sericea, red-osier dogwood: Bright red-orange stems all winter; *C. sericea* 'Flavirama' has yellow stems. Zones 2–8.

Corylus avellana 'Contorta', Harry Lauder's walking stick: Twisted branches make a winter garden sculpture. Zones 4–8.

Cotoneaster spp.: Bright red berries persist into winter. Hardiness varies with species.

(continued)

Trees and Shrubs for Seasonal Interest *(cont'd)*

Daphne odora, winter daphne: Fragrant rose-purple flowers in late winter to very early spring. Zones 7–10.

Eucalyptus spp.: Outer bark peels to reveal yellow inner bark. Zones 9–11.

Hamamelis spp., witch hazel: Fragrant yellow or orange ribbony flowers in late winter to very early spring. Hardiness varies; most are hardy in Zones 5–8.

Ilex spp., holly: Red berries remain in winter, glossy leaves are attractive all year. Hardiness varies with species.

Jasminum nudiflorum, winter jasmine: Waxy yellow flowers (not fragrant) in mid to late winter. Zones 5 or 6–10.

Leucothoe fontanesiana, fetterbush, drooping leucothoe: Bronzy purple fall foliage remains in winter. Zones 5–8.

Pernettya mucronata, Chilean pernettya: Clusters of purple, red, pink, or white fruits persist in winter. Zones 8–10.

Photinia spp.: New growth produced in autumn and winter is bright red. Hardiness varies with species.

Prunus serrula, flowering cherry: Peeling reddish-brown bark; unfortunately, this species is susceptible to borers and other problems. Zones 5–6.

Pyracantha spp.: Clusters of yellow, orange, or red fruits persist in winter. Hardiness varies with species.

Rhus spp., sumac: Brown seed heads persist well into winter. Zones 3 or 4 to 8 or 9.

Viburnum

V. opulus, European cranberry bush (Zones 3–8) and *V. trilobum*, American cranberry bush (Zones 2–7): Red fruits remain into late winter.

MAJOR AZALEA HYBRID GROUPS

There are many, many azalea hybrids. Some of the most important groups of hybrids are described here.

Exbury hybrids (a subgroup of the Knap Hill hybrids): Deciduous plants with good autumn color; upright form. Large (3 inches across or more) flowers in cream, yellow, orange, pink, rose, and red. Hardy to USDA Zone 5.

Gable hybrids: Evergreen, to 3 or 4 feet tall. Medium flowers (to 2 inches) in red, violet-red, salmon pink, and white. Hardiest of the evergreen azaleas, hardy to Zone 6, some to Zone 5.

Ghent hybrids: Deciduous, upright form, to 6 to 10 feet. Flowers are generally of medium size, and may be single or double; colors include white, pink to red, yellow, orange, and combinations of two colors. Hardiest of the azaleas, to Zone 4.

Glenn Dale hybrids: Evergreen; form and leaf size vary. Medium to large flowers in white, pink, rose, and purple. Hardy to Zone 6, some to Zone 5.

Kaempferi hybrids: semievergreen (except in the coldest parts of their range), some fall color, upright and somewhat open form, relatively tall plants reach 6 feet. Flowers are usually single, small to medium (to 2 inches across); colors range from white to rose to purple and orange to red. Hardy to Zone 6, some to Zone 5.

Knap Hill hybrids: Deciduous, usually upright in form. Large flowers (3 to 4 inches across), generally single, in colors ranging from cream to pink, rose, red, salmon, orange, and yellow. Hardy to Zone 5, some to Zone 4.

Kurume hybrids: Evergreen, compact form, to 4 feet tall; small leaves. Flowers are small (to 2 inches) but massed, single or double, usually pink to scarlet. Hardy to Zone 7.

Mollis hybrids: Deciduous, upright form, 3 to 5 feet. Medium flowers (usually 3 inches) ranging from yellow to bright red. Hardy to Zone 5.

Southern Indica hybrids: Evergreen, the classic azaleas for southern gardens. Plants grow larger than other evergreen azaleas. Large flowers may be double or single, in white, pink, lavender, and red. Hardy to Zone 8, a few to Zone 7.

Other Rhododendron Hybrids

Other rhododendrons are not classified into the same distinct groupings as azaleas. Cultivars are usually listed individually along with species or grouped by color. The informal groupings below include a wide variety of plants.

Catawba hybrids: Evergreen, 6 to 10 feet. Medium flowers range from white to rose to purple. Hardy to Zone 5.

Dexter hybrids: Evergreen, to 8 feet, dense foliage. Large flowers are often fragrant, pink and other colors. Hardy to Zone 5.

Fortunei hybrids: Evergreen, to 12 feet. Large flowers in shades of pink, red, and yellow with pink. Most are hardy to Zone 6.

P. J. M. hybrids: Evergreen, excellent fall color, compact, rounded form, to 6 feet tall. Flowers are bright lavender-pink. Hardy to Zone 4 and tolerant of heat, sun, and shade.

DROUGHT-TOLERANT TREES AND SHRUBS

Following are listings of trees and shrubs that tolerate varying degrees of drought. They are grouped into three broad climate categories: Cool climates include Zones 2 through cooler parts of Zone 5 (although not all the plants listed will survive in Zone 2); temperate climates include Zones 5 through 7; warm climates are Zones 8 through 11. Weather conditions vary widely within each zone, and it is important to understand the climate in your area, and the microclimate in and immediately around your garden. See chapter 1 for information on climate and weather.

COOL CLIMATES (ZONE 2 TO NORTHERN ZONE 5)

Amelanchier alnifolia, western serviceberry, hardy to Zone 3
Caragana arborescens, Siberian peashrub
Chrysothamnus spp., rabbitbrush, hardy to Zone 3
Elaeagnus angustifolia, Russian olive, Zone 3
Juniperus virginiana, eastern red cedar
Ligustrum obtusifolium var. *regelianum*, Regel's privet, Zone 3
Lonicera maackii, Amur honeysuckle, Zone 3
Myrica pensylvanica, bayberry, Zone 3
Physocarpus spp., ninebark, Zone 3
Picea, spruce
- *P. abies*, Norway spruce
- *P. glauca*, white spruce, Zone 3
- *P. pungens*, Colorado spruce, Zone 3

Pinus, pine
- *P. cembra*, Swiss stone pine
- *P. mugo*, mugo pine
- *P. resinosa*, red pine

Potentilla fruticosa, bush cinquefoil
Prunus virginiana, chokecherry, Zone 3
Rhus, sumac, most are hardy to Zone 3
- *R. aromatica* is hardy to Zone 2

Robinia spp., black locust
Rosa, rose
- *R. rubrifolia*, redleaf rose
- *R. rugosa*, saltspray rose, Zone 3

Salix humilis, prairie willow, Zone 3
Shepherdia canadensis, russet buffalo berry
Symphoricarpos orbiculatus, coralberry, Zone 3
Vaccinium angustifolium, lowbush blueberry

TEMPERATE CLIMATES (ZONES 5 TO 7)

Albizia julibrissin, silk tree
Amelanchier alnifolia, western serviceberry
Arbutus unedo, strawberry tree (does best in dry, not humid, climates)
Aronia arbutifolia, red chokeberry
Atriplex spp., saltbush (for desert and seashore conditions)
Berberis spp., barberry
Buddleia spp., butterfly bush
Caragana spp., pea shrub
Caryopteris spp., blue-mist shrub
Catalpa spp.
Cedrus atlantica, atlas cedar, hardy to Zone 6
Celtis spp., hackberry
Cercis occidentalis, western redbud
Cercocarpus spp., mountain mahogany
Cotoneaster spp.
Crataegus crus-galli, cockspur hawthorn
Elaeagnus angustifolia, Russian olive, autumn olive
Euonymus alatus, burning bush
Fallugia paradoxa, apache plume
Fendlera rupicola, false mock orange
Forestiera spp., desert olive
Genista, broom
- *G. sagittalis*, arrow broom
- *G. tinctoria*, woadwaxen

Ginkgo, maidenhair tree
Gleditsia triacanthos var. *inermis*, thornless honey locust
Gymnocladus dioica, Kentucky coffee tree

Hippophae spp., sea buckthorn
Hypericum, St.-John's-wort
  H. calycinum, hardy to Zone 6
  H. frondosum, to Zone 6
  H. prolificum
Juniperus, juniper, numerous species
Koelreuteria paniculata, goldenrain tree
Kolkwitzia amabilis, beautybush
Ligustrum, privet, numerous species
Lonicera maackii, Amur honeysuckle
Myrica spp., bayberry
Phellodendron amurense, Amur cork tree
Picea pungens, Colorado spruce
Pinus, pine
  P. flexilis, limber pine
  P. mugo, mugo pine
  P. nigra, Austrian pine
  P. ponderosa, ponderosa pine
Potentilla fruticosa, bush cinquefoil
Prunus
  P. americana, wild plum
  P. besseyi, sand cherry
  P. padus, European bird cherry
Quercus, oak
  Q. gambelii, scrub oak
  Q. macrocarpa, bur oak
Rhus spp., sumac
Ribes cereum, squaw currant
Robinia, locust
  R. neomexicana, New Mexico locust
  R. pseudoacacia, black locust
Rosa, rose
  R. foetida var. *bicolor*, Austrian copper rose
  R. rugosa, saltspray rose
Syringa, lilac
  S. meyeri, Meyer lilac
  S. × persica, Persian lilac
Tamarix, tamarisk, salt cedar
Viburnum lantana, wayfaring tree
Yucca spp.

WARM CLIMATES (ZONES 8 TO 11)

Acacia spp.
Artemisia spp., sagebrush
Atriplex spp., saltbush (for desert and seashore gardens)
Aucuba spp., gold dust plant
Baccharis spp., desert broom
Berberis darwinii, Darwin barberry
Brachychiton populneus, bottle tree
Callistemon citrinus, lemon bottlebrush, Zone 9 and south
Cassia artemisioides, feathery cassia
Ceanothus spp., California lilac
Cedrus, cedar
  C. atlantica 'Glauca', Zone 9 and north
  C. deodara, deodar cedar
Cercis occidentalis, western redbud, Zone 9 and north
Cercocarpus spp., mountain mahogany
Chamaebatiaria millefolium, fernbush
Chilopsis linearis, desert willow
Cistus spp., rock rose
Colutea spp., bladder senna
Coprosma repens, mirror plant
Cytisus, broom
  C. × praecox, Warminster broom
  C. scoparius, Scotch broom
Elaeagnus pungens, thorny elaeagnus
Eucalyptus spp., gum tree
Euonymus japonica, evergreen euonymus
Fallugia paradoxa, apache plume
Feijoa sellowiana, pineapple guava
Fendlera rupicola, false mock orange
Foresteira, desert olive
Fouquiera splendens, ocotillo
Fremontodendron spp., flannelflower
Genista, broom
  G. hispanica, Spanish broom, Zone 9 and north
  G. monosperma

(continued)

Drought-Tolerant Trees and Shrubs *(cont'd)*

G. pilosa, silky-leaved woadwaxen
G. sagittalis, arrow broom
Grevillea robusta, silk oak, Zones 10–11 only
Hypericum, St.-John's-wort
H. calycinum
H. frondosum
H. × moseranum
H. patulum, goldencup St.-John's-wort
Ilex, holly
I. cornuta, Chinese holly
I. vomitoria, yaupon
Juniperus, juniper, numerous species
Lagerstroemia indica, crape myrtle
Lantana camara
Larryea spp., creosote bush
Leptospermum scoparium, New Zealand tea tree
Ligustrum, privet
L. japonicum, Japanese privet
L. vulgare, common privet
Myrtus spp., myrtle
Nandina domestica, heavenly bamboo
Nerium oleander, oleander
Osmanthus fragrans, sweet olive
Philadelphus microphyllus, littleleaf mock orange
Photinia spp.
Prosopis glandulosa, honey mesquite
Punica granatum, pomegranate
Pyracantha spp., firethorn
Quercus macrocarpa, bur oak
Raphiolepis indica, Indian hawthorn
Rhus spp., sumac
Ribes cereum, squaw currant
Romneya coalteri, Matilija poppy
Rosa, rose
R. foetida var. *bicolor*, Austrian copper rose
R. rugosa, saltspray rose
Rubus deliciosus, flowering raspberry
Spartium junceum, Spanish broom
Symphoricarpos orbiculatus, coralberry
Tamarix spp., tamarisk, salt cedar
Xylosma spp.
Yucca spp.

Trees and Shrubs for Wet Places

COOL CLIMATES (ZONE 2 TO NORTHERN ZONE 5)

Acer rubrum, red swamp maple
Alnus, alder
A. glutinosa, black alder
A. incana, white alder
Amelanchier spp., serviceberry, hardy to Zone 4
Betula nigra, river birch, to Zone 4
Carpinus caroliniana, American hornbeam
Chamaedaphne calyculata, leatherleaf
Chionanthus spp., fringe tree, to Zone 3
Clethra alnifolia, sweet pepperbush, to Zone 3
Cornus, dogwood
C. alba, Tatarian dogwood
C. sericea, red-osier dogwood
Eucalyptus leucoxylon, white ironbark
Fraxinus, green ash, red ash, to Zone 3
Halesia carolina, Carolina silverbell, to Zone 4
Ilex, holly
I. glabra, inkberry, to Zone 4
I. verticillata, winterberry, to Zone 3
Larix spp., eastern larch
Ledum groenlandicum, Labrador tea
Nyssa spp., tupelo, to Zone 4
Potentilla fruticosa, bush cinquefoil
Quercus bicolor, swamp white oak, to Zone 3
Rhododendron
R. maximum, rosebay rhododendron, to Zone 3
R. periclymenoides, pinxterbloom azalea, to Zone 3
R. viscosum, swamp azalea, to Zone 3
Salix alba, white willow
Sambucus canadensis, American elder, to Zone 3

Taxodium distichum, bald cypress, to Zone 4
Thuja occidentalis, American arborvitae
Vaccinium
- *V. angustifolium*, lowbush blueberry
- *V. corymbosum*, highbush blueberry, to Zone 3
- *V. macrocarpon*, cranberry

Viburnum
- *V. opulus*, European cranberrybush
- *V. trilobum*, American cranberrybush

TEMPERATE CLIMATES (ZONES 5 TO 7)

Acer rubrum, red swamp maple
Alnus, alder
- *A. cordata*, Italian alder
- *A. glutinosa*, black alder
- *A. incana*, white alder

Amelanchier, serviceberry
- *A. canadensis*
- *A. laevis*

Aronia spp., red chokeberry
Betula nigra, river birch
Calluna spp., heather
Calocedrus spp., incense cedar
Calycanthus spp., Carolina allspice
Carpinus caroliniana, American hornbeam
Cephalanthus occidentalis, buttonbush
Chamaecyparis thyoides, white cedar, false cypress
Chamaedaphne calyculata, leatherleaf
Chionanthus spp., fringe tree
Cornus, dogwood
- *C. alba*, Tatarian dogwood
- *C. sericea*, red-osier dogwood

Enkianthus spp.
Fraxinus, green ash, red ash
Halesia carolina, Carolina silverbell
Hamamelis vernalis, vernal witch hazel
Hypericum densiflorum
Ilex
- *I. glabra*, inkberry
- *I. verticillata*, winterberry

Kalmia spp., mountain laurel
Leucothoe fontanesiana, fetterbush
Lindera spp., spicebush
Liquidambar spp., sweet gum
Lyonia mariana, staggerbush
Magnolia virginiana, sweet bay magnolia
Metasequoia glyptostroboides, dawn redwood
Nyssa spp., tupelo
Potentilla fruticosa, bush cinquefoil
Quercus, oak
- *Q. bicolor*, swamp white oak
- *Q. palustris*, pin oak

Rhododendron
- *R. arborescens*, sweet azalea
- *R. maximum*, rosebay rhododendron
- *R. periclymenoides*, pinxterbloom azalea
- *R. vaseyi*, pinkshell azalea
- *R. viscosum*, swamp azalea

Salix, willow
- *S. alba*, white willow
- *S. babylonica*, weeping willow
- *S. gracilistyla*, rosegold pussy willow

Sambucus canadensis, American elder
Vaccinium
- *V. angustifolium*, lowbush blueberry
- *V. corymbosum*, highbush blueberry
- *V. macrocarpon*, cranberry, Zone 6 and north

Viburnum
- *V. cassinoides*, witherod
- *V. opulus*, European cranberrybush
- *V. trilobum*, American cranberrybush

WARM CLIMATES (ZONES 8 TO 11)

Amelanchier arborea, downy serviceberry, Zone 9 and north
Carpinus caroliniana, American hornbeam, Zone 9 and north
Chionanthus spp., fringe tree, Zone 9 and north
Clethra alnifolia, sweet pepperbush
Fraxinus, green ash, red ash, Zone 9 and north
Gaultheria veitchiana

(continued)

Trees and Shrubs for Wet Places *(cont'd)*

Ilex

I. glabra, inkberry, Zone 9 and north

I. verticillata, winterberry, Zone 9 and north

Itea spp., sweetspire

Kalmia spp., mountain laurel

Leucothoe fontanesiana, fetterbush

Lindera spp., spicebush

Liquidambar spp., sweet gum

Lyonia mariana, staggerbush

Magnolia virginiana, sweetbay magnolia

Melaleuca quinquenervia, broad-leaved paperbark, Zones 10–11 only

Metasequoia glyptostroboides, dawn redwood

Nyssa spp., tupelo

Pernettya mucronata

Rhododendron

R. arborescens, sweet azalea

R. viscosum, swamp azalea

Rosa palustris, swamp rose

Sabal minor, dwarf palmetto

Salix spp., willows, Zone 9 and north

Sambucus canadensis, American elder, Zone 9 and north

Spiraea tomentosa, hardhack

Taxodium distichum, bald cypress, Zone 9 and north

Viburnum cassinoides, witherod viburnum, Zone 9 and north

Zenobia pulverulenta, dusty zenobia, Zone 9 and north

Trees and Shrubs for Acid Soil

These trees and shrubs prefer soil with a pH in the acid range, below 7.0.

Abies spp., fir

Aesculus × *carnea*, red horse chestnut

Alnus incana, white alder

Calluna spp., heather

Camellia spp.

Chamaecyparis thyoides, white cedar

Chionanthus spp., fringe tree

Choisya ternata, Mexican orange

Clethra alnifolia, sweet pepperbush

Corema conradii, broom crowberry

Cornus spp., dogwood

Daboecia spp., Irish heath

Enkianthus spp.

Erica spp., heath

Exochorda spp., pearlbush

Fothergilla spp.

Gardenia jasminoides

Ilex spp., holly

Illicium floridanum, Florida anise tree

Juniperus communis, common juniper

Kalmia spp., mountain laurel

Ledum groenlandicum, Labrador tea

Leucothoe spp.

Lyonia ligustrina, maleberry

Magnolia

M. grandiflora, southern magnolia

M. virginiana, sweet bay magnolia

Mahonia spp.

Myrica pensylvanica, bayberry

Nyssa sylvatica, tupelo

Oxydendrum arboreum, sourwood

Paxistima canbyi

Pinus spp., pines

Quercus spp., oaks

Rhododendron spp., azaleas and rhododendrons

Sorbus americana, American mountain ash

Vaccinium spp., blueberries

Viburnum acerifolium, dockmackie

Xanthorhiza simplicissima, yellowroot

Zenobia pulverulenta, dusty zenobia

Trees and Shrubs for Hedges and Screens

When planted in a row, these plants can be used to define boundaries or create a screen. Some can be sheared and maintained as neat, formal hedges; others are best when allowed to grow to their natural form in informal hedgerows.

Abelia spp.
Acer, maple
- *A. campestre*, hedge maple
- *A. ginnala*, Amur maple

Berberis spp., barberry
Buxus spp., boxwood
Carpinus, hornbeam
- *C. caroliniana*, American hornbeam
- *C. betulus*, European hornbeam

Cotoneaster lucidus, hedge cotoneaster
Cupressus spp., cypress
Deutzia gracilis, slender deutzia
Elaeagnus pungens, thorny elaeagnus
Eugenia spp.
Euonymus
- *E. alatus*, burning bush, winged euonymus
- *E. japonica*, evergreen euonymus

Fagus sylvatica, European beech
Forsythia spp.
Hibiscus
- *H. rosa-sinensis*
- *H. syriacus*, rose of Sharon

Hydrangea paniculata 'Grandiflora', peegee hydrangea
Ilex, holly
- *I.* × *attenuata*, hybrid holly
- *I. cornuta*, Chinese holly
- *I. crenata*, Japanese holly
- *I. glabra*, inkberry
- *I. opaca*, American holly
- *I. vomitoria*, yaupon

Juniperus, juniper; narrow cultivars of various species are good for screening. *J. virginiana*, red cedar, is also used for screening
Ligustrum spp., privet
Lonicera nitida, box honeysuckle
Malus spp., flowering crab apple
Myrtus communis, myrtle
Nerium oleander, oleander
Osmanthus spp.
Photinia spp.
Phyllostachys spp., bamboo
Picea, spruce
- *P. abies*, Norway spruce
- *P. pungens*, Colorado spruce

Pittosporum crassifolium
Poncirus trifoliata, hardy orange
Prunus
- *P. laurocerasus*, cherry laurel
- *P. tomentosa*, Nanking cherry

Pyracantha coccinea, scarlet firethorn
Quercus imbricaria, shingle oak
Rhododendron spp., azaleas
Rosmarinus officinalis, rosemary
Rosa spp., shrub roses
Spiraea × *vanhouttei*, bridal wreath
Syringa spp., lilac
Taxus spp., yew
Thuja spp., arborvitae
Tsuga spp., hemlock
Viburnum tinus
Xylosma congestum

TREES AND SHRUBS WITH PARTICULAR SHAPES

Cultivar names often offer a clue to the character of the plant. If you are looking for a plant with a weeping habit, look for cultivars named *Pendula* (or consult the list below). Narrow, columnar forms are often named *Columnaris* or *Fastigiata*. Dwarf forms may have *Nana* or *Compacta* as part of their botanical names. *Prostrata* indicates a low-growing, spreading shrub.

Columnar Trees and Shrubs

Acer, maple
- *A. campestre* 'Fastigiatum', hedge maple
- *A. platanoides* 'Columnare', 'Crimson Song', and 'Olmsted', Norway maple
- *A. rubrum* 'Columnare', 'Armstrong', and 'Scarlet Sentinel', red maple
- *A. saccharinum* 'Pyramidale', silver maple
- *A. saccharum* 'Lanco Columnar', 'Newton Sentry', 'Slavin's Upright', and 'Temple's Upright', sugar maple

Alnus glutinosa 'Pyramidalis' (a.k.a. 'Fastigiata'), common alder

Betula pendula 'Fastigiata' and 'Obelisk', European white birch

Carpinus betulus 'Columnaris', European hornbeam

Cedrus atlantica 'Fastigiata', Atlas cedar

Crataegus phaenopyrum 'Fastigiata', Washington thorn

× *Cupressocyparis leylandii* 'Green Spire', 'Leighton Green', and 'Robinson's Gold', leyland cypress

Fagus sylvatica 'Dawyck', 'Dawyck Gold', and 'Dawyck Purple', European beech

Fraxinus americana 'Greenspire' and 'Manitoo', white ash

Ginkgo biloba 'Fastigiata', 'Mayfield', and 'Princeton Sentry', maidenhair tree

Ilex crenata 'Fastigiata', Japanese holly

Juniperus, juniper
- *J. chinensis* 'Columnaris Glauca', 'Obelisk', 'Spartan', and 'Spearmint', Chinese juniper
- *J. communis* 'Gold Cone' and 'Sentinel', common juniper
- *J. scopulorum* 'Skyrocket' and 'Weichii', Rocky Mountain juniper
- *J. squamata* 'Loderii', singleseed juniper
- *J. virginiana* 'Emerald Sentinel', 'Glauca', 'Hillii', 'Nova', 'Princeton Sentry', 'Pseudocupressus', and 'Stover', eastern red cedar

Koelreuteria paniculata 'Fastigiata', goldenrain tree

Larix decidua 'Fastigiata', European larch

Liriodendron tulipifera 'Fastigiatum', tulip tree

Magnolia grandiflora 'Russet', southern magnolia

Malus, flowering crab apple
- *M. baccata* 'Columnaris', Siberian crab apple
- hybrid cultivars 'Harvest Gold', 'Red Baron', 'Sentinel', and 'Velvet Pillar'

Picea orientalis 'Nigra Compacta', oriental spruce

Pinus, pine
- *P. cembra* 'Columnaris', Swiss stone pine
- *P. flexilis* 'Columnaris', limber pine
- *P. nigra* 'Pyramidalis', Austrian pine
- *P. strobus* 'Fastigiata', eastern white pine
- *P. sylvestris* 'Fastigiata', Scotch pine

Populus, poplar
- *P. alba* 'Pyramidalis', white poplar
- *P. nigra* 'Italica', lombardy poplar (susceptible to disease)
- *P. tremula* 'Erecta', European aspen

Pseudotsuga menziesii 'Fastigiata', Douglas fir

Quercus robur 'Attention', 'Fastigiata', and 'Skyrocket', English oak

Robinia pseudoacacia 'Pyramidalis', black locust

Sophora japonica 'Columnaris', Japanese pagoda tree

Sorbus aucuparia 'Fastigiata', rowan

Taxodium ascendens 'Prairie Sentinel', pond cypress

Taxus, yew
- *T. baccata* 'Cheshuntensis', 'Fastigiata', and 'Fastigiata Aurea', English yew
- *T.* × *media* 'Anthony Wayne', 'Meadowbrook', 'Sentinelis', and 'Viridis'

Thuja, arborvitae
- *T. orientalis* 'Elegantissima' and 'Minima glauca', American arborvitae
- *T. plicata* 'Fastigiata', giant arborvitae

Tilia, linden
- *T. americana* 'Fastigiata' and 'Legend', basswood
- *T. cordata* 'Swedish Upright', littleleaf linden
- *T. platyphylla* 'Fastigiata', bigleaf linden
- *T. tomentosa* 'Erecta', silver linden

Weeping Trees and Shrubs

Abies alba 'Pendula', weeping white fir

Acer, maple
- *A. campestre* 'Eastleigh Weeping', hedge maple
- *A. palmatum* 'Dissectum Atropurpureum', Japanese maple
- *A. saccharinum* 'Wieri', silver maple

Alnus incana 'Pendula', white alder

Betula pendula 'Gracilis' and 'Youngii', European white birch

Buddleia alternifolia 'Argentea', silver buddleia

Buxus sempervirens 'Pendula', common boxwood

Caragana arborescens 'Pendula' and 'Walker', Siberian peashrub

Carpinus betulus 'Pendula', European hornbeam

Cedrus, cedar
- *C. atlantica* 'Glauca Pendula', blue atlas cedar
- *C. deodara*, deodar cedar
- *C. libani* 'Pendula', cedar of Lebanon

Cercidiphyllum japonicum 'Pendula', katsura tree

Chamaecyparis nootkatensis 'Pendula', nootka false cypress

Cornus, dogwood
- *C. florida* 'Pendula', flowering dogwood
- *C. kousa* 'Pendula' and 'Weaver's Weeping', kousa dogwood

Corylus avellana 'Pendula', European filbert

Cotinus coggygria 'Pendula', smokebush

Crataegus monogyna 'Pendula', singleseed hawthorn

Fagus sylvatica 'Pendula' and 'Purpurea Pendula', European beech

Forsythia
- *F.* × *intermedia* 'Densiflora'
- *F. suspensa* var. *sieboldii*, weeping forsythia

Fraxinus excelsior 'Pendula', European ash

Ginkgo biloba 'Pendula', maidenhair tree

Ilex vomitoria 'Pendula', yaupon

Juniperus, juniper
- *J. scopulorum* 'Tolleson's Weeping Juniper', Rocky Mountain juniper
- *J. virginiana* 'Pendula', eastern red cedar

Larix, larch
- *L. decidua* 'Pendula', European larch
- *L. kaempferi* 'Dervaes' and 'Pendula'

Lonicera fragrantissima, winter honeysuckle

Malus, flowering crab apple
- hybrid cultivars 'Autumn Treasure', 'Candied Apple' (a.k.a. 'Weeping Candied Apple'), 'Coral Cascade', 'Coralene', 'Egret', 'Firedance', 'Little Troll', 'Louisa', 'Lullaby', 'Luwick', 'Maria', 'Molten Lava', 'Pagoda', 'Red Jade', 'Red Swan', 'Royal Splendor', 'Sea Foam', and 'Sinai Fire'

Picea, spruce
- *P. omorika* 'Pendula', Serbian spruce
- *P. orientalis* 'Weeping Dwarf' (a.k.a. 'Pendula'), oriental spruce
- *P. pungens* 'Glauca Pendula', blue spruce

Pinus, pine
- *P. densiflora* 'Pendula', Japanese red pine
- *P. flexilis* 'Pendula', limber pine
- *P. strobus* 'Pendula', eastern white pine

(continued)

Weeping Trees and Shrubs *(cont'd)*

Prunus subhirtella var. *pendula*, weeping Higan cherry; also hybrid cultivar 'White Fountain'

Pseudotsuga menziesii 'Pendula', Douglas fir

Quercus robur 'Pendula', English oak

Salix, willow

- *S. alba* 'Tristis', golden weeping willow
- *S. babylonica*, weeping willow
- *S. caprea* 'Pendula', goat willow
- *S.* 'Prairie Cascade'
- *S. purpurea* 'Pendula'

Sophora japonica 'Pendula', Japanese pagoda tree

Sorbus aucuparia 'Pendula', rowan

Spiraea × *vanhouttei*, bridal wreath (fountain shape)

Styrax japonicus 'Pendula', Japanese snowbell

Syringa pekinensis 'Pendula', Pekin lilac

Taxodium distichum 'Pendens', bald cypress

Thuja occidentalis 'Filiformis' and 'Pendula', American arborvitae

Trees and Shrubs with Colorful Leaves

Trees and shrubs with colorful autumn foliage can be found in the list of plants for seasonal interest, under autumn, on page 271. The plants listed here have colored leaves in other seasons.

Abelia × *grandiflora* 'Francis Mason', glossy abelia, yellow-green leaves with yellow edges on new leaves

Acacia baileyana, Cootamundra wattle, the young leaves of 'Purpurea' are deep purple

Acanthopanax sieboldianus 'Variegatus', five-leaf aralia, white-edged leaves

Acer, maple

- *A. japonicum*, full moon maple, 'Aureum' has yellow leaves
- *A. negundo*, box elder
  - 'Auratum', yellow leaves
  - 'Aureo-marginatum', yellow edges
  - 'Elegans', yellow edges
  - 'Flamingo', leaves edged with white, young shoots are pink
  - 'Variegatum', variegated with white
- *A. palmatum*, Japanese maple
  - 'Bloodgood', reddish purple
  - 'Burgundy Lace', burgundy
  - 'Moonfire', reddish purple
  - var. *atropurpureum*, reddish purple
- *A. palmatum*, Dissectum Group, Japanese cutleaf maple
  - 'Bloodgood', burgundy leaves
  - 'Butterfly', green leaves with pink edges in spring
  - 'Crimson King', red
  - 'Crimson Queen', red
  - 'Dissectum Atropurpureum', young leaves are burgundy, fading to green in summer
  - 'Flavescens', yellow-green
  - 'Filigree', yellow-green
  - 'Garnet', red
  - 'Ornatum', red
  - 'Osakazuki', yellow
  - 'Purpureum', dark red
  - 'Red Filigree Lace', maroon
  - 'Reticulatum', variegated with pink and yellow
- *A. platanoides*, Norway maple
  - 'Crimson King', burgundy
  - 'Crimson Sentry', burgundy
  - 'Drummondii', white edges

'Faasen's Redleaf', red
'Royal Red', red
A. pseudoplatanus, sycamore maple
'Atropurpureum', undersides of leaves are purple
'Brilliantissimum', young leaves are pink, turn cream, then yellow
A. rubrum, red maple
'Variegatum', variegated with white
A. saccharinum, silver maple, has silvery leaves
'Lutescens' has yellow leaves in spring that turn to yellow-green as they age
Alnus, alder
A. glutinosa, common alder
'Aurea', yellow
'Charles Hewitt', variegated
A. incana, white alder, 'Aurea' has yellow leaves
Aucuba japonica, gold dust plant
'Crotonifolia', 'Maculata', 'Picturata', and 'Variegata' are all spotted and splashed with golden yellow
'Sulphur' has yellow edges
'Fructo Albo' is variegated with white
Berberis thunbergii, Japanese barberry
red-leaved cultivars include 'Red Bride', 'Red Chief', 'Red Pillar', and 'Sheridan's Red'
'Aurea', yellow leaves
'Silver Beauty', green variegated with white
'Variegata', green splashed or spotted with white and yellow
var. *atropurpurea* has reddish purple leaves
var. *atropurpurea* 'Crimson Pygmy', red leaves
var. *atropurpurea* 'Crimson Velvet', rosy red deepening to maroon
var. *atropurpurea* 'Golden Ring', burgundy with yellow edge
var. *atropurpurea* 'Harlequin', new leaves are a combination of cream, pink, and purple
var. *atropurpurea* 'Pink Queen', rose-pink with splotches and spots of red and white. 'Rose Glow' develops purple spots
Betula pendula, European white birch
'Purple Rain', 'Purpurea', purple leaves
Buddleia davidii, butterfly bush, 'Harlequin' has green leaves variegated with cream
Buxus sempervirens, boxwood
'Argenteo-variegata', variegated with white
'Aureo-variegata', variegated with yellow
'Elegantissima', cream edges
Calluna vulgaris, Scotch heather
'Gold Haze', 'Robert Chapman', yellow leaves
Catalpa bignonioides, 'Aurea' has yellow leaves
Cedrus atlantica, Atlas cedar
'Argentea', bluish
'Aurea', yellowish
'Glauca', bluish
Chamaecyparis, false cypress
C. lawsoniana, lawson false cypress
'Forsteckensis', grayish green
'Pygmaea Argentea', yellow
C. obtusa, Hinoki false cypress
'Cripsii', yellow
'Mariesii', white-tipped green foliage
'Nana Aurea', yellow
C. pisifera, Japanese false cypress
'Aurea Nana', yellow
'Boulevard', silvery in summer, bluish in winter
'Filifera Aurea', yellow
'Nana Variegata', green and white
'Plumosa Aurea', yellow
Cornus, dogwood
C. alba, Tatarian dogwood
'Argenteo-marginata' ('Elegantissima'), leaves have creamy white margins
C. controversa, giant dogwood
'Variegata', pale yellow edge
C. florida, flowering dogwood
'Cherokee Sunset', variegated with yellow and copper

(continued)

Trees and Shrubs with Colorful Leaves *(cont'd)*

C. kousa, kousa dogwood

'Snowboy', leaves edged in white

Corylus maxima 'Purpurea', purple giant filbert, purple leaves

Cotinus coggygria, smokebush

'Daydream', 'Notcutt's Variety', 'Royal Purple', and 'Velvet Cloak' have burgundy leaves

'Red Beauty', purplish red

× *Cupressocyparis leylandii*, leyland cypress

'Castlewellan Gold', yellow

'Naylor's Blue', blue-green

'Robinson's Gold', yellow

'Silver Dust', variegated with white

Daphne × *burkwoodii* 'Carol Mackie', white edges

Daphne odora, winter daphne

'Aureo-marginata', pale yellow edges

'Variegata', yellow edges

Elaeagnus pungens, thorny elaeagnus

'Maculata' (or 'Aureo-variegata'), variegated with yellow

'Marginata', white edges

'Aurea', yellow edges

Euonymus japonicus, Japanese euonymus

cultivars variegated with yellow include 'Aureus' and 'Ovatus Aureus'

cultivars variegated with white include 'Albomarginatus', 'Silver King', and 'Silver Queen'

Fagus sylvatica, European beech

purple-leaved cultivars include 'Atropurpurea', 'Dawyck Purple', 'Purple Fountain', 'Purpurea Nana', 'Purple Pendula', and 'Riversii'

yellow-leaved cultivars include 'Aurea Pendula', 'Dawyck Gold', and 'Rohan Gold'

'Aurea-variegata', edged in yellow

'Luteo-variegata', variegated with yellow

'Follis Variegatus', variegated with white and yellow

'Roseo-marginata' (a.k.a. 'Purpurea Tricolor'), purplish leaves edged and variegated with pink and white

Fraxinus excelsior, European ash

'Aurea', 'Aurea Pendula', and 'Gold Cloud' have yellow leaves

Ginkgo biloba 'Variegata', maidenhair tree, variegated with white

Hydrangea macrophylla, bigleaf hydrangea

'Tricolor', leaves are green, edged with creamy white or pale yellow

'Variegata', a lacecap type with white-edged leaves

Ilex, holly

I. aquifolium, English holly

'Argenteo-marginata', edged with white

'Aurea-marginata', edged with yellow

I. cornuta Chinese holly

'Cajun Gold', gold edges

'O'Spring', cream leaves

I. crenata, Japanese holly

'Golden Gem', yellow leaves

'Midas Touch', yellow-green

Juniperus, juniper

J. chinensis, Chinese juniper

blue leaved cultivars include 'Angelica Blue', 'Aquarius', 'Arctic Blaauw', 'Blue Cloud', 'Blue Point', 'Blue Vase', 'Glauca', and 'Pfitzeriana Glauca'

yellow-leaved cultivars include 'Aurea', 'Gold Coast', 'Old Gold', 'Pisifera Aurea', 'Pfitzeriana Aurea', and 'Saybrook Gold'

'Milky Way', 'Sulphur Spray', and 'Variegata' are variegated with white

J. communis, common juniper

'Depressa Aurea' and 'Gold Cone' have yellow foliage

J. conferta, shore juniper, 'Blue Pacific' has blue-green foliage

J × *media*, 'Pfitzerana Aurea' has yellow foliage

J. sabina, Savin juniper

'Blue Danube', 'Blue Forest', and 'Pepin' have blue-green foliage

'Variegata' is variegated with white

J. scopulorum, Rocky Mountain juniper

blue-leaved cultivars include 'Blue Heaven', 'Chandler's Silver', 'Dewdrop', 'Erecta Glauca', 'Moonglow', 'Skyrocket', 'Winter Blue', and 'Wichita Blue'

Kerria japonica, Japanese kerria

'Aureo-variegata', variegated with yellow

'Picta', variegated with white

Leptospermum scoparium, New Zealand tea tree

'Gaiety Girl' and 'Waringi' have red leaves

Leucothoe fontanesiana, fetterbush, 'Girard's Rainbow' has green leaves variegated with pink and white

Ligustrum, privet

L. japonicum, Japanese privet

'Silver Star' and 'Variegatum' are variegated with white

L. ovalifolium, California privet

'Aureum' is variegated with yellow

L. × *vicaryi*, golden privet, has yellow leaves

Liquidambar styraciflua, sweet gum

'Aurea' is marked with yellow

'Aurora' and 'Golden Treasure' are variegated with yellow

'Matthew's Gold' has yellow leaves

Liriodendron tulipifera, tulip tree, leaves of 'Aurea-marginatum' are edged in yellow

Lonicera nitida, box honeysuckle, 'Baggesen's Gold' has yellow leaves

Myrtus communis, myrtle

'Compacta Variegata' and 'Variegata' are both variegated with white

Nandina domestica, heavenly bamboo

'Atropurpurea Nana', 'Gulf Stream', and 'Moon Bay' have red leaves in winter

'Moyers Red' is purplish red in winter

'Nana Purpurea' has purple leaves

'Variegatus' is variegated with white

Osmanthus heterophyllus, holly olive

'Aureomarginatus', yellow edges

'Purpureus', purple-green leaves

'Variegatus', white-edged leaves

Philadelphus coronarius, mock orange

'Aureus', yellow leaves

'Variegatus', white-edged leaves

Photinia × *fraseri* has red leaves

Physocarpus opulifolius, eastern ninebark, 'Dart's Gold' has yellow leaves

Picea pungens, Colorado spruce

'Fat Albert' and 'Mission Blue' are bluer than most

'Argentea' is silvery

Pieris japonica, Japanese pieris, 'Variegata' has white edges

Pinus sylvestris, Scotch pine

'Aurea' has yellow-green new growth

'French Blue' is bluish

Pittosporum tobira, 'Variegata' has white edges

Prunus

P. × *blireiana*, flowering plum, leaves are reddish purple when young, bronzy green in summer, and bronzy red in fall

P. cerasifera, cherry plum

'Atropurpurea' and 'Diversifolia' have burgundy leaves

'Mt. St. Helen' and 'Thundercloud' have purple leaves

'Newport' and 'Nigra' are dark purple

P. laurocerasus, cherry laurel, 'Variegata' is variegated with white

P. virginiana, chokecherry

leaves of 'Canada Red' and 'Shubert' turn red in summer

Robinia pseudoacacia, black locust, 'Frisia' has yellow leaves

(continued)

Trees and Shrubs with Colorful Leaves *(cont'd)*

Sambucus, elder
- *S. canadensis*, American elder, 'Aurea' has yellow leaves
- *S. niger*, European elder
  - 'Aureo-marginata', pale yellow edges
  - 'Marginata', cream edges
  - 'Purpurea', purple leaves
- *S. racemosa*, European red elder, 'Plumosa Aurea' has feathery yellow leaves

Spiraea
- *S.* × *bumalda*
  - 'Goldflame', new leaves are orange, fading to bronze, then yellow, finally turning green
  - 'Limemound' has yellow to lime green leaves
- *S. japonica*
  - 'Goldmound' and 'Golden Princess' have yellow leaves

Taxus, yew
- *T. baccata*, English yew
  - 'Aurea', 'Standishii' and 'Washingtonii' have yellow leaves
- *T. cuspidata*, Japanese yew, 'Aurescens' has yellow leaves

Thuja, arborvitae
- *T. occidentalis*, American arborvitae
  - 'Aurea', 'Lutea', and 'Rheingold' are yellow
  - 'Umbraculifera' is blue-gray
- *T. orientalis*, oriental arborvitae
  - 'Aurea Nana', 'Golden Ball' and 'Golden Globe' are yellow
  - 'Sunkist' has golden tips
- *T. plicata*, western arborvitae
  - new growth of 'Canadian Gold' and 'Stoneham Gold' is yellow

Tilia tomentosa, silver linden, the undersides of the leaves are covered with white hairs, giving a silvery appearance

Weigela florida
- 'Variegata' and 'Variegata Nana' are edged with white

Shrubs and Small Trees for Mixed Borders

These trees and shrubs are compact in size, or grow slowly and remain small for years, making them good choices to combine with perennials, groundcovers, and other plants.

Abies fraseri, fraser fir, grows very slowly

Acer, maple
- *A. griseum*, paperbark maple
- *A. japonicum*, full moon maple
- *A. palmatum*, Dissectum Group, dwarf cultivars of Japanese cutleaf maple

Amelanchier spp., serviceberry

Aucuba japonica, gold dust plant

Berberis spp., barberry

Buddleia
- *B. alternifolia* 'Argentea', silver buddleia
- *B. davidii* 'Pygmy Purple' and 'Lochinch', butterfly bush
- *B. japonica*

Buxus spp., boxwood

Callicarpa spp., beautyberry

Camellia spp.

Caryopteris spp., blue mist shrub

Ceanothus americanus, New Jersey tea

Ceanothus spp., California lilac

Cercis canadensis, redbud

Chamecyparis spp., false cypress

Chionanthus retusus, Chinese fringe tree; *C. virginicus*, white fringe tree, is larger but grows slowly

Cistus spp., rock rose

Cornus, dogwood
- *C. alba*, Tatarian dogwood
- *C. florida*, flowering dogwood
- *C. kousa*, kousa dogwood
- *C. mas*, cornelian cherry
- *C. × rutgersensis*, hybrid dogwood

Corylus maxima 'Purpurea', purple hazel

Cotinus
- *C. cogyggria*, smokebush
- *C. obovatus*, American smoketree (for large borders)

Cytisus spp., broom

Daphne
- *D. × burkwoodii*, 'Carol Mackie'
- *D. cneorum*, garland flower
- *D. odora*, winter daphne
- *D. retusa*

Enkianthus spp.

Eucryphia glutinosa

Forsythia spp.

Fothergilla gardenii

Franklinia alatamaha

Hamamelis spp., witch hazel

Hydrangea
- *H. macrophylla*
- *H. quercifolia*, oakleaf hydrangea

Ilex spp., holly

Juniperus, juniper, dwarf and columnar juniper cultivars
- *J. scopulorum* 'Gray Gleam' and 'Lavender Chip', Rocky Mountain juniper
- *J. squamata* 'Meyeri'
- *J. virginiana* 'Skyrocket' and other cultivars, eastern red cedar

Kalmia spp., mountain laurel

Kerria japonica, Japanese kerria

Leucothoe spp.

Magnolia
- *M. × loebneri*, Loebner magnolia
- *M. × soulangiana*, saucer magnolia
- *M. stellata*, star magnolia
- *M. virginiana*, sweet bay magnolia

Mahonia
- *M. aquifolium*, Oregon grape holly
- *M. nervosa*, longleaf mahonia

Malus spp., flowering crab apple

Philadelphus spp., mock orange

Pieris spp.

Pinus, pine
- *P. cembra*, Swiss stone pine (grows slowly)
- *P. mugo* and var. *mugo*
- *P. thunbergiana*, Japanese black pine

Prunus spp., flowering cherry

Pyracantha spp.

Raphiolepis indica, Indian hawthorn

Rhododendron spp., azalea and rhododendron

Robinia pseudoacacia 'Frisia', black locust

Salix, willow
- *S. gracilistyla*, roseglow pussy willow
- *S. purpurea* 'Nana'

Sarcococca spp.

Spiraea spp.

Styrax spp., snowbell

Symphoricarpos
- *S. albus*, snowberry
- *S. orbiculatus*, coralberry

Symplocos paniculata, sapphire berry

Syringa spp. lilac

Taxus spp. yew

Viburnum spp.

Weigela florida

Fragrant Trees and Shrubs

The fragrant parts of the plants listed below are flowers, except where otherwise indicated.

Abelia
- *A. chinensis*, sweet-scented
- *A. × grandiflora*, glossy abelia, mildly fragrant

Acer ginnala, Amur maple

Buddleia davidii, butterfly bush, mildly fragrant

(continued)

Fragrant Trees and Shrubs *(cont'd)*

Buxus sempervirens, sweet-scented flowers, aromatic leaves

Calycanthus floridus, Carolina allspice, mildly scented, fruity flowers, seedpods aromatic when crushed

Caryopteris × *clandonensis*, blue mist shrub, leaves smell pungent when crushed

Ceanothus spp., California lilac, sweet

Chamaecyparis, false cypress

- *C. obtusa*, Hinoki false cypress, 'Kosteri', 'Nana', and 'Nana Aurea' have sweet-scented foliage
- *C. thyoides*, 'Ericoides' and 'Rubicon' have a spicy aroma

Chimonanthus praecox, wintersweet, spicy scent

Chilopsis linearis, desert willow, fragrant flowers in summer

Choisya ternata, Mexican orange, sweet-scented flowers, leaves have pungent, citrusy smell when crushed

Cinnamomum camphora, camphor tree, fragrant flowers in spring

Cladrastis kentuckea (*C. lutea*), yellowwood, sweetly fragrant flowers

Clethra alnifolia, sweet pepperbush, sweet, slightly spicy fragrance

Corylopsis pauciflora, buttercup winterhazel, sweet

Cupressus macrocarpa 'Lutea', Monterey cypress, foliage smells lemony when crushed

Daphne spp., sweetly fragrant flowers; *D. odora*, winter daphne, has the strongest scent

Elaeagnus

- *E. angustifolia*, Russian olive
- *E. pungens*, thorny elaeagnus

Fothergilla major, large fothergilla, sweet

Gardenia jasminoides, intensely sweet

Hamamelis spp., witch hazel, sweet

Helichrysum angustifolia, curry plant, leaves are spicily aromatic, like curry

Hovenia dulcis, Japanese raisin tree, sweetly fragrant flowers

Itea spp. sweetspire, sweet

Juniperus communis, common juniper, 'Compressa', 'Hibernica', and 'Repandum', foliage releases fruity, applelike scent when crushed

Koelreuteria bipinnata, Chinese flame tree, fragrant flowers in late summer

Laburnum × *watereri*, golden chain tree, sweet

Laurus nobilis, bay tree, leaves are aromatic

Lavandula spp., lavender, flowers and leaves have refreshing scent

Lonicera, honeysuckle

- *L. fragrantissima*, winter honeysuckle, lemony

Magnolia

- *M. denudata*, Yulan magnolia, fruity
- *M. grandiflora*, southern magnolia, fruity
- *M. virginiana*, sweet bay magnolia, lemony

Malus spp., crab apple, numerous species and varieties have sweet-scented blossoms

Michelia figo, banana shrub, flowers smell like bananas

Myrtus communis, myrtle, intensely sweet flowers, aromatic leaves

Nerium oleander, sweet, almondlike

Osmanthus

- *O. delavayi*, sweet
- *O. fragrans*, sweet olive, very sweet
- *O. heterophyllus*, holly olive, very sweet

Oxydendrum arboreum, sourwood, sweetly fragrant white flowers

Paulownia tomentosa, empress tree, vanilla-scented flowers

Philadelphus, mock orange, numerous species and cultivars have a sweet scent similar to orange blossoms

Pittosporum spp., sweet

Poncirus trifoliata, hardy orange, sweet, like orange blossoms

Prunus, the blossoms of a number of flowering cherries have a sweet, almondy scent. Fragrant cherries include:

- *P. padus* 'Grandiflora'
- *P. tomentosa*, Nanking cherry
- *P. yedoensis*, Yoshino cherry

Rhododendron, azaleas. Many deciduous azaleas have sweetly fragrant flowers. Fragrant species include:

- *R. arborescens*, sweet azalea
- *R. luteum*
- *R. prinophyllum*, roseshell azalea
- *R. nudiflorum*, pinxterbloom azalea
- *R. vaseyi*, pinkshell azalea

Ribes odoratum, flowering currant, spicy-sweet

Robinia pseudoacacia, black locust, sweet

Rosa spp., rose. See chapter 3 for a list of fragrant roses.

Rosmarinus officinalis, rosemary, leaves have a fresh, piney scent

Skimmia japonica 'Fragrans', slightly fragrant

Sophora secundiflora, mescal bean, fragrant spring flowers

Spartium junceum, Spanish broom, sweet honey scent

Styrax obassia, fragrant snowbell, fragrant white flowers

Symplocos paniculata, sapphire berry, sweetly fragrant flowers

Syringa spp., lilac. The common lilac, *S. vulgaris*, has the most fragrant flowers, with a sweet scent

Thuja, arborvitae

- *T. occidentalis*, American arborvitae, 'Danica', 'Hetz Midget', 'Holmstrupii', and 'Rheingold' give off a fruity, applelike scent when leaves are crushed
- *T. plicata*, foliage smells pineappley when crushed

Tilia, linden

- *T. cordata*, littleleaf linden, and *T. tomentosa*, silver linden, both have fragrant but inconspicuous flowers

Viburnum, numerous species have sweetly fragrant flowers, including:

- *V.* × *burkwoodii*
- *V.* × *carlcephalum*
- *V. carlesii*, Koreanspice viburnum
- *V. farreri*
- *V. grandiflorum*
- *V.* × *juddii*
- *V. opulus*
- *V. tinus*, laurustinus

Yucca spp., sweet

FORCING BRANCHES INDOORS

For an early taste of spring, you can cut branches of some spring-blooming trees and shrubs and force them into early bloom. Forced branches will bloom a month or two ahead of their normal outdoor blooming time.

Cut branches that you would normally prune, to avoid harming the plant's shape. Look for branches with nice, fat flower buds. When to cut is a judgment call. If you cut the branches too early, the buds may not open. Cut too late, the branches won't flower any earlier than their outdoor counterparts.

Here are a few guidelines to keep in mind:

- Shrubs that produce flowers before leaves are easier to force than those that send out foliage first.

(continued)

Forcing Branches Indoors *(cont'd)*

- The later the plant blooms outdoors, the longer it will take to force into bloom indoors. The best time to cut branches for forcing is late winter to very early spring. Branches cut in fall will probably not bloom, because the plants need a cold period before their buds will open.
- Cut branches for forcing on a mild day, around noon when they are full of sap. To maximize the branch's ability to take up water, scrape the outer bark from the cut end of the branch, and cut 3-inch-long slits in the wood, or split the end of the stem with a hammer (but be careful not to crush the stems).
- Stand the cut ends of the branches in a tall container of room-temperature water for 24 hours. If possible, submerge the entire branch, buds and all. Then change to cool water, stand the branches upright, submerged to the lowest buds, and put the container in a dimly lit place where the temperature is about 60° to 65°F, such as a basement or attached garage. You can put some filtering charcoal (not barbecue briquettes) in the water to keep it fresh.
- Three or four days later, change the water, add fresh charcoal, and bring the container to a north window or other location that receives light but not direct sun. Mist the branches with room-temperature water several times a week.
- When the flowers start to open, put the branches in full sun. This helps the blossoms develop good color.
- To speed the forcing process, put the branches in warmer water (100° to 110°F), and replace it with fresh warm water once a day. Mist daily. If you want the flowers for a special occasion and find that they are ready to open too soon, you can slow them down by moving them to a cooler location, where the temperature is 55° to 65°F.
- Throughout the forcing process and when the flowers are in bloom, once a week cut an inch off the bottom of each stem, and give the branches fresh water with new charcoal.

Some branches that force readily are listed below. Cutting times are approximate and will vary with location and weather conditions.

Amelanchier canadensis, serviceberry, cut branches in late January

Cercis canadensis, redbud, cut in early March

Chaenomeles spp., flowering quince, cut in mid-February

Cornus

  C. florida, flowering dogwood, cut in mid to late March

  C. mas, cornelian cherry, cut in late January or early February

Crataegus spp., hawthorn, cut in mid to late March

Forsythia, spp., cut in late January or February
Hamamelis spp., witch hazel, cut in January
Leucothoe spp., cut in March
Malus, apple, flowering crab apple, cut in mid-March or April; time of bloom varies, so cut when buds are plump and just beginning to show color
Philadelphus spp., mock orange, cut in mid to late March
Prunus
- *P. maritima*, beach plum, cut in late January or February
- *P. persica*, flowering peach, cut in late January or February
- *P. serrulata* and other species, flowering cherry, cut in late January or February
- *P. triloba*, flowering plum, cut in late January or February

Rhododendron spp., azalea, cut in late January or February
Ribes odoratum, flowering currant, cut in April when buds show color
Salix discolor, pussy willow, cut in February

TREES AND SHRUBS THAT ATTRACT WILDLIFE

As more and more of our open land is developed, habitat for wildlife is disappearing at an alarming rate. Gardeners can help by creating places for wildlife on their properties, and enjoy the flutter of butterfly wings, the songs of birds, and the many other benefits of sharing one's land with wildlife.

Backyard wildlife habitats can attract birds, butterflies, moths, bees, and other insects, mammals, reptiles, and amphibians.

A landscape designed for wildlife looks rather different from the neatly groomed garden beds and borders so many of us are used to. Wildlife gardens are less manicured, more wild and natural-looking. A mixture of plants of different heights and types is essential, as is a source of water. Trees and shrubs play an important role in wildlife gardens. They provide cover and nesting sites, as well as food in the form of fruits, seeds, and nuts. Those with nectar-rich flowers also nourish butterflies, moths, and bees.

If you would like information on developing a backyard wildlife habitat, contact the National Wildlife Federation, 1400 Sixteenth Street, N.W., Washington, D.C. 20036. To order a copy of their Backyard Wildlife Habitat information packet (which costs $5.50, shipping and handling included), write to the address above or call 1-800-822-9919.

Below are trees and shrubs that are especially attractive to wildlife. They are listed by region because many of the best wildlife plants are regional natives.

NORTHEAST

Acer, maple
- *A. rubrum*, red maple
- *A. saccharum*, sugar maple

Amelanchier canadensis, serviceberry
Berberis spp., barberry
Buddleia davidii, butterfly bush

(continued)

Trees and Shrubs that Attract Wildlife *(cont'd)*

Calycanthus caroliniana, Carolina allspice
Ceanothus americanus, New Jersey tea
Cornus, dogwood
- *C. amomum*, silky dogwood
- *C. sericea*, red-osier dogwood

Cotoneaster spp.
Crataegus spp., hawthorn
Elaeagnus umbellata, autumn olive
Fagus grandifolia, American beech
Ilex spp. holly
- *I. verticillata*, winterberry

Juniperus virginiana, eastern red cedar
Lindera benzoin, spicebush
Liriodendron tulipifera, tulip tree
Mahonia aquifolium, Oregon grape holly
Myrica pensylvanica, bayberry
Nyssa sylvatica, tupelo
Picea glauca, white spruce
Pinus strobus, white pine
Prunus maritima, beach plum
Quercus, oak
- *Q. alba*, white oak
- *Q. rubra*, red oak

Rhododendron spp.
Rhus, sumac
- *R. copallina*, shining sumac
- *R. typhina*, staghorn sumac

Rosa rugosa, saltspray rose
Sambucus canadensis, American elder
Sassafras albidum
Symphoricarpos orbiculatus, coralberry
Syringa spp., lilac
Thuja occidentalis, American arborvitae
Tsuga canadensis, Canadian hemlock
Viburnum dentatum, arrowwood viburnum

SOUTHEAST

Aesculus pavia, red buckeye
Amelanchier canadensis, serviceberry
Aralia spinosa, Hercules' club
Berberis spp., barberry
Buddleia davidii, butterfly bush
Callicarpa americana
Calycanthus caroliniana, Carolina allspice
Carya
- *C. illinoinensis*, pecan
- *C. ovata*, shagbark hickory

Celtis laevigata, hackberry
Cornus florida, flowering dogwood
Cotoneaster spp.
Diospyros virginiana, persimmon
Ilex
- *I. cassine*, dahoon
- *I. opaca*, American holly

Juniperus virginiana, eastern red cedar
Liriodendron tulipifera, tulip tree
Magnolia grandiflora, southern magnolia
Myrica cerifera, wax myrtle
Pinus, pine
- *P. palustris*, longleaf pine
- *P. taeda*, loblolly pine

Quercus, oak
- *Q. phellos*, willow oak
- *Q. virginiana*, live oak

Rhus glabra, smooth sumac
Rubus spp., blackberry
Sabal palmetto, cabbage palmetto
Sambucus canadensis, American elder
Serenoa repens, saw palmetto
Taxodium distichum, bald cypress
Tsuga caroliniana, Carolina hemlock
Vaccinium spp., blueberry
Viburnum
- *V. dentatum*, arrowwood viburnum
- *V. prunifolium*, blackhaw viburnum
- *V. rufidulum*, southern blackhaw

NORTH CENTRAL

Acer saccharum, sugar maple
Amelanchier canadensis, serviceberry
Berberis spp., barberry

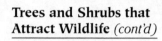

Buddleia davidii, butterfly bush
Carya ovata, shagbark hickory
Ceanothus americanus, New Jersey tea
Cornus sericea, red-osier dogwood
Fagus grandfolia, American beech
Ilex verticillata, winterberry
Juniperus, juniper
 J. chinensis var. *pfitzeriana*, Pfitzer juniper
 J. virginiana, eastern red cedar
Lindera benzoin, spicebush
Mahonia aquifolium, Oregon grape holly
Myrica pensylvanica, bayberry
Nyssa sylvatica, tupelo
Picea glauca, white spruce
Pinus, pine
 P. resinosa, red pine
 P. strobus, white pine
Prunus pumila, sand cherry
Quercus, oak
 Q. alba, white oak
 Q. borealis, northern red oak
Rhus typhina, staghorn sumac
Ribes spp., currant
Sassafras albidum
Symphoricarpos albidum, snowberry
Thuja occidentalis, American arborvitae
Tsuga canadensis, Canadian hemlock
Vaccinium spp., blueberry
Viburnum
 V. dentatum, arrowwood viburnum
 V. lentago, nannyberry
 V. prunifolium, blackhaw viburnum
 V. trilobum, American cranberrybush

MOUNTAIN–GREAT BASIN REGION

Abies, fir
 A. grandis, white fir
 A. lasiocarpa, subalpine fir
Acer glabrum, Rocky Mountain clump maple
Amelanchier alnifolia, serviceberry
Artemisia ludoviciana, prairie sagebrush
Betula fontinalis, western red birch
Buddleia davidii, butterfly bush
Cercocarpus spp., mountain mahogany
Chrysothamnus nauseosus, rabbitbrush
Cornus sericea, red-osier dogwood
Ephedra trifurca, Mormon tea
Ilex verticillata, winterberry
Juniperus, juniper
 J. osteosperma, Utah juniper
 J. scopulorum, Rocky Mountain juniper
Pinus, pine
 P. contorta, lodgepole pine
 P. edulis, piñon pine
 P. flexilis, limber pine
 P. ponderosa, ponderosa pine
Populus
 P. fremontii, Fremont cottonwood
 P. tremuloides, quaking aspen
Prunus, cherry
 P. besseyi, sand cherry
 P. virginiana, chokecherry
Pseudotsuga menziesii, douglas fir
Quercus emoryi, emory oak
Rhus glabra, smooth sumac
Ribes aureum, golden currant

SOUTHWEST

Acer grandidentatum, bigtooth maple
Amelanchier spp., serviceberry
Arbutus menziesii, madrone
Beloperone californica
Celtis pallida, hackberry
Cercidium floridum, palo verde
Chilopsis linearis, desert willow
Chrysothamnus nauseosus, rabbitbrush
Encelia farinosa, brittlebush
Juniperus scopulorum, Rocky Mountain juniper
Larrea tridentata, creosote bush
Olneya tesota, ironwood
Picea pungens, blue spruce

(continued)

Trees and Shrubs that Attract Wildlife *(cont'd)*

Pinus, pine
- *P. edulis*, piñon pine
- *P. ponderosa*, ponderosa pine

Platanus wrightii, Arizona sycamore
Prosopis juliflora var. *velutina*, velvet mesquite
Prunus virginiana, chokecherry
Purshia tridentata, bitterbush
Quercus, oak
- *Q. emoryi*, emory oak
- *Q. gambelii*, gambel oak
- *Q. turbinella*, shrub live oak

Rhamnus crocea, redberry buckthorn
Rhus, sumac
- *R. ovata*, sugar sumac
- *R. trilobata*, skunkbush

Robinia neomexicana, New Mexico locust
Shepherdia rotundifolia, buffaloberry
Tecoma stans, trumpetbush

NORTHWEST

Abies grandis, grand fir
Acer, maple
- *A. circinatum*, vine maple
- *A. macrophyllum*, bigleaf maple

Alnus rubra, red alder
Amelanchier alnifolia, serviceberry
Arbutus menziesii, madrone
Arctostaphylos columbiana, manzanita
Berberis spp., barberry
Buddleia davidii, butterfly bush
Ceanothus prostratus, mahala mat
Chrysothamnus nauseosus, rabbitbrush
Cornus, dogwood
- *C. nuttallii*, Pacific dogwood
- *C. sericea*, red-osier dogwood

Crataegus spp., hawthorn
Gaultheria shallon, salal
Mahonia aquifolium, Oregon grape holly
Malus spp., crab apple
Oemleria cerasiformis, osoberry
Pinus monticola, western white pine
Prunus pumila, sand cherry
Pseudotsuga taxifolia, douglas fir
Quercus garryana, Oregon white oak
Rhamnus purshiana, cascara buckthorn
Ribes sanguineum, red currant
Sambucus caerulea, blue elderberry
Sorbus spp., mountain ash
Thuja plicata, western red cedar
Tsuga heterophylla, western hemlock
Vaccinium ovatum, evergreen huckleberry
Viburnum spp.

STATE TREES

Alabama: Southern pine (*Pinus caribaea*, slash pine, *P. palustris*, longleaf pine and *P. taeda*, loblolly pine)

Alaska: Sitka spruce (*Picea sitchensis*)

Arizona: Palo verde (*Cercidium floridum*)

Arkansas: Pine (*Pinus* spp.)

California: Redwood (*Sequoia sempervirens*)

Colorado: Colorado spruce (*Picea pungens* var. *glauca*)

Connecticut: White oak (*Quercus alba*)

Delaware: American holly (*Ilex opaca*)

District of Columbia: Scarlet oak (*Quercus coccinea*)

Florida: Cabbage palmetto (*Sabal palmetto*)

Georgia: Live oak (*Quercus virginiana*)

Hawaii: Kuki or candlenut (*Aleurites moluccana*)

Idaho: Western white pine (*Pinus monticola*)

Illinois: White oak (*Quercus alba*)

Indiana: Tulip tree (*Liriodendron tulipifera*)

Iowa: Oak (*Quercus* spp.)

Kansas: Cottonwood (*Populus deltoides, P. balsamifera*)

Kentucky: Tulip tree (*Liriodendron tulipifera*)

Louisiana: Bald cypress (*Taxodium distichum*)

Maine: White pine (*Pinus strobus*)

Maryland: White oak (*Quercus alba*)

Massachusetts: American elm (*Ulmus americana*)

Michigan: Eastern white pine (*Pinus strobus*)

Minnesota: Red pine (*Pinus resinosa*)

Mississippi: Southern magnolia (*Magnolia grandiflora*)

Missouri: Flowering dogwood (*Cornus florida*)

Montana: Western yellow pine (*Pinus ponderosa*)

Nebraska: American elm (*Ulmus americana*)

Nevada: Singleleaf pine (*Pinus cembroides* var. *monophylla*)

New Hampshire: Canoe birch (*Betula papyrifera*)

New Jersey: Red oak (*Quercus rubra*)

New Mexico: Piñon pine (*Pinus edulis*)

New York: Sugar maple (*Acer saccharum*)

North Carolina: Pine (*Pinus* spp.)

North Dakota: American elm (*Ulmus americana*)

Ohio: Ohio buckeye (*Aesculus glabra*)

Oklahoma: Redbud (*Cercis canadensis*)

Oregon: Douglas fir (*Pseudotsuga menziesii*)

Pennsylvania: Canadian hemlock (*Tsuga canadensis*)

Rhode Island: Red maple (*Acer rubrum*)

South Carolina: Cabbage palmetto (*Sabal palmetto*)

(continued)

State Trees *(cont'd)*

South Dakota: Black Hills spruce (*Picea glauca* 'Densata')

Tennessee: Tulip tree (*Liriodendron tulipifera*)

Texas: Pecan (*Carya illinoinensis*)

Utah: Colorado blue spruce (*Picea pungens* var. *glauca*)

Vermont: Sugar maple (*Acer saccharum*)

Virginia: Flowering dogwood (*Cornus florida*)

Washington: Western hemlock (*Tsuga heterophylla*)

West Virginia: Sugar maple (*Acer saccharum*)

Wisconsin: Sugar maple (*Acer saccharum*)

Wyoming: Plains cottonwood (*Populus sargentii*)

TREES OF DIFFERENT SIZES

Small Trees

The trees listed here grow 30 feet or less in height and are good choices for small yards and gardens.

Acer, maple
- *A. buergeranum*, trident maple
- *A. ginnala*, Amur maple
- *A. griseum*, paperbark maple (may eventually reach 40 feet, but grows slowly)
- *A. japonicum*, full moon maple
- *A. palmatum*, Japanese maple

Amelanchier spp., serviceberry

Bauhinia variegata, orchid tree

Callistemon citrinus, lemon bottlebrush

Carpinus caroliniana, American hornbeam

Cercidium floridum, palo verde

Cercis, redbud
- *C. canadensis*, eastern redbud
- *C. occidentalis*, western redbud

Chilopsis linearis, desert willow

Chionanthus, fringe tree
- *C. retusus*, Chinese fringe tree
- *C. virginicus*, white fringe tree

Cornus, dogwood
- *C. florida*, flowering dogwood
- *C. kousa*, kousa dogwood
- *C.* × *rutgersensis*, hybrid dogwood

Cotinus obovatus, American smoke tree

Crataegus, hawthorn
- *C. crus-galli*, cockspur hawthorn
- *C. laevigata*
- *C.* × *lavallei*, lavalle thorn
- *C. phaenopyrum*, Washington thorn

Elaeagnus angustifolia, Russian olive

Eriobotrya japonica, loquat

Feijoa sellowiana, pineapple guava

Franklinia alatamaha

Ilex spp., holly

Koelreuteria (may eventually reach 35 feet)
- *K. bipinnata*, Chinese flame tree
- *K. paniculata*, goldenrain tree

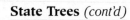

Magnolia

- *M.* × *soulangiana*, saucer magnolia
- *M. tomentosa*, star magnolia
- *M. virginiana*, sweet bay magnolia

Malus, flowering crab apple, most species and cultivars are under 30 feet

Oxydendrum arboreum, sourwood

Pinus

- *P. cembra*, Swiss stone pine
- *P. mugo*, mugo pine
- *P thunbergiana*, Japanese black pine

Prunus, flowering cherry

- *P.* 'Okame'
- *P. sargentii*, Sargent flowering cherry
- *P. serrulata*, Japanese flowering cherry, species form is taller, but there are numerous cultivars under 30 feet
- *P. yedoensis* 'Akebono'

Prunus cerasifera 'Atropurpurea', purple leaf plum

Sophora secundiflora, mescal bean

Styrax

- *S. japonicus*, Japanese snowbell
- *S. obassia*: Fragrant snowbell

Syringa reticulata, Japanese tree lilac

Tsuga canadensis 'Pendula', weeping Canadian hemlock

Big Trees for Large Spaces

These trees are large and need lots of space. Feature them as specimens—focal points—on a broad lawn, or use them elsewhere in an expansive landscape. The trees on this list grow at least 60 feet tall (most are substantially taller), and some have a wide-spreading canopy as well.

Abies, fir

- *A. concolor*, balsam fir
- *A. homolepis*, nikko fir
- *A. procera*, noble fir

Acer, maple

- *A. macrophyllum*, bigleaf maple
- *A. pseudoplatanus*, sycamore maple
- *A. rubrum*, red maple
- *A. saccharum*, sugar maple

Aesculus hippocastanum, horse chestnut

Araucaria

- *A. araucana*, Chilean pine
- *A. bidwillii*, bunya-bunya pine

Cedrus, cedar

- *C. atlantica*, Atlas cedar
- *C. deodara*, deodar cedar

Chamaecyparis, false cypress

- *C. nootkatensis*, Nootka false cypress
- *C. obtusa*, Hinoki false cypress

Fagus, beech

- *F. grandifolia*, American beech
- *F. sylvatica*, European beech

Fraxinus, ash

- *F. americana*, white ash
- *F. excelsior*, European ash

Ginkgo biloba, maidenhair tree

Gymnocladus dioica, Kentucky coffee tree

Larix decidua, European larch

Liquidambar styraciflua, sweet gum

Liriodendron tulipifera, tulip tree

Magnolia grandiflora, southern magnolia

Metasequoia glyptostroboides, dawn redwood

Picea, spruce

- *P. asperata*, Chinese spruce
- *P. engelmannii*, Engelman spruce
- *P. orientalis*, eastern spruce
- *P. pungens*, Colorado spruce
- *P. sitchensis*, Coast spruce

(continued)

Big Trees for Large Spaces *(cont'd)*

Pinus, pine
- *P. pinea*, Italian stone pine
- *P. ponderosa*, ponderosa pine
- *P. radiata*, Monterey pine
- *P. sylvestris*, Scotch pine

Platanus
- *P.* × *acerifolia*, London plane
- *P. occidentalis*, eastern sycamore

Populus deltoides, eastern cottonwood

Pseudotsuga menziesii, Douglas fir

Quercus, oak
- *Q. alba*, white oak (wide spreading)
- *Q. macrocarpa*, bur oak
- *Q. rubra*, red oak (wide spreading)
- *Q. virginiana*, live oak (wide spreading)

Thuja plicata, giant cedar

Tilia tomentosa, silver linden

Zelkova serrata, Chinese zelkova

Shade Trees

The trees listed here are good for shade, and also generally amenable to garden use, that is, growing happily with other plants. The shade they cast is not so heavy that it prohibits the growth of understory plants.

Acer, maple: Classic shade trees for street and lawn planting. Smaller species, such as Amur, paperbark, and Japanese maples are handsome in small yards and mixed borders

- *A. platanoides*, Norway maple: Plant by itself or as a street tree, roots are invasive
- *A. macrophyllum*, bigleaf maple
- *A. rubrum*, red maple
- *A. saccharum*, sugar maple

Ailanthus altissima, tree of heaven: Useful in poor, dry soil, but not recommended with other plants

Albizia julibrissin, silk tree: Ferny leaves give light, dappled shade, especially good in dry climates

Alnus glutinosa, black alder: Especially useful as a screen or divider

Betula spp., birch: Small leaves provide dappled shade

Caragana arborescens, Siberian pea tree: Compound leaves provide shade of medium density, can itself tolerate quite a bit of shade

Cercis canadensis, redbud: Medium shade, tolerates underplanting

Chamaecyparis obtusa, Hinoki false cypress: Pleasant shade and more amenable to underplanting than most false cypresses

Chilopsis linearis, desert willow: Excellent shade tree for desert gardens

Cladrastis kentuckea, yellowwood: Nice shade tree for lawn or street planting; permits underplanting

Cornus spp., dogwoods: Handsome in lawns, cast medium shade, and permit underplanting

C. florida, flowering dogwood: Many are suffering from an anthracnose disease in the East, and a gamble, but still one of the most beautiful shade trees for home use where the disease is not prevalent

C. kousa, kousa dogwood

C. mas, cornelian cherry

C. nuttallii, Pacific dogwood: Lovely for the West Coast, but hard to grow

C × rutgersensis, hybrid dogwood

Crataegus spp., hawthorn: Handsome trees with medium shade, allow underplanting

Elaeagnus angustifolia, Russian olive: Good shade tree for windy, dry, exposed locations, but not recommended for underplanting

Fagus, beech, regal: Classic shade trees to plant by themselves; mature trees are not kind to nearby plants

F. grandifolia, American beech

F. sylvatica, European beech

Fraxinus spp., ash: Spreading trees cast lovely shade for people; not recommended for underplanting

Gleditsia triacanthos, honey locust: Light, dappled shade, but roots tend to spread; if you want to plant near it, grow var. *inermis*, which is thornless

Grevillea robusta, silk oak: Ferny leaves cast shade of medium density; amenable to underplanting if lower limbs are removed to raise the canopy

Halesia carolina, Carolina silverbell: Graceful, arching form, shade of medium density; takes well to underplanting

Jacaranda mimosifolia: Ferny leaves cast dappled to medium shade; for warm climates only

Koelreuteria paniculata, goldenrain tree: Spreading canopy casts deep shade—nice for people but not recommended for underplanting

Liquidambar styraciflua, sweet gum: Fine on its own, but not amenable to underplanting; fairly dense shade, and greedy roots when mature

Liriodendron tulipifera, tulip tree: Big, pretty tree for specimen use; moderate shade; not recommended for underplanting

Magnolia spp.: As a group, they cast medium shade and take underplanting reasonbly well

Malus spp., flowering crab apple: Nice shade trees for small yards, but not recommended for underplanting

(continued)

Shade Trees *(cont'd)*

Melia azedarach, chinaberry: Good shade tree for desert gardens

Metasequoia glyptostroboides, dawn redwood: Ferny leaves; fine for underplanting when young, mature trees will shade out plants growing close to trunk

Nyssa sylvatica, tupelo: Broad crown provides nice shade, will tolerate underplanting

Oxydendrum arboreum, sourwood: Good for lightly shaded places, casts medium shade itself

Pinus spp., pine: Pleasant shade for people, permit underplanting when young; remove lower branches of mature trees to allow plants to grow underneath

Populus tremuloides, quaking aspen: Nice shade and less invasive roots than most other poplars and cottonwoods, making it a better choice for gardens

Prosopis glandulosa, honey mesquite: Casts light, dappled shade in desert gardens

Prunus spp., flowering cherry: Good as lawn trees, or planted near the house where the spring flowers can be enjoyed

Pseudotsuga menziesii, Douglas fir: One of the best needled evergreens to use in shady gardens; if lower branches are removed from mature trees to raise the canopy, underplanting can succeed

Quercus spp., oak: Oaks are among the best shade trees for people, and generally amenable to underplanting

Robinia pseudoacacia, black locust: Dappled to medium shade; they tend to sucker and grow in groups, so plan on having a clump

Salix babylonica: Lovely shade tree for moist soil, especially along a stream, but not good for underplanting with other plants

Schinus molle, California pepper tree: Good shade tree for poor soil in dry, warm climates, but messy, and roots become invasive in time

Sophora japonica, Japanese pagoda tree: Excellent for home use; compound leaves cast shade of medium density; permits underplanting

Sorbus spp., mountain ash: Compound leaves cast shade of medium density; fine for underplanting, especially if lower branches of older trees are removed

Stewartia pseudocamellia, Japanese stewartia: Small leaves cast shade that permits underplanting

Taxodium distichum, bald cypress: Quite tall when mature, but a nice shade tree that will grow in most parts of the United States

Tough Trees and Shrubs for City Conditions

City conditions are difficult for plants. Light is often limited, soil is generally poor, and there are strong winds, dramatic swings in temperature, and air pollution. Street trees have the added problems of limited root runs, inadequate water, exposure to road salt in winter, and damage from animals, vehicles, and vandals. The plants listed here are among the best performers in these conditions.

Acer, maple
- *A. campestre*, hedge maple
- *A. rubrum*, red maple

Aesculus × *carnea*, red horse chestnut
Amerlanchier spp., serviceberry
Berberis thunbergii, Japanese barberry
Carpinus, hornbeam
- *C. betulus*, European hornbeam
- *C. caroliniana*, American hornbeam

Celtis occidentalis, hackberry
Chamaecyparis, false cypress
- *C. nootkatensis*, Nootka false cypress
- *C. pisifera*

Corylus colurna, Turkish filbert
Crataegus viridis 'Winter King', Winter King hawthorn
Elaeagnus umbellata, autumn olive
Eucommia ulmoides, hardy rubber tree
Euonymus alatus, burning bush, winged euonymus
Forsythia spp.
Fraxinus excelsior, European ash
Ginkgo biloba, maidenhair tree
Gleditsia triacanthos var. *inermis*, thornless honey locust
Gymnocladus dioica, Kentucky coffee tree
Hibiscus syriacus, rose of Sharon
Hydrangea paniculata 'Grandiflora', peegee hydrangea
Juniperus spp., juniper
Koelreuteria paniculata, goldenrain tree
Ligustrum spp., privet
Malus spp., flowering crab apple
Potentilla fruticosa, shrubby cinquefoil
Pyrus calleryana, callery pear
Quercus, oak
- *Q. imbricaria*, shingle oak
- *Q. rubra*, red oak
- *Q. shumardii*, shumard oak

Rhamnus frangula, alder buckthorn
Sophora japonica, Japanese pagoda tree
Syringa reticulata, Japanese tree lilac
Taxodium distichum, bald cypress
Taxus spp., yew
Tilia tomentosa, silver linden
Ulmus parviflora, Chinese elm, lacebark elm
Zelkova serrata, Japanese zelkova

Trees and Shrubs with Ornamental Bark

Some trees have interesting bark that is an asset to the garden year-round, and which can be especially valuable in winter when the landscape in all but warm climates is barren and at rest. Bark may be interesting because of its color, like that of the white birches; a particularly smooth or lumpy or patterned texture; or because the outer layer peels (or exfoliates) to reveal differently colored inner bark. The trees and shrubs listed here are noted for their decorative bark.

Acer, maple
- *A. buergeranum*, trident maple, exfoliating scaly brown to grayish to orangey bark

(continued)

Trees and Shrubs with Ornamental Bark *(cont'd)*

A. davidii, David maple, white-striped bark in winter; rare in the United States, but best-suited to the Pacific Northwest

A. griseum, paperbark maple, brown bark exfoliates to reveal orangey brown to golden inner bark

A. palmatum 'Sangokaku' (a.k.a. 'Senkaki'), coralbark maple, young stems on young trees are coral-colored, stunning in winter

Amelanchier arborea, downy serviceberry, smooth grayish bark, often slightly reddish, with vertical cracks; as tree ages bark becomes interestingly furrowed

Arbutus menziesii, madrone, and *A. unedo*, strawberry tree, both have peeling orange-brown bark

Betula, birch

B. alleghaniensis, yellow birch, flaky yellowish gray bark changes to reddish brown as tree matures, and forms large plates

B. nigra 'Heritage', Heritage river birch, white bark peels in plates to reveal cinnamon, russet, or grayish inner bark

B. papyrifera, canoe birch, white bark striped and streaked with deep gray or black; bark peels in large sheets to reveal orange inner bark

B. pendula, European white birch, white bark striped with gray, becoming black as tree ages; very susceptible to borer damage

B. populifolia, gray birch, grayish white bark with dark triangular markings where branches meet trunk

Carpinus, hornbeam

C. betulus, European hornbeam, furrowed gray bark on mature trees

C. caroliniana, American hornbeam, smooth, gray, twisted bark

Carya ovata, shagbark hickory, bark peels in long strips, giving trunk a shaggy appearance

Clethra

C. acuminata, cinnamon clethra, brown to reddish brown bark, sometimes exfoliates

C. barbinervis, Japanese clethra, smooth gray, lustrous bark that sometimes exfoliates

Cryptomeria japonica, Japanese cedar, reddish brown bark that exfoliates in long strips

Eucalyptus spp., gray-green outer bark peels to reveal yellow inner bark

Fagus sylvatica, European beech, smooth gray bark develops a lovely texture over time

Franklinia alatamaha, smooth gray bark with vertical cracks

Lagerstroemia indica, crape myrtle, smooth gray outer bark peels to expose inner bark that's a mixture of grays and browns

Parrotia persica, Persian parrotia, on mature trees bark exfoliates, revealing a mixture of gray, green, brown and white

Pinus bungeana, lacebark pine, bark of mature tree peels in plates to expose lighter inner bark

Platanus

P. × *acerifolia*, London plane, exfoliating gray-green to cream bark

P. occidentalis, sycamore, reddish to grayish brown bark exfoliates to reveal creamy white inner bark

Prunus, flowering cherry

P. maackii, Amur cherry, shiny, exfoliating reddish brown bark striped in black

P. serrula, peeling reddish brown bark; unfortunately susceptible to borers and other problems

Stewartia pseudocamellia, Japanese stewartia, exfoliating bark of grayish brown, sometimes with a red-orange sheen

Ulmus parvifolia, lacebark elm, mottled bark of gray, brown, green, and orange peels in patches to reveal lighter inner bark

Problematic Trees

Here are some trees with undesirable characteristics. If you are planning to plant some new trees on your property, you may want to avoid these, depending upon your location and dedication.

Acer negundo, box elder, attracts the box elder bug, looks weedy, and has weak wood

Acer saccharinum, silver maple, messy, brittle, branches are prone to breaking, invasive roots; also susceptible to insect problems

Aesculus hippocastanum, horse chestnut, invasive roots, prone to disease

Birches, European white birch (*Betula pendula*), canoe birch (*B. papyrifera*) and gray birch (*B. populifolia*) are all being attacked by leaf miners and borers, and it is best to avoid planting them at this time. European white birch is most susceptible. A good substitute is river birch, *B. nigra* 'Heritage'.

(continued)

Trees and Shrubs with Ornamental Bark *(cont'd)*

Cornus florida, flowering dogwood, an anthracnose disease has killed many throughout the eastern United States. The disease seems to be less severe in dry years, and good care helps home specimens ward it off. Water the trees in dry weather and keep fallen leaves cleared up. *Cornus kousa* and *C.* × *rutgersensis*, a hybrid between *C. florida* and *C. kousa*, both appear to be more resistant to the disease than flowering dogwood.

Cupressus macrocarpa, Monterey cypress, tends to blow over

Malus, flowering crab apples, notoriously prone to scab disease; look for resistant cultivars

Paulownia tomentosa, empress tree, lovely flowers but very messy, with very dense shade and invasive roots

Pinus thunbergiana, Japanese black pine, dying in droves on Long Island due to insect problems. If you live where insects are a problem for black pines, substitute a native species such as eastern red cedar, *Juniperus virginiana*.

Populus, poplars, as a group, susceptible to numerous pest and disease problems. Lombardy poplar (*P. nigra* 'Italica') is especially problematic. Plains cottonwood (*P. deltoides* var. *occidentalis*) has messy seeds and invasive roots, so be forewarned if you plant it.

Pyrus calleryana, callery pear, often has weak branch structure and tends to split. Look for trees with wide-angled branches instead of narrow crotches.

Salix, willows, susceptible to numerous pests and diseases, wood is weak, roots are greedy for water, and invasive

Tsuga canadensis, eastern hemlock, *T. caroliniana*, Carolina hemlock, have been ravaged by the hemlock woolly adelgid in the eastern United States. Dormant oil sprays have been effective in controlling the insect, and the western hemlock (*T. heterophylla*) appears to be resistant and shows promise as a possible substitute

Ulmus pumila, Siberian elm, invasive roots, self-sows with abandon, weak wood

Trees and Shrubs with Contorted Branches

Trees and shrubs with twisted, gnarled branches can serve as focal points in winter gardens. When the leaves have fallen, the plants appear as strange sculptures in the barren landscape. Here are some trees and shrubs with contorted branches.

Arbutus unedo 'Compacta', strawberry tree

Chaenomeles speciosa 'Contorta', flowering quince

Corylus avellana 'Contorta', Harry Lauder's walking stick

× *Cupressocyparis leylandii* 'Contorta' (a.k.a. *Cupressus macrocarpa* 'Contorta'), leyland cypress

Morus bombycis 'Unryu', mulberry (rare and hard to find)

Poncirus trifoliata 'Flying Dragon', hardy orange, has twisted stems and curved thorns

Prunus mume 'Contorta', flowering apricot (hard to find)

Salix, willows

S. babylonica 'Crispa', ram's horn willow, has weeping branches and curled leaves

S. erythroflexuosa, the leaves as well as the weeping branches are twisted; yellow bark

S. × 'Golden Curls', has yellow bark on twisted, weeping branches. 'Scarlet Curls' has red bark.

S. matsudana 'Tortuosa', corkscrew willow

TREE AND SHRUB MISCELLANY

Here are some interesting tree and shrub facts, from *The Guinness Book of World Records*:

- The oldest known shrub is a creosote bush (*Larrea tridentata*) found in California. It is estimated to be 11,700 years old.
- The tallest rhododendron is a specimen of *Rhododendron arboreum* growing on a mountain in India; it is 65 feet tall.
- The oldest known type of tree still living today is the ginkgo or maidenhair tree (*Ginkgo biloba*), which has been with us since the Jurassic era, 160 million years ago.
- The oldest tree known to be living today in the United States is the bristlecone pine (*Pinus longaeva*), which is found in the Nevada and California deserts. The oldest recorded specimen, found in Nevada, was 5,100 years old. The oldest one living today is 4,700 years old and grows in California. It's called Methusaleh.
- Scientists believe the giant sequoia (*Sequoiadendron giganteum*) could live as long as 6,000 years, although no specimen that old has yet been found.
- The biggest tree in the world in terms of mass is the General Sherman giant sequoia in Sequoia National Park in California. In 1991 it measured 83 feet in circumference and had an estimated weight of 2,756 tons. It's still growing.

(continued)

Trees and Shrub Miscellany *(cont'd)*

- The tree with the biggest recorded circumference was a European chestnut (*Castanea sativa*) on Mount Etna that measured 190 feet.
- The tree with the broadest-spreading canopy is a great banyan (*Ficus benghalensis*) in the Indian Botanical Garden in Calcutta. It spreads over three acres.
- The tallest tree ever measured was a eucalyptus (*Eucalyptus regnans*) in Australia, which was believed to be 470 feet tall in 1885. Another specimen found in 1872, also in Australia, was 435 feet at the time but was estimated to have topped 500 feet at its tallest.
- The tallest tree living today is the National Geographic Society coast redwood (*Sequoia sempervirens*) in Humboldt Redwoods State Park in California. In 1991 it was 365 feet tall.

Chapter 5
GRASSES AND GROUNDCOVERS

LAWN GRASSES

This chapter provides information on lawn grasses, ornamental grasses, and low-growing plants used for groundcover.

REGIONAL LAWN GRASSES

NORTHEAST AND UPPER MIDWEST

Bentgrass (*Agrostis* spp.). Suitable for New York State and the Northeast, and north into Canada. Not recommended for the Midwest. Tolerates poor soil but best with reasonably fertile soil and regular water. Usually mixed with other grasses. Attractive but needs frequent mowing and tends to develop thatch. Not good in hot, humid conditions. Cultivars include Astoria, Cohansey, Emerald, Exeter, Highland, Penneagle, Seaside, Toronto.

Buffalo grass (*Buchloe dactyloides*). For arid locations in the Upper Midwest. Native American species, tolerant of heat, cold, drought, heavy soil. In Upper Plains, plant with redtop (*Agrostis alba*). Cultivars include Prairie, Sharp's Improved, 609, Texoka.

(continued)

Regional Lawn Grasses *(cont'd)*

Fine fescue (*Festuca rubra, F. longifolia*). Tolerates shade and drought. Recommended cultivars include Atlanta, Banner, C-26, Flyer, Fortress, Highlight, Jamestown, Pennlawn, Reliant, Ruby, Scaldis, Shadow, Waldina.

Kentucky bluegrass (*Poa pratensis*). Most widely planted lawn grass across the northern two-thirds of the continental United States. Produces a thick, lush lawn. Needs watering in dry weather. Good cultivars include Adelphi, America, Bensun, Bristol, Columbia, Eclipse, Liberty, Majestic, Midnight, Nugget, Parade.

Perennial ryegrass (*Lolium perenne*). Germinates quickly and can anchor soil while bluegrass gets established. Short-lived. Recommended cultivars include Palmer, Pennfine, Repell, Yorktown II.

Zoysia grass (*Zoysia* spp.). Usually grown in the South, but also recommended for dry parts of the Midwest. Takes time to become established but tolerates drought and pests. Goes dormant in winter. Cultivars include Emerald, Jade, Meyer (Z-52).

SOUTHEAST

Bahia grass (*Paspalum notatum*). Good in South, especially coastal locations with poor soil. Low maintenance needs. Cultivars include Argentine, Paraguay, Pensacola.

Bermuda grass (*Cynodon dactylon* and other spp.). Full sun. Needs less water and fertilizer than many grasses, but prone to thatch buildup. Goes dormant in winter; overseed with ryegrass in fall. Cultivars include Cheyenne, Midiron, MIdway, Ormond, Sahara, Sundevil, Tifway, Tufcote, Vamont.

Centipede grass (*Eremochloa ophiuroides*). Low in maintenance—doesn't need as much fertilizing or mowing as most lawn grasses in the South. Good in acid soil, poor to average fertility. Does not do well in dry climates. Overseed with ryegrass for winter. Cultivars include Oaklawn, Tennessee Hardy.

Tall fescue (*Festuca arundinacea*). Useful in shady locations in the upper South. Tolerates heat and drought. A blend of two or more cultivars works best. Cultivars include Adventure, Apache, Bonanza, Falcon, Finelawn I, Houndog, Mustang, Olympic, Rebel II, Shannon, Silverado.

Ryegrass (*Lolium* spp.). Used to overseed grasses like Bermuda that go dormant in winter. Ryegrassses can become pests when they persist after the dormant summer grass returns to active growth. Oregon intermediate ryegrass (*L.* × *hybridum*), a hybrid between an annual and a perennial ryegrass, is considered better for overseeding than the annual type. Or look for turf-type cultivars of perennial ryegrass (*L. perenne*), such as All Star, Birdie, Blazer, Derby, Manhattan II, Omega II, Palmer, Pennfine, Prelude, Yorktown II.

St. Augustine grass (*Stenotaphrum secundatum*). Most widely planted lawn grass in Florida. Good for the humid Gulf Coast region, moderate shade as well as full sun. Needs watering in dry climates. Cannot tolerate cold. Prone to thatch. Look for cultivars resistant to St. Augustine decline (SAD). Floratam resists chinch bugs. Seville is salt-tolerant. Other cultivars include Bitter Blue, Floratine, Roselawn.

Zoysia grass (*Zoysia* spp.). Takes time to become established, but tolerates drought and pests. Tough and durable. Prone to thatch. Goes dormant in winter and is difficult to overseed. Cultivars include Emerald, Jade, Meyer (Z-52).

MIDWEST–GREAT PLAINS

Bermuda grass (*Cynodon dactylon* and other spp.). Suitable for the lower Midwest. Full sun. Needs less water and fertilizer than many other grasses. Goes dormant in winter; overseed with ryegrass in fall. Cultivars include Cheyenne, Guymon, Midiron, Midway, PeeDee, Sahara, Sundevil, Tifway, Vamont.

Blue grama (*Bouteloua gracilis*). Native to the Plains, good in arid locations with alkaline soil. Tolerates heat and drought; low maintenance needs.

Buffalo grass (*Buchloe dactyloides*). A native American species, tolerant of heat, cold, drought, and heavy soil. In the upper Plains plant it with redtop (*Agrostis alba*), a bentgrass. Where soil is alkaline, mix it with blue grama. Cultivars include Prairie, Sharp's Improved, 609, Texoka.

Fine fescue (*Festuca rubra*, *F. longifolia*). Tolerates shade, drought, poor soil. Cultivars include Aurora, Jamestown (for shade), Pennlawn, Reliant, Scaldis.

Tall fescue (*Festuca arundinacea*). Sometimes called Kentucky 31. Grown in the lower Midwest. Tolerates heat and drought. Cultivars include Apache, Clemfine, Falcon, Midnight, Rebel.

Kentucky bluegrass (*Poa pratensis*). Most widely grown lawn grass in the northern two-thirds of the continental United States. Needs watering in dry weather. Cultivars include America, Cheri, Dawn, Glade, Harmony, Merion, Nassau, Pennstar.

Perennial ryegrass (*Lolium perenne*). Use to overseed Bermuda grass in winter. Fast-growing and short-lived. Cultivars include Blazer, Palmer, Yorktown II.

Zoysia grass (*Zoysia* spp.). Recommended for arid parts of the Midwest. Takes time to become established, but tolerates drought and pests. Goes dormant in winter and is difficult to overseed. Cultivars include Emerald, Jade, Meyer (Z-52).

(continued)

Regional Lawn Grasses *(cont'd)*

SOUTHWEST AND CALIFORNIA

Alkali grass (*Puccinellia* spp.). For highly alkaline soils only.

Bermuda grass (*Cynodon dactylon* and other spp.). Full sun. Needs less water and fertilizer than many other grasses. Goes dormant in winter; overseed with ryegrass in fall. Cultivars include Cheyenne, Midiron, Santa Ana, Texturf 10, Tifway, Tifway II.

Buffalo grass (*Buchloe dactyloides*). Tolerant of heat and drought. Look for turf-type varieties. Cultivars include Falcon, Houndog, Mustang, Olympic, Rebel II, Shannon, Silverado.

Perennial ryegrass (*Lolium perenne*). Fast-growing and short-lived. Use to overseed Bermuda grass in fall. Cultivars include Citation II, Manhattan II, Palmer, Repell, Tat.

Zoysia grass (*Zoysia* spp.). Takes time to become established, but tolerates drought and pests. Goes dormant in winter and is difficult to overseed. Cultivars include Emerald, Jade, Meyer (Z-52).

NORTHWEST (INCLUDES NORTHERN CALIFORNIA)

Bentgrass (*Agrostis* spp.). Recommended for coastal locations in the Northwest. Cultivars include Astoria, Cohansey, Congressional, Emerald, Exeter, Highland, Penneagle, Seaside, Toronto.

Fine fescue (*Festuca rubra*, *F. longifolia*). Tolerates shade. Usually mixed with other grasses. Cultivars include Aurora, Enjoy, Jamestown (for shade), Reliant, Scaldis.

Tall fescue (*Festuca arundinacea*). Tolerates heat and drought. Look for turf-type varieties. Cultivars include Falcon, Houndog, Mustang, Olympic, Rebel II, Shannon, Silverado.

Kentucky bluegrass (*Poa pratensis*). Most widely planted lawn grass across upper two-thirds of the continental United States. Needs watering in dry weather. Cultivars include Adelphi, America, Bensun, Bristol, Columbia, Eclipse, Liberty, Majestic, Midnight, Parade.

LIGHT NEEDS

LAWN GRASSES FOR FULL SUN

Bahia grass: Full sun to partial shade

Bentgrass: Full sun to partial shade

Bermuda grass: Full sun

Buffalo grass: Full sun

Centipede grass: Full sun to light shade

Tall fescue: Full sun to light shade

Kentucky bluegrass: Full sun to partial shade

Ryegrass: Full sun to light shade

Zoysia grass: Full sun to light shade

LAWN GRASSES FOR SHADE

Bahia grass: Tolerates partial to light shade

Centipede grass: Tolerates partial to light shade

Fine fescue: Tolerates light shade (the most shade-tolerant)

Tall fescue: Tolerates light shade

St. Augustine grass: Tolerates light shade

Zoysia grass: Tolerates light shade

DROUGHT-TOLERANT LAWN GRASSES

Alkali grass: Drought-tolerant, suitable for desert climates

Bahia grass: Can tolerate drought, but grows best in climates with regular rainfall

Bermuda grass: Tough and drought-tolerant

Buffalo grass: Once established, can get by on low water—as little as 12 inches a year

Centipede grass: Tolerates brief dry spells, but needs water in a drought

Fine fescue: The species known as hard fescue (*Festuca longifolia*) is moderately drought-tolerant, cultivar Aurora in particular. FRT-30149 fine fescue (*F. rubra*) and Shademaster creeping fescue can also tolerate drought.

Tall fescue: Moderately drought-tolerant, more so in cooler climates.

Kentucky bluegrass: Not drought-tolerant as a rule, although cultivars Bristol, Challenger, and Wabash hold up well during dry spells

Perennial ryegrass: Moderately drought-tolerant

Zoysia grass: Drought-tolerant

WHEN TO PLANT

In all regions, the best time to seed a lawn is early fall or early spring, when weather conditions are moderate and least stressful for plants.

Sod, plugs, and sprigs can be planted anytime during the growing season.

ESTABLISHING A NEW LAWN

You can start a new lawn with seed, sod, sprigs, or plugs (the last two are used mainly in the South).

SEEDING A LAWN

This is the least expensive method, but it requires the most work to get a lawn established.

- Buy fresh, name-brand seed. Read the label carefully. It should list not just the types of grasses contained in the mix, such as Kentucky bluegrass and fine

(continued)

Seeding a Lawn *(cont'd)*

fescue, but also the cultivars the mix contains, such as America (bluegrass) and Pennlawn (fine fescue). The label should also list germination rates. Look for 75% or better for Kentucky bluegrass, and at least 85% for fine fescue, tall fescue, and ryegrass.

- Test the soil for pH and nutrient content. The best pH range for most lawn grasses is 6.2 to 6.8 or 7.0. If the pH is below 6.2, add lime to raise it. Apply 50 pounds of lime per 1,000 square feet. If more lime is needed to raise or maintain the pH in the desired range, apply at the same rate two or three times a year instead of applying more lime at one time.
- Cultivate the soil 4 to 6 inches deep. If the soil is poorly drained, spread 4 to 6 inches of good topsoil and till it in well.
- Rake to smooth out high and low spots and level the surface, and to remove stones, twigs, and large lumps and clods.
- Broadcast seed evenly over the soil surface; a mechanical spreader provides the most uniform coverage. Put half the seed in the spreader and go over the area in one direction. Then spread the rest of the seed at a 90-degree angle to the first direction.
- Rake the seed lightly into the soil, then water lightly to settle the soil. If the soil is light and powdery when dry, roll it before watering.
- Mulch with straw or burlap to prevent the seed from washing or blowing away or being eaten by birds.

You can have the lawn hydroseeded by a professional. In hydroseeding, a blend of seed, fertilizer, and mulch is pressure-blown onto the soil. The mixture sticks to the soil, so less seed is likely to be washed away by rain or blown away by wind.

Keep the soil evenly moist until the seeds germinate. When the seedlings are up, water more deeply and less often.

OVERSEEDING

To overseed a lawn (that is, to plant new seed in an existing lawn) with cool-season grasses for winter greenery in warm climates or to repair thin spots, first mow the existing grass closely.

- If thatch or weeds are present, remove them. Rake away all debris to leave the soil surface bare between the grass plants that remain.
- Apply lime or fertilizer if needed.
- Sow seed by hand or with a slit seeder (you may be able to rent one instead of purchasing it).

- Rake lightly, and top-dress with a thin layer of good-quality soil. Roll or tamp.
- Water gently but thoroughly, and keep moist 4 to 6 weeks.

SOD

To lay sod, prepare the soil as directed above for seeding.

- Unroll strips of sod and lay them in a staggered pattern (the way bricks are laid) so the short ends of adjoining strips are not in line with one another. Butt the edges of the sod strips tightly against one another, but do not overlap them.
- When the sod is in place, roll it to ensure good contact with the soil.
- Water thoroughly, soaking the sod well so the water penetrates all the way through.
- Give the sod a good soaking every day (unless it rains) for 1 to 2 weeks. After the first 2 weeks, keep the sod moist (but not saturated) for another 4 weeks, until it establishes good roots.

SPRIGS AND PLUGS

Prepare the soil as directed for seeding.

- Space sprigs evenly over the area, and plant by hand or with special equipment designed for this purpose. Set sprigs about 6 inches apart, plugs 6 to 12 inches apart.
- Top-dress with a thin layer of good-quality soil.
- Keep evenly moist until growth begins (4 to 6 weeks) as for seed, but do not saturate as for sod.

LAWN MAINTENANCE

MOWING

- Keep lawn mower blades sharp. Dull blades leave ragged edges that look messy and invite disease.
- Never remove more than one-third of the grass blade at a time when mowing. Mowing a bit too high is better than mowing too low.

(continued)

Mowing *(cont'd)*

- Do not mow when the grass is wet; clippings will clump up and clog the mower.
- Mow higher in hot weather or shady conditions, lower in cool weather and full sun.
- Leave the clippings on the lawn after mowing. They feed the grass, do not cause thatch, and can cut fertilizer needs in half.

MOWING HEIGHTS FOR DIFFERENT GRASSES

Bahia grass: 2 to 3 inches
Bentgrass: 1/3 to 1 inch
Bermuda grass: 3/4 to 1 1/2 inches
Blue grama: 2 to 3 inches
Buffalo grass: 1 inch, or let it reach full height of 3 to 4 inches
Centipede grass: 1 to 2 inches
Fine fescue: 2 inches
Tall fescue: 2 to 3 inches
Kentucky bluegrass: 1 1/2 to 2 1/2 inches
Annual ryegrass: 1 1/2 to 2 inches
Perennial ryegrass: 1 1/2 to 2 inches
St. Augustine grass: 1 1/2 to 3 inches
Zoysia grass: 1 to 1 1/2 inches

WATERING

Traditional practice is to give lawns one to two inches of water per week, except in the case of drought-tolerant grasses (see page 317).

A more recent—and water-conserving—recommendation is to water only during prolonged drought, and then to water deeply, so water penetrates 6 to 8 inches into the soil. During brief spells of dry weather, the grass will go dormant and lose color, but will begin growing and regain its green color with rain.

FERTILIZING

Northeast: Apply high-nitrogen lawn fertilizer in autumn when the grass stops growing, or in spring.

Southeast: Fertilize warm-season grasses in early summer and again in late summer. Fertilize Bermuda and zoysia lawns in spring when they turn green, and again in summer. You may also fertilize lightly in fall. If your lawn does not go dormant in winter, feed in early spring as well.

Fertilize winter lawns in autumn. If you forget, fertilize them in spring.

Midwest–Great Plains: Fertilize in early fall, or in spring.

Southwest and southern California: Fertilize warm-season grasses lightly three or four times from late spring to late summer. If the lawn includes cool-season grasses that begin growing in late winter, fertilize in early spring and fall as well.

Fertilize drought-tolerant lawns in spring and again in late summer.

Fertilize winter lawns in autumn.

Northwest (including northern California): Fertilize in autumn when the grass stops growing, or in spring.

All regions: To minimize leaching and runoff of excess fertilizer, use a slow-release formula and follow the package directions.

If you lime the lawn, do not apply lime and fertilizer together—they can bind one another up and prove ineffective.

Organic Fertilizers

Top-dress lawns with compost and aged manure or activated sewage sludge. Cottonseed meal is another good organic source of nitrogen, but is expensive for a large area. Seaweed and fish products are also effective.

Corn gluten meal supplies nitrogen and kills germinating seeds of annual weeds.

WEED CONTROL

To avoid herbicides, accept some weeds in the lawn. Good cultural practices that produce dense, healthy turf should result in fewer weeds.

Pull weeds by hand as much as time and energy permit. A weed-popping tool makes the job easier.

To minimize herbicide effects on the environment, use a glyphosphate product that breaks down quickly, and perform spot applications directly to individual weeds.

Use any herbicides only when absolutely necessary, and explicitly follow the package directions regarding handling, use, storage, and disposal. Do not pour unused products down the drain or onto the ground, and do not dispose of empty or nearly empty containers along with ordinary household trash. Find out what procedures your community has for disposal of toxic household wastes and follow them.

Apply preemergent herbicides in spring, before weed seeds germinate and plants begin to grow.

Spot-apply other weedkillers during the growing season as plants emerge, or while they are still in the early stages of growth. Weeds are most vulnerable when they are young.

Most weedkillers are most effective in warm weather.

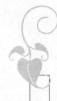

PEST AND DISEASE CONTROL

Responsible gardeners must strive to minimize the use of toxic pesticides, fungicides, and other materials. Many of the substances traditionally used to treat lawns are suspected carcinogens, and overuse results in runoff that causes water pollution.

Careful choice of lawn grasses and good cultural practices reduce pest and disease problems.

Look for cultivars resistant to pests and diseases common in your area. Look for cultivars that contain endophytes, which are beneficial fungi that live in the grass plants and produce substances that repel or kill such pests as armyworms, billbugs, chinchbugs, harmful nematodes, and sod webworms.

Check the lawn often for signs of problems so you can catch them early. When you notice symptoms, such as brown patches, consider environmental and cultural causes first, before assuming pests or diseases are the cause.

Use pesticides and fungicides only when absolutely necessary, and explicitly follow package directions regarding their handling, application, storage, and disposal.

Pests

Armyworm: Use biological controls (Trichogramma wasp) or Diazinon.

Beetles (Japanese beetle, Asiatic garden beetle, Oriental beetle): Cut and pull up sections of sod and handpick grubs.

Japanese beetle grubs: Use milky spore disease to control (takes 2 to 3 years to take effect but provides excellent long-term control). Or use Diazinon.

Billbugs: Use rotenone, diatomaceous earth, carbaryl, or Diazinon.

Chinch bugs: Plant resistant varieties. Keep lawn well-nourished. Use sabadilla dust, carbaryl, or Diazinon.

Nematodes: Use good cultural practices, keeping lawn well nourished and adequately watered.

Sod webworm: Use insecticidal soap, *Bacillus thuringiensis* (Bt), milky spore disease, carbaryl, or Diazinon.

Diseases

- Amend heavy soil to improve drainage before planting new lawns.
- Aerate lawn regularly.
- Do not water at night.
- Don't mow when wet and leave heavy clumps of clippings on lawns.

- Avoid fertilizing in midsummer.
- Plant a mix of grasses.

Try the organic controls below for specific diseases, or use fungicides when necessary.

Brown patch: Do not overwater. Do not fertilize heavily. Mow high.

Chlorosis: Centipede grass is prone to chlorosis (yellowing) caused by iron deficiency. Keep fertility levels relatively low, and pH below 6.0.

Dollar spot: Keep thatch to a minimum. Fertilize to maintain soil in fertile condition. Water only during drought. Mow high.

Fairy ring: Avoid high-nitrogen fertilizers. Remove infected soil and replace with fresh soil; replant area.

Leaf spot: Plant resistant varieties. If the soil is poorly drained, take up problem areas, add organic matter to the soil to lighten it, and replant. Good air circulation is important—prune low tree branches, open up dense plantings that block air passage. Do not overfertilize with nitrogen.

DE-THATCHING

Thatch is a dense layer of tough dead grass stems and roots that build up at the base of the sod faster than they can decay. Thatch prevents water and fertilizer from reaching plant roots.

In a small area, use a heavy metal rake to break up and remove thatch. For a large area, rent a power rake, or hire a professional to remove thatch.

Earthworms afford an excellent means of controlling thatch. Organic cultural practices encourage earthworm populations.

AERATING

Aeration is the practice of poking many tiny holes in the ground to loosen compacted soil and allow air and water to penetrate. Every couple of years, go over the lawn with a step-on aerating tool, or special spikes that you attach to your shoes before walking on the lawn. Or rent an aerating machine.

Sources of Information

For more information on lawn grasses and lawn care, contact your County Cooperative Extension office, or the Lawn Institute, 1509 Johnson Ferry Rd. NE, Suite 190, Marietta, GA 30062.

ORNAMENTAL GRASSES

Specimen Plants

Specimen plants are especially attractive species and cultivars that lend additional color and texture to a garden when grown with other plants. They are also grown either singly or in groups, usually isolated or arranged along with rocks or other natural items in the landscape. The ornamental grasses listed here make good specimen plants.

Alopecurus pratensis, foxtail grass
  A. pratensis 'Aureus'
Andropogon gerardii, big bluestem
Arundo donax, giant reed
  A. donax var. *versicolor*
Calamagrostis
  C. acutiflora var. *stricta*, feathered grass
  C. arundinacea var. *brachytricha*, Korean feather reed grass
  C. arundinacea 'Karl Foerster', Korean feather reed grass
Chasmanthium latifolium, spangle grass
Cortaderia selloana, pampas grass
  C. selloana 'Argenteum'
  C. selloana 'Bertini'
  C. selloana 'Gold Band'
  C. selloana 'Silver Stripe'
Deschampsia caespitosa, hair grass
  D. caespitosa 'Goldstaub'
  D. caespitosa 'Fairy's Joke'
Elymus glaucus, wild rye
Erianthus ravennae, plume grass
Glyceria maxima 'Variegata', manna grass
Miscanthus, all species and cultivars, silver grass, eulalia
Molinia caerulea, purple moor grass
  M. caerulea, 'Karl Foerster'
  M. caerulea 'Skyracer'
  M. caerulea 'Windspiel'
Pennisetum, fountain grass
  P. alopecuroides
  P. alopecuroides 'Hameln'
  P. setaceum 'Cupreum'
  P. villosum, feathertop
Spartina pectinata 'Aureo-marginata', slough grass
Stipa, feather grass
  S. gigantea, giant feather grass
  S. pennata, European feather grass

Ornamental Grasses for Groundcover

Groundcovers are usually perennial plants that spread to cover the ground like a lawn, but require far less maintenance than lawn grasses. The ornamental grasses listed here are especially useful for covering areas of land where lawn grasses would be difficult to maintain. They are also far more interesting to look at than mown grass.

FOR WET SITES

Alopecurus alpinus, foxtail grass
Arrhenatherum elatius var. *bulbosum* 'Variegata', bulbous oats grass
Calamagrostis arundinacea, Korean reed grass
Dactylis glomerata, cock's foot orchard grass
Deschampsia caespitosa, hair grass
  D. caespitosa 'Bronzeschleir'
  D. caespitosa 'Goldenhaenge'
  D. caespitosa 'Goldstaub'
Elymus canadensis, Canadian wild rye
Erianthus ravennae, ravenna grass
  E. ravennae var. *purpurascens*

Glyceria maxima 'Variegata', manna grass
Hakonechloa macra 'Aureola', hakone grass
Miscanthus, all species and cultivars, silver grass, eulalia
Molinia caerulea, purple moor grass
- *M. caerulea* 'Karl Foerster'
- *M. caerulea* 'Skyracer'
- *M. caerulea* 'Variegata'
- *M. caerulea* 'Windspiel'

Oplismenus hirtellus, ribbon grass
Panicum virgatum, switch grass
- *P. virgatum* 'Rubrum'
- *P. virgatum* 'Strictum'

Phalaris arundinacea var. *picta*, perennial ribbon grass
Phragmites australis, common reed (invasive)
Spartina pectinata 'Aureo-marginata', slough grass
Stenotaphrum secundatum 'Variegatum', striped St. Augustine grass
Zizania aquatica, wild rice

FOR DRY SITES

Alopecurus pratensis, foxtail grass
Andropogon gerardii, big bluestem
Briza maxima, annual quaking grass
Bromus secalinus, brome grass
Eragrostis, love grass
- *E. curvula*, perennial love grass
- *E. tef*, annual love grass

Festuca, fescue
- *F. rubra*
- *F. tenuifolia*
- *F. vivipara*

Hordeum jubatum, squirreltail barley
Miscanthus sacchariflorus 'Variegatus', Amur silver grass
Pennisetum, fountain grass
- *P. alopecuroides*
- *P. setaceum* 'Cupreum'

Poa alpina, alpine bluegrass
Sorghastrum nutans, Indian grass
Spartina pectinata 'Aureo-marginata', slough grass
Stipa
- *S. arundinacea*
- *S. calamagrostis*, silver grass
- *S. capillata*, feather grass
- *S. elegantissima*
- *S. gigantea*, giant feather grass

Grasses to Naturalize

When naturalizing grasses, plant them so that they look as though they belong in the landscape, then allow them to colonize the area. Plant them in masses or in large, flowing drifts. Combine them with low-maintenance perennials or wildflowers in meadow and prairie gardens. Use them as a transition between a wild field or woodland and more controlled garden areas. Plant them around the edge of a pond.

Except for occasional cleanups, or replacement of dead or dying plants, naturalized grasses need little or no maintenance. The ornamental grasses listed here are good for naturalizing.

Andropogon gerardii, big bluestem
Arundo donax, giant reed
- *A. donax* var. *veriscolor*

Bouteloua, grama
- *B. curtipendula*, side oats grama
- *B. gracilis*, blue grama

Briza media, quaking grass
Bromus secalinus, brome grass
Chasmanthium latifolium, spangle grass
Cortaderia selloana, pampas grass, all cultivars
Deschampsia flexuosa, crinkled hair grass
Elymus canadensis, Canadian wild rye

(continued)

Grasses to Naturalize *(cont'd)*

Eragrostis, love grass

- *E. curvula*
- *E. spectabilis*
- *E. tef*, annual love grass

Festuca, fescue

- *F. amethystina*
- *F. rubra*
- *F. scoparia*
- *F. tenuifolia*

Holcus, velvet grass

- *H. lanatus* 'Variegatus'
- *H. mollis* 'Variegatus'

Koeleria cristata, hair grass

Melica altissima, melic grass

- *M. altissima* 'Atropurpurea'

Miscanthus

- *M. sacchariflorus*, American silver grass
- *M. sacchariflorus* 'Giganteus'
- *M. sinensis*, eulalia
- *M. sinensis* 'Gracillimus'
- *M. sinensis* 'Zebrinus'

Molinia caerulea 'Variegata', variegated purple moor grass

Pennisetum, fountain grass

- *P. alopecuroides*
- *P. alopecuroides* 'Hameln'
- *P. setaceum* 'Cupreum'
- *P. setaceum* 'Rubrum'

Phalaris arundinacea var. *picta*, ribbon grass, gardener's garters

Phragmites australis, common reed (invasive)

Setaria italica, foxtail millet

Sorghastrum nutans, Indian grass

Spartina pectinata 'Aureo-marginata', slough grass

Stipa arundinacea, feather grass

Grasses for Shade

Most ornamental grasses are sun lovers. But a number of grasses—especially in their variegated forms—will grow well in partial to light shade. The plants listed here are suited to shady conditions, though none of them will tolerate full or dense shade.

Agrostis nebulosa, cloud grass

Arrhenatherum elatius var. *bulbosum* 'Variegatum', bulbous oats grass

Chasmanthium latifolium, spangle grass

Deschampsia caespitosa, tufted hair grass

- *D. caespitosa* 'Goldstaub'
- *D. caespitosa* var. *vivipara*

Festuca, fescue

- *F. gigantea*
- *F. rubra*

Hakonechloa macra 'Aureola'

Helictotrichon sempervirens, blue oat grass

Holcus lanatus 'Variegatus', variegated velvet grass

Hystrix patula, bottlebrush grass

Koeleria cristata, hair grass

Lagurus ovatus, hare's tail grass

Melica, melic grass

- *M. altissima*
- *M. ciliata*

Milium effusum 'Aureum', wood millet

Miscanthus sacchariflorus 'Variegatus'

Oplismenus hirtellus, ribbon grass

Phalaris arundinacea var. *picta*, ribbon grass, gardener's garters

Stenotaphrum secundatum 'Variegatum', striped St. Augustine grass

Ornamental Grasses for Cutting and Drying

CUT FLOWERS

Agrostis nebulosa, cloud grass
Arundo donax, giant reed
Briza, quaking grass
  B. maxima, annual quaking grass
  B. media, quaking grass
  B. minor, little quaking grass
Chasmanthium latifolium, spangle grass
Cortaderia, all species and cultivars, pampas grass
Deschampsia caespitosa, all cultivars, hair grass
Eragrostis, love grass
  E. curvula
  E. spectabilis
  E. tef, annual love grass
Erianthus ravennae, ravenna grass
Hystrix patula, bottlebrush grass
Lagurus ovatus, hare's tail grass
Lamarckia aurea, goldentop
Miscanthus, all species and cultivars, silver grass, eulalia
Panicum virgatum, switchgrass
Pennisetum, fountain grass
  P. alopecuroides
  P. setaceum, all cultivars, annual fountain grass
Setaria italica, foxtail millet
Sorghastrum nutans, Indian grass
Stipa pennata, European feather grass
Vetiveria zizanioides, vetiver
Zizania aquatica, wild rice

DRIED ARRANGEMENTS

Agrostis nebulosa, cloud grass
Arundo donax, giant reed
Briza, quaking grass
  B. maxima, annual quaking grass
  B. media, quaking grass
  B. minor, little quaking grass
Chasmanthium latifolium, spangle grass
Cortaderia, all species and cultivars, pampas grass
Eragrostis, love grass
  E. curvula
  E. spectabilis
  E. tef, annual love grass
Hystrix patula, bottlebrush grass
Lagurus ovatus, hare's tail grass
Lamarckia aurea, goldentop
Melica, melic grass
  M. altissima
  M. ciliata
Miscanthus, all species and cultivars, silver grass, eulalia
Panicum virgatum, switchgrass
Pennisetum, fountain grass
  P. alopecuroides
  P. setaceum, all cultivars
Phragmites australis, common reed (invasive)
Setaria italica, foxtail millet
Sorghastrum nutans, Indian grass
Stipa pennata, European feather grass
Triticum, wheat
  T. aestivum
  T. turgidum
Vetiveria zizanioides, vetiver
Zea mays, ornamental corn
  Z. mays 'Strawberry Corn'
  Z. mays var. *japonica*
Zizania aquatica, wild rice

Ornamental Grasses for Fall Color

Andropogon gerardii, big bluestem
Arundo donax, giant reed
Chasmanthium latifolium, spangle grass
Cortaderia, all species and cultivars, pampas grass

(continued)

Ornamental Grasses for Fall Color *(cont'd)*

Eragrostis tef, annual love grass
Erianthus ravennae, ravenna grass
Hakonechloa macra 'Aureola'
Helictotrichon sempervirens, blue oat grass
Imperata cylindrica var. *rubra*, Japanese blood grass
Koeleria cristata, hair grass
Miscanthus, all species and cultivars, silver grass, eulalia
Molinia, all species and cultivars, moor grass
Panicum virgatum, switchgrass
Pennisetum, fountain grass
  P. alopecuroides
  P. setaceum
Phragmites australis, common reed (invasive)
Sorghastrum nutans, Indian grass
Spartina pectinata 'Aureo-marginata', slough grass
Stipa arundinacea, feather grass

CALENDAR OF CARE FOR ORNAMENTAL GRASSES

Northeast, Mid-Atlantic, Midwest, Northwest

Spring. In early spring, start the seeds of annual grasses indoors.

Cut back to the ground perennial grasses left standing over winter, before they show new growth.

When the soil is workable, plant bareroot and dormant grasses.

When danger of frost is past, plant homegrown seedlings (harden them off first) and garden-center plants.

Direct-seed fast-growing annuals where the season is long enough. Thin the seedlings when a few inches high.

Summer. Continue planting container-grown plants as long as the weather is mild.

When the young plants reach 6 inches in height, mulch for the summer.

During dry weather, water grasses that cannot tolerate drought, and grasses growing in containers.

Cut grasses for fresh arrangements or drying when they bloom or produce seed heads.

Autumn. Collect seeds of nonhybrid grasses to save and plant next year.

Cut back broken stems and remove damaged leaves of perennials. Let the plants stand for winter interest.

Pull annual grasses as the season ends.

Divide and transplant crowded perennial grasses.

Work compost, old mulches, or other organic matter into the soil.

Winter. Mulch perennial grasses when the soil freezes to prevent heaving over winter.

Prepare for next year's garden: Plan seed and plant orders, revise garden plans, and gather seed-starting supplies.

Southeast and Southwest

Spring. Plant perennial grasses when they arrive from mail-order nurseries.

Plant container-grown grasses from the garden center before the weather turns hot. Give transplants shade and moisture until they become established.

Direct-sow annuals or transplant homegrown seedlings. Thin when the seedlings are a few inches high.

When the plants reach 6 inches in height, mulch for the summer.

Summer. Water grasses not tolerant of drought, and those growing in containers.

As mulches break down and become thin, add more.

Cut grasses for fresh arrangements or drying when they bloom or produce seed heads.

Autumn. Plant cool-season grasses.

Collect seeds of nonhybrid grasses to save and plant next year.

Cut back broken stems and remove damaged leaves of perennial grasses.

Pull annuals when the plants become fatigued.

Divide and transplant crowded perennials.

Work compost, old mulches, or other organic matter into the soil.

Winter. Cut perennial grasses back to the ground before they show new growth.

Revise garden plans; order seeds and plants.

Start seeds indoors for planting out in early spring.

Plant bareroot perennials when they arrive from mail-order nurseries in late winter or early spring.

GROUNDCOVERS

WAYS TO USE GROUNDCOVERS

Groundcovers can serve many functions in the garden. Here are some of them.

- Unify the landscape. Visually connect island beds of trees, flowers, shrubs, and other plants.
- Provide a transition from manicured gardens to wild open space beyond your property boundary (ornamental grasses and other tall groundcover plants work best). Or create a transition between gardens and lawn or other open space.
- Anchor groups of trees and tall shrubs to the ground. If space permits, using two or three groundcovers in a gradation of heights can be an especially effective way to draw the eye gradually downward (or upward).
- Dramatize the terrain—carpeting ridges and troughs emphasizes their contours. A groundcover on a flat area can create the effect of a pool of water.
- Act as the floor or carpet in an outdoor garden "room" enclosed by hedges or other tall plants (which act as the "walls").

(continued)

Ways to Use Groundcovers *(cont'd)*

- Create abstract patterns of color and texture in a broad open area.
- Provide an alternative to lawn in low-traffic areas.
- Control erosion on a slope.
- Substitute for lawn on a steep slope or other places difficult to mow.
- Occupy locations too shady for lawn grasses.
- Grow around the base of trees, where lawn grass is difficult to establish and mow.
- Grow around decks and patios.
- Grow around boulders and rocks that are part of the landscape.
- Grow between stepping stones in a path (small-leaved plants work best for this purpose).

GROUNDCOVERS FOR DIFFERENT USES

Flowering Groundcovers

Alchemilla vulgaris, lady's mantle: Fluted, lobed leaves with pointed tips; sprays of small chartreuse flowers late spring. To 12 inches high. Sun or shade. Spreads slowly. To Zone 3.

Ajuga reptans, bugleweed, carpet bugle: Spatulate leaves to 4 inches long with scalloped edges; spikes of small blue-violet, purple, or pink flowers mid to late spring. To 12 inches high. Sun or shade. Will invade a lawn if not confined. To Zone 4.

Antennaria spp., pussytoes: Fuzzy gray or white leaves; clusters of white or pink flowers on slender stalks in spring. To 12 inches high. To Zone 3.

Arctotheca calendula, capeweed: Yellow daisy flowers bloom for much of the year above a carpet of gray-green leaves. Spreads quickly. Tolerates heat and drought. To Zone 9.

Astilbe chinensis var. *pumila*: A dwarf spreading astilbe. Ferny, toothed leaves; small spikes of tiny lavender-pink flowers in late summer. To 8 inches high. Sun to light shade. To Zone 5.

Calluna vulgaris, Scotch heather: Evergreen leaves, spikes of pink, white, or red flowers in summer. Poor, acid soil, moist but not wet. To Zone 4.

Cerastium tomentosum, snow-in-summer: Low, spreading mounds of silvery gray-green leaves; small white flowers in spring and early summer. To 6 inches high. Well-drained soil. To Zone 2 or 3.

Ceratostigma plumbaginoides, blue leadwort: Low mat of leaves turn reddish bronze in fall; glowing deep blue flowers in fall. To 8 inches tall. To Zone 6.

Chamaemelum nobile, Roman chamomile: Finely cut, feathery, apple-scented leaves; small white daisy flowers with large yellow center in summer. To 12 inches high. To Zone 4.

Chrysogonum virginianum, green-and-gold, goldenstar: Toothed, oval, deep green leaves; starry golden flowers in spring and summer. To 12 inches high. Rich soil, shade. To Zone 6.

Conradina verticillata: Small, narrow, deep-green leaves; covered with two-lipped, purple-blue flowers in spring. To 6 inches high. Sandy soil; full sun. To Zone 6.

Convallaria majalis, lily of the valley: Spikes of small, sweetly fragrant, white bell-shaped flowers in mid-spring. Upright pointed oblong leaves turn yellow and look ratty in late summer. To 8 inches tall. Vigorous and invasive. Sun or shade. To Zone 2.

Delosperma 'Alba', white ice plant: Triangular grayish green leaves, small white flowers. To 8 inches tall. Tolerates drought and heat. To Zone 9.

Drosanthemum hispidum, rosea ice plant: Low mat of leaves, lavender-pink flowers in spring. To 6 inches high. Tolerates drought and heat. To Zone 10.

Epimedium spp., barrenwort: Light to bright green leaves turn color in fall. Sprays of white, yellow, pink, or red flowers in mid-spring. To 10 inches high. Most to Zone 3 or 4.

Erica carnea, spring heath: Needlelike leaves, rose-red or white flowers late winter to early spring, depending on location. 6 to 12 inches tall. Full sun to partial shade, acid soil. To Zone 5.

Galax urceolata: Shiny round to heart-shaped leaves, wands of small white flowers late spring to summer. Moist soil. To Zone 4.

Galium odoratum, sweet woodruff: Whorled leaves with slender, pointed leaflets; clusters of little white flowers mid-spring; fresh, haylike scent. To 8 inches high. Moist shade. Can be invasive once established. To Zone 4.

Gaultheria shallon, salal: Dark green, leathery leaves, clusters of waxy white flowers in late spring to early summer, edible purple-black fruit. To 18 inches tall. Fertile, acid soil, sun or shade. Grown on the West Coast. To Zone 5.

Gazania hybrids: Oblong grayish green leaves, daisy flowers in yellow, bronze, orange, orange-red, white. Tolerates drought and poor soil. Sun. To Zone 9.

(continued)

Flowering Groundcovers *(cont'd)*

Hemerocallis spp. and cultivars, daylily: Clumps of straplike leaves; trumpet flowers in many shades of red, pink, yellow, and orange in summer. 6 inches to 3 feet tall, depending on variety. Sun or shade, tolerates a range of soil and moisture conditions. To Zone 3.

Hypericum calycinum, Aaron's beard, St.-John's-wort: Oblong leaves, bright yellow flowers mid to late summer. To 18 inches high. Does well in sandy soil and other difficult locations. To Zone 6.

Iris cristata, crested iris: Bluish green sword-shaped leaves, lilac-blue flowers in early spring. To 6 inches tall. Sun or shade. To Zone 3.

Lamiastrum galeobdolon, yellow archangel: Oval leaves to 3 inches long; clusters of small yellow flowers in mid-spring. To 20 inches high. Light to deep shade, well-drained soil. Invasive. 'Variegatum' has variegated leaves. To Zone 4.

Lamium maculatum, dead nettle: Small oval leaves with scalloped edges have silver to white spots or overlay. Small pink, white, or purple flowers bloom through much of summer. To 8 inches tall. To Zone 3.

Lampranthus, ice plant: All are hardy Zone 9 and south; all tolerate heat and drought.

L. aurantiacus: Daisylike flowers of yellow, gold, or orange in early spring. To 15 inches high.

L. productus, purple ice plant: Bright purple flowers late winter through spring. To 12 inches tall.

L. spectabilis, trailing ice plant: Gray-green leaves; red, rose, pink, lavender, or purple flowers. To 12 inches tall.

Liriope, lilyturf

L. muscari, big blue lilyturf: Clumps of narrow, grassy leaves; slender upright spikes of violet, white, or lavender flowers late summer to early fall. To 18 inches tall. Sun or shade. Drought-tolerant. To Zone 6.

L. spicata, creeping lilyturf: Clumps of grassy leaves; spikes of purple or white flowers mid to late summer. To 12 inches high. To Zone 4.

Lysimachia nummularia, creeping Jenny: Small rounded leaves, small yellow flowers from late spring to fall. To 2 inches high. Moist soil. To Zone 3.

Phlox

P. stolonifera, creeping phlox: Low mats of foliage; mid to late spring flowers in lavender-blue, pink, or white. To 12 inches tall. Shade. To Zone 2 or 3.

P. subulata, moss pink: Low mats of small, narrow leaves; in early to mid spring covered with white, lavender, pink, or rose flowers. To 6 inches tall. Full sun to partial shade. To Zone 2 or 3.

Pulmonaria saccharata, Bethlehem sage: Pointed leaves spotted with white; tubular flowers of purple, pink, or blue in early spring. To 18 inches tall. Moist soil, shade. To Zone 3 or 4.

Rosmarinus officinalis 'Prostratus', prostrate rosemary: Aromatic, needlelike leaves; light blue flowers in spring and summer. Full sun, well-drained soil. Hardy only to Zone 8.

Sarcococca hookerana var. *humilis*, sweet box: Glossy evergreen leaves, sweetly fragrant white flowers late winter or early spring. To 3 feet tall. Zones 5 to 7.

Sedum, stonecrop

S. acre, goldmoss: Small, narrow, succulent light green leaves on trailing stems; small yellow flowers in late spring. To 2 inches high. Grows practically anywhere and can become a pest. Full sun to light shade. To Zone 3.

S. reflexum, jenny stonecrop: Dense mat of blue-green leaves; yellow flowers in summer. To 10 inches tall. Well-drained soil, tolerates drought. To Zone 3.

S. × *rubrotinctum*: Small, succulent, club-shaped bronzy red leaves; yellow flowers in summer. To 8 inches tall. To Zone 9.

S. spurium 'Dragon's Blood': Rosettes of bronzy succulent leaves; rose-red flowers in summer. Drought-tolerant. To Zone 3.

Teucrium chamaedrys, germander: Small spike of rose to purple flowers in summer; small oblong leaves with serrated edges. To 10 inches high (var. *prostratus* is lower). Takes shearing well. To Zone 5.

Tiarella cordifolia, foamflower: Broad, hairy, lobed and toothed leaves; spikes of small fluffy-looking white flowers mid-spring to midsummer. 6 to 12 inches tall. Partial to light shade; moist, rich soil. To Zone 4.

Uvularia grandiflora, big merrybells: Bright green leaves, bell-shaped yellow flowers in spring. To 18 inches tall. To Zone 3.

Verbena canadensis, trailing verbena, rose verbena: Narrow, dark green, deeply toothed leaves; trailing stems turn up at the tips. Clusters of small flowers in shades of pink, red, and purple bloom all summer. Full sun. Perennial to Zone 8, grow as annual elsewhere.

Vinca, periwinkle

V. major 'Variegata', big periwinkle: Broad oval leaves variegated with cream. To 18 inches high, trailing. Blue-violet flowers in spring. Full sun to light shade. To Zone 7; elsewhere grow as annual.

V. minor, periwinkle: Glossy oval leaves, 5-petaled purple flowers early to mid-spring. White, pink, and double-flowered forms also available. To 6 inches high. Sun or shade, many soils. To Zone 4.

(continued)

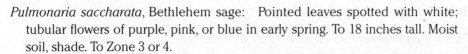

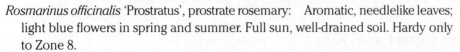

ANNUAL GROUNDCOVERS

Low-growing annuals that self-sow, such as *Lobularia maritima* (sweet alyssum) and *Portulaca grandiflora* (moss rose) can also be used as groundcovers.

Foliage Groundcovers

Aegopodium podagraria var. *variegatum*, bishop's weed: Compound leaves variegated with cream. To 12 inches tall. For poor, dry soil only; extremely invasive in better conditions. Sun or shade. To Zone 5.

Ajuga reptans, bugleweed, carpet bugle: Toothed oval leaves, variegated or colored in some varieties; small spikes of violet flowers in spring. Burgundy Glow has leaves of green, cream and purple-pink. Bronze Beauty, Giant Bronze, and Jungle Bronze have bronze leaves. To about 6 inches tall. Sun or shade. To Zone 4.

Alchemilla vulgaris, lady's mantle: Fluted, lobed leaves with pointed tips capture drops of rain or dew; sprays of small chartreuse flowers in late spring. To 12 inches tall. Sun or shade. Spreads slowly. To Zone 3.

Artemisia stellerana, beach wormwood: Silvery, deeply divided leaves; clusters of small yellow flowers in summer. For sunny, sandy, seashore conditions. Drought-tolerant. To Zone 2 or 3.

Asarum, wild ginger

A. canadense: Heart-shaped green leaves to 6 inches across, inconspicuous flowers. Shade. Moist, fertile soil. To Zone 3.

A. europaeum, European wild ginger: Glossy, deep green, heart-shaped leaves to 3 inches across, inconspicuous flowers. Moist, fertile soil. Shade. To Zone 4.

Baccharis pilularis, coyote bush: Evergreen shrub with toothed dark green leaves and inconspicuous flowers. To 12 inches high and 10 inches across. Best in dry conditions, but can tolerate moist soil if well-drained. Native to coastal California. To Zone 8.

Cerastium tomentosum, snow-in-summer: Low, spreading mounds of silvery gray-green leaves; small white flowers in spring and early summer. To 6 inches high. Well-drained soil, tolerates drought. To Zone 2.

Dichondra micrantha: Small, rounded leaves on creeping stems to about 4 inches tall. A lawn substitute in warm climates. Sun or shade. Tolerates heat. To Zone 10.

Epimedium spp., barrenwort: Light to bright green leaves turn bronze or coppery in fall. Sprays of white, yellow, pink, or red flowers in mid-spring. To 10 inches high. Most to Zone 3 or 4.

Euonymus fortunei, wintercreeper: Small, oblong evergreen leaves on trailing stems; numerous variegated cultivars with white, cream, or yellow. To 12 inches high. Vigorous and adaptable, sun or shade. 'Coloratus' spreads quickly. To Zone 4.

Fragaria, strawberry

F. chiloensis, ornamental strawberry: Round leaves with toothed edges, in groups of three; white flowers with yellow centers; small red fruit. To 6 inches high. Spreads by runners. Sun or shade. A West Coast plant. To Zone 4 or 5.

F. virginiana, wild strawberry: Round leaves with toothed edges, in groups of three; white flowers with yellow center in spring; small, tasty red fruit in early summer. To 12 inches high. Spreads by runners. Sun or shade. An eastern plant. To Zone 3.

Galax urceolata: Glossy, round to heart-shaped, evergreen leaves; wands of small white flowers late spring to summer. To 6 inches high. Moist soil, shade. To Zone 4.

Galium odoratum, sweet woodruff: Whorled leaves with slender, pointed leaflets; clusters of little white flowers in mid-spring; fresh, haylike scent. To 8 inches high. Moist shade. Can be invasive once established. To Zone 4.

Gaultheria shallon, salal: Leathery dark green leaves; clusters of waxy white flowers late spring to early summer; edible blue-black fruit. To 18 inches high. Grown on the West Coast. Fertile, acid soil; sun or shade. To Zone 5.

Glechoma hederacea 'Variegata', creeping charlie, ground ivy: Small, rounded, lobed leaves are variegated with cream; sparse clusters of little blue-violet flowers spring and summer. To 3 inches tall. Sun or shade. Can be an invasive pest unless confined. To Zone 3.

Hedera, ivy

H. canariensis, Algerian ivy: Large, dark green leaves to 6 inches across, with 3 or more pointed lobes. Some cultivars variegated with cream, some have purplish stems. Sun or shade. To Zone 7 or 8.

H. helix, English ivy: Lustrous, dark green, evergeen leaves, usually with 5 pointed lobes, to 3 inches long. Cultivars are variegated with yellow or creamy white; some have small leaves or crinkled leaves. Sun or shade, adapts to a range of soil and moisture conditions. To Zone 5.

Hosta spp. and cultivars, plantain lily: Clumps of upright lance-shaped to broadly oval leaves can be lime green to blue-green, smooth or puckered, plain or variegated with white or gold. Bell-shaped flowers on vertical stalks, white or

(continued)

lavender, some fragrant, bloom in summer, but plants are grown primarily for their foliage. 4 inches to 3 feet tall, depending on variety. Sun or shade. To Zone 3.

Houttuynia cordata 'Chameleon': Oval leaves with irregular edges, a blend of cream, green, and pink. Sun or shade, moist soil. Can be invasive. To Zone 5.

Juniperus, juniper

J. chinensis var. *sargentii*, Sargent juniper: Needled evergreen forms a dense, low mat to 18 inches high and 8 feet across. Sun, well-drained soil. Tolerates poor soil and seashore conditions. To Zone 4.

J. conferta, shore juniper: Low mat of needled branches to 15 inches high and 7 feet across. Sun, well-drained soil. Tolerates drought, road salt, and seashore conditions. To Zone 5.

J. horizontalis, creeping juniper: Low, dense mat of needled branches to just 4 inches high, 2 feet across. Tolerates drought. 'Blue Rug' is reliable and durable. To Zone 2.

J. squamata 'Blue Carpet': Low, spreading cultivar with blue-green needles. Sun, well-drained soil. To Zone 5.

Lamiastrum galeobdolon 'Variegatum', silver frost lamiastrum: Green and white variegated leaves; small yellow flowers mid-spring. Well-drained soil, shade. Invasive when established. To Zone 4.

Lamium maculatum, dead nettle: Small oval leaves with scalloped edges have silver to white spots or overlay. Small pink, white, or purple flowers bloom in summer. To 8 inches tall. 'Beacon Silver' and 'White Nancy' especially recommended. Aureum has yellow-green leaves. Shade. To Zone 3.

Lysimachia nummularia 'Aurea', creeping Jenny: Small, rounded, yellow-green leaves; small yellow flowers late spring to fall. To 2 inches tall. Moist soil. To Zone 3.

Mahonia repens, creeping mahonia: Compound evergreen leaves with oval leaflets. To 12 inches tall. To Zone 5.

Pachysandra

P. procumbens, Allegheny pachysandra: Toothed oblong leaves to 3 inches long, in whorls. To 12 inches tall. To Zone 6.

P. terminalis, Japanese spurge: Glossy green, toothed leaves to 4 inches long, in whorls. 'Variegata' has leaves edged in cream. To 6 inches high. Shade, moist soil. To Zone 5.

Paxistima canbyi: Small evergreen leaves in a dense mat turn bronze in fall. To 12 inches tall. Acid soil, shade. Tolerates drought. To Zone 5.

Rosmarinus officinalis 'Prostratus', prostrate rosemary: Aromatic dark green needle-like leaves; light blue flowers spring and summer. To 2 feet high. Tolerates drought and wind. Sun. To Zone 8.

Sarcococca hookerana var. *humilis*, sweet box: Glossy evergreen leaves; fragrant white flowers late winter. To 3 feet high. Shade. To Zone 5.

Sempervivum spp., houseleek, hen-and-chicks: Rosettes of succulent green leaves, some tinged with red or bronze. To 12 inches high. To Zone 4 or 5.

Soleirolia soleirolii, baby's tears: Tiny round green leaves carpet the ground. To 3 inches tall. Any moist soil. Shade. To Zone 9.

Stachys byzantina, lamb's ears: Oblong leaves covered with soft white hairs. Spikes of purple flowers in summer, not terribly ornamental. To 18 inches high. Full sun, well-drained soil. Nice as an edging or border. To Zone 4.

Teucrium chamaedrys, germander: Small oval silver leaves with serrated edges. Small spikes of rose to purple flowers in summer. To 10 inches tall (var. *prostratum* is lower). To Zone 5.

Thymus, thyme

T. lanatus, woolly thyme: Small aromatic leaves on fuzzy stems; clusters of tiny rose-pink flowers in early summer. To 4 inches high. Tolerates heat and drought. Sun. To Zone 3.

T. serpyllum, creeping thyme, mother of thyme: Very small aromatic leaves; clusters of tiny purple-pink flowers. Hugs the ground. Tolerates heat and drought. Sun. To Zone 3.

Vinca major 'Variegata': Broad oval leaves variegated with cream, on trailing stems that root; blue-violet flowers. To 24 inches tall. Sun or shade. To Zone 7; elsewhere grow as annual.

Xanthorhiza simplicissima, yellowroot: Dense mat of leaves that turn yellow to orange in fall. To 2 feet tall. Tolerates wet or dry, sunny or shady conditions. To Zone 4.

Ferns for Groundcover

Adiantum pedatum, maidenhair fern: Bright green fronds of slender leaflets on wiry dark stems. Light shade; fertile, moist but well-drained soil. To Zone 3.

Athyrium

A. filix-femina, lady fern: Finely divided fronds of many slender leaflets. To 20 inches. Best in moist soil but tolerates some drought. Partial shade. To Zone 3.

A. goeringianum 'Pictum', Japanese painted fern: Slow to spread, but sturdy. Fronds are purplish green with central silver coloring. To 18 inches. Deciduous. Light to full shade. To Zone 3.

(continued)

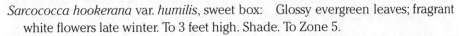

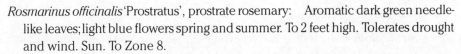

Ferns for Groundcovers *(cont'd)*

Cyrtomium falcatum, holly fern: Glossy evergreen leaves, to 30 inches long. 12 to 24 inches high. Moist but well-drained soil, slightly acid pH. Partial shade; also tolerates some salt and drought. Zones 9 and 10.

Cystopteris fragilis: Deciduous fronds to 10 inches long. Spreads quickly. Cool, moist, shady conditions. To Zone 3.

Dennstaedtia punctilobula, hay-scented fern: Delicate, finely cut fronds to 30 inches long. Sun or shade. Moist conditions, tolerates a range of soils. To Zone 3.

Onoclea sensibilis, sensitive fern, bead fern: Fronds to 4 feet long; inner fronds carry beadlike spore cases that stand all winter. Sun or shade, prefers moist, even marshy, soil. Take care to buy propagated, not wild-collected, plants. To Zone 3.

Osmunda cinnamomea, cinnamon fern: Dark green, deeply cut fronds to 3 feet long; central sterile fronds look like cinnamon sticks. Moist, acid soil, partial shade. To Zone 3.

Polypodium

P. aureum, golden polypody, hare's foot fern: Fuzzy, scaly rhizomes creep along soil surface. Deeply cut fronds to 3 feet long. To Zone 10.

P. vulgare, common polypody: Deeply cut leathery fronds to 10 inches long. Shade. To Zone 3.

Polystichum acrostichoides, Christmas fern: Leathery dark green fronds to 24 inches long. Moist conditions, shade or some sun. To Zone 3.

Rumohra adiantiformis, leatherleaf fern: Leathery dark green fronds to 3 feet long, much used by florists. Partial shade. Tolerates some salt and drought. To Zone 9.

Groundcovers with Ornamental Fruit

Arctostaphylos uva-ursi, bearberry: Small evergreen leaves turn reddish bronze in fall; red berries in autumn. To 5 inches high. Sun or shade. Tolerates sandy soil and seashore conditions, as long as soil is acid, pH 5.0 or below. To Zone 2.

Cornus canadensis, bunchberry: Whorled evergreen leaves with oval leaflets. Small yellow flowers in spring, bunches of red berries late summer and fall. Moist, shady conditions. To Zone 2.

Cotoneaster

C. apiculatus, cranberry cotoneaster: Small leaves turn reddish purple in fall; red autumn berries persist into winter. Forms dense mats to 24 inches high. Sun, well-drained soil. To Zone 4.

C. dammeri: Small evergreen oval leaves; small white to pinkish flowers in spring; red berries in fall. To 15 inches tall and 10 feet across. Tolerates seashore conditions. To Zone 5.

C. horizontalis, rockspray cotoneaster: Small leaves turn reddish purple in fall; small red berries in autumn persist into winter. To 3 feet high. To Zone 5.

Fragaria, strawberry

F. chiloensis, ornamental strawberry: Round leaves with toothed edges, in groups of three; white flowers with yellow center; red fruit. To 6 inches high. Spreads by runners. Sun or shade. A West Coast plant. To Zone 4 or 5.

F. virginiana, wild strawberry: Round leaves with toothed edges, in groups of three; white flowers with yellow center in spring; small red fruit in early summer. To 12 inches high. Spreads by runners. Sun or shade. An eastern plant. To Zone 3.

Gaultheria shallon, salal: Leathery dark green leaves; clusters of waxy white flowers late spring to early summer; edible purplish black fruit. Grown on the West Coast. Fertile, acid soil. Sun or shade. To Zone 5.

Mitchella repens, partridgeberry: Small, rounded, evergreen leaves; tubular white flowers in summer; bright red berries in fall. To 10 inches high. Moist, acid soil, shady woodland conditions. To Zone 3 or 4.

Pernettya mucronata, Chilean pernettya: Glossy evergreen leaves; berries in shades of purple, pink, red, or white (depending on variety) persist into winter. To 18 inches high. Full sun, but tolerates partial shade. Zones 6 to 7.

Evergreen Groundcovers

Arctostaphylos uva-ursi, bearberry

Baccharis pilularis, coyote bush

Calluna vulgaris, Scotch heather

Cornus canadensis, bunchberry

Cotoneaster spp.

Erica carnea, spring heath

Euonymus fortunei, wintercreeper

Galax urceolata

Gaultheria shallon, salal

Hedera helix, English ivy

Hypericum calycinum, Aaron's beard, St.-John's-wort

Juniperus spp., juniper

Mahonia repens, creeping mahonia

Mitchella repens, partridgeberry

Paxistima canbyi

Pernettya mucronata, Chilean pernettya

Phlox subulata, moss pink

Rosmarinus officinalis 'Prostratus', prostrate rosemary

Sarcococca hookerana var. *humilis*, sweet box

Vinca minor, periwinkle

Groundcovers for Full Sun

The plants listed below perform best in full sun.

Achillea tomentosa, yarrow
Antennaria spp., pussytoes
Arctotheca calendula, capeweed
Artemisia stellerana, beach wormwood
Baccharis pilularis, coyote bush
Calluna vulgaris, Scotch heather
Cerastium tomentosum, snow-in-summer
Chamaemelum nobile, Roman chamomile, best in full sun but tolerates partial shade
Delosperma 'Alba', white ice plant
Drosanthemum hispidum, rosea ice plant
Erica carnea, spring heath, best in sun but tolerates partial shade
Gazania hybrids
Juniperus spp., juniper
Lampranthus spp., ice plant
Pernettya mucronata, Chilean pernettya, best in sun but tolerates partial shade
Phlox subulata, moss pink, best in sun but tolerates partial shade
Rosmarinus officinalis 'Prostratus', prostrate rosemary
Sedum spp., stonecrop
Sempervivum spp., houseleek, hen-and-chicks
Stachys byzantina, lamb's ears
Teucrium chamaedrys, germander
Thymus spp., thyme
Verbena canadensis, creeping verbena, rose verbena

Groundcovers for Shade

These plants will grow in varying degrees of shade.

Aegopodium podagraria, bishop's weed, full sun to light shade
Ajuga spp., bugleweed, full sun to light shade
Alchemilla vulgaris, lady's mantle, full sun to light shade
Arctostaphylos uva-ursi, bearberry, full sun to light shade
Asarum spp., wild ginger
Astilbe chinensis var. *pumila*, full sun to light shade
Ceratostigma plumbaginoides, blue leadwort, full sun to light shade
Chrysogonum virginianum, green-and-gold, goldenstar
Convallaria majalis, lily of the valley, full sun to full shade
Cornus canadensis, bunchberry, partial to full shade
Cotoneaster spp., full sun to light shade
Dichondra micrantha, full sun to light shade
Epimedium spp., barrenwort, partial to full shade
Eounymus fortunei, wintercreeper, full sun to full shade
Fragaria spp., strawberry, full sun to light shade
Galax urceolata, partial to light shade
Galium odoratum, sweet woodruff, partial to full shade
Gaultheria shallon, salal, full sun to light shade
Glechoma hederacea 'Variegata', variegated creeping charlie, full sun to light shade
Hedera spp., ivy, partial to full shade; English ivy grows in deep shade
Hemerocallis spp. and varieties, daylily, full sun to light shade
Hosta spp. and varieties, plantain lily, partial to light shade
Houttuynia cordata 'Chameleon', partial to light shade
Hypericum calycinum, Aaron's beard, St.-John's-wort, partial to light shade
Iris cristata, crested iris, full sun to light shade

Lamiastrum galeobdolon, yellow archangel, partial to full shade
Lamium maculatum, dead nettle, partial to full shade
Liriope spp., lilyturf, full sun to full shade
Lonicera spp., honeysuckle, full sun to light shade
Lysimachia nummularia 'Aurea', creeping jenny, full sun to partial shade
Mahonia repens, creeping mahonia, partial to light shade
Mitchella repens, partridgeberry, partial to full shade
Pachysandra spp., partial to deep shade
Paxistima canbyi, light to deep shade
Phlox stolonifera, creeping phlox, partial to light shade
Pulmonaria saccharata, Bethlehem sage, partial to light shade
Sarcococca hookerana var. *humilis*, sweet box, partial to full shade
Soleirolia soleirolii, baby's tears, partial to light shade
Uvularia grandiflora, big merrybells, light to full shade
Vinca spp., periwinkle, full sun to light shade
Xanthorhiza simplicissima, yellowroot, partial to light shade; also tolerates sun

Groundcovers for Poor Soil

The plants listed here succeed in poor soil where many other plants would fail.

Aegopodium podagraria, bishop's weed, highly invasive in all but poor soils
Artemisia stellerana, beach wormwood
Calluna vulgaris, Scotch heather
Convallaria majalis, lily of the valley
Euonymus fortunei, wintercreeper
Gazania hybrids
Hedera helix, English ivy
Juniperus chinensis var. *sargentii*, Sargent juniper
Lonicera japonica 'Halliana', Hall's honeysuckle, highly invasive in all but poor soils
Pachysandra terminalis, Japanese spurge

Groundcovers for Slopes and Banks

Ajuga spp., bugleweed
Baccharis pilularis, coyote bush
Cotoneaster spp.
Drosanthemum hispidum, rosea ice plant
Euonymus fortunei, wintercreeper
Gazania hybrids
Hedera spp., ivy
Juniperus spp., juniper
Lonicera spp., honeysuckle
Pachysandra spp.
Phlox subulata, moss pink
Rosmarinus officinalis 'Prostratum', prostrate rosemary
Vinca major 'Variegata'

Taller Plants to Use as Groundcover

We tend to think of groundcovers as low, creeping plants. But taller plants that spread can also be used to cover an expanse of ground. The plants listed below all grow taller than 1 foot. Also consider the ornamental grasses on the list of "Ornamental Grasses for Groundcover" on page 324.

Artemisia stellerana, beach wormwood
Athyrium filix-femina, lady fern
Cotoneaster lucidus, hedge cotoneaster
Cyrtomium falcatum, holly fern
Cystopteris fragilis

(continued)

Taller Plants to Use as Groundcovers *(cont'd)*

Dennstaedtia punctilobula, hay-scented fern
Diervilla lonicera, bush honeysuckle
Hemerocallis spp. and varieties, daylily
Hosta spp. and varieties, plantain lily
Juniperus spp., juniper
Liriope spp., lilyturf
Lonicera spp., honeysuckle
Onoclea sensibilis, sensitive fern
Osmunda cinnamomea, cinnamon fern
Polemonium caeruleum, Jacob's ladder
Polystichum acrostichoides, Christmas fern
Potentilla fruticosa, bush cinquefoil
Rhus spp., sumac
Rumohra adiantiformis, leatherleaf fern
Sarcococca hookerana var. *humilis*, sweet box
Uvularia grandiflora, big merrybells
Xanthorhiza simplicissima, yellowroot

TIPS ON CARING FOR GROUNDCOVERS

- Match the plants to the available growing conditions.
- Prepare the soil carefully before planting, as you would for any other garden plants. Good soil preparation is especially important when planting under trees.
- Before planting, check the rate of spread of the groundcover. If the plant spreads slowly, space plants close together (4 to 8 inches is a good rule of thumb). If the plant fills in quickly, you can set plants farther apart (on 1-foot centers), and save some money.
- Cover some runners of new plants with soil or peg down trailing stems to encourage rooting and development of new plants.
- Keep the soil moist until the plants become fully established, so runners can root easily and begin new plants quickly. It can take as long as two or three years for some groundcovers to fully establish themselves, so don't stop watering too soon.
- Weed groundcovers until they fill in. Continue to remove any weeds that pop up in less vigorous groundcovers.
- Mulch to conserve soil moisture in summer, and to prevent soil heaving in winter.
- Fertilize established groundcovers in spring, or top-dress in fall with sieved compost.
- Many low, nonwoody groundcovers can be mowed, trimmed, or edged to keep them neat or to rejuvenate them. Mow once a year, just before the plants begin active growth, or during the growing season when the plants look messy. Mow at a height of 2 to 4 inches. Trimmings of some can be treated like cuttings—rooted and planted to fill gaps or cover a new area.

Chapter 6
VINES

TYPES OF VINES

There are three different means by which vining plants climb, and the method of climbing determines the type of support the vine needs.

Twining vines twist their stems around a vertical support. Grow them on trellises, arbors, latticework, posts, vertical strings or wires, or chain-link fences.

Vines with tendrils coil the tendrils (or sometimes their leaf stalks) around a horizontal support. Grow these vines on latticework, grow netting, trellises with horizontal bars or wires, or chain-link fences.

Clinging vines grasp a rough surface with aerial rootlets or small disks on the ends of their stems. These vines will hold onto a brick, stone, or cement wall and need no assistance. Some will climb a tree trunk without harming the tree, but do not train these vines onto clapboard or wood shingle buildings—they can lift the siding from the wall.

Annual Vines

This list describes true annuals and vines that are often grown as annuals.

Adlumia fungosa, mountain fringe: Biennial with small, three-part leaves that give a lacy effect. Small white bell-shaped flowers in midsummer. Tolerates sandy soil.

(continued)

Annual Vines *(cont'd)*

Anredera cordifolia, Madeira vine, mignonette vine: Tendrilled vine that grows quickly to 20 feet or more. Glossy, oblong, evergreen leaves. Long clusters of small, fragrant white flowers in late summer. Perennial in Zones 10 and 11. Roots are hardy somewhat farther north, but top growth dies back in winter. Will grow in sandy soil.

Asarina antirrhinifolia, twining snapdragon: Vigorous twiner growing to 6 feet in one season. Light green, lobed, triangular leaves. Tubular two-lipped flowers similar to snapdragons or violets, in purple, white, or rose-pink, midsummer to fall. Perennial in Zones 8 to 11; grown as annual farther north. Tolerates sandy soil and very alkaline soil.

Basella alba, Malabar spinach: Twining tender vine growing 10 feet or more in a hot summer; grows rampantly in the South. Fleshy, broadly oval leaves are edible but bland, used as summer spinach substitute. Very small purple or pink flowers in midsummer. 'Rubra' has reddish purple stems and red-violet flowers.

Benincasa hispida, wax gourd, ash gourd, Chinese watermelon: Tender annual trailing or climbing by tendrils, growing about 15 feet in a hot summer. Broad-lobed, toothed leaves to 6 inches wide. Yellow flowers in midsummer. Cylindrical fruits about 2 inches in diameter and 8 to 10 inches long, used in pickles or curries, produced where frost-free growing season is at least 100 days long.

Cardiospermum halicacabum, balloon vine, heart pea, love-in-a-puff: Tendrilled tender vine to 10 feet long; perennial in Zones 10 and 11, elsewhere grown as annual. May self-sow in warm climates. Deeply cut leaves. Clusters of small white flowers. Seedpods look like little balloons, seeds have heart-shaped marking.

Cobaea scandens, cup-and-saucer vine: Tendrilled tender perennial grown as annual north of Zone 9. Grows to 25 feet in a summer. Smooth, oval leaves. Cup-shaped lavender to violet flowers have five-part green calyx that forms the "saucer," produced midsummer to frost.

Cucumis dipsaceus, hedgehog gourd, teasel gourd: Prickly stems, broadly oval to heart-shaped leaves, smaller than those of most cucumbers and melons. Yellow flowers. Small oblong fruits to about 2 inches long, covered with prickly bristles; begin green and ripen to yellowish beige.

Cucumis melo, Dudaim Group, Queen Anne's pocket melon, pomegranate melon: Small vine with broadly triangular, toothed leaves. Yellow flowers to 3 inches across. Oval fruit ripening to brown with yellow stripes, very fragrant.

Cucumis melo, Flexuosus Group, snake cucumber, serpent melon: Tender annual with broad, toothed leaves and yellow flowers. Fruit is narrow and long, to 3 feet, often curled and coiled.

Cucurbita pepo var. *ovifera*, gourds: Tender annual vine to about 12 feet. Large, coarse leaves. Yellow flowers. Hard-shelled fruits are varied shapes and sizes: egg-shaped, pumpkin-shaped, slender and cylindrical, some with curved necks, some with warty skin, in cream, yellow, green-and-yellow striped, green-and-white striped, and assorted combinations of these.

Dioscorea batatas, cinnamon vine, Chinese yam: Twining. Broadly oval leaves. Small clusters of flowers that smell like cinnamon. Edible tubers to 3 feet long. Roots hardy to Zone 5, vine to Zone 6; tubers produced only in Zones 10 and 11.

Diplocyclos palmatus, marble vine: Tendrilled annual growing to 10 feet in one summer. Green leaves have three deep lobes. Clusters of unremarkable greenish flowers bloom atop small fruits that begin as marblelike balls of light green with white stripes, maturing to red-orange with cream stripes.

Dolichos lablab (*Lablab purpureus*), hyacinth bean: Twining tender perennial usually grown as annual, to 15 feet or more in a summer. Can be grown as perennial in Zones 10 and 11. Oval to triangular leaves in groups of three. Spikes of fragrant, purple, pealike flowers followed by red-violet pods that are edible but not very tasty.

Ecballium elaterium, squirting cucumber: Herbaceous perennial grown as annual. Trailing stems with hairy triangular leaves. Yellow flowers. Oblong, hairy green fruit to about 2 inches long. When fruit matures, it drops from stem and shoots out its seeds. Certainly a novelty.

Eccremocarpus scaber, glory flower: Tendrilled, twining, evergreen perennial to about 12 feet long. Hardy in Zones 9 to 11; elsewhere grown as annual, and blooms the first year from seed. Compound leaves with three oval leaflets. Clusters of small, tubular, orange-red flowers. 'Aureus' has yellow flowers. 'Carmineus' has carmine flowers. Tolerates very alkaline soil.

Echinocystis lobata, wild cucumber, wild balsam apple: Tendrilled hardy annual to 20 feet. Lobed leaves similar to grape foliage. Clusters of small white flowers. Spiny oval fruits to 2 inches long.

Gloriosa superba, gloriosa lily: To 12 feet. Narrowly oblong leaves. Flowers are yellow, changing to red, with narrow, twisted, wavy-edged petals; bloom in fall in warm climates. Zones 10 and 11. Farther north treat as annual; dig and store tubers indoors over winter. 'Lutea' has yellow flowers. Tolerates sandy soil.

Humulus japonicus, Japanese hop vine: Fast-growing twining annual to 30 feet. Deeply lobed, dark green leaves, toothed stems. Small green flowers followed by scaly, greenish, conelike fruits. Grown for the foliage.

(continued)

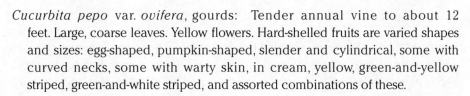

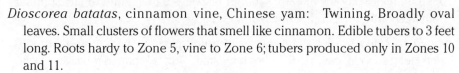

Annual Vines *(cont'd)*

Ipomoea alba, moonflower: Twining tender perennial grown as annual, to about 10 feet. Broad oval to heart-shaped leaves. Large, white, sweetly fragrant flowers with wide petals and long tubular throat, open in late afternoon and remain open all night. Blooms in early summer in Zones 9 to 11, mid to late summer until frost farther north. Tolerates sandy soil.

Ipomoea coccinea, scarlet starglory, red morning glory: Twining annual to 10 feet. Heart-shaped leaves to 6 inches long; small, funnel-shaped red flowers with yellow throat bloom almost all summer. Tolerates sandy soil.

Ipomoea × *multifida*, cardinal climber: Twining annual to 10 feet. Broad, arrow-shaped leaves are very deeply cut, to about 4 inches wide. Bright crimson flowers with white eye and tubular throat have pentagon shape when viewed face-on, bloom through most of summer. Tolerates sandy soil.

Ipomoea nil, morning glory: Annual or tender perennial twiner to 10 feet. Heart-shaped leaves to 6 inches wide have three lobes. Funnel-shaped flowers with wide petals about 4 inches across, violet, purple, rose-pink, white, or blue, sometimes double-petalled or fringed. Imperial Japanese morning glories belong to this species. Tolerates sandy soil.

Ipomoea purpurea, common morning glory: Annual twiner to about 8 feet. Heart-shaped leaves to 5 inches long. Funnel-shaped flowers may be single or double, red, pink, purple, blue-violet, or white. May self-sow and become a pest. 'Alba' has white flowers. 'Huberi' has variegated leaves with silvery markings. White flowers of 'Madame Anne' are striped with red. 'Violacea' has double purple flowers. Tolerates sandy soil.

Ipomoea quamoclit (formerly *Quamoclit pennata*), cypress vine: Annual twiner to 20 feet. Ferny, delicate leaves to 3 inches long are deeply divided into many narrow segments. Bright scarlet flowers about 1½ inches long are star-shaped with tubular throat. Tolerates sandy soil.

Ipomoea tricolor, morning glory: Twining tender perennial to 10 feet, grown as annual. Large heart-shaped to oval leaves about 4 inches wide. Funnel-shaped flowers to 4 inches across, violet in the species, with pale yellow to white throat. Flowers open in the morning and close by late afternoon. Plants bloom from midsummer to frost. 'Heavenly Blue' has true sky-blue flowers with pale yellow throat. 'Pearly Gates' has white flowers. 'Flying Saucers', blue-and-white-striped flowers. 'Wedding Bells', lavender-pink flowers. Tolerates sandy soil.

Lagenaria siceraria, calabash gourd, white-flowered gourd, bottle gourd: Tendrilled, tender annual to 25 feet. Large, broad, oval to kidney-shaped leaves up to 12 inches across. Large, funnel-shaped, fragrant white flowers to

5 inches across open late afternoon or at night. Pale green fruit can be round, oblong, or long-necked, from 3 inches to 3 feet long, with hard shell; once used for dippers and spoons. Needs hot weather and long growing season for fruit to mature.

Lathyrus odoratus, sweet pea: Tendrilled annual to about 8 feet, dwarf varieties to 2 feet. Oval to rounded leaves. Pealike flowers in shades of purple, lavender, red, pink, salmon, and white, sweetly fragrant in some (especially old) varieties. Grows best when temperature is below 75°F. Blooms all summer in northern and cool coastal gardens; elsewhere peters out when weather turns hot in summer. Grown for winter flowers in Zones 10 and 11. Purple flowers generally most fragrant. Fragrant varieties include 'Antique Fantasy Mixed', 'Old Spice', and 'Painted Lady'.

Luffa aegyptiaca (*L. cylindrica*), loofah, dishcloth gourd: Tendrilled, tender annual. Broad, lobed leaves to 12 inches long. Large yellow flowers to 3 inches across. Cylindrical fruit to 2 feet long; edible when young; peeled, dried fibrous interior of mature fruit used as bath sponge. Needs long, warm growing season to produce mature fruit.

Mina lobata, flag of Spain, crimson starglory: Twining, tender perennial to about 10 feet, usually grown as annual except in Zones 10 and 11. Large leaves with three lobes. Spikes of tubular flowers about 3/4 inch long are red in bud stage and when open, slowly fade to yellow as they age.

Momordica balsamina, balsam apple: Tendrilled, tender perennial grown as annual north of Zone 10. Grows quickly to about 6 feet. Deep green, lobed, sharply toothed leaves to 4 inches across. Yellow or white flowers about 1 inch across. Oval, warty, orange fruits to 3 inches long split open when mature to reveal red interior.

Momordica charantia, balsam pear: Tendrilled, tender perennnial grown as annual; may be perennial in Zones 10 and 11. Vines can reach 12 feet in a season. Deeply lobed leaves somewhat larger than those of balsam apple. Large yellow or white flowers. Warty, oval, yellow-orange fruits to 8 inches long, split open when ripe to reveal bright scarlet seed coats.

Muehlenbeckia complexa, wire vine: Twining, fast-growing tender perennial grown outdoors in Zones 10 and 11, as annual or greenhouse plant elsewhere. Elliptical to fiddle-shaped leaves on wiry stems. Inconspicuous clusters of small flowers.

Phaseolus coccineus, scarlet runner bean: Twining, tender perennial grown as annual. Vines grow to about 8 feet in a summer. Dark green oval leaves in groups of three. Clusters of brilliant scarlet 1-inch flowers. Coarse-skinned pods are edible when very young; better used later for shell beans. Keep pods picked to encourage more flowers.

(continued)

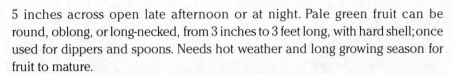

Annual Vines *(cont'd)*

Thunbergia alata, black-eyed Susan vine, clock vine: Twining, tender perennial grown as annual north of Zone 10. Trailing vines to about 6 feet will climb if attached to trellis. Oval to triangular leaves to 3 inches long, with toothed edges. Gold, cream, or yellow-orange flowers with dark centers in mid to late summer; blooms much of the year in warm climates. Grows best in warm weather. Tolerates sandy soil.

Thunbergia grandiflora, Bengal clock vine, sky flower: Twining, tender perennial is evergreen in Zones 10, 11, and protected locations in Zone 9. Toothed oval leaves to 8 inches long. Drooping clusters of sky-blue flowers to about 3 inches across in mid to late summer in the North, mid-spring with continuing sporadic bloom throughout the year in warm climates.

Tropaeolum majus, nasturtium: Twining annual vine with long stems that climb to 8 feet or more when given support, or trail across the ground without support. Disc-shaped deep green leaves. Fragrant, five-petalled, funnel-shaped, spurred flowers in shades of red, mahogany, orange, gold, yellow, and creamy white, all summer. Flowers and leaves are edible, with peppery flavor; buds can be pickled like capers. Needs average to poor soil to bloom well. A pest in southern California where it self-sows.

Tropaeolum peregrinum, canary creeper: Twining annual to 8 to 10 feet. Light green, deeply lobed leaves. Small (1-inch), yellow, fringed flowers.

Perennial Vines

Abrus precatorius, rosary pea: Twiner to 10 feet, trailing or climbing. Compound leaves of pairs of small leaflets 1/2 inch long. Small rosy-purple, pink, or red flowers. Red seeds with black spot are poisonous if eaten, used for beads. Zones 9 and south.

Actinidia arguta, bower actinidia, tara vine: Twiner to 25 feet or more. Lustrous, oval, toothed leaves about 5 inches long. Clusters of white flowers. Edible greenish yellow fruits. Zones 4 to 8. Need both male and female plants to produce fruit.

Actinidia chinensis (*A. deliciosa*), Chinese gooseberry, kiwifruit, yangtao: Twiner to 15 feet. Broad leaves about 6 inches across. Yellow-orange flowers. Edible fruit has hairy brown skin and green interior; only matures in the warmest climates. Zones 7 to 11.

Actinidia kolomikta: Twiner to 15 feet. Oval leaves, often variegated with pink and white. White flowers, edible fruit. Grown for foliage. Zones 4 to 8. Tolerates very alkaline soil.

Actinidia polygama, silver vine, silvervine actinidia: Twiner to 15 feet. Oval leaves may be splashed with white. Small white, fragrant flowers. Edible yellow fruit. Grown for foliage; male plants have most attractive leaves. Zones 5 or 6 to 8.

Akebia quinata, five-leaf akebia, chocolate vine: Twiner to 40 feet. Compound leaves made up of five leaflets. Clusters of small, fragrant, brownish to purplish flowers. Edible (but very bland) bluish or purple fruits. Zones 5 to 8. Can be invasive. Tolerates very alkaline soil.

Allamanda cathartica, golden trumpet vine: To 40 feet. Glossy oblong leaves about 6 inches long, in groups of four. Yellow trumpet-shaped flowers. Zones 10 and 11. Farther north, purchase blooming-size plants and treat as annual, or overwinter plants in greenhouse. Cultivars include 'Grandiflora', 'Hendersonii', and 'Nobilis'.

Ampelopsis arborea, pepper vine: Tendrilled, to 15 feet or more. Dark green, semievergreen, pinnate leaves. Clusters of small greenish flowers followed by pink berries ripening to blue-black. Zones 7 to 9; Zone 6 with winter protection. Can be rampant in Zone 9. Native to southeastern United States.

Ampelopsis brevipedunculata, porcelain ampelopsis: Tendrilled, to 10 feet. Three-lobed dark green leaves, inconspicuous flowers. Grown for its berries, which ripen from lavender to yellow to bright turquoise blue. Zones 4 to 8. Tolerates very alkaline soil. 'Elegans' has leaves splashed with white and sometimes pink; better behaved than species, which is invasive in the Northeast, where it has escaped from cultivation.

Antigonon leptopus, coral vine: Tendrilled, to 30 feet or more. Dark green heart-shaped leaves to 3 inches long. Clusters of bright pink or white flowers, more or less continuously in warm climates. Edible tubers. Zones 8 to 11.

Apios americana, groundnut vine: Twiner, to 8 feet. Pinnate leaves similar to wisteria. Fragrant, brownish orange pealike flowers in late summer. Edible tubers produced in fall. Zones 5 to 9.

Aristolochia durior (*A. macrophylla*), Dutchman's pipe: Twining and fast-growing, to 30 feet. Large, broad, heart-shaped leaves to 12 inches long. Oddly shaped long-tubed yellowish flowers resemble a clay pipe. Zones 5 to 8. Native to the Midwest. Tolerates clay soil.

Aristolochia elegans, calico flower: Tender woody twiner. Triangular leaves to 3 inches long. White flowers veined or spotted with purple on the outside, purplish brown inside, have long tubular throat. Zones 10 and 11.

Bauhinia corymbosa, orchid tree, phanera: Tendrilled tender vine. Two-lobed leaves to 2 inches long. Loose clusters of pinkish, rose-pink, or white flowers about 1 inch across, with frilly petals, in winter or very early spring. Zones 10 and 11.

(continued)

Perennial Vines *(cont'd)*

Beaumontia grandiflora, herald's trumpet, Easter lily vine: To 10 feet. Drooping, deep green, oblong to oval leaves to 9 inches long. Clusters of large, fragrant, white trumpet-shaped flowers, sometimes with pink tips and/or green veining, 5 inches long, in spring. Zones 10 and 11.

Bignonia capreolata, cross vine: Clinging tendrilled vine to 30 feet or more. Evergreen pointed oval leaves. Clusters of funnel-shaped yellow-red to buff-colored flowers in spring. Zones 6 to 9, but top growth dies back in winter in northern part of range. Common name comes from cross-shaped tissue visible in center of stem when cut open. Spreads by underground runners; plant where roots can be confined.

Bougainvillea spp. and hybrids: Twining, spiny, woody vines to 30 feet long. Oval leaves. Grown for colorful papery bracts which surround the inconspicuous flowers. Bracts are shades of magenta, red, pink, orange, salmon, gold, white, and purple. Pink and white-flowered hybrids tend to be least vigorous growers, while red and magenta varieties are strongest growers. Zones 10 and 11.

Campsis radicans, trumpet creeper: Clinging vine to 40 feet or more. Compound leaves composed of oval leaflets. Trumpet-shaped orange or red flowers to 2 inches wide, mid to late summer, attractive to hummingbirds. Zones 5 (perhaps 4 in a sheltered location) to 8. Native to the Southeast. 'Flava' has yellow flowers. *C.* × *tagliabuana* 'Madame Galen' is very similar to *C. radicans* but has larger flowers. Tolerates clay soil.

Celastrus scandens, American bittersweet: Twining, to 25 feet. Deciduous oval leaves, clusters of small flowers. Grown for colorful red to red-orange seed cases. Zones 4 to 8. Tolerates clay, sandy, and very alkaline soils. Oriental bittersweet, *C. orbiculatus*, is similar but very invasive.

Cissus antarctica, kangaroo vine: Tendrilled tender vine. Leathery, toothed, glossy green leaves. Rampant in warm climates. Zones 10 and 11. Farther north, grow in hanging baskets and bring indoors as houseplant in cold weather.

Cissus hypoglauca: Palmately compound leaves made up of oblong leaflets. Tiny but ornamental yellow flowers. New growth is copper-colored. Zones 9 to 11, or farther north as a houseplant.

Cissus incisa, marine ivy: Tendrilled climber to 30 feet. Deciduous or semievergreen compound or deeply lobed leaves with coarsely toothed edges. Zones 7 to 11.

Cissus rhombifolia, grape ivy: Tendrilled, trailing or climbing vine with hairy stems. Toothed oval leaves in clusters of three. Zones 10 and 11. Farther north, grow in hanging baskets and bring indoors as houseplant in cold weather.

Clematis, large-flowered hybrids: Tendrilled vines to 10 to 25 feet. Deep green oval leaves. Most have disc-shaped flowers, up to 6 inches across, with wide, flat petals. Colors include many shades of purple, blue, red, and pink, also yellow and white. Zones 4 to 9.

Florida Group (of hybrids) blooms in summer on old wood. Includes 'Belle of Woking', 'Duchess of Edinburgh', 'Enchantress', and 'Kathleen Dunford'.

Jackmanii Group blooms in summer and autumn on new wood, more cold-hardy than other large-flowered hybrids. Included here in this group are hybrids derived from *C. lanuginosa* and *C. viticella*, which also bloom in summer on new wood. 'Ascotiensis', 'Blue Gem', 'Comtesse de Bouchard', 'Crimson King', 'Crimson Star', 'Duchess of Albany', 'Elsa Spath', 'Ernest Markham', 'Etoile Violette', 'Fairy Queen', 'Gipsy Queen', 'Hagley Hybrid', 'Huldine', 'King Edward VII', 'Lady Betty Balfour', 'Lady Northcliffe', 'Little Nell', 'Lord Neville', 'Margot Koster', 'Minuet', 'Mme. Edouard Andre', 'Nelly Moser', 'Perle d'Azur', 'Prins Hendrik', 'Ramona', 'Star of India', 'Ville de Lyon', 'W. E. Gladstone', and 'William Kennett'.

Patens Group blooms in spring on old wood. Includes 'Bees Jubilee', 'Barbara Dibley', 'Barbara Jackman', 'Daniel Deronda', 'Guiding Star', 'Kathleen Wheeler', 'Lincoln Star', 'Marie Bousselot', 'Miss Bateman', 'Percy Picton', and 'The President'.

C. apiifolia, October clematis: To 9 feet. Compound leaves of three lobed or toothed leaflets. Clusters of small white flowers in fall. Zones 3 to 9.

C. armandii, armand clematis: Grows quickly to 20 feet or more, taller in favorite conditions like the Pacific Northwest. Leathery, deep green leaves. Clusters of fragrant white flowers 2 inches across in spring. Zones 7 to 11. Top growth may be damaged in a severe winter in Zone 7, but plant will recover.

C. crispa, curly clematis: To 9 feet. Pinnate leaves with small oval leaflets. Bell-shaped pale violet flowers in late summer. Zones 7 to 10.

C. × *jackmanii*, Jackman clematis: To 10 feet. Pinnate leaves. Violet to reddish purple flowers to 6 inches across, midsummer to fall. To Zone 5. The first of the large-flowered hybrids.

C. × *lawsoniana*: Large, rosy purple flowers with dark veins in mid to late summer. 'Henryi' has cream-colored flowers.

C. ligusticifolia: Western virgin's bower. Vigorous grower to 15 feet. Compound leaves with lobed leaflets. Clusters of white flowers in late summer to early fall. To Zone 4. Native to the western United States.

(continued)

Perennial Vines *(cont'd)*

C. montana, anemone clematis: Grows from 10 to 25 feet. Compound leaves with three toothed oval leaflets. Clusters of lightly fragrant white flowers in spring to early summer turn pink as they age. Aggressive but blooms on new wood and can be controlled by hard pruning. Zones 5 to 8. Var. *rubens*, pink clematis, has purplish leaves and rose or pink flowers.

C. paniculata (*C. terniflora*), sweet autumn clematis: Grows to 20 or 30 feet. Compound leaves with three lobed or scalloped leaflets. Clusters of fragrant white flowers in early fall, followed by berries. Zones 5 to 9.

C. tangutica, golden clematis: To 15 feet. Compound leaves of oblong leaflets. Bell-shaped yellow flowers 1½ inches long in midsummer to early fall. Zones 5 to 9.

C. texensis, scarlet clematis: To about 10 feet. Pinnate leaves. Bell-shaped scarlet or rosy flowers, late summer to early fall. Zones 4 to 9.

C. virginiana, virgin's bower, woodbine: To 18 to 20 feet. Compound leaves of three oval leaflets. Cluster of creamy white flowers in late summer to early fall. Zones 4 to 8.

C. vitalba, traveler's joy: To 25 feet. Pinnate leaves. Clusters of mildly fragrant greenish white flowers in late summer to early fall. Zones 4 to 9.

C. viticella, Italian clematis: To 12 feet. Pinnate leaves. Blue, purple, or red-violet flowers in mid to late summer. Zones 4 to 9.

Clerodendrum thomsoniae, bleeding-heart glorybower: Twining evergreen. Oval to oblong leaves to about 5 inches. Clusters of small, deep red flowers backed by large white calyx, in summer or nearly continuously in warmest parts of the continental United States; plants bloom winter or spring in Hawaii. Zones 10 and 11.

Clianthus puniceus, glory pea, parrot's beak: To 6 feet. Semiwoody; pinnate leaves with many leaflets. Red pealike flowers to 3 inches, in drooping clusters. Zones 10 and 11. Rambles but will climb if fastened to support. Tolerates sandy soil.

Clytostoma callistegioides (*Bignonia violacea*), Argentine trumpet vine, orchid trumpet vine: Tendrilled, to 20 feet. Glossy evergreen leaves to 3 inches long. Masses of pinkish lavender trumpet flowers in late spring and summer. Zones 9 to 11.

Cocculus carolinus, Carolina moonseed, snailseed: Twining, 6 to 12 feet high. Oval leaves to 4 inches long, sometimes lobed. Clusters of inconspicuous flowers followed by showy red fruits in summer. Zones 7 to 11. Native to the southeastern United States.

Cryptostegia grandiflora, rubber vine, purple allamanda: Twining, tender woody vine. Glossy, leathery, oblong leaves to 5 inches long. Clusters of lilac-purple bell-shaped 3-inch flowers. Plant contains a milky sap once used as a rubber substitute. Zones 10 and 11.

Decumaria barbara: To 30 feet, climbs by aerial rootlets. Glossy, narrow, elliptical leaves to 4 inches long. Round-topped clusters of small white flowers similar to hydrangea. Peeling bark. Zones 6 to 11. Native to southeastern United States.

Dioscorea batatas, cinnamon vine, Chinese yam: Twining. Broadly oval leaves. Small clusters of cinnamon-scented flowers. Edible tubers to 3 feet long. Roots hardy to Zone 5, vine to Zone 6; tubers produced only in Zones 10 and 11. Can also be grown as an annual.

Distictis buccinatoria, Mexican blood trumpet vine, red trumpet vine: Tendrilled, clinging, fast growing, to 50 feet or more. Dark green, glossy, oblong leaves. Large clusters of deep orange-red flowers with yellow throat, fading to deep rose, blooming all summer into autumn. Zones 9 to 11. Tolerates clay soil.

Distictis lactiflora, vanilla-scented trumpet vine: Tendrilled. Compound leaves with oblong leaflets. Clusters of funnel-shaped, light bluish purple flowers with yellow throat, fading to pale lavender, summer to autumn. Zones 10 and 11.

Distictis 'Rivers', royal trumpet vine: To 20 feet. Like *D. buccinatoria*, but flowers are rosy purple with yellow-orange throat, blooming late summer and fall. Foliage is less dense and plant grows more slowly than red trumpet vine.

Euonymus fortunei, wintercreeper: Trails or clings and climbs by rootlets, to 30 feet. Small oval to elliptic evergreen leaves with scalloped or toothed edges. Many cultivars with variegated foliage. Greenish white flowers. Ornamental red or orange berries late summer to autumn. Zones 5 to 9. 'Minima' has small leaves to 1/2 inch long. 'Sarcoxie' has glossy leaves and bright orange berries. 'Silver Queen' has leaves with irregular ivory edging. Var. *vegeta*, bigleaf wintercreeper, has larger, more rounded leaves and lots of red to orange fruit.

Ficus pumila, creeping fig: Clinging, to 30 feet. Small, broadly oval, deep green evergreen leaves to 2 or 3 inches long, on thin stems. Zones 9 to 11.

Gelsemium sempervirens, Carolina jessamine: Vigorous twiner to 20 feet. Glossy evergreen lance-shaped leaves. Clusters of pleasant-scented, tubular yellow flowers in spring and summer. Zones 7 to 9; may survive as far north as New York City with winter protection. Poisonous, so treat with care. 'Plena' and 'Pride of Augusta' have double flowers.

Hardenbergia comptoniana: Evergreen twiner to 8 feet. Compound pealike leaves with three to five leaflets to 3 inches long. Drooping clusters of pealike blue-violet flowers in late winter and spring. Zones 10 and 11. Can be grown in greenhouse farther north.

Hedera canariensis, Algerian ivy, Canary Island ivy: Clinging. Oval or heart-shaped lobed deep green leaves to 6 inches long, on burgundy stems. Numerous cultivars are variegated with creamy white, some with dark veins. Zones 8 to 11.

(continued)

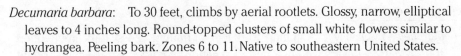

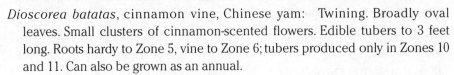

Perennial Vines *(cont'd)*

Hedera helix, English ivy: Clinging, to 80 feet, or trailing. Glossy dark green, often lobed. Many cultivars with assorted variegation of gold, creamy white, or light green. Zones 5 to 9, depending on the variety.

Hoya carnosa, wax vine, honey plant: Twining. Smooth, succulent, dull green oval leaves to 3 inches long. Clusters of small, fragrant, star-shaped white or pale pink flowers with red center. Zones 10 and 11; farther north grow in greenhouse.

Humulus lupulus, common hop vine: Fast-growing twiner. Dark green leaves with three to five lobes. Scaly greenish, conelike flowers; female flowers are source of commercial hops. Tolerates clay soil. Zones 5 to 9. 'Aureus' has golden to yellow-green foliage.

Hydrangea anomala subsp. *petiolaris* (*H. petiolaris*), climbing hydrangea: Clings by aerial rootlets, growing slowly to 50 or 60 feet. Broad, oval, dark green leaves to 4 inches long. Large clusters, 6 to 10 inches long, of small white flowers in early to midsummer. Zones 5 to 9. Tolerates clay soil and very alkaline soil.

Jasminum grandiflorum, Spanish jasmine: To about 4 feet high. Pairs of oval leaves on arching branches. Very fragrant tubular white flowers. Zones 10 and 11, perhaps protected locations in Zone 9.

Jasminum officinale, poet's jasmine: To 15 feet or more. Pairs of oval leaves. Clusters of fragrant white tubular flowers. 'Aureo-variegatum' has leaves variegated with yellow; the form *affine* has larger flowers. Mildest parts of Zone 7 to Zone 11. Tolerates alkaline soil.

Jasminum sambac, Arabian jasmine: Tender evergreen. Glossy, broadly oval leaves. Clusters of fragrant white tubular flowers. 'Grand Duke of Tuscany' has double flowers. Zones 10 and 11. Farther north, grow in pots or hanging baskets and bring indoors over winter.

Kadsura japonica, scarlet kadsura: Twining, to 10 or 12 feet, evergreen in the South and deciduous in the North. Slender oblong leaves. Inconspicuous cup-shaped flowers, followed by clusters of bright red berries in fall. Zones 6 or 7 to 11.

Lapageria rosea, Chilean bellflower: Drooping, dark green, leathery leaves to 3 inches long. Bell-shaped red flowers to 4 inches long in summer. Needs acid soil. Zones 10 and 11.

Lathyrus grandiflorus, everlasting pea: Twining tendrilled perennial to 6 feet. Pairs of oval leaflets. Slightly fragrant, rosy purple pealike flowers. Tolerates very alkaline soil. Zones 6 to 9.

Lathyrus latifolius, perennial pea: Rampant-growing tendrilled perennial to 9 feet. Pairs of oval leaflets. Rosy pink or white pealike flowers. 'Splendens' has red and deep purple flowers. Tolerates clay soil and very alkaline soil. Zones 4 to 8.

Lonicera flava, yellow honeysuckle: Spreading twiner to 12 feet. Elliptical leaves. Clusters of fragrant, orangey yellow two-lipped flowers in late spring. Red fruits attractive to birds. Zones 5 to 8. Native to the southeastern United States.

Lonicera heckrottii: Everblooming honeysuckle. Elliptical leaves. Spikes of tubular flowers, rosy red outside and yellow inside, in early summer, with sporadic bloom all summer. Red fruit. To Zone 5, Zone 4 with winter protection.

Lonicera henryi: Semievergreen, twining or prostrate. Oblong to lance-shaped leaves. Pairs of yellowish red or purple-red flowers, early to late summer. Black fruit. To Zone 5.

Lonicera perfoliatae: Fragrant pink blossoms in summer, followed by orange berries.

Lonicera periclymenum, woodbine: Twiner to 30 feet. Oval to oblong,bluish to grayish green leaves, evergreen in warm regions. Clusters of fragrant yellowish white flowers in early to late summer. Red fruit. Zones 5 to 9. 'Aurea' has variegated leaves. 'Graham Thomas' blooms long, with very fragrant flowers.

Lonicera sempervirens, trumpet honeysuckle: Twiner to 50 feet. Oval to oblong leaves, evergreen in the South. Clusters of 2-inch scarlet-red flowers, yellow on the inside, late spring to late summer, attractive to hummingbirds. Red fruit. Zones 4 to 9. 'Magnifica' is vigorous and blooms late. 'Sulphurea' has yellow flowers. 'Superba' has scarlet flowers.

Lonicera × tellmanniana, Tellmann honeysuckle: Hybrid between *L. sempervirens* and *L. tragophylla*. Twining. Clusters of deep yellow flowers tinged with red in bud stage, early summer to early fall. Zones 5 to 9.

Lonicera tragophylla, Chinese honeysuckle: Twining. Oblong leaves. Clusters of bright yellow flowers in early summer. Red fruit. To Zone 6.

Lycium chinense, Chinese matrimony vine: May be shrubby with arching branches, or trailing, to 12 feet long. Oval to lance-shaped leaves usually, although size and shape vary. Small purple flowers develop at nodes or in leaf axils, early to late summer. Bright red or orange berries in late summer to early fall. Plants spread by suckers. To Zone 5.

Macfadyena unguis-cati, catclaw vine: To 25 feet. Clinging, clawlike tendrils. Oblong to lance-shaped leaves to 2 inches long. Bright yellow flowers. Zone 7 or 8 to 11. Can become invasive in warm climates.

Mandevilla × amabilis: Woody twiner to 20 feet. Oblong ribbed leaves. Large funnel-shaped flowers, pale pink at first, darkening to deep rose as they age, bloom all summer. Zones 10 and 11; elsewhere grow in a large tub and bring indoors over winter. 'Alice du Pont', the most common variety, has bright pink flowers with deeper pink throat.

(continued)

Perennial Vines *(cont'd)*

Mandevilla laxa (*M. suaveolens*), Chilean jasmine: Woody twiner to 20 feet. Oval or heart-shaped leaves. Clusters of fragrant, funnel-shaped white to cream flowers 2 inches across, in summer. Flower scent resembles gardenia. Zones 8 to 11.

Menispermum canadense, moonseed: Woody twiner to 12 feet. Circular to oval lobed leaves, fuzzy on the underside, to 8 inches long. Clusters of white to yellowish flowers in late spring. Dark fruits similar to grapes are poisonous. Grown for its foliage in the eastern United States. Spreads by underground runners and can become a pest. To Zone 4.

Millettia reticulata, evergreen wisteria: Woody twiner to 15 feet. Leathery, bright green, evergreen compound leaves with oval to lance-shaped leaflets. Terminal clusters of fragrant pealike reddish purple flowers in late summer. Zones 8 to 11.

Pandorea jasminoides, bower plant: Woody climber. Light green evergreen pinnate leaves composed of oval to lance-shaped leaflets. Small clusters of funnel-shaped, pinkish white flowers with deep pink throat, to 2 inches long, in summer and autumn. Zones 10 and 11, perhaps to Zone 9 with winter protection. 'Alba' has white flowers. 'Rosea' has lavender-pink flowers.

Pandorea pandorana, wonga-wonga vine: Woody climber. Evergreen pinnate leaves composed of oval to broadly lance-shaped leaves. Clusters of yellowish white flowers with purple-spotted throat. Zones 10 and 11. 'Rosea' has pale rose flowers.

Parthenocissus henryana, silvervein creeper: Deciduous woody vine, clinging and tendrilled. Compound leaves made of oval leaflets, with white vein and purple underside. Clusters of small greenish white flowers. Dark blue berries in fall, attractive to birds. Zones 8 to 11.

Parthenocissus quinquefolia, Virginia creeper: Clinging, tendrilled vine to 30 feet or more. Compound leaves to 6 inches long, made of five toothed oval leaflets arranged like fingers on a hand. Inconspicuous flowers. Blue-black berries in late summer or fall are attractive to birds. Leaves turn bright red-orange in fall. Zones 3 to 9. 'Engelmannii' has smaller leaflets. 'Hirsuta' has leaves with hairy underside.

Parthenocissus tricuspidata, Boston ivy: Clinging climber to 50 feet. Lobed leaves to 8 inches long, turn dark red in autumn. Inconspicuous flowers. Blue-black berries in late summer or fall. Zones 4 to 8. Leaves of 'Lowii' are small, and purple when young. 'Minutifolia' has small leaves. 'Purpurea' has dark purple leaves.

Passiflora caerulea, blue passionflower: Tendrilled climber. Deeply lobed leaves. Flowers usually white, to 4 inches across, with fringelike corona that is violet at the tip, white in middle, and purple at base, blooming early summer to early fall. Edible fruit where growing season is long enough. Tolerates clay soil and alkaline soil. Zones 8 to 11; elsewhere grow in pots and overwinter in greenhouse. 'Grandiflora' has larger flowers to 6 inches across. 'Constance Elliott' has white flowers.

Passiflora incarnata, maypop: Tendrilled climber, hardiest of the passionflowers. Deeply lobed, toothed leaves 4 to 6 inches long. Flowers white to pale lavender, 2 to 3 inches across, with pink to purple corona, blooming in summer in the North, much of the year in warm climates. Edible yellow fruit where season is long enough. Tolerates clay soil. Zones 7 to 11.

Periploca graeca, silk vine: Twining, deciduous woody climber to 40 feet. Oblong to lance-shaped leaves. Clusters of greenish flowers, purple inside, ending in a crown of threadlike filaments. Zones 7 to 11; provide winter protection in Zone 7. Can be invasive.

Philodendron spp.: Large genus of clinging herbaceous epiphytic plants grown for their foliage. Fleshy deep green leaves may be heart-shaped, lobed, or compound, from about 2 inches to 3 feet long, depending on the species. Grown outdoors in Zones 10 and 11, as houseplants elsewhere.

Pileostegia viburnoides, tanglehead: Clinging vine to 25 feet. Evergreen elliptical leaves to 5 inches long are glossy dark green. Clusters of small white flowers late summer to early fall. Zones 7 to 10.

Plumbago auriculata, Cape plumbago: Shrubby climber. Lance-shaped leaves to 2 inches long. Clusters of pale blue flowers, 1 inch across, all summer, or nearly year-round in some locations. Zones 10 and 11.

Polygonum aubertii, silver-lace vine, silver-fleece vine: Twiner, grows quickly to 20 feet or more. Oval to lance-shaped leaves to 2$^1/_2$ inches long. Clusters of small, mildly fragrant white flowers look lacy in late summer to early fall. Tolerates alkaline soil. Zones 4 to 9.

Pyrostegia venusta, flame vine, orange trumpet: Clinging, tendrilled vine. Evergreen compound leaves with oval leaflets to 3 inches long. Clusters of brilliant orange tubular flowers in winter. Zones 10 and 11.

Rhoicissus capensis, Cape grape, African grape: Tendrilled evergreen. Round to kidney-shaped evergreen leaves, some deeply lobed, to 8 inches across, with scalloped edges. Clusters of reddish purple berries. New growth is bronzy or rusty-colored. Zones 10 and 11.

Rosa, climbing and rambler roses: See chapter 3, "Annuals," for information on these varieties.

Rosa banksiae, Lady Banks rose: Evergreen, to 20 feet or more. Compound leaves in groups of three or five leaflets. Small white or yellow flowers mid-spring or slightly later. Red hips. Zones 8 to 10. 'Alba Plena' has double white flowers. 'Lutea' has double yellow flowers. 'Lutescens' has single yellow blossoms.

(continued)

Perennial Vines *(cont'd)*

Rosa laevigata, Cherokee rose: Evergreen, to 20 feet. Compound leaves in groups of three. Fragrant white flowers to $3^1/_2$ inches across, in late spring. Orange hips. Zones 7 to 10.

Rosa wichuraiana, memorial rose: Semievergreen trailer or climber. Compound leaves of five or more leaflets. Clusters of small white fragrant flowers mid to late summer to early fall. To Zone 5.

Schisandra chinensis, Chinese magnolia vine: Twiner to 25 feet. Glossy oval to oblong leaves to 4 inches long, with toothed or serrated edges. Fragrant white to pinkish flowers in late spring to early summer. Clusters of ornamental berry-like red fruits in fall. Plant male and female plants to get berries. To Zone 5.

Schisandra propinqua, Himalayan magnolia vine: Twining evergreen. Oval to slender oblong leaves. Orange flowers. Clusters of red berrylike fruits to 6 inches long in fall. Plant male and female plants to get berries. Zones 9 to 11.

Schizophragma hydrangeoides, Japanese hydrangea vine: Clinging vine to 18 feet or more. Broad oval leaves to 4 inches long, with toothed edges. Flat-topped clusters of white flowers, somewhat similar to lacecap hydrangea, in midsummer. Zones 5 to 7.

Senecio confusus, Mexican flame vine: Twining tender herbaceous perennial to 8 feet. Oval to triangular leaves to about 2 inches long. Clusters of small orange to orange-red daisylike flowers. Zones 9 to 11, grown mostly along the Gulf Coast.

Senecio macroglossus, wax vine, natal ivy: Twining evergreen. Triangular, lobed leaves to $2^1/_2$ inches long. Yellow daisylike flowers. Zones 10 and 11; elsewhere grow as houseplant. 'Variegatus' has green-and-yellow variegated leaves.

Smilax glauca, catbrier, wild sarsaparilla: Tendrilled climbing shrub. Wiry, prickly stems. Oval to kidney-shaped leaves to 4 inches long. Small white to greenish flowers. Blue to black fruits. Zones 5 to 9. Hard to get rid of once established. The closely related *S. rotundifolia* is similar but more invasive, extremely difficult to eradicate once established.

Solanum jasminoides, potato vine, jasmine nightshade: Fast-growing twiner to 20 feet or more. Dark green oval to lance-shaped leaves to 3 inches long, evergreen in mild winters. Clusters of star-shaped bluish white flowers to 1 inch across, blooming in spring and sporadically through the year. Zones 9 to 11. 'Grandiflorum' has larger flower clusters.

Solanum wendlandii, Costa Rican nightshade, paradise flower: Shrubby climber. Prickly stems, glossy, compound, pinnate leaves to 10 inches long. Clusters of lavender-blue flowers midsummer to fall. Tolerates sandy soil. Zones 10 and 11.

Stauntonia hexaphylla, Japanese staunton vine: Woody evergreen twiner to 40 feet. Compound leaves of oval to elliptical leaflets. Clusters of fragrant white flowers tinged with purple. Edible small purple fruits. Zones 8 to 11.

Stephanotis floribunda, Madagascar jasmine: Evergreen twiner, to 15 feet or more. Dark green, glossy, elliptical leaves to 4 inches long. Clusters of intensely fragrant, tubular, waxy white flowers in all summer. Zones 10 and 11.

Tecomaria capensis, Cape honeysuckle: Extremely vigorous climbing or rambling shrub to 20 feet, can be grown as a vine or pruned and used as a shrub. Compound light green evergreen leaves to 6 inches long. Clusters of funnel-shaped scarlet flowers about 2 inches long, late summer into winter. Zones 9 and 11. 'Aurea' and 'Lutea' have yellow flowers (and may actually be the same cultivar).

Trachelospermum jasminoides, Confederate jasmine, star jasmine: Vigorous twiner to 15 feet or more, or will sprawl as groundcover. Small evergreen, oblong to elliptical leaves of dark green. Fragrant, creamy white star-shaped, tubular flowers in summer. Tolerates very alkaline soil. Zones 8 to 11. Elsewhere grow in pots brought indoors for winter. 'Japonicum' has white-veined leaves that turn bronze in fall. 'Variegatum' has green-and-white variegated leaves.

Tripterygium regelii, Regel's three-wing nut: Deciduous woody twiner to 8 feet. Bright green elliptical to oval leaves with scalloped edges, to 6 inches long. Pyramidal clusters of greenish white flowers, to 10 inches long, in mid to late summer. Small purplish red to brown fruits with three wings. Zones 5 to 10.

Vitis spp., grape: Tendrilled vines with broad, lobed leaves; clusters of berry fruits of many species are used for eating or winemaking. Species are available for all climates.

Vitis coignetiae, crimson glory vine: The best ornamental grape. Large round to oval leaves turn bright red in autumn. Purple-black, poorly flavored fruit. Tolerates clay soil. Zones 5 to 11.

Wisteria floribunda, Japanese wisteria: Deciduous woody twiner to 25 feet. Bright green pinnate leaves with oval leaflets. Hanging clusters of sweet-scented, pealike violet flowers can be 18 inches long, bloom a week or two after Chinese wisteria. Cultivars have flowers in white and shades of pink, red, and violet. Tolerates clay soil. Zones 4 or 5 to 10. Var. *macrobotrys* flower clusters can be 3 feet long. Buy grafted plants (unless you are prepared to wait up to 10 years for plants to bloom).

Wisteria sinensis, Chinese wisteria: Deciduous woody twiner to 30 feet. Pinnate leaves of oval leaflets. Hanging clusters of lightly fragrant, pealike blue-violet flowers to 12 inches long, in mid to late spring. Tolerates clay soil and very alkaline soil. Zones 5 to 10, but less hardy than Japanese wisteria. 'Alba' has fragrant white flowers. 'Purpurea' has violet-purple flowers. Buy grafted plants (unless you are prepared to wait up to 10 years for plants to bloom).

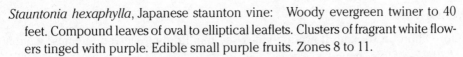

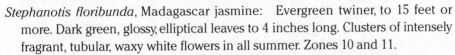

Flowering Vines

For information on pruning flowering vines, see the "Pruning Flowering Vines" section on pages 370–372 of this chapter.

Abrus precatorius, rosary pea
Akebia quinata, five-leaf akebia (fragrant)
Allamanda cathartica, golden trumpet vine
Anredera cordifolia, Madeira vine (fragrant)
Antigonon leptopus, coral vine
Apios americana, groundnut vine (fragrant)
Aristolochia durior, Dutchman's pipe
Aristolochia elegans, calico flower
Asarina antirrhinifolia, twining snapdragon
Bauhinia corymbosa, orchid tree
Beaumontia grandiflora, Easter lily vine (fragrant)
Bignonia capreolata, cross vine
Bougainvillea spp. and hybrids
Campsis radicans, trumpet creeper
Cissus hypoglauca
Clematis spp. and hybrids (*C. armandii*, *C. montana*, and *C. paniculata* are fragrant)
Clerodendrum thomsoniae, bleeding-heart glorybower
Clianthus puniceus, glory pea
Clytostoma callistegioides, Argentine trumpet vine
Cobaea scandens, cup-and-saucer vine
Cocculus carolinus, Carolina moonseed
Cryptostegia grandiflora, rubber vine
Decumaria barbara
Dioscorea batatas, cinnamon vine (fragrant)
Distictis buccinatoria, Mexican blood trumpet vine
Distictis lactiflora, vanilla-scented trumpet vine (fragrant)
Dolichos lablab, hyacinth bean
Eccremocarpus scaber, glory flower
Gelsemium sempervirens, Carolina jessamine (fragrant)
Gloriosa superba, gloriosa lily
Hardenbergia comptoniana
Hoya carnosa, wax vine (fragrant)
Hydrangea anomala subsp. *petiolaris*, climbing hydrangea
Ipomoea alba, moonflower (fragrant)
Ipomoea coccinea, scarlet starglory
Ipomoea × *multifida*, cardinal climber
Ipomoea nil, morning glory
Ipomoea purpurea, common morning glory
Ipomoea quamoclit, cypress vine
Ipomoea tricolor, morning glory
Jasminum grandiflorum, Spanish jasmine (fragrant)
Jasminum officinale, poet's jasmine (fragrant)
Jasminum sambac, Arabian jasmine (fragrant)
Lapageria rosea, Chilean bellflower
Lathyrus grandiflorus, everlasting pea (slightly fragrant)
Lathyrus latifolius, perennial pea
Lathyrus odoratus, sweet pea (fragrant)
Lonicera flava, yellow honeysuckle (fragrant)
Lonicera heckrottii, everblooming honeysuckle
Lonicera henryi
Lonicera periclymenum, woodbine (fragrant)
Lonicera sempervirens, trumpet honeysuckle
Lonicera × *tellmanniana*, Tellmann honeysuckle
Lonicera tragophylla, Chinese honeysuckle
Lycium chinense, Chinese matrimony vine
Macfadyena unguis-cati, catclaw vine
Mandevilla × *amabilis*
Mandevilla laxa, Chilean jasmine (fragrant)
Mina lobata, flag of Spain
Pandorea jasminoides, bower plant
Pandorea pandorana, wonga-wonga vine
Passiflora caerulea, blue passionflower

Passiflora incarnata, maypop

Periploca graeca, silk vine

Phaseolus coccineus, scarlet runner bean

Pileostegia viburnoides, tanglehead

Plumbago auriculata

Polygonum aubertii, silver-lace vine (lightly fragrant)

Pyrostegia venusta, orange trumpet

Rosa, climbing roses (some are fragrant)

Rosa, rambler roses (some are fragrant)

Rosa banksiae, Lady Banks rose

Rosa laevigata, Cherokee rose (fragrant)

Rosa wichuraiana, memorial rose (fragrant)

Schisandra chinensis, Chinese magnolia vine (fragrant)

Schisandra propinqua, Himalayan magnolia vine

Schizophragma hydrangeoides, Japanese hydrangea vine

Senecio confusus, Mexican flame vine

Senecio macroglossus, wax vine

Solanum jasminoides, potato vine

Solanum wendlandii, Costa Rican nightshade

Stauntonia hexaphylla, Japanese staunton vine (fragrant)

Stephanotis floribunda, Madagascar jasmine (fragrant)

Tecomaria capensis, Cape honeysuckle

Thunbergia alata, black-eyed Susan vine

Thunbergia grandiflora, Bengal clock vine

Trachelospermum jasminoides, Confederate jasmine (fragrant)

Tripterygium regelii, Regel's three-wing nut

Tropaeolum majus, nasturtium (fragrant)

Tropaeolum peregrinum, canary creeper

Wisteria floribunda, Japanese wisteria (fragrant)

Wisteria sinensis, Chinese wisteria (lightly fragrant)

Vines with Ornamental and Interesting Fruit

Actinidia
- *A. arguta*, bower actinidia
- *A. chinensis*, Chinese gooseberry
- *A. kolomikta*
- *A. polygama*, silver vine

Akebia quinata, five-leaf akebia

Ampelopsis
- *A. arborea*, pepper vine
- *A. brevipedunculata*, porcelain ampelopsis

Benincasa hispida, wax gourd

Cardiospermum halicacabum, balloon vine

Celsatrus scandens, American bittersweet

Clematis spp. and hybrids (interesting seed heads)

Cocculus carolinus, Carolina moonseed

Cucumis
- *C. dipsaceus*, hedgehog gourd
- *C. melo*, Dudaim Group, Queen Anne's pocket melon
- *C. melo*, Flexuosus Group, snake cucumber

Cucurbita pepo var. *ovifera*, gourds

Diplocyclos palmatus, marble vine

Dolichos lablab, hyacinth bean

Ecballium elaterium, squirting cucumber

Echinocystis lobata, wild cucumber

Euonymus fortunei, wintercreeper

Kadsura japonica, scarlet kadsura

Lagenaria siceraria, calabash gourd

Lonicera spp., honeysuckle

Luffa aegyptiaca, loofah

Lycium chinense, Chinese matrimony vine

Menispermum canadense, moonseed

Momordica
- *M. balsamina*, balsam apple
- *M. charantia*, balsam pear

Parthenocissus
- *P. henryana*, silvervein creeper
- *P. quinquefolia*, Virginia creeper
- *P. tricuspidata*, Boston ivy

Passiflora
- *P. caerulea*, blue passionflower
- *P. incarnata*, maypop

(continued)

Vines with Ornamental and Interesting Fruit *(cont'd)*

Rhoicissus capensis, Cape grape
Rosa
- *R. banksiae*, Lady Banks rose
- *R. laevigata*, Cherokee rose

Schisandra
- *S. chinensis*, Chinese magnolia vine
- *S. propinqua*, Himalayan magnolia vine

Stauntonia hexaphylla, Japanese staunton vine
Tripterygium regelii, Regel's three-wing nut
Vitis spp., grape

Foliage Vines

These vines are grown primarily for foliage interest.

Actinidia kolomikta
Akebia quinata, five-leaf akebia
Aristolochia durior, Dutchman's pipe
Basella alba, Malabar spinach
Cissus
- *C. antarctica*, kangaroo vine
- *C. hypoglauca*
- *C. incisa*, marine ivy
- *C. rhombifolia*, grape ivy

Euonymus fortunei, wintercreeper
Ficus pumila, creeping fig
Hedera
- *H. canariensis*, Canary Island ivy
- *H. helix*, English ivy

Humulus
- *H. japonicus*, Japanese hop vine
- *H. lupulus*, common hop vine

Menispermum canadense, moonseed
Muehlenbeckia complexa, wire vine
Parthenocissus
- *P. henryana*, silvervein creeper
- *P. quinquefolia*, Virginia creeper
- *P. tricuspidata*, Boston ivy

Philodendron spp.
Rhoicissus capensis, Cape grape
Vitis coignetiae, crimson glory vine

Evergreen Vines

Abrus precatorius, rosary pea
Allamanda cathartica, golden trumpet vine
Anredera cordifolia, Madeira vine
Antigonon leptopus, coral vine
Beaumontia grandiflora, Easter lily vine
Bignonia capreolata, cross vine
Bougainvillea spp. and hybrids
Cissus
- *C. antarctica*, kangaroo vine
- *C. hypoglauca*
- *C. incisa*, marine ivy
- *C. rhombifolia*

Clerodendrum thomsoniae, bleeding-heart glorybower
Clianthus puniceus, glory pea
Clytostoma callistegioides, Argentine trumpet vine
Decumaria barbara
Dioscorea batatas, cinnamon vine
Distictis
- *D. buccinatoria*, Mexican blood trumpet vine
- *D. lactiflora*, vanilla-scented trumpet vine

Euonymus fortunei, wintercreeper
Ficus pumila, creeping fig
Gelsemium sempervirens, Carolina jessamine
Gloriosa superba, gloriosa lily (where perennial)
Hardenbergia comptoniana
Hedera helix, English ivy
Hoya carnosa, wax vine
Jasminum
- *J. grandiflorum*, Spanish jasmine
- *J. officinale*, poet's jasmine
- *J. sambac*, Arabian jasmine

Kadsura japonica, scarlet kadsura
Lapageria rosea, Chilean bellflower
Macfadyena unguis-cati, catclaw vine
Mandevilla
- *M.* × *amabilis*
- *M. laxa*, Chilean jasmine

Pandorea
- *P. jasminoides*, bower plant
- *P. pandorana*, wonga-wonga vine

Pileostegia viburnoides, tanglehead
Pyrostegia venusta, flame vine
Rhoicissus capensis, Cape grape
Schisandra
- *S. chinensis*, Chinese magnolia vine
- *S. propinqua*, Himalayan magnolia vine

Senecio
- *S. confusus*, Mexican flame vine
- *S. macroglossus*, wax vine

Stauntonia hexaphylla, Japanese staunton vine
Tecomaria capensis, Cape honeysuckle
Thunbergia grandiflora, Bengal clock vine
Trachelospermum jasminoides, Confederate jasmine

Vines for Shade

The following vines all tolerate at least some shade. See pages 49–50 for definitions of partial, light, full, and dense shade.

Actinidia
- *A. arguta*, bower actinidia, partial shade
- *A. chinensis*, Chinese gooseberry, partial shade
- *A. kolomikta*, partial shade
- *A. polygama*, silvervine, partial shade

Adlumia fungosa, mountain fringe, partial shade
Akebia quinata, five-leaf akebia, partial to light shade
Ampelopsis
- *A. arborea*, pepper vine, partial shade
- *A. brevipedunculata*, porcelain ampelopsis, partial shade

Apios americana, groundnut vine, partial to light shade
Aristolochia durior, Dutchman's pipe, partial to light shade
Bignonia capreolata, cross vine, tolerates partial to light shade but blooms best in full sun
Celastrus scandens, American bittersweet, partial to light shade
Cissus
- *C. antarctica*, kangaroo vine, partial to light shade
- *C. hypoglauca*, partial to light shade
- *C. incisa*, marine ivy, partial to light shade
- *C. rhombifolia*, partial to light shade

Clematis spp. and hybrids, partial to light shade; they especially like shade on their roots
Clytostoma callistegioides, Argentine trumpet vine, partial to light shade
Cobaea scandens, cup-and-saucer vine, partial shade
Distictis buccinatoria, Mexican blood trumpet vine, partial shade
Euonymus fortunei, wintercreeper, partial to full shade
Ficus pumila, creeping fig, partial to full shade
Gelsemium sempervirens, Carolina jessamine, partial shade
Hardenbergia comptoniana, partial to light shade
Hedera
- *H. canariensis*, Canary Island ivy, partial to full shade
- *H. helix*, English ivy, partial to dense shade

Hoya carnosa, wax vine, partial to light shade; can cope with full shade but will not bloom as well

(continued)

Vines for Shade *(cont'd)*

Humulus spp., hops, partial to light shade

Hydrangea anomala subsp. *petiolaris*, climbing hydrangea, partial to light shade

Lapageria rosea, Chilean bellflower, partial shade

Lonicera spp., honeysuckle, partial to light shade

Lycium chinense, Chinese matrimony vine, partial to light shade

Mandevilla × *amabilis*, partial shade

Menispermum canadense, moonseed, partial to light shade

Parthenocissus

- *P. henryana*, silvervein creeper, partial to light shade
- *P. quinquefolia*, Virginia creeper, partial to light shade
- *P. tricuspidata*, Boston ivy, partial to light shade

Philodendron spp., light to full shade

Pileostegia viburnoides, tanglehead, light to full shade

Polygonum aubertii, silver-lace vine, partial shade

Rhoicissus capensis, Cape grape, partial shade

Schizophragma hydrangeoides, Japanese hydrangea vine, partial to light shade

Stauntonia hexaphylla, Japanese staunton vine, partial to light shade

Stephanotis floribunda, Madagascar jasmine, ideal location is where roots are shaded and vine gets sun for half the day

Tecomaria capensis, Cape honeysuckle, partial shade

Thunbergia

- *T. alata*, black-eyed Susan vine, partial to light shade
- *T. grandiflora*, Bengal clock vine, partial to light shade

Trachelospermum jasminoides, Confederate jasmine, partial to light shade

Vitis spp., grape

Vines That Tolerate Dry Soil

Ampelopsis

- *A. arborea*, pepper vine
- *A. brevipedunculata*, porcelain ampelopsis

Bougainvillea spp. and hybrids

Campsis radicans, trumpet creeper

Celastrus scandens, American bittersweet

Cissus antarctica, kangaroo vine

Clematis

- *C. apiifolia*, October clematis
- *C. texensis*, scarlet clematis
- *C. virginiana*, virgin's bower

Ficus pumila, creeping fig

Lonicera sempervirens, trumpet honeysuckle

Parthenocissus

- *P. quinquefolia*, Virginia creeper
- *P. tricuspidata*, Boston ivy

Plumbago auriculata

Polygonum aubertii, silver-lace vine

Smilax glauca, catbrier

Four Vines That Tolerate Wet Soil

Campsis radicans, trumpet creeper

Clematis virginiana, virgin's bower

Menispermum canadense, moonseed

Trachelospermum jasminoides, Confederate jasmine

Vines for Groundcover

These vining plants will trail and ramble across the ground when not fastened to a support. They are good choices for planting on a bank, hillside, or other hard-to-reach location, to control erosion, eliminate the need to mow grass, or add color and interest.

Abrus precatorius, rosary pea

Akebia quinata, five-leaf akebia (can be invasive when allowed to trail)

Ampelopsis arborea, pepper vine

Celastrus scandens, American bittersweet

Cissus

- *C. antarctica*, kangaroo vine
- *C. rhombifolia*, grape ivy

Clematis

- *C. apiifolia*, October clematis
- *C. paniculata*, sweet autumn clematis
- *C. vitalba*, traveler's joy
- *C. viticella*, Italian clematis

Cucumis

- *C. dipsaceus*, hedgehog gourd
- *C. melo*, Dudaim Group, Queen Anne's pocket melon
- *C. melo*, Flexuosus Group, snake cucumber

Cucurbita pepo var. *ovifera*, gourds

Ecballium elaterium, squirting cucumber

Euonymus fortunei, wintercreeper

Hedera

- *H. canariensis*, Canary Island ivy
- *H. helix*, English ivy (can be rampant and invasive in the South)

Lagenaria siceraria, calabash gourd

Lonicera henryi

Luffa aegyptiaca, loofah

Lycium chinense, Chinese matrimony vine

Menispermum canadense, moonseed

Muehlenbeckia complexa, wire vine

Parthenocissus

- *P. henryana*, silvervein creeper
- *P. quinquefolia*, Virginia creeper

Plumbago auriculata

Rosa wichuraiana, memorial rose

Senecio macroglossus, wax vine

Tecomaria capensis, Cape honeysuckle

Trachelospermum jasminoides, Confederate jasmine

Tropaeolum majus, nasturtium

Vitis spp., grape

Vines to Grow in Containers

These vines can be grown in hanging baskets or other types of containers. Many of these are annuals, or treated as annuals where they are not hardy.

Asarina antirrhinifolia, twining snapdragon

Bougainvillea spp. and hybrids, can be grown in containers with regular severe pruning

Cissus spp.

Hardenbergia comptoniana

Hedera helix, English ivy

Hoya carnosa, wax vine

Ipomoea spp., morning glories, moonflower

Jasminum

- *J. officinale*, poet's jasmine
- *J. sambac*, Arabian jasmine

Lapageria rosea, Chilean bellflower

Mandevilla × *amabilis*, grow in a large pot or tub

Muehlenbeckia complexa, wire vine

Passiflora caerulea, blue passionflower

(continued)

Vines to Grow in Containers *(cont'd)*

Philodendron spp.

Senecio macroglossus, wax vine

Stephanotis floribunda, Madagascar jasmine

Thunbergia alata, black-eyed Susan vine

Wisteria spp., can be grown in container with regular severe pruning

Vines for Screening

Use these vines for screening and quick cover, to camouflage a shed or outbuilding, or to hide an undesirable view.

Actinidia

- *A. arguta*, bower actinidia
- *A. chinensis*, Chinese gooseberry
- *A. kolomikta*
- *A. polygama*, silver vine

Akebia quinata, five-leaf akebia (can be invasive)

Ampelopsis spp. (use for quick cover, but too light for screening; can be invasive)

Antigonon leptopus, coral vine

Aristolochia

- *A. durior*, Dutchman's pipe
- *A. elegans*, calico flower

Bignonia capreolata, cross vine

Campsis radicans, trumpet creeper

Celastrus scandens, American bittersweet

Cissus antarctica, kangaroo vine

Clematis

- *C. montana*, anemone clematis
- *C. paniculata*, sweet autumn clematis
- *C. texensis*, scarlet clematis
- *C. virginiana*, virgin's bower
- *C. vitalba*, traveler's joy
- *C. viticella*, Italian clematis

Cobaea scandens, cup-and-saucer vine

Distictis buccinatoria, Mexican blood trumpet vine

Ficus pumila, creeping fig

Hedera

- *H. canariensis*, Canary Island ivy
- *H. helix*, English ivy

Humulus lupulus 'Aureus', golden hops

Lonicera sempervirens, trumpet honeysuckle

Lycium chinense, Chinese matrimony vine

Macfadyena unguis-cati, catclaw vine

Menispermum canadense, moonseed

Momordica

- *M. balsamina*, balsam apple (where perennial)
- *M. charantia*, balsam pear (where perennial)

Muehlenbeckia complexa, wire vine

Parthenocissus

- *P. quinquefolia*, Virginia creeper
- *P. tricuspidata*, Boston ivy

Passiflora

- *P. caerulea*, blue passionflower
- *P. incarnata*, maypop

Polygonum aubertii, silver-lace vine

Smilax glauca, catbrier (excellent barrier)

Trachelospermum jasminoides, Confederate jasmine

Vitis spp., grape

Wisteria

- *W. japonica*, Japanese wisteria
- *W. sinensis*, Chinese wisteria

Vines to Grow on Trellises, Arbors, and Vertical Supports

These twining vines will wrap their stems around a vertical support.

Abrus precatorius, rosary pea
Actinidia
- *A. arguta*, bower actinidia
- *A. chinensis*, Chinese gooseberry
- *A. kolomikta*
- *A. polygama*, silver vine

Akebia quinata, five-leaf akebia
Anredera cordifolia, Madeira vine
Aristolochia
- *A. durior*, Dutchman's pipe
- *A. elegans*, calico flower

Asarina antirrhinifolia, twining snapdragon
Basella alba, Malabar spinach
Bougainvillea spp. and hybrids
Celastrus scandens, American bittersweet
Cissus hypoglauca
Clematis spp. and hybrids
Clerodendrum thomsoniae, bleeding-heart glorybower
Clianthus puniceus, glory pea (must attach to support)
Cocculus carolinus, Carolina moonseed
Cryptostegia grandiflora, rubber vine
Decumaria barbara
Dioscorea batatas, cinnamon vine
Dolichos lablab, hyacinth bean
Eccremocarpus scaber, glory flower
Gelsemium sempervirens, Carolina jessamine
Hardenbergia comptoniana
Hoya carnosa, wax vine
Humulus
- *H. japonicus*, Japanese hops
- *H. lupulus*, common hops
- *H. lupulus* 'Aureus', golden hops

Ipomoea
- *I. alba*, moonflower
- *I. coccinea*, scarlet starglory
- *I.* × *multifida*, cardinal climber
- *I. nil*, morning glory
- *I. purpurea*, common morning glory
- *I. quamoclit*, cypress vine
- *I. tricolor*, morning glory

Jasminum
- *J. grandiflorum*, Spanish jasmine
- *J. officinale*, poet's jasmine
- *J. sambac*, Arabian jasmine

Kadsura japonica, scarlet kadsura
Lapageria rosea, Chilean bellflower
Lonicera spp., honeysuckle
Mandevilla
- *M.* × *amabilis*
- *M. laxa*, Chilean jasmine

Menispermum canadense, moonseed
Mina lobata, flag of Spain
Muehlenbeckia complexa, wire vine (where perennial)
Periploca graeca, silk vine
Phaseolus coccineus, scarlet runner bean
Polygonum aubertii, silver-lace vine
Rosa, climbing roses
Schisandra
- *S. chinensis*, Chinese magnolia vine
- *S. propinqua*, Himalayan magnolia vine

Senecio confusus, Mexican flame vine
Solanum
- *S. jasminoides*, potato vine
- *S. wendlandii*, Costa Rican nightshade

Stauntonia hexaphylla, Japanese staunton vine
Stephanotis floribunda, Madagascar jasmine
Tecomaria capensis, Cape honeysuckle
Thunbergia
- *T. alata*, black-eyed Susan vine
- *T. grandiflora*, Bengal clock vine

(continued)

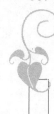

Vines to Grow on Trellises, Arbors, and Vertical Supports *(cont'd)*

Trachelospermum jasminoides, Confederate jasmine
Tripterygium regelii, Regel's three-wing nut
Tropaeolum
- *T. majus*, nasturtium
- *T. peregrinum*, canary creeper

Wisteria
- *W. floribunda*, Japanese wisteria
- *W. sinensis*, Chinese wisteria

Vines to Grow on Trees

These clinging vines are good choices for climbing a tree trunk.

Campsis radicans, trumpet creeper
Clematis spp. and hybrids
Euonymus fortunei, wintercreeper
Ficus pumila, creeping fig
Hydrangea anomala subsp. *petiolaris*, climbing hydrangea
Philodendron spp.
Schizophragma hydrangeoides, Japanese hydrangea vine

Clinging Vines to Grow on Buildings

These vines will cling to the wall of a building.

Campsis radicans, trumpet creeper
Distictis buccinatoria, Mexican blood trumpet vine
Euonymus fortunei, wintercreeper
Ficus pumila, creeping fig
Hedera
- *H. canariensis*, Canary Island ivy
- *H. helix*, English ivy

Hydrangea anomala subsp. *petiolaris*, climbing hydrangea
Macfadyena unguis-cati, catclaw vine
Parthenocissus
- *P. henryana*, silvervein creeper
- *P. quinquefolia*, Virginia creeper
- *P. tricuspidata*, Boston ivy

Philodendron spp.
Pileostegia viburnoides, tanglehead
Pyrostegia venusta, flame vine
Schizophragma hydrangeoides, Japanese hydrangea vine

Tendrilled Vines to Grow on Fences and Horizontal Supports

These vines like to coil their tendrils around horizontal strings or wires, netting, or gridlike supports.

Ampelopsis
- *A. arborea*, pepper vine
- *A. brevipedunculata*, porcelain ampelopsis

Anredera cordifolia, Madeira vine
Antigonon leptopus, coral vine
Bauhinia corymbosa, orchid tree
Benincasa hispida, wax gourd
Bignonia capreolata, cross vine
Cardiospermum halicacabum, balloon vine
Cissus
- *C. antarctica*, kangaroo vine
- *C. incisa*, marine ivy
- *C. rhombifolia*, grape ivy

Clematis spp. and hybrids

Clytostoma callistegioides, Argentine trumpet vine

Cobaea scandens, cup-and-saucer vine

Distictis lactiflora, vanilla-scented trumpet vine

Eccremocarpus scaber, glory flower

Echinocystis lobata, wild cucumber

Lagenaria siceraria, calabash gourd (support heavy fruit with cloth slings)

Lathyrus

- *L. grandiflorus*, everlasting pea
- *L. latifolius*, perennial pea
- *L. odoratus*, sweet pea

Luffa aegyptiaca, loofah (support heavy fruit with cloth slings)

Macfadyena unguis-cati, catclaw vine

Momordica

- *M. balsamina*, balsam apple
- *M. charantia*, balsam pear

Parthenocissus

- *P. henryana*, silvervein creeper
- *P. quinquefolia*, Virginia creeper

Passiflora

- *P. caerulea*, blue passionflower
- *P. incarnata*, maypop

Polygonum aubertii, silver-lace vine

Rhoicissus capensis, Cape grape

Rosa, climbing and rambler roses (flexible canes can be fastened to fences)

Vines to Spill Over a Wall

These vines will cascade over a wall when planted along the top of it.

Ampelopsis

- *A. arborea*, pepper vine
- *A. brevipedunculata*, porcelain ampelopsis

Cissus rhombifolia, grape ivy (where perennial)

Clematis

- *C. armandii*, October clematis
- *C. montana*, anemone clematis
- *C. paniculata*, sweet autumn clematis

Rosa

- *R. laevigata*, Cherokee rose
- *R. wichuraiana*, memorial rose

Tecomaria capensis, Cape honeysuckle

Vines to Shade a Porch

These vines are especially nice when trained around a porch. Most have fairly large leaves or thick growth that provides shade. See also the list of "Vines for Screening" for other possibilities.

Antigonon leptopus, coral vine

Aristolochia durior, Dutchman's pipe

Bougainvillea spp. and hybrids

Campsis radicans, trumpet creeper

Cobaea scandens, cup-and-saucer vine

Gelsemium sempervirens, Carolina jessamine

Humulus lupulus, common hops

Momordica balsamina, balsam apple

Pyrostegia venusta, flame vine

Thunbergia

- *T. alata*, black-eyed Susan vine (where perennial)
- *T. grandiflora*, Bengal clock vine (where perennial)

Vines to Keep Out of the Garden

These vines are invasive and can be difficult to eradicate once established. Some of them have become terrible pests in parts of the United States, and some are problematic only under certain conditions.

Akebia quinata, five-leaf akebia: Rampant and invasive under good conditions, strangles other plants. Best when grown in shady conditions and rather poor soil.

Ampelopsis brevipedunculata, porcelainberry: Has escaped from cultivation in parts of the Northeast and is crowding out other plants in woodlands. Grow it with caution.

Celastrus orbiculatus, oriental bittersweet: Rampant and invasive under practically any conditions. Girdles small trees and kills them. Instead plant *C. scandens*, the native species.

Convolvulus arvensis, *C. sepium*, bindweed: Grows anywhere. Invasive; the vines climb on any available support and strangle other plants.

Lonicera japonica, Japanese honeysuckle, Hall's honeysuckle (*L.* 'Halliana'): Still often sold in nurseries, but spreads all over the place and chokes out other plants. Nearly impossible to contain when established.

Macfadyena unguis-cati, catclaw vine: A real pest in the Deep South, it spreads rapidly, damages walls on which it climbs, and is generally hard to get rid of. Less problematic in dry climates.

Pueraria lobata, kudzu: Introduced from the Orient to control erosion and cover ground, it has taken over the Southeast. Grows rapidly and covers anything—plants, trees, even houses. Not as troublesome in the North, where cold winters help to control it.

Rhus radicans, poison ivy: Pretty fall color, but causes serious rashes and blisters in susceptible people, and difficult to eradicate when established. Regular repeated mowing or herbicides will get rid of it eventually.

Rosa multiflora, wild rose: Grows like a weed, and difficult to eradicate—pieces of rootstock will produce new plants. Seeds are spread by birds. Will take over unless valiant efforts are made to control it.

Wisteria spp.: The flowers are lovely, and the plants are difficult to establish, but once it takes hold it seeds itself with abandon and can become problematic.

PRUNING FLOWERING VINES

WHAT TO PRUNE

- Cut back shoots that have bloomed, cutting back to a vigorous shoot lower on the plant.

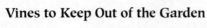

- Remove dead and damaged growth.
- Remove weak shoots to thin out dense growth.

WHEN TO PRUNE

Prune vines that bloom on new wood in late winter or early spring:

Anredera cordifolia, Madeira vine

Antigonon leptopus, coral vine

Bignonia capreolata, cross vine

Campsis radicans, trumpet creeper

Clerodendrum thomsoniae, bleeding-heart glorybower

Clianthus puniceus, glory pea

Clytostoma callistegioides, Argentine trumpet vine

Distictis spp.

Ipomoea (species grown as perennials in warm climates)

Lapageria rosea, Chilean bellflower

Lonicera spp. honeysuckle

Mandevilla spp.

Parthenocissus spp.

Passiflora spp.

Pileostegia viburnoides, tanglehead

Plumbago auriculata, Cape plumbago

Polygonum aubertii, silver-lace vine

Pyrostegia venusta, flame vine

Solanum jasminoides, potato vine

Stephanotis floribunda, Madagascar jasmine

Vitis spp., grape

Prune vines that flower on last year's wood right after they bloom:

Actinidia spp.

Allamanda cathartica, golden trumpet vine

Aristolochia spp.

Beaumontia grandiflora, herald's trumpet

Bougainvillea spp. and hybrids

Decumaria barbara

Gelsemium sempervirens, Carolina jessamine

Hoya carnosa, wax vine

Hydrangea anomala subsp. *petiolaris*, climbing hydrangea

Jasminum spp., jasmine

Pandorea spp.

Schizophragma hydrangeoides, Japanese hydrangea vine

HOW TO PRUNE CLEMATIS

Large-Flowered Hybrids

Florida Group: Bloom in summer on old wood. Prune lightly and not too often. Prune after blooming.

Patens Group: Bloom in spring on old wood. Prune same as Florida Group, when plants finish blooming.

Jackmanii Group: Bloom in summer and autumn on new wood. Prune back to the ground when dormant. These hybrids are more cold-hardy than other large-flowered hybrids.

Species

Prune according to when they bloom: Prune late bloomers that flower on new wood in spring, and prune those that bloom on old wood (usually early bloomers) when they finish flowering.

If you don't know which type of clematis you have, examine the plants to find the remains of last season's blooms; see if they are on the youngest, thinnest stems or the oldest, thickest ones.

HOW TO PRUNE WISTERIA

Wisteria needs regular pruning to control its rampant growth and to encourage flowering. In the North, two prunings should suffice. In the South, more frequent pruning—up to five or six times—is necessary to keep this vine under control.

In summer, prune all the long, straggly stems except the ones the plant needs to climb. Also shorten the lateral stems. Cut back by one-third to one-half when pruning.

In late winter, cut back the shoots pruned last summer to two or three buds. Cut back to about 6 inches any long shoots that developed after last summer's pruning.

Chapter 7
HERBS

WHAT IS AN HERB?

To botanists, an herb is a nonwoody plant. To herbalists and herb gardeners, however, an herb is a plant with a current or historical practical use. Herbs are used in cooking, for healing, to make dyes, and for their fragrances. The herb garden may contain annuals, herbaceous perennials, bulbs, shrubs, and trees. This chapter is devoted to useful plants that are widely grown in herb gardens.

PERENNIAL HERBS

Aloe (*Aloe vera*), Zones 10 to 11; elsewhere grow as houseplant

Angelica (*Angelica archangelica*), Zones 4 to 9. Not a true perennial; dies after blooming, usually in second or third year, then self-sows

Anise hyssop (*Agastache foeniculum*), Zones 5 to 9

Bay (*Laurus nobilis*), Zones 8 to 11; elsewhere grow in pots and bring indoors for winter

Bee balm, bergamot (*Monarda didyma*), Zones 4 to 9

Betony (*Stachys officinalis*), Zones 4 to 10

Caraway (*Carum carvi*), Zones 3 to 7. Biennial or sometimes annual that self-sows

Catmint (*Nepeta × faassenii*), Zones 4 to 9

(continued)

Perennial Herbs *(cont'd)*

Catnip (*Nepeta cataria*), Zones 4 to 9

Chamomile, Roman (*Chamaemelum nobile*), Zones 3 to 8

Chicory (*Cichorium intybus*), Zones 3 to 10

Chives (*Allium schoenoprasum*), Zones 3 to 9

Clary (*Salvia sclarea*), Zones 4 to 7. Biennial or short-lived perennial that self-sows

Coltsfoot (*Tussilago farfara*), Zones 4 to 6

Comfrey (*Symphytum officinale*), Zones 3 to 9

Costmary, Bible leaf (*Tanacetum balsamita*), Zones 4 to 8

Dock (*Rumex* spp.), Zones 5 to 9

Elecampane (*Inula helenium*), Zones 3 to 9

Fennel (*Foeniculum vulgare*), Zones 4 to 10; can also be grown as annual

Feverfew (*Tanacetum parthenium*), Zones 5 to 7

Foxglove (*Digitalis purpurea*), Zones 3 to 11. Biennial that self-sows. Poisonous

Garlic (*Allium sativum*), Zones 5 to 10

Garlic chives (*Allium tuberosum*), Zones 5 to 9

Germander (*Teucrium chamaedrys*), Zones 5 to 10

Ginger (*Zingiber officinale*), Zones 9 to 11; elsewhere grow in pots and bring indoors over winter

Goldenrod (*Solidago* spp.), Zones 4 to 9

Goldenseal (*Hydrastis canadensis*), Zones 4 to 8

Horehound (*Marrubium vulgare*), Zones 4 to 8

Horsetail (*Equisetum* spp.), Zones 4 to 9

Hyssop (*Hyssopus officinalis*), Zones 3 to 11

Indigo (*Indigofera suffruticosa* and *I. tinctoria*), Zones 9 to 11; for warm climates only

Lady's bedstraw (*Galium verum*), Zones 3 to 7

Lavender (*Lavandula* spp.)

- English lavender (*L. angustifolia*), Zones 5 to 8
- French lavender (*L. dentata*), Zones 8 to 9

Lavender cotton (*Santolina chamaecyparissus*), Zones 6 to 8

Lemon balm (*Melissa officinalis*), Zones 4 to 9

Lemongrass (*Cymbopogon citratus*), Zones 9 to 11; elsewhere grow in pots and bring indoors over winter

Lemon verbena (*Aloysia triphylla*), Zones 9 to 11; elsewhere grow in pots and bring indoors over winter

Licorice (*Glycyrrhiza glabra*), Zones 7 to 9

Lovage (*Levisticum officinale*), Zones 4 to 8

Marsh mallow (*Althaea officinalis*), Zones 3 to 9

Meadowsweet, queen-of-the-meadow (*Filipendula ulmaria*), Zones 3 to 9

Mint (*Mentha* spp.), Zones 5 to 11

Apple mint (*M. suaveolens*)

Corsican mint, creeping mint (*M. requienii*)

Orange mint (*M.* × *piperita* var. *citrata*)

Peppermint (*M.* × *piperita*)

Pineapple mint (*M. suaveolens* 'Variegata')

Spearmint (*M. spicata*)

Mugwort (*Artemisia vulgaris*), Zones 4 to 9

Mustard (*Brassica* spp.), Zones 2 to 9

Black mustard (*B. nigra*)

White mustard (*B. hirta*)

Oregano (*Origanum* spp.), Zones 3 to 11

Orris (*Iris* × *germanica* var. *florentina*), Zones 3 to 11

Pennyroyal, European pennyroyal (*Mentha pulegium*), Zones 5 to 9

Rosemary (*Rosmarinus officinalis*), Zones 8 to 11; elsewhere grow in pots and bring indoors over winter

Rue (*Ruta graveolens*), Zones 4 to 11

Saffron (*Crocus sativus*), Zones 6 to 9

Sage (*Salvia officinalis*), Zones 4 to 8

Salad burnet (*Poterium sanguisorba*), to Zone 3

Savory, winter (*Satureja montana*), Zones 6 to 9

Soapwort (*Saponaria officinalis*), Zones 3 to 11

Southernwood (*Artemisia abrotanum*), Zones 6 to 11

Sweet cicely (*Myrrhis odorata*), Zones 3 to 7

Sweet flag (*Acorus calamus*), Zones 3 to 11

Sweet woodruff (*Galium odoratum*), Zones 3 to 9

Tansy (*Tanacetum vulgare*), Zones 3 to 9

Tarragon (*Artemisia dracunculus*), Zones 4 to 8

(continued)

Perennial Herbs *(cont'd)*

Thyme (*Thymus* spp.), Zones 5 to 11

Common thyme, garden thyme (*T. vulgaris*)

Lemon thyme (*T.* × *citriodorus*)

Mother of thyme, creeping thyme (*T. serpyllum*)

Valerian (*Valeriana officinalis*), Zones 5 to 11

Vervain (*Verbena officinalis*), Zones 5 to 9

Violet, sweet violet (*Viola odorata*), Zones 5 to 9

Wintergreen (*Gaultheria procumbens*), to Zone 4

Yarrow (*Achillea millefolium*), Zones 3 to 11

ANNUAL HERBS

This list includes tender perennials often grown as annuals where they are not hardy.

Anise (*Pimpinella anisum*)

Basil (*Ocimum basilicum*)

Borage (*Borago officinalis*)

Calendula, pot marigold (*Calendula officinalis*)

Castor bean (*Ricinus communis*). Seeds are source of castor oil, but are poisonous if eaten

Cayenne pepper (*Capsicum annuum*, Longum Group). Tender perennial grown as annual

Chamomile, German (*Matricaria recutita*)

Chervil (*Anthriscus cerefolium*)

Coriander, cilantro (*Coriandrum sativum*)

Cumin (*Cuminum cyminum*)

Dill (*Anethum graveolens*)

Horseradish (*Armoracia rusticana*). Perennial (Zones 5 to 8), but usually grown as annual or biennial for roots of best quality

Marjoram, sweet marjoram (*Origanum majorana*). Perennial in Zones 9 to 11, but usually grown as annual

Mexican marigold mint (*Tagetes lucida*)

Parsley (*Petroselinum crispum*). Biennial grown as annual

Pineapple sage (*Salvia elegans*). Perennial in Zones 9 to 11, but usually grown as annual

Safflower (*Carthamus tinctorius*)

Savory, summer (*Satureja hortensis*)

Scented geraniums (*Pelargonium* spp.). Perennial in Zones 10 and 11; elsewhere grow as annuals (start with cuttings or plants) or in pots moved indoors in winter

- Apple geranium (*P. odoratissimum*)
- Coconut geranium (*P. grossularioides*)
- Lemon geranium (*P. crispum*)
- Nutmeg geranium (*P. × fragrans*)
- Orange geranium (*P. × citrosum*)
- Peppermint geranium (*P. tomentosum*)
- Rose geranium (*P. graveolens*)
- Rose-scented geranium (*P. capitatum*)

HERBS FOR DIFFERENT SITUATIONS

DRY SOIL

Betony (*Stachys officinalis*)

Catmint (*Nepeta × faassenii*)

Chamomile

- German chamomile (*Matricaria recutita*)
- Roman chamomile (*Chamaemelum nobile*)

Clary (*Salvia sclarea*)

Costmary (*Tanacetum balsamita*)

Fennel (*Foeniculum vulgare*)

Feverfew (*Tanacetum parthenium*)

Foxglove (*Digitalis purpurea*)

Horehound (*Marrubium vulgare*)

Hyssop (*Hyssopus officinalis*)

Lady's bedstraw (*Galium verum*)

Lavender (*Lavandula* spp.)

Lavender cotton (*Santolina chamaecyparissus*)

Marjoram, sweet marjoram (*Origanum majorana*)

Mexican mint marigold (*Tagetes lucida*)

Mugwort (*Artemisia vulgare*)

Mullein (*Verbascum thapsus*)

Oregano (*Origanum* spp.)

Rosemary (*Rosmarinus officinalis*)

Rue (*Ruta graveolens*)

Salad burnet (*Poterium sanguisorba*)

Savory, winter (*Satureja montana*)

Southernwood (*Artemisia abrotanum*)

St.-John's-wort (*Hypericum perforatum*)

Tansy (*Tanacetum vulgare*)

Thyme (*Thymus* spp.)

Vervain (*Verbena officinalis*)

Wormwood (*Artemisia absinthium*)

MOIST SOIL

These herbs grow well in soil that is moist but not soggy.

Aconite, monkshood (*Aconitum napellus*), poisonous

Bee balm, bergamot (*Monarda didyma*)

Castor bean (*Ricinus communis*)

Chervil (*Anthriscus cerefolium*)

Clary (*Salvia sclarea*)

Coltsfoot (*Tussilago farfara*)

Foxglove (*Digitalis purpurea*)

Horseradish (*Armoracia rusticana*)

Lemon balm (*Melissa officinalis*)

Lemon verbena (*Aloysia triphylla*)

Lovage (*Levisticum officinale*)

(continued)

Herbs for Different Situations *(cont'd)*

Meadowsweet, queen-of-the-meadow (*Filipendula ulmaria*)
Mustard, black (*Brassica nigra*)
Sweet cicely (*Myrrhis odorata*)
Violet, sweet violet (*Viola odorata*)
Wintergreen (*Gaultheria procumbens*)

These herbs will grow in damp locations, where the soil can become quite wet.

Angelica (*Angelica archangelica*)
Comfrey (*Symphytum officinale*)
Elecampane (*Inula helenium*)
Goldenseal (*Hydrastis canadensis*)
Horsetail (*Equisetum* spp.)
Licorice (*Glycyrrhiza glabra*)
Marsh mallow (*Althaea officinalis*)
Pennyroyal, European (*Mentha pulegium*)
Soapwort, bouncing bet (*Saponaria officinalis*)
Sweet flag (*Acorus calamus*)
Valerian (*Valeriana officinalis*)
Water mint (*Mentha aquatica*)

POOR SOIL

These herbs will grow in soil of low fertility.

Anise (*Pimpinella anisum*)
Chamomile, Roman (*Chamaemelum nobile*)
Chicory (*Cichorium intybus*)
Dill (*Anethum graveolens*)
Dock, curled (*Rumex crispus*)
Goldenrod (*Solidago* spp.)
Lavender cotton (*Santolina chamaecyparissus*)
Mugwort (*Artemisia vulgare*)
Mullein (*Verbascum thapsus*)
Rue (*Ruta graveolens*)
Safflower (*Carthamus tinctorius*)
Soapwort, bouncing bet (*Saponaria officinalis*)
St.-John's-wort (*Hypericum perforatum*)
Thyme (*Thymus* spp.)

RICH SOIL

The herbs listed here grow best in soil that is fertile and rich in organic matter.

Aconite, monkshood (*Aconitum napellus*), poisonous
Angelica (*Angelica archangelica*)
Basil (*Ocimum basilicum*)
Bee balm (*Monarda didyma*)
Castor bean (*Ricinus communis*)
Cayenne pepper (*Capsicum annuum*, Longum Group)
Comfrey (*Symphytum officinale*)
Costmary, bible leaf (*Tanacetum balsamita*)
Foxglove (*Digitalis purpurea*)
Ginger (*Zingiber officinale*)
Goldenseal (*Hydrastis canadensis*)
Horseradish (*Armoracia rusticana*)
Lemon verbena (*Aloysia triphylla*)
Licorice (*Glycyrrhiza glabra*)
Lovage (*Levisticum officinale*)
Marjoram, sweet marjoram (*Origanum majorana*)
Mustard, black (*Brassica nigra*)
Orris (*Iris × germanica* var. *florentina*)
Pennyroyal, European (*Mentha pulegium*)
Scented geranium (*Pelargonium* spp.)
Sweet flag (*Acorus calamus*)
Tarragon (*Artemisia dracunculus*)
Valerian (*Valeriana officinalis*)
Violet, sweet violet (*Viola odorata*)

SHADE

The herbs listed here tolerate or prefer varying degrees of shade. See pages 49–50 for definitions of partial, light, and full shade.

Aconite, monkshood (*Aconitum napellus*). Partial shade
Angelica (*Angelica archangelica*). Prefers partial to light shade

Basil (*Ocimum basilicum*). Best in full sun but tolerates partial shade
Bee balm, bergamot (*Monarda didyma*). Partial shade
Betony (*Stachys officinalis*). Partial shade
Caraway (*Carum carvi*). Partial to light shade
Cardamom (*Elettaria cardamomum*). Partial to full shade
Castor bean (*Ricinus communis*). Partial shade
Catmint (*Nepeta* × *faassenii*). Partial shade
Catnip (*Nepeta cataria*). Partial shade
Chamomile. Partial shade
  German chamomile (*Matricaria recutita*)
  Roman chamomile (*Chamaemelum nobile*)
Chervil (*Anthriscus cerefolium*). Prefers partial shade
Chives (*Allium schoenoprasum*). Partial shade
Comfrey (*Symphytum officinale*). Partial shade
Coriander (*Coriandrum sativum*). Partial to light shade
Costmary, bible leaf (*Tanacetum balsamita*). Partial shade
Elecampane (*Inula helenium*). Partial to light shade
Foxglove (*Digitalis purpurea*). Partial shade. Poisonous
Garlic chives (*Allium tuberosum*). Partial shade
Germander (*Teucrium chamaedrys*). Partial shade
Ginger (*Zingiber officinale*). Partial shade
Ginseng (*Panax* spp.). Partial shade
Lady's bedstraw (*Galium verum*). Partial to light shade
Lemon balm (*Melissa officinalis*). Partial shade
Licorice (*Glycyrrhiza glabra*). Partial shade
Lovage (*Levisticum officinale*). Partial shade
Mint (*Mentha* spp.). Partial shade
Parsley (*Petroselinum crispum*). Partial shade
Pennyroyal, European (*Mentha pulegium*). Partial to full shade
Rosemary (*Rosmarinus officinalis*). Develops strongest flavor in full sun, but also grows well in partial shade
Saffron (*Crocus sativus*). Partial to light shade
Salad burnet (*Poterium sanguisorba*). Partial shade
Soapwort, bouncing bet (*Saponaria officinalis*). Partial shade
Sweet cicely (*Myrrhis odorata*). Partial shade
Sweet flag (*Acorus calamus*). Partial shade
Sweet woodruff (*Galium odoratum*). Partial to full shade, prefers shade
Tansy (*Tanacetum vulgare*). Partial shade
Tarragon (*Artemisia dracunculus*). Partial shade
Valerian (*Valeriana officinalis*). Partial to full shade
Violet, sweet violet (*Viola odorata*). Partial to full shade, prefers shade
Wintergreen (*Gaultheria procumbens*). Partial shade

HERBS TO GROW IN CONTAINERS

Aloe (*Aloe barbadensis*)
Basil (*Ocimum basilicum*)
Bay (*Laurus nobilis*)
Calendula, pot marigold (*Calendula officinalis*)
Catnip (*Nepeta cataria*)
Cayenne pepper (*Capsicum annuum*, Longum Group)
Chervil (*Anthriscus cerefolium*)
Chives (*Allium schoenoprasum*)
Coriander, cilantro (*Coriandrum sativum*)
Dill (*Anethum graveolens*)
Garlic chives (*Allium tuberosum*)
Ginger (*Zingiber officinale*)
Lemon balm (*Melissa officinalis*)
Lemongrass (*Cymbopogon citratus*)
Lemon verbena (*Aloysia triphylla*)
Marjoram, sweet marjoram (*Origanum majorana*)
Mint (*Mentha* spp.)
Oregano (*Origanum* spp.)
Rosemary (*Rosmarinus officinalis*)
Sage (*Salvia officinalis*)
Savory, summer (*Satureja hortensis*)
Scented geranium (*Pelargonium* spp.)
Tarragon (*Artemisia dracunculus*)
Thyme (*Thymus* spp.)

HERBS FOR COOKING

Angelica (*Angelica archangelica*): Candied stems—cakes, desserts; chopped leaves—salads, fruit

Anise (*Pimpinella anisum*): Fish, chicken, pork, carrots, spinach, fruit, breads, cookies, liqueur

Basil (*Ocimum basilicum*): Fish, poultry, beef, lamb, veal, pasta, eggs, rice, salad dressings, pesto sauce, tomatoes, green beans, broccoli, cabbage, carrots, cauliflower, eggplant, potatoes, spinach, squash

Bay (*Laurus nobilis*): Fish, chicken, beef, lamb, veal, tomatoes, paté, soups and stews

Borage (*Borago officinalis*): Fish, chicken, salads, soups, iced tea and other cold drinks

Calendula, pot marigold (*Calendula officinalis*): Flower petals add saffronlike color to soups and rice dishes.

Caraway (*Carum carvi*): Fish, beef, pork, cheese, eggs, cabbage and sauerkraut, green beans, cauliflower, peas, potatoes, spinach, squash, breads (especially rye)

Chervil (*Anthriscus cerefolium*): Fish, chicken, veal, eggs, carrots, corn, peas, spinach, tomatoes, salads

Chives (*Allium schoenoprasum*) and garlic chives (*A. tuberosum*): Fish, poultry, veal, asparagus, carrots, cauliflower, corn, peas, potatoes, spinach, tomatoes, eggs, soups, salads

Coriander, cilantro (*Coriandrum sativum*): Fish, poultry, pork, lamb, game, mushrooms, potatoes, tomatoes, eggs, sauces, salsas, curries, pickles, soups, paté

Cumin (*Cuminum cyminum*): Chicken, beef, lamb, dry beans, cabbage, carrots, cauliflower, curries, salsas

Ginger (*Zingiber officinalis*): Fish, chicken, beef, lamb, pork, veal, carrots, squash, fruit

Horseradish (*Armoracia rusticana*): The roots, grated and mixed with vinegar, are condiment for smoked fish, roast beef, sausages, red beets, carrots

Hyssop (*Hyssopus officinalis*): Game birds (duck, goose, pheasant), paté

Lemon balm (*Melissa officinalis*): Chicken, lamb, asparagus, broccoli, corn, fruit, soups, sauces

Lemongrass (*Cymbopogon citratus*): Soups

Lemon thyme (*Thymus × citriodorus*): Fish, asparagus

Lemon verbena (*Aloysia triphylla*): Fish, chicken, fruit, teas and punches

Lovage (*Levisticum officinale*): Poultry, meats, potatoes, tomatoes, soups, stews, paté, stuffings

Marjoram, sweet marjoram (*Origanum majorana*): Fish, poultry, beef, lamb, veal, game, sausages, pasta, eggs, green beans, broccoli, cabbage, carrots, cauliflower, eggplant, mushrooms, potatoes, squash, tomatoes, stuffings

Mint (*Mentha* spp.): Lamb, veal, dry beans, green beans, carrots, eggplant, peas, fruit, desserts, sauces

Apple mint (*M. suaveolens*): Fruit sorbets, ices, sherbets

Peppermint (*M. × piperita*): Fruit salads, sorbets, iced tea

Spearmint (*M. spicata*): Sauces, salads, vegetables

Oregano (*Origanum* spp.): Fish, chicken, beef, pork, eggs, pasta, dry beans, broccoli, eggplant, mushrooms, potatoes, squash, tomatoes

Parsley (*Petroselinum crispum*): Practically everything. Fish, poultry, beef, lamb, veal, dry beans, carrots, cauliflower, eggplant, potatoes, tomatoes, soups and stews, sauces, salads (especially tabbouli), stuffings

Pineapple sage (*Salvia elegans*): Fruits, cold beverages

Rosemary (*Rosmarinus officinalis*): Fish, poultry, pork, lamb, beef, veal, eggs, cauliflower, mushrooms, peas, squash, fruit, soups and stews, breads, stuffings

Saffron (*Crocus sativus*): Fish, chicken, lamb, pork, eggs, rice, corn

Sage (*Salvia officinalis*): Fish, poultry, game, beef, pork, veal, eggs, asparagus, dry beans, green beans, cabbage, carrots, corn, eggplant, potatoes, squash, tomatoes, stuffings, paté

Savory, summer (*Satureja hortensis*) and winter (*S. montana*): Fish, poultry, beef, veal, sausage, game, eggs, asparagus, dry beans, green beans, cabbage, carrots, cauliflower, eggplant, peas, squash, tomatoes

Sweet cicely (*Myrrhis odorata*): Cabbage, fruit

Tarragon (*Artemisia dracunculus*): Fish, chicken, beef, lamb, eggs, asparagus, broccoli, carrots, cauliflower, mushrooms, peas, potatoes, tomatoes, rice, sauces (especially béarnaise), salad dressings

Thyme (*Thymus* spp.): Fish, poultry, beef, veal, lamb, game, eggs, asparagus, dry beans, green beans, broccoli, carrots, corn, eggplant, mushrooms, peas, potatoes, spinach, tomatoes, rice, stuffings

Which Oregano Is Best?

Oregano is one of the most-used culinary herbs, and one of the most confusing for gardeners. Many kinds of plants are sold as oregano, and they differ in flavor and pungency.

Probably the least desirable is wild oregano or wild marjoram (*Origanum vulgare*), which grows into a coarse, floppy plant with dull green, poorly flavored leaves and purple flowers on 2-foot stems. Varieties and cultivars of the species are a better bet. One often sold as Italian oregano has a shrubbier habit, white flowers, and a stronger flavor. Golden oregano (*O. vulgare* 'Aureum') is a more compact plant with yellow leaves.

The oregano most widely considered to have the best taste is Greek oregano (usually listed as *O. heracleoticum* or *O. vulgare* subsp. *hirtum*). It grows to 1½ feet high, with grayish green leaves and a strong scent and flavor.

Mexican oregano (*Lippia graveolens*), which has a similar flavor, actually belongs to the verbena family, and is more closely related to lemon verbena than to true oreganos.

The best way to choose oregano plants at an herb farm or garden center is to stroke a leaf between your fingers to release the scent (without bruising or crushing the leaf). Buy the type that smells best to you.

Culinary Herb Mixtures

FINES HERBES

Chervil, chives, parsley, and tarragon

HERBS DE PROVENCE

A blend of basil, fennel, lavender, rosemary, savory, tarragon, and thyme

BOUQUETS GARNIS

Try the following combinations for bouquets garnis:

Bay, marjoram, parsley, and thyme
Bay, parsley, and tarragon
Bay, parsley, and fennel
Bay, chives, parsley, and chervil
Bay, sage, and thyme
Bay, parsley, thyme, and/or rosemary

GENERAL SEASONING

Try these combinations for general-purpose seasoning, or as a salt substitute:

Basil, oregano, and parsley

Chives, marjoram, parsley, and thyme

Basil, marjoram, sage, savory, and thyme

Herbs to Season Ethnic Cuisines

Cajun: Bay, cayenne, basil, black pepper, garlic, and thyme

Chinese: Star anise, coriander, fennel, garlic, ginger, and pepper

French: Bay, chervil, fennel, garlic, parsley, sorrel, tarragon, and thyme

German: Anise, bay, caraway, dill, fennel, horseradish, lovage, parsley, summer savory, and thyme

Indian: Cayenne, cardamom, coriander, cumin, fennel, garlic, ginger, lemongrass, mint, saffron, and turmeric

Italian: Basil, chives, fennel, garlic, Italian parsley, oregano, rosemary, and thyme

Mexican: Coriander (cilantro), cumin, garlic, and oregano

Thai: Anise, basil, coriander, lemongrass, and mint

HERBS FOR TEA

Angelica (*Angelica archangelica*)

Anise (*Pimpinella anisum*)

Anise hyssop (*Agastache foeniculum*)

Basil (*Ocimum basilicum*), especially cinnamon basil

Bee balm, bergamot (*Monarda didyma*)

Borage (*Borago officinalis*)

Catnip (*Nepeta cataria*)

Chamomile

- German chamomile (*Matricaria recutita*)
- Roman chamomile (*Chamaemelum nobile*)

Echinacea (*Echinacea purpurea*)

Fennel seed (*Foeniculum vulgare*)

Goldenseal (*Hydrastis canadensis*)

Horehound (*Marrubium vulgare*)

Hyssop (*Hyssopus officinalis*)

Lemon balm (*Melissa officinalis*)

Lemongrass (*Cymbopogon citratus*)

Lemon verbena (*Aloysia triphylla*)

Marjoram, sweet marjoram (*Origanum majorana*)

Mexican mint marigold (*Tagetes lucida*)

Mint (*Mentha* spp.)

Oregano (*Origanum* spp.)

Parsley (*Petroselinum crispum*)

Pineapple sage (*Salvia elegans*)

Rosemary (*Rosmarinus officinalis*)

Sage (*Salvia officinalis*)

Salad burnet (*Poterium sanguisorba*)

Thyme (*Thymus* spp.)

Valerian (*Valeriana officinalis*)

Wintergreen (*Gaultheria procumbens*)

HERBS WITH EDIBLE FLOWERS

Anise hyssop (*Agastache foeniculum*)

Basil (*Ocimum basilicum*)

Bee balm (*Monarda didyma*)

Borage (*Borago officinalis*)

Calendula (*Calendula officinalis*)

Chamomile, German (*Matricaria recutita*)

Chives (*Allium schoenoprasum*)

Coriander (*Coriandrum sativum*)

Fennel (*Foeniculum vulgare*)

Garlic chives (*Allium tuberosum*)

Lavender (*Lavandula angustifolia*)

Mexican mint marigold (*Tagetes lucida*)

Mint (*Mentha* spp.)

Oregano (*Origanum* spp.)

Pineapple sage (*Salvia elegans*)

Sage (*Salvia officinalis*)

Thyme (*Thymus* spp.)

Violet (*Viola odorata*)

HERBS WITH ORNAMENTAL FLOWERS

Aconite, monkshood (*Aconitum napellus*), blue-violet

Anise hyssop (*Agastache foeniculum*), purple

Bee balm, bergamot (*Monarda didyma*), red, purple, pink, white

Betony (*Stachys officinalis*), red-violet

Borage (*Borago officinalis*), blue

Calendula, pot marigold (*Calendula officinalis*), yellow, orange

Catmint (*Nepeta × faassenii*), purple

Chamomile (*Chamaemelum nobile*, *Matricaria recutita*), white with gold center

Chives (*Allium schoenoprasum*), purplish pink

Clary (*Salvia sclarea*), lavender, pink, white

Coltsfoot (*Tussilago farfara*), yellow

Costmary (*Tanacetum balsamita*), white with large yellow center

Elecampane (*Inula helenium*), yellow

Feverfew (*Tanacetum parthenium*), white with yellow center

Foxglove (*Digitalis purpurea*), lavender, pink, white

Garlic chives (*Allium tuberosum*), white

Goldenrod (*Solidago* spp.), golden yellow

Hyssop (*Hyssopus officinalis*), violet

Lavender (*Lavandula* spp.), purple

Lavender cotton (*Santolina chamaecyparissus*), yellow

Marsh mallow (*Althaea officinalis*), pink, white

Meadowsweet, queen-of-the-meadow (*Filipendula ulmaria*), white

Mexican mint marigold (*Tagetes lucida*), yellow

Orris (*Iris × germanica* var. *florentina*), white to pale lilac-purple

Pineapple sage (*Salvia elegans*), scarlet

Rosemary (*Rosmarinus officinalis*), blue

Safflower (*Carthamus tinctorius*), yellow

Saffron (*Crocus sativus*), white, lavender, purple

Sage (*Salvia officinalis*), violet, blue, white

Scented geranium (*Pelargonium* spp.), pink, lavender, white

Soapwort, bouncing bet (*Saponaria officinalis*), pink

Sweet woodruff (*Galium odoratum*), white

Tansy (*Tanacetum vulgare*), yellow

Thyme (*Thymus* spp.), lavender, pink, or white

Violet, sweet violet (*Viola odorata*), purple, pink, white

Yarrow (*Achillea millefolium*), white

FRAGRANT HERBS

The herbs listed here are fragrant or aromatic.

- Angelica (*Angelica archangelica*)
- Anise (*Pimpinella anisum*)
- Anise hyssop (*Agastache foeniculum*)
- Basil (*Ocimum basilicum*)
- Bay (*Laurus nobilis*)
- Bee balm, bergamot (*Monarda didyma*)
- Chamomile
  - German chamomile (*Matricaria recutita*)
  - Roman chamomile (*Chamaemelum nobile*)
- Clary (*Salvia sclarea*)
- Coriander (*Coriandrum sativum*)
- Costmary (*Tanacetum balsamita*)
- Fennel (*Foeniculum vulgare*)
- Hyssop (*Hyssopus officinalis*)
- Lavender (*Lavandula* spp.)
- Lavender cotton (*Santolina chamaecyparissus*)
- Lemon balm (*Melissa officinalis*)
- Lemon thyme (*Thymus × citriodorus*)
- Marjoram, sweet marjoram (*Origanum majorana*)
- Mint (*Mentha* spp.)
- Pennyroyal, European pennyroyal (*Mentha pulegium*)
- Pineapple sage (*Salvia elegans*)
- Rosemary (*Rosmarinus officinalis*)
- Sage (*Salvia officinalis*)
- Scented geranium (*Pelargonium* spp.)
- Southernwood (*Artemisia abrotanum*)
- Sweet cicely (*Myrrhis odorata*)
- Sweet goldenrod (*Solidago odorata*)
- Sweet woodruff (*Galium odoratum*)
- Thyme (*Thymus* spp.)
- Valerian (*Valeriana officinalis*)
- Violet, sweet violet (*Viola odorata*)
- Yarrow (*Achillea millefolium*)

HERBS FOR DYEING

These herbs are used to color yarns and textiles. Some of them impart different colors depending on the mordant used.

- Angelica (*Angelica archangelica*), green
- Betony (*Stachys officinalis*), green, yellow-green
- Calendula, pot marigold (*Calendula officinalis*), gold, brownish gold
- Chamomile, Roman (*Chamaemelum nobile*), yellow
- Coltsfoot (*Tussilago farfara*), green
- Comfrey (*Symphytum officinale*), green, brown
- Dock (*Rumex* spp.), yellow, green, red
- Elecampane (*Inula helenium*), blue
- Fennel (*Foeniculum vulgare*), green, yellow, brown
- Goldenrod (*Solidago* spp.), yellow, gold, green
- Indigo (*Indigofera suffruticosa*), blue
- Lady's bedstraw (*Galium verum*), yellow, red, purple
- Lavender cotton (*Santolina chamaecyparissus*), golden yellow
- Madder (*Rubia* spp.), orange, red, brown
- Mullein (*Verbascum thapsus*), yellow, green
- Safflower (*Carthamus tinctoria*), yellow, russet
- Tansy (*Tanacetum vulgare*), green, yellow
- Woad (*Isatis tinctoria*), blue, pink
- Yarrow (*Achillea millefolium*), yellow, green, black, gray

HERBS FOR BATHING

To add herbs to bathwater, place a handful of fresh or dried herbs in a muslin bag or tea strainer and suspend it under the faucet so water flows through as the tub is filled. Or make a strong infusion of the herb in boiling water (like tea) and pour it into the bath.

Along with each herb is a listing of the quality or qualities it imparts when used in bathing.

Bay (*Laurus nobilis*): Stimulating, good for sore muscles and joints, astringent
Calendula, pot marigold (*Calendula officinalis*): Stimulating
Catnip (*Nepeta cataria*): Calming
Chamomile (*Chamaemelum nobile, Matricaria recutita*): Calming
Clary (*Salvia sclarea*): Astringent
Comfrey (*Symphytum officinale*): Emollient, calming, good for sore muscles and joints
Dock (*Rumex* spp.): Astringent
Fennel (*Foeniculum vulgare*): Stimulating
Ginger (*Zingiber officinale*): Stimulating, good for circulation
Horseradish (*Armoracia rusticana*): Stimulating
Hyssop (*Hyssopus officinalis*): Calming
Lady's mantle (*Alchemilla vulgaris*): Astringent
Lavender (*Lavandula* spp.): Stimulating
Lemon balm (*Melissa officinalis*): Calming
Lemongrass (*Cymbopogon citratus*): Astringent
Lemon verbena (*Aloysia triphylla*): Stimulating
Marjoram, sweet marjoram (*Origanum majorana*): Stimulating
Meadowsweet, queen-of-the-meadow (*Filipendula ulmaria*): Stimulating, astringent
Mullein (*Verbascum thapsus*): Calming, astringent
Oregano (*Origanum* spp.): Good for sore muscles and joints
Peppermint (*Mentha × piperita*) and other mints: Stimulating
Rosemary (*Rosmarinus officinalis*): Astringent, stimulating
Sage (*Salvia officinalis*): Stimulating, good for sore muscles and joints
Savory (*Satureja* spp.): Stimulating
Sweet flag (*Acorus calamus*): Calming
Tansy (*Tanacetum vulgare*): Calming
Thyme (*Thymus* spp.): Antiseptic, deodorant, stimulating
Valerian (*Valeriana officinalis*) roots: Calming
Vervain (*Verbena officinalis*): Calming
Violet, sweet violet (*Viola odorata*): Calming
Yarrow (*Achillea millefolium*): Astringent

HEALING HERBS

CHINESE HEALING HERBS

Thousands of herbs are used by traditional healers in China. Listed here are some that are familiar to American gardeners.

Aconite, monkshood (*Aconitum napellus*)
Burdock (*Arctium lappa*)
Comfrey (*Symphytum officinale*)
Curly dock (*Rumex crispus*)
Elecampane (*Inula helenium*)
Garlic (*Allium sativum*)
Ginger (*Zingiber officinalis*)
Ginseng (*Panax* spp.)
Joe-pye weed (*Eupatorium purpureum*)
Lavender (*Lavandula* spp.)
Licorice (*Glycyrrhiza glabra*)
Mugwort (*Artemisia vulgaris*)
Mustard (*Brassica* spp.)
Peony roots (*Paeonia* spp.)
Peppermint (*Mentha* × *piperita*)
Raspberry leaf (*Rubus* spp.)
Rosemary (*Rosmarinus officinalis*)
Sage (*Salvia officinalis*)
Wild ginger (*Asarum* spp.)
Violet (*Viola* spp.)
Yarrow (*Achillea millefolium*)

ANCIENT GREECE

During the time of Hippocrates—and before—these herbs were part of the pharmacopoeia in Greece.

Anise (*Pimpinella anisum*)
Burdock (*Arctium lappa*)
Chamomile (*Chamaemelum nobile*)
Fennel (*Foeniculum vulgare*)
Holy thistle (*Silybum marianum*)
Horehound (*Marrubium vulgare*)
Lemon balm (*Melissa officinalis*)
Mint (*Mentha* spp.)
Mullein (*Verbascum* spp.)
Rosemary (*Rosmarinus officinalis*)
Thyme (*Thymus vulgaris*)

MEDIEVAL MONASTERIES

During the Middle Ages, European monks grew herbs for healing, cooking, and other uses. All the plants listed here could be found in monastery gardens.

Betony (*Stachys officinalis*)
Burdock (*Arctium lappa*)
Chamomile
  German chamomile (*Matricaria recutita*)
  Roman chamomile (*Chamaemelum nobile*)
Chervil (*Anthriscus cerefolium*)
Clary (*Salvia sclarea*)
Coriander (*Coriandrum sativum*)
Cumin (*Cuminum cyminum*)
Dill (*Anethum graveolens*)
Fennel (*Foeniculum vulgare*)
Garlic (*Allium sativum*)
Horehound (*Marrubium vulgare*)
Hyssop (*Hyssopus officinalis*)
Lavender (*Lavandula* spp.)
Lovage (*Levisticum officinale*)
Marsh mallow (*Althaea officinalis*)
Marjoram (*Origanum* spp.)
Mint (*Mentha* spp.)
Mugwort (*Artemisia vulgaris*)
Parsley (*Petroselinum crispum*)
Pennyroyal, European (*Mentha pulegium*)
Rosemary (*Rosmarinus officinalis*)
Rue (*Ruta graveolens*)
Sage (*Salvia officinalis*)
Savory, winter (*Satureja montana*)
Tarragon (*Artemisia dracunculus*)
Thyme (*Thymus* spp.)
Violet (*Viola* spp.)
Wormwood (*Artemisia absinthium*)
Yarrow (*Achillea millefolium*)

(continued)

Healing Herbs *(cont'd)*

NATIVE AMERICAN

These plants are part of the healing traditions of Native Americans. The bark of a number of trees has also played an important role in healing.

Bearberry (*Arctostaphylos uva-ursi*)
Blackberry (*Rubus* spp.)
Burdock (*Arctium lappa*)
Comfrey (*Symphytum officinale*)
Dock (*Rumex* spp.)
Echinacea (*Echinacea angustifolia*)
Garlic (*Allium sativum*)
Ginseng (*Panax* spp.)
Goldenseal (*Hydrastis canadensis*)
Horsetail (*Equisetum* spp.)
Joe-pye weed (*Eupatorium purpureum*)
Licorice (*Glycyrrhiza glabra*)
Mints (*Mentha* spp.)
Mullein (*Verbascum thapsus*)
Nettle (*Urtica dioica*)
Oregon grape (*Mahonia aquifolium*)
Plantain (*Plantago major*)
Tansy (*Tanacetum vulgare*)
Wild ginger (*Asarum canadense*)
Wintergreen (*Gaultheria procumbens*)

THE DOCTRINE OF SIGNATURES

For centuries European medicine was based on an idea known as the Doctrine of Signatures. Paracelsus was perhaps the greatest proponent of the Doctrine, but its influence is seen in all the great herbals of medieval Europe and England.

According to the Doctrine of Signatures, every plant that could be used in healing revealed its healing properties by a "sign"—some aspect of its physical appearance, scent, or habitat. The sign indicated the disease the plant could cure, or the part of the body it could be used to treat. Thus, a yellow flower would be used to treat jaundice, or a plant with leaves shaped like an ear or a hand would be used to treat ailments of that part of the body.

HERBS IN MAGIC

The herbs listed here belong to magic and folklore. If you aspire to become a witch, seer, enchanter, or magician (or to protect yourself from one), these herbs will be of interest. The uses given in the list have traditionally been assigned to these herbs.

Anise (*Pimpinella anisum*): Keeps away nightmares

Bay (*Laurus nobilis*): Burn the leaves to see visions

Betony (*Stachys officinalis*): Prevents nightmares and intoxication

Calendula, pot marigold (*Calendula officinalis*): To revitalize yourself

Chamomile (*Chamaemelum nobile*): Draws money, aids sleep

Caraway (*Carum carvi*): Strengthens the memory

Clove pink (*Dianthus caryophyllus*): For power and energy

Clover (*Trifolium* spp.): Keeps you young-looking; four-leaf clover prevents madness

Comfrey (*Symphytum officinale*): For a safe journey

Dill (*Anethum graveolens*): Protects children

Ferns: Bring rain. Putting fern seed (spores) in your shoes makes you invisible

Garlic (*Allium sativum*): Prevents drowning and shipwrecks, wards off evil spirits and vampires

Holly (*Ilex* spp.): Protects one's home from lightning

Hops (*Humulus lupulus*): Induces sleep

Hyssop (*Hyssopus officinalis*): For purification

Lavender (*Lavandula* spp.): For purification, to promote sleep, to see ghosts

Lovage (*Levisticum officinale*): Cleanses the spirit and psyche

Mayapple (*Podophyllum peltatum*): Cures impotence, promotes fertility

Meadowsweet, queen-of-the-meadow (*Filipendula ulmaria*): Brings peace to the household

Mugwort (*Artemisia vulgaris*): Prevents fatigue

Mullein (*Verbascum thapsus*): Gives courage, keeps away wild animals

Pennyroyal (*Mentha pulegium*): Prevents fatigue

Rosemary (*Rosmarinus officinalis*): For memory or remembrance, to increase mental alertness, to purify

Rue (*Ruta graveolens*): Prevents illness, gets rid of bad thoughts

Saffron (*Crocus sativus*): To call forth the winds

Sage (*Salvia officinalis*): For prosperity

St.-John's-wort (*Hypericum perforatum*): To banish spirits and become invincible

Sweet woodruff (*Galium odoratum*): For victory, to get a fresh start

Thyme (*Thymus vulgaris*): For renewal and cleansing, to prevent nightmares, to banish evil spirits

Vervain (*Verbena officinalis*): For cleansing and purification, to attract wealth; used at Candlemas to see the future

Violet (*Viola* spp.): Can change your luck

Wormwood (*Artemisia absinthium*): For clairvoyance and divination

Yarrow (*Achillea millefolium*): Prevents negativity, enhances divination, quells fear

Herbs to Use in Love Potions

Caraway (*Carum carvi*)
Catnip (*Nepeta cataria*)
Coriander (*Coriandrum sativum*)
Dill (*Anethum graveolens*)
Elecampane (*Inula helenium*)
Lemon verbena (*Aloysia triphylla*)
Lovage (*Levisticum officinale*)
Marjoram, sweet marjoram (*Origanum majorana*)
Meadowsweet, queen-of-the-meadow (*Filipendula ulmaria*)
Orris (*Iris × germanica* var. *florentina*)
Rosemary (*Rosmarinus officinalis*)
Spearmint (*Mentha spicata*)
Valerian (*Valeriana officinalis*)
Vervain (*Verbena officinalis*)
Yarrow (*Achillea millefolium*)

For Protection

Angelica (*Angelica archangelica*)
Bay (*Laurus nobilis*)
Betony (*Stachys officinalis*)
Burdock (*Arctium lappa*)
Caraway (*Carum carvi*)
Dill (*Anethum graveolens*)
Ferns
Horehound (*Marrubium vulgare*)
Hyssop (*Hyssopus officinalis*)
Marjoram (*Origanum majorana*)
Mugwort (*Artemisia vulgaris*)
Nettle (*Urtica dioica*), to remove a curse
Rosemary (*Rosmarinus officinalis*)
St.-John's-wort (*Hypericum perforatum*)
Vervain (*Verbena officinalis*)
Wormwood (*Artemisia absinthium*)

To Induce or Enhance Clairvoyance and Prophetic Ability

Calendula, pot marigold (*Calendula officinalis*)
Mugwort (*Artemisia vulgaris*)
Saffron (*Crocus sativus*)
Wormwood (*Artemisia absinthium*)
Yarrow (*Achillea millefolium*)

To Fly

According to folklore, witches used these herbs in ointments that enabled them to fly. These plants are quite poisonous when ingested, and undoubtedly induced hallucinations. In addition, basil, parsley, and sweet flag are also supposed to help one fly.

Belladonna (*Atropa belladonna*)
Datura, jimsonweed (*Datura stramonium*)
Hellebore (*Helleborus niger*), better known to perennial gardeners as the Christmas rose
Henbane (*Hyoscyamus niger*)
Poison hemlock (*Conium maculatum*)

PEST-REPELLENT HERBS

Certain plants are believed by gardeners to repel insects. Most of this information comes from folklore rather than science, but some of the plants, such as peppermint, have been studied scientifically and found to contain volatile oils or other compounds that may well deter some pests.

Basil (*Ocimum basilicum*): Asparagus beetle; 'Dark Opal' basil is said to repel tomato hornworm

Bay (*Laurus nobilis*): Fleas

Borage (*Borago officinalis*): Tomato hornworm

Castor bean (*Ricinus communis*): Moles

Catnip (*Nepeta cataria*): Aphids, Colorado potato beetle, cucumber beetle, flea beetle, Japanese beetle, squash bug

Chives (*Allium schoenoprasum*): Aphids

Coriander (*Coriandrum sativum*): Aphids, Colorado potato beetle, spider mites

Dill (*Anethum graveolens*): Cabbage looper, imported cabbage worm, tomato hornworm

Fennel (*Foeniculum vulgare*): Aphids, slugs and snails

Garlic (*Allium sativum*): Aphids,cabbage looper, cabbage maggot, codling moth, imported cabbage worm, Japanese beetle, rabbits, pear borer, slugs and snails

Hyssop (*Hyssopus officinalis*): Cabbage looper, imported cabbage worm

Mustard (*Brassica* spp.): Aphids

Parsley (*Petroselinum crispum*): Asparagus beetle

Pennyroyal (*Mentha pulegium*): Cabbage looper, imported cabbage worm, fleas

Peppermint (*Mentha × piperita*): Ants, aphids, cabbage looper, flea beetle, imported cabbage worm, moths, squash bug, whitefly

Rosemary (*Rosmarinus officinalis*): Carrot fly, Mexican bean beetle, moths, slugs and snails

Rue (*Ruta graveolens*): Cucumber beetle, flea beetle

Sage (*Salvia officinalis*): Cabbage looper, cabbage maggot, carrot fly, imported cabbage worm

Savory, summer and winter (*Satureja hortensis, S.montana*): Mexican bean beetle

Southernwood (*Artemisia abrotanum*): Cabbage butterfly, cabbage looper, flea beetle, imported cabbage worm

Spearmint (*Mentha spicata*): Ants, aphids, cabbage looper, flea beetle, squash bug

(continued)

Pest-Repellent Herbs *(cont'd)*

Tansy (*Tanacetum vulgare*): Ants, Colorado potato beetle, flea beetle, imported cabbage worm, Japanese beetle, squash bug

Thyme (*Thymus vulgaris*): Cabbage looper, imported cabbage worm, moths, whitefly

Wormwood (*Artemisia absinthium*): Ants, cabbage looper, cabbage maggot, carrot fly, codling moth, fela beetle, mice, whitefly

HARVESTING AND PRESERVING HERBS

HARVESTING TIPS

- Pick sprigs or leaves as needed throughout the growing season.
- Harvest branched plants like basil by pinching from the tips, to promote bushier growth and more leaf production.
- Pick off flowers of basil and mints to promote continued production of good-quality leaves.
- When harvesting leaves, cut stems or branches; do not strip leaves from the stem and leave the bare stem on the plant. You can take up to three-fourths of the topgrowth without harming the plant.
- Harvest only healthy leaves.
- Generally speaking, herb leaves have the maximum scent and flavor right before a plant starts to bloom.
- Harvest seed heads of anise, caraway, dill, fennel, coriander, and other umbellifers when the color darkens but before they shatter and drop the seeds.
- Harvest lavender when the buds are colored but before they open.
- When harvesting whole plants or large amounts of herbs, try to harvest in the morning on a clear, sunny day, when the dew has dried. At this time of day the plants contain the highest concentration of the volatile oils that give them their flavor.
- Keep picking annual herbs until the plants are killed by frost.
- Stop major harvesting of perennial herbs a month or six weeks before you expect the first fall frost, so the plant growth has time to harden before winter.

DRYING TIPS

Dried herbs should be brittle and easily crumbled, but not so dry that they turn into powder when crumbled.

- Dry small quantities of leaves or flowers on screen racks. Air-dry, or spread on cookie sheets and place in the oven on the lowest setting, with the door open, for several hours or until dry. In a gas oven, the heat of the pilot light will dry herbs in a couple of days.
- To air-dry larger quantities of leaves, gather stems in bunches, fasten them with a rubber band, and hang them upside down in an attic or other dark, dry, well-ventilated place.
- Collect seed heads when the seeds ripen. Place them in paper bags (one kind of herb to a bag). When the seed heads shatter, the seeds will be caught in the bottom of the bag.
- To dry herbs in a microwave, place a layer of clean leaves between paper towels and microwave on high for 3 minutes. Turn the leaves every 30 seconds if your microwave does not have a turntable. If the herbs are not yet dry after 3 minutes, microwave for 20 to 30 seconds more. Continue with 20- or 30-second intervals until the herbs are dry.
- Microwave herbs on a clear day when the humidity is low, or the herbs may reabsorb moisture after microwave drying.
- Store dried herbs out of light, or in brown glass jars. Storage containers should be tightly capped to keep out air.

FREEZING TIPS

- Keep leaves of small plants, such as thyme, on the stems to freeze. Detach larger leaves from the stems before freezing.
- Spread whole or chopped leaves on cookie sheets and place in the freezer. When frozen, store in a freezer bag or container.
- Basil must be blanched before freezing or it will turn black. Other herbs can be frozen without blanching.
- Most frozen herbs are good for six months—long enough to get through the winter.
- Use frozen herbs in soups, casseroles, and cooked dishes. Thaw and pat dry before using in salads or as garnish.
- Another way to freeze is to puree herbs with enough water to make a mushy liquid. Pour into ice-cube trays and freeze. When frozen, store in freezer bags or containers. Use the frozen cubes in soups and stews.

Chapter 8

VEGETABLES

SEASONAL VEGETABLES

COOL-SEASON CROPS

HARDY

These vegetables can tolerate temperatures below freezing and are the earliest to go into the garden. Those marked with an asterisk (*) can also be planted in summer for fall harvest, or in fall for winter harvest in warm climates.

Asparagus	Garlic	Onions	Spinach*
Broccoli*	Kale*	Peas*	Turnips*
Brussels sprouts	Kohlrabi*	Radishes*	
Cabbage*	Leeks	Rhubarb	
Collards*	Mustard*	Rutabaga	

HALF-HARDY

These crops can stand some light frost and short-term exposure to freezing temperatures. They can go into the garden shortly before the last frost date.

Artichoke, globe	Celery	Endive	Potatoes
Beets*	Chard	Escarole	Salsify
Carrots*	Chicory	Lettuce, head	
Cauliflower	Chinese cabbage*	Lettuce, looseleaf*	
Celeriac	Cress*	Parsnips	

WARM-SEASON VEGETABLES

TENDER

The leaves and fruit of these crops are damaged by light frosts. They are usually planted on or shortly after the last frost date.

Beans, shell (bush and pole)
Beans, snap (bush and pole)
Corn
Southern peas (black-eye, crowder)
Tomatoes

VERY TENDER

These crops need a temperature of at least 70°F to grow well. Plant them a few weeks after the last frost, when soil and weather are warm.

Beans, lima (bush and pole)
Cucumbers
Eggplant
Melons
Okra
Peppers (hot and sweet)
Pumpkins
Squash, summer
Squash, winter
Sweet potatoes

WHEN TO PLANT

Note: This table (in common with many seed catalogs) directs you to plant some early crops "as soon as the soil can be worked." This is usually about 4 weeks before the last frost date, depending on the type of soil. The heavier the soil, the later it becomes workable, especially during a cool, wet spring. See the list of frost dates in chapter 1 to find the last frost date for your area. Vegetables for which no indoor planting date is given are best sown directly in the garden.

CROP	WEEKS BEFORE (-) OR AFTER (+) LAST FROST TO PLANT OUT	WEEKS BEFORE PLANTING OUT TO SOW INDOORS
Artichoke (*Cynara scolymus*)	Plant suckers in spring or fall (warm climates) Transplants or direct-sow -2 to 0 weeks	4
Arugula (*Eruca sativa*)	As soon as soil can be worked.	

CROP	WEEKS BEFORE (-) OR AFTER (+) LAST FROST TO PLANT OUT	WEEKS BEFORE PLANTING OUT TO SOW INDOORS
Asparagus (*Asparagus officinalis*)	-2 to 4 weeks (crowns) +4 (seedlings)	12 to 14
Beans, snap and shell (*Phaseolus vulgaris*)	0 to +2	
Beans, lima (*Phaseolus limensis*)	+2	
Beets (*Beta vulgaris*)	-2 to 4 (successions every 3 weeks until midsummer) 10 weeks before fall frost	4
Broccoli (*Brassica oleracea*, Botrytis Group)	-4 to +2 (seedlings) -4 to -6 (seeds) 12 to 14 weeks before first fall frost	4 to 6
Brussels sprouts (*Brassica oleracea*, Gemmifera Group)	-4 (but better planted for late harvest) Sow 10 to 12 weeks before first fall frost	6
Cabbage (*Brassica oleracea*, Capitata Group)	Early varieties, -5 to +3 Midseason, 0 Late varieties, +4 Sow 18 weeks before first fall frost	5 to 7
Carrots (*Daucus carota* var. *sativus*)	-4 to -6 Sow 12 weeks before fall frost	
Cauliflower (*Brassica oleracea*, Botrytis Group)	-3 to +2 Sow 12 weeks before fall frost	5 to 7
Celeriac (*Apium graveolens* var. *rapaceum*)	Anytime after danger of heavy frost is past	8

(continued)

When to Plant *(cont'd)*

CROP	WEEKS BEFORE (-) OR AFTER (+) LAST FROST TO PLANT OUT	WEEKS BEFORE PLANTING OUT TO SOW INDOORS
Celery (*Apium graveolens* var. *dulce*)	-3 to +4 In warm climates, can direct-sow at 0	6 to 8
Chard, Swiss chard (*Beta vulgaris* var. *cicla*)	-1 to -3 In warm climates, 10 weeks before first fall frost or in midsummer for fall harvest	
Chicory, cutting (*Cichorium intybus*)	As soon as soil can be worked, or in midsummer for fall harvest	
Chicory, radicchio	17 weeks before first fall frost	
Chicory, witloof (*Cichorium intybus* 'Witloof')	17 weeks before first fall frost	
Chinese cabbage (*Brassica rapa*)	-4 to -6. 12 weeks before first fall frost	4
Collards (*Brassica oleracea*, Acephala Group)	-4 to +2 (seedlings) -3 to -4 (seeds) 10 to 12 weeks before first fall frost	6 to 8
Corn (*Zea mays*)	+2 to +3	
Corn salad, mache (*Valerianella locusta*)	As soon as soil can be worked	
Cress (*Lepidium sativum*)	As soon as soil can be worked	
Cucumbers (*Cucumis sativus*)	+1	
Eggplant (*Solanum melongena* var. *esculentum*)	+2 to +3	8 to 10
Endive and escarole (*Cichorium endivia*)	-4 to +2 (seedlings) -2 to -4 (seeds) 15 weeks before first fall frost	4 to 6

CROP	WEEKS BEFORE (-) OR AFTER (+) LAST FROST TO PLANT OUT	WEEKS BEFORE PLANTING OUT TO SOW INDOORS
Florence fennel (*Foeniculum vulgare* var. *azoricum*)	+2	4 to 6
Garlic (*Allium sativum*)	-4 to +1 (seedlings or cloves) -4 to -6 (seeds)	4 to 6 (cloves)
Jerusalem artichoke (*Helianthus tuberosus*)	-2 to -4 (tubers)	
Kale (*Brassica oleracea* var. *acephala*)	-4 to +2 (seedlings) -4 to -5 (seeds) Sow 10 weeks before first fall frost	6 to 8
Kohlrabi (*Brassica oleracea* Gongylodes Group)	-4 to -5 10 weeks before first fall frost	
Leeks (*Allium ampeloprasum*, Porrum Group)	-4 to +2 Warm climates, sow in summer or early fall	8 to 10
Lettuce, head (*Lactuca sativa*)	-4 to +2	4 to 6
Lettuce, leaf (*Lactuca sativa*)	-4 to +2 Sow 8 weeks before first fall frost	4 to 6
Melons	+1 to +3 (transplant when seedlings have no more than 3 leaves)	3 to 4
Mustard (*Brassica juncea*)	-2 to -4 6 to 8 weeks before first fall frost	
Okra (*Abelmoschus esculentus*)	+4 (seedlings) +1 to +2 (seeds) Zones 10–11, sow anytime in winter	6 to 8

(continued)

When to Plant *(cont'd)*

CROP	WEEKS BEFORE (-) OR AFTER (+) LAST FROST TO PLANT OUT	WEEKS BEFORE PLANTING OUT TO SOW INDOORS
Onions (*Allium cepa*)	-4 to 0 (seedlings) -4 to -6 (seeds) -2 to +2 (sets)	6 to 8
Parsnips (*Pastinaca sativa*)	-3 to +3 (seedlings) -2 to -4 (seeds) Zones 9–11, sow late fall to early winter	4 to 6
Peas (*Pisum sativum*)	-3 to -4 Sow 10 to 12 weeks before first fall frost	
Peppers (*Capsicum annuum*)	+3 to +4 (seedlings)	8 to 10
Potatoes (*Solanum tuberosum*)	-1 to -3 (seed potatoes)	
Radishes (*Raphanus sativus*)	-3 to -4 Sow 4 weeks before first fall frost Zones 9–11, sow 8 weeks before last frost, or in fall Winter radishes: 10 weeks before first fall frost	
Rhubarb (*Rheum rhaponticum*)	As soon as soil can be worked, or in fall (crowns)	
Rutabaga (*Brassica napus*)	15 weeks before first fall frost (seeds)	
Salsify (*Tragopogon porrifolius*)	-1 to -3 (seeds)	
Shallots (*Allium cepa*, Aggregatum Group)	-2 to -4 (sets) Warm climates, plant in fall	
Sorrel (*Rumex acetosella*)	As soon as soil can be worked (seeds)	
Southern peas (*Vigna unguiculata*)	+1 (seeds)	

CROP	WEEKS BEFORE (-) OR AFTER (+) LAST FROST TO PLANT OUT	WEEKS BEFORE PLANTING OUT TO SOW INDOORS
Spinach (*Spinacia oleracea*)	-2 to -4 (seedlings) -4 to -5 (seeds) 6 weeks before first fall frost	4 to 6
Squash, summer (*Cucurbita pepo* var. *melopepo*)	+1 to +3	
Squash, winter, and pumpkins (*Cucurbita maxima*, *C. mixta*, *C. moschata*, *C. pepo* var. *pepo)*	+1 to +3	
Tomatoes (*Lycopersicon lycopersicum*)	+1 to +3 (seedlings)	8 to 10
Turnips (*Brassica rapa*, Rapifera Group)	-2 to -4 (seeds) Sow 8 weeks before first fall frost	

SPACING DISTANCES FOR VEGETABLES

This table gives the spacing plants need to mature. Distances are given for both conventional rows and for intensive beds (in which plants are spaced equidistant in all directions). For some plants, such as cucumbers or beans, the choice is between planting in rows or in hills (see chapter 2, "Gardening Techniques," for how to do this). The soil in intensive beds must be fertile and rich in organic matter to support a greater number of plants per amount of space available.

VEGETABLE	PLANT IN ROWS	PLANT IN BEDS (or hills)
Artichoke	24 inches apart, rows 36 inches apart	
Arugula	6 inches apart, rows 18 inches apart	6 inches apart

(continued)

Spacing Distances for Vegetables *(cont'd)*

VEGETABLE	PLANT IN ROWS	PLANT IN BEDS (or hills)
Asparagus	24 inches apart, rows 36 to 48 inches apart	14–18 inches apart
Beans, Bush Snap and Shell varieties	3–4 inches apart, rows 18–30 inches apart	in hills 36 inches apart
Beans, Pole Snap	4–6 inches apart, rows 24–36 inches apart	in hills 36 inches apart
Beans, Bush Lima	3–6 inches apart, rows 24–30 inches apart	8 inches apart
Beans, Pole Lima	6–10 inches apart, rows 30–36 inches apart	
Beets	3–4 inches apart, rows 8–12 inches apart	6 inches apart
Broccoli	15–18 inches apart, rows 24–36 inches apart	18 inches apart
Brussels Sprouts	18–24 inches apart, rows 30–36 inches apart	18 inches apart
Cabbage	Early varieties 14–18 inches apart Late varieties 18–24 inches apart Rows 30–36 inches apart	15–18 inches apart 15–18 inches apart
Carrots	3–4 inches apart, rows 12 inches apart	3 inches apart
Cauliflower	24 inches apart, rows 36 inches apart	18 inches apart
Celeriac	6–8 inches apart, rows 18 inches apart	12 inches apart
Celery	6 inches apart, rows 24 inches apart	9 inches apart

VEGETABLE	PLANT IN ROWS	PLANT IN BEDS (or hills)
Chard, Swiss chard	9 inches apart, rows 18 inches apart	9 inches apart
Chicory, Cutting	6–8 inches apart, rows 30 inches apart	8 inches apart
Chicory, Radicchio	12–18 inches apart, rows 24 inches apart	18 inches
Chicory, Witloof	6–8 inches apart, rows 18 inches apart	8 inches
Chinese Cabbage	Nonheading varieties 9 inches apart Heading varieties 16 inches apart Rows 12–18 inches apart	
Collards	15 inches apart, rows 36 inches apart	15 inches
Corn	12 inches apart, rows 30 inches apart	18 inches apart in beds, or in hills 6 feet apart
Corn Salad, Mache	16 inches apart, rows 24 inches apart	18 inches apart
Cress	2 inches, rows 12 inches apart	4 inches apart
Cucumbers	6 inches apart, rows 6 feet apart	18 inches apart in beds, or 3–4 plants in hills 4 feet apart
Eggplant	24 inches apart, rows 36 inches apart	24 inches apart
Endive and Escarole	18 inches apart, rows 24 inches apart	18 inches apart
Florence fennel	8 inches apart, rows 18 inches apart	12 inches apart

(continued)

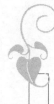

Spacing Distances for Vegetables *(cont'd)*

VEGETABLE	PLANT IN ROWS	PLANT IN BEDS (or hills)
Garlic	3–4 inches apart, rows 12–16 inches apart	6 inches apart
Jerusalem Artichoke	12 inches apart, rows 36–48 inches apart	in hills 12 inches apart
Kale	12–15 inches apart, rows 18–24 inches apart	15–18 inches apart
Kohlrabi	9 inches apart, rows 30 inches apart	9 inches apart
Leeks	4 inches apart, rows 20 inches apart	6 inches apart
Lettuce, Head	12 inches apart, rows 14 inches apart	12 inches apart
Lettuce, Leaf	9 inches apart, rows 14 inches apart	9 inches apart
Melons		3–5 feet apart in beds, or in hills 3–5 feet apart
Mustard	9 inches apart, rows 18 inches apart	9 inches apart
Okra	Dwarf varieties 10 inches apart, rows 24–48 inches apart	18 inches apart
	Standard varieties 14 inches apart, rows 48 inches apart	18 inches apart
Onions	Scallions 2 inches apart, rows 12–18 inches apart	
	Mature bulbs 4–6 inches apart, rows 12–18 inches apart	4–6 inches apart

VEGETABLE	PLANT IN ROWS	PLANT IN BEDS (or hills)
Parsnips	4–6 inches apart, rows 18 inches apart	6 inches apart
Peas	Dwarf or bush varieties 1–2 inches apart, rows 24 inches apart Standard varieties 1–2 inches apart, rows 30–36 inches apart, or double rows 8 inches apart with trellis between them	6 inches apart (all types)
Peppers	18–24 inches apart, rows 36 inches apart	15 inches apart
Potatoes	12–15 inches apart, rows 24–30 inches apart	15 inches apart
Radishes	Early varieties 2–3 inches apart, rows 10–12 inches apart Winter varieties 6 inches apart, rows 18 inches apart	3 inches apart 6–8 inches apart
Rhubarb	36 inches apart, rows 48 inches apart	36 inches apart
Rutabagas	8 inches apart, rows 18 inches apart	9 inches apart
Salsify	4 inches apart, rows 12–15 inches apart	6 inches apart
Shallots	4–6 inches apart, rows 9 inches apart	6 inches apart
Sorrel	18 inches apart, rows 18 inches apart	18 inches apart
Southern peas	2–3 inches apart, rows 24–40 inches apart	in hills 36 inches apart

(continued)

Spacing Distances for Vegetables *(cont'd)*

VEGETABLE	PLANT IN ROWS	PLANT IN BEDS (or hills)
Spinach	6 inches apart, rows 14 inches apart	6 inches apart
Squash, Summer and Bush varieties, Winter, and Pumpkins	2–3 feet apart, rows 4–6 feet apart	in hills 4–6 feet apart Beds: summer squash 2 feet apart, winter squash and pumpkins 3 feet apart
Squash, Vining varieties	3–4 feet apart, rows 8–12 feet apart	in hills 6–8 feet apart, pumpkins 10–12 feet apart
Tomatoes	18–24 inches apart, rows 36 inches apart	24 inches apart
Turnips	4–6 inches apart, rows 12–15 inches apart	6 inches apart

PLANTING DEPTH

Depths are for seeds unless otherwise specified.

Artichoke: 4 inches (suckers)
Arugula: 1/2 inch
Asparagus: seeds 1/2 inch
  Crowns: 6–8 inches (6 inches in most soils, 8 inches in sandy soil)
Beans, all types: 1-1 1/2 inches
Beets: 1/2–1 inch
Broccoli: 1/4 inch
Brussels sprouts: 1/2 inch
Cabbage: 1/2 inch
  Chinese cabbage: 1/2 inch
Carrots: 1/4–1/2 inch
Cauliflower: 1/2 inch
Celeriac: 1/8–1/4 inch
Celery: 1/8–1/4 inch
Chard, Swiss chard: 1/2–1 inch
Chicory, cutting: 1/2 inch
Chicory, witloof: 1/4 inch
Collards: 1/2 inch
Corn: 1 1/2 inches
Corn salad, mache: 1/2 inch
Cress: 1/4–1/2 inch

Cucumbers: 1–1½ inch
Eggplant: ¼ inch
Endive and escarole: ¼–½ inch
Kale: ½ inch
Kohlrabi: ½ inch
Leeks: ½ inch
Lettuce, head: ½ inch
Lettuce, leaf: ¼ inch
Melons: ½–1½ inches
Okra: ½ inch
Onions: Seeds ¼–½ inch
Sets: ½ inch
Parsnips: ¼–½ inch
Peas: 1–1½ inches
Peppers: ½ inch
Pumpkins: 1 inch
Radishes: ½ inch
Rhubarb: Crowns 2–3 inches
Rutabagas: ½–1 inch
Salsify: ½ inch
Spinach: ½ inch
Squash, summer: ½–1 inch
Squash, winter: 1 inch
Tomatoes: 1 inch
Turnips: ¼–½ inch

TRANSPLANTING TOLERANCE OF VEGETABLES

Transplant Easily

Broccoli
Brussels sprouts
Cabbage
Cauliflower
Collards
Endive and escarole
Garlic
Kale
Kohlrabi
Leeks
Lettuce, head and leaf
Mustard
Shallots
Tomatoes

Transplant Reasonably Well

Beets
Celery
Chard, Swiss chard
Eggplant
Onions
Parsnips
Peppers

Transplant with Care

If you have a short growing season and must start these vegetables indoors, start them in individual peat pots and transplant carefully to minimize root disturbance.

Artichoke
Carrots
Corn
Cucumbers
Melons
Okra
Spinach
Squash, summer
Squash, winter
Turnips
Watermelon

Vegetables to Direct-Seed

These vegetables grow best when sown directly in the garden.

Beans, snap, shell, and lima
Peas
Radishes (transplant well, but grow quickly so indoor sowing is unnecessary)
Rutabagas
Salsify

HOW MUCH TO PLANT

The following table suggests planting rates for common vegetables to supply an individual's annual needs. These amounts assume that certain vegetables will be canned or frozen for winter use. If you do not plan to store vegetables, cut the rate for vegetables that can and freeze well by half; amounts stay the same for vegetables best used when fresh.

An asterisk, *, indicates vegetables that can or freeze well.

Artichoke: 1–3 plants
Asparagus*: 10 crowns, 10–15 feet of row
Beans, Bush Snap*: 1/2 lb. of seed, 10–15 plants, or 25–50 feet of row
Beans, Pole Snap*: 1/4 lb. of seed, 20 plants, or 15–25 feet of row
Beans, Bush Lima*: 1/4 lb. of seed, 30 plants, or 10–15 feet of row
Beans, Pole Lima*: 1 pkt. of seed, or 12 plants
Beets*: 1/2 pkt., 20–25 plants, or 5–10 feet of row
Broccoli*: 1/4 pkt. of seed, 5–10 plants, or 8–12 feet of row
Brussels Sprouts*: 1/4 pkt., 5–10 plants, or 8–12 feet of row
Cabbage
  Early varieties: 1/4 pkt., 5–10 plants, or 8–12 feet of row
  Late varieties: 1/2 pkt., 20 plants, or 28–38 feet of row
Carrots*: 1/2 pkt. of seed, 50–60 plants, 5–10 feet of row
Cauliflower: 1/4 pkt. of seed, 8–10 plants, 5–10 feet of row
Celery: 6–8 plants, or 3–5 feet of row
Chard, Swiss chard*: 1/4 pkt. of seed, 5–10 plants, or 5–10 feet of row
Chinese cabbage: 6–7 plants
Collards*: 1/4 pkt. of seed, 4–6 plants, or 6 feet of row
Corn*: 1/2 lb. of seed, 40–50 plants, 25–50 feet of row
Cucumbers: 1/4 pkt. of seed, 6–9 plants, or 2–3 hills
Eggplant: 2–3 plants, or 4–6 feet of row
Endive and Escarole: 3–4 plants
Garlic: 5–10 bulbs, or 3 feet of row
Jerusalem artichoke: 3–5 plants
Kale*: 1/4 pkt. of seed, 10–15 plants, or 5–10 feet of row
Kohlrabi: 1/4 pkt. of seed, 8 plants, or 3–5 feet of row
Leeks: 1/4 pkt. of seed, 3 feet of row
Lettuce, head: 1/2 pkt. of seed, 7 plants, or 5–10 feet of row
Lettuce, leaf: 1/2 pkt. of seed, 15–20 plants, or 5–10 feet of row
Melons: 1/4 pkt. of seed, 3–5 hills
Mustard*: 1/4 pkt. of seed, 7 plants, 3–5 feet of row
Okra: 1/4 pkt. of seed, 4–6 feet of row
Onions*: 1/4 pkt. of seed, 1lb. of sets, 40 plants, or 10–15 feet of row
Parsnips: 1/4 pkt. of seed, 25 plants, or 3–5 feet of row
Peas*: 1/4 lb. of seed, 50 plants, 15–25 feet of row
Peppers*: 1/4 pkt. of seed, 2–3 plants, 4–6 feet of row
Potatoes: 5–10 lbs. seed potatoes, 10–15 plants, or 50–100 feet of row
Radishes: 1/2 pkt. of seed, 30 plants, or 5–10 feet of row
Rhubarb: 2–3 roots, or 5–10 feet of row
Rutabagas: 1/4 pkt. of seed, 10 plants, or 5–10 feet of row
Salsify: 15–20 plants
Spinach*: 1/2 pkt. of seed, 30 plants, or 5–10 feet of row
Squash, summer*: 1/4 pkt. of seed, 4–6 plants, 5–10 feet of row, or 2–3 hills
Squash, winter*: 1/4 pkt. of seed, 4–6 plants, 12–18 feet of row, or 2–3 hills
Sweet potatoes: 10–18 plants, or 20–24 feet of row
Tomatoes*: 1/4 pkt. of seed, 3–5 plants, or 10–15 feet of row
Turnips: 1/4 oz. of seed, 20–30 plants, or 10–15 feet of row

NUTRIENT NEEDS

Heavy Feeders

For best performance, these vegetables need a fertile soil high in nutrients and organic matter.

- Artichoke
- Asparagus
- Beets
- Broccoli
- Brussels sprouts
- Cabbage
- Cauliflower
- Celeriac
- Celery
- Chinese cabbage
- Collards
- Corn
- Cucumbers
- Eggplant
- Endive and Escarole
- Kale
- Kohlrabi
- Lettuce (head and leaf)
- Melons
- Okra
- Pumpkins
- Radishes
- Rhubarb
- Spinach
- Squash, summer
- Squash, winter
- Tomatoes

Light Feeders

These crops grow well in most average garden soils.

- Carrots
- Chard
- Garlic
- Leeks
- Mustard
- Onions
- Parsnips
- Peppers
- Potatoes
- Rutabaga
- Shallots
- Sweet Potatoes
- Turnips

Soil Enhancers

Legumes fix nitrogen in the soil and actually boost fertility.

- Alfalfa and clover (often grown as cover crops)
- Beans (all kinds)
- Peas (all kinds)

CRITICAL WATERING TIMES

Most vegetables have the greatest need for water during particular phases of their development. They can get along with less water at other times without reducing or otherwise damaging the harvest. When water is scarce, these are the most important times to water vegetables.

Artichokes: Need ample moisture all season

Asparagus: After harvest ends, while foliage grows actively

Beans: When plants bloom, flowers are pollinated, and pods swell

Broccoli: As heads develop

Cabbage: As heads develop

Carrots: While roots enlarge

Cauliflower: As heads develop, especially during blanching just prior to harvest

Corn: During tasseling and silking, as ears develop

Cucumbers: When plants bloom and set fruit

Eggplants: Throughout growth and fruit development

(continued)

Critical Watering Times *(cont'd)*

Garlic: As bulbs enlarge

Leeks: Throughout their growth and development of enlarged stem bases

Lettuce

Head: As heads develop

Leaf: Throughout growth and development

Onions: As bulbs enlarge

Peas: When plants bloom, flowers are pollinated, and pods swell

Peppers: Throughout season

Potatoes: As the tubers grow, after plants flower

Pumpkins: During budding, and flowering

Radishes: As roots enlarge

Spinach: Throughout growth and development

Squash (summer and winter): During budding, and flowering

Tomatoes: Throughout, especially blooming, fruit set, and as fruits develop

Turnips: As roots expand

VEGETABLE VARIETIES FOR COOL CLIMATES

The varieties listed below are recommended for northern gardens with a short growing season. To find other possibilities, check seed catalogs for early-maturing and cold-tolerant varieties.

BEANS, SNAP AND SHELL

Bert Goodwin's
Beurre de Rocquencourt
Blue Lake
Bush Blue Lake
Contender
Earliserve Bush
Fortex
Gold Crop Wax
Golden Rocky
Great Northern
Green Crop
Improved Tendergreen
Jacob's Cattle
Kentucky Wonder
Kentucky Wonder Wax
Low's Champion
Maine Yellow Eye
Montana Green
Northeaster
Oregon Giant
Provider
Royal Burgundy
Scarlet Beauty Elite 7 Pod
Soldier
Spartan Arrow
Tongue of Fire
Tender Crop
Top Crop
Venture
Vermont Cranberry

BEETS

Burpee Golden
Crosby's Egyptian
Detroit Dark Red
Early Wonder
Red Ace
Red Ball

BROCCOLI

Green Comet
Green Goliath
Park's Early Emerald Hybrid

CABBAGES

Blue Max Savoy
Copenhagen Market
Danish Roundhead
Early Jersey Wakefield
Early Marvel
Emerald Acre
Golden Acre
Heads Up
Lasso Red
Luna
Market Prize
Polar Green
Primax
Red Acre
Sanibel

CARROTS

Baby Finger Nantes
Chantenay Long
Danvers Half Long
Nantes Half Long
Short 'n' Sweet

CAULIFLOWER

Alert
Amazing
Andes
Candid Charm
Early Snowball
Snow Crown
Snow King
Super Snowball

CHINESE CABBAGE

Blues F-l
Dynasty
Michihli
Nozaki Early
Springtide

CORN

Ashworth
Earlivee
Early Golden Giant
Extra Early Bantam
Extra Early Super Sweet
Fisher's Earliest
Golden Midget
Grant
King Arthur
Lyric
Northern Super Sweet
Northernvee
Northern Xtra Sweet
Platinum Lady
Polar Super Sweet
Polarvee
Quickie
Seneca Horizon
Skyline
Spartan
Sugar Buns
Sweet Dreams
Sweet Heart

CUCUMBERS

Bush Champion
Conquest
Early Russian
General Lee
Jazzer
Marketer
Marketmore 76
Marketmore 86
Northern Pickling
Pioneer
Revenue
Saladin
Slice King
Spacemaster
Straight Eight
Supersett
Sweet Success

EGGPLANT

Dusky Hybrid
Early Black Egg
Easter Egg
Ichiban Hybrid
Orient Express
Pirouette
Tycoon

LETTUCE

Black-Seeded Simpson
Buttercrunch
Butter King
Great Lakes
Oakleaf
Ruby
Salad Bowl
many other loose leaf varieties

MELONS

Alaska
Burpee Hybrid
Canada Gem Hybrid
Earli-dew
Earligold
Earliqueen
Earlisweet
Far North
Flyer
Minnesota Midget
Passport
Sweet Granite

WATERMELONS

Canada Supersweet
Mickylee
New Hampshire Midget
Stokes Sugar Hybrid
Sugar Baby
Sweet Favorite
Yellow Baby Hybrid

ONIONS

Northern gardeners should seek out long-day onion varieties.

Bingo
Buffalo
Canada Maple
Capable
Copra
Downing Yellow Globe
Eskimo
Evergreen Hardy
Giant White Sweet Spanish
Norsemen
Norstar
Prince
Purplette
Quicksilver Pearl
Red Giant
Riverside Sweet Spanish
Southport Red Globe
Southport White Globe
Snowbaby
Spartan Banner 80
Sweet Sandwich

(continued)

Vegetable Varieties for Cool Climates *(cont'd)*

ONIONS *(cont'd)*
Walla Walla
White Sweet Spanish
Yellow Sweet Spanish

PEAS
Alaska
Bounty
Daybreak
Dwarf Grey Sugar
Early Frosty
Early Sweet
Knight
Maestro
Montana Narvel
Oregon Sugar Pod II
Sparkle
Sugar Ann
Thomas Laxton
Wando

PEPPERS, HOT
Caliente
Cayenne Long
Early Jalapeño
Hot Stuff
Hungarian Hot Wax
Inferno
Karlo
Pretty in Purple
Twilight

PEPPERS, SWEET
All Hybrid
Big Bertha
California Wonder
Cubanelle
Earliest Red Sweet
Elisa Hybrid
Giant Szegedi
Gypsy Hybrid
Islander
Italia
Jingle Bells
Klondike Bell
Lady Bell
Lipstick
Ma Belle
Merrimack Wonder
North Star
Orobelle
Staddon's Select
Sweet Cherry
Sweet Chocolate
Vanguard
Yankee Bell
Yellow Bell

POTATOES
Alaska Frostless
Alaska Red
Alaska Sweetheart
Anoka
Bliss Triumph (a.k.a. Red Bliss)
Caribe
Cariboo
Centennial Russet
Chieftain
Dazoc
Denali
Glacier
Idita Red
Irish Cobbler
Kennebec
Norkota Russet
Norland
Onaway
Russian Banana
Sangre Red
Yukon Gold

SQUASH, SUMMER
Ambassador
Black Beauty
Butterbar
Cocozelle
Condor
Early Prolific Straightneck
Gold Rush
Grey Zucchini
Raven
Scallopini
Seneca
Sunburst
Sundance
Yellow Crookneck
Zucchini Select

SQUASH, WINTER, AND PUMPKINS
Autumn Queen
Baby Bear
Burpee Butterbush
Buttercup
Butternut
Connecticut Field
Early Golden Summer Crookneck
Ebony Acorn
Gold Nugget
Gold Rush
Jersey Golden Acorn
Mountaineer
New England Pie
Scallopini
Spaghetti
Sunburst
Table King
Tivoli
Waltham

TOMATOES
Bonner
Bonny Best
Daybreak
Dona
Earlirouge
Early Cascade

Early Girl
Farthest North
Fireball
Gem State
Glacier
Gold Dust
Ida Gold
Kotlas (Spirit)
Latah
Manitoba
Moira
Mountain Spring
Oregon Spring
Pixie Hybrid
Prairie Fire
Rocket
Sandpoint
Shoshone
Siberia
Starshot
Stokes Alaska
Stupice
Sub-Arctic Maxi
Sub-Arctic Plenty
Summerset
Swift
Whippersnapper

VEGETABLE VARIETIES FOR THE PACIFIC NORTHWEST

These varieties are suited to the cool, moist summers of this region.

ARTICHOKES

Green Globe

ASPARAGUS

Larac
UC 157

BEANS, SNAP AND SHELL

Blue Lake Pole
Blue Lake Venture
Cascade Giant
EZ Pick
Fortex
Golden Rocky
Goldmarie
Kentucky Blue
Kentucky Wonder Brown
Musica
Rapier
Royal Burgundy
Scarlet Emperor
Violet-Podded Stringless

BEETS

Detroit Supreme
Early Wonder Tall Top
Forono
Little Ball
Red Ace
Winterkeeper

BROCCOLI

Green Valiant
Minaret (romanesco)
Packman
Purple Sprouting
Rosalind
Shogun
Southern Comfort
White Sprouting Late

BRUSSELS SPROUTS

Lunet
Prince Marvel
Rider
Tardis
Vincent

CABBAGE

Charmant
Chieftain Savoy
Danish Ballhead
January King
Julius
Meteor
Ruby Ball
Salarite
Savonarch
Springtime
Winterstar
Wivoy

CARROTS

Armstrong
Danvers
Estelle
Merida
Mokum
Royal Chantenay
Thumbelina

CAULIFLOWER

Alpha Fortados
Arbon
Purple Cape
Ravella
Snow Crown
Vernon
Walcherin Varieties (a series)
White Rock

(continued)

Vegetable Varieties for the Pacific Northwest *(cont'd)*

CORN

Bodacious
D'Artagnan
Golden Jubilee
Precocious
Reward
Seneca Dawn
Seneca Horizon
Seneca Starshine
Sugar Buns
Sugar Dots
Sugar Snow
Sweet Treat

CUCUMBERS

Armenian
Cascade
GY 200
Lemon
Marketmore 76
Slicemaster Select
SMR 58

EGGPLANT

Bambino
Dusky Hybrid
Early Bird
Short Tom

KALE

Siberian
Westland Winter
Winterbor
Winter Red

LETTUCE

Buttercrunch
Continuity
Canasta
Little Gem
Majestic Red
Mascara
Red Sails
Salinas
Salad Bowl
Sierra
Slobolt
Valmaine
Winter Density

MELONS

Crimson Sweet
Earlidew
Earligold
Garden Baby
Iroquois
Jade Star
Passport
Pulsar
Sugar Baby
Yellow Doll

ONIONS

Buffalo
Cardinal
Crystal Wax
Early Yellow Globe
Foxy
Hi-Ball
Red Man
Stockton Early Red
Walla Walla
White Lisbon

PEAS

Alderman (Tall Telephone)
Dwarf White Sugar
Maestro
Mega
Oregon Giant
Oregon Pioneer
Oregon Sugar Pod
Oregon Trail
Snappy
Sugar Ann
Sugar Snap (and other snap peas)

PEPPERS, HOT

Early Jalapeño
Hungarian Hot Wax
Long Thin Cayenne
Serrano
Surefire

PEPPERS, SWEET

Chocolate Beauty
Early Cal Wonder
Golden Bell
Gypsy
Northstar
Peto Wonder
Purple Beauty
Staddon's Select

POTATOES

All Blue
Desiree
Yellow Finn

SQUASH, SUMMER

Black Beauty Zucchini
Butterstick
Gold Rush
Scallopini
Sunburst
Yellow Crookneck

SQUASH, WINTER, AND PUMPKINS

Buttercup
Cream of the Crop
Delicata
Hubbard
Jack Be Little
Small Sugar
Spirit
Sugar Loaf

Sweet Meat
Table King
Zenith

TOMATOES

Big Beef
Celebrity
Early Cascade
Early Cherry
Fantastic
Golden Delight
Golden Treasure
Kootenai
Large
Oregon Pride
Oregon Spring
Oregon Star
Prairie Fire
Stupice
Sweetie
Sweet Million

VEGETABLE VARIETIES FOR WARM CLIMATES

The varieties listed here are especially tolerant of heat, and are good choices for southern gardens.

BEANS, SNAP AND SHELL

Alabama Pole No. 1
Appaloosa
Aztec Scarlet Runner
Black Valentine
Commodore Improved
Dade (bred for South Florida)
Derby Bush
Kentucky Wonder
McCaslan
Pinto varieties
Poamoho
Rattlesnake
Romano
State White Half Runner
Tennessee Green Pod
Tepary bean varieties
Topcrop

BEANS, LIMA

Christmas (Giant Speckled Pole Lima)
Dixie Speckled Butter Pea (does well in hot, humid conditions)
Florida Butter (hot, humid)
Florida Speckled (hot, dry)
Fordhook 242
Henderson
Hopi Red
Hopi White
Jackson Wonder
Pima Beige

BEETS

Big Red
Detroit Dark Red
Early Wonder Tall Top
Pacemaker III

BROCCOLI

Baccus
Green Comet
Packman
Premium Crop
Waltham 29

BRUSSELS SPROUTS

Jade Cross
Royal Marvel
Valiant

CABBAGE

Early Jersey Wakefield
Green Cup
King Cole
Ruby Ball
Savoy King
Stonehead

CARROTS

Chantenay
Danvers Half Long
Gold Pak
Imperator
Lady Finger
Nantes
Royal Chantenay
Texas Gold Spike
Thumbelina
Touchon

CORN

Acoma Blue
Acoma White
Alamo-Navajo Blue
Ashworth
Calumet
Cocopa
Gila River
Golden Bantam
Golden Midget
Hopi Blue
Hopi Pink
Hopi Speckled
How Sweet It Is
Illini Chief
Isleta Blue

(continued)

Vegetable Varieties for Warm Climates *(cont'd)*

CORN *(cont'd)*

Merit
Navajo Gold
Navajo White
Navajo Yellow
Papago
Silver Queen
Texas Shoepeg
Yaqui
Yuman
Yuman Yellow

CUCUMBERS

Armenian
Dasher
Fancipak
Fanfare
Lemon
Little Leaf
Lucky Strike
Poinsett
Salad Bush
Slicemaster
Spacemaster
Straight Eight
Sweet Salad
Sweet Success

EGGPLANT

Black Beauty
Florida Market
Ichiban
Long Purple
Midnite
White Dourgas

LETTUCE

Anuenue
Bibb
Black-Seeded Simpson
Buttercrunch
Iceberg
Kagran Summer
Montello
Oakleaf
Parris Island Cos
Premier Great Lakes
Red Sails
Salad Bowl
Simpson Elite
Slobolt
Summer Bibb

MELONS

Ananas
Banana
Black Diamond (watermelon)
Bush Star Hybrid Cantaloupe
Caravelle
Chaca No. 1
Charleston Gray (watermelon)
Chimayo
Dixie Jumbo
Golden Beauty
Green Nutmeg
Hale's Best
Jumbo Hale's Best
Jubilee (watermelon)
Mission Hybrid
Navajo Yellow
New Mexico Melon
Perlita
Resistant
Rocky Ford
San Juan
Santo Domingo Mixed
Sugar Baby (watermelon)

MUSTARD

Florida Broadleaf
Savannah
Southern Giant Curled
Tendergreen (mustard spinach)

OKRA

Annie Oakley
Blondy
Burgundy
Clemson Spineless
Cowhorn
Dwarf Green Long Pod
Emerald Green
Lee
Louisiana Green Velvet
Perkins Long Pod Ribbed
Spineless Green Velvet

ONIONS

Gardeners in southern locations should grow short-day varieties.

California
Colossal PRR
Creole C-5
Granex 429
Granex Yellow PRR
New Mexico White Grano
Red Burgundy
Red Creole
Sweet Sandwich
Texas 1015Y Supersweet
Texas Grano 502
Texas Grano Valley Sweet
Vidalia Sweet
White Bermuda
White Granex
White Lisbon
White Sweet Spanish
Yellow Sweet Spanish

PEAS

Green Arrow
Little Marvel
Miragreen
Novella
Snow Flake
Sugar Ann

Sugar Snap
Wando

PEAS, SOUTHERN

Big Boy
Calico Crowder
California No. 5 Black Eye
Colossus
Cream 8
Dixie Lee
Lady
Magnolia
Mississippi Silverskin
Pink Eye Purple Hull
Suzanne
Texas Cream 40
Whipoorwill
White Acre
White Purple Hull Crowder
Zipper Cream

PEPPERS, HOT

Most chili peppers grow well in the hot, dry conditions of the Southwest. Those listed here can also take high humidity.

Anaheim
Ancho
Cayenne
Charleston Hot
Chilaca
Chimayo
Habanero
Hungarian Yellow Wax
Jalapeño
Jaloro
Long Slim Cayenne
MexiBell
Mirasol
New Mexico Big Jim
Pico de Gallo
Red Cherry Hot
Santo Domingo
Scotch Bonnet
Serrano
Tabasco

PEPPERS, SWEET

Big Bertha
Biscayne
California Wonder
Cal Wonder 300
Camelot
Cubanelle
Elisa
Gator Belle Hybrid
Gypsy Hybrid
Jupiter
Keystone Resistant Giant Sweet
Park's Whopper
Pimiento Sweet
Staddon's Select
Sweet Banana

SQUASH, SUMMER

Butterbar
Cocozelle
Dixie Hybrid Yellow Crookneck
Early Prolific Straightneck
Early Summer Crookneck
Early Yellow Straightneck
Goldbar
Gold Rush
Multipik
Peter Pan
President
Scallopini
Senator
Sunburst
Sun Drops
Tatume Summer
White Bush Scallop
Yellow Bush

SQUASH, WINTER, AND PUMPKINS

Acoma
Baby Bear
Big Max
Big Moon
Butternut
Cream of the Crop
Delicata
Hopi
Jack Be Little
Papalote Ranch Cushaw
Pink Banana
Red Kuri
Mayo Blusher
Mayo Segualca
Santo Domingo
Sweet Mama
Table Ace
Tahitian
Triple Treat
Turk's Turban

TOMATOES

Ace-Hy VFN (especially good in California)
Arkansas Traveler Improved (performs well in hot, humid conditions)
Bonny Best
Brandywine
Celebrity
Chico III
Earlirouge
Hayslip
Heatwave
Homestead
Hybrid Ace VFN
Kootenai
Landrey's
Manalucie F

(continued)

Vegetable Varieties for Warm Climates *(cont'd)*

TOMATOES *(cont'd)*

Manapal F (hot, humid conditions)
Oregon Spring
Porter's Pride
Rebel Red
Red Cherry Large
Solar Set
Stakebreaker
Surefire
Tropic (bred for Florida)
Walter
Whirlaway

BIGGEST VEGETABLES

These vegetables hold the current world records for size, according to *The Guinness Book of World Records:*

Cabbage: 124 pounds, grown in Great Britain in 1989

Carrot: 15 pounds, 7 ounces, grown in New Zealand in 1978. A carrot 6 feet $10^1/_2$ inches long was grown in Great Britain in 1991.

Celery: 46 pounds, 1 ounce, Great Britain, 1990

Cucumber: 20 pounds, 1 ounce, Great Britain, 1991

Garlic: 2 pounds, 10 ounces, California, 1985

Onion: 11 pounds, 2 ounces, Great Britain, 1992

Parsnip: $171^3/_4$ inches long, Great Britain, 1990

Potato: 7 pounds, 1 ounce, a tie. Both were grown in Great Britain, one in 1982 and one in 1963.

Pumpkin: 827 pounds, Washington, 1992

Radish: 37 pounds, 15 ounces, South Australia, 1992

Rutabaga: 48 pounds, 12 ounces, Great Britain, 1980

Squash: 821 pounds, New York, 1990

Tomato: 7 pounds, 12 ounces, Oklahoma, 1986

Zucchini: 64 pounds, 8 ounces, Great Britain, 1990

U.S. Records

Beet: 45 pounds, 8 ounces California, 1984

Collard: 35 feet tall, 62 inches wide, North Carolina, 1980

Corn: 31 feet tall, Iowa, 1946

Eggplant: 5 pounds, $5^1/_4$ ounces, South Carolina, 1984

Kohlrabi: 36 pounds, Michigan, 1979

Lima Bean: 14 inches, North Carolina, 1979

Onion: $7^1/_2$ pounds, Arizona, 1984

Pepper: $13^1/_2$ inches, New Mexico, 1975

Rutabaga: 39 pounds, Oregon, 1979

Sweet Potato: $40^3/_4$ pounds, Georgia, 1982

Zucchini: 19.92 pounds, Wisconsin, 1984

ALL-AMERICA SELECTIONS WINNERS

All-America Selections is an independent organization established in 1932 to test new varieties of vegetables, flowers, and bedding plants grown from seed. Plants are grown in a network of trial gardens across the United States, and evaluated by judges using a point scale. There are also public AAS display gardens across the country.

1933	Stringless Black Valentine bean
1933 *(cont'd)*	Stringless Green Pod bean
	Ohio Canner beet

1933 (cont'd)	Honey Rock cantaloupe
	Improved Perfecto cantaloupe
	Imperator carrot
	Clark's Special cucumber
	Giant Nobel spinach
	Pritchard tomato
	Graystone watermelon
1934	Asgrow Wonder beet
	Good for All beet
	Little Marvel beet
	Perfected Detroit beet
	Penn State Ballhead cabbage
	Morse's Bunching carrot
	Kingscrost Bantam corn
	Stowell's Evergreen Hybrid corn
	Barteldes cucumber
	Batavian Full Heart endive
	Peerless parsley
	Glowing Ball radish
1935	Just Right cabbage
	Imperial cantaloupe
	Hybrid Bantam corn
	Colorado cucumber
	Straight-8 cucumber
	L. S. White Boston lettuce
	Giant Southern Curled L. S. mustard
	Asgrow King pepper
	White Pearl radish
	Viking spinach
	Scarlet Dawn tomato
1936	Asgrow Canner beet
	Golden Colonel corn
1936 (cont'd)	Paramount parsley
	Confidence pea
	Comet radish
	Jewel radish
	Burpee Globe tomato
	Penn State tomato
1937	Earliest of All red cabbage
	Moskow Market Pride cabbage
	Claudia carrot
	Supreme Half-Long carrot
	Prizewinner endive
	Triumph of Prague kohlrabi
	Atlantic lettuce
	Yellow Valencia onion
	Canner King pea
	Teton pea
	Windsor A pepper
	Bloomsdale No. 5 spinach
	Darkie spinach
	Resisto spinach
	Summer Savory spinach
	Winter King spinach
1938	The Commodore bean
	Perfect Model beet
	Chieftan cabbage
	Sauerkraut King cabbage
	Spearhead lettuce
	Rocky Ford pepper
	Billiard Ball radish
	Del Monte spinach
	Early Prolific Straightneck squash
	Cardinal tomato
	Harkness tomato

(continued)

All-America Selections Winners *(cont'd)*

1939	Granada bean
	Plentiful bean
	Queen of Colorado cantaloupe
	Aristogold Bantam No. 1 corn
	EarPack Bantam 12-Row corn
	New Hampshire Hybrid eggplant
	Clemson Spineless okra
	White Lightning okra
	Top Notch pea
	Connecticut Straightneck squash
	Golden Table Queen
1940	Baby Potato lima bean
	Ioana corn
	Deep-Heart Fringed endive
	Evergreen parsley
	Fordhook pepper
	Mingold tomato
1941	Tenderpod bean
	Honey Gold cantaloupe
	Allegheny Hybrid corn
	Spancross Hybrid corn
	Cos-type Batavian endive
	Louisiana Green Velvet okra
	Sweet Banana pepper
	Yankee Hybrid squash
	Victor tomato
1942	Long Island Long pod bean
1942 *(cont'd)*	Medal Refugee bean
	Decatur bean
	Lincoln Hybrid Sweet corn
	Topflight Bantam Hybrid corn
	Cosbert 600 lettuce
	New York PW55 lettuce
	Fordhook Zucchini squash
1943	Cangreen Bush lima bean
	Potomac bean
	Marketer cucumber
	Early Pimiento pepper
	Jubilee tomato
1944	Keystonian bean
	Cubit cucumber
1945	Bush Early Market lima bean
	Bush Fordhook 242 lima bean
	Florida Belle bean
	Improved Commodore bean
	Goldengrain Hybrid corn
1946	Longreen bean
1947	Ranger Snapbean
	Erie corn
	Bronze Beauty lettuce
1948	Peerless lima bean
	Cherokee Wax bean
	Puregold Wax bean
	Supergreen bean
	Excel Bermuda onion

1948 (cont'd)	Freezonian pea
	Victory Freezer pea
1949	Triumph lima bean
	Ideal Snowball cauliflower
	Flagship corn
	Penlake lettuce
	Premier Great Lakes lettuce
	Cherry Belle radish
	Caserta squash
1950	Topcrop bean
	Unconn squash
	Congo watermelon
1951	O. S. Cross cabbage
	Granite State cantaloupe
	Big Mo corn
	Golden State corn
	Io chief corn
	Surecrop cucumber
	Prizewinner, C. L. S. mustard
	Urbana tomato
	New Hampshire Midget watermelon
1952	Stringless Hort Snapbean
	Wade bean
	Golden Delight cantaloupe
	Salad Bowl lettuce
	Vinedale pepper
	Allneck Cushaw pumpkin
	America spinach
1953	*no winners*
1954	*no winners*
1955	Seminole bean
	Pennsweet cantaloupe
	Golden Beauty Hybrid corn
1956	Gold Pak carrot
1957	Greencrop bean
	Ruby Queen beet
	Smoothie cucumber
	Greenwave mustard
	Champion radish
	Black Beauty squash
1958	Choctaw Wax bean
	Pearlgreen bean
	Ruby lettuce
1959	Gardengreen Snap bean
	Jade Cross brussels sprouts
1960	Just Right turnip
1961	*no winners*
1962	*no winners*
1963	Executive bean
	Emerald Cross cabbage
	Buttercrunch (Bibb) lettuce
	Greyzini zucchini squash
	Hercules Butternut squash
1964	Cleopatra broccoli
	Zenith broccoli
1965	Savoy King cabbage
	Samson cantaloupe
	Triumph cucumber
	Chefini squash

(continued)

All-America Selections Winners *(cont'd)*

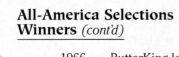

1966	ButterKing lettuce
	Gold Nugget squash
1967	Bell Boy pepper
	Spring Giant tomato
1968	Spartan Valor cucumber
1969	Green Comet broccoli
	Harvester Queen cabbage
	Stonehead cabbage
	Snow King cauliflower
	Kindred squash
	St. Pat Scallop squash
	Tokyo Cross turnip
1970	Waltham Butternut squash
	Small Fry tomato
1971	Red Head Cabbage
	Early Xtra Sweet corn
1972	Ruby Ball cabbage
	Victory cucumber
1973	Aristocrat Zucchini squash
1974	Goldcrop bean
	Bush Acorn Table King squash
1975	Premium Crop broccoli
	Snow Crown cauliflower
	Yellow Baby watermelon
1976	*no winners*
1977	Savoy Ace cabbage
	Spirit pumpkin
	Melody spinach
	Scallopini squash
1978	Liberty cucumber
	Floramerica tomato
	Sweet Favorite watermelon
1979	Saladin cucumber
	Grand Duke kohlrabi
	Sugar Snap pea
	Dutch Treat pepper
	Early Butternut squash
	Sweet Mama squash
1980	Gold Rush squash
1981	Gypsy pepper
1982	Jersey Golden Acorn squash
	Peter Pan squash
1983	Sweet Success cucumber
1984	Sugar Ann pea
	Celebrity tomato
1985	Red Sails lettuce
	Sunburst squash
1986	How Sweet It Is corn
	Blondy okra
1987	Autumn Gold pumpkin
1988	Honey 'n Pearl corn
	Salad Bush cucumber
	Burgundy okra
	MexiBell pepper
	Super Chili pepper
1989	*no winners*
1990	Derby bean
	Super Cayenne pepper
	Cream of the Crop squash
	Sun Drops squash

1991	Kentucky Blue bean	1993	Baby Bear pumpkin
	Tivoli squash		Husky Gold tomato
	Golden Crown watermelon	1994	Fanfare cucumber
1992	Thumbelina carrot		Big Beef tomato
	Fernleaf dill	1995	*no winners*

BEST-TASTING TOMATOES

Taste is subjective, of course, but here are 15 tomato varieties noted for especially good flavor. Most are heirlooms (introduced before 1940), but a few contemporary hybrids also make the cut.

Bonny Best
Brandywine, an Amish heirloom variety widely acclaimed as the best-tasting tomato of all
Burpee's Delicious
Celebrity VFFNTA Hybrid
Costoluto Genovese
Dona VFFNT Hybrid
Johnny's 361
Marglobe
Marmande
Persimmon
Pink Ponderosa
Pruden's Purple
Rutgers
Sweet 100
Tappy's Finest

HOW HOT ARE HOT PEPPERS?

There are chili peppers and there are chili peppers. Some are mildly pungent, some are hot, and some are downright incendiary. Here is a basic guide to the relative heat of 40 chili pepper varieties available from American seed companies.

MILDLY HOT

Anaheim
Ancho (called "poblano" when picked green)
Big Jim
Hungarian Yellow Wax
Italian White Wax
Karlo
Mexi Bell Hybrid
Mulatto
New Mexico #6
Pimiento

MEDIUM HOT

Ancho 101
Caliente
Cascabel
Guajillo

(continued)

How Hot Are Hot Peppers? *(cont'd)*

MEDIUM HOT *(cont'd)*

Hungarian Cherry
Hungarian Rainbow Wax
Hungarian Wax
NuMexico Sunrise
NuMexico Sunset
Vallero

FIERY

Aji
Cherokee
Centennial
Dr. Greenleaf Red Hot Tabasco
Fire!
Fresno
Habanero (the hottest of all; many times hotter than jalapeño)
Jalapeño
Large Red Thick Cayenne (cayennes are hotter than jalapeño, but not as hot as habanero)
Long Red Slim Cayenne
Louisiana Hot
Peter Pepper
Pretty Purple Pepper (hotter than jalapeño when ripe)
Serrano
Stripe
Super Cayenne Hybrid
Super Chili (hotter than jalapeño, but not as hot as cayenne)
Tabasco
Tiny Samoa
Twilight

COLLECTING AND SAVING SEEDS

You can save seeds of nonhybrid varieties of vegetables and other plants to preserve heirloom varieties no longer available commercially, to enjoy incomparable flavor or better hardiness or characteristics not available in modern hybrids, or to develop a strain that is particularly well adapted to your location (by saving seeds of the best plants in your garden over several plant generations).

WHICH SEEDS TO SAVE?

You can collect and save seeds of nonhybrid or open pollinated varieties. Such plants reproduce by self-pollination (if the plants contain both male and female flowers or the flowers contain both male and female parts), or by pollination with pollen from others of their kind.

Do not collect seed from F-1 hybrids. These hybrids are produced by crossing two parent species, and their seed will not produce a second generation of plants identical to its parents. (See chapter 2 for additional information.)

TIPS ON COLLECTING AND SAVING SEEDS

1. If you are growing more than one variety of a species, in most cases you must isolate the variety for which you want to save seeds, to prevent cross-pollination between the varieties. To isolate a variety:

    - Plant varieties that mature at different times and will not be blooming together.

- Plant the variety far away from other varieties of the species (1/4 mile is enough for most vegetables and flowers).
- Enclose the plants in wire mesh cages or cover them with cheesecloth or floating row covers to prevent cross-pollination. Pollinate the plants yourself, or introduce appropriate pollinators into the enclosure if feasible. Cover the plants before the flowers open and do not uncover them until seeds have formed.

2. Collect seeds when they are fully mature.
    - Take seeds from fruiting crops (such as tomatoes, melons, and eggplant) when the fruit is very ripe—even overripe—but before it starts to rot.
    - Collect seeds of beans, peas, and grains when they (and the pods) are fully dry.
    - Gather seed heads from herbs and other seeds in small capsules before they shatter and drop from the plant. Check every day as the seeds ripen, or tie paper bags (with a few holes for aeration) around the seed containers to catch the seeds when they fall.
3. Clean seeds carefully before storage. Remove them from the fruit or pods, and wash them in clear water.
4. Let seeds dry thoroughly before storing, or they may rot.
5. Store seeds in airtight containers, labeled, in a cool, dry place (the refrigerator works fine).

STORAGE LIFE OF VEGETABLE SEEDS

Below is the average number of years seeds remain viable if properly stored.

Asparagus	3 years	Corn	2	Parsnips	1
Beans	3	Corn salad (mache)	5	Peas	3
Beets	4	Cress	5	Peppers	2
Broccoli	3	Cucumbers	5	Radishes	5
Brussels sprouts	4	Eggplant	4	Rutabagas	4
Cabbage	4	Endive	5	Salsify	1
Carrots	3	Kale	4	Scorzonera	2
Cauliflower	4	Kohlrabi	3	Sorrel	4
Celeriac	3	Leeks	2	Southern peas	3
Celery	3	Lettuce	6	Spinach	3
Chard, Swiss chard	4	Muskmelon	5	Squash and pumpkins	4
Chicory	4	Mustard	4	Tomatoes	4
Chinese cabbage	3	Okra	2	Turnips	4
Collards	5	Onions	1	Watermelon	4

Source: Knott's Handbook for Vegetable Growers, *2nd edition, Oscar A. Lorenz and Donald N. Maynard. John Wiley & Sons, 1980*

OPEN-POLLINATED AND HEIRLOOM VARIETIES

An excellent source of information on nonhybrid vegetable varieties and their availability is *Garden Seed Inventory*, compiled by Kent Whealy, 3rd edition, 1992. The book lists all nonhybrid varieties known to be available in the United States, along with sources of seeds. Order from Seed Saver Publications, 3076 N. Winn Rd., Decorah, IA 52101. $22 paperback, $28 hardcover, postpaid.

Below are listed some readily available varieties from which you can save seeds.

ARTICHOKE

Green Globe

ASPARAGUS

Mary Washington

BEANS, SNAP AND SHELL

Appaloosa Goose
Blue Lake, Blue Lake Stringless
Bountiful
Canada Wild Goose
China Yellow (Sulphur)
Commodore
Contender (Buff Valentine)
Cranberry
Dragon Tongue
French Navy
Golondrinas
Great Northern
Green Crop
Hopi Black
Hopi Pinto
Hopi Purple
Hopi Yellow
Jacob's Cattle
Kentucky Wonder
Kentucky Wonder Wax
King Mammoth Horticultural
Landreth Stringless
Low's Champion
Maine Yellow Eye
Pencil Pod Black Wax
Pinto
Potomac
Ram's Horn
Red Lazy Wife
Red Montezuma
Rocquencourt
Romano
Royal Burgundy
Royalty Purple Pod
Scarlet Runner
Soldier
Stringless Black Valentine
Taos Red
Taylor's Dwarf Horticultural
Tenderette
Tongues of Fire
Topcrop
Turkey Craw
Venture
Vermont Cranberry
White Dutch Runner
Yaqui String

BEANS, LIMA

Christmas (Large Speckled Calico)
Cliff Dweller
Fordhook 242
Henderson's Bush
Hopi Gray
Hopi Red
Hopi White
Hopi Yellow
Illinois Giant
Jackson Wonder Butterbean
King of the Garden
Pima Beige
Willow Leaf White
Worchester Indian Red Pole

BEETS

Albino
Chioggia
Crosby's Egyptian
Cylindra
Detroit Dark Red
Early Wonder
Edmund's Blood
Golden
Long Season
Ruby Queen

BROCCOLI

De Cicco
Italian Green Sprouting (Calabrese)
Romanesco
Spartan Early
Waltham 29

BRUSSELS SPROUTS

Long Island Improved (Catskill)
Rubine Red

CABBAGE

April Green
Blue Max (savoy type)
Charleston Wakefield
Chieftain Savoy
Copenhagen Market

Danish Ballhead
Early Dutch Round
Early Jersey Wakefield
Early Marvel
Emerald Acre
Golden Acre
Greyhound
January King (savoy)
Lasso (red)
Meteor (red)
Premium Late Flat Dutch
Primax Early
Quick Green Storage
Red Acre (red)

CARROTS

Chantenay
Danvers 126
Danvers Half Long
Imperator
Little Finger
Minicor (Amsterdam Minicor)
Nantes
Nantes Touchon
Oxheart
Scarlet Nantes
Sucram

CAULIFLOWER

Alert
Dominant
Early Snowball
Purple Giant
Self Blanche
Snow's Overwintering

CHICORY

Castelfranco
Catalogna
Grumolo Dark Green
Rossa di Treviso (Red Treviso)
Rossa di Verona (Red Verona)
Variegata di Castelfranco
Witloof

COLLARDS

Georgia Blue Stem
Morris Improved Heading
Southern
Vates

CORN

Acoma Blue
Acoma White
Apache Red
Ashworth
Black Aztec
Black Mexican
Bloody Butcher
Chemehuevi
Cocopah
Early Pearl
Extra Early Bantam
Fisher's Earliest
Gila River
Golden Bantam
Golden Jubilee
Guarijio Red
Hickory King
Hopi Blue
Hopi Chinmark
Hopi Pink
Hopi Speckled
Jemez Blue
Jemez White
Navajo Gold
Navajo White
Navajo Yellow
Shoepeg (Country Gentleman)
Stowell's Evergreen
Tennessee Red Cob
Texas Shoepeg
Tom Thumb
Yaqui Blue

CUCUMBERS

Armenian
Black Diamond
Boston Pickling
Chicago Pickling
Lemon
Marketmore 76
Marketmore 80
Marketmore 86
National Pickling
Poinsett 76
Small Paris
Spacemaster
Straight Eight
Suyo Long
White Wonder

EGGPLANT

Baby White Tiger
Black Beauty
Casper
Chinese White
Early Black Egg
Early Long Purple
Florida Market
Italian Pink Bicolor
Long White Sword
Pallida Romanesca
Rosa Bianca
Snake Eye
Sweet Red
Thai Green
White Egg

ENDIVE

Broad-leaved Batavian (escarole)
Green Curled Ruffec
President

KALE

Blue Siberian
Green Marrowstem
Greenpeace
Marrowstem
Ragged Jack
Russian Red

(continued)

Open-Pollinated and Heirloom Varieties *(cont'd)*

KALE *(cont'd)*

Vates Dwarf Blue-Curled Scotch
Walking Stick

KOHLRABI

Early Purple Vienna
White Vienna

LETTUCE

All-Year-Round (butterhead)
Black-Seeded Simpson (looseleaf)
Buttercrunch (butterhead)
Butterking (butterhead)
Capitan (butterhead)
Cosmo (romaine)
Deer Tongue, a.k.a. Matchless (looseleaf)
Grandpa Admires (butterhead)
Grand Rapids (looseleaf)
Hanson (crisphead)
Kagran Summer (butterhead)
Little Gem, a.k.a. Sugar Cos (romaine)
Lollo Rossa (looseleaf)
Marvel of Four Seasons (butterhead)
May King (butterhead)
Mignonette Bronze (butterhead)
Mignonette Green (butterhead)
New York, a.k.a. Wonderful (crisphead)
Oak Leaf (looseleaf)
Parris Island Cos (romaine)
Prizehead (looseleaf)
Red Grenoble (looseleaf)
Reine de Glace (crisphead)
Ruby (looseleaf)
Salad Bowl (looseleaf)
Sierra (crisphead)
Slobolt (looseleaf)
Summertime (crisphead)
Tennis Ball (butterhead)
Tom Thumb (butterhead)
White Boston (butterhead)
Winter Density (romaine)

MELONS

Ananas
Blenheim Orange
Casaba
Charantais
Chimayo
Crenshaw
Delicious
Edisto 47
Golden Gopher
Hale's Best Jumbo
Harvest Queen
Honeydew
Iroquois
Jenny Lind
Kangold
Kansas
Marygold
Medium Persian
Minnesota Midget
Navajo Yellow
Nutmeg
Old Time Tennessee
Pike
San Juan
Sweet Granite

WATERMELON

Charleston Gray
Dixie Queen
Hopi Red
Hopi Yellow
Ice Cream
Mayo
Moon and Stars
Mountain Hoosier
Stone Mountain
Strawberry
Yellow Crimson

MUSTARD

Florida Broadleaf
Fordhook Fancy
Green-in-Snow
Osaka Purple
Red Giant
Southern Giant Curled

OKRA

Burgundy
Clemson Spineless
Dwarf Green Long Pod
Gold Coast
Perkins Mammoth Long Pod
Star of David
White Velvet

ONIONS

Beltsville Bunching
Burgundy
Creole C-5
Crystal Wax
Downing Yellow Globe
Evergreen Long White Bunching
Italian Red Torpedo
New York Early
Purplette
Red Giant
Red Mac
Red Wethersfield
Ruby
Southport White Globe
Texas Grano 502
Vidalia Sweet
Walla Walla Sweet
White Bermuda
White Lisbon
Wonder of Pompeii

PEAS

Alaska
Blue Pod
Corvalette Bush
Dwarf Grey Sugar
Golden Sweet Vine
Improved Laxton's Progress
Lincoln
Little Marvel
Mammoth Melting Sugar
Novella
Oregon Sugar Pod
Sugar Snap
Tall Telephone
Wando

PEPPERS, HOT

Anaheim Chili
Ancho
Aurora
Chilaca
Chimayo
Cochiti
Hades Hot
Hungarian Wax
Jalapeño
Large Red Cherry Hot
Long Red Cayenne
Louisiana Hot
Mirasol
Negro
Pico de Gallo
Ring of Fire
Sandia
Tabasco
Vallero

PEPPERS, SWEET

Bull Nose (Large Bell, Sweet Mountain)
California Wonder
Cubanelle
Earlired
Early California
Gambro
Red Cherry (Large Sweet Cherry)
Rooster Spur
Roumanian Sweet
Staddon's Select
Sweet Chocolate
Sweet Pimiento
World Beater (Ruby Giant)
Yankee Bell
Yellow Cheese

POTATOES

Abnaki
Acadia Russet
All-Blue
Aylesbury Gold
Belle de Fontenay
Beltsville
Bevelander
Blue Christie
Caribe Sport
Caribou
Cascade
Champion
Conestoga
Cowhorn Purple Flesh
Dark Levitt's Pink
Early Gem
Early Vermont
Epicure Red Banana
Erstling
Eureka Purple
Favorite Red
French Yellow
Gold Coin
Green Mountain
Housa
Hindenberg
Hudson
Huron
Irish Treasure
Kerry Blue
Long Blue Andean
Lonlac
Minnesota Russet
Newfoundland Elephant
Newfoundland Jumbo
Norway
Ogonok
Pioneer
Poorlander
Pressman's German
Prestile
Purple Baker
Purple Rose
Red Beauty
Red Thumb
Rhine Red
Rosa Yellow Pear
Rose Gold
Saginaw Gold
Ute Russet
Viking Red
Ware's Pride
White Bliss
White Elephant
White Rose
Yellow Dutch
Yellow Finn
Yellow Idaho
Yukon Gold

RADISHES

Champion
Cherry Bell
China Rose
Comet
Early Scarlet Globe
Flame
French Breakfast
Giant White Globe
Long Black Spanish
Long White Icicle
Mammoth White
Round Black Spanish
Sparkler

(continued)

Open-Pollinated and Heirloom Varieties *(cont'd)*

SPINACH

America
Bloomsdale Dark Green
Bloomsdale Long Standing
Broadleaved Summer
Giant Noble
King of Denmark

SQUASH, SUMMER

Benning's Green Tint
Black Zucchini
Dark Green Zucchini
Early Prolific Straightneck
Golden Bush Scallop
Golden Zucchini
Patty Pan (White Bush Scallop)
Wood's Earliest Prolific
Yellow Crookneck
Yellow Custard

SQUASH, WINTER, AND PUMPKINS

Acoma Pumpkin
Atlantic Giant
Big Max
Blue Banana
Blue Hubbard
Buttercup
Chesnut
Connecticut Field
Delicata
Elfrida
Etampes
Fordhook Acorn
Golden Cushaw
Golden Hubbard
Gold Nugget
Hopi Pumpkin
Idaho Gem
Little Gem
Jack Be Little
Magdalena Big Cheese
Mooregold
Pima Bajo
Pink Banana
Sibley
Small Sugar (New England Pie)
Spaghetti
Sugar Baby
Table Queen
Waltham Butternut
Young's Beauty

TOMATOES

Arkansas Traveler
Beefsteak (Crimson Cushion)
Bonny Best
Brandywine
Burbank
Cherokee Purple
Dad's Mug
Dad's Sunset
Delicious
Dinner Plate
Dutchman
Gem State
German
Giant Paste
Golden Queen
Goldie
Great White
Green Grape
Hayslip
Ida Gold
Lemon Boy
Marglobe
Marmande
Mortgage Lifter
Nepal
Nova
Oxheart
Peron
Persimmon
Pineapple
Ponderosa Red
Ponderosa Yellow
Principe Borghese
Pruden's Purple
Red Cherry
Red Currant
Red Pear
Roma
Ruffled Yellow
Rutgers
San Marzano
Stone
Striped German
Stupice
Sundrop
Super Italian Paste
Tappy's Finest
Tigerella
Tiny Tim
Valencia
Watermelon Beefsteak
Yellow Belgium
Yellow Currant
Yellow Marble
Yellow Pear

TURNIPS

All Seasons
Amber Globe
Ohno Scarlet
Presto
Purple Top White Globe
White Egg
Yellow Globe

SOURCES OF NONHYBRID SEEDS

Seeds of heirloom and open-pollinated varieties of vegetables and other plants are available from the following sources. Read catalogs carefully—open-pollinated varieties can be found in the catalogs of other companies as well. Addresses for these companies are given in Appendix 5.

- Abundant Life Seed Foundation
- Bountiful Gardens
- The Cook's Garden
- Deep Diversity
- Down on the Farm Seed
- Fox Hollow Herb and Heirloom Seed Co.
- Garden City Seeds
- Gleckler's Seedmen
- Heirloom Garden Seeds
- High Altitude Gardens
- J. L. Hudson, Seedsman
- Liberty Seed Company
- Native Seeds/SEARCH
- Nichols Garden Nursery
- Old Sturbridge Village Museum Gift Shop
- Plants of the Southwest
- Redwood City Seed Company
- Ronninger's Seed Potatoes
- Seed Savers Exchange
- Seeds Blum
- Seeds of Change
- Shepherd's Garden Seeds
- Southern Exposure Seed Exchange
- Thomas Jefferson Center for Historic Plants
- Tomato Grower's Supply Company

ORNAMENTAL VEGETABLES

The varieties listed here are especially decorative in the garden, and interesting in the kitchen as well.

ARTICHOKE

Purple Sicilian and Violetto: Large edible flower buds are deep reddish purple

BEANS

Dragon Tongue: Yellow pods striped in bronze
Scarlet Runner Bean: Brilliant scarlet flowers and deep green leaves
Royal Burgundy and Royalty: Purple pods and lavender blossoms
Trionfo Violetto: Deep lavender flowers, purple-veined leaves, purple pods

(continued)

Ornamental Vegetables *(cont'd)*

BEETS

Albino: White roots

Burpee's Golden: Golden-yellow roots

BROCCOLI

King Purple and Purple Sprouting: Purple heads

Romanesco: Conical chartreuse heads with florets arranged in a spiral pattern

BRUSSELS SPROUTS

Rubine or Rubine Red: Deep burgundy leaves

CARDOON (*Cynara cardunculus*)

Large silvery leaves with toothed, deeply cut edges

CAULIFLOWER

Purple Cape, Purple Giant, and Violet: Purple heads

CHARD

Rhubarb: Red stems and red-veined leaves

CHICORY

Radicchio chicories such as Giulio, Palla Rossa, Rouge de Verone (Red Verona), Early Treviso, and Red Treviso produce deep burgundy heads, with white-veined leaves. Castelfranco is marbled red and white.

CORN

Variegata: Variegated leaves

Chinook, Red Stalker, and Wampum: Have colored kernels. Wampum also has purple and red stalks.

Zea mays var. *japonica* and var. *japonica* 'Quadri-color': These are ornamental corns with leaves striped with white and yellow, and sometimes pink

CUCUMBER

Lemon ripens to bright yellow

EGGPLANT

Black Prince: Dark lavender fruit

Pink Bride: Lavender and white

Pinky: Large, purple-pink fruits on small plants

Rosa Bianca: Lavender to white

Small Sweet Red: Ripens to rich red

Violette de Firenze: Lavender, sometimes with white stripes

White Beauty, White Egg, White Knight, and Bush White: White fruit

Eggplants also have pretty lavender-purple flowers

FLORENCE FENNEL (*Foeniculum vulgare* var. *dulce*)

Fine, feathery foliage that can act like a theater scrim in the garden

FLOWERING CABBAGE AND KALE

Also known as ornamental cabbage and kale: The plants form large rosettes of blue-green leaves flushed and veined with creamy white or bright red-violet, the colors intensifying in cold autumn weather. Kale varieties have frillier leaves. Not as tasty as conventional garden varieties, but edible.

GREENS

Curly Mallow (*Malva verticillata*): 4 to 6 feet tall, large lobed leaves have curly edges

KALE

Coral Queen: Deep red leaves

Ragged Jack: Red leaves

KOHLRABI

Early Purple Vienna, Purple Danube, Purple Vienna, and Rapid have dusty purple bulbs

LETTUCE

Red-leaved varieties include Lollo Rossa, Red Deer Tongue, Red Grenoble, Red Majestic, Red Riding Hood, Red Sails, Red Salad Bowl, Rosy, Rouge d'Hiver, Ruby, and Selma Lollo

MUSTARD

Giant Red and Osaka have burgundy-colored leaves

Mizuna: Narrow, light green leaves with toothed, frilly, deeply cut edges

Red Giant: Crinkly leaves are dark red-purple with white midrib

OKRA

Burgundy: Deep purple-red pods and stems, pretty yellow flowers

ORACH

Red Orach: Leaves of rich, deep red

(continued)

Ornamental Vegetables *(cont'd)*

PEAS

Golden Sweet: Yellow pods

PEPPERS

Albino and Alwin: White fruit ripens to orange where the growing season is long enough

Aurora: Hot pepper that changes from lavender to orange to red as it ripens

Earliest Red Sweet and Earlired: Ripen to red earlier and in a shorter season than most peppers

Islander, Lilac Belle, and Purple Beauty: Purple, eventually ripening to red. Lorelei, Purple Bell, and Violetta are also purple

Golden Bell and Tequila Sunrise: Orange fruit

Twilight: Chili pepper that begins purple, changes to yellow, and turns red when ripe

POTATOES

Blossom: Tubers are red inside; plants have large pink or white flowers

RADISHES

Easter Egg: Roots are shades of pink, lavender, white, or purple, with white flesh

Pink Beauty: Rosy pink skin and white interior

Plum Purple: Dark purple skin and white flesh

RHUBARB

Plants have decorative red stalks and large, sculptural leaves.

Victoria: If you let it bloom it sends up tall plumes of little ivory flowers

SEA KALE (*Crambe maritima*)

Large blue-green leaves and sprays of small white flowers

SQUASH

Golden and Goldrush zucchini are yellow

Jersey Golden Acorn and Orobelle: Ripen orange

TOMATOES

Golden Boy, Golden Jubilee, Goldie, Gold Nugget, Hybrid Lemon Boy, Mandarin Yellow Cross, Persimmon, Ponderosa Yellow, and Yellow Pear: Yellow to orange fruit

Golden Pygmy: A yellow-fruited cherry tomato

Tigerella: Red-and-yellow-striped fruit

White Beauty: White fruit

BABY VEGETABLES

Listed here are some varieties suitable for use as baby vegetables. Some produce small fruits; others can be harvested when quite young.

BEANS, SNAP
Camile
Dandy
Finaud
Fin des Bagnols
Label
Marbel
Royal Burgundy
Triomphe de Farcy

BEETS
Burpee's Golden
Dwergina
Little Ball (Little Mini Ball)
Spinel

CARROTS
Baby Orange
Baby Sweet Hybrid
Kinko
Lady Finger
Little Finger
Minicor
Parmex
Planet
Sucram
Sweet Cherry Ball
Sweetness

CORN
Baby Corn

CUCUMBERS
French cornichon varieties (can be picked quite young)

EGGPLANT
Baby White Tiger
Easter Egg
Little Fingers
Mini Finger
Pirouette
Purple Pickling
Slim Jim

FLOWERING CABBAGE AND KALE
Miniature Flowering Kale
Miniature Japanese Ornamental Cabbage

LETTUCE
Baby Oak
Little Gem
Sucrine
Summer Baby Bibb
Tom Thumb

PAC CHOY
Mei Quing Choy (Baby Pac Choy)

PEPPER
Canape

PUMPKIN
Jack Be Little

SQUASH, SUMMER
Aristocrat
French White Bush
Gold Rush
Peter Pan
Seneca
Sunburst
Sun Drops

TOMATOES
Gem State
Gold Nugget
Pixie Hybrid
Red Cherry
Red Currant
Sundrop
Tiny Tim
Yellow Currant

CONTAINER VEGETABLES

Here are some vegetable varieties especially well suited to the confined conditions of container growing.

BEANS
Romano
Royal Burgundy
Venture

BEETS
Most beet varieties grow well in pots; small-rooted and round types work better than the longer slicing varieties

CABBAGE
Blue Max
Earliana
Lasso

(continued)

Container Vegetables *(cont'd)*

CABBAGE *(cont'd)*

Primax
Ruby Ball

CARROTS

Baby Finger
Gold Pak
Kinko
Little Finger
Minicor
Parmex
Planet
Sweet Cherry Ball
Thumbelina

CUCUMBERS

Bush Pickle
Bush Whopper
Park's Burpless Bush
Patio Pik
Pot Luck
Salad Bush
Spacemaster

EGGPLANT

Bambino
Neon
Orient Express
Pirouette
Slim Jim
Thai Green

GREENS

Most leafy greens grow well in pots. Consider:

Arugula
Chicory
Collards
Corn salad (mache)
Cress
Kale
Lettuce (especially looseleaf varieties)
Mustard
Sorrel

PEPPERS

Most sweet and hot pepper varieties are suitable for container culture. Especially good ones include:

Ace
Bell Boy
Keystone Resistant
New Ace
Red Cherry
Sweet Banana
Thai Hot

RADISHES

Early small-rooted radishes are great for containers. Winter storage radishes can also be grown in pots but need deep containers (at least 12 inches deep).

SQUASH

Look for bush varieties, such as:

Burpee Golden Zucchini
Burpee Butterbush
Butter Swan
Cream of the Crop
Green Magic
Table King

TOMATOES

Determinate varieties are better for containers than indeterminate types. Consider the following in particular:

Better Bush
Bitsy VF
Cherry Gold
Dwarf Champion
Husky Gold
Husky Pink
Husky Red
Lunch Box
Pixie Hybrid II
Red Robin
Stakeless
Tiny Tim
Yellow Canary

WATERMELON

Garden Baby
Golden Midget

Vegetables for Shade

For definitions of partial and light shade, see pages 49–50.

Arugula, partial shade
Beans, best in full sun, but tolerate partial shade
Beets, partial shade
Broccoli, partial shade
Brussels sprouts, partial shade
Cabbage, partial shade
Cauliflower, partial shade
Celery, partial shade
Chard, partial to light shade
Cress, partial to light shade
Endive and escarole, partial to light shade
Garlic, partial shade
Kale, partial shade
Kohlrabi, partial shade

Leeks, partial shade

Lettuce

- Head, partial shade
- Leaf, partial to light shade

Parsnips, partial shade

Peas, partial shade

Potatoes, partial shade

Radishes, partial to light shade

Rutabagas, partial shade

Salsify, partial shade

Spinach, partial to light shade

Squash, summer, best in full sun but tolerates partial shade

Turnips, partial shade

FASTEST MATURING VEGETABLES

The following vegetables are the quickest to mature. The list gives the approximate number of days from seed to the beginning of the harvest. In addition to the vegetables listed here, look for early varieties of other crops when you want to start picking as soon as possible.

Arugula: 35–40 days

Beans: Early bush varieties, 50

Beets: 55–65

Broccoli: Early varieties, 55

Carrots: Early varieties, 50

Cauliflower: Early varieties, 50

Chard: 50

Cress: 30–40

Cucumbers: Early pickling varieties, 50

Kohlrabi: 50–60

Lettuce, looseleaf varieties: 40–50

Mustard: 35–55

Okra: 50–60

Onions, for use as scallions: 45–60

Peas: Early varieties, 55

Radishes: 20–30

Spinach: 35–45

Squash: Summer, 40–50

SEASON-EXTENDING TECHNIQUES

To extend the growing season, you must create a protected environment where conditions are more moderate than those in the open garden. Creating a warmer environment lets you plant earlier in spring and continue harvesting later in fall. You can also extend the season for spring crops into summer by creating a cooler environment with protection from the sun.

GARDEN DESIGN

Plant on a gentle south-facing slope, or make a series of raised garden beds angled toward the south. Do not plant in the sunken areas between beds—cold air will collect there. A 5 percent slope (one that falls 5 feet over a distance of 100 feet) creates garden conditions equivalent to those 30 miles south of your location, and gains you a couple of days of extra growing time in spring and fall.

COLD FRAMES

A cold frame—a bottomless box with a clear or translucent cover, that is set on the ground or over a sunken bed—can extend the growing season by 1 to 3 months.

Spring: Use the frame to start seedlings, grow early crops, harden off seedlings.

Summer: Remove the lid and use as a nursery bed to start fall crops or perennials from seed.

Autumn: Extend the harvest of summer crops, grow salad greens and other compact cool-weather crops.

Winter: Extend the harvest of autumn crops, propagate trees and shrubs from cuttings; fill the cold frame with dry leaves or straw and use it to store root vegetables.

You can buy a cold frame but it is simple to build your own. The sides can be wood, cinder block, or brick. Portable frames have wood or aluminum frames and clear sides.

The covers (and clear sides) can be acrylic, Plexiglass, UV-stabilized polyethylene attached to a frame, or glass. Old storm windows are excellent tops and last longest. Polyethylene lasts only a few seasons. A heavier-duty option is PolyWeave—8 mil polyethylene reinforced with woven nylon mesh; it transmits 90 percent of available sunlight, lasts up to five seasons, and protects to 25°F.

Cold frames should face south. The back wall should be a few inches higher than the front wall, so the top will be angled for maximum sun exposure. Good drainage is essential—standing water is deadly to plants. A thermometer inside is helpful. The frame should be opened when the temperature insides reaches 65°–75°F.

Cold Frame Modifications

Soil heating cables (with a built-in preset thermometer) create a warmer environment, ideal for starting seeds in spring.

Insulating the sides and top in very cold weather extends the harvest well into winter. Insulate with foam panels inside, bags of leaves, bales of hay, or old blankets outside.

An automatic, solar-powered vent opener—available from various mail-order sources—will open the lid automatically when the temperature inside is too warm.

Temporary cold frame. Stack bales of hay around plants you want to prot^ct; cover with old storm windows.

PLASTIC TUNNELS

Called "hoop greenhouses" when made on a large scale, these can extend the season 6 to 8 weeks in spring and in fall.

To make one, stretch plastic sheeting over a series of sturdy wire or plastic hoops. Use 4 or 6 mil polyethylene or copolymer sheeting with an ultraviolet inhibitor. Cut slits in the sides for ventilation or leave ends open for ventilation except on very cold or windy nights.

PLASTIC TENTS

Throw a sheet of plastic over a trellis or frame made of wood or metal poles, to make a tent to protect a group of plants. Less convenient than tunnels, but creates similar effects.

STORM WINDOWS

Lean old storm windows against the south wall of the house to create small protected areas.

FLOATING ROW COVERS AND GARDEN BLANKETS

Made of lightweight fabric, these covers are simply laid loosely over plants. They protect the plants from frost damage to 28°F (though damage may occur to parts of plants touching the fabric), transmit 85 percent of the available sunlight, and are also permeable to air and water. After about 20 weeks of use, light begins to weaken the fibers, and the covers need to be replaced.

When danger of frost is past, temperatures under the covers are about 10°F warmer than the open air at night, 5°F warmer during the day.

Cover Materials

Reemay: Spunbonded polyester
Agryl P17: Spunbonded polypropylene
Agronet: Fine mesh made of polypropylene and nylon

Uses for Covers

- To speed growth of young plants early in the season, when the soil is warm enough for planting. They do not warm the soil but provide a protected environment for seedlings, producing a harvest 1 to 2 weeks earlier than normal.
- To slow evaporation of moisture from the soil
- To protect plants from damage due to strong wind and heavy rain
- To keep pests off of plants.
- To protect late summer crops from light fall frost, extending the harvest. (Note: Keep tomatoes and other fruit from touching the fabric)

Installation

- Cut the covers to fit the area you want to protect.
- Drape the covers loosely over plants, to allow room for growth.
- Fasten the edges with U-shaped metal pins, or weight them down with stones, bricks, boards, or soil.

INFRARED MULCH

Infrared mulch is a transparent but dark-colored plastic mulch that absorbs heat to warm the soil and also keeps down weeds. It is useful for giving an early start to tender crops such as melons, tomatoes, peppers, corn, and squash in cool climates.

Cut planting holes big enough to allow water to penetrate to the plant roots, because the plastic is impermeable to moisture.

CLOCHES AND HOT CAPS

These devices protect individual plants, or just a few plants at a time. Using them can add 3 to 4 weeks to the growing season. You simply set them over the plants when it's cold, and lift them off in warm weather. The smaller the cloche, the faster it will overheat. Remove on sunny or mild days.

Glass cloches. Made from two panes of glass held together with special metal clips in an A-frame structure. Line them up to protect a row of plants. Place a pane of glass at either end during very cold weather to make a closed structure. Bell jar cloches to protect individual plants are also available.

Plastic jugs. Cut the bottom out of plastic milk or spring water jugs for homemade cloches. Unscrew the cap to allow ventilation when the outdoor temperature is 32°F or higher. In very cold weather, cover cloche and all with loose mulch 1 to 1½ feet deep for extra protection.

Protective cylinders. Make cylinders or tall boxes of wire mesh fencing and wrap with polyethylene sheeting (4, 6, or 8 mil). Or wrap plastic around a tomato cage. Or make cylinders from plastic with wire mesh embedded in it. Or you can make cylinders or tunnels from sheets of bendable fiberglass.

Wall O'Water. Tepee made of a series of hollow polyethylene tubes joined together. You set the tepee over the plant to enclose it, and fill the tubes with water (each device holds about 3 gallons). During the day, the water absorbs heat from the sun, so temperatures inside the tepee don't get too high. Wall O'Water is supposed to be able to hold up to 900,000 calories of heat. At night, the water slowly releases the heat, keeping temperatures inside the device warmer than the outside air. Gather the top of the tepee together on very cold nights. If the water starts to freeze, it releases additional heat. Wall O'Water protects plants to a temperature of 10°F and lasts three to five years with proper use.

SHADE NETTING

Shade netting shields plants from intensely hot sun, to postpone bolting and prolong the harvest of spring crops in summer. Netting made of polyethylene or polypropylene provides 50 percent shade. Look for UV-treated netting for longer life.

Knitted shade fabrics are available to provide 30, 40, 50, 60, 70, 80, or 90 percent shade, and come in white, green, blue, or black.

Support shade netting on wire or plastic hoops, or a series of low wood stakes.

Chapter 9

FRUIT

BEST SITE

The best location for fruit is a place in full sun, with deep, well-drained, fertile soil rich in organic matter. Avoid a location exposed to frequent strong wind, or frost pockets at the bottom of a hill. If you live in the North, where the growing season is short, a gentle slope facing south to southeast will provide maximum sun exposure and make the most of the short season. In more southerly regions, a north-facing slope is a better bet. It will discourage plants from beginning to grow in the first spells of mild weather and lessen the chance that fruit blossoms will be damaged by a late frost.

The ideal soil pH for apples and pears is mildly acid to neutral, 6.0 to 7.0. Cherries, peaches, and plums prefer acid soil with a pH of 5.5 to 6.5

PLANTING SYSTEMS FOR FRUIT

BUSH AND SMALL FRUITS

- Plant in rows or hedgerows (double rows); train grapes and trailing brambles on wire trellises.
- Treat individual plants as specimens (stake brambles).
- Plant strawberries by the matted row or hill method (see "Planting and Caring for Bush and Small Fruits," next).

TREE FRUIT

If you are planning an orchard, several accepted methods of laying it out ensure both that you plant trees at the recommended distance apart, and that no space is wasted.

- Square: Divide the orchard into a grid of squares, and plant a tree in each corner of the squares. The size of the squares is determined by space needed for each tree.
- Quincunx: Like the square, but with an additional tree planted in the center of each square.
- Triangular: Plant one tree in each corner of an equilateral triangle. This allows more trees per acre than square or quincunx spacing.
- Hedgerow: Dwarf trees can be planted in a double row; allow enough space between them to harvest, prune, and do other maintenance.
- Contour or terrace planting: For a hillside orchard, use a series of level terraces running across the slope (you will need professional help to construct the terraces).
- Self-fruitful varieties can be planted by themselves as specimen trees (see page 453).

PLANTING AND CARING FOR BUSH AND SMALL FRUITS

Blackberry (*Rubus* spp.). Includes dewberry, loganberry, youngberry

Planting: Plant 1 to 3 feet apart in rows.
Tolerates most soils except acid or soggy and poorly drained.

Growing: Keep plants mulched throughout the growing season.

Pruning: When first-year canes of erect-growing varieties grow 3 to 5 feet tall, cut back tips by 3 to 4 inches, to stimulate branching.

When canes finish bearing in their second year, cut back to the ground. Remove the prunings to prevent disease.

Allow canes of trailing varieties to trail over the ground in their first year. In the late winter, before the second year of growth begins, prune canes to 10 feet and fasten to a trellis of one or two wires. Arrange the canes in large loops to allow maximum sun exposure.

When canes bear fruit, prune back to the ground as soon as harvest is complete.

Gardeners growing dewberries (southern blackberries) may prune all canes—both first and second year—back to ground after harvest to prevent disease.

Problems: If a virus or other disease strikes, immediately remove and dispose of infected plants.

Blueberry (*Vaccinium ashei*, rabbiteye; *V. corymbosum*, *V. australe*, highbush blueberry). Growing range: rabbiteye blueberry in the southeastern United States, highbush blueberries in the eastern United States, from Maine to Florida and west to Arkansas up to Michigan.

Planting: Plant in reasonably fertile, moist but well-drained acid soil—pH below 5.0 for highbush, pH to 5.5 for rabbiteye.

Plant in spring, rabbiteye plants 7 to 8 feet apart, highbush 6 feet apart.

Growing: Mulch with oak leaves or other acid material.

Pruning: At planting, prune back bushes by one-quarter, and remove any bushy growth near base of plants.

When plants mature, each year prune off oldest canes (5 or 6 years old). Remove twiggy growth from younger canes. Also remove any shoots that form late in summer.

Currant (*Ribes nigrum*, black currant; *R. sativum*, red currant). Currants are a host for white pine blister rust and growing them is prohibited in parts of the United States. Check with your County Cooperative Extension agent, and if necessary, obtain a growing permit from the nursery where you purchase plants.

Planting: Plant in spring or fall, 5 to 6 feet apart. Prune back at planting time to 5 to 6 inches.

Currants tolerate a range of soil types from sandy loam to clay, and mildly acid to mildly alkaline pH. A moist but well-drained soil is ideal. Plants tolerate partial to light shade, but may develop mildew in less than full sun.

Pruning: After 3 years, remove the oldest branches while plants are dormant, in late winter. Remove 3-year-old branches each year to keep a constant supply of productive younger growth.

Problems: Buy certified disease-free stock. Do not plant currants within 900 feet of any white pines.

Raspberry (*Rubus occidentalis*, eastern black raspberry; *R. leucodermis*, western black raspberry; *R. strigosus*, red raspberry).

Planting: If planting both red and black varieties, locate them at least 300 feet apart to prevent cross-pollination.

Raspberries tolerate a range of soil types, as long as the soil is well-drained. Mildly acid pH is best.

Plants grow best on a single-wire trellis with the wire 3 feet above the ground. Space plants 2 to 3 feet apart in rows 6 feet apart. Or the plants can be set as close as 15 inches apart to shade out weeds.

Plant with the crown just below the soil surface. Firm the soil around the plant and water well. When plants show new growth, remove the old cane.

Planting in raised beds prevents phytophthora root rot and increases yields.

Growing: Mulch during the growing season, and in late fall for winter protection. Plants need sun to partial shade.

Water thoroughly once a week in midsummer if weather is dry.

Pruning: Black raspberries: Prune the tips so the canes do not bend over and root. When the harvest is completed, cut the fruiting canes back to the ground. When this year's canes grow 3 feet tall, prune the tips to encourage formation of lateral stems. The following spring, prune back the laterals to 10 inches. If necessary, thin new canes to allow 3 or 4 per foot of row.

Red and yellow raspberries, summer-bearing: When the harvest is finished, cut all the old fruiting canes back to the ground. If necessary, thin young canes to allow 3 or 4 per foot of row. Remove suckers. In spring, thin the plants again to leave canes 6 inches apart. Cut back the canes to 36–40 inches.

Red and yellow raspberries, everbearing: When summer harvest is complete, cut the fruiting canes to the ground, or wait until fall. Also remove the weakest younger canes. After fall harvest, either cut all canes back to the ground, or tip prune the canes just finished bearing to leave them about 36 inches high.

Strawberry (*Fragaria* spp.). Everbearing varieties are appropriate only where summers are not too severe and the season is not too short—Zones 5 to 8.

Planting: Plant in light, fertile, moist but well-drained soil rich in organic matter, with a mildly acid pH. Soil should be well tilled to reduce the threat of problems from weeds, grass, and insect larvae in the soil.

Plant in spring, as soon as the soil can be worked.

Matted row method: Space the plants 18 inches apart in rows 3 feet apart, with the crowns right at soil level. Allow runners to form. After plants bear in their second year, remove or plow under the plants and start with new plants the third year.

Hill method: Set the plants 12 inches apart in 3 rows 12 inches apart, to create a bed. Remove runners as soon as they form. Mulch well. This method requires more work, but plants continue to produce for several years.

Everbearing varieties: Plant as you would regular varieties.

Growing: With either method, remove flowers during the first year so the plants do not set fruit (which would seriously weaken the plants).

Everbearing varieties: In the first year, pick off all flowers until mid-summer, then allow the plants to bloom to produce a fall harvest.

Mulch strawberries deeply in winter, starting when the temperature dips to 15° to 20°F and continuing until it remains above 25°F in spring. Use straw or other loose mulch. Cover the plants during late spring frosts, especially if the plants are blooming.

SMALL FRUIT VARIETIES

For the North

BLACKBERRIES

Ebony King, hardy to Zone 5
El Dorallo, to Zone 4
Darrow, Zone 4
Illini, Zone 5

BLUEBERRIES

Bluecrop, hardy to Zone 4
Bluegold, to Zone 4
Bluehaven, Zone 5
Bluejay, Zone 4
Dwarf Tophat, Zone 4
Herbert, Zone 4
Jersey, Zone 5
Late Blue, Zone 4
Lowbush blueberry (*Vaccinium angustifolium*), Zone 2
Nelson, Zone 4
Northblue, Zone 3
Northcountry, Zone 3 or 4
Northland, Zone 3
Ornablue, Zone 4
Patriot, Zone 3
Rancocas, Zone 3
Saskatoon, Zone 3
Sierra, Zone 4
Tophat, Zone 4

CURRANTS

Alpine currant (*Ribes alpinum*), hardy to Zone 2
Black September, to Zone 4
Cherry (Cherry Red), Zone 3
Consort, Zone 4
Golden currant (*R. aureum*), Zone 2
Red Lake, Zone 2
White Imperial, Zone 3
White Pearl, Zone 3
Wilder, Zone 3

RASPBERRIES

Amity, hardy to Zone 3
August Red, to Zone 4
Boyne, Zone 2 or 3
Brandywine, Zone 4
Canby, Zone 4
Fall Gold, Zone 4
Fall Red, Zone 4
Festival, Zone 3
Heritage, Zone 4
Jewel, Zone 4
Latham, Zone 3
Mammoth Red Thornless, Zone 4
Munger, Zone 4
Nootka, Zone 3
Nordic, Zone 3

(continued)

Small Fruit Varieties *(cont'd)*

For the North *(cont'd)*

RASPBERRIES *(cont'd)*

Redwing, Zone 3 or 4
Royalty, Zone 4
Sunrise, Zone 4

STRAWBERRIES

Alpine strawberries (*Fragaria vesca*), hardy to Zone 4
Blomiden, to Zone 3
Catskill, Zone 3 or 4
Crimson King, Zone 4
Cyclone, Zone 4
Dunlap, Zone 4
Empire
Fort Laramie, Zone 4
Gilbert
Glooscap
Holiday, Zone 4
Honeoye, Zone 3 or 4
Jewel
Kent, Zone 3
Pink Panda, Zone 3
Red Coat, Zone 3
Red Glow, Zone 3
Sparkle
Surecrop, Zone 4
Sweetheart, Zone 3
Trumpeter, Zone 4
Veestar, Zone 3

For the South

These varieties are recommended for gardens in warm climates.

BLACKBERRIES

Black Satin, hardy as far south as Zone 9
Brazos, to Zone 9
Comanche, Zone 9
Dirksen, Zone 10
Flordagrand, Zone 10
Navaho, Zone 10
Roseborough, Zone 9
Smooth Stem, Zone 9
Thornfree, Zone 9

BLUEBERRIES (HIGHBUSH VARIETIES)

Avonblue, hardy south to Zone 9
Burlington, to Zone 10
Cape Fear, Zone 10
Sharpblue, Zone 10
Sunshine Blue, Zone 10

BLUEBERRIES (RABBITEYE VARIETIES)

Zone 6 or 7 is the northern limit of the rabbit-eye range, depending upon the variety.

Aliceblue, hardy south to Zone 9
Beckyblue, to Zone 9
Bluebell, Zone 10
Brightwell, Zone 9
Briteblue, Zone 10
Centurion, Zone 9
Chaucer, Zone 9
Choice, Zone 9
Climax, Zone 9
Delite, Zone 10
Powder Blue, Zone 9
Premier, Zone 9
Southland, Zone 10
Tifblue, Zone 9
Woodard, Zone 9

RASPBERRIES

Cumberland, hardy south to Zone 9
Dormanred, to Zone 9

STRAWBERRIES

Arking, hardy south to Zone 8
Atlas, to Zone 9
Cardinal, Zone 9
Chandler, Zone 9
Florida 90, Zones 8–9 only

Floridabelle, Zone 9
Pajaro, Zone 9
Pink Panda, Zone 9
Sequoia, Zone 9
Surecrop, Zone 8
Tennessee Beauty, Zone 8
Tioga, Zone 9

Disease-Resistant Small Fruit

BLUEBERRIES
Brazos
Dirksen
Premier
Snyder
Currants
Cherry
Coronet
Crusader

RASPBERRIES
Amity
Black Hawk
Bristol
Dundee
Everbearing Fall Red
Fall Gold
Jewel
Killarney
Latham
Royalty (resistant to aphid that carries virus)
Taylor

STRAWBERRIES
Cardinal
Dunlap
Earliglow
Glooscap
Guardian
Honeoye
Ogallala
Ozark Beauty
Red Chief
Selva
Surecrop

GRAPES

Vitis spp. and hybrids, American grapes, European-American hybrids, muscadine grapes; *V. vinifera* hybrids, French wine grapes

Planting: Look for one-year-old plants when purchasing stock. The best soil is loamy, fertile, and rich in organic matter, and is well-drained, with a slightly acid to neutral pH. Viniferas need a long growing season and semi-arid conditions.

Plant in late winter or early spring, as soon as the soil can be worked. Space muscadines 9 to 10 feet apart, or grow on an arbor. Space other varieties 8 feet apart in rows 6 feet apart, or follow spacing directions from nursery.

Trim back the roots to 6 inches. Spread out the lowest group of roots in the bottom of the planting hole, cover with fine soil, and tamp. Spread the upper roots over the soil, cover them, and tamp. Water well to settle the soil around roots, then fill the rest of the hole with soil.

At planting time, prune off all but the 2 or 3 strongest canes on each plant, and cut back the remaining canes to 2 to 4 buds.

Growing: Water only during dry spells, if the leaves begin to droop. Mulch for winter protection north of Zone 9.

Pruning: The first winter, cut off all but the sturdiest cane on each plant. Cut back the remaining cane to 3 or 4 buds. In spring, when the new shoots are a foot long, remove all but the strongest shoot growing from each bud.

THE KNIFFEN SYSTEM OF GRAPE CULTURE

You will need a two-wire trellis to train the vines. Position the first wire 2 feet above the ground, and the second wire 5 feet above the ground.

During the second year of growth, allow 4 side branches to develop, 2 in each direction from the main stem. Train the branches on the trellis wires. Remove all buds that will encourage growth in other directions.

In the third year, let 4 more stems grow from buds on the main stem. Last year's canes should bear fruit this year. Late in the following winter, prune off the old canes that produced fruit. Fasten the third-year stems to the wires and let 4 new canes grow in the fourth year.

Each year you will train 4 new canes to replace the old ones after they bear.

GRAPE VARIETIES

Disease-Resistant Varieties

Aurora
Baco Noir
Buffalo
Concord
Cowart
Daytona
Dixie
Glenora
Jumbo
Lake Emerald
Lakemont Seedless
Mars
Ontario
Reliance
Steuben
Stover
Suffolk Red Seedless
Venus
Villard Blanc

Wine Grapes

By general agreement, European wine grapes—viniferas—grow well only in particular areas of the country, primarily parts of the West Coast and the California wine country, the lake country in upstate New York, and the North Fork of eastern Long Island. Wine grapes are also grown in parts of Pennsylvania, New Jersey, and Maryland. American varieties and French-American hybrids are better choices for gardeners in most of the United States.

The varieties listed here are recommended for winemaking.

- Aurora
- Baco Noir (Baco No. 1)
- Beta
- Cabernet Sauvignon
- Catawba
- Cayuga
- Chardonnay
- Concord
- Edelweiss
- Foch (Kuhlmann 1882)
- Fredonia
- Gewurztraminer
- Grey Riesling
- Merlot
- Moore's Diamond
- Niagara
- Pinot Chardonnay
- Seibel 5279
- Seibel 9549
- Seyve (Seyve-Villard 5276)
- Stover
- Villard Blanc
- White Riesling

Table Grapes

These varieties are excellent for fresh use.

- Alden
- Buffalo
- Canadice
- Concord, Concord Seedless
- Daytona
- Delaware
- Edelweiss
- Fredonia
- Golden Muscat
- Glenora
- Himrod
- Interlaken
- Lake Emerald
- Lakemont
- Mars
- Mississippi Blue
- Muscadine varieties (see list of grapes for the South)
- Niagara
- Ontario
- Red Flame
- Reliance
- Remaily
- Romulus
- Saturn
- Schuyler
- Seneca
- Steuben
- Stover
- Suffolk Red
- Van Buren
- Vanessa
- Venus
- Worden

Grape Varieties for the North

Canadice, Zones 4–7 or northern 8
Cayuga, Zones 4–7
Concord, Zones 4–8
Concord Seedless, Zones 4–9
Delaware, Zones 4–7
Edelweiss, Zones 4–8
Foch, Zones 4–7
Himrod, Zones 5 or southern 4–8
Ontario, Zones 4–7
Red Canadice, Zones 4–8
Reliance, Zones 4–8
Reliance Pink Seedless, Zones 4–8
Schuyler, Zones 4–7
Seyve, Zones 4–7
Swenson Red, Zones 4–8
Valiant, Zones 3–8
Van Buren, Zones 3 or 4–7
Worden, Zones 4–7

Grape Varieties for the South

Blue Lake, Zones 5–9
Carlos (muscadine), Zones 7–9
Cowart (muscadine), Zones 7–9
Daytona, Zones 8–10
Dixie (muscadine), Zones 7–9
Fry (muscadine), Zones 7–9
Higgins (muscadine), Zones 7–9
Jumbo (muscadine), Zones 7–9
Lake Emerald, Zones 7–9
Magnolia (muscadine), Zones 8–9
Magoon (muscadine), Zones 7–9
Noble (muscadine), Zones 7–9
Red Flame (Flame), Zones 8–9
Scuppernong (muscadine), Zones 7–9
Southland (muscadine), Zones 7–9
Stover, Zones 7–9
Summit (muscadine), Zones 7–9
Triumph (muscadine), Zones 7–9
Villard Blanc, Zones 6–9
Welder (muscadine), Zones 8–9

TREE FRUIT VARIETIES

For the North

Hardiness depends in part on the root stock on which the fruiting top growth is grafted. Varieties not listed here may be available on hardy root stocks that allow them to be grown farther north than usual. Look for other hardy varieties in regional nursery catalogs.

APPLES

Adanac, hardy to Zone 2
Alexander, to Zone 2
Ashmead's Kernel, Zone 3
Autumn Arctic, Zone 2
Beacon, Zone 3
Breakey, Zone 2
Chenango Strawberry, Zone 3
Connell Red, Zone 3
Cortland, Zone 4
Crimson Beauty, Zone 2
Duchess of Oldenburg, Zone 3
Early Harvest, Zone 2
Egremont Russet, Zone 3
Fireside, Zone 3
Freedom, Zone 3
Golden Russet, Zone 3
Haralson, Zone 2
Heyer 20, Zone 2
Hibernal, Zone 2
Honeygold, Zone 2
Jonamac, Zone 2

(continued)

PRODUCTION, TREE LIFE, AND START OF BEARING OF VARIOUS FRUIT TREES

FRUIT TREE	YEARS FROM PLANTING TO BEARING	USEFUL LIFE IN YEARS	ESTIMATED PRODUCTION PER TREE AT		
			3 years	6 years	10 years
Apples					
Dwarf	2 to 4	10 to 15	0 to 2 pecks	1 to 2 bushels	3 to 5 bushels
Semi-dwarf	3 to 4	15 to 20	0 to 2 pecks	1 to 3 bushels	4 to 10 bushels
Spur type	3 to 4	15 to 20	0 to 2 pecks	1 to 3 bushels	2 to 4 bushels
Standard	4 to 6	15 to 20	none	0 to 2 bushels	5 to 15 bushels
Apricot					
Standard	3 to 5	15 to 20	0 to 1 peck	1 to 2 bushels	2 to 4 bushels
Nectarine					
Standard	2 to 3	10 to 15	1 to 2 pecks	1 to 3 bushels	3 to 5 bushels
Peach					
Standard	2 to 3	10 to 15	1 to 2 pecks	1 to 3 bushels	3 to 5 bushels
Pear					
Dwarf	3 to 4	10 to 15	0 to 2 pecks	1 to 2 bushels	1 to 3 bushels
Plum					
Standard	3 to 5	15 to 20	0 to 2 pecks	1 to 2 bushels	3 to 5 bushels
Sour cherries					
Meteor, North Star, and Suda Hardy	2 to 3	10 to 15	0 to 1 peck	1 to 2 pecks	2 to 3 pecks
Standard	3 to 5	15 to 20	0 to 1 peck	2 to 4 pecks	8 to 12 pecks
Sweet cherry					
Standard	4 to 7	15 to 20	none	0 to 3 pecks	8 to 16 pecks

Tree Fruit Varieties *(cont'd)*

For the North *(cont'd)*

APPLES *(cont'd)*

Lord's Seedling, Zone 3
Macoun, Zone 4
Maiden's Blush, Zone 2
McIntosh, Zone 4
Morden 363, Zone 2
Niagara, Zone 2
Norland, Zone 3
Northern Lights
Northwestern Greening, Zone 2
Oriole, Zone 3
Parkland, Zone 2
Peach, Zone 3
Prairie Spy, Zone 2
Primate, Zone 2
Red Astrachan, Zone 3
Red Duchess of Oldenburg, Zone 3
Red Gravenstein, Zone 2
Rosthern 15, Zone 2
Rosthern 18, Zone 2
Spartan, Zone 4
State Fair, Zone 3
Sweet Sixteen, Zone 2
Tolman Sweet, Zone 2
Viking, Zone 3
Vista Bella, Zone 2
Wealthy, Zone 2
Westland, Zone 3
Williams, Zone 3
Wolf River, Zone 2
Yellow Transparent, Zone 2

APRICOTS

Manchu, hardy to Zone 4, or warmer parts of Zone 3
Moonglow, to Zone 4 or southern Zone 3
Scout, Zone 4
Sungold, Zone 4 or southern Zone 3

CHERRIES

Meteor, hardy to Zone 4, or protected locations in Zone 3
Montmorency, to Zone 4
Morello, Zone 4
North Star, Zone 4
Richmond, Zone 4 or southern Zone 3
Suda Hardy, Zone 4

PEACHES

Reliance, hardy to Zone 5 or protected locations in Zone 4
Sunapee, to Zone 4
Veteran, Zone 5

PEARS

Bartlett, hardy to Zone 5 or southern Zone 4
Clapps Favorite, to Zone 4
Flemish Beauty, Zone 3
Golden Sweet, Zone 4 or southern Zone 3
Harvest Queen, Zone 4
Kosui, Zone 4
Lincoln, Zone 4
Luscious, Zone 4 or southern Zone 3
Maxine, Zone 3
Mendel, Zone 3
Nova, Zone 3
Parker, Zone 3
Patton, Zone 3
Seckel, Zone 5 or protected locations in Zone 4
Ure, Zone 3
Yakumo, Zone 4

PLUMS

Ember, hardy to Zone 3
Pipestone, to Zone 3
Redcoat, Zone 3
South Dakota, Zone 4
Toka, Zone 3
Underwood, Zone 3
Waneta, Zone 3

For the South

APPLES

Anna, hardy south to Zone 9
Black Twig
Dorsett Golden, to Zone 9
Ein Sheimer, Zones 8–9 only
Golden Delicious, Zone 9
Gordon, Zone 9
Granny Smith, Zone 9
McIntosh, Zone 9
Red Delicious, Zone 9
Reverend Morgan, Zone 9
Stayman Winesap, Zone 8
Tropical Beauty
White Winter Pearmain
Winesap, Zone 8
Yates, Zone 9

FIGS

Black Mission, Zones 7–10 only
Brown Turkey, Zones 7–10
Celeste, Zones 7–10
Texas Everbearing, Zones 7–10

NECTARINES

Desert Dawn, hardy south to Zone 9
Durbin, to Zone 9
Sun Red, Zones 8–9 only

PEACHES

Flordahome, Zones 8–9 only
Florida King, Zones 8–9 only
Junegold, hardy south to Zone 9
La Feliciana, Zones 8–9 only
Suwanee, Zones 7–9 only

PEARS

Baldwin, hardy south to Zone 9
Pineapple, Zones 8–9 only

PERSIMMONS

Fuyugaki, Zones 8–9 only
Giant Fuyu, Zones 8–9 only
Hachiya, Zones 8–9 only
Jiro, Zones 7–9 only
Saijo, Zones 7–9 only
Tanenashi, Zones 8–9 only

PLUMS

Bruce, Zones 7–9 only
Burbank, hardy south to Zone 9
Crimson, to Zone 9
Methley, Zone 9
Ozark Premier, Zone 9
Santa Rosa, Zone 9
Satsuma, Zone 9
Shiro, Zone 9

Self-Fruitful Varieties

The varieties listed below do not require a pollinator variety in order to set fruit.

APPLES

Ein Sheimer (produces better when 2 trees are planted)
Grimes Golden
Jon-A-Red
Jonathan
Moorpark (produces better when 2 trees are planted)
Stark Golden Delicious
Starkspur Red Roma Beauty
Yellow Delicious

APRICOTS

Giant Sureset
Goldcot
Goldkist
Hungarian Rose
Katy
Manchu
Manchurian Bush Apricot
Moongold

(continued)

Self-Fruitful Varieties *(cont'd)*

APRICOTS *(cont'd)*

Parfait Plumcot (apricot–plum hybrid)
Sungold
Wilson Delicious

CHERRIES

Black Beauty
Earlimont
Hansen
Lapins
Meteor
Montmorency
Nanking
North Star
Starkrimson
Stella

NECTARINES

Gulf Pride
Mericrest
Nectacrest
Stark Delicious
Stark Sunglo

PEACHES

Belle of Georgia
Champion White
Desertgold
Elberta
Flordahome
Florida King
Golden Jubilee
Gulf Queen
Hale Haven
Junegold
La Feliciana
Madison
Old Fashioned Rochester
Polly
Red Globe
Red Haven
Reliance
Rich Haven
Starking Delicious

PEARS

Kieffer
Seckel (produces better with cross-pollination)
Stark Honeysweet

PLUMS

Big Blue
Damson
Dwarf Mount Royal
Earliblue
Fellemberg
Green Gage
Methley
Stanley
Yellow Egg

POLLINATOR VARIETIES

Apples

Yields are better, even for self-fruitful varieties, when two or more are planted.

Crab apples, Cortland, Golden Delicious, Jonathan, Red Delicious, Rome Beauty, and Starkspur EarliBlaze are good pollinators. In warmer regions Dorsett Golden and Granny Smith are two good pollinators.

Baldwin, McIntosh, Mutsu, Northern Spy, and Winesap should not be planted as pollinators for other varieties.

Apricots

Most apricots are self-fruitful and can be planted by themselves.

Perfection and Riland need a pollinator.

Cherries

Sour or pie cherries are self-fruitful.

Stella, Lapins, and Starkrimson are self-fruitful sweet cherries. Two especially good pollinators are Van and Stark Gold.

Bing will not cross-pollinate with Emperor Francis or Napoleon (Royal Anne).

Peaches and Nectarines

Most peaches are self-fruitful except for J. H. Hale, but even self-fruitful varieties produce bigger crops when another variety is planted nearby. Plant J. H. Hale with any other variety.

Nectarines are generally self-fruitful and do not need a pollinator.

Pears

Most pears need cross-pollination, and even self-fruitful varieties produce better with a pollinator.

All pear varieties will pollinate each other except for Bartlett and Seckel. Do not plant these two varieties together unless you also plant a third variety for pollination.

If you grow Asian pears, plant another Asian variety for pollination.

Plums

Many plums need pollinators.

European and Japanese plums do not cross-pollinate well; plant two European varieties or two Japanese varieties.

DWARF AND GENETIC DWARF VARIETIES

Many standard tree fruits are available in dwarf form, grafted onto dwarfing rootstocks. The varieties listed here are specially bred for compact size, and most can be grown in containers.

APPLES

Apple Babe
Garden Delicious
Stark Royal Gala
Spur-type varieties

APRICOT

Aprigold
Garden Annie
Stark Goldenglo

CHERRIES

Garden Bing
Hansen's Bush Cherry
North Star

(continued)

Dwarf and Genetic Dwarf Varieties *(cont'd)*

PEACHES AND NECTARINES

Bonanza (peach)
Com-Pact Redhaven (peach)
Dwarf Fingerlakes (peach)
Dwarf Mericrest (nectarine)
Garden Beauty (nectarine)
Garden Delight (nectarine)
Garden King (nectarine)
Garden Sun (peach)
Gold Treasure (peach)
Honey Babe (peach)
Nectacrest (nectarine)
Nectar Babe (nectarine)
Stark HoneyGlo (nectarine)
Stark Sensation (peach)

PEAR

Shinseiki

DISEASE-RESISTANT TREE FRUIT

APPLES

Anoka
Beacon
Bonnie-Best
Bramley's Seedling
Calville Blanc d'Hiver
Dayton
Duchess of Oldenburg
Freedom
Golden Russet
Haralson
Jefferis
Jerseymac
Jonafree
Jonathan
Keepsake
King David
Liberty
Lodi
MacFree
Macoun
Mutsu Crispin
Red Baron
Roxbury Russet
Spartan
Summer Rambo
Wealthy
York Imperial

CHERRIES

Compact Stella
Meteor
Montmorency
North Star

NECTARINES

Durbin
Mericrest

PEACHES

Belle of Georgia
Curlfree
Elberta
Junegold
La Feliciana
Red Haven
Sweethaven
White Champion

PEARS

Ayers
Harrow Delight
Kieffer
Luscious
Maxine
Moonglow
Nova
Orient
Pineapple
Seckel
Tyson

HEIRLOOM APPLES

Interested in old-fashioned apples? Consider the varieties listed below. All are readily available from U.S. sources.

Alexander
Ashmead's Kernel
Baker Sweet
Blue Pearmain
Bottle Greening
Bramley's Seedling
Calville Blanc d'Hiver
Champlain
Chenango Strawberry
Claygate Pearmain
Cornish Gilliflower
Cox's Orange Pippin
Davey
Discovery
Doctor Matthews
Duchess of Oldenburg
Dudley
Dyer
Early Harvest
Early Joe
Edward VII
Egremont Russet
Gloria Mundi
Golden Noble
Golden Pearmain
Golden Russet
Gravenstein
Grimes Golden
High Top Sweet
Hubbardston Nonesuch
Irish Peach
James Grieve
Jefferis
Kandil Sinap
Katja
Kidd's Orange Red
Lady
Laxton Superb
Lords Seedling
Lowland Raspberry
Lubsk Queen
Lyman's Large Summer
Maiden's Blush
Mother
Opalescent
Peck's Pleasant
Pink Pearl
Pound Sweet
Primate
Ralls Janet
Ramsdell Sweet
Red Astrachan
Red June
Rhode Island Greening
Ribston Pippin
Richard Delicious
Roman Stem
Ross Nonpareil
Roxbury Russet
Sheepnose (Black Gilliflower)
Smokehouse
Snow Apple (Fameuse)
Somerset of Maine
Sops of Wine
Spitzenberg
Summer Rambo
Summer Rose
Sutton Beauty
Tolman Sweet
Tompkins Country King
Twenty Ounce Pippin
Tydeman's Early
Wagener
Wealthy
Westfield Seek-No-Further
Williams
Winter Banana
Winter White Pearmain, oldest known English apple, grown since at least A.D. 1200

(continued)

Heirloom Apples *(cont'd)*

Wismer's Dessert
Wolf River
Yates
Yellow Newtown Pippin (Newtown Pippin)
York Imperial

APPLE FLAVORS

Tart Apple Varieties

Almata
Ashmead's Kernel
Black Twig
Bramley's Seedling
Duchess of Oldenburg
Edward VII
Gloster
Granny Smith
Haralson
Jonathan
Lodi
Lubsk Queen
McIntosh (very mild)
Newtown Pippin
Northern Lights
Patton
Pink Pearmain
Red Baron
Red Duchess of Oldenburg
Rhode Island Greening
Sierra Beauty
Stayman Winesap
Summer Red
Viking
Winter Banana
Yellow Pippin

Sweet Apple Varieties

Baker Sweet
Calville Blanc d'Hiver
Connell Red
Fireside
Fuji
Golden Delicious
Golden Nugget
High Top Sweet
Honey Gold
Idared
Irish Peach
Jonagold
Kidd's Orange Red
King
Pink Pearl
Pound Sweet
Ramsdell Sweet
Raritan
Red Fuji
Redgold
Sheepnose (Black Gilliflower)
Spigold
Summer Scarlet
Sweet Sixteen
Tolman Sweet
Yellow Gold Delicious
Yellow Newtown Pippin

Some Other Apples Noted for Fine Flavor

Ashmead's Kernel
Cornish Gilliflower
Cox's Orange Pippin
Egremont Russet
Mutsu (Crispin)
Spitzenberg
Westfield Seek-No-Further
Winesap

Apples for Cooking and Baking

The apple varieties listed here are all excellent for use in cooking and baking.

Anoka
Baldwin
Belle de Boskoop
Black Gilliflower (Sheepnose)
Calville Blanc d'Hiver
Connell Red
Cox's Orange Pippin
Duchess of Oldenburg
Early Harvest
Garden Delicious
Golden Noble
Granny Smith
Gravenstein
Idared
Irish Peach
Lodi
Porter
Pound Apple (Old-Fashioned)
Redfield
Rhode Island Greening
Rockingham Red
Rome Beauty
Sweet Sixteen
Tolman Sweet
Twenty Ounce
Westland
Winesap
Wolf River
Yellow Transparent
York Imperial

HALL OF FAMERS

According to *The Guinness Book of World Records*, these fruits hold the current world records for size.

Apple: 3 pounds 2 ounces (Michigan)
Cantaloupe: 62 pounds (North Carolina)
Grapefruit: 6 pounds 8½ ounces (Arizona)
Grapes: 20 pounds 11½ ounces (Chile)
Lemon: 8 pounds 8 ounces (California)
Pineapple: 17 pounds 8 ounces (Philippines)
Strawberry: 8.17 ounces (Great Britain)
Watermelon: 262 pounds

Chapter 10

CONTAINER GARDENS

Containers have a multiplicity of uses, whether or not you also have a garden in the ground. For northern gardeners, containers offer the additional benefit of allowing you to grow plants not normally hardy in your area by bringing the pots indoors for winter.

DESIGN TIPS FOR CONTAINER GARDENS

- For visual impact, group containers together. Plan a gradation of heights, as in a garden in the ground, to create a sense of depth.
- Set pots in groups, with the tallest plants in the back and shortest ones in front. Or display smaller pots of plants on tiered shelving to achieve a gradation of heights.
- In a large tub or planter set in front of a wall and viewed from one side, place a tall plant in the back, then several medium-size plants, then some smaller plants, and finally, cascading or trailing plants around the edges to spill over the sides of the container.
- In a large planter that is freestanding and can be viewed from all sides, place the tall plant in the center and position plants of gradually decreasing size in concentric rings, working out toward the edges of the container.
- Combine plants with foliage of different textures and forms for added interest.
- Keep color schemes simple: Rely on just a few colors. Use white and pastel shades in containers in shady locations.

(continued)

Design Tips for Container Gardens *(cont'd)*

- Choose containers in proportion to the plant. A large plant in a small pot looks top-heavy; a small plant in a large pot gets lost. In smaller pots, plant one or two plants.
- Use a group of tall plants or trellised vines in large tubs to form a privacy screen, enclose an outdoor seating area, or divide space in the garden.
- Place a row of potted plants—or several windowboxes—atop a retaining wall to soften the hard edge.
- Set potted houseplants in the garden to create surprising effects or add a tropical touch.
- Group small plants in individual pots in a windowbox, Victorian fernery, or rectangular planter to create a massed effect on a porch or patio.
- Cover tops of individual pots grouped in a planter with moist sphagnum moss (sheet type, not milled type) to hide them and create a finished look.

PLANTS FOR POTS AND WINDOWBOXES

For the environmental needs of the plants listed below, see the appropriate chapters. See also the lists of container vegetables in chapter 8, "Vegetables," and dwarf and extra-dwarf varieties of fruit in chapter 9, "Fruit," for more plants that can be grown in containers.

ANNUALS

Agapanthus orientalis, *A.* hybrids, lily-of-the-Nile, can be grown as perennial in warm climates
Antirrhinum majus, snapdragon
Arctotis stoechadifolia, African daisy
Argyranthemum frutescens (*Chrysanthemum frutescens*), marguerite daisy, perennial best grown as annual in containers
Begonia × *semperflorens-cultorum*, wax begonia
Bellis perennis, English daisy, grow as annual or biennial in containers
Browallia speciosa, sapphire flower
Calendula officinalis, pot marigold
Callistephus chinensis, China aster
Catharanthus roseus, Madagascar periwinkle, perennial in warm climates
Celosia cristata, *C. cristata* var. *plumosa*, cockscomb, woolflower
Centaurea cyanus, bachelor's button, cornflower
Cheiranthus spp., wallflower, biennial usually grown as annual
Cineraria maritima, dusty miller
Cleome hasslerana, spider flower
Coleus hybrids
Cosmos bipinnatus, *C. sulphureus*, cosmos daisy
Dianthus chinensis, China pink
Dimorphotheca sinuata, Cape marigold, tender perennial grown as annual
Dorotheanthus bellidiformis, Livingstone daisy
Eschscholzia californica, California poppy
Euphorbia marginata, snow-on-the-mountain
Felicia
  F. amelloides, blue marguerite
  F. bergerana, kingfisher daisy
Fuchsia hybrids, shrubs in warm climates; grown as annuals in hanging baskets

Gazania spp., tender perennial usually grown as annual in containers

Gerbera jamesonii, Transvaal daisy, tender perennial usually grown as annual in containers

Gomphrena globosa, globe amaranth

Helichrysum petiolare, 'Limelight' has yellow-green leaves

Heliotropium arborescens, heliotrope

Iberis umbellata, globe candytuft

Impatiens

- *I. balsamina*, balsam impatiens
- *I.* hybrids, bedding impatiens

Lobelia erinus, edging lobelia

Lobularia maritima, sweet alyssum

Matthiola incana, stock

Myosotis sylvatica, annual forget-me-not

Nicotiana alata cultivars, flowering tobacco

Nierembergia hippomanica, cupflower

Nigella damascena, love-in-a-mist

Papaver, poppy

- *P. nudicaule*, Iceland poppy
- *P. rhoeas*, field poppy, Shirley poppy

Pelargonium, geranium

- *P.* × *domesticum*, Lady Washington geranium
- *P. graveolens*, rose geranium
- *P.* × *hortorum*, zonal geranium
- *P. peltatum*, ivy geranium
- *P. tomentosum*, peppermint geranium (and other scented varieties)

Petunia × hybrida

Phlox drummondii, annual phlox

Portulaca grandiflora, moss rose

Salvia

- *S. farinacea*, mealycup sage, perennial south of Zone 7, but best as annual in containers
- *S. splendens*, scarlet sage

Tagetes, marigold

- *T. erecta*, African marigold, American marigold
- *T. patula*, French marigold
- *T. tenuifolia*, signet marigold

Torenia fournieri, wishbone flower

Trachymene caerulea, blue lace flower

Tropaeolum, nasturtium

- *T. majus*
- *T. minus*

Verbena

- *V. canadensis*, trailing verbena, rose verbena
- *V.* × *hybrida*, garden verbena

Viola

- *V. tricolor*, Johnny-jump-up
- *V.* × *wittrockiana*, pansy

Zinnia elegans

PERENNIALS

Achillea spp., yarrow

Agave spp.

Alchemilla vulgaris, lady's mantle

Aloe spp.

Aurinia saxatilis, basket-of-gold

Bergenia cordifolia, heartleaf bergenia

Campanula spp., bellflower, harebell

Crassula spp.

Dendrathema × *grandiflorum* (*Chrysanthemum* × *morifolium*), garden chrysanthemum

Dianthus spp., perennial garden pinks

Echeveria spp., hen-and-chicks

Echinocactus spp.

Echinocereus spp., hedgehog cactus

Ferns, many species

Geranium spp., cranesbill, hardy geranium

Helianthemum nummularium, rock rose

Hemerocallis hybrids, daylily, especially 'Stella d'Oro' and other dwarfs

Heuchera sanguinea, coralbells

Hosta spp. and hybrids, plantain lily; small and medium size varieties work best in containers, avoid the largest

Iberis sempervirens, perennial candytuft

Leucanthemum × *superbum* (*Chrysanthemum* × *superbum*), shasta daisy

Nepeta spp., catmint

Primula spp., primrose

Saxifraga × *urbium*, London pride

(continued)

Plants for Pots and Windowboxes *(cont'd)*

PERENNIALS *(cont'd)*

Sedum

S. 'Autumn Joy'

S. acre, goldmoss

S. sieboldii

S. spathulifolium

S. spurium, dragon's blood sedum

Sempervivum spp., hen-and-chicks, houseleek

Tanacetum parthenium, pyrethrum

Tradescantia spp., spiderwort

Veronica spp., speedwell

Viola

V. cornuta, horned violet

V. odorata, sweet violet

BULBS

Begonia × *tuberhybrida*, tuberous begonia

Bletilla hyacinthina, hardy orchid

Caladium × *hortulanum*, fancy-leaved caladium, often grown as annual

Chionodoxa spp., glory-of-the-snow

Colchicum spp.

Crocus, spp.

Cyclamen spp., hardy cyclamen

Dahlia, dwarf varieties

Galanthus nivalis, snowdrop

Gladiolus, miniature varieties

Hyacinthus orientalis, hyacinth

Iris cristata, crested iris

Lilium spp., lily

Muscari spp., grape hyacinth

Narcissus spp., daffodil and narcissus

Scilla siberica, Siberian squill

Tulipa spp., tulip

HERBS

Basil (*Ocimum basilicum*)

Bay (*Laurus nobilis*)

Borage (*Borago officinalis*)

Chives (*Allium schoenoprasum*)

Coriander, cilantro (*Coriandrum sativum*)

Dill (*Anethum graveolens*)

Garlic chives (*Allium tuberosum*)

Lavender (*Lavandula* spp.)

Marjoram (*Origanum majorana*)

Mints (*Mentha* spp.)

Oregano (*Origanum heracleoticum*, *O. vulgare*)

Parsley (*Petroselinum crispum*)

Rosemary (*Rosmarinus officinalis*)

Sage (*Salvia officinalis*)

Tarragon (*Artemisia dracunculus*)

Thyme (*Thymus* spp.)

TREES AND SHRUBS

Aucuba japonica, gold dust plant

Buxus sempervirens, boxwood

Camellia japonica

Cephalotaxus drupacea 'Fastigiata', plum yew

Chamaecyparis lawsoniana, Lawson cypress

'Aurea Densa'

'Ellwoodii'

'Ellwoodii Variegata'

'Gimborni'

'Lutea Nana'

'Minima'

'Minima Aurea'

Chamaecyparis obtusa, Hinoki cypress

'Filicoides'

'Juniperoides Compacta'

'Mariesi'

'Minima'

'Nana'

'Nana Contorta'

'Nana Gracilis'

'Nana Lutea'

Chamaecyparis pisifera, Sawara cypress

'Boulevard'

'Gold Dust'

'Plumosa Aurea'

Chamaecyparis thyoides 'Andelyensis', white cedar

Cryptomeria japonica, Japanese cedar
- 'Spiralis Elongata'
- 'Vilmoriniana'

Euonymus fortunei, wintercreeper (trailing)

Gardenia jasminoides

Hydrangea macrophylla

Juniperus chinensis, Chinese juniper
- 'Aurea'
- 'Blaauw's Variety'
- 'Pyramidalis'

Juniperus communis, common juniper
- 'Columnaris'
- 'Compressa'
- 'Echiniformis'

Juniperus scopulorum, Rocky Mountain juniper
- 'Gray Gleam'
- 'Lakewood Globe'
- 'Skyrocket'
- 'Welchii'

Phormium tenax, New Zealand flax

Picea abies 'Little Gem', Norway spruce

Picea glauca 'Conica', dwarf Alberta spruce

Picea orientalis 'Nigra Compacta', oriental spruce

Pieris spp.

Rosa hybrids, miniature roses

Taxus baccata 'Columnaris', English yew

Thuja occidentalis, American arborvitae
- 'Ericoides'
- 'Hetz Midget'
- 'Holmstrup'
- 'Little Gem'
- 'Rheingold'

Thuja orientalis, Oriental arborvitae
- 'Baker'
- 'Bonita'
- 'Elegantissima'
- 'Golden Globe'
- 'Meldensis'
- 'Minima Glauca'

Yucca spp.

VINES

Actinidia kolomikta, kolomikta vine

Cobaea scandens, cup-and-saucer vine

Hedera helix, English ivy, especially small-leaved varieties

Ipomoea
- *I. alba*, moonflower
- *I. nil*, morning glory
- *I. purpurea*, morning glory
- *I. tricolor*, morning glory

Lathyrus odoratus, sweet pea

Passiflora spp., passionflower

Phaseolus coccineus, scarlet runner bean

Thunbergia alata, black-eyed Susan vine

Tropaeolum majus, nasturtium, will climb if given support

Tropaeolum peregrinum, canary creeper

Vinca
- *V. major* 'Variegata'
- *V. minor*, periwinkle

PLANTS FOR HANGING BASKETS

Arctotis stoechadifolia, African daisy

Begonia × *tuberhybrida*, tuberous begonia

Brachycome iberidifolia, Swan River daisy

Browallia speciosa, sapphire flower

Campanula isophylla, Ligurian bellflower

Fuchsia × *hybrida*

Hedera spp., ivy

Impatiens hybrids, bedding impatiens

Lantana spp.

(continued)

Plants for Hanging Baskets *(cont'd)*

Lobelia erinus, edging lobelia

Lobularia maritima, sweet alyssum

Pelargonium

- *P.* × *hortorum*, cascading varieties of zonal geranium
- *P. peltatum*, ivy geranium

Petunia × *hybrida*

Phlox drummondii, annual phlox

Portulaca grandiflora, moss rose

Sanvitalia procumbens, creeping zinnia

Thunbergia alata, black-eyed Susan vine

Torenia fournieri, wishbone flower

Tropaeolum majus, nasturtium

Verbena canadensis, trailing verbena, rose verbena

Vinca

- *V. major* 'Variegata'
- *V. minor*, periwinkle

POTTING MIXES

ALL-PURPOSE MIXES

1 part soil (potting soil, pasteurized topsoil, or garden loam)
1 part sharp builder's sand
1 part peat moss

2 parts soil
1 part crumbled compost
1 part sharp sand, perlite, or vermiculite

2 parts commercial growing mix
1 part potting soil or garden loam

1 part potting soil or garden loam
1 part sharp sand, vermiculite, or perlite
1 part peat moss

PENN STATE MIX

1 part clay loam
2 parts sphagnum peat moss
2 parts perlite

or

equal parts sandy clay loam, sphagnum peat moss, and perlite

or

equal parts sandy loam and sphagnum peat moss

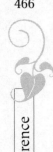

UNIVERSITY OF CALIFORNIA MIX

Equal parts fine sand and peat moss, plus, per cubic yard of mix:

4 ounces potassium nitrate

4 ounces potassium sulfate

2½ pounds 20% superphosphate

7½ pounds dolomitic limestone

2½ pounds ground limestone

JOHN INNES COMPOST

The famous British growing mix. Here's what it contains:

7 parts composted loam

3 parts peat moss

2 parts coarse sand

1½ parts ground limestone

8½ parts fertilizer (a mix of 2 parts hoof and horn meal, 2 parts superphosphate, and 1 part sulfate of potash) *or* 12 parts 5–10–10 fertilizer

HUMUSY MIX

1 part potting soil or garden loam

2 parts crumbled compost

1 part peat moss or vermiculite

SOILLESS MIXES

3 parts peat moss

1 part sharp sand, perlite, or vermiculite

¾ cup ground limestone per bushel (for acid-loving plants, do not add lime)

equal parts sphagnum peat moss and vermiculite

GROWING PLANTS IN CONTAINERS

PLANTING TIPS

- Fill the container with moist potting mix to ½ inch from the top. Water to settle the mix, add more mix to bring up the level, and water again. Repeat this procedure as needed until the level of the mix is ½ inch from the top of the container after watering.

(continued)

Planting Tips *(cont'd)*

- Dig a hole large enough to accommodate the plant's root ball. Set the plant in the hole. Firm the soil around the roots, and water. Fill in any holes that remain.
- When planting several plants in a large container, plant the largest first and work down in size and outward in the container to the smallest plant.
- Keep soil evenly moist—not soggy—until plants establish new roots. When a gentle pull on the plant meets with resistance, roots have formed.
- Mulch, if you wish, to conserve soil moisture. Use cocoa bean hulls or other fine-textured material.

MAINTENANCE TIPS

- Clean containers after use, or every two years, to remove fertilizer salts and lime deposits. Scrub empty pots in soapy water with stiff brush. Rinse well with clear water.
- To reuse a pot after disposing of a diseased plant, scrub as directed above. Then let the pot soak for several hours in a solution of 1 part liquid household chlorine bleach to 9 parts water. Rinse thoroughly with clear water.
- Water plants in flowerpots and small planters daily in summer. Plants in small pots or in hot, dry, or windy locations may need water more than once a day.
- Check tubs and large containers by poking a finger into the soil. When the soil is dry 1 to 2 inches below the surface, water.
- Water thoroughly, so that excess water drains out from the holes in the bottom of the container. Pour off any water that remains in drainage saucers 15 minutes after watering.
- To revive a plant wilted from serious lack of water, plunge the pot into a bucket of water to completely submerge the pot. When bubbling ceases, remove the pot from the water and let it drain. Mist the plant foliage. Set the plant in a shady place to recover.
- Add half-strength soluble fertilizer to the water for the plants once a week, or use at the strength directed on the package label every 2 to 3 weeks when the plants are in active growth.
- Stake tall plants in windy locations.
- Deadhead flowering plants regularly to keep them neat; for annuals, to keep them blooming.

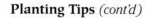

- Pull weeds that sprout in pots.
- Check often for signs of pests and disease; take action promptly when you notice symptoms.

PREPARING FOR WINTER

- At the end of the growing season, clean out containers of annuals. Put spent plants that were healthy on the compost pile, along with the used potting mix, or spread the potting mix on the garden.
- Brush loose soil from the empty pots, scrub them out, and store them indoors, in the basement, garage, or shed for the winter.
- Cut back container perennials to a few inches above ground at the end of the growing season. Move containers in exposed locations to a sheltered place, perhaps next to the wall of a building.
- Move tender plants that summered outdoors back inside when the weather grows cooler. Set them in a shady outdoor location for a week to help them begin adjusting to lower light levels. Keep them away from other houseplants for the first few weeks indoors as you monitor for pests or diseases that might be carried in from outdoors.
- Make sure perennial vines are securely fastened to their supports as they go into winter.
- Spray broad-leaved evergreens with antidesiccant where cold winter winds may be a problem.
- When soil in containers freezes, mulch to prevent thawing during winter mild spells. Cover or weight down mulches to keep them in place.
- Be sure that trees, shrubs, and perennials in containers are well watered going into winter.

Appendix 1

ABOUT PLANT NAMES

Plants are classified into groups according to similarities in their structure. Botany is the study of the structure and classification of plants. The system of botanical nomenclature used internationally was developed primarily by an eighteenth-century Swedish scientist named Carl von Linne. Latin is used for botanical nomenclature as it is for other scientific languages. After his death in 1778, von Linne was honored by having his name Latinized to Carolus Linnaeus.

Botanical nomenclature is not static. Names must be found for newly discovered and newly bred plants, and sometimes the names of plants are changed. Not too many years ago botanists reclassified most of the plants in the genus *Chrysanthemum* into several other newly created genera. Much to the dismay of gardeners, the familiar garden chrysanthemum is no longer a chrysanthemum. Its scientific name is now *Dendrathema*.

Although botanical nomenclature does change occasionally, it is still the most sensible and reliable means of identifying plants. Plants' common names or nicknames vary from country to country, region to region, and even neighborhood to neighborhood. The plant southern gardeners know as green-and-gold is called goldenstar farther north. The name hen-and-chicks is given to plants of at least two different genera—*Echeveria* and *Sempervivum*, and could refer to any of dozens of species. But botanical names are the same all over the world, and gardeners who become familiar with them will find it much easier to get the plants they want from garden centers and mail-order catalogs.

Here is a brief introduction to botanical nomenclature.

Plant families are groups of related plants that share certain characteristics. For example, the Rose Family, Rosaceae, contains about 2,000 species grouped into about 100 genera. Roses, strawberries, apples, and spiraea are all members of the family. At first glance, these plants all look quite different.

Some bear their flowers singly, others in clusters. Some of the flowers are single, with one tier of petals, while others—like many hybrid roses—have many more petals. But upon closer examination, the flowers are similar in structure. Most of them, at least in their unimproved wild form, have four or five petals. The single flowers of species roses do indeed look a lot like the blossoms of strawberry plants.

In botanical nomenclature, the Latin family names end in *-ae*, and are printed in Roman type with an initial capital letter. Labiatae, Compositae, Umbelliferae, and Leguminosae are a few more examples.

A genus (the plural is genera) is a group of closely allied plant species that belong to the same family. Plants that belong to the same genus are similar to one another in many ways, and they are different from other members of the family in many ways. A few genera contain only one species. Genus names often describe the plants' appearance in some way, or they commemorate the person who first named the group of plants.

The simplest form of identification for a particular plant consists of two names, the first of which is the genus name. The genus name is printed in italics with the first letter capitalized. The genus name of columbine is *Aquilegia*, which is derived from the Latin word *aquila*, meaning eagle. Columbine flowers are noted for the long spurs on the petals, which must have suggested to Linnaeus the sharp talons of a bird of prey. The second name given to a plant is its species name, which further differentiates it from other plants.

A species is a plant or group of very closely related plants (called varieties or cultivars) that are alike except for small differences such as flower color, leaf variegation, or plant size (dwarf plants are usually varieties or cultivars). The species name also describes the plant. To return to the example of the columbine, the name of one species, *caerulea*, indicates that the flower is blue, as indeed it is. A very loose approximation of the columbine's botanical name in English might be "blue flower with eagle's claws." (The common name columbine, by the way, is from the Latin *columba*, meaning "dove," probably because the flowers reminded someone of a flock of gentle birds clustered together.)

Species names are printed in italics. In the past many species names were capitalized, but it is now widely accepted that all may be lowercase, although reference works such as *Hortus Third* preserve the capitals as a matter of historical interest. The word *species* is often abbreviated as sp. or, when more than one species is referred to, spp.

A variety is a variation of a species that has occurred as a natural mutation. The name is printed in italics, following the abbreviation var., which appears in Roman type. A cultivar is a variety developed in cultivation. It is written in Roman type, with an initial capital letter, and enclosed in single quotation marks.

PLANT FAMILIES

Here are most of the major families of ornamental plants, along with the names of familiar genera they contain.

ACERACEAE, MAPLE FAMILY

Acer

AGAVACEAE, AGAVE FAMILY

Agave, *Cordyline*, *Dracaena*, *Phormium*, *Sansevieria*, *Yucca*

AIZOACEAE, CARPETWEED FAMILY

Carpobrotus, *Delosperma*, *Dorotheanthus*, *Drosanthemum*, *Lampranthus*, *Mesembryanthemum*

AMARANTHACEAE, AMARANTH FAMILY

Alternanthera, *Amaranthus*, *Celosia*, *Gomphrena*, *Iresine*

AMARYLLIDACEAE, AMARYLLIS FAMILY

Agapanthus, *Amaryllis*, *Brodiaea*, *Clivia*, *Crinum*, *Eucharis*, *Galanthus*, *Haemanthus*, *Hippeastrum*, *Hymenocallis*, *Ipheion*, *Leucojum*, *Lycoris*, *Narcissus*, *Nerine*, *Sprekelia*, *Sternbergia*, *Tulbaghia*, *Zephyranthes*

ANACARDIACEAE, CASHEW FAMILY

Anacardium, *Cotinus*, *Pistacia*, *Rhus*

APOCYNACEAE, DOGBANE FAMILY

Allamanda, *Amsonia*, *Catharanthus*, *Mandevilla*, *Nerium*, *Plumeria*, *Trachelospermum*, *Vinca*

ARALIACEAE, ARALIA FAMILY

Acanthopanax, *Aralia*, *Brassaia*, *Fatsia*, *Hedera*, *Panax*, *Schefflera*

ARISTOLOCHIACEAE, BIRTHWORT FAMILY

Aristolochia, *Asarum*

ASCLEPIADACEAE, MILKWEED FAMILY

Asclepias, *Hoya*, *Oxypetalum*, *Periploca*, *Stapelia*, *Stephanotis*

BEGONIACEAE, BEGONIA FAMILY

Contains 3 genera, but only *Begonia*, which has over 1,000 species, is well known

BERBERIDACEAE, BARBERRY FAMILY

Berberis, *Epimedium*, *Mahonia*, *Nandina*, *Podophyllum*, *Vancouveria*

BETULACEAE, BIRCH FAMILY

Alnus, *Betula*, *Carpinus*, *Corylus*, *Ostrya*

BIGNONIACEAE, BIGNONIA FAMILY

Bignonia, *Campsis*, *Catalpa*, *Chilopsis*, *Distictis*, *Eccremocarpus*, *Incarvillea*, *Jacaranda*, *Macfadyena*, *Paulownia*, *Tecomaria*

(continued)

Plant Families *(cont'd)*

BORAGINACEAE, BORAGE FAMILY

Anchusa, *Borago*, *Brunnera*, *Cynoglossum*, *Echium*, *Heliotropium*, *Lithodora*, *Lithospermum*, *Mertensia*, *Myosotis*, *Omphalodes*, *Pulmonaria*, *Symphytum*

BUXACEAE, BOXWOOD FAMILY

Buxus, *Pachysandra*, *Sarcococca*

CACTACEAE, CACTUS FAMILY

Over 200 genera, including *Cereus*, *Echinocactus*, *Echinocereus*, *Echinopsis*, *Ferocactus*, *Lobivia*, *Mammillaria*, *Melocactus*, *Notocactus*, *Opuntia*, *Pereskia*, *Rhipsalis*, *Schlumbergera*

CAMPANULACEAE, BELLFLOWER FAMILY

Adenophora, *Campanula*, *Jasione*, *Platycodon*, *Trachelium*

CAPRIFOLIACEAE, HONEYSUCKLE FAMILY

Abelia, *Diervilla*, *Kolkwitzia*, *Linnaea*, *Lonicera*, *Sambucus*, *Symphoricarpos*, *Viburnum*, *Weigela*

CARYOPHYLLACEAE, PINK FAMILY

Agrostemma, *Cerastium*, *Dianthus*, *Gypsophila*, *Lychnis*, *Saponaria*, *Silene*

COMPOSITAE, COMPOSITE OR SUNFLOWER FAMILY

Achillea, *Ageratum*, *Ammobium*, *Anacyclus*, *Anaphalis*, *Antennaria*, *Anthemis*, *Arctotis*, *Artemisia*, *Aster*, *Baileya*, *Bellis*, *Boltonia*, *Brachycome*, *Calendula*, *Callistephus*, *Catananche*, *Centaurea*, *Chrysanthemum*, *Chrysogonum*, *Cichorium*, *Cirsium*, *Cladanthus*, *Coreopsis*, *Cosmos*, *Crepis*, *Dahlia*, *Dendrathema*, *Dimorphotheca*, *Doronicum*, *Dyssodia*, *Echinacea*, *Echinops*, *Erigeron*, *Eupatorium*, *Felicia*, *Gaillardia*, *Gazania*, *Gerbera*, *Helenium*, *Helianthus*, *Helichrysum*, *Heliopsis*, *Inula*, *Lactuca*, *Layia*, *Leontopodium*, *Leucanthemum*, *Liatris*, *Ligularia*, *Matricaria*, *Osteospermum*, *Petasites*, *Ratibida*, *Rudbeckia*, *Santolina*, *Sanvitalia*, *Senecio*, *Solidago*, *Stokesia*, *Tagetes*, *Tanacetum*, *Tithonia*, *Tussilago*, *Vernonia*, *Xeranthemum*, *Zinnia*

CRUCIFERAE, MUSTARD FAMILY

Alyssum, *Arabis*, *Aubrieta*, *Aurinia*, *Brassica*, *Cardamine*, *Cheiranthus*, *Crambe*, *Draba*, *Hesperis*, *Iberis*, *Lobularia*, *Lunaria*, *Malcolmia*, *Matthiola*

CUCURBITACEAE, GOURD FAMILY

Cucumis, *Cucurbita*, *Ecballium*, *Lagenaria*, *Luffa*, *Momordica*

CUPRESSACEAE, CYPRESS FAMILY

Calocedrus, *Chamaecyparis*, *Cupressus*, *Juniperus*, *Platycladys*, *Thuja*, *Thujopsis*

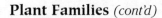

ERICACEAE, HEATH FAMILY

Andromeda, Arbutus, Arctostaphylos, Calluna, Chamaedaphne, Daboecia, Enkianthus, Erica, Gaultheria, Kalmia, Ledum, Leucothoe, Oxydendrum, Pernettya, Pieris, Rhododendron, Vaccinium

GENTIANACEAE, GENTIAN FAMILY

Eustoma, Exacum, Gentiana

GERANIACEAE, GERANIUM FAMILY

Erodium, Geranium, Pelargonium

GRAMINAE, GRASS FAMILY

Contains 700 genera, including *Agrostis, Ammophila, Andropogon, Arundinaria, Arundo, Bambusa, Briza, Bromus, Chasmanthium, Coix, Cortaderia, Cymbopogon, Cynodon, Deschampsia, Elymus, Eragrostis, Festuca, Helictotrichon, Holcus, Koeleria, Lagurus, Milium, Miscanthus, Molinia, Oryza, Panicum, Pennisetum, Phalaris, Phragmites, Phyllostachys, Sasa, Setaria, Sorghum, Sporobolus, Stipa, Triticum, Uniola, Vetiveria, Zea, Zizania, Zoysia*

HAMAMELIDACEAE, WITCH HAZEL FAMILY

Corylopsis, Fothergilla, Hamamelis, Liquidambar, Parrotia

IRIDACEAE, IRIS FAMILY

Belamcanda, Crocosmia, Crocus, Dietes, Freesia, Gladiolus, Iris, Ixia, Schizostylis, Sisyrinchium, Sparaxis, Tigridia, Tritonia, Watsonia

LABIATAE, MINT FAMILY

Agastache, Ajuga, Amethystea, Calamintha, Coleus, Collinsonia, Glechoma, Hyssopus, Lamiastrum, Lamium, Lavandula, Marrubium, Melissa, Mentha, Ocimum, Origanum, Perilla, Perovskia, Phlomis, Physostegia, Prunella, Pycnostachys, Rosmarinus, Salvia, Satureja, Stachys, Teucrium, Thymus

LEGUMINOSAE, PEA OR PULSE FAMILY

Acacia, Albizia, Baptisia, Caesalpinia, Caragana, Cassia, Cercidium, Cercis, Cladrastis, Coronilla, Cytisus, Dolichos, Genista, Gleditsia, Glycyrrhiza, Gymnocladus, Indigofera, Laburnum, Lathyrus, Lotus, Lupinus, Mimosa, Phaseolus, Robinia, Sophora, Thermopsis, Wisteria

LILIACEAE, LILY FAMILY

Aloe, Asparagus, Bulbocodium, Calochortus, Camassia, Chionodoxa, Colchicum, Convallaria, Endymion, Eremurus, Erythronium, Fritillaria, Galtonia, Hemerocallis, Hesperocallis, Hosta, Hyacinthus, Kniphofia, Lachenalia, Lilium, Liriope, Muscari, Ophiopogon, Ornithogalum, Polygonatum, Puschkinia, Scilla, Smilacina, Tricyrtis, Trillium, Tulipa, Uvularia, Veltheimia

(continued)

Plant Families *(cont'd)*

LYTHRACEAE, LOOSESTRIFE FAMILY
Cuphea, Lagerstroemia, Lythrum

MALVACEAE, MALLOW FAMILY
Abelmoschus, Abutilon, Alcea, Althaea, Callirhoe, Hibiscus, Lavatera, Sidalcea

MYRTACEAE, MYRTLE FAMILY
Callistemon, Eucalpytus, Eugenia, Feijoa, Leptospermum, Melaleuca, Myrtus, Syzygium

NYCTAGINACEAE, FOUR-O'CLOCK FAMILY
Abronia, Bougainvillea, Mirabilis

OLEACEAE, OLIVE FAMILY
Abeliophyllum, Chionanthus, Fontanesia, Forsythia, Fraxinus, Jasminum, Ligustrum, Olea, Osmanthus, Syringa

PAPAVERACEAE, POPPY FAMILY
Argemone, Eschscholzia, Glaucium, Hunnemannia, Macleaya, Meconopsis, Papaver, Platystemon, Romneya, Sanguinaria, Stylophorum

PINACEAE, PINE FAMILY
Abies, Cedrus, Larix, Picea, Pinus, Pseudolarix, Pseudotsuga, Tsuga

PLUMBAGINACEAE, PLUMBAGO OR LEADWORT FAMILY
Armeria, Ceratostigma, Limonium, Plumbago

POLEMONIACEAE, PHLOX FAMILY
Cobaea, Gilia, Linanthus, Phlox, Polemonium

POLYPODIACEAE, POLYPODY FAMILY
Acrostichum, Adiantum, Asplenium, Athyrium, Blechnum, Cyrtomium, Cystopteris, Davallia, Dennstaedtia, Dryopteris, Matteuccia, Nephrolepis, Onoclea, Pellaea, Phyllitis, Platycerium, Polypodium, Polystichum, Pteris, Rumohra, Woodwardia

PORTULACACEAE, PORTULACA FAMILY
Calandrinia, Claytonia, Lewisia, Portulaca, Talinum

PRIMULACEAE, PRIMROSE FAMILY
Androsace, Cyclamen, Dodecatheon, Lysimachia, Primula

RANUNCULACEAE, CROWFOOT OR BUTTERCUP FAMILY
Aconitum, Actaea, Adonis, Anemone, Aquilegia, Caltha, Cimicifuga, Clematis, Consolida, Delphinium, Eranthis, Helleborus, Hepatica, Hydrastis, Nigella, Ranunculus, Thalictrum, Trollius, Xanthorhiza

ROSACEAE, ROSE FAMILY

Alchemilla, Amelanchier, Aronia, Aruncus, Chaenomeles, Cotoneaster, Crataegus, Eriobotrya, Filipendula, Fragaria, Geum, Kerria, Malus, Photinia, Physocarpus, Potentilla, Prunus, Pyracantha, Pyrus, Raphiolepis, Rhodotypos, Rosa, Rubus, Sanguisorba, Sorbus, Spiraea

RUBIACEAE, MADDER FAMILY

Bouvardia, Coffea, Galium, Gardenia, Ixora, Mitchella, Pentas

RUTACEAE, RUE FAMILY

Choisya, Citrus, Dictamnus, Fortunella, Poncirus, Ruta, Skimmia

SAXIFRAGACEAE, SAXIFRAGE FAMILY

Astilbe, Bergenia, Decumaria, Deutzia, Escallonia, Heuchera, Hydrangea, Kirengeshoma, Peltiphyllum, Philadelphus, Pileostegia, Ribes, Rodgersia, Saxifraga, Schizophragma, Tiarella

SCROPHULARIACEAE, FIGWORT FAMILY

Antirrhinum, Asarina, Calceolaria, Castilleja, Chelone, Collinsia, Cymbalaria, Digitalis, Erinus, Hebe, Leucophyllum, Linaria, Mazus, Mimulus, Nemesia, Penstemon, Scrophularia, Torenia, Verbascum, Veronica

SOLANACEAE, NIGHTSHADE FAMILY

Browallia, Brugmansia, Brunfelsia, Capsicum, Cestrum, Datura, Lycopersicon, Nicandra, Nicotiana, Nierembergia, Petunia, Physalis, Salpiglossis, Schizanthus, Solanum

TAXODIACEAE, TAXODIUM FAMILY

Cryptomeria, Glyptostrobus, Metasequoia, Sciadopitys, Sequoia, Taxodium

THEACEAE, TEA FAMILY

Camellia, Franklinia, Stewartia

ULMACEAE, ELM FAMILY

Celtis, Ulmus, Zelkova

UMBELLIFERAE, PARSLEY OR CARROT FAMILY

Aegopodium, Ammi, Anethum, Angelica, Astrantia, Cuminum, Daucus, Eryngium, Foeniculum, Heracleum, Levisticum, Myrrhis, Petroselinum, Pimpinella, Trachymene

VERBENACEAE, VERVAIN OR VERBENA FAMILY

Aloysia, Callicarpa, Caryopteris, Clerodendrum, Lantana, Verbena, Vitex

VITACEAE, GRAPE FAMILY

Ampelopsis, Cissus, Parthenocissus, Rhoicissus, Vitis

MEANINGS OF FREQUENTLY USED BOTANICAL NAMES

The words defined below are part of the botanical names—usually species or variety names—of many plants. All of these words describe some characteristic of the plants they name.

acaulis stemless
alba, albus white
amabile, amabilis beautiful
arborescens treelike
aurantiaca orange
aurea, aureum gold
azurea blue
blanda pleasant
caerulea deep blue
canadensis from Canada or America
chinensis from China
coccinea scarlet
communis common
cordata heart-shaped
crispa finely waved, curled
dulce sweet
elata tall
elegans elegant
erecta upright, erect
flava, flavum yellow
florida, floridus flowering
fragrans fragrant
fragrantissima very fragrant
fruticosa shrublike
gracilis graceful
grandiflora large-flowered
griseum gray
hortensis of the garden
humilis low-growing
hybridus hybrid
incana gray-haired
japonica, japonicum from Japan
lactea milky
laevis smooth
lanceolata lance-shaped
longifolia long-leaved
lutea, luteus yellow
macrophylla large-leaved
maculata spotted
majus larger
maritima from near the sea
maxima largest
microphylla small-leaved
millefolium thousand-leaved
minor, minus smaller
mollis soft
montana from the mountains
multiflora many-flowered
nana dwarf
nigra black
nitida, nitidum shining
odorata scented
officinalis used as an herb (medicinally)
palmatum palmate, shaped like a hand
palustris from marshes or wet places
parvifolia small-leaved
pendula drooping, pendulous
perenne, perennis perennial
pictum painted
procumbens prostrate
pulchella pretty
pumila low-growing, dwarf
punctata spotted
purpurea purple
repens, reptans creeping
rosea rose-colored
rotundifolia round-leaved
rubra, rubrum red
sanguinea blood-red
scandens climbing
semperflorens everblooming
sempervirens evergreen
speciosa showy
spectabilis spectacular
spinosus spiny
spinosissimus spiniest

superbum superb
tomentosa, tomentosum hairy
umbellata having flowers in umbels (see Glossary, page 488)
variegata variegated
villosa, villosum softly hairy
virginiana from Virginia
vulgaris common

PLANT NICKNAMES

Although the common names of plants are not a reliable means of precise indentification, many of them are quite interesting. Some plants got their nicknames from mythology and folklore, some were named for the way they look, or where they grow. Below are 50 interesting plant nicknames and their origin.

Angel's trumpet (*Datura* spp.): The large, white trumpet-shaped flowers are poisonous—in fact, eating any part of the plant can be deadly.

Baby's breath (*Gypsophila* spp.): Plants produce clouds of tiny white flowers as delicate as a baby's soft breath.

Bachelor's button, cornflower (*Centaurea cyanus*): The flower was popular as a boutonniere in Victorian days. "Cornflower," because it grew wild in fields of grain in England (corn was used to refer to any grain).

Balloon flower (*Platycodon grandiflorus*): Flower buds look like old-fashioned hot air balloons.

Birdfoot violet (*Viola pedata*): Deeply divided leaves resemble a bird's foot.

Blackberry lily (*Belamcanda chinensis*): Flowers are followed by fruit capsules that open to expose seeds resembling black berries.

Bleeding heart (*Dicentra spectabilis*): Flowers are heart-shaped, with white petals projecting down from the center, and thought to resemble drops of blood.

Bloodroot (*Sanguinaria canadensis*): The root contains a red sap that makes it appear to "bleed" when cut.

Catchfly (*Silene* spp.): Leaves of some species secrete a sticky substance that can trap insects on the leaves.

Cockscomb, woolflower (*Celosia cristata*): Some plants bear fan-shaped red flowers thought to resemble a rooster's comb. All the varied flowers found in this species have a woolly texture.

Columbine (*Aquilegia* spp.): *Columba* is Latin for "dove"; the flowers supposedly look like a group of doves gathered together.

Cranesbill (*Geranium* spp.): The pointed seed capsules are shaped like a crane's or stork's beak.

Cup-and-saucer vine (*Cobaea scandens*): Cup-shaped flowers are backed by a flat, saucerlike calyx.

(continued)

Plant Nicknames *(cont'd)*

Cupid's dart (*Catananche caerulea*): The ancient Greeks believed the flower could inspire passion, as did the mythological darts of Cupid.

Daylily (*Hemerocallis* spp.): Each lilylike flower blooms for just one day.

Dutchman's breeches (*Dicentra cucullaria*): Two-part white flowers look like pantaloons hung out on a line to dry.

Dutchman's pipe (*Aristolochia durior*): Unusual yellowish brown flowers are U-shaped, and do look rather like a pipe.

Fleabane (*Erigeron* spp.): American pioneers burned it to repel fleas and other insects.

Four-o'clock (*Mirabilis jalapa*): Flowers open in late afternoon.

Foxglove (*Digitalis* spp.): Legend has it that fairies made the flowers as gloves for their friends, the foxes, to wear over their paws so they could steal into the henhouse.

Gas plant (*Dictamnus albus*): Leaves and flowers emit a vapor that will ignite if you hold a lit match to the plant on a windless summer night.

Harry Lauder's walking stick (*Corylus avellana* 'Contorta'): Named after a Scottish actor who always carried a gnarled wooden cane.

Joe-pye weed (*Euptorium purpureum*): Supposedly named for a Native American medicine man who used the plant for healing.

Johnny-jump-up (*Viola tricolor*): Plants self-sow and pop up all over the garden.

Lilac (*Syringa vulgaris*): From the Persian word for blue, to describe the flower color.

Love-in-a-mist (*Nigella damascena*): Pastel flowers float above a mass of delicate, fernlike foliage.

Love-in-a-puff (*Cardiospermum halicacabum*): This vine's balloonlike fruits hold seeds marked with a heart.

Love-lies-bleeding (*Amaranthus caudatus*): Bears long, drooping clusters of tiny, deep red flowers that must have reminded someone of blood flowing.

Lungwort (*Pulmonaria* spp.): Was prescribed for lung problems according to the Doctrine of Signatures (the spotted leaves were thought to be shaped like lungs). Also called soldiers-and-sailors or boys-and-girls because plants often bear both pink and blue flowers.

Moonflower (*Ipomoea alba*): Has large white moonlike flowers that open in the afternoon and stay open all night.

Monkshood (*Aconitum* spp.): Flowers are shaped like a monk's cowl or a helmet.

Morning glory (*Ipomoea* spp.): Was so named because the flowers open in the morning with the dawn and fade and wilt by midafternoon.

Partridgeberry (*Mitchella repens*): Partridges and other wild fowl eat the berries.

Pheasant's eye (*Adonis annua*): Flowers are red with a dark central spot, like the eye of a pheasant.

Pussytoes (*Antennaria* spp.): Soft puffy flower heads look like kittens' paws.

Quaking grass (*Briza* spp.): Small panicles on thin stems tremble with every passing breeze.

Roof iris (*Iris tectorum*): In Imperial Japan, irises were not permitted to be grown in gardens. Some gardeners got around the ban by planting them on the roofs of their houses.

Scarlet pimpernel, poor man's weather glass (*Anagallis arvensis*): Red flowers close when rain is coming.

Shadblow, shadbush (*Amelanchier* spp.): Blooms in spring when the shad (a type of fish) run.

Shooting star (*Dodecatheon* spp.): Flowers have stamens fused into a cone that points toward the ground, extending beyond the reflexed petals—it looks like the way a child would draw a comet.

Snapdragon (*Antirrhinum majus*): When the flowers are pinched on the sides, the two parts open and shut like an animal's jaws. Somehow the flower came to be associated with the legend of St. George and the dragon.

Snow-in-summer (*Cerastium tomentosum*): Leaves have woolly white hairs, and the plants bear white flowers in summer.

Soapwort (*Saponaria officinalis*): The leaves make a foamy lather when you crush them in water. Another name, bouncing bet, was bestowed because the white flowers with their reflexed petals looked like a peek up the skirts of a woman bending over a washtub.

Spider flower (*Cleome hasslerana*): Flower petals have long thin claws like a spider's legs.

Sunflower (*Helianthus* spp., *Heliopsis* spp.): Disk-shaped flowers with golden rays resemble the sun, and some turn to follow the sun across the sky as the day progresses.

Tickseed (*Coreopsis* spp.): Seed capsules are small and black, and look like bugs when they are dry.

Tidytips (*Layia platyglossa*): Yellow flower petals have neat white edges.

Trout lily (*Erythronium americanum*): The flowers look like small lilies, and the leaves are spotted like a trout.

Wishbone flower (*Torenia fournieri*): Two joined stamens in the flower's throat look like a wishbone.

Yarrow (*Achillea* spp.): Thought to come from the Anglo-Saxon *gearwe*, meaning "ready to heal." The plant was used to stop bleeding, according to legend originally by Achilles on the battlefields of Troy (which gave rise to the genus name).

Appendix 2
GLOSSARY

Acid soil Soil having a pH below 7.0 and containing no limestone.

Adventitious Plant parts that grow in unusual locations, such as roots that grow aboveground from a stem or leaf, or shoots that grow from callus tissue formed where a plant was injured.

Aerial roots Roots growing from aboveground portions of a stem. Many epiphytic plants have aerial roots (*see* Epiphyte).

Air-layering A method of propagation used for some woody-stemmed plants, in which the bark is wounded and covered with damp sphagnum moss and plastic to induce roots to form at the site of the injury.

Alkaline soil Soil having a pH above 7.0, usually found where limestone is present and/or rainfall is sparse.

Allée A walkway or drive lined on both sides with trees that are usually carefully pruned and often tall.

Alternate Term used to describe leaves (or buds) produced at intervals on either side of a stem, with no two leaves being directly across from one another.

Annual A plant that completes its entire life cycle—germinating, growing to maturity, and producing seeds—in one growing season.

Anther The part of a flower stamen that produces pollen.

Apex The growing tip of a shoot, or end of a leaf.

Aphid Common small insect that sucks plant juices and damaged plants, and excretes sweet honeydew harvested by ants. Often found clustered on young shoots and in leaf axils.

Arboretum A collection of trees.

Awn A stiff, hairlike extension on a seed, fruit, flower petal, or leaf, most often found on the ends of grass seeds, a feature of many ornamental grasses.

Axil The point where a leaf or petiole joins a stem. Many plants form growth buds in leaf axils that grow into new shoots when the stem above that point is pinched back.

Bed A freestanding garden area that can be viewed from all sides, called an island bed when surrounded by a lawn.

Bedding plants Plants set out in masses to provide color for just one season, then removed. Annuals are often used as bedding plants.

Biennial A plant that lives for two years, blooming and producing seeds in its second year. Many biennials will bloom the first year if seeds are sown early indoors, and may be treated as annuals.

Blade The flat part of a leaf, often used in reference to the leaves of grasses.

Blanching A process of excluding light from a plant to keep it from turning green. Blanching is used to produce pale white cauliflower, Belgian endive, and asparagus, to increase tenderness or reduce bitterness.

Bolt Bloom or produce seeds prematurely, often in response to warm temperatures, drought, or long daylength. Lettuce and spinach are prone to bolting.

Bordeaux mixture A fungicide containing hydrated lime and copper sulfate, used primarily on grapevines.

Border A garden area along the edge of a property or next to a fence, wall, or building. Borders are generally longer than they are wide, and viewed mainly from one side.

Bract A modified leaf, usually found at the base of a flower, flower stem, or cluster of flowers. Some plants with insignificant flowers are noted for their colorful bracts—poinsettia is one example.

Broadleaf evergreen A plant with evergreen leaves that are broad rather than needlelike. Azaleas, hollies, camellias, and rhododendrons are examples.

Budding A method of grafting in which a bud and small bit of bark are inserted into a cut in the bark of another plant to join top growth from the bud plant to the root system of a stronger or hardier plant. Most often used for roses and fruit trees.

Bulb A storage organ, usually underground, consisting of a modified short stem, often enclosed in protective swollen leaf bases. A bulb contains enough nutrients to support the plant through a season of growth.

Bulbil A small bulblike structure, produced aboveground, that can be used to propagate a new plant. Many lilies develop bulbils in their leaf axils.

Bulblet A small bulb produced at the base of a mature bulb. Bulblets can be removed and used in propagation.

Callus Tissue formed by a plant to seal an injury to a stem or root. Cuttings form callus where they are severed from the plant and then are able to produce roots instead of rotting.

Calyx Protective outer layer of a flower, usually made of modified leaves, that encloses the flower bud as it develops; the collective name for sepals. The calyx is green in many plants, colorful in others. In some plants, the calyx looks like the petals.

Cambium Thin layer of tissue between the protective woody tissue (bark) and water-conducting tissues of a tree or shrub. The cambium produces new cells that increase the size of both the inner and outer tissues; injury to the cambium thus interferes with growth.

Cane Stiff stem of a shrubby plant, used to describe main stems of roses, bramble fruits, and bamboo.

Capillary matting Matting made of synthetic fibers and placed under potted plants to supply continuous moisture. The matting draws water from a reservoir by capillary action; the moisture is absorbed through drainage holes in the bottom of the pots.

Chlorosis Yellowing or lightening of plant tissues caused by nutrient deficiency (especially iron or potassium) or disease.

Clone A plant that is genetically identical to its parent, produced by vegetative (asexual) methods of propagation.

Cold frame A bottomless box with a glass or plastic lid that provides a sheltered environment for plants in cold weather.

Complete flower A flower that contains petals and sepals, and both male (stamen) and female (pistil) reproductive organs.

Compost Decomposed remains of plants and other organic materials used to supply organic matter and nutrients to garden soil.

Compound Made up of more than one part, used to describe leaves composed of two or more leaflets, or flowers consisting of more than one floret.

Conifer A tree or shrub that produces cones or, in some cases, fruits. Most conifers are evergreens with narrow, needlelike or scalelike leaves.

Cordate Heart-shaped, term used to describe leaves.

Cordon A style of espalier in which a plant is trained to grow as one main stem by removing all side branches. A double cordon, or U, has two branches, a multiple cordon has more.

Corm A bulblike storage structure that is actually the modified base of an underground stem. Unlike a true bulb, a corm lives just one year and is then replaced by a new corm.

Cormlet Small corm that develops at the base of a mature corm, or sometimes on a stem aboveground. Also known as a cormel.

Corolla Collective term for a flower's petals.

Corona A part of some flowers that grows between the corolla and the stamens and pistil, such as the cup of a daffodil or the fringed structure in a passionflower.

Corymb A round or flat-topped cluster of flowers with the outer flowers on longer stalks than the inner flowers.

Cotyledon Seed leaf, the first leaf or leaves a plant develops. Dicotyledons (dicots) have two cotyledons; monocotyledons (monocots) have one.

Crisped Finely waved edge (of a leaf or flower).

Crown The point of a plant where the roots meet the stem, at or immediately below the surface of the soil.

Culm The hollow jointed stem of a bamboo or grass.

Cultivar A plant variety developed in cultivation, short for cultivated variety.

Cutting A part of a plant removed and induced to form roots and shoots, eventually growing into a new plant genetically identical to the parent.

Cyme A rounded or flat-topped cluster of flowers in which the central flower opens first.

Damping-off A fungus disease that attacks seedlings, girdling and weakening the stem and causing the plants to collapse.

Deadhead Remove faded, spent flowers to keep them from forming seeds.

Deciduous Term describing plants that lose all their leaves at some time during each year, at the end of their growing season.

Dentate Term describing a leaf with evenly toothed edges, the teeth facing outward.

Dieback When tips of shoots die because of disease or frost damage.

Dioecious Plants, such as hollies, that produce male and female flowers on separate plants. Both male and female plants are needed to produce fruit.

Disbud Remove some of a plant's flower buds to produce fewer but larger flowers. Often done to plants being grown for exhibition.

Disk flower A small, often insignificant, flower that is part of the central portion of a composite (daisylike) flower. *See also* Ray flower.

Division Method of vegetative propagation in which a plant clump is cut apart into several sections, which are replanted to produce new plants.

Double A flower that has more than the usual number of petals.

Drill Shallow, straight, narrow furrow in which seeds are sown.

Drupe Fruit that has one or more seeds surrounded by fleshy tissue. Stone fruits (cherries, peaches, plums) are drupes, as are raspberries (which are a cluster of drupes).

Entire Leaves having smoooth edges without teeth or indentations.

Epiphyte Plant that grows on another plant for support, but does not parasitize it.

Ericaceous Plants belonging to the Heath Family, Ericaceae, which grow in acid soil.

Espalier Method of training trees, usually fruit trees, to grow in particular patterns with all the growth in a flat plane.

Evergreen Plant that keeps its foliage longer than one growing season, remaining green year-round. Semievergreen plants lose some of their leaves each growing season while retaining others.

Eye Dormant bud from which new growth can develop under the right conditions.

F1 hybrid A first-generation hybrid produced by cross-pollinating two compatible parent plants. Seeds for F1 hybrids must be produced by crossing the parent plants anew each time; the hybrids will not come true from seed (*see* True).

Fall Lower petal, especially of an iris, that droops downward.

Family Group of related plant genera that share certrain characteristics and differ in others.

Fastigiate Trees and shrubs on which the branches grow vertically instead of spreading horizontally.

Filament Slender stalk which supports the anthers of a flower. Anther and filament collectively are called the stamen.

Floret One of the small individual flowers that make up a composite flower or flower cluster.

Force Induce a plant to grow, bloom, or set fruit out of its natural season.

Friable Term describing soil that crumbles readily and is easy to work.

Gall Abnormal growth on a plant caused by insects or disease.

Genus Group of related plant species that share many common characteristics and are believed to have evolved from the same ancestor.

Glaucous Blue-green or gray-green leaf. Also used to describe a fruit with a waxy whitish bloom (coating), such as a grape or blueberry.

Grafting Method of joining top growth of one plant (called the scion) to the roots of another plant (the stock or rootstock) so they unite into one plant.

Green manure Fast-growing crop, often a legume, grown in empty areas of the garden then cut down and tilled in or left to decompose, to add organic matter to the soil.

Groundcover Spreading plants grown to cover an expanse of soil.

Hardening off A process of adapting plants started indoors to outdoor garden conditions by placing them outdoors for gradually increasing lengths of time over a period of days.

Hardy Able to withstand the coldest winter temperatures normal in a given location without protection. In warm climates, hardiness is also used to describe a plant's ability to tolerate the hottest summer temperatures normally experienced.

Heel A piece of main stem or older tissue taken along with some cuttings to help them root more easily.

Heeling-in Temporarily planting a bare-root tree or shrub to keep the roots from drying out until it can be planted in its permanent location.

Herbaceous Nonwoody perennial plants whose top growth dies back to the ground each winter while the roots live on underground.

Humus Fully decomposed organic matter, produced naturally or as a result of composting.

Hybrid *See* F1 hybrid.

Inflorescence Group of flowers arranged on a stem, such as a corymb, cyme, panicle, raceme, or umbel.

Lanceolate Lance-shaped.

Lateral Shoot or stem growing from a bud on the side of a stem or root.

Layering Method of vegetative propagation in which a stem is pegged to the ground, forms roots, and is then severed from the parent plant and transplanted.

Leaching Process by which nutrients are lost from soil when they are dissolved in water and carried away from the root zone as the water drains.

Leaflet One section of a compound leaf.

Loam Soil containing a mixture of sand, silt, and clay. Loam is generally fertile and well-drained, ideal for gardening.

Lobe Portion of a leaf or flower petal separated from the rest of the structure by an indentation.

Monocarpic A plant that blooms and sets seed only once, then dies. Used to describe plants, such as century plant (*Agave*), that live several years before blooming.

Monoecious Plants that produce both male and female flowers on the same plant, such as squash.

Mulch Organic or inorganic covering laid over garden soil to discourage weeds and slow evaporation of moisture from the soil.

Naturalized A plant established in a garden in congenial conditions and allowed to grow and reproduce as it would in the wild.

Neutral Soil with a pH of 7.0, that is neither acid nor alkaline.

Nodes Points on a stem from which leaves, shoots, or flowers grow.

Offset Young plant that grows from the base of the parent plant and may be separated and transplanted. Or a young bulb that forms at the base of the parent bulb, and may be separated and planted to eventually grow to blooming size.

Opposite Leaves produced directly across from each other on two sides of a stem.

Ovary A female flower organ located at the base of the pistil, that holds ovules and will eventually grow into a fruit if fertilized.

Palmate A leaf that has lobes resembling fingers on a hand.

Panicle Branched inflorescence, with the branches carried along an axis; a branched raceme.

Parterre Flat garden area with geometric beds of ornamental plants, often in elaborate patterns, the beds enclosed by low hedges. Parterres are meant to be viewed from above.

Peat, peat moss Partially decayed plant remains that collect in bogs. Sphagnum peat comes from sphagnum moss; sedge peat from decayed sedges and other plants. Peat moss adds organic matter but no nutrients to garden soils.

Perennial A plant that lives three growing seasons or more.

Perianth Collective name for the corolla and calyx of a flower.

Petal A part of a flower's colorful corolla. Petals are actually modified leaves.

Petiole The stem on which a leaf is carried, a leaf stalk.

pH A measurement of soil's acidity or alkalinity. Measured on a 14-point scale; 7.0 is neutral, readings above 7.0 are alkaline, and below 7.0 are acid. Each number on the pH scale indicates a degree of acidity or alkalinity 10 times the value of the number preceding it.

Photosynthesis Chemical process by which plants use energy from sunlight and chlorophyll to convert carbon dioxide and water into sugars that fuel growth.

Pinnate Compound leaf made up of individual leaflets arranged in pairs on opposite sides of a stem.

Pistil Female organs of a flower, comprised of the stigma, style, and ovary.

Pollination Fertilization of a flower by the transfer of ripe pollen from anthers to a receptive stigma (*see* "Parts of a Flower" on page 58 in chapter 2, "Gardening Techniques").

Pome A fleshy fruit formed by the union of the ovary and the fused base of the corolla and calyx. Apples and pears are pomes.

Procumbent Term describing a low-growing plant that creeps along the ground, is prostrate.

Pruning Removing branches, stems, or roots, or parts thereof, to remove damaged or diseased tissue, or to rejuvenate or reshape the plant.

Raceme An unbranched elongated cluster of flowers with the flowers carried along a central stalk; the youngest flowers are at the tip of the raceme.

Radicle An embryonic root contained in a seed; the first root to emerge as the seed germinates.

Ray flower Part of a composite flower, one of the elongated flowers that form an outer ring around the central disk flowers. Ray flowers often look like petals.

Recurved Curved backward (describes flower petals).

Reflexed Bent sharply backward (flower petals).

Rhizome Swollen, creeping underground stem that stores nutrients like a bulb. Roots and shoots grow from the rhizome.

Root ball Root system and the soil that clings to it when a plant is dug up or unpotted.

Rootstock Plant that supplies the root system of a grafted plant.

Rosette Cluster of leaves that fan out from a point. A rosette is usually at or near ground level, at the base of the stem.

Runner Slender horizontal stem that trails across the soil surface and roots at each node that makes contact with the soil.

Scandent Vining plant that develops long stems which climb loosely over supports, without attaching themselves.

Scarify Nick or abrade a hard seed coat to make it easier for the seed to absorb the moisture it needs to germinate.

Scion Plant grafted to another plant to supply the top growth of a new plant.

Self-seed When a plant expels mature seeds that germinate and grow into new plants on their own, with no help from the gardener.

Semihardwood Cutting taken late in the season from current year's growth that has begun to turn woody. Also called semiripe.

Sepal One part of a flower's calyx (*see* Calyx). Sepals may be green and insignificant, or as showy as petals.

Sessile Describes leaves or flowers that have no stalk and grow directly from the stem.

Shrub Woody plant with many stems that usually branch near the base.

Simple Describes a leaf that is one piece, not divided into leaflets (*see also* Entire).

Sodic soil Highly alkaline soil with a pH above 8.5, found in some desert areas. Also called alkali soil.

Species Group of closely related plants that differ only in small ways. The basic unit of plant classification; species are in turn gathered into genera. Some genera contain only one species.

Sphagnum Type of very porous moss found in bogs, used after it has been compressed into peat, or in green or dried form, as an addition to growing media.

Spike Narrow, elongated, unbranched cluster of sessile flowers (*see* Sessile) produced along a central axis.

Spore Reproductive structure of a plant that has no flowers (and thus, no seeds)—ferns, mosses, and fungi.

Sport Plant mutation that results in a shoot or new plant different from the rest of the plant or other plants of its kind. The mutation is caused by a genetic change that is spontaneous or accidental, or induced intentionally.

Spur Short side stem growing from another branch, usually on a fruit tree, from which flowers and eventually fruit grow. Also the name of a long, hollow extension on the end of a flower petal.

Stamen A flower's male reproductive organ, which consists of one or more anthers and filaments.

Standard Tree or shrub trained to grow as a bushy ball of foliage atop a straight, bare stem. Also the name of the upright petal of a legume flower, and the three upright petals of an iris flower.

Stigma Part of the female reproductive organ of a flower, the stigma is located at the top of the style, and becomes sticky to receive ripe pollen grains during fertilization.

Stolon Stem that grows horizontally aboveground, or hangs downward, and roots when the tip touches the ground, forming a new plant.

Stomate, plural **stomata** Pore in a leaf through which carbon dioxide, oxygen, and water vapor pass during photosynthesis and transpiration.

Stratify Place seeds in a cold environment to break their dormancy and enable them to germinate. A necessary pretreatment for seeds of many trees and shrubs being sown indoors.

Style Part of the female reproductive structure of a flower, the style supports the stigma.

Subshrub Plant with a woody base whose green shoots die back each winter.

Succulent Plant with fleshy, swollen leaves and stems that contain sap and store moisture to supply the plant during dry weather. Also used to describe the fleshy tissues.

Sucker Extra shoot growing from a plant's roots or the underground part of its stem. Suckers can weaken the plant, but may often be rooted to produce a new plant after their removal.

Taproot Large straight root that grows downward into the soil to bring up water from deep underground. The taproot may be enlarged into a storage organ, as in a carrot, to hold nutrients for the plant.

Tender Term describing a plant that is damaged or killed by cold temperatures. Frost-tender describes plants harmed by frost and freezing temperatures.

Tendril Long, thin modified leaf, stem, or leaf stalk that twists or coils itself around a support to enable a plant to climb.

Thatch Layer of dead stems and leaves that can build up at the base of the turf in a lawn faster than the material can decay. Thatch hinders the passage of water and fertilizers to the soil beneath the lawn.

Tilth Condition of the surface layer of soil when it is suitable for cultivation. Soil that has good tilth, or is friable, is crumbly, fine-textured without being powdery, and easy to work.

Top-dress Spread compost, fertilizers, or other soil-enhancing material on top of the soil around plants, without working the material into the soil.

Topiary Painstaking process of pruning, clipping, and training trees and shrubs into precise decorative shapes, and maintaining them that way by frequent clipping.

Trifoliate Compound leaf made up of three leaflets, or leaves produced in groups of three.

True, come true from seed Ability of a plant to produce offspring very similar to itself from seed when self-pollinated.

Truss Compact, branching cluster of flowers or fruit.

Tuber Swollen bulbous storage organ, usually located underground, that develops from a modified stem or root.

Umbel Flower cluster in which the florets are produced on stalks arising from a single central point. Umbels can be globular or flat-topped.

Variegated Plant whose leaves are irregularly marked with a second color, most often yellow, ivory, or white. Variegation is due to a lack of chlorophyll in the colored areas.

Variety A variant of a species that originally occurred in nature rather than as a result of intentional breeding.

Vegetative Asexual. Vegetative propagation methods produce new plants genetically identical to the parent without pollination and seeds. Also used to describe leafy, nonblooming growth.

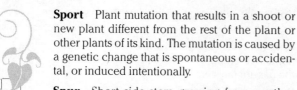

Vermiculite Lightweight, water-absorbent material used in potting mixtures and manufactured from heat-expanded mica.

Water sprout Long, upright shoot produced by a tree or shrub, often after pruning. Water sprouts will not bloom or bear fruit, and are usually removed to conserve the plant's strength.

Whip Young, unbranched tree.

Whorl Group of three or more flowers, stems, or branches that radiate from a single point on the stem, branch, or trunk.

Appendix 3

DIRECTORY OF ARBORETA AND BOTANIC GARDENS

Below are listed names and addresses of major public gardens in the United States. There are many more public gardens in addition to those listed here. Check with local tourism offices when planning trips to particular areas, to find out about other gardens worth seeing.

ALABAMA

Donald E. Davis Arboretum
Auburn University
Auburn, AL 36830
(205) 826-5755

Birmingham Botanical Garden
2612 Lane Park Rd.
Birmingham, AL 35223
(205) 879-1227

Huntsville Botanical Gardens
4747 Bob Wallace Ave.
Huntsville, AL 35223
(205) 830-4447

Mobile Botanical Gardens
P.O. Box 8382
Mobile, AL 36608
(205) 342-0555

Bellingrath Gardens
Rt. 1, Box 60
Theodore, AL 36582
(205) 973-2217

ALASKA

Alaska Botanical Garden
P.O. Box 202202
Anchorage, AK 99520
(907) 265-3165

The Gardens at the Museum of Alaska Transportation and Industry
P.O. Box 909
Palmer, AK 99645
(907) 745-4493

ARIZONA

Desert Botanical Garden
1201 N. Galvin Parkway
Phoenix, AZ 85008
(602) 941-1225

Boyce Thompson Southwestern Arboretum
37615 U.S. 60
Superior, AZ 85273
(520) 689-2811

Arizona-Sonora Desert Museum
2021 N. Kinney Rd.
Tucson, AZ 85743
(602) 883-1380

Tucson Botanical Garden
2150 N. Alvernon Way
Tucson, AZ 85712
(602) 326-9686

CALIFORNIA

Los Angeles State and County Arboretum
301 N. Baldwin Ave.
Arcadia, CA 91006
(818) 446-8251

Regional Parks Botanic Garden
Tilden Regional Park
Berkeley, CA 94708
(415) 841-8732

University of California at
Berkeley Botanical Garden
Centennial Dr.
Berkeley, CA 94720
(415) 642-3343

Rancho Santa Ana Botanic
Garden
1500 N. College Ave.
Claremont, CA 91711
(714) 625-8767

Fullerton Arboretum
California State University
800 N. State College
Fullerton, CA 92634
(714) 773-3579

Descanso Gardens
1418 Descanso Dr.
La Canada, CA 91011
(213) 790-5571

Muir Woods National Monument
Rt. 1 and Panoramic Hwy.
Mill Valley, CA 94941
(415) 388-2595

The Living Desert
47-900 Portola Ave.
P.O. Box 1775
Palm Desert, CA 92261
(619) 346-5694

Strybing Arboretum and
Botanical Gardens
9th Avenue and Lincoln Way
San Francisco, CA 94122
(415) 753-70891

Huntington Botanical Gardens
1151 Oxford Rd.
San Marino, CA 91108
(818) 405-2100

Lotusland (Ganna Walska
Lotusland)
695 Ashley Rd.
Santa Barbara, CA 93108
(805) 969-3767

Santa Barbara Botanic Garden
1212 Mission Canyon Rd.
Santa Barbara, CA 93105
(805) 682-4726

Filoli Center
Canada Rd.
Woodside, CA 94062
(415) 364-8300

COLORADO

Horticultural Arts Society
Demonstration Garden
900 N. Glen Ave.
Colorado Springs, CO 80907
(719) 475-0250

Denver Botanic Gardens
909 York St.
Denver, CO 80206
(303) 331-4000

CONNECTICUT

Mianus River Gorge Wildlife
Refuge and Botanical
Preserve
151 Brookside Dr.
Greenwich, CT 06831

New Canaan Nature Center
144 Oenoke Ridge
New Canaan, CT 06840
(203) 966-9577

Connecticut College Arboretum
Williams St.
New London, CT 06320
(203) 447-1911, ext. 7700

Bartlett Arboretum
151 Brookdale Rd.
Stamford, CT 06903
(203) 322-6971

DELAWARE

Mt. Cuba Center for the Study of
Piedmont Flora
P.O. Box 3570
Greenville, DE 19807
(302) 239-4244

Eleutherian Mills
P.O. Box 3630, Rt. 141
Wilmington, DE 19735
(302) 658-2400

Nemours Mansion and Gardens
P.O. Box 109, Rockland Rd.
Wilmington, DE 19899
(302) 651-6912

Winterthur Museum and
Gardens
Kennett Pike, Rt. 52
Winterthur, DE 19735
(302) 654-1548

DISTRICT OF COLUMBIA

Dumbarton Oaks
1703 32nd St., N.W.
Washington, DC 20007
(202) 342-3200

United States Botanic Garden
Maryland Ave., S.W.
Washington, DC 20024
(202) 225-8333

United States National
Arboretum
3501 New York Ave., N.E.
Washington, DC 20002
(202) 475-4815

FLORIDA

Flamingo Gardens
3750 Flamingo Rd.
Fort Lauderdale, FL 33330
(305) 473-2955

Bok Tower Gardens
P.O. Drawer 3810
Burns Ave. and Tower Blvd.
Lake Wales, FL 33859
(813) 676-1408

Fairchild Tropical Garden
10901 Old Cutler Rd.
Miami, FL 33156
(305) 667-1651

Marie Selby Botanical Gardens
811 S. Palm Ave.
Sarasota, FL 34236
(813) 366-5730

GEORGIA

The State Botanical Garden of Georgia
2450 S. Milledge Ave.
Athens, GA 30605
(706) 542-1244

Atlanta Botanical Garden
P.O. Box 77246
Atlanta, GA 30357
(404) 876-5858

Callaway Gardens
U.S. Highway 27 South
P.O. Box 2000
Pine Mountain, GA 31822
(706) 663-2281

HAWAII

Waimea Falls Park Arboretum and Botanical Gardens
55-864 Kamehameha Hwy.
Haleiwa, HI 96712
(808) 638-8511

Hawaii Tropical Botanic Garden
248 Kahoa Rd.
Hilo, HI 96720
(808) 964-5233

Foster Botanical Garden
180 N. Vineyard Blvd.
Honolulu, HI 96817
(808) 533-3406

Honolulu Botanical Gardens
50 N. Vineyard Blvd.
Honolulu, HI 96817
(808) 522-7060

Harold L. Lyon Arboretum
University of Hawaii at Manoa
3860 Manoa Rd.
Honolulu, HI 96822
(808) 988-3177

Moir's Gardens
R.R. 1, P.O. Box 73
Koloa, HI 96756
(808) 742-6411

Kula Botanical Gardens
R.R. 2, Box 288
Kula, HI 96790
(808) 878-1715

National Tropical Botanical Garden
P.O. Box 340
Lawai, HI 96765
(808) 332-7361

IDAHO

Idaho Botanical Garden
2355 Old Penitentiary Rd.
Boise, ID 83712
(208) 343-8649

ILLINOIS

Garfield Park Conservatory
300 N. Central Park Blvd.
Chicago, IL 60624
(708) 533-1281

Lincoln Park Conservatory
2400 N. Stockton Dr. and Fullerton Pkwy.
Chicago, IL 60614
(708) 294-4770

Chicago Botanic Garden
P.O. Box 400
Glencoe, IL 60022
(708) 835-5440

The Morton Arboretum
Rt. 53
Lisle, IL 60532
(708) 968-0074

Washington Park Horticultural Center
Fayette and Chatham Rds.
Springfield, IL 62704

INDIANA

Foster Gardens
3900 Broadway
Fort Wayne, IN 46807

Hayes Regional Arboretum
801 Elks Rd.
Richmond, IN 47374
(317) 962-3745

IOWA

Bickelhaupt Arboretum
340 S. 14th St.
Clinton, IA 52732
(319) 242-4771

Des Moines Botanical Center
909 East River Dr.
Des Moines, IA 50316
(515) 283-4148

Ewing Park Lilac Arboretum
McKinley Ave. and
Indianola Rd.
Des Moines, IA 50315
(515) 283-4227

KANSAS

The Bartlett Arboretum
Box 39
Belle Plaine, KS 67013
(316) 488-3451

Kansas Landscape Arboretum
Rt. 5
Wakefield, KS 67487
(913) 263-2540

Botanica, The Wichita Gardens
701 N. Amidon
Wichita, KS 67203
(316) 264-0448

KENTUCKY

Bernheim Forest Arboretum
Claremont, KY 40110

LOUISIANA

Jungle Gardens
General Delivery
Avery Island, LA 70513
(318) 365-8173

Louisiana State Arboretum
Linton Rd.
Benton, LA 71006

Hodges Gardens
P.O. Box 900
Many, LA 71449
(318) 586-3523

Longue Vue House and Gardens
7 Bamboo Rd.
New Orleans, LA 70124
(504) 488-5488

Rosedown Plantation and
Gardens
P.O. Box 1816
St. Francisville, LA 70775
(504) 635-3332

MAINE

Wild Gardens of Acadia
Acadia National Park
Sieur de Monts Spring
Bar Harbor, ME 04609
(207) 288-3338

Merryspring
P.O. Box 893
Camden, ME 04843
(207) 236-8831

Deering Oaks Rose Circle
55 Portland St.
Portland, ME 04101
(207) 874-8871

MARYLAND

William Paca Garden
1 Martin St.
Annapolis, MD 21401
(410) 267-6656 or
(410) 269-0601

Ladew Topiary Gardens
3535 Jarrettsville Pike
Monkton, MD 21111
(301) 557-9466

Brookside Gardens
1500 Glenallan Ave.
Wheaton, MD 20902
(301) 949-8230

MASSACHUSETTS

Isabella Stewart Gardner
Museum
280 The Fenway
Boston, MA 02115
(617) 566-1401

Garden in the Woods
180 Hemenway Rd.
Framingham, MA 01701
(508) 877-7630

The Arnold Arboretum of
Harvard University
125 Arborway
Jamaica Plain, MA 02130
(617) 524-1718

Botanic Garden of Smith
College
Northampton, MA 01063
(413) 584-2700

Berkshire Garden Center
P.O. Box 826
Stockbridge, MA 02162
(413) 298-3926

Old Sturbridge Village
1 Old Sturbridge Village Rd.
Sturbridge, MA 61566
(508) 347-3362

MICHIGAN

Mattaei Botanical Garden
University of Michigan
1800 N. Dixboro Rd.
Ann Arbor, MI 48105
(313) 764-1168

Nichols Arboretum
University of Michigan
Ann Arbor, MI 48104
(313) 763-6632

W. J. Beal Botanic Garden
Michigan State University
East Lansing, MI 48823
(517) 355-0348

Dow Gardens
1018 W. Main St.
Midland, MI 48640
(517) 631-2677

Fernwood
1720 Range Line Rd.
Niles, MI 49120
(616) 695-6491

MINNESOTA

Minnesota Landscape Arboretum and Horicultural Research Center
University of Minnesota
3687 Arboretum Dr.
P.O. Box 39
Chanhassen, MN 55317
(612) 489-1740

Como Park Conservatory
Midway Parkway and Kaufman Drive
St. Paul, MN 55103
(612) 489-1740

MISSISSIPPI

The Crosby Arboretum
3702 Hardy St.
Hattiesburg, MS 39401
(601) 264-5249

Jackson State University Botanical Garden
1400 John R. Lynch St.
Jackson, MS 39209
(601) 968-2595

MISSOURI

Shaw Arboretum
I-44 and Rt. 100
Gray Summit, MO 63039
(314) 577-5138

University of Missouri Department of Horticulture
I-43 Agricultural Bldg.
Columbia, MO 65211
(314) 882-2745

Missouri Botanical Garden
P.O. Box 299
St. Louis, MO 63166
(314) 577-5100

MONTANA

The Gatiss Gardens
4790 Montana 35, Rt. 5
Kalispell, MT 59901
(406) 755-2950

Memorial Rose Garden
Brooks Ave.
Missoula, MT 59801

NEBRASKA

Nebraska Statewide Arboretum
111 Forestry Sciences Laboratory
University of Nebraska, East Campus
Lincoln, NE 68508
(402) 472-2971

Omaha Botanical Center
1605 S. 113th Plaza
Omaha, NE 68114
(402) 333-2359

NEVADA

Wilbur D. May Arboretum and Botanical Garden
1502 Washington St.
Reno, NV 89503
(702) 785-4153

NEW HAMPSHIRE

Saint Gaudens National Historic Site
R.R. 2, Box 73
Cornish, NH 03745
(603) 675-2175

Rhododendron State Park
Fitzwilliam, NH 03452
(603) 532-8862

Fuller Gardens
10 Willow Ave.
North Hampton, NH 03862
(603) 964-5414

Moffatt-Ladd House and Garden
154 Market St.
Portsmouth, NH 03801
(603) 436-8221

Strawbery Banke
P.O. Box 300
Portsmouth, NH 03801
(603) 433-1100

NEW JERSEY

Leaming's Run Botanical Gardens
1845 Rt. 9 North
Cape May Court House, NJ 08210
(609) 465-5871

Leonard J. Buck Garden
Far Hills, NJ 07931
(908) 234-2677

Frelinghuysen Arboretum
53 E. Hanover Ave., P.O. Box 1295
Morris Township, NJ 07962
(201) 326-7600

Willowwood Arboretum
P.O. Box 129R
Morristown, NJ 07960
(201) 829-0474

Rutgers Research and Display Gardens
U.S. 1 at Ryders Lane
New Brunswick, NJ 08902
(201) 932-9639

Skylands Botanical Gardens
Ringwood State Park
Box 302
Ringwood, NJ 07456
(201) 962-9534

Reeves-Reed Arboretum
165 Hobart Ave.
Summit, NJ 07901
(201) 273-8787

NEW YORK

New York Botanical Garden
Bronx, NY 10458
(718) 817-8705

Wave Hill
675 W. 252nd St.
Bronx, NY 10471
(718) 549-3200

Brooklyn Botanic Garden
1000 Washington Ave.
Brooklyn, NY 11225
(718) 622-4433

Bayard Cutting Arboretum
Montauk Hwy.
Great River, NY 11739
(516) 581-1002

Mary Flagler Cary Arboretum
Milbrook, NY 12545
(914) 677-5358 or 5359

Mohonk Mountain House
Lake Mohonk
New Paltz, NY 12561
(914) 255-4500

Central Park Conservatory Garden
830 Fifth Ave.
New York, NY 10021
(212) 360-2766

Old Westbury Gardens
P.O. Box 430
Old Westbury, NY 11568
(516) 333-0048

Planting Fields Arboretum
P.O. Box 58
Oyster Bay, NY 11771
(516) 922-9200

Highland Botanical Park
375 Westfall Rd.
Rochester, NY 14620
(716) 244-8079

NORTH CAROLINA

The Botanical Gardens at Asheville
151 W. T. Weaver Blvd.
Asheville, NC 28804
(704) 252-5190

The North Carolina Arboretum
P.O. Box 6617
Asheville, NC 28816
(704) 665-2492

North Carolina Botanical Garden
University of North Carolina
Chapel Hill, NC 27514
(919) 967-2246

North Carolina State University Arboretum
Horticulture Dept., Kilgore Hall
Raleigh, NC 27695
(919) 737-3132

NORTH DAKOTA

International Peace Garden
Rt. 1
Dunseith, ND 58329
(701) 263-4390

Agassiz Nursery
4201 S. University Dr.
Fargo, ND 58103
(701) 232-8188

OHIO

Garden Center of Greater Cleveland
11030 East Blvd.
Cleveland, OH 44106
(216) 721-1600

James M. Cox, Jr. Arboretum
6733 Springboro Pike
Dayton, OH 45449
(513) 434-9005

Kingwood Center
900 Park Ave. W
Mansfield, OH 44906
(419) 522-0211

Holden Arboretum
9500 Sperry Rd.
Mentor, OH 44060
(216) 946-4400

The Dawes Arboretum
7770 Jacksontown Rd., SE
Newark, OH 43056
(800) 44DAWES or (614) 323-2355

Toledo Botanical Garden
5403 Elmer Dr.
P.O. Box 7430
Toledo, OH 43615
(419) 536-8365

OKLAHOMA

Oklahoma Botanical Garden and Arboretum
Oklahoma State University
Stillwater, OK 74078
(405) 744-5415

Cherokee Gardens
Tahlequah, OK 74464

OREGON

Greer Gardens
1280 Goodpasture Island Rd.
Eugene, OR 97401
(503) 686-8266

Mount Pisgah Arboretum
P.O. Box 5621
Eugene, OR 97405
(503) 747-3817

The Berry Botanic Garden
11505 S.W. Summerville Ave.
Portland, OR 97219
(503) 636-4112

Hoyt Arboretum
4000 S.W. Fairview Blvd.
Portland, OR 97221
(503) 228-8732

International Rose Test Garden at Washington Park
400 S. W. Kingston Ave.
Portland, OR 97201
(503) 248-4302

Leach Botanical Garden
6704 S. E. 122nd Ave.
Portland, OR 97236
(503) 761-9503

PENNSYLVANIA

Hershey Rose Gardens and Arboretum
621 Park Ave.
Hershey, PA 17033
(717) 534-3492

Longwood Gardens
P.O. Box 501, Rt. 1
Kennett Square, PA 19348
(215) 388-6741

Swiss Pines
R.D. 1, Box 127
Charlestown Rd.
Malvern, PA 19355
(610) 933-6916

Bartram's Garden
54th St. and Lindbergh Blvd.
Philadelphia, PA 19143
(215) 729-5281

Morris Arboretum of the University of Pennsylvania
9414 Meadowbrook Ave.
Philadelphia, PA 19118
(215) 247-5777

Phipps Conservatory
Schenley Park
Pittsburgh, PA 15213
(412) 255-2370

Bowman's Hill Wildflower Preserve
Washington Crossing Historic Park
P.O. Box 103
Washington Crossing, PA 18977
(215) 862-2924

RHODE ISLAND

Blithewold Mansion and Gardens
Ferry Rd., P.O. Box 716
Bristol, RI 02809
(401) 253-2707

Green Animals Topiary Garden
Cory's Lane
Portsmouth, RI 02871
(401) 847-1000

Roger Williams Park
Elmwood Ave.
Providence, RI 02905
(401) 785-9450

SOUTH CAROLINA

Magnolia Plantation and Gardens
Rt. 4, Hwy. 61
Charleston, SC 29407
(803) 571-1266

Middleton Place
Ashley River Rd.
Charleston, SC 29407
(803) 556-6020

South Carolina Botanical Garden
Clemson University
Clemson, SC 29634
(803) 656-4964

SOUTH DAKOTA

McCrory Gardens
South Dakota State University
Dept. of Horticulture and Forestry
6th St.
Brookings, SD 57007
(605) 688-5136

Great Plains Botanical Society
P.O. Box 461
Hot Springs, SD 57747
(605) 745-3397

TENNESSEE

Memphis Botanic Garden
Goldsmith Garden Center
750 Cherry Rd.
Memphis, TN 38117
(901) 685-1566

Tennessee Botanical Garden and Fine Arts Center at Cheekwood
1200 Forrest Park Dr.
Nashville, TN 37205
(615) 352-5310

Opryland Hotel
2800 Opryland Dr.
Nashville, TN 37214
(615) 889-6600

University of Tennessee Arboretum
901 Kerr Hollow Rd.
Oak Ridge, TN 37830
(615) 483-3571

TEXAS

The National Wildflower Research Center
2600 FM 973 North
Austin, TX 78725
(512) 929-3600

Dallas Arboretum and Botanic Garden
8617 Garland Rd.
Dallas, TX 75218
(214) 327-8263

Fort Worth Botanic Garden
3220 Botanic Garden Dr.
Fort Worth, TX 76107
(817) 871-7686

Houston Arboretum and Nature Center
4501 Woodway
Houston, TX 77024
(713) 681-8433

Valley Botanical Garden
Rt. 3, Box 1388
McAllen, TX 78501

San Antonio Botanical Center
555 Funsten Place
San Antonio, TX 78209
(512) 821-5143

Tyler Municipal Rose Garden
W. Front and Boone Sts.
P.O. Box 390
Tyler, TX 75710
(214) 592-1661

UTAH

Joan Hardle Arboretum
Murray City Park
Murray, UT 84157
(801) 264-2614

State Arboretum of Utah
University of Utah
100 South and 1400 East
Salt Lake City, UT 84112
(801) 581-5322

VERMONT

University of Vermont Agricultural Experiment Station
College of Agriculture and Life Sciences
Rt. 7
Burlington, VT 05405
(802) 656-2980

Shelburne Museum
Shelburne, VT 05482
(802) 985-3346

VIRGINIA

River Farm
American Horticultural Society
7931 E. Boulevard Dr.
Alexandria, VA 22308
(703) 768-5700

Monticello
P.O. Box 386
Charlottesville, VA 22902
(804) 979-1489

Norfolk Botanical Gardens
Airport Rd.
Norfolk, VA 23518
(804) 853-6972

Lewis Ginter Botanical Garden
P.O. Box 28246
Richmond, VA 23228
(804) 262-9887

WASHINGTON

Bloedel Reserve
7571 NE Dolphin Dr.
Bainbridge Island, WA 98110
(206) 842-7631

The Herbfarm
32804 Issaquah-Fall City Rd.
Fall City, WA 98024
(206) 784-2222

Rhododendron Species Foundation
P.O. Box 3798
Federal Way, WA 98063
(206) 661-9377

Washington Park Arboretum
2300 Arboretum Drive East
Seattle, WA 98112
(206) 543-8800

John A. Finch Arboretum
3404 Woodland Blvd.
Spokane, WA 99204
(509) 456-4331

Manito Park Conservatory and Gardens
4 W. 21st Ave.
Spokane, WA 99203
(509) 456-4331

Ohme Gardens
3327 Ohme Rd.
Wenatchee, WA 98801
(509) 662-5785

WEST VIRGINIA

West Virginia Arboretum
Dept. of Biology
West Virginia University
Morgantown, WV 26506
(304) 293-5201

WISCONSIN

Green Bay Botanical Garden
P.O. Box 1913
624 Doty St.
Green Bay, WI 54305
(414) 432-4224

Alfred L. Boerner Botanical Gardens
5879 S. 92nd St.
Hales Corners, WI 53130
(414) 425-1130

University of Wisconsin Arboretum
1207 Seminole Way
Madison, WI 53711
(608) 263-7888

Schlitz Audubon Center
1111 E. Brown Deer Rd.
Milwaukee, WI 53217
(414) 352-2880

River Edge Nature Center
Newburg, WI 53060
(414) 675-6888

WYOMING

Cheyenne Botanic Gardens
710 S. Lions Park Dr.
Cheyenne, WY 82001
(307) 637-6458

Appendix 4
PLANT SOCIETIES

Below are listed some of the plant societies devoted to outdoor plants. Local garden clubs will be able to tell you which societies have chapters active in your area. The information below was current at the time this book was written, but be advised that plant society contacts tend to change frequently.

Alabama Wildflower Society
Mrs. Dottie Elam
240 Ivy Lane
Auburn, AL 36830
(205) 339-2541

Alaska Native Plant Society
Verna Pratt
P.O. Box 141613
Anchorage, AK 99514
(907) 333-8212

American Bamboo Society
Richard Haubrich
P.O. Box 640
Springville, CA 93265
(209) 539-2145

American Bonsai Society
Anne D. Moyle
P.O. Box 358
Keene, NH 03431
(603) 352-9034

American Camellia Society
C. David Scheibert
P.O. Box 1217
Fort Valley, GA 31030
(912) 967-2358

American Conifer Society
Mrs. Maxine Schwartz
P.O. Box 242
Severna Park, MD 21146

American Daffodil Society, Inc.
Mary Lou Gripshover
1686 Grey Fox Trails
Milford, OH 45150
(513) 248-9137

American Dahlia Society
Michael Martinolich
159 Pine St.
New Hyde Park, NY 11040

American Fern Society, Inc.
James D. Caponettti, Treasurer
Dept. of Botany, University of Tennessee
Knoxville, TN 37996
(615) 974-6219

American Gourd Society
John Stevens
P.O. Box 274
Mount Gilead, OH 43338
(419) 946-3302

American Hemerocallis Society
Elly Launius, Executive Secretary
1454 Rebel Dr.
Jackson, MS 39211
(601) 366-4362

American Herb Association
P.O. Box 353
Rescue, CA 95672

American Horticultural Society
7931 E. Boulevard Dr.
Alexandria, VA 22308
(703) 768-5700

American Hosta Society
Dennis Savory
5300 Whiting Ave.
Edina, MN 55435

American Iris Society
Jeane Stayer
7414 E. 60th St.
Tulsa, OK 74145

American Ivy Society
Elizabeth Carrick
P.O. Box 520
West Carrollton, OH 45449
(513) 434-7069

American Peony Society
Greta M. Kessenich
250 Interlachen Rd.
Hopkins, MN 55343
(612) 935-4706

American Pomological Society
Dr. R. M. Crassweller
103 Tyson Bldg.
University Park, PA 16802
(814) 865-2571

American Primrose Society
Jay G. Lunn
Rt. 5, Box 93
Hillsboro, OR 97124
(503) 640-4582

American Rhododendron Society
Barbara R. Hall, Executive Secretary
P.O. Box 1380
Gloucester, VA 23061
(804) 693-4433

American Rock Garden Society
Buffy Parker
15 Fairmead Rd.
Darien, CT 06820

American Rose Society
Membership Secretary
P.O. Box 30,000
Shreveport, LA 71130
(318) 938-5402

Arizona Native Plant Society
David Ingram
P.O. Box 41206
Tucson, AZ 85717

Arkansas Native Plant Society
Dr. James Gulden
Dept. of Forest Resources, UAM
Monticello, AR 71655
(501) 460-1049

Azalea Society of America, Inc.
Mrs. Marjorie Taylor
5203 Queensbury Ave.
Springfield, VA 22151
(703) 321-7053

Bio-Dynamic Farming & Gardening Association
Roderick Shouldice
P.O. Box 550
Kimberton, PA 19442
(215) 935-7797

Bio-Integral Resource Center (BIRC)
P.O. Box 7414
Berkeley, CA 94707
(415) 524-2567

Bonsai Clubs International
Virginia Ellermann
2636 W. Mission Rd.
Tallahassee, FL 32304

Botanical Club of Wisconsin
Rudy G. Koch, Dept. of Biology
University of Wisconsin, La Crosse
La Crosse, WI 54601

Cactus & Succulent Society of America
Louise Lippold
P.O. Box 3010
Santa Barbara, CA 93130

California Horticultural Society
Mrs. Elsie Mueller
1847 34th Ave.
San Francisco, CA 94122
(415) 566-5222

California Native Plant Society
Kristina Schierenbeck
909 12th St., #116
Sacramento, CA 95814
(916) 447-2677

California Rare Fruit Growers
Dianne M. Hand
California State Arboretum
Fullerton, CA 92634

Colorado Native Plant Society
Myrna P. Steinkamp
P.O. Box 200
Fort Collins, CO 80522

Friends of the Trees
Michael Pilarski
P.O. Box 1466
Chelan, WA 98816

Georgia Botanical Society
Suzanne S. Jackson, Treasurer
3461 Ashwood Lane
Chamblee, GA 30341

Hardy Plant Society—
Mid-Atlantic Group
Mrs. Peg Elliott
710 Hemlock Rd.
Media, PA 19063
(215) 566-0861

Hardy Plant Society of Oregon
Connie Hanni
33530 S.E. Bluff Rd.
Boring, OR 97009
(501) 663-9201

Hawaiian Botanical Society
University of Hawaii, Botany Dept.
3190 Maile Way
Honolulu, HI 96822

Herb Society of America, Inc.
Leslie Rascan
9019 Kirtland Chardon Rd.
Mentor, OH 44060
(216) 256-0514

Heritage Rose Group
Miriam Wilkins
925 Galvin Dr.
El Cerrito, CA 94530
(415) 526-6960

Hobby Greenhouse Association
HGA Membership
1432 Templeton Hills Rd.
Templeton, CA 93465
(805) 434-2692

Holly Society of America, Inc.
Mrs. E. H. Richardson, Secretary
304 North Wind Rd.
Baltimore, MD 21204
(301) 825-8133

Home Orchard Society
Winnifred M. Fisher
P.O. Box 776
Clackamas, OR 97015
(503) 630-3392

Horticultural Alliance of the Hamptons
P.O. Box 202
Bridgehampton, NY 11932

Horticultural Society of New York
128 W. 58th St.
New York, NY 10019
(212) 757-0915

Idaho Native Plant Society
P.O. Box 9451
Boise, ID 83707

International Dwarf Fruit Tree Association
303 Dept. of Horticulture
Michigan State University
East Lansing, MI 48824
(517) 355-5200

International Geranium Society
4610 Druid St.
Los Angeles, CA 90032

International Lilac Society
Walter W. Oakes
P.O. Box 315
Rumford, ME 04276
(207) 562-7453

International Palm Society
Mrs. Lynn McKarney
P.O. Box 368
Lawrence, KS 66044
(913) 843-1235

International Water Lily Society
Charles B. Thomas
P.O. Box 104
Buckeystown, MD 21717
(301) 874-5373

Kansas Wildflower Society
Virginia Hocker
Mulvane Art Center, Washburn University
Topeka, KS 66611
(913) 296-6324

Long Island Horticultural Society
Donald Brodman, President
44 N. Kings Ave.
Lindenhurst, NY 11757
(516) 884-1679

Louisiana Native Plant Society
Richard Johnson, President
Rt. 1, Box 151
Saline, LA 71070

The Magnolia Society, Inc.
Phelan A. Bright
907 S. Chestnut St.
Hammond, LA 70403
(504) 542-9477

Marigold Society of America, Inc.
Jeannette Lowe
P.O. Box 5112
New Britain, PA 18901
(215) 348-5273

Massachusetts Horticultural Association
300 Massachusetts Ave.
Boston, MA 02115
(617) 536-9280

Master Gardeners International Corp. (MaGIC)
2904 Cameron Mills Rd.
Alexandria, VA 22302
(703) 683-6485

Michigan Botanical Club
Matthaei Botanical Gardens
1800 Dixboro Rd.
Ann Arbor, MI 48105

Minnesota Native Plant Society
Robin Fox, University of Minnesota
1445 Gortner Ave.
220 BioSci Center, MNPS
St. Paul, MN 55108

Minnesota State Horticultural Society
161 Alderman Hall
University of Minnesota
1970 Folwell Ave.
St. Paul, MN 55108
(612) 624-7752

Mississippi Native Plant Society
Victor A. Rudis
P.O. Box 2151
Starkville, MS 39759
(601) 324-0430

Missouri Native Plant Society
John Darel, Treasurer
P.O. Box 176, Dept. of Natural Resources
Jefferson City, MO 65102

National Chrysanthemum Society, Inc.
Galen L. Goss
10107 Homar Pond Dr.
Fairfax Station, VA 22039
(703) 978-7951

National Gardening Association
Depot Square
Peterborough, NH 03458
(802) 863-1308

Native Plant Society of New Mexico
Jean Heflin
443 Live Oak Loop Northeast
Albuquerque, NM 87122
(505) 356-3942

Native Plant Society of Oregon
Mary Falconer, Membership Chair
1920 Engel Avenue Northwest
Salem, OR 97304

Native Plant Society of Texas
Dana Tucker
P.O. Box 891
Georgetown, TX 78627
(512) 863-7794

New England Botanical Club
Botanical Museum
Oxford St.
Cambridge, MA 02138

New England Wild Flower Society
Bee Entwisle
180 Hemenway Rd.
Framingham, MA 01701
(508) 877-7630

New Jersey Native Plant Society
Freylinghuysen Arboretum
P.O. Box 1295 R
Morristown, NJ 07960

North American Fruit Explorers
Jill Vorbek, Membership Chair
Rt. 1, Box 94
Chapin, IL 62628
(217) 245-7589

North American Gladiolus Council
Peter Weicenbach
11102 W. Calumet Rd.
Milwaukee, WI 53224
(414) 354-7859

North American Heather Society
Alice E. Knight
62 Elma-Monte Rd.
Elma, WA 98541
(206) 482-3258

North American Lily Society, Inc.
Dr. Robert Gilman, Secretary-Treasurer
P.O. Box 272
Owatonna, MN 55060
(507) 451-2170

North Carolina Wild Flower Preservation Society
Mrs. S. M. Cozart
900 W. Nash St.
Wilson, NC 27893
(919) 243-2048

Northern Nevada Native Plant Society
Loring Williams
P.O. Box 8965
Reno, NV 89507
(702) 358-7759

Northern Nut Growers Association
Kenneth Bauman
9870 S. Palmer Rd.
New Carlisle, OH 45344
(513) 878-2610

Northwest Horticultural Society
Mrs. Leo Cunningham
V. Isaacson Hall, University of Washington, GF-15
Seattle, WA 98195
(206) 527-1794

Northwest Perennial Alliance
Bob Lilly
P.O. Box 45574, University Station
Seattle, WA 98145
(206) 525-6245

Ohio Native Plant Society
A. K. Malmquist
6 Louise Dr.
Chagrin Falls, OH 44022
(216) 338-6622

The Pennsylvania Horticultural Society
325 Walnut St.
Philadelphia, PA 19106
(215) 625-8250

Pennsylvania Native Plant Society
1806 Commonwealth Bldg.
316 Fourth Ave.
Pittsburgh, PA 15222

Rare Fruit Council International, Inc.
Carolyn Welch Betts
P.O. Box 561914
Miami, FL 33256
(305) 663-2852

Rhododendron Species Foundation
Pam Elms, P.O. Box 3798
Federal Way, WA 98063
(206) 661-9377

The Royal Horticultural Society
Membership Secretary
80 Vincent Square
London SW1P 2PE, England

Seed Savers Exchange
c/o Kent Whealy
R.R. 3, Box 239
Decorah, IA 52101
(319) 382-5990

Tennessee Native Plant Society
Dept. of Botany
University of Tennessee
Knoxville, TN 37996
(615) 974-225

Texas State Horticultural Society
Norman Winter
4348 Carter Creek, Suite 101
Bryan, TX 77802
(409) 846-1752

Tropical Flowering Tree Society
Dolores Fugina
Fairchild Tropical Garden
10901 Old Cutler Rd.
Miami, FL 33156
(305) 248-0818

Utah Native Plant Society
Pam Poulsen, Treasurer
3631 S. Carolyn St.
Salt Lake City, UT 84106

Virginia Native Plant Society
P. H. White
P.O. Box 844
Annandale, VA 22003

Washington Native Plant Society
Dept. of Botany, KB-15
University of Washington
Seattle, WA 98195
(206) 543-1942

Western Horticultural Society
Robert Young
P.O. Box 60507
Palo Alto, CA 94306
(415) 369-2358

Woody Plant Society
Betty Ann Mech
1315 66th Ave. Northeast
Minneapolis, MN 55432
(612) 574-1197

World Pumpkin Federation
Ray Waterman, Vice President
14050 Gowando State Rd.
Collins, NY 14034
(716) 532-5995

Wyoming Native Plant Society
Robert Dorn
P.O. Box 1471
Cheyenne, WY 82003

Appendix 5

SEED, NURSERY, AND GARDEN SUPPLY CATALOGS

This is a listing of mail-order seed, nursery, and garden supply companies currently doing business in the United States. Space does not permit a complete listing of mail-order catalogs in this book. Two good sources of more complete information on mail-order suppliers are *Gardening By Mail 4*, by Barbara J. Barton (Houghton Mifflin Company, 1994), and *The Complete Guide to Gardening and Landscaping by Mail* (published annually by the Mailorder Association of Nurseries, 8683 Doves Fly Way, Laurel, MD 20723, (301)490-9143). Many companies must charge for sending out their catalog, so inquire if there is a charge when you request the catalog, even if no charge is listed below.

Abundant Life Seed Foundation
P.O. Box 772
Port Townsend, WA 98358
Heirloom and open-pollinated varieties of vegetables, grains, herbs, flowers, wildflowers, trees and shrubs, also books.
Catalog $2

Bear Creek Nursery
P.O. Box 411
Northport, WA 99157
Fruits, nuts, ornamental trees, and a few ornamental shrubs and perennials.

Bluestone Perennials
7205 Middle Ridge Rd.
Madison, OH 44057
(800) 852-5243
Large selection of perennials.

Lee Bristol Nursery
Bloomingfields Farm
Gaylordsville, CT 06755
(203) 354-6951
Daylilies.

Bountiful Gardens
Ecology Action
5798 Ridgewood Rd.
Willits, CA 95490
(707) 459-6410
Heirloom vegetables, cover crops, grains, herbs, flowers, books. Also a rare seed catalog.
Catalog $3

W. Atlee Burpee & Co.
Warminster, PA 18974
(800) 888-1447
Seeds and plants of flowers, vegetables, and herbs, fruits, ornamental trees and shrubs, bulbs, supplies.

Collector's Nursery
16804 N.E. 102nd Ave.
Battle Ground, WA 98604
(206) 574-3832
Unusual and interesting plants, including many native to the Northwest.
Catalog $2

Comstock, Ferre & Co.
263 Main St.
Box 125-0125
Wethersfield, CT 06109
(203) 529-6255
Vegetables, herbs, annuals, perennials, wildflowers, organic fertilizers.
Catalog $1

The Cook's Garden
P.O. Box 535
Londonderry, VT 05148
(802) 824-3400
Gourmet vegetables, excellent selection of salad crops, herbs, flowers, books.
Catalog $1

The Daffodil Mart
Rt. 3, Box 794
Gloucester, VA 23061
(804) 693-3966
Daffodils, narcissus, tulips, and specialty bulbs.
Catalog $1

Daylily Discounters International
Rt. 2, Box 4
Alachua, FL 32615
(904) 462-1539
Daylilies, companion perennials, accessories, books.
Catalog $2

Deep Diversity
P.O. Box 190
426 Box Canyon Rd.
Gila, NM 88038
Seeds of trees, shrubs, vegetables, perennials, annuals, herbs, grasses, fruits, all open-pollinated. Catalog includes seeds produced by Peace Seeds and Seeds of Change.
Catalog $4

DeGiorgi Seed Company
6011 N Street
Omaha, NB 68117
(402) 731-3901
Annuals, perennials, wildflowers, grasses, herbs, vegetables, books, and supplies.

Down on the Farm Seed
P.O. Box 184
Hiram, OH 44234
Heirloom and open-pollinated vegetables, herbs, and flowers.

Fairweather Gardens
P.O. Box 330
Greenwich, NJ 08323
(609) 451-6261
Ornamental tree and shrub plants.
Catalog $3

Henry Field's Seed & Nursery Co.
415 North Burnett
Shenandoah, IA 51602
(605) 665-4491
Vegetables, fruits, annuals, perennials, herbs, houseplants, shrubs, vines, and supplies.

ForestFarm
990 Tethrow Rd.
Williams, OR 97544
(503) 846-7269
Large selection of trees, shrubs, vines, ferns, grasses, and perennials.
Catalog $3

Fox Hollow Herb and Heirloom Seed Co.
P.O. Box 148
McGrann, PA 16236
Heirloom and open-pollinated varieties of herbs and other plants.
Catalog $1

Garden City Seeds
1324 Red Crow Rd.
Victor, MT 59875
(406) 961-4837
Vegetables, flowers, herbs, grasses, wildflowers, organic fertilizers, books, and garden supplies. Open-pollinated varieties as well as hybrids, varieties for the North.
Catalog $2

Gardener's Eden
P.O. Box 7307
San Francisco, CA 94120
(800) 822-9600
Upmarket garden accessories and supplies.

Gardens Alive!
5100 Schenley Place
Lawrenceburg, IN 47025
(812) 537-8651
Organic fertilizers and pest and disease controls, cover crops, supplies.

Gardener's Supply Company
128 Intervale Rd.
Burlington, VT 05401
(802) 863-1700
Organic fertilizers and pest and disease controls, large selection of tools and supplies.

Gleckler's Seedmen
Metamora, OH 43540
Vegetable seeds and plants, unusual varieties, large selection of tomatoes.

The Gourmet Gardener
8650 College Blvd., Dept. 205AH
Overland Park, KS 66210
(913) 345-0490
Gourmet and European vegetable varieties, herbs, edible flowers, and books.
Catalog $2, refundable with order

Gurney's Seed & Nursery Co.
110 Capital St.
Yankton, SD 57079
(605) 665-1671
Vegetables, herbs, annuals, houseplants, trees, shrubs, bulbs, perennials, fruits, nuts, tools, and supplies.

Hastings
1036 White St., S.W.
P.O. Box 115535
Atlanta, GA 30310
(404) 755-6580
Vegetables, fruits, trees, shrubs, vines, a few perennials, and gardening supplies. Varieties suited to southern gardens.

Heirloom Garden Seeds
P.O. Box 138
Guerneville, CA 95446
Heirloom and open-pollinated varieties.
Catalog $2.50

High Altitude Gardens
P.O. Box 4238
Ketchum, ID 83340

P.O. Box 1048
Hailey, ID 83333
Wildflowers, native grasses, open-pollinated and gourmet vegetables, and herbs, suited to tough high-altitude conditions; tools, supplies, and books.
Catalog $3

Holbrook Farm & Nursery
115 Lance Rd.
P.O. Box 368
Fletcher, NC 28732
(704) 891-7790
Good selection of perennials, and some trees and shrubs.

J. L. Hudson, Seedsman
P.O. Box 1058
Redwood City, CA 94064
Large selection of unusual, heirloom, and open-pollinated vegetables, annuals, perennials, herbs, trees, and shrubs.
Catalog $1

Ed Hume Seeds, Inc.
P.O. Box 1450
Kent, WA 98035
Vegetables, annuals, and perennials for cool, short-season climates, also books and supplies.
Catalog $1

Jackson & Perkins
P.O. Box 1028
Medford, OR 97501
(800) 872-7673
Roses, perennials, a few shrubs, gift plants, accessories.

Johnny's Selected Seeds
Foss Hill Rd.
Albion, ME 04910
(207) 437-4301
Vegetables, herbs, and flowers, including gourmet and cold-climate varieties, tools, supplies, and books.

J. W. Jung Seed Co.
Randolph, WI 53956
(414) 326-3123
Vegetables, fruits, annuals, perennials, houseplants, lilies, summer bulbs, tools, and supplies. Many cold-climate varieties.

Klehm Nursery
Rt. 5, Box 197 Penny Rd.
South Barrington, IL 60010
(800) 553-3715
Peonies, tree peonies, hostas, daylilies, ornamental grasses, and other perennials.
Catalog $4

Lake County Nursery
Rt. 84, Box 122
Perry, OH 44081
(216) 259-5571
Ornamental trees and shrubs, grasses, perennials, ferns, and books.

Landis Valley Museum
2451 Kissel Hill Rd.
Lancaster, PA 17601
(717) 569-0401
Their Heirloom Seed Project offers a catalog of open-pollinated heirloom vegetables, grains, herbs, and a few flowers, also scion wood for several heirloom apple varieties.
Catalog $2

A. M. Leonard, Inc.
241 Fox Dr.
P.O. Box 816
Piqua, OH 45356
(800) 543-8955
Huge assortment of tools and equipment.

Henry Leuthardt
P.O. Box 666
East Moriches, NY 11940
(516) 878-1387
Specialize in dwarf, semi-dwarf, and espaliered fruit trees, also grapes and berries.

Liberty Seed Co.
P.O. Box 806
New Philadelphia, OH 44663
(216) 364-1611
Vegetables, annuals, and perennials, including hybrid and open-pollinated varieties, also some supplies.

McClure & Zimmerman
108 W. Winnebago
P.O. Box 368
Friesland, WI 53935
Bulb specialists. Large selection of bulbs, both common and unusual, along with supplies and books.

Mellinger's Inc.
2310 W. South Range Rd.
North Lima, OH 44452
(216) 549-9861
Trees, shrubs, wildflowers, ornamental grasses, fruits, vegetables, herbs, bulbs, perennials, tropical plants, lawn grasses, cover crops, books, and supplies.

Milaeger's Gardens
4838 Douglas Ave.
Racine, WI 53402
(414) 639-2371
Perennials, herbs, hardy roses, wildflowers, prairie grasses, and books.
Catalog $1

Miller Nurseries
5060 West Lake Rd.
Canandaigua, NY 14424
(800) 836-9630
Fruit varieties for northern gardens, some roses, perennials, ornamental trees and grasses, and supplies.

Moon Mountain Wildflowers
P.O. Box 34
Morro Bay, CA 93443
(805) 772-2473
Wildflowers and regional wildflower mixes.
Catalog $1.50

Native Seeds/SEARCH
2509 N. Campbell Ave. #325
Tucson, AZ 85719
(602) 327-9123
A nonprofit seed bank selling seeds of many heirloom and open-pollinated vegetables for southwestern gardens, and handcrafted baskets and other items.
Catalog $1

Necessary Trading Co.
New Castle, VA 24127
(703) 864-5103
Organic fertilizers and pest and disease controls, supplies, equipment, and books.
Catalog $2

Nichols Garden Nursery
1190 North Pacific Hwy.
Albany, OR 97321
(503) 928-9280
Gourmet and unusual vegetables, herbs, flowers, wildflowers, lawn grasses.

Walt Nicke Co.
36 McLeod Lane
P.O. Box 433
Topsfield, MA 01983
(508) 887-3388
Large selection of tools and equipment, along with books and bird feeders.

NORTHPLAN/Mountain Seed
P.O. Box 9107
Moscow, ID 83843
(208) 882-8040
Seeds of hybrid and open-pollinated vegetables for northern gardens, also some annuals.
A companion company, Northplan Seed Producers, sells seed of native wildflowers, shrubs, trees, and grasses.
Catalog $1

Old Sturbridge Village Museum Gift Shop
1 Old Sturbridge Village Rd.
Sturbridge, MA 01566
Seeds of heirloom flowers, vegetables, and herbs.
Catalog $1

Owen Farms
2951 Curve-Nankipoo Rd.
Rt. 3, Box 158-A
Ripley, TN 38063
(901) 635-1588
Trees, shrubs, and perennials.
Catalog $2

Park Seed Co.
Cokesbury Rd.
Greenwood, SC 29647
(803) 941-4480
Vegetables, fruits, annuals, perennials, shrubs, herbs, wildflowers, houseplants, summer bulbs, and supplies.

Peaceful Valley Farm Supply
P.O. Box 2209
Grass Valley, CA 95945
(916) 272-4769
Organic, open-pollinated vegetables, fruits, bulbs, cover crops, lawn grasses, wildflowers, books, tools, and supplies, including organic fertilizers and pest and disease controls.

Pinetree Garden Seeds
Box 300
New Gloucester, ME 04260
(207) 926-3400
Vegetables, flowers, herbs, bulbs, tools, supplies, and books.

Plants of the Southwest
Agua Fria, Rt. 6 Box 11A
Santa Fe, NM 87505
(505) 471-2212
Vegetables, grasses, large selection of wildflowers, trees, and shrubs, all for southwestern gardens. Many native and open-pollinated varieties. Also books.
Catalog $3.50

Porter & Son, Seedsmen
1510 Washington St.
P.O. Box 104
Stephenville, TX 76401
Vegetables, herbs, flowers, bulbs, and supplies. Many varieties for southern climates.

Redwood City Seed Company
Box 361
Redwood City, CA 94064
Large selection of open-pollinated seeds.
Catalog $1

Rocknoll Nursery
1639 Hess Rd.
Sardinia, OH 45171
(513) 288-2304
Perennials, shrubs, and ornamental grasses.

Ronniger's Seed Potatoes
Star Route 91
Moyie Springs, ID 83845
Seed potatoes, including many heirloom varieties, garlic, onions, cover crops, and books.
Catalog $2

The Roseraie at Bayfields
P.O. Box R
Waldoboro, ME 04572
(207) 832-6330
Specialize in hardy low-maintenance roses.

John Scheepers, Inc.
P.O. Box 700
Bantam, CT 06750
(203) 567-0838
Bulb specialists; large selection of narcissus, tulips, lilies, and other bulbs.

Seed Savers Exchange
3076 N. Winn Rd.
Decorah, IA 52101
Heirloom and open-pollinated seeds. Send $1 for information.

Seeds Blum
Idaho City Stage
Boise, ID 83706
Large selection of heirloom and open-pollinated vegetables, also annuals, perennials, wildflowers, herbs, grains, and books. Catalog $3

Seeds of Change
P.O. Box 15700
Santa Fe, NM 87506
Large selection of organic, open-pollinated seed for vegetables (including heirloom and native varieties), grains, and flowers, plus how-to information and interesting reading on environmental concerns in the back of the catalog.

Seeds * West
P.O. Box 27057
Albuquerque, NM 87125
(505) 242-7474
Organic seeds for vegetables, herbs, wildflowers, and garden flowers, heirloom and open-pollinated varieties as well as hybrids, all drought-tolerant and suited to gardens in the western United States.

Select Seeds Antique Flowers
180 Stickney Rd.
Union, CT 06076
Seeds for old-fashioned annuals and perennials.

Shepherd's Garden Seeds
30 Irene St.
Torrington, CT 06790
(203) 482-3638
Gourmet vegetable seeds from around the world, good selection of herbs, plus old-fashioned, edible, fragrant, and cutting flowers. Catalog $1

Smith & Hawken
25 Corte Madera
Mill Valley, CA 94941
(415) 383-2000
Upscale garden tools and accessories.

Southern Exposure Seed Exchange
P.O. Box 170
Earlysville, VA 23936
Large selection of heirloom vegetables, also gardening supplies and books. Catalog $3

Southern Seeds
P.O. Box 2091
Melbourne, FL 32902
Open-pollinated vegetables and herbs for southern gardens.

Spring Hill Nurseries
110 W. Elm St.
Tipp City, OH 45371
Perennials, groundcovers, vines, and a few trees and shrubs.

Stark Bro's Nurseries
Louisiana, MO 63353
Good selection of tree fruits and small fruits, nuts, also some ornamental trees and shrubs, and supplies.

Stokes Seeds Inc.
Box 548
Buffalo, NY 14240
(716) 695-6980
Large selection of vegetables and annuals, also perennials and ornamental grasses, supplies and accessories.

Territorial Seed Co.
P.O. Box 157
20 Palmer Ave.
Cottage Grove, OR 97424
Hybrid and open-pollinated vegetables, herbs, annuals and perennials for northwestern gardens. Also books, tools, and supplies.

Thomas Jefferson Center for Historic Plants
P.O. Box 316
Charlottesville, VA 22902
Seeds of varieties in the gardens at Monticello. Catalog $1

Thompson & Morgan
P.O. Box 1308
Jackson, NJ 08527
(908) 363-2225
U.S. arm of the British seed company. Large selection of annuals and perennials, vegetables and herbs.

Tomato Growers Supply Co.
P.O. Box 2237
Fort Myers, FL 33902
(813) 768-1119
Huge selection of tomatoes, including many heirloom varieties, also good assortment of sweet and hot peppers, and some books and supplies.

Van Bourgondien Bros.
P.O. Box 1000
245 Farmingdale Rd., Rt. 109
Babylon, NY 11702
(800) 622-9959
Large assortment of bulbs and perennials.

Van Engelen Inc.
Stillbrook Farm
313 Maple St.
Litchfield, CT 06759
(203) 567-8734 or 567-5662
Bulb specialists. Large selection of narcissus, tulips, and lilies, and many other bulbs.

The Vermont Wildflower Farm
P.O. Box 5, Rt. 7
Charlotte, VT 05445
(802) 425-3504
Wildflower seeds and seed mixes for different regions.

Andre Viette Farm & Nursery
Rt. 1, Box 16
Fishersville, VA 22939
(703) 943-2315
Large selection of perennials, ornamental grasses, ferns, and herbs; many hostas, daylilies, iris, and peonies.
Catalog $2

Wayside Gardens
Hodges, SC 29695
(800) 799-7275
Perennials, bulbs, trees, shrubs, vines, roses, and ornamental grasses.

White Flower Farm
Litchfield, CT 06759
(203) 496-9600
Long known for perennials, they also carry annuals, bulbs, and shrubs.
Catalog $5

Wildseed Farms, Inc.
1101 Campo Rosa Rd.
P.O. Box 508
Eagle Lake, TX 77434
(800) 848-0078
Wildflowers, regional wildflower mixes, and herbs.

INDEX

A

B

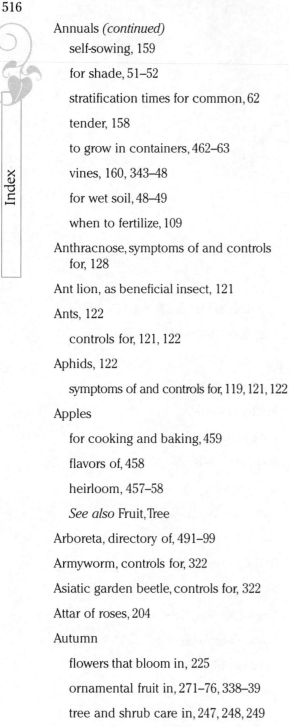

C

D

E

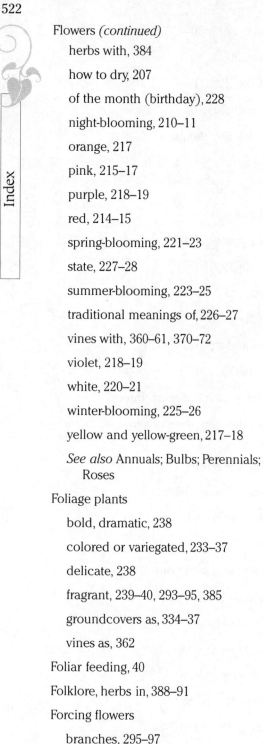

G

H

I

J

K

L

M

N

O

P

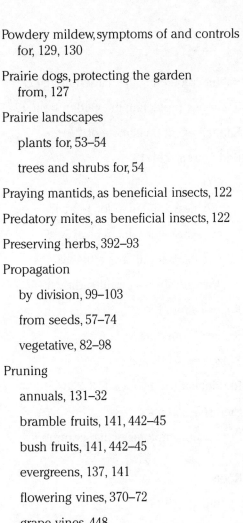

R

S

T

U

V

W

Y

Z

NOTES

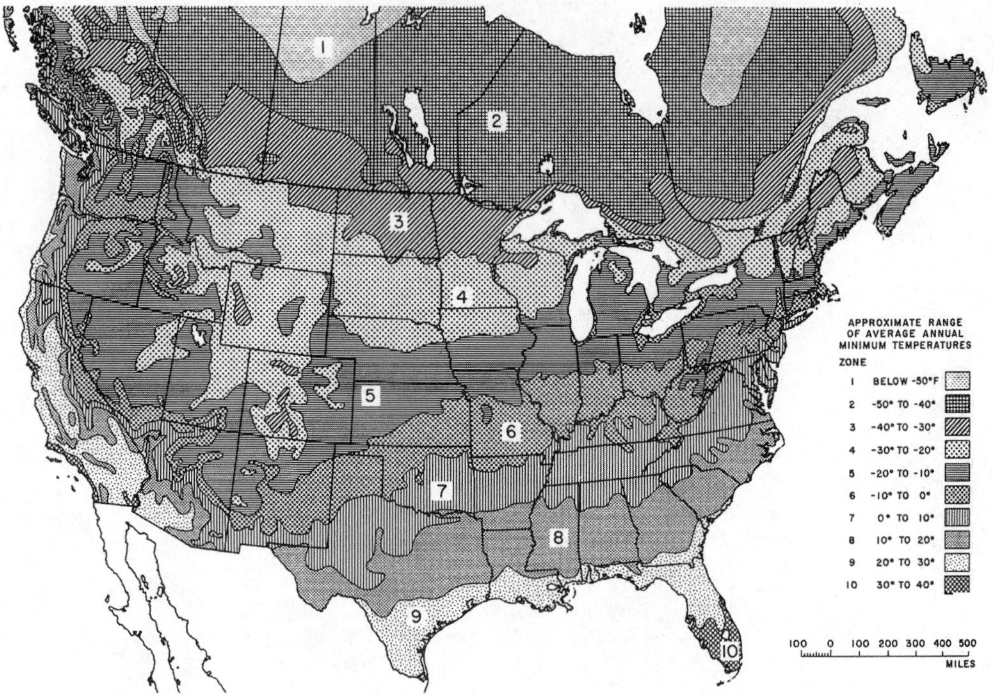

*The USDA currently offers a color zone map with an additional zone, 11, for southern parts of Florida, California, and Hawaii. The color version subdivides Zones 1–10 into "a" and "b" sections, with the "a" portion of each zone being an average of 5°F cooler than the "b" portion.